Research Advances in the Integration of Big Data and Smart Computing

Pradeep Kumar Mallick
Institute for Research and Development, India

A volume in the Advances in Computational Intelligence and Robotics (ACIR) Book Series

Published in the United States of America by
Information Science Reference (an imprint of IGI Global)
701 E. Chocolate Avenue
Hershey PA, USA 17033
Tel: 717-533-8845
Fax: 717-533-8661
E-mail: cust@igi-global.com
Web site: http://www.igi-global.com

Library of Congress Cataloging-in-Publication Data

Research advances in the integration of big data and smart computing / Pradeep Kumar Mallick, editor.
pages cm
Includes bibliographical references and index.
ISBN 978-1-4666-8737-0 (hardcover) -- ISBN 978-1-4666-8738-7 (ebook) 1. Big data. I. Mallick, Pradeep Kumar, 1984-
QA76.9.B45R43 2016
005.7--dc23
2015019730

This book is published in the IGI Global book series Advances in Computational Intelligence and Robotics (ACIR) (ISSN: 2327-0411; eISSN: 2327-042X)

British Cataloguing in Publication Data
A Cataloguing in Publication record for this book is available from the British Library.

All work contributed to this book is new, previously-unpublished material. The views expressed in this book are those of the authors, but not necessarily of the publisher.

For electronic access to this publication, please contact: eresources@igi-global.com.

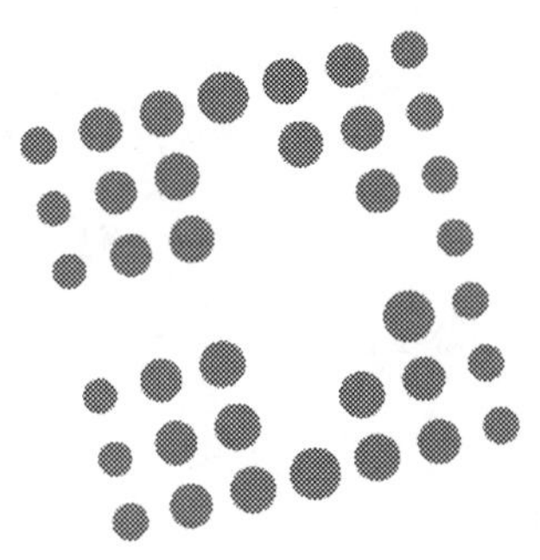

Advances in Computational Intelligence and Robotics (ACIR) Book Series

ISSN: 2327-0411
EISSN: 2327-042X

Mission

While intelligence is traditionally a term applied to humans and human cognition, technology has progressed in such a way to allow for the development of intelligent systems able to simulate many human traits. With this new era of simulated and artificial intelligence, much research is needed in order to continue to advance the field and also to evaluate the ethical and societal concerns of the existence of artificial life and machine learning.

The **Advances in Computational Intelligence and Robotics (ACIR) Book Series** encourages scholarly discourse on all topics pertaining to evolutionary computing, artificial life, computational intelligence, machine learning, and robotics. ACIR presents the latest research being conducted on diverse topics in intelligence technologies with the goal of advancing knowledge and applications in this rapidly evolving field.

Coverage

- Synthetic Emotions
- Cognitive Informatics
- Machine Learning
- Algorithmic Learning
- Natural Language Processing
- Heuristics
- Computational Logic
- Pattern Recognition
- Evolutionary computing
- Intelligent control

IGI Global is currently accepting manuscripts for publication within this series. To submit a proposal for a volume in this series, please contact our Acquisition Editors at Acquisitions@igi-global.com or visit: http://www.igi-global.com/publish/.

The Advances in Computational Intelligence and Robotics (ACIR) Book Series (ISSN 2327-0411) is published by IGI Global, 701 E. Chocolate Avenue, Hershey, PA 17033-1240, USA, www.igi-global.com. This series is composed of titles available for purchase individually; each title is edited to be contextually exclusive from any other title within the series. For pricing and ordering information please visit http://www.igi-global.com/book-series/advances-computational-intelligence-robotics/73674. Postmaster: Send all address changes to above address.

Titles in this Series

For a list of additional titles in this series, please visit: www.igi-global.com

Handbook of Research on Emerging Perspectives in Intelligent Pattern Recognition, Analysis, and Image Processing
Narendra Kumar Kamila (C.V. Raman College of Engineering, India)
Information Science Reference • copyright 2016 • 484pp • H/C (ISBN: 9781466686540) • US $255.00 (our price)

Innovative Research in Attention Modeling and Computer Vision Applications
Rajarshi Pal (Institute for Development and Research in Banking Technology, India)
Information Science Reference • copyright 2016 • 370pp • H/C (ISBN: 9781466687233) • US $200.00 (our price)

Research Advances in the Integration of Big Data and Smart Computing
Pradeep Kumar Mallick (Institute for Research and Development, India)
Information Science Reference • copyright 2016 • 324pp • H/C (ISBN: 9781466687370) • US $210.00 (our price)

Handbook of Research on Swarm Intelligence in Engineering
Siddhartha Bhattacharyya (RCC Institute of Information Technology, India) and Paramartha Dutta (Visva-Bharati University, India)
Engineering Science Reference • copyright 2015 • 744pp • H/C (ISBN: 9781466682917) • US $335.00 (our price)

Handbook of Research on Advancements in Robotics and Mechatronics
Maki K. Habib (The American University in Cairo, Egypt)
Engineering Science Reference • copyright 2015 • 993pp • H/C (ISBN: 9781466673878) • US $515.00 (our price)

Handbook of Research on Advanced Intelligent Control Engineering and Automation
Ahmad Taher Azar (Benha University, Egypt) and Sundarapandian Vaidyanathan (Vel Tech University, India)
Engineering Science Reference • copyright 2015 • 795pp • H/C (ISBN: 9781466672482) • US $335.00 (our price)

Handbook of Research on Artificial Intelligence Techniques and Algorithms
Pandian Vasant (Universiti Teknologi Petronas, Malaysia)
Information Science Reference • copyright 2015 • 796pp • H/C (ISBN: 9781466672581) • US $495.00 (our price)

Handbook of Research on Synthesizing Human Emotion in Intelligent Systems and Robotics
Jordi Vallverdú (Universitat Autònoma de Barcelona, Spain)
Information Science Reference • copyright 2015 • 469pp • H/C (ISBN: 9781466672789) • US $245.00 (our price)

Recent Advances in Ambient Intelligence and Context-Aware Computing
Kevin Curran (University of Ulster, UK)
Information Science Reference • copyright 2015 • 376pp • H/C (ISBN: 9781466672840) • US $225.00 (our price)

www.igi-global.com

701 E. Chocolate Ave., Hershey, PA 17033
Order online at www.igi-global.com or call 717-533-8845 x100
To place a standing order for titles released in this series, contact: cust@igi-global.com
Mon-Fri 8:00 am - 5:00 pm (est) or fax 24 hours a day 717-533-8661

Editorial Advisory Board

Table of Contents

Detailed Table of Contents

Preface xvi

Chapter 1

Big Data: The Data Deluge 1

Jayshree Ghorpade-Aher, University of Pune, Pune
Reena Pagare, University of Pune, Pune
Anita Thengade, University of Pune, Pune
Santaji Ghorpade, IBM India Pvt. Ltd., India
Manik Kadam, Allana Institute, India

Today is the Computer Era, where the data is increasing exponentially. Managing such a huge data is a challenging job. Under the explosive increase of global data, the term of big data is mainly used to describe enormous datasets. The state-of-the-art of big data is discussed here. The discussions aim to provide a comprehensive overview and big-picture to readers of this existing research area. This chapter discusses the different models and technologies for Big Data; It also introduces Big data Storage. Big data has been a potential topic in various research fields and areas like healthcare, public sector, retail, manufacturing personal data, etc.

Chapter 2

Transmission Control Protocol for Mobile Ad Hoc Network 22

Sukant Kishoro Bisoy, C. V. Raman College of Engineering, India
Prasant Kumar Pattnaik, KIIT University, India

The Transmission Control Protocol (TCP) is a reliable protocol of transport layer which delivers data over unreliable networks. It was designed in the context of wired networks. Due to popularity of wireless communication it is made to extend TCP protocol to wireless environments where wired and wireless network can work smoothly. Although TCP work in wireless and wired-cum-wireless network, the performance is not up to the mark. In literature lot of protocols has been proposed to adopt TCP in wireless mobile ad hoc network. In this, we present an overall view on this issue and detailed discussion of the major factors involved. In addition, we survey the main proposals which aim at adapting TCP to mobile and static Ad hoc environments. Specifically, we show how TCP can be affected by mobility and its interaction with routing protocol in static and dynamic wireless ad hoc network.

Breast cancer is the second largest cause of cancer deaths among women. Mainly, this disease is tumor related cause of death in women. Early detection of breast cancer may protect women from death. Various computational methods have been utilized to enhance the diagnoses procedures. In this paper, we have presented the genetic algorithm (GA) based association rule mining method which can be applied to detect breast cancer efficiently. In this work, we have represented each solution as chromosome and applied to genetic algorithm based rule mining. Association rules which imply classification rules are encoded with binary strings to represent chromosomes. Finally, optimal solutions are found out by develop GA-based approach utilizing a feedback linkage between feature selection and association rule.

Some high speed IP networks, which involve interior gateway protocols, such as OSPF, are not capable of finding the new routes to bypass the effect like failure in time. At the point when the failure occurs the network must converge it before the traffic has the capacity to go to and from the network segment that caused a connection disconnect. The duration of the convergence period of these protocols vary from hundred of milliseconds to 10 seconds, which creates unsteadiness and results high packet loss rate. This issue may be determined by proposing an algorithm that can rapidly react to the topology change and reduce the convergence time by providing back up path which is already stored in routing table before the failover occurs.

Cotton leaf diseases have occurred all over the world, including India. They adversely affect cotton quality and yield. Technology can help in identifying disease in early stage so that effective treatment can be given immediately. Now, the control methods rely mainly on artificial means. This paper propose application of image processing and machine learning in identifying three cotton leaf diseases through feature extraction. Using image processing, 12 types of features are extracted from cotton leaf image then the pattern was learned using BP Neural Network method in machine learning process. Three diseases have been diagnosed, namely Powdery mildew, Downy mildew and leafminer. The Neural Network classification performs well and could successfully detect and classify the tested disease.

Chapter 6
The Pedagogy of English Teaching-Learning at Primary Level in Rural Government Schools: A Data Mining View 105
P. Sunil Kumar, BPUT, India
Sateesh Kumar Pradhan, Utkal University, India
Sachidananda Panda, BPUT, India

English language is accepted as the global language in all walks of life today. Hence it becomes mandatory for everyone to learn English in order to be successful at the individual as well as social levels. Although Government has taken number of initiatives, it is necessary to mention that our rural schools at the primary level are adversely affected in this aspect, as the children are not properly taken care of in English teaching and learning skills. This paper is based on a survey work done amongst the students, parents and teachers by using data mining techniques like association rule mining measures and other interesting measures to reveal the facts for better implementation.

Chapter 7
Indic Language: Kannada to Braille Conversion Tool Using Client Server Architecture Model....... 120
Shaila H. Koppad, Bangalore University, India
T. M. Shwetha, Bangalore University, India

The aim of this research paper is to convert Kannada script to Braille, to enable the visually-impaired lead a better life by means of providing better learning aides. It proposes a possibility of facilitating the regional teachers to teach Kannada through Braille. "Braille Lipi" is instrumental in providing an able platform for the visually-impaired to habituate studying. This paper addresses the various aspects of "Braille Lipi", it throws light on the origin and various levels, which depends on user-type (either simple, moderate or expert) explained with architecture of Braille system. Kannada to Braille Conversion Tool mainly focuses on elaborating the conversion of Kannada script to Braille script. An attempt to better understand, by a brief insight to Kannada script, Kannada alphabets is made and the whole intention of the contribution is a humble gesture to humanity. The main advantage of the model is visually-impaired can also have access to e-governance.

Chapter 8
Baseline Drift Removal of ECG Signal: Comparative Analysis of Filtering Techniques 134
Akash Kumar Bhoi, Sikkim Manipal Institute of Technology (SMIT), India
Karma Sonam Sherpa, Sikkim Manipal Institute of Technology (SMIT), India
Bidita Khandelwal, Central Referral Hospital and SMIMS, India

The filtering techniques are primarily used for preprocessing of the signal and have been implemented in a wide variety of systems for Electrocardiogram (ECG) analysis. It should be remembered that filtering of the ECG is contextual and should be performed only when the desired information remains undistorted. Removal of baseline drift is required in order to minimize changes in beat morphology that do not have cardiac origin, which is especially important when subtle changes in the ''low-frequency'' ST segment are analyzed for the diagnosis of ischemia. Here, for baseline drift removal different filters such as Median, Low Pass Butter Worth, Finite Impulse Response (FIR), Weighted Moving Average and Stationary Wavelet Transform (SWT) are implemented. The fundamental properties of signal before and after baseline drift removal are statistically analyzed.

Chapter 9
Signal Processing: Iteration Bound and Loop Bound 153
Deepika Ghai, PEC University of Technology, India
Neelu Jain, PEC University of Technology, India

Digital signal processing algorithms are recursive in nature. These algorithms are explained by iterative data-flow graphs where nodes represent computations and edges represent communications. For all data-flow graphs, time taken to achieve output from the applied input is referred as iteration bound. In this chapter, two algorithms are used for computing the iteration bound i.e. Longest Path Matrix (LPM) and Minimum Cycle Mean (MCM). The iteration bound of single-rate data-flow graph (SRDFG) can be determined by considering the Multi-rate data-flow graph (MRDFG) equivalent of the SRDFG. SRDFG contain more nodes and edges as compared to MRDFG. Reduction of nodes and edges in MRDFG is used for faster determination of the iteration bound.

Chapter 10
Application of Big Data in Economic Policy 178
Brojo Kishore Mishra, C.V. Raman College of Engineering, India
Abhaya Kumar Sahoo, C.V. Raman College of Engineering, India

Now-a-days main factor of any information in different fields is data. Different database like relational, object-oriented database is very different from traditional database in case of data retrieval, data management and data updation. So, Data mining is a process of extracting hidden knowledge or useful pattern from huge amount of data in case of efficient databases. As amount of data increases day by day, so it is very difficult to manage related data to different fields. Big data analysis takes a major role for accessing, managing and manipulating of both structured and unstructured data. It is possible to transform business, government and other aspects of the economy by big data. In this chapter, we discuss how big data analytics can be applied in economic policy of government and private sector for making better decision. Here we can use map-reduce programming model provided by Hadoop for analysis of big data in economic policy management.

Chapter 11
Advanced Dimensionality Reduction Method for Big Data 198
Sufal Das, North-Eastern Hill University, India
Hemanta Kumar Kalita, North-Eastern Hill University, India

The growing glut of data in the worlds of science, business and government create an urgent need for consideration of big data. Big data is a term that describes large volumes of high velocity, complex and variable data that require advanced techniques and technologies to enable the capture, storage, distribution, management, and analysis of the information. Big data challenge is becoming one of the most exciting opportunities for the next years. Data mining algorithms like association rule mining perform an exhaustive search to find all rules satisfying some constraints. it is clear that it is difficult to identify the most effective rule from big data. A novel method for feature selection and extraction has been introduced for big data using genetic algorithm. Dimensionality reduction can be considered a problem of global combinatorial optimization in machine learning, which reduces the number of features, removes irrelevant, noisy and redundant data, to obtain the accuracy and saves the computation time and simplifies the result. A genetic algorithm was developed based approach utilizing a feedback linkage between feature selection and association rule using MapReduce for big data.

The power system has undergone multifold growth in its generation, transmission and distribution in past few decades. The types of conductors used for transmission system in India are ACSR / AAAC. These conductors have several constraints. The Ampacity of these conductors is less and hence they cannot be operated at high temperature also the losses in these type of conductors are more. To overcome the drawbacks of ACSR / AAAC conductors, this paper proposes a new approach of using High Tension Low Sag (HTLS) conductors, also a comparison is made between ACSR, AAAC and HTLS conductors on the basis of voltage drop and power loss for benefit evaluation of HTLS conductor over traditionally used conductors.

Facial recognition is the most natural means of biometric identification as it deals with the measurement of a biological relevance. Since, faces varies from each and every person, therefore, it can be used for security purpose. Face recognition is a very challenging problem, where the human face changes over time, as it depends on the pose, expression, occlusion, aging, etc. It can be used in many areas such as for surveillance purposes, security, general identity verification, criminal justice system, smart cards, etc. The most important part of the face recognition is the evaluation of facial features. With the help of facial feature, the system usually looks for the position of eyes, nose and mouth and distances between them can be detected and computed. This chapter will discuss some of the techniques that can be used to extract important facial features.

Personal identification from the iris images acquired under less-constrained imaging environment is highly challenging. Such environment requires the development of efficient iris segmentation approach and recognition strategy which can exploit multiple features available for the potential identification. So, along with the iris features periocular features have increasing attention in biometrics technology. For the recognition purpose iris and periocular information are collected from both the eyes of same person simultaneously. The term periocular refers to the facial region in the immediate vicinity of the eye. Acquisition of image for periocular biometric is expected to require less subject cooperation. In this chapter, a dual iris based multimodal biometric system that increases the performance and accuracy of the typical iris recognition system is proposed.

Usage of General Purpose Graphics Processing Units (GPGPUs) in high-performance computing is increasing as heterogeneous systems continue to become dominant. CUDA had been the programming environment for nearly all such NVIDIA GPU based GPGPU applications. Still, the framework runs only on NVIDIA GPUs, for other frameworks it requires reimplementation to utilize additional computing devices that are available. OpenCL provides a vendor-neutral and open programming environment, with many implementations available on CPUs, GPUs, and other types of accelerators, OpenCL can thus be regarded as write once, run anywhere framework. Despite this, both frameworks have their own pros and cons. This chapter presents a comparison of the performance of CUDA and OpenCL frameworks, using an algorithm to find the sum of all possible triple products on a list of integers, implemented on GPUs.

Synthetic Aperture Radar (SAR) are imaging Radar, it uses electromagnetic radiation to illuminate the scanned surface and produce high resolution images in all-weather condition, day and night. Interference of signals causes noise and degrades the quality of the image, it causes serious difficulty in analyzing the images. Speckle is multiplicative noise that inherently exist in SAR images. Artificial Neural Network (ANN) have the capability of learning and is gaining popularity in SAR image processing. Multi-Layer Perceptron (MLP) is a feed forward artificial neural network model that consists of an input layer, several hidden layers, and an output layer. We have simulated MLP with two hidden layer in Matlab. Speckle noises were added to the target SAR image and applied MLP for speckle noise reduction. It is found that speckle noise in SAR images can be reduced by using MLP. We have considered Log-sigmoid, Tan-Sigmoid and Linear Transfer Function for the hidden layers. The MLP network are trained using Gradient descent with momentum back propagation, Resilient back propagation and Levenberg-Marquardt back propagation and comparatively evaluated the performance.

Biometrics refers to metrics related to human characteristics and Traits. Face Recognition is the process of identification of a person by their facial image. It has been an active area of research for several decades, but still remains a challenging problem because of the complexity of the human face. The objective is to authenticate a person, to have a FAR and FRR very low. This project introduces a new approach for face recognition system using FFT algorithm. The database that contains the images is named as train database and the test image which is stored in test database is compared with the created train database.

For further processing RGB data is converted into grayscale, thus reduces the matrix dimension. FFT is applied to the entire database and mean value of the images is computed and the same is repeated on test database also. Based on the threshold value of the test image, face recognition is done. Performance evaluation of Biometrics is done for normal image, skin color image, ageing image and blur image using False Acceptance Rate(FAR), False Rejection Rate(FRR), Equal Error Rate(EER) and also calculated the accuracy of different images.

Chapter 18
White Patch Detection in Brain MRI Image Using Evolutionary Clustering Algorithm 323
Pradeep Kumar Mallick, St. Peter's University, India
Mihir Narayan Mohanty, SOA University, India
S. Saravana Kumar, Sree Vidyanikethan Engineering College, India

Though image segmentation is a fundamental task in image analysis; it plays a vital role in the area of image processing. Its value increases in case of medical diagnostics through medical images like X-ray, PET, CT and MRI. In this chapter, an attempt is taken to analyze an MRI brain image. It has been segmented for a particular patch in the brain MRI image that may be one of the tumors in the brain. The purpose of segmentation is to partition an image into meaningful regions with respect to a particular application. Image segmentation is a method of separating the image from the background, read the contents and isolating it. In this chapter both the concept of clustering and thresholding technique have been used. The standard methods such as Sobel, Prewitt edge detectors is applied initially. Then the result is optimized using GA for efficient minimization of the objective function and for improved classification of clusters. Further the segmented result is passed through a Gaussian filter to obtain a smoothed image.

Compilation of References 340

About the Contributors 364

Index 372

Preface

INTRODUCTION

Since last decade, smart Computing has become a formal area of research in Computer Science. It covers computational techniques in machine learning, computer science and engineering disciplines, which investigate, simulate, and analyze very complex issues and phenomena. Unlike conventional computing schemes. Recent trend in big data phenomenon and the emerging fourth paradigm in computing - the data-intensive science discovery - accelerate the research interest and momentum of smart Computing. With the four V's viz. volume, velocity, variety, and veracity of big data from sensor network and Internet of things, intelligent systems are now being challenged with new data description models and management tasks for data integration, transformation, visualization, querying and real-time analysis. Cognitive computing adds another level of potentials, by emphasizing on the role of human mind especially in the business and marketing scenarios.

THE CHALLENGES

The main challenges in handling Big Data lie not only in the four V's, namely, Volume, Variety, Velocity and Veracity, but also its Variability in content and structure which calls for new approaches for interpretation and understanding of the data. Big Data demands are evolutionary change in research methodology and in tools to be employed. Traditional Computational Intelligence techniques need a complete re-haul to handle these challenges. Smart Computing techniques can play a significantly important role in this due to their inherent capabilities of dealing with imprecision and uncertainty. Machine learning (ML) algorithms are computationally expensive, especially on the typical central processing unit (CPU) environment. The growing births of new intelligent system architectures are often due to the multi strategy learning and adaptation of advanced soft computing techniques in various fields such as pattern recognition, and data mining, particularly to address the issues of Big Data.

ISSUES WITH BIG DATA

The ideal infrastructure for big data shares common characteristics with the shift toward software-defined IT environments. The challenges around big data in many ways are the impetus for software-defined data centres. According to the 2012 IDC Data Centre Infrastructure Survey, data centre capacity is slated to grow by more than 50% over the next 5 years. But this new capacity must serve an emerging, diverse set of workloads: Big data analytics, content serving, archiving and mobility together are eclipsing traditional transactional workloads. Because of the business opportunity, big data analytics are playing a major role in emerging architectures. The data mix has changed along with the workloads. Traditionally, data was predominately structured. In other words, could be organized in rows and columns (think relational databases, bank and credit card transactions, purchaseorders, and so forth). Global data is now 80% or more unstructured (think photos, X-rays, videos, emails, tweets, and so forth). Unstructured data rely on file systems to translate sequences of bits or bytes stored on disks in fixed lengths or "blocks" into user- or client-understandable formats. A data block by itself has no knowledge of the file to which it belongs. Structured data stored in databases understand (read and write) blocks directly because they contain their own "filing systems." Both data types must be analyzed, often together and concurrently, to meet big data business objectives. Big data business opportunities are usually time and event dependent. For example, to improve sales, a business may wish to predict and influence customer behaviour by making offers as targeted and personalized as possible. Or, a business may need to identify an anomaly, such as a product defect, quickly, before it causes revenue loss. As such, multiple data sources must come together real time or at least within a designated window of time. More than one application might require access to multiple data sources. Big data infrastructure must deliver the right type of compute resources when data, applications and end users need them, or business opportunities might be missed. Big data requires a top-down approach to information infrastructure where requests from business owners are translated into compute resources tailored to the job at hand. It requires a new approach to infrastructure, one that is more programmable, or, if you will, software-defined. The core information infrastructure characteristics shared by the needs of big data and software-defined IT are abstraction, extensibility and automation. Look for these characteristics throughout this white paper. These characteristics are not easy to deliver, but technology is advancing to get us there. Many solutions are already firmly established in today's IT environment. Others, newer to IT, are essential to your big data information infrastructure.

EFFICIENCY AND FLEXIBILITY

Optimization at every level of the big data stack is an imperative. Big data analytics projects are notoriously unpredictable and can involve very large, complex data sets from many sources. At the infrastructure layer, there are opportunities to inject both efficiency and flexibility that serve the entire stack. Virtualization is the *abstraction* of infrastructure and other IT resources. Server virtualization has become universally accepted as a way to make dramatically more efficient and flexible use of physical servers: Physical servers can be carved into many virtual servers, which can be created nearly instantaneously and deleted when no longer required, making the physical resources available once again. Storage virtualization brings a similar level of efficiency and flexibility to big data infrastructures. It makes it much easier and more cost-effective to access large volumes of structured and unstructured data. The virtualized storage resources are presented as pools of on-demand data to big data analytics applications. Using *automation*, the utilization rate of well-managed, virtualized tiered storage can approach 100%, making it very cost-effective. Likewise, network virtualization or software-defined networks take a number of physical network connections and present them as pools of connections, *abstracting* underlying network complexity. Bottom line: Virtualization addresses big data challenges by allowing your infrastructure to move constantly changing big data workloads flexibly to the right compute and storage resources. It also allows resources to expand quickly and efficiently to meet the volume, velocity and variety of big data.

PERFORMANCE AND SCALE

If virtualization is the efficiency and flexibility superhero of big data infrastructure, then performance and scale are the dynamic duo of extensibility. A sometimes-misunderstood feature of big data is that it can start small and grow bigger. Or, its "bigness" can originate with the notion that it must be obtained from many sources and analyzed together. In other words, sometimes the "big" in big data is not the sheer volume of data, but the variety and/or the velocity. Therefore, the ability to scale linearly for capacity and performance is important to big data infrastructure.

ISSUES WITH SMART COMPUTING

While there is standalone value in each of the innovations in software systems, server infrastructure, network infrastructure, and client devices, it is the combination of all these innovations that will allow computing technologies to become smarter. Smart Computing can do this because it combines five key functions of intelligence — what we call the five A's of Smart Computing. If we think about any concept of smart behaviour or smart actions, these consist of five stages of activity. Smart Computing uses digital business architecture technologies, either brand new ones or new deployments of existing technologies

New technologies for pervasive interactions such as radio frequency identification (RFID), sensors, video cameras, global positioning system (GPS) chips, smart cards, and other tools will capture data on the identity, status, condition, and/or location of people and physical assets — data that indicates anomalies that present a business opportunity, activity, threat, or risk. Unified communications technologies such as third-generation (3G) wireless networks will transport this data from these client devices back to central servers for analysis.

Business intelligence and specialized analytical software such as data mining and predictive analytics, video image analysis, pattern recognition, and artificial intelligence algorithms will determine whether businesses or governments should act on or ignore a pattern or an anomaly. Businesses and governments have already been using these analytical tools for making sense of historical data, as well as for starting to make predictions about what may happen next. But now, they will be deployed against the real-time data being transmitted from the new awareness devices. Analyzing and storing the massive amounts of data that will be received is only possible with the more flexible and adaptable servers and storage devices enabled by server virtualization, data center automation, and storage life-cycle management — as well as the potential for more flexible processing expansion and storage capacity through cloud computing. Expect more of the basic processing that sifts out meaningful information from background noise to happen at the fringes of the unified wireline and wireless broadband networks that connect to the awareness devices. For this analysis to have business value, though, it will need to present alternatives.

Rules engines and workflow are the existing technologies for deciding which alternative courses to pursue, either automatically through the application of a rule that says "if this happens, do this," or through human review based on workflow engines that route the anomaly and alternative courses to the right person to make a decision.8 The basic function of rules engines and workflow will stay constant

— seismic leaps will be necessary in the data flow and analytical inputs in a world of vastly expanded real-time awareness. For example, rules engines will need to adapt and change their rules on the fly (based on new analysis of what the best alternatives should be), and workflow engines will need to change rapidly what alternatives should be presented to which people based on the seriousness of the issue. In either case, once a human being or a rules engine makes a decision on what to do, that decision should trigger the requisite actions.

The action may be as simple as quoting a different price, placing a new order, making a new offer to a customer, or initiating a customer service contact. Or the action may be as complex as adjusting thermostats in tens of thousands of households and businesses to avoid an electricity brownout. These actions will be executed through integrated links to the appropriate process applications. The spreading conversion of process apps to service-oriented architectures will allow these process apps to be adapted to business scenarios, with specific app components pushed down to the awareness devices where they can execute that action, whether that is alerting a citizen on her smartphone to the updated arrival time of a bus that was stuck in traffic, notifying a doctor on a tablet device about the drug allergies of a patient he is about to see, or directing the thermostat in an individual home to raise the temperature by turning up the air conditioner by three degrees.

Tracking all steps in the process to aid in regulatory compliance, compliance with company policies and goals, and improvement opportunities is critical. Any definition of "smartness" includes elements of monitoring activity and learning how to do it better. Technology needs to capture, track, and analyze information on each stage of this cycle to make sure that the right actions were taken and to learn how to improve the analysis and identify better alternatives.

THE TRENDS IN COMPUTING TECHNOLOGIES

Mainframe computing helped automate high-frequency transactions. High-frequency transactions include booking an airline reservation, making a bank deposit or payment, generating a utility or telephone bill, underwriting an insurance policy or processing a claim, or paying a government benefit. So, that problem has been largely solved.

Personal computing helped automate individual transactions. Individual transactions include writing a letter, memo, or report; analyzing financial data in a spreadsheet; or preparing a presentation for an audience of managers, employees, or customers. So, that problem has largely been solved.

Network computing helped automate key business processes. Business processes include paying a supplier, billing a customer, taking an order, buying from a supplier, hiring and paying an employee, and manufacturing a product or designing one. While opportunities still exist to automate other processes (for example, generating a contract or creating a sales proposal) as well as to link related processes, most of the big efficiency gains from process efficiency have already been realized. New business processes are arising to take advantage of what technology can enable, such as customer-driven product innovation; crowd-based problem solving; and contract-driven pricing, quoting, configuration, or services. And while many business processes have become more efficient (thanks to network computing technologies), there is still room for making them more effective by applying rules engines, workflow, analytics, and business process management to help processes deliver better, more optimal results. These are all areas where Smart Computing solutions can deliver real value to the business, through the introduction of

Smart Computing process applications based on the design principles that Forrester has called Dynamic Business Applications.

THE TARGET AUDIENCE

The abilities of Smart Computing to optimize the management of the balance sheet will meet a ready audience because the current recession has heightened CEO awareness of the importance of the balance sheet. The 2008 to 2009 recession was in many ways a balance-sheet-driven downturn. The housing crisis that was the trigger for the downturn was the result of consumer mortgage liabilities getting way ahead of the sustainable value of the home assets that consumers borrowed against. Similarly, the financial crisis that pushed the global economy to the brink of a depression occurred because of major imbalances between bank liabilities and assets — imbalances that had to be closed through massive infusions of government support. CEOs understand that they need to pay much more attention to the balance sheet, and the risks and opportunities that lurk in it, and not just the income statement of revenues and costs. Better technology generates more revenues when it allows businesses and governments to do new things with technology by addressing and solving problems that older technology could not solve.

Businesses will adopt Smart Computing technologies because they help them address the key challenge of optimizing the value of their balance sheets, allowing them to move beyond financial assets and liabilities to their physical assets and liabilities (like electric grids or hospitals) and then to their intangible assets and liabilities (like a skilled workforce or brand). Assets and liabilities tend to be very industry-specific, even more so than processes that may be common across industries. And the task of optimizing the value of these assets and liabilities is definitely industry-specific because what optimization means will vary dramatically from industry to industry.

Financial services firms focus on financial assets and liabilities. A financial services company will place most emphasis on optimizing the value of its financial assets and liabilities, a medium emphasis on optimizing the value of its human assets, and a low value on optimizing the value of its physical assets. Telecommunications and transportation firms emphasize physical assets. Companies in these industries rely on vast quantities of physical assets, which require large capital investment. Business returns in these industries depend heavily on how extensively these assets are leveraged, as well as how firms can predict, minimize, and manage breakdowns in these physical assets more effectively when they do happen.· Professional services firms value human assets the most. A professional services firm that does primarily consulting will place most emphasis on optimizing the value of human assets, medium on financial assets, and little on physical assets; while a professional services firm that does outsourcing may place most of its emphasis on its physical assets, then its financial assets, and finally on its human assets.

Big data and use of smart computing techniques has been a potential topic in various research fields and areas like health care, public sector, retail, manufacturing personal data, etc. The research works on the said topic is to pull together the hardware, software, and network elements of Smart Computing. To get expertise in the skills and technologies that will be differentiators in Smart Computing. To have the ability to play the angles between horizontal and vertical solutions in an organization handling large volumes of data. In-depth understanding of the balance sheet issues facing specific industries.

A description of the importance of each of the chapter submissions:

- Chapter1: Big data offers huge potential to positively impact on the functioning of commercial organizations and governments by providing them a competitive advantage. To support Big Data, high performance computing platforms are required which impose systematic designs to unleash the full power of the Big Data. With Big Data technologies, we will hopefully be able to provide most relevant and most accurate social sensing feedback to better understand our society at real-time.
- Chapter 2: Although TCP work in wireless and wired-cum-wireless network, the performance is not up to the mark. After this the challenges that TCP faces in ad hoc network is presented. At last different proposals to make TCP work better in MANETs was presented.
- Chapter 3: An automatic diagnosis system for detecting breast cancer based on association rules and genetic algorithm is introduced. Feature extraction is the key for pattern recognition and classification. The best classifier will perform poorly if the features are not chosen well. Normally association rule mining does not work well for large data set. It is required to select proper threshold values for different objectives which is also a challenging task. Our method is free from all these limitations as genetic algorithm gives an exhaustive search for large input spaces.
- Chapter 4: An analytical approach is presented in this paper, which focus on reduction in convergence delay and packet loss. In this paper we conclude that whenever the breakage or failure occurs in network, OSPF regenerate routing table and routing tree according to the topology by finding the path having minimum cost. The time that is required by OSPF for regeneration is referred to as convergence delay. The duration of the convergence period of these protocols vary from hundred of milliseconds to tens of seconds which results into instability, leads to high packet loss rate. Quick convergence time is necessary to meet network based application requests and quality of service (QoS) prerequisites of modern dynamic vast-scale routing domains, such as data centres.
- Chapter 5: This paper propose application of image processing and machine learning in identifying three cotton leaf diseases through feature extraction. Using image processing, 12 types of features are extracted from cotton leaf image then the pattern was learned using BP Neural Network method in machine learning process. Three diseases have been diagnosed, namely powdery mildew, Downy mildew and leaf miner. The Neural Network classification performs well and could successfully detect and classify the tested disease.
- Chapter 6: Association rules are used for finding the association between two elements and shows relationship between them. The conclusion is extracted from confidence, cosine, AV analysis, lift, correlation and conviction analysis is that most of the people commented on teaching competency as well as the course designed. From the above analysis it can be concluded that the pedagogy of English teaching learning is affected more due to teaching incompetency and late learning at primary level in rural government schools.
- Chapter 7: The development of low cost Kannada text to Braille is necessary for Braille teaching people and help to visually impaired community in Karnataka. It will show the new way of conversion method for people working in computer environment. The software algorithm which is coded reads the sentence from the Input box of the Braille software tool and breaks them into characters and are counted up to the value of the enter key. The Braille code equivalent of each character is generated in the output box of the tool. The same technique can be used in various languages like Bengali, Hindi, Tamil, etc., The Braille code conversion process is a single step and the data transfer rate is normal and it is controllable. It is one of the best tool for visually impaired people and Braille learning people using computer technology.

- Chapter 8: The electrocardiogram is a noninvasive and the record of variation of the bio-potential signal of the human heartbeats. The ECG detection which shows the information of the heart and cardiovascular condition is essential to enhance the patient living quality and appropriate treatment. Filtering of ECG signal to remove this baseline wander while preserving the low frequency ECG clinical information is necessary. In the present paper effort has been made to perform the comparative analysis of five different filters that were statically analyzed and WMA filter performance is found to be sought for removal of baseline drift.
- Chapter 9: Many DSP algorithms are recursive in nature and represented by DFG's. In these, the maximum sampling frequency is dependent on the topology of the DFG. Iteration bound is the reciprocal of the maximum sampling frequency, which tells how fast DSP program can be implemented in hardware. Two algorithms (Longest Path Matrix and Minimum Cycle Mean) are used for computing iteration bound. The Minimum Cycle Mean algorithm is usually faster than the Longest Path Matrix algorithm. The iteration bound of Single Rate DFG is same as that of Multi Rate DFG. The Single Rate DFG contains more nodes and edges as compared to Multi Rate DFG.
- Chapter 10: Big Data will change the landscape of economic policy and economic research using Hadoop. As no of economic policy to be implemented by Government, it will be easy to handle e-Governance system by use of recent advances in Big Data. Big Data analysis tools like Map Reduce over Hadoop and HDFS, promise to help organizations better understand their customers and the marketplace, hopefully leading to better business decisions, economic policy and competitive advantages.
- Chapter 11: There is an incredible investment both in the business and in the research groups around enormous information. Since its introduction, association rule mining has become an important research area in data mining. It is troublesome to users or even specialists to suitably point out minimum support as a threshold. The utilization of a multi-objective evolutionary structure for association rule mining offers an enormous adaptability to endeavor in further work. In this chapter, a Pareto based genetic algorithm has been utilized to illuminate the multi-objective rule mining issue utilizing two measures - accuracy and comprehensibility. Using MapReduce platform, distributed parallel processing has been achieved for big data to find out the optimal association rules which can be as a role of dimensionality reduction method for big data.
- Chapter 12: It can be concluded that, judiciary selection of the conductor will lead to save energy in the transmission system as reduction of loss is nothing but saving of energy. Also saving of 1 MW of energy leads to save 800 tons of coal and 2000 tons of CO_2 emission reduction. So reconductoring the existing system with new HTLS conductor will lead to save energy with minimum impact on environment.
- Chapter 13: This chapter discusses about different facial feature extraction scheme. All of these schemes are implemented in Matlab. Based on the implementation, we have prepared a comparison table. After careful comparison of all of these approaches, we have found that the best performance can be achieved by using a hybrid approach, which is a combination of different techniques applied in the other approaches, as we can see that extraction of local and global features are both required for face recognition.
- Chapter 14: The purpose of Iris recognition, a biometrical based technology for personal identification and verification, is to recognize a person from his/her iris prints. In this chapter, an attempt has been made to present of different iris and periocular recognition methods separately. The study of different techniques provides a development of new technique in this area as combining

the iris and periocular features of both the eyes of same person and expected the more recognition accuracy than that of the existing approaches. The primary objective of this chapter is to improve the iris recognition accuracy by exploiting the iris and periocular information from both eyes simultaneously. Since this chapter provides idea of combining the iris and periocular features from both the eyes of same person works efficiently and expected better recognition accuracy compared to literature for the distantly acquired noisy iris images.

- Chapter 15: OpenCL is in no way a bad choice compared to CUDA, given a fair comparison. The performance gaps initially noted are stated due to API implementations, native kernel optimizations and the efficient use of memory. OpenCL also has portability as its main benefits, while CUDA continues to be refined by developers at NVIDIA. We also observed that OpenCL model (14) does not support architecture of CPU in terms of parallel operating and (6) has a different memory model.
- Chapter 16: Synthetic Aperture Radar (SAR) are imaging Radar, it uses electromagnetic radiation to illuminate the scanned surface and produce high resolution images in all-weather condition, day and night. Interference of signals causes noise and degrades the quality of the image, it causes serious difficulty in analyzing the images. Speckle is multiplicative noise that inherently exist in SAR images. Artificial Neural Network (ANN) have the capability of learning and is gaining popularity in SAR image processing. Multi-Layer Perceptron (MLP) is a feed forward artificial neural network model that consists of an input layer, several hidden layers, and an output layer
- Chapter 17: Biometrics refers to metrics related to human characteristics and Traits. Face Recognition is the process of identification of a person by their facial image. It has been an active area of research for several decades, but still remains a challenging problem because of the complexity of the human face. The objective is to authenticate a person, to have a FAR and FRR very low. This paper introduces a new approach for face recognition system using FFT algorithm. The database that contains the images is named as train database and the test image which is stored in test database is compared with the created train database.
- Chapter 18: Though image segmentation is a fundamental task in image analysis; it plays a vital role in the area of image processing. Its value increases in case of medical diagnostics through medical images like X-ray, PET, CT and MRI. In this paper, an attempt is taken to analyse a CT brain image. It has been segmented for a particular patch in the brain CT image that may be one of the tumours in the brain. The purpose of segmentation is to partition an image into meaningful regions with respect to a particular application. Image segmentation is a method of separating the image from the background, read the contents and isolating it.In this paper both the concept of clustering and thresholding technique with edge based segmentation methods like sobel, prewitt edge detectors is applied

CONCLUSION

The chapters furnished in the book have sighted the scope, utility and holistic role of Big data when integrated with smart computing techniques thus enriching the research areas like data mining, distributed network environment and literature.

Chapter 1
Big Data:
The Data Deluge

Jayshree Ghorpade-Aher
University of Pune, Pune

Anita Thengade
University of Pune, Pune

Reena Pagare
University of Pune, Pune

Santaji Ghorpade
IBM India Pvt. Ltd., India

Manik Kadam
Allana Institute, India

ABSTRACT

Today is the Computer Era, where the data is increasing exponentially. Managing such a huge data is a challenging job. Under the explosive increase of global data, the term of big data is mainly used to describe enormous datasets. The state-of-the-art of big data is discussed here. The discussions aim to provide a comprehensive overview and big-picture to readers of this existing research area. This chapter discusses the different models and technologies for Big Data; It also introduces Big data Storage. Big data has been a potential topic in various research fields and areas like healthcare, public sector, retail, manufacturing personal data, etc.

I. INTRODUCTION

Since last two decades, there is a huge amount of data collection and we need something to handle that, so as the development process we are moving from file to database, data-ware house, datacenters, and now the big term Big Data. Big data is data that exceeds the processing capacity of conventional database systems. The data is too big, moves too fast, or doesn't fit the structures of your database architectures. One must choose an appropriate way to gain value from this huge data. According to a report from International Data Corporation (IDC), in 2011; the overall created and copied data volume in the world was 1.8ZB ($\approx 10^{21}$B), which increased by nearly nine times within 5 years (Min, Shiwen, Yunhao, 2014). The various source for collection of such data are generated from online transactions, emails, videos, audios, images, click streams, logs, posts, search queries, health records, social networking interactions, science data, sensors and mobile phones and their applications. According to the recent survey, a personal computer holds about 500 terabytes. Various other sources like Facebook (log data of over 10 PB per

DOI: 10.4018/978-1-4666-8737-0.ch001

month), Google (processes 100 PB of data) electricity board, telecom industries, organizations, twitter (12 TB), railway, airlines (black box), stock exchange market etc. also add to the huge amount of data (≈5 EB of data was created by humans until 2003). Today this amount of information is created in just a day. Figure 1 specifies the various components of Big data. Today working with conventional databases and other software tools have not proven efficient while handling the large datasets.

Definition: *Big data is a term for massive data sets having large, more varied and complex structure with the difficulties of storing, analyzing and visualizing for further processes or results.*

In 2010, Apache Hadoop defined big data as datasets which could not be captured, managed, and processed by general computers within an acceptable scope.

May 2011, McKinsey & Company, a global consulting agency announced Big Data as the next frontier for innovation, competition, and productivity.

Doug Laney, an analyst of META (presently Gartner) defined challenges and opportunities brought about by increased data with a 3Vs model as shown in figure 1 [Seref & Duygu, 2013], that is the increase of Volume (*size of data increasing day by day*), Velocity (*processing of data*), and Variety (*Structured data inserts a data warehouse already tagged and easily sorted but, Unstructured data is random and difficult to analyze, Semi-structured data does not conform to fixed fields but contains tags to separate data elements*).

Figure 1. The 3 V's of Big Data

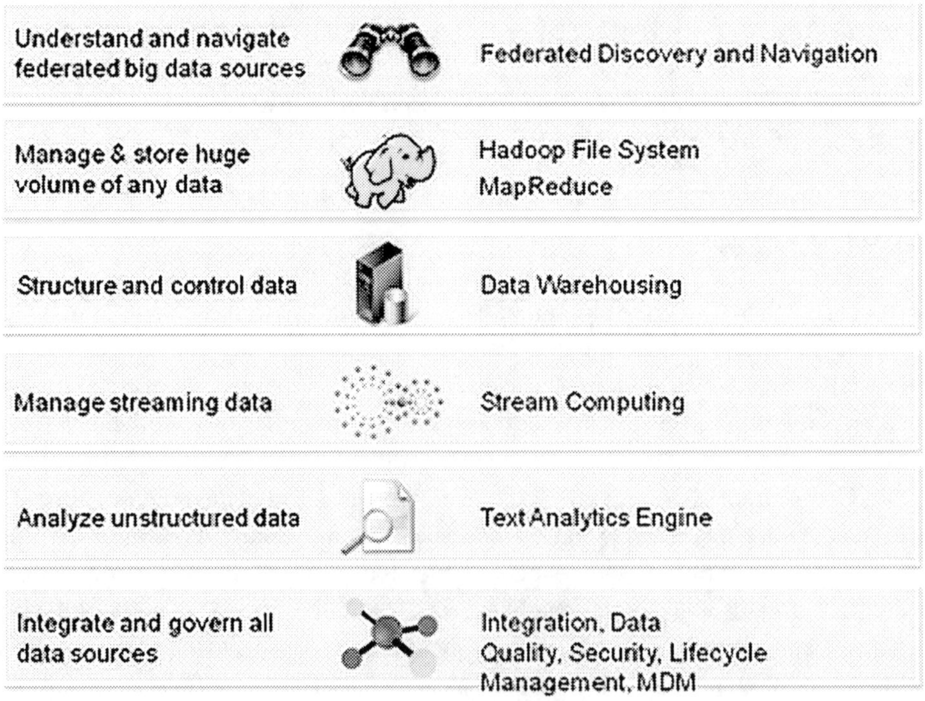

- **High-Volume:** It is the amount and size of the data. Enterprises are awash with ever-growing data of all types, moving from TBs to even PBs of information.

Memory unit	Size	Binary size
kilobyte (kB/KB)	10^3	2^{10}
megabyte (MB)	10^6	2^{20}
gigabyte (GB)	10^9	2^{30}
terabyte (TB)	10^{12}	2^{40}
petabyte (PB)	10^{15}	2^{50}
exabyte (EB)	10^{18}	2^{60}
zettabyte (ZB)	10^{21}	2^{70}
yottabyte (YB)	10^{24}	2^{80}

For example, turn 12 terabytes of Tweets created each day into improved product sentiment analysis and convert 350 billion annual meter readings to better predict power consumption.

- **High-Velocity:** It is the speed rate in collecting or acquiring or generating or processing of data. For time-sensitive processes such as catching fraud, big data must be used as it streams into the enterprise in order to maximize its value. The processing of the data should be efficient to increase the performance of the system. Even a delay of few nano seconds will affect the output of the system. For example, scrutinizing nearly 5 million trade events created each day to identify potential fraud.
- **High-Variety:** Big data is any type of data - structured and unstructured data such as text, sensor data, audio, video, click streams, log files and more. New insights are created while analyzing these data types together. For example, monitoring 1000's of live video feeds from surveillance cameras to target points of interest and exploiting the 90+% data growth in images, video and documents to improve customer satisfaction.

II. TECHNOLOGIES AND MODELS

Technologies

Big data has become of the important part of the computerized world, so let us understand the various technologies which are closely associated with big data.

DACHE

Dache is a *data-aware cache system* for big-data applications, which uses the MapReduce framework. Dache (Yaxiong, Jie & Cong, 2014) aims at extending the MapReduce framework by incorporating a cache layer, which efficiently identifies and accesses the cache items in a MapReduce job. The cache-manager manages the cache items and answers the queries for mappers and reducers. In Dache, tasks submit their intermediate results to the cache manager. A task queries the cache manager before executing the actual computing work. Dache is implemented by extending Hadoop and it designs the cache request-reply protocol.

Cache Description Scheme: The cache description scheme has two parts, i.e. map and reduce.

Map Phase Cache Description

Figure 2 (Yaxiong, Jie & Cong, 2014) describes the architecture of Dache. A cache item is obtained from the source input and various operations are applied on the input to properly index the cache item produced by the workers in the map phase. Cache refers to the intermediate data that is produced by worker nodes/processes during the execution of a MapReduce task. The steps are as follows:

- Store a piece of cached data in a Distributed File System (DFS).
- Describe a cache item is by a 2-tuple: { Origin, Operation }.
  where, Origin = name of a file in the DFS and
  Operation = a linear list of available operations performed on the Origin file.

The exact format of the cache description of different applications varies according to their specific semantic contexts. Cache descriptions can be recursive when multiple worker nodes/processes are sequentially processing a data file. On the other hand, this recursive description could be expanded to an iterative one by directly appending the later operations to the older ones.

Reduce Phase Cache Description

In the reduce phase, a mechanism is devised to take into consideration the partition operations applied on the output in the map phase. A method is used for reducers to utilize the cached results in the map

Figure 2. Architecture of Dache

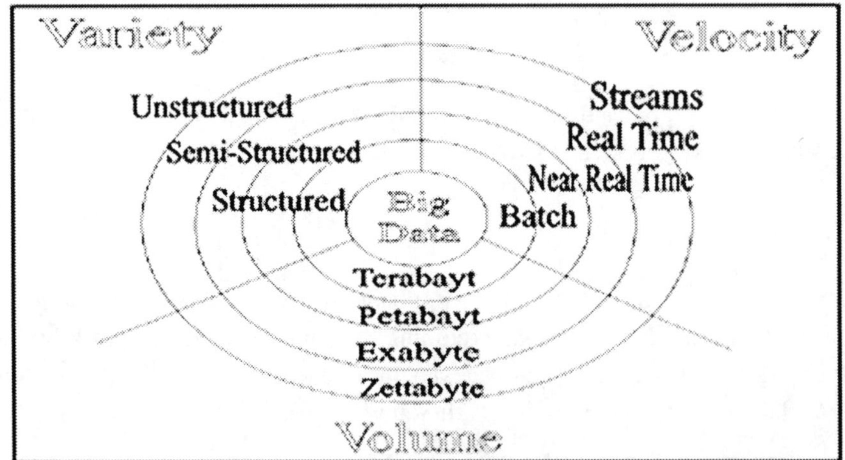

phase to accelerate the execution of the MapReduce job. The input for the reduce phase is also a list of key-value pairs, where the value could be a list of values. Also, in the reduce phase, the original input and the applied operations are required.

- Original input = stored intermediate results of the map phase in the DFS.
- Applied operations = operations with unique IDs that are specified by the user.

The cached results, unlike those generated in the Map phase, cannot be directly used as the final output. Hence, a finer description (original data files generated in the Map phase) of the original input of the cache items in the reduce phase is applied.

MapReduce Advantages

- Automatic Parallelization:
    - Size of RAW INPUT DATA ➔ instantiate multiple MAP tasks
    - Number of intermediate <key, value> partitions ➔ instantiate multiple REDUCE tasks
- Run-time:
    - Data partitioning
    - Task scheduling
    - Handling machine failures
    - Managing inter-machine communication
- Completely transparent to the programmer/analyst/user

Hadoop

Hadoop is widely used in big data applications in the industry, for example spam filtering, network searching, clickstream analysis, and social recommendation. Extremely large datasets found in Big Data projects are difficult to work with using conventional databases, statistical software, and visualization tools. Massively parallel software, such as Hadoop, running on tens, hundreds, or even thousands of servers is more suitable for Big Data challenges.

The Map/Reduce architecture provides a parallel processing framework that might be a better solution than multithreading, whereas Hadoop Distributed File System (HDFS) is an essential innovation to the performance of the Hadoop framework. Parallel programming can be implemented using multithreading and carefully handling/co-ordinating the access of each thread to the shared data. Hadoop eliminates the shared state completely and reduces the issues such as no race or deadlock conditions. Hadoop is a Java based framework and heterogeneous open source platform. It is not a replacement for database, warehouse or ETL (Extract, Transform, Load) strategy, but it includes a distributed file system, analytics and data storage platforms and a layer that manages parallel computation, workflow and configuration administration. HDFS runs across the nodes in a Hadoop cluster and connects together the file systems on many input and output data nodes to make them into one big file system. Map/reduce is a specialized directed acyclic graph which can be used for many purposes (Ho, R., 2008). It is organized as a "*map*" function which transforms a piece of data into some number of key/value pairs. Each of these elements will then be sorted by their key and reach to the same node, where a "*reduce*" function is used to merge the values (of the same key) into a single result as shown below in figure 3 (Ho, R., 2008).

Figure 3. Map/Reduce Directed Acyclic Graph

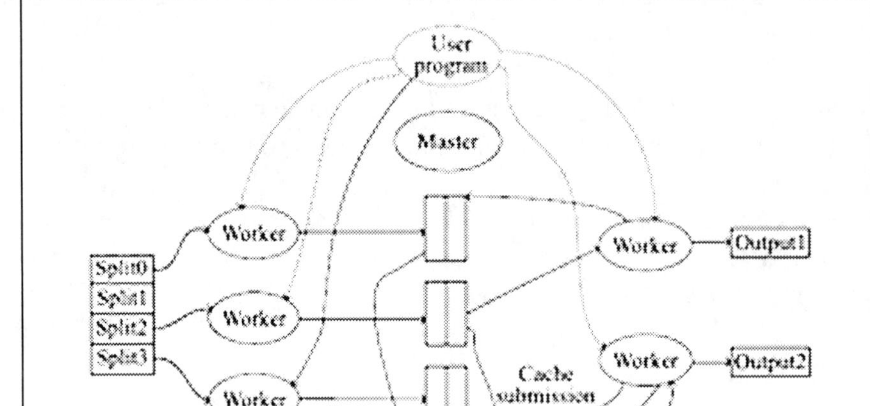

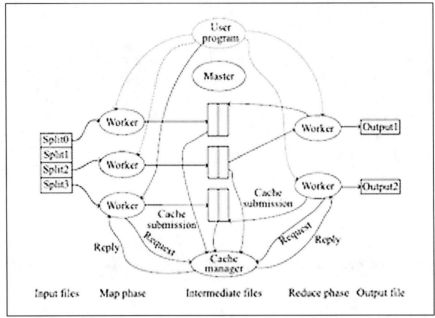

The code snippet below shows typical map and reduce functions. Several may be chained together to implement a parallel algorithm for different use cases.

```
map (input_record)
{
...
emit(k1, v1)
...
emit(k2, v2)
...
}
reduce (key, values)
{
aggregate = initialize()
while (values.has_next)
{
aggregate = merge(values.next)
}
collect(key, aggregate)
}
```

Platforms for Large-Scale Data Analysis

- Parallel DBMS technologies
    - Popularly used for more than two decades
        - Research Projects: Gamma, Grace, etc.
        - Commercial: Multi-billion dollar industry but access to only a privileged few
    - Relational Data Model
    - Indexing
    - Familiar SQL interface
    - Advanced query optimization
    - Well understood and studied
- MapReduce
    - Overview:
        - Data-parallel programming model
        - An associated parallel and distributed implementation for commodity clusters
    - Pioneered by Google -Processes 20 PB of data per day
    - Popularized by open-source Hadoop - Used by Yahoo!, Facebook, Amazon, and the list is growing

Internet-Of-Things (IOT)

… a new phase of the Information Society – the Internet of Things in which the web will not only link computers but potentially every object created by mankind. – Viviane Reding.

The semantic origin of the expression *IoT* is composed by two words and concepts: "Internet" and "Thing", where "Internet" can be defined as "The world-wide network of interconnected computer networks which is based on a standard communication protocol", while "Thing" is "an object not precisely identifiable". Thus, semantically, "*Internet of Things*" means "*a world-wide network of interconnected objects uniquely addressable, based on standard protocol.* 'The Internet of Things' is a concept originally coined and introduced by MIT, Auto-ID Center and intimately linked to RFID and electronic product code (EPC).

As shown in figure 4, from any time, any place connectivity for anyone, we will now have connectivity for anything!

Large amount of networking sensors are embedded into various devices and machines in the real world and deployed in different fields which collect various kinds of data, such as environmental data, geographical data, astronomical data, and logistic data. A report from Intel pointed out that big data in IoT has three features that conform to the big data paradigm:

- abundant terminals generating masses of data;
- data generated by IoT is usually semi-structured or unstructured;
- data of IoT is useful only when it is analyzed (Chen et al. 2014).

As the data is collected from various sources, it differs from the normal data and has classical characteristics such as heterogeneity, variety, unstructured feature, noise, and high redundancy. Proficient big

Figure 4. Internet of Things (source - ITU adapted from Nomura Research Institute)

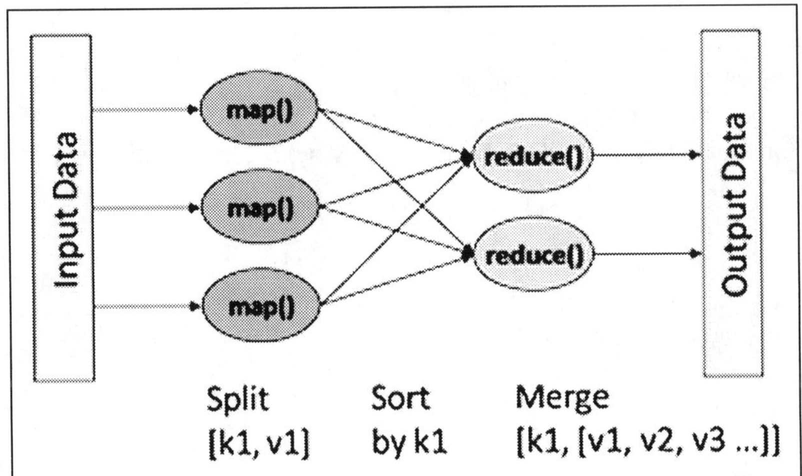

data technologies should be used to promote the development of IoT. The extensive and prevalent deployment of IoT drives the high growth of data both in quantity and category, thus it gives the opportunity for the application and development of big data. Also, the research advances, new trends, challenges and business models of IoT are accelerated by the application of big data technology. According to a report by Lyndsey Gilpin (June 2014), Intel is looking to be a leader in the food and agriculture industry with projects to address water and food security, safety, and sustainability by using the two technologies- big data and IoT [Lyndsey Gilpin June 13, 2014). Intel is driving the movement to use big data to solve large-scale food security problems, starting with those in California. Through its short term projects, the company is increasing research initiatives and data access, but long-term, Intel wants to create an accessible, reliable reference platform for scientists around the world

Cloud

Cloud computing is an extremely successful paradigm of service oriented computing, which has revolutionized the use of computing infrastructure (Divyakant & Amr El, 2011). Cloud has three important paradigms:

- Infrastructure as a Service (IaaS),
- Platform as a Service (PaaS), and
- Software as a Service (SaaS).
- Also, now-a-days we have Database as a Service or Storage as a Service.

Elasticity, reliability, efficiency, agility, performance, pay-per-use, low upfront investment, low time to market, virtualization and security are some of the key features that make CC a ubiquitous paradigm for deploying extensively large applications. These applications result in a tremendous increase in the scale of the data generated. Thus, consumption of this heavy data is also a challenge. The big data differs from the traditional data in following aspects (Robert, 2012):

Traditional Data:

- Large scale
- Highly centralized
- Structured
  - files / records / databases
- Sequential
- Indexed
- Processing Transactions

Big Data:

- Massive scale
- Highly distributed
- Unstructured (processed using ETL – *Extract, Translate and Load* tool)
  - emails / audio-video / spreadsheets / documents / blogs / journals / books / search data / chat sessions / sensor data / geo-spatial data / log files etc.
- Random
- Patterns and relationships

Cloud Computing (CC) and big data go hand-in-hand. Big data is the object of the computation-intensive operation and stresses the storage capacity of a cloud system. CC uses huge computing and storage resources, thus providing big data applications with fine-grained computing capacity. Cloud computing transforms the IT architecture while big data influences business decision-making. The emergence of big data accelerates the development of cloud computing. The distributed storage technology based on CC effectively manages big data; whereas the parallel computing capacity of CC improves the efficiency of data acquisition and data analysis. Cloud Computing and Big Data work together to have *Stream Computing*, providing the improved forecasting and predictive analysis across all scientific disciplines. It includes individually tailored/personalized solutions, services and experiences.

Models

A phenomenon known as the *data deluge* explains the immense increase in the quantity of data/information generated by business, government, and science. The various Big data models, used for different applications are:

Virtual Data Space: VDS Model

Big Data usually includes data sets with sizes beyond the ability of commonly used software tools to capture, curate, manage, and process the data within a tolerable elapsed time. Big data sizes are a constantly moving target, ranging from a few dozen terabytes to many petabytes of data in a single data set. The explosive growth of information has taken us into the era of big data. For such a massive scale of data, semantic integration rather than simple storage is necessary. Also, the diversity of data schema and format hinders the unification of data model, especially for non-structured data such as images and audios.

The massive, distributed, heterogeneous and diverse features of big data have raised challenges to the traditional data management systems. Considering these circumstances, the dataspace was put forward as

Figure 5. Virtual Dataspace Framework

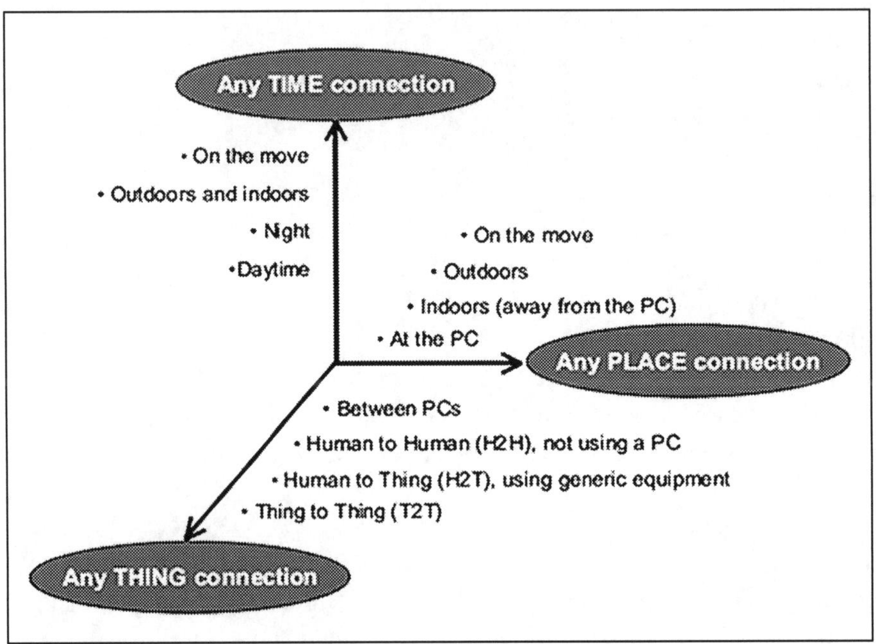

a new service mode for big data management. Thus, the development and innovation of *DataSpace*, virtual dataspace (*VDS*) (Wei, Changjun, Yang, & Xin, 2013) model is proposed for big data management. The model incorporates data management methods according to the actual need in scientific domain. VDS is business intelligence in Big Data and constructed in virtual technologies. As shown in figure 6 [Lin et al. 2013], VDS refers to a set of subject, data, and flexible services constructed by virtual technologies. The VDS framework mainly comprises a very important aspect called *virtualization*, wherein it masks the complexity of data integration, data relationship, format diversity and provides various flexible data services. Here, the local ontologies are created from data sources and are mapped to form a global ontology. As per the ontology mapping, the access log and user feedback are considered for data evolution. The effectiveness of VDS is used for data management in material domain.

Big Data Model for Recommender Systems

Today social media generates more and more information in a short period of time. Social networks and enterprise social software has two key features:

- The connections between the people that use them and
- The information they share.

As shown in figure 6, the intersection of social media and big data (Dion, 2011) will result in:

- Big data-enabled applications that are plugged into consumer and enterprise social networks.

Figure 6. Social Media and big data

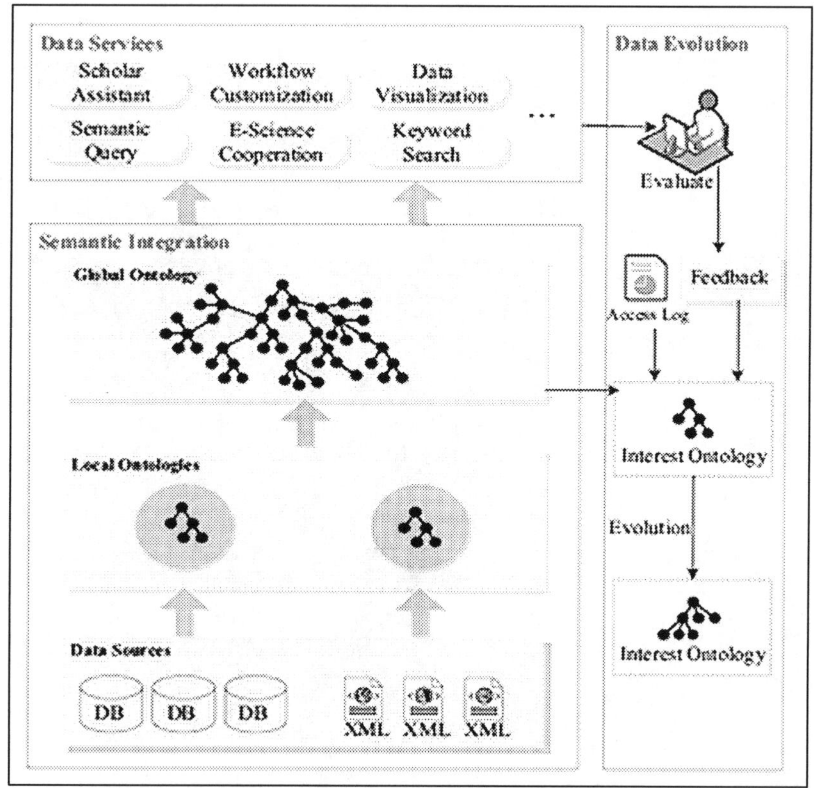

- The blurring of external and internal big data.
- Privacy, governmental, and regulatory concerns will grow.
- Analytics that finds you.
- Cloud big data analytics emerges.

Social networking services and cloud computing has gained a great popularity amongst its users. As information systems are becoming sophisticated and mobile, the amount of data is rapidly increasing every year. The model incorporates factors related to social networks and is applied to information recommendation with respect to various social behaviors, which increase the reliability of the recommended information. The big data model has the flexibility to expand for incorporating more sophisticated additional factors, as per the requirement. The big data model is used for storing and processing data used in information recommendation, and processing the data with Map-Reduce.

The analysis of big data helps us to understand the organization of the social networking system, which serves as a method of communication between users, the role of it in the community and the way and the path of communication. As seen in Figure 7 (Xiaoyuen, Lianhua, Minjoo, & Minsoo, 2012) the data of the friendship between users in social media, clubs, contents or comments is considered to make a data model to recommend information. Among big data, clubs or contents of related items or categories is used to make a data model, so that the accuracy of the recommendation system can be improved,

Figure 7. Data Model for Information Recommendation

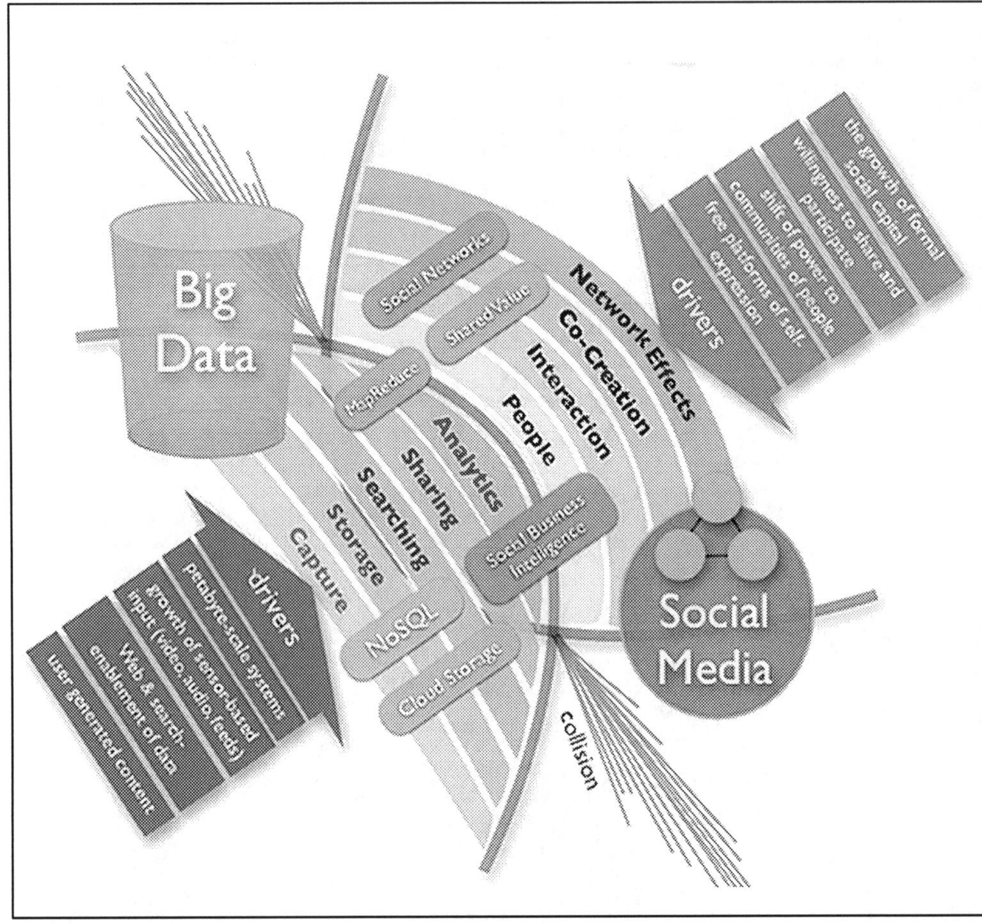

based on the preference of the individual. The research on the big data model has different key features that affect the degree of confidence in information recommendation and increases the understanding of basic reliability.

The Store, Schedule and Switch (SSS) Model

The SSS model is a new data delivery model in the Big Data Era. The Store, Schedule and Switch (SSS) model provides scheduled data delivery services to different applications, handling the QoS in the network. SSS (Weiqiang, Fengqin, Wei, Yaohui & Weisheng, 2013) networks give the timeless delivery of data as per the requirement, thus able to make use of resources in more balanced and controlled way. Here, the data storage becomes part of the network, uses the dynamic virtual circuit switching technique to provide the scheduled data delivery services to various applications. In today's data networks, fragmentation and packetization are the two important aspects for data delivery. The applications packetized the data before entering the network and then deliver it on a per-packet basis in the network until all pieces have reached their destination. This makes packet processing/forwarding the only function the network has to perform, simplifies the application/network interaction and consequently, drives application innovations. But, the performance of data transfer (i.e. moving of big data from one side of the network to another) is affected by the higher traffic volume and larger data size. the movement of data files is difficult, in a congested network, without the use of concurrent TCP flows, or other transport level optimizations.

Also the network operators find it difficult to deploy a new service on top of a shared packet switched network, which is prone to unpredictable congestion at all times. As a result, performing consistent and differentiated services to big data, which have already been packetized, is difficult. This delivery model makes use of mass storage and fast (virtual) circuit switching. Data sources assign a delivery priority to each piece of big data. The priority is used by the network to decide at which moment the data should be delivered or moved.

An SSS network, as shown in figure 8 is capable of providing scheduled network services in the form of standard APIs. The two types of interfaces are:

- Interface between the scheduler and all data sources/sinks, and
- Interface between the scheduler and all switching nodes,

Figure 8. Scheduled Network Services

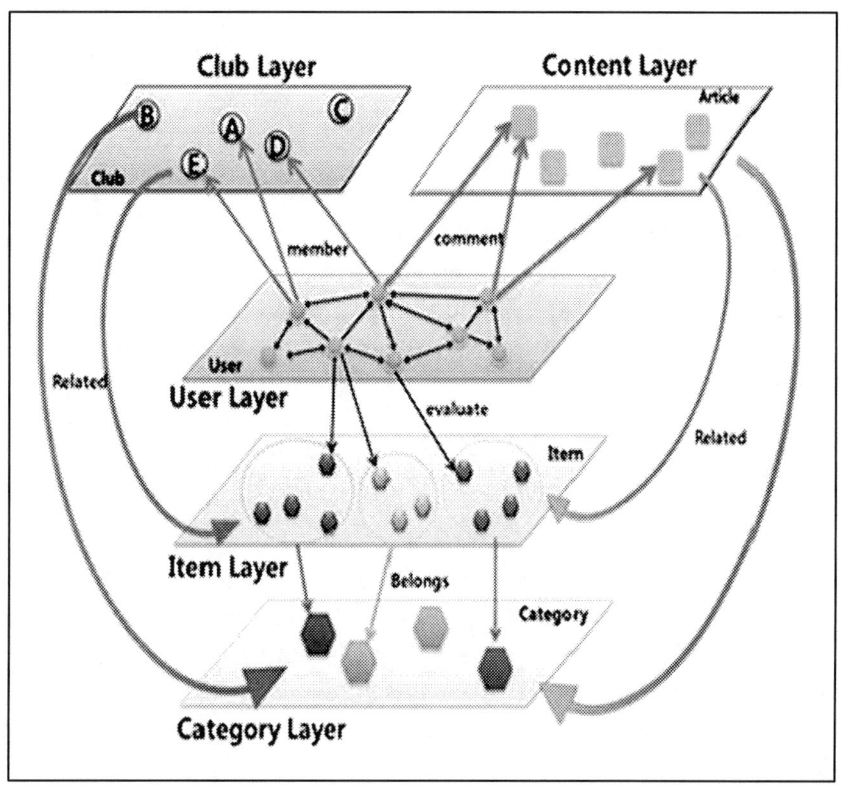

The data in the batch are delivered to their destination applications through their respective procedures. SSS does not require storage on every switching node, but those switching nodes which are close to the data source/sinks need to be equipped with storage. Also, when the network is too large, it is difficult to establish a high capacity (virtual) circuit across the whole network. In such case, installing storage on intermediate nodes improves the network performance by delivering data in 2 or more stops.

III. BIGDATA STORAGE

HACE theorem: Big Data starts with large-volume, **h**eterogeneous, **a**utonomous sources with distributed and decentralized control, and seeks to explore **c**omplex and **e**volving relationships among data [Xindong, Xingquan, Gong-Qing, & Wei, 2014].

Some of the key features of the Big Data are listed below:

- *Huge Data with Heterogeneous and Diverse Dimensionality:*

Each information collector uses its own schemata for data recording and nature of each application also result in diverse representation of the data. e.g. CT scan of an individual, DNA or genomic related test.

- *Autonomous sources with Distributed and Decentralized Control:*

Being autonomous each data sources is able to generate and collect information without involving any centralized control. e.g. Google & Facebook are the Big Data related applications.

- *Complex and Evolving Relationships:*

As the volume of Big Data increases, so the complexity in the relationships will increase. e.g. Facebook(friend connections) or Twitter(followers)

Big data storage (Chen et. al. 2014) refers to the storage and management of large-scale datasets while achieving reliability and availability of data. Massive storage technologies can be used for storing a huge amount of data.

Massive Storage Technology and Architecture Evolution

Today the data is increasing at an exponential speed, which is created by the different users and organizations. This data should be stored in an appropriate format so that it is easily accessible for further processing. In a computing environment, devices designed for storing data are termed storage devices or simply storage. There are various types of storages such as internal hard disks, external disk arrays and tapes. The use of storages varies based on the type of data and the rate at which it is created. This technology evolution is supported by the intelligent networked storage as shown in figure 9 (G. Somasundaram & Alok Shrivastava, 2009).

Figure 9. Storage Technology and Architecture Evolution

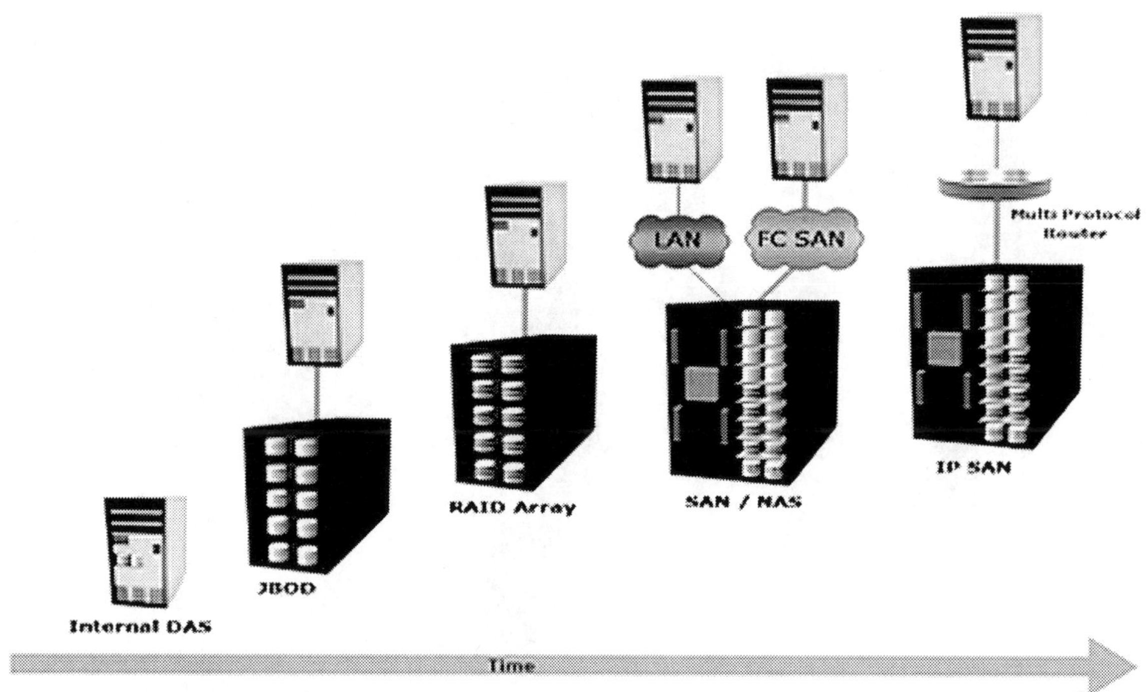

Direct Attached Storage (DAS): In DAS various hard disks are directly connected with servers, and data management is server-centric, such that storage devices are peripheral equipment's, each of which takes a certain amount of I/O resource and is managed by individual application software. For this reason, DAS is only suitable to interconnect servers with a small scale.

DAS is ideal for local data provision with quick deployment for small environments. It has very simple deployment process. Small organization or industries can have DAS Set up with low capital expense. There are few Challenges with DAS like scalability, more downtime for maintenance and limited resources. Scalability is limited in terms of number of connectivity ports to hosts, number of addressable disks and distance limitations. DAS needs more downtime required for maintenance with internal system of DAS. It has limited ability to share resources.

Now a day's Business need is to make Just-in-time information available to the users i.e high availability of data. It demands the integration of information infrastructure with business processes and flexible and resilient storage architecture. But, DAS could not meet these challenges and hence Storage Networking like FC SAN, NAS, IP SAN emerged as a solution.

Network Attached Storage (NAS): NAS is actually an auxillary storage equipment of a network. It is directly connected to a network through a hub or switch through TCP/IP protocols. In NAS, data is transmitted in the form of files. Figure 10 shows the evolution of file sharing technology (G. Somasundaram, Alok Shrivastava, 2009).

Figure 10. File Sharing Technology Evolution

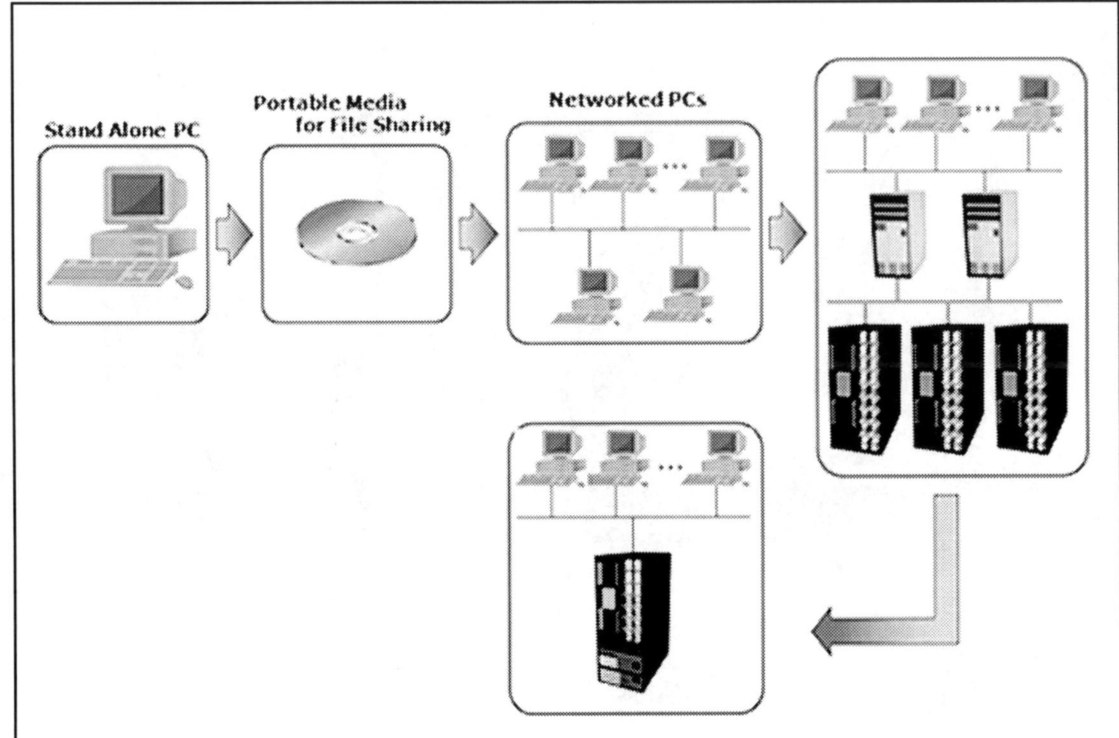

NAS Benefits

- NAS has centralized storage architecture.
- Improved flexibility: Compatible with Unix and Windows
- Scalability: It enables organizations to maximize their data center real estate with a scalable system that can start small and grow to multiple petabytes
- High availability through native clustering
- Provides security integration to environment (user authentication and authorization).

NAS File Sharing Protocols are CIFS and NFS. NAS is implemented as Integrated NAS and Gateway NAS. As shown in figure 11 (G. Somasundaram, Alok Shrivastava, 2009), the various components of NAS are NAS Head and Storage Array.

Storage Area Network (SAN): SAN is especially designed for data storage with a scalable and bandwidth intensive network, for example a high-speed network with optical fiber connections. In SAN, data storage management is relatively independent within a storage local area network, where multipath based data switching among any internal nodes is utilized to achieve a maximum degree of data sharing and data management.

Figure 11. File Components of NAS

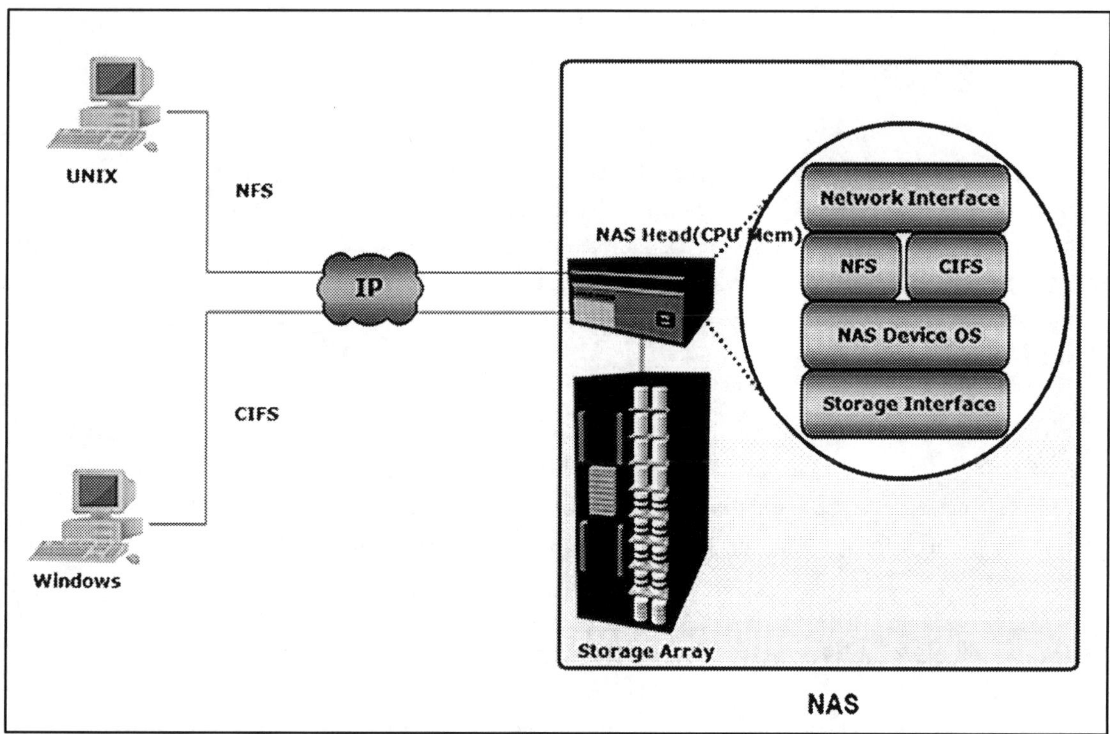

Salient Features of SAN

- Dedicated high speed network of servers and shared storage devices
- Provide block level data access
- Resource Consolidation: Centralized storage and management
- Scalability: Theoretical limit is approximately 15 million devices
- Secure Access

Components of SAN

- ***Node ports:*** Ports are available on HBA in host, each port has transmit (Tx) link and receive (Rx) link. HBAs perform low-level interface functions automatically to minimize impact on host performance. Examples of nodes are hosts, storage and tape library.
- ***Cabling:*** SAN implementation uses Copper cables for short distance and Optical fiber cables for long distance.

Two Types of Optical Cables

Single-mode: It can carry single beams of light and useful with distance up to 10 KM.

Multi-mode: It can carry multiple beams of light simultaneously and useful with distance up to 500 meters

- ***Interconnecting devices:*** Basis for SAN communication needs Hubs, Switches and directors.
- ***Storage array: It*** provides storage consolidation and centralization. Features of an array are high Availability/Redundancy, high Performance, Business Continuity and Multiple host connectivity.
- ***SAN management software:*** A suite of tools used in a SAN to manage the interface between host and storage arrays. They provide integrated management of SAN environment and web based GUI or CLI.

The important factors for a distributed system to store massive data are Consistency, Availability and Partition Tolerance. The research on big data promotes the development of storage mechanisms for big data. Existing storage mechanisms like DAS, NAS and SAN of big data may be classified into three bottom-up levels: (i) file systems, (ii) databases, and (iii) programming models.

IV. KEY APPLICATIONS

Big data is considered to be the next frontier for Innovation, Competition and Productivity. There are many applications of big data analytics for retailers to manage supply chain and logistics, merchandising, pricing, marketing, and advertising. Advanced analysis of Big data helps to identify the hidden patterns, unknown correlations, etc. Thus, provides a better business decision power – strategic and operational for effective marketing, customer satisfaction and finally the increase in revenue.

The term big data has come to be used to describe multi-terabytes of data sets. As more and more organizations are stepping out of the traditional boundaries of the enterprise to understand the impact of the environment on their business, big data keeps growing bigger day-by-day. Social media channels, websites, automatic censors at the workplace and robotics are producing a plethora of structured, unstructured and semi-structured data. Advanced analytics based on big data is the art of putting all these fragmented and often disconnected pieces together and generate actionable insights for the enterprise.

The astonishing growth and diversity in connected data continues to profoundly affect how people make sense of this data. The virtuous circle (Wei, M.Brian, Iman, & Schahram, 2013) represents the interconnection between these various sources of data. Connected people produce a data stream that's analyzed by connected computers, thus the raw data is processed to induce knowledge, which generates the intelligence and it proliferates back to the connected people.

V. CHALLENGES

Big Data also has its own set of problems and challenges (Avita, Mohammad, RHGoudar, 2013). Some of them are listed below:

Data representation: Many datasets have certain levels of heterogeneity in type, structure, semantics, organization, granularity, and accessibility. Data representation makes data more meaningful for computer analysis and user. Improper data representation will reduce the value of the original data.

Redundancy reduction and data compression: Generally, there is a high level of redundancy in datasets. Redundancy reduction and data compression is effective to reduce the indirect cost of the entire system on the premise that the potential values of the data are not affected.

Data life cycle management: Big data stores large volume of data, so during accessing data the life cycle of data should be maintained properly.

Data confidentiality: Big data service providers could not effectively maintain and analyze huge datasets because of their limited capacity. They use tools to analyze such data, which increase the potential safety risks.

Domain and application knowledge: Domain and application knowledge provides essential information for designing Big Data mining algorithms and systems, as it identifies the right features for modeling the underlying data.

Expendability and scalability: the analytical system of big data must support present and future datasets.

Availability of enterprise-ready products and tools

VI. CONCLUSION

Big data triggers the revolution of thinking. It offers huge potential to positively impact on the functioning of commercial organizations and governments by providing them a competitive advantage. To support Big Data, high performance computing platforms are required which impose systematic designs to unleash the full power of the Big Data. With Big Data technologies, we will hopefully be able to provide most relevant and most accurate social sensing feedback to better understand our society at real-time.

REFERENCES

Chen, Mao, & Liu. (2014). *Big Data: A Survey.* Springer.

Divyakant & El Abbadi. (2011). *Big Data and Cloud Computing: Current State and Future Opportunities*. ACM.

Han, Tian, Yoon, & Lee. (2012). *A Big Data Model supporting Information Recommendation in Social Networks*. IEEE.

Hinchcliffe, D. (2011). *How social media and big data will unleash what we know*. Retrieved from http://www.zdnet.com/blog/hinchcliffe/how-social-media-and-big-data-will-unleash-what-we-know/1533

Ho, R. (2008). *How Hadoop Map/Reduce works*. Retrieved April 2013, from http://architects.dzone.com/articles/how-hadoopmapreduce-work

June, L. G. (2014). *How Intel is using IoT and big data to improve food and water security*. Retrieved from www.techrepublic.com/article/how-intel-is-using-iot-and-big-data-to-improve-food-and-water-security/

Katal, Wazid, & Goudar. (2013). *Big Data: Issues, Challenges, Tools and Good Practices*. IEEE.

Keahey, R. (2012). *Cloud Computing and Big Data*. Retrieved from http://www.slideshare.net/rkeahey/cloud-computing-and-big-data

Lin, W., Hu, C., Li, Y., & Cheng, X. (2013). Virtual Dataspace-A Service Oriented Model for Scientific Big Data. *IEEE Fourth International Conference on Emerging Intelligent Data and Web Technologies*. doi:10.1109/EIDWT.2013.5

Sagiroglu, S., & Sinanc, D. (2013). *Big Data: A Review*. IEEE.

Somasundaram, Shrivastava, & EMC Educational Services. (2009), *Information Storage and Management - Storing, Managing, and Protecting Digital Information*. Wiley India.

Sun, W., Li, F., Guo, W., Jin, Y., & Hu, W. (2013). *Store, Schedule and Switch – A New Data Delivery Model in the Big Data Era. In Proceedings of IEEE ICTON* (p. 13). IEEE.

Wei Tan, M., Blake, Saleh, & Dustdar. (2013). Social-Network-Sourced Big Data Analytics. *IEEE Internet Computing*, 62-69.

Wu, Zhu, Wu, & Ding. (2014). Data Mining with Big Data. *IEEE Transactions on Knowledge and Data Engineering, 26*(1).

Zhao, Wu, & Liu. (2014). Dache- A Data Aware Caching for Big-Data Applications Using the Map Reduce Framework. *Tsinghua Science and Technology, 19*(1), 39-50.

KEY TERMS AND DEFINITIONS

Big Data: "Big Data are high-volume, high-velocity, and/or high-variety information assets that require new forms of processing to enable enhanced decision making, insight discovery and process optimization" (Gartner 2012).

Cloud Computing: "Cloud computing is an emerging computing technology that uses the internet and central remote servers to maintain data and applications."

DAS: Direct Attached Storage (e.g. storage controller on motherboards handling IDE/ATA, USB drives). It refers to a digital storage system directly attached to a server or workstation, without a storage network in between. It is mainly used to differentiate non-networked storage from the concepts of storage area network (SAN) and network-attached storage (NAS) (Wikipedia).

Internet of Things: " The Internet of Things, also called The Internet of Objects, refers to a wireless network between objects, usually the network will be wireless and self-configuring, such as household appliances" (Wikipedia).

NAS: Network Attached Storage (e.g. SaMBa, NFS, FTP). NAS is file-level computer data storage connected to a computer network providing data access to a heterogeneous group of clients. NAS not only operates as a file server, but is specialized for this task either by its hardware, software, or configuration of those elements (Wikipedia).

Recommender System: Recommender systems or recommendation systems are a subclass of information filtering system that seek to predict the 'rating' or 'preference' that user would give to an item or social element they had not yet considered, using a model built from the characteristics of an item or the user's choice.

SAN: Storage Area Network (e.g. SCSI, Fibre Channel, iSCSI). SAN is a high-speed network of storage devices that connects the various storage devices with servers. It provides block-level storage that can be accessed by the applications running on any networked servers.

Chapter 2
Transmission Control Protocol for Mobile Ad Hoc Network

Sukant Kishoro Bisoy
C. V. Raman College of Engineering, India

Prasant Kumar Pattnaik
KIIT University, India

ABSTRACT

The Transmission Control Protocol (TCP) is a reliable protocol of transport layer which delivers data over unreliable networks. It was designed in the context of wired networks. Due to popularity of wireless communication it is made to extend TCP protocol to wireless environments where wired and wireless network can work smoothly. Although TCP work in wireless and wired-cum-wireless network, the performance is not up to the mark. In literature lot of protocols has been proposed to adopt TCP in wireless mobile ad hoc network. In this, we present an overall view on this issue and detailed discussion of the major factors involved. In addition, we survey the main proposals which aim at adapting TCP to mobile and static Ad hoc environments. Specifically, we show how TCP can be affected by mobility and its interaction with routing protocol in static and dynamic wireless ad hoc network.

1. INTRODUCTION

In military domain the wireless communication happens through point-to-point radio links. Wireless network can be categorized into wired-cum-wireless networks, that is wireless network at the periphery of wired network and totally wireless networks also called the mobile ad hoc networks. In case of the wired-cum-wireless network, the wired networks provide a high-speed backbone and the wireless LAN is attached at the periphery of the wired network. The wireless network area is divided into smaller regions called cells. A fixed base station provides an interface between the wired and wireless part of the network and controls each cell. The Mobile Hosts (MH) can move freely from one cell to another. Any call originating from one wireless network to another wireless network, passes through the wired backbone. In case of mobile ad hoc networks there are no fixed base stations. Each MH movement is independent of the movement of other hosts and it can enter or leave the system at any time. There is no fixed backbone and the MHs cooperate to deliver the messages from one MH to another.

DOI: 10.4018/978-1-4666-8737-0.ch002

Ad Hoc Networks are complex distributed systems that consist of wireless mobile or static nodes that can freely and dynamically self-organize. In this way they form arbitrary, and temporary "Ad hoc" networks topologies, allowing devices to seamlessly interconnect in areas with no pre-existing infrastructure. MANETs are self-configuring infrastructure-less networks that adapt dynamically to changing environments. In contrast to cellphone technology, MANETs are able to support multi-hop wireless communication over a shared medium. However, the capacity and performance of MANETs are much lower, compared to cellphone networks, and informing future users and service developers on the limitations as well as the advantages of this technology is essential for proliferation of the MANET technology. While MANET technology is very suitable for tactical communication, many IP-based protocols are not directly usable in MANETs. These protocols were developed in a strictly wire-based network domain, where attributes like interference and packet loss are less dominant and better controlled than in wireless multi-hop networks. For instance, queue loss is the sole contributor to packet loss, while medium-based bit errors are but non-existent. In MANETs, the Bit Error Rate (BER) is much higher than in wired networks (several orders of magnitude). Protocols that anticipate the cause of packet loss to be caused by queue drop-tail may make the wrong assumption in MANETs, reacting badly in this situation.

2. TCP OVERVIEW

TCP (Transmission Control Protocol) (Postel,1981) was designed to provide reliable end-to-end delivery of data over unreliable networks. The Transmission Control Protocol (TCP) has become an essential protocol for Internet communication due to most of the internet traffic carries by TCP. It provides important function like rate control, flow control and traffic congestion without which the Internet is useless. However, TCP makes several assumptions about the network. It assumes the packet loss is the only reason of network congestion, and not transmission errors. It also assumes that the Round Trip Time (RTT) is relatively constant (little jitter) and that rerouting happens very quickly. This assumption is limited to wired network.

Since bit error rates are very low in wired networks, nearly all TCP versions nowadays assume that packets losses are due to congestion. Consequently, when a packet is detected to be lost, either by timeout or by multiple duplicated ACKs, TCP slows down the sending rate by adjusting its congestion window. Although this assumption is reasonable for wired networks, it is questionable for wireless networks especially MANETs. All those causes that are not related to congestion can result in unnecessary congestion control, which will degrade the TCP performance. In wireless networks packet loss may be due to high bit error rate, mobility, path asymmetry, multi hop communication and interference by neighbor nodes where losses are not related to congestion. So TCP cannot adapt to this environment. In last few decades many researchers have been tried to enhance and optimize the performance of TCP over wireless networks. These improvements include infrastructure based WLANs(Balakrishnan,1997; Bakre,1997; Balakrishnan,1995) mobile cellular networking environments(Brown,1997; Balakrishnan,1995) and satellite networks(Hinderson,1999;Durst,1996). In fact TCP has variants of protocols: Tahoe, Reno, Newreno, Sack1 and Vegas. All these protocols were proposed to improve their congestion control techniques and perform differently in Ad hoc networks(Xu,2002). However, all these versions suffer from the same problem of inability to distinguish packet losses due to congestion or due to the specific features of Ad hoc networks. These proposals are not directly useful for the employment of TCP in MANETs. However, there has become more interest during the last decade in improving TCP for communication in multi-hop wireless networks(Holand,2002). The increased research effort on TCP in MANETs bodes well for a future where TCP and its excellent qualities is part of extending wire-based services into the wireless multi-hop domain(Wang,2002).

3. MYTH OF TCP

In order to make communication between different packet networks TCP-like protocol were proposed in 1974(Cerf,1974). Then three way handshaking method were introduced in 1975(Tomlinson,1975). The specification of TCP is given in RFC 793(Postel,1981). The specification has later been amended and changed, which has been documented through a large number of IETF RFCs(Braden,1989;Deering,1998;Xiao,2000;Allman,2009;Paxson,2011) and a roadmap to the different documents specifying and extending TCP is presented by M. Duke et al.(2006). Several researchers extended TCP protocol by modifying at the sender side, which makes compatible with earlier versions. A milestone in the work on TCP was New Year's Day 1983, when the Advanced Research Projects Agency Network (ARPANET) had officially completed its migration to the TCP/IP protocol suite. In 1984, John Nagle proposed an algorithm now known as Nagle's algorithm(Nagle,1984). The algorithm concatenates a number of small buffer messages. This increases the network efficiency through reducing the number of packets that must be sent. This again greatly reduces the overhead of small packets. The work predicted congestion collapse in the ARPANET. The problems predicted by Nagle began occurring in October 1986, when the ARPANET saw several collapses caused by congestion. This spurred initiatives to address the problem. In 1987, Karn's algorithm(Karn,1987) to better estimate the RTT in TCP was proposed, and in 1988, Van Jacobson and Michael Karels enforced TCP with congestion control. This was an extension to the existing flow control, which protected the receiver from being overrun. Today, the congestion control functionality has made TCP to be widely regarded as the protocol that "saved the Internet". The congestion algorithm proposed by Jacobson and Karels opened a new field of research, focusing on the optimization of the congestion control mechanism. The next part of this report presents the most important TCP variants from the literature up until 1996 in chronological order.

4. TCP MECHANISM

This section describes the key mechanism used by basic TCP protocol. The following mechanism is used for TCP operation.

4.1 Connection Set Up

TCP provides a connection-oriented service over packet switched networks for providing reliable data transfer. It requires virtual connection between two end points (called handshaking process) before any data transfer. There are three phases in any virtual connection. These are the connection establishment, data transfer and connection termination phases. To establish the connection, either end nodes (hosts) may start the procedure by sending a request packet to the opposed side. The full procedure is commonly referred to as "three-way handshake" because it involves the exchange of three packets in total. The details of three-way handshaking are given in (Postel,1981). Once connection is established, communicating applications can transmit data between each other. After successful data transfer the connection terminates.

4.2 Flow Control

Flow control is a technique whose primary purpose is to properly match the transmission rate of sender to that of the receiver and the network. It is important for the transmission to be at a high enough rates to ensure good performance, but also to protect against overwhelming the network or receiving host. TCP uses the window field, briefly described previously, as the primary means for flow control. During the data transfer phase, the window field is used to adjust the rate of flow of the byte stream between communicating TCPs. Flow control is implemented to avoid that a TCP sender overflows the receiver's buffer. Thus, the receiver advertises in every ACK transmitted a window limit to the sender. This window is named receiver advertised window (*rwin*) and changes over time depending on both the traffic conditions and the application speed in reading the receiver's buffer. Therefore, the sender may not increase its window at any time beyond the value specified in *rwin*.

4.3 Congestion Control

Congestion control algorithm is used to prevent sender overloads the network and is concerned with the traffic inside the network. Its purpose is to prevent collapse inside the network when the traffic source (sender) is faster than the network in forwarding data. To this end, the TCP sender also uses a limiting window called congestion window (cwnd). Assuming that the receiver is not limiting the sender, cwnd defines the amount of data the sender may send into the network before an ACK is received.

5. CONGESTION CONTROL MECHANISMS

Generally Internet traffic management with buffer management for fair service and TCP congestion control issues is an active area of research and experimentation. Congestion typically occurs where multiple links feed into a single link, such as where internal LANs are connected to WAN links. Congestion also occurs at routers in core networks where nodes are subjected to more traffic than they are designed to handle. TCP/IP networks such as the Internet are especially susceptible to congestion because of their basic connection- less nature. Jacobson and Karels developed a congestion control mechanism for TCP following a congestion collapse on the internet. Prior to this no congestion control mechanism was specified for TCP. Their method is based on ensuring the 'conservation of packets,' i.e., that the packets are entering the network at the same rate that they are exiting with a full window of packets in transit. This section brief summary of the standard congestion control algorithms widely used in TCP implementations today. The congestion control algorithms are defined in(Jacobson,1988;Jacobson,1990). The four algorithms, Slow Start, Congestion Avoidance, Fast Retransmit and Fast Recovery are described below.

5.1 Slow Start

It is the mechanism used by the sender to control the transmission rate, otherwise known as sender-based flow control. The rate of acknowledgements returned by the receiver determines the rate at which the sender can transmit data. During the initial phase of a TCP connection, the Slow Start algorithm is used. When a TCP connection begins, the Slow Start algorithm initializes congestion window to one segment, which is the maximum segment size (MSS) initialized by the receiver during the connection establishment phase. When acknowledgements are returned by the receiver, the congestion window increases by one segment for each acknowledgement returned. Thus, the sender can transmit the minimum of the congestion window and the advertised window of the receiver, which is simply called the transmission window i.e. [min (*cwnd*, *awnd*)].

After the first successful transmission and acknowledgement of a TCP the segment increases the window to two segments. After successful transmission of these two segments and acknowledgements completes, the window is increased to four segments. Then eight segments, then sixteen segments and so on, doubling from there on out up to the maximum window size advertised by the receiver or until congestion finally does occur. In slow start congestion window increases exponentially up to some defined threshold value called *ssthresh.*

5.2 Congestion Avoidance

As shown in figure 1, once the congestion window reaches *ssthresh*, Congestion Avoidance phase is used to slow the transmission rate. During this period, congestion window increases linearly rather exponentially. In the Congestion Avoidance algorithm a retransmission timer expiring or the reception of duplicate ACKs can implicitly signal the sender that a network congestion situation is occurring. The sender immediately sets its transmission window to one half of the current window size (the minimum of the congestion window and the receiver's advertised window size), but to at least two segments. If congestion was indicated by a timeout, the congestion window is reset to one segment, which automatically puts the sender into Slow Start mode. If congestion was indicated by duplicate ACKs, the Fast Retransmit and Fast Recovery algorithms are invoked as shown in figure 2. As data is received during Congestion Avoidance, the congestion window is increased. However, Slow Start is only used up to the halfway point where congestion originally occurred. This halfway point was recorded earlier as the new transmission window. After this halfway point, the congestion window is increased by one segment for all segments in the transmission window that are acknowledged. This mechanism will force the sender to more slowly grow its transmission rate, as it will approach the point where congestion had previously been detected.

5.3 Fast Retransmit

TCP receiver may get duplicate ACK due to two reasons. One is Segment lost and second one is segment was delayed and received out of order at the receiver. If the receiver can re-order segments, it should not be long before the receiver sends the latest expected acknowledgement. Typically no more than one or two duplicate ACKs should be received when simple out of order conditions exist. If however more than two duplicate ACKs are received by the sender, it is a strong indication that at least one segment has been lost. The TCP sender will assume enough time has lapsed for all segments to be properly reordered by the fact that the receiver had enough time to send three duplicate ACKs.

When three or more duplicate ACKs are received, the sender does not even wait for a retransmission timer to expire before retransmitting the segment (as indicated by the position of the duplicate ACK in the byte stream). This process is called the Fast Retransmit algorithm. Immediately following Fast Retransmit is the Fast Recovery algorithm.

Figure 1. Slow start and Congestion avoidance mechanism

Slow Start

```
initialize: cwnd = 1
for (each segment ACKed)
    cwnd++
until (congestion event OR cwnd
> ssthresh)
If cwnd > ssthresh
Enter congestion avoidance
phase
```

Congestion avoidance

```
/* slowstart is over        */
/* cwnd > ssthresh */
Until (timeout) { /* loss event */
  every ACK:
     cwnd += 1
  }
ssthresh = cwnd/2
cwnd = 1
perform slowstart
```

Figure 2. Fast retransmit and fast recovery mechanism

```
After receiving 3 dupACKS:
            Retransmit the lost segment.
            Set ssthresh = cwnd size/2.
            Set cwnd = ssthresh.
If dupACK arrives:
          ++ ndupacks
          Transmit new segment, if allowed.
If new ACK arrives:
          ndupacks = 0
        Exit fast recovery.
If RTO expires:
        ndupacks = 0
      Perform slow-start - (ssthresh = cwnd size/2,
cwnd = 1 )
```

5.4 Fast Recovery

Since the Fast Retransmit algorithm is used when duplicate ACKs are being received, the TCP sender has implicit knowledge that there is data still flowing to the receiver. Why? The reason is because duplicate ACKs can only be generated when a segment is received. This is a strong indication that serious network congestion may not exist and that the lost segment was a rare event. So instead of reducing the flow of data abruptly by going all the way into Slow Start, the sender only enters Congestion Avoidance mode.

Rather than start at a window of one segment as in Slow Start mode, the sender resumes transmission with a larger window, incrementing as if in Congestion Avoidance mode. This allows for higher throughput under the condition of only moderate congestion. These algorithms are described in below figure.

6. TCP VARIANTS PROTOCOL

6.1 TCP Tahoe

TCP Tahoe(Karn,1987) is first version of TCP with congestion control. The "Tahoe" algorithm first appeared in 4.3BSD-Tahoe and was made available to non-AT&T licensees as part of the "4.3BSD Networking Release 1"; this ensured its wide distribution and implementation. The TCP Tahoe congestion control strategy consists of multiple mechanisms. When a connection is initialized, TCP uses a mechanism called slow start to put more data into the network by increasing the congestion window. Initially it starts with a window of one Maximum Segment Size (MSS). For every acknowledgement, the congestion window increases by one MSS so that effectively the congestion window doubles for every RTT. The window is doubled as follows: If the congestion window has two packets outstanding, and one packet is acknowledged, this means that the congestion window is increased to three packets, and only one packet is outstanding. I.e. the sender may now send two new packets. When the final packet (of the original two) is acknowledged, this allows the sender to increase the congestion window with one MSS yet again, bringing the total congestion window to four, and of these two are free. In other words, the congestion window has doubled. When the congestion window exceeds a threshold *ssthresh*, the algorithm enters a new state, called congestion avoidance. In the state of congestion avoidance, the congestion window is additively increased by one MSS every RTT, instead of the previous one MMS per acknowledged packet, as long as non-duplicate ACKs are received. Triple duplicate ACKs are interpreted in the same way as a timeout. In such a case, Tahoe performs a "fast retransmit", reduces the congestion window to one MSS, and resets to the slow-start state.

6.2 Reno

In 1990 improvements to Tahoe were made in 4.3BSD-Reno and subsequently released to the public as "Networking Release 2" and later 4.4BSD-Lite. This version of TCP introduced a fast recovery phase. If three duplicate ACKs are received by the sender, it will halve the congestion window size, perform a fast retransmit, and enter a state called fast recovery. In this state, TCP retransmits the missing packet that was signaled by three duplicate ACKs, and waits for an acknowledgment of the entire transmit window before returning to congestion avoidance. If there is no acknowledgment, i.e., if an ACK times out, TCP Reno experiences a timeout and enters the slow-start state, just like Tahoe.

6.3 TCP NewReno

TCP-Reno has been modified in two versions. The first version is Newreno and second version is SACK. Floyd et al(2012) proposed TCP NewReno in 1996 which is a modification of TCP Reno. It improves retransmissions during the fast recovery phase. In this phase, a new unsent packet from the end of the congestion window is sent for every duplicate ACK that is returned, to keep the transmit window full. For every ACK that makes partial progress in the sequence space, the sender assumes that the ACK points to a new hole, and the next packet beyond the acknowledged sequence number is sent. The progress in the transmit buffer resets the timeout timer, and this allows New-Reno to fill large or multiple holes in the sequence space. High throughput is maintained during the hole-filling process, because New-Reno can send new packets at the end of the congestion window during fast recovery. While entering fast recovery, TCP records the highest outstanding unacknowledged packet sequence number. Upon the acknowledgment of this sequence number, TCP returns to the congestion avoidance state. New-Reno will misinterpret the situation if there are no losses, but instead reordering of packets by more than 3 packet sequence numbers. In such a case, New-Reno mistakenly enters fast recovery, but when the reordered packet is delivered, ACK sequence-number progress occurs and from there until the end of fast recovery, every bit of sequence number progress produces a duplicate and needless retransmission that is immediately acknowledged. Through its new improved fast recovery algorithm, it recovers multiple packet losses per window and minimizes as many as transmission timeout events. Therefore Newreno version is more suitable than Reno in the mobile wireless environment where packet losses may occur in bursts.

6.4 TCP Sack1

Selective Acknowledgment (SACK) TCP was another improvement to TCP proposed in 1996, in RFC 2018(Mathis,1996). It retains the basic properties of TCP Reno. It is suitable for a network where multiple segments lost in a single window of TCP. In Sack, the receiver uses the option fields of TCP header (Sack option) for notifying the sender of up to usually three blocks of non-contiguous set of data received and queued by the receiver. The first block reports the most recent packet received at the receiver, and the next blocks repeat the most recently reported Sack blocks. The sender keeps a data structure called scoreboard to keep track of the Sack options (blocks) received so far. In this way, the sender can infer whether there are missing packets at the receiver. If so, and its congestion window permits, the sender retransmits the next packet from its list of missing packets. In case there are no such packets at the receiver and the congestion window allows, the sender simply transmits a new packet. Like TCP Reno, the Sack implementation also enters fast recovery upon receipt of generally three duplicate acknowledgments. Then, its sender retransmits a packet and halves the congestion window. During fast recovery, Sack monitors the estimated number of packets outstanding in the path (transmitted but not yet acknowledged) by maintaining a variable called pipe. This variable determines if the sender may send a new packet or retransmit an old one, in that the sender may only transmit if pipe is smaller than the congestion window. At every transmission or retransmission, pipe is incremented by one, and it is decremented by one when the sender receives a duplicate ACK packet containing a Sack option informing it that a new data packet has been received by the receiver.

6.5 TCP Vegas

TCP Vegas(Brakmo,1994) was proposed in 1994. It uses packet delay, as a signal to determine the rate at which to send packets in congestion avoidance algorithm. In Tahoe, Reno, Newreno, Sack1 congestion is detected by packet drops only after it has actually happened. Based on increasing RTT values of the packets Vegas detect congestion at an incipient stage and measure the queuing delay. Based on this Vegas adjust congestion window size for each connection. The difference between expected traffic and actual traffic is used to adjust the size of the congestion window. Both the increase and decrease of the rate is additive (Additive Increase, Additive Decrease (AIAD)). The Vegas algorithm depends heavily on accurate calculation of the base RTT value. If it is too small, then the throughput of the connection will be less than the bandwidth available, while if the value is too large, it will push too much traffic over the network path. Another challenge is the problem of rerouted paths, where the algorithm will have problems knowing the base RTT value. Finally, when TCP Vegas is run on a network that is running other variants of TCP that are less able to detect and act upon congestion, e.g., Reno, TCP Vegas will also get an unfairly small share of the bandwidth.

6.6 Bic Tcp

Binary Increase Congestion control (BIC)-TCP(Xu,2004), proposed in 2004. It is an implementation of TCP with an optimized congestion control algorithm for high speed networks with high latency: so-called "long fat networks". It has a unique congestion window algorithm which tries to find the maximum where to keep the window at for a long period of time, by using a binary search algorithm. BIC-TCP was the default TCP variant for the Linux kernels 2.6.8 through 2.6.18.

6.7 Cubic Tcp

Ha et al. described and explained CUBIC8 in (Ha,2008) in 2008. CUBIC is a less aggressive and more systematic derivative of BIC-TCP. In CUBIC, the window is a cubic function of time since the last congestion event, with the inflection point set to the window prior to the event. CUBIC has been the default TCP variant for Linux since kernel 2.6.19 (2006), replacing BIC-TCP, but the CUBIC implementation has since gone through several upgrades. These are documented in(Ha,2008).

6.8 Compound TCP

Compound TCP (CTCP) (Tan,2005) proposed in 2005, and is designed to aggressively adjust the sender's congestion window to optimize TCP for connections with large bandwidth-delay products while trying not to harm fairness. It is implemented as standard TCP version in Windows Server 2008, and is also available (but disabled by default) in Windows Vista and Windows 7. The CTCP is claimed to be a synergy of delay-based and loss-based approach, where a scalable delay-based component is added into the standard TCP Reno congestion avoidance algorithm (a.k.a., the loss-based component). The sending rate of CTCP is controlled by both components. The new delay-based component can rapidly increase sending rate when the network path is underutilized, but gracefully retreat in a busy network when a bottleneck queue is built. The authors argue that augmented with this delay-based component, CTCP provides very good bandwidth scalability and at the same time achieves good TCP-fairness.

7. CHALLENGES OF TCP IN AD-HOC NETWORK

TCP face some tough challenges in ad hoc networks due to the fact that it was not designed to operate in such a highly dynamic scenario in terms of topology. In reality, even though TCP has evolved significantly over the years toward a robust and reliable service protocol, the focus has been primarily on wired networks or wired-cum-wireless network. Ad hoc network pose new challenges to TCP due to several reasons: lossy channels, hidden and exposed stations, path asymmetry, network partitions, route failures, and power constraints.

7.1 Lossy Channels

The main causes of errors in wireless channel are shown in figure 3.

Signal attenuation: This is due to a decrease in the intensity of the electromagnetic energy at the receiver (e.g. due to long distance), which leads to low signal-to-noise ratio (SNR).

Doppler shift: This is due to the relative velocities of the transmitter and the receiver. Doppler shift causes frequency shifts in the arriving signal, thereby complicating the successful reception of the signal.

Multipath fading: Electromagnetic waves reflecting off objects or diffracting around objects can result in the signal traveling over multiple paths from the transmitter to the receiver. Multipath propagation can lead to fluctuations in the amplitude, phase, and geographical angle of the signal received at a receiver.

In order to increase the success of transmissions, link layer protocols implement the following techniques: Automatic Repeat reQuest (ARQ), or Forward Error Correction (FEC), or both. For example, IEEE 802.11 implements ARQ, so when a transmitter detects an error, it will retransmit the frame, error detection is timer based. Bluetooth implements both ARQ and FEC on some synchronous and asynchronous connections.

7.2 Hidden and Exposed Stations

In Ad hoc networks, stations may rely on physical carrier-sensing mechanism to determine idle channel, such as in the IEEE 802.11 DCF function. This sensing mechanism does not solve completely the *hidden station* and the *exposed station* problems (Tobagi,1975). Before explaining these problems, we need to clarify the "transmission range" term. The transmission range is the range, with respect to the transmitting station, within which a transmitted packet can be successfully received.

A typical hidden terminal situation is shown in Figure 3. Suppose stations A and C have a data to transmit to station B. Station A cannot detect C's transmission because it is outside the transmission

Figure 3. Causes of errors in wireless channel.

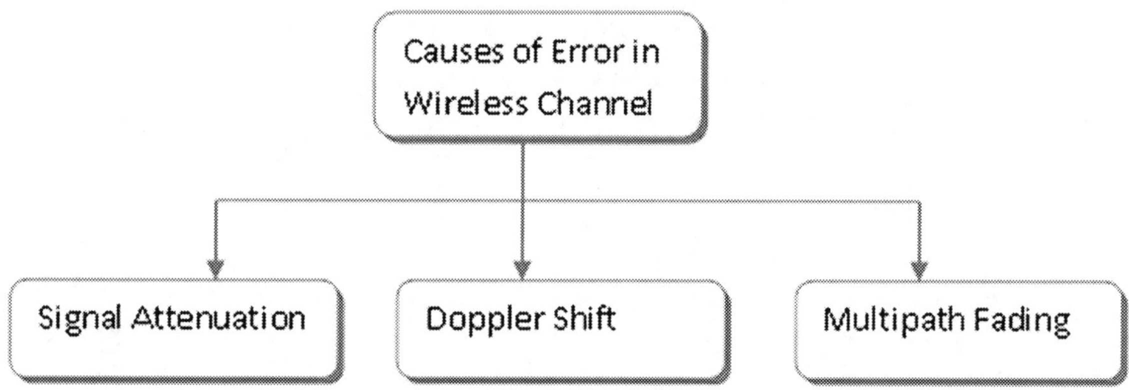

range of C. Station C is therefore "hidden" to station A and station A is hidden from station C. Since A and C transmission are through same wireless channel, there will be packet collisions at B. To alleviate the hidden terminal problem, virtual carrier sensing mechanism has been introduced (Bharghavan,1994). It is based on a two-way handshaking that precedes data transmission. Specifically, the source station transmits a short control frame, called Request-To-Send (RTS), to the destination station. Upon receiving the RTS frame, the destination station replies by a Clear-To-Send (CTS) frame, indicating that it is ready to receive the data frame. Both RTS and CTS frames contain the total duration of the data transmission. All stations receiving either RTS or CTS will keep silent during the data transmission period. However, as pointed out in(Fu,2003;Xu,2003) the hidden station problem may persist in IEEE 802.11 Ad hoc networks even with the use of the RTS/CTS handshake. This is due to the fact that the power needed for interrupting a packet reception is much lower than that of delivering a packet successfully. In other words, node's transmission range is smaller than the sensing node range. For more details see the model of the physical layer implemented in NS-2 and Glomosim simulators .

An exposed node is the one that is within the sensing range of the transmitter but out of the interfering range of the receiver. The exposed station problem results from a situation where a transmission has to be delayed because of the transmission between two other stations within the sender's transmission range. In Figure 4, we show a typical scenario where the exposed terminal problem occurs. Let us assume that A and C are within B's transmission range, and A is outside C's transmission range. Let us also assume that B is transmitting to A, and C has a frame to be

transmitted to D. According to the carrier sense mechanism, C senses a busy channel because of B's transmission. Therefore, station C will refrain from transmitting to D, although this transmission would not cause interference at A. The exposed station problem may thus result in a reduction of channel utilization. It is worth noting that hidden terminal and exposed terminal problems are correlated with

Figure 4. Hidden Terminal Problem

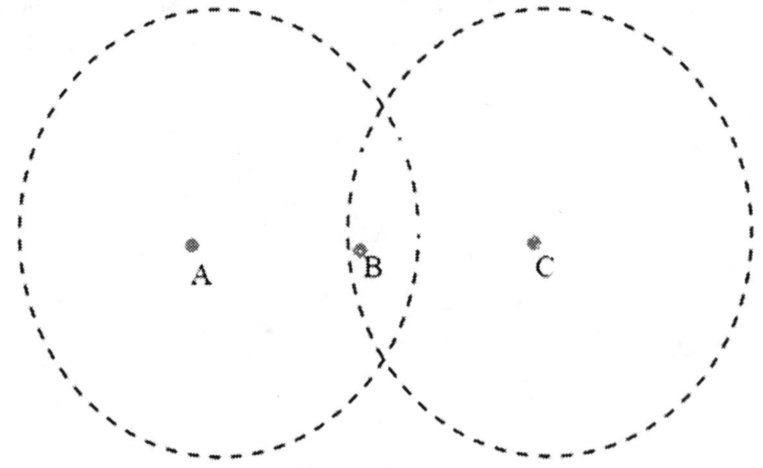

the transmission range. By increasing the transmission range, the hidden terminal problem occurs less frequently. On the other hand, the exposed terminal problem becomes more important as the transmission range identifies the area affected by a single transmission.

7.3 Path Asymmetry

Path asymmetry in Ad hoc networks may appear in several forms like bandwidth asymmetry, loss rate asymmetry, and route asymmetry.

Bandwidth asymmetry: Satellite networks suffer from high bandwidth asymmetry, resulting from various engineering tradeoffs (such as power, mass, and volume), as well as the fact that for space scientific missions, most of the data originates at the satellite and flows to the earth. The return link is not used, in general, for data transferring. On the other hand in Ad hoc networks, the degree of bandwidth asymmetry is not very high. For example, the bandwidth ratio lies between 2 and 54 in Ad hoc networks that implement the IEEE 802.11 version g protocol(online). The asymmetry results from the use of different transmission rates. Because of this different transmission rates, even symmetric source destination paths may suffer from bandwidth asymmetry.

Loss rate asymmetry: This type of asymmetry takes place when the backward path is significantly more lossy than the forward path. In Ad hoc networks, this asymmetry is due to the fact that packet losses depend on local constraints that can vary from place to place. Note that loss rate asymmetry may produce bandwidth asymmetry. For example, in multi-rate IEEE 802.11 protocol versions, senders may use the Auto-Rate-Fallback (ARF) algorithm for transmission rate selection(Kamerman,1997). With ARF, senders attempt to use higher transmission rates after consecutive transmission successes, and revert to lower rates after failures. So, as the loss rate increases the sender will keep using low transmission rates.

Route asymmetry: Unlike the previous two forms of asymmetry, where the forward path and the backward path can be the same, route asymmetry implies that distinct paths are used for TCP data and TCP ACKs. This asymmetry may be artifact of the routing protocol used. Route asymmetry increases routing overheads and packet losses in case of high degree of mobility1. Because when nodes move, using distinct forward and reverse routes increases the probability of route failures experienced by TCP connections. However, this is not the case of static networks or networks that have low degree of mobility, like the case of a network with routes of high lifetime compared to the session transfer time. So, it is up to the routing protocols to select symmetric paths when such routes are available in the case of Ad hoc networks of high mobility. In the context of satellite networks, there has been a lot of research on how to improve TCP performance. But since satellite networks are out of the scope of the report, we will limit ourselves to list three techniques introduced by these proposals, which we believe might be useful in Ad hoc networks. The first one is "TCP header compression" that reduces the size of the TCP ACKs on the backward path (Jacobson,1990). The second one is "ACK filtering" that reduces the number of TCP ACKs transmitted, by taking advantage of the fact that TCP ACKs are cumulative (Balakrishnan,2001). The third one is "ACK congestion control" that let the receiver also control the congestion on the backward path. This is done by dynamically maintaining a delayed-ACK factor *d* by the receiver, and by sending one ACK for every *d* data packet received (Balakrishnan,2001). The difference between ACK filtering and ACK congestion control is that the first one is a link layer technique that can be implemented at intermediate nodes, however the second one is a TCP layer technique that is implemented at the TCP sink. Unfortunately, these techniques alone cause problems such as increasing sender's burst traffic and also slowing down the sender's congestion window growth. So, it is necessary to adapt the sender congestion control algorithm to avoid these problems. For details about the sender adaptation techniques, we refer to (Balakrishnan,2001). The adaptive delayed-ACK proposed in (Altman,2003) aims to reduce the contention on the channel, by reducing the number of TCP ACKs transmitted. We have not found any other proposal dealing with the asymmetry problem in Ad hoc networks.

7.4 Network Partition

An Ad hoc network can be represented by a simple graph *G*. Mobile stations are the "vertices". A successful transmission between two stations is an undirected "edge". Network partition happens when *G* is disconnected. The main reason of this disconnection in MANETs is node mobility. Another factor the can lead to network partition is energy constrained operation of nodes.

An example of network partition is illustrated in Figure 5 where dashed lines represent the links between nodes and red arrow mark represent node movement. When node D moves away from node C this results in a partition of the network into two separate components. Clearly, the TCP agent of node A cannot receive the TCP ACK transmitted by node F. If the disconnectivity persists for duration greater than the retransmission timeout (RTO) of node A, the TCP agent will trigger the *exponential backoff* algorithm (Paxson,2000), which consists of doubling the RTO whenever the timeout expires. Originally, TCP does not have indication about the exact time of network reconnection. This lack of indication may lead to long idle periods during which the network is connected again, but TCP is still in the backoff state.

7.5 Routing Failures

In wired networks route failures occur very rarely. In MANETs they are frequent events. The main cause of route failures is node mobility. Another factor that can lead to route failures is the link failures due to the contention on the wireless channel, which is the main cause of TCP performance degradation

Figure 5. Exposed Terminal Problem

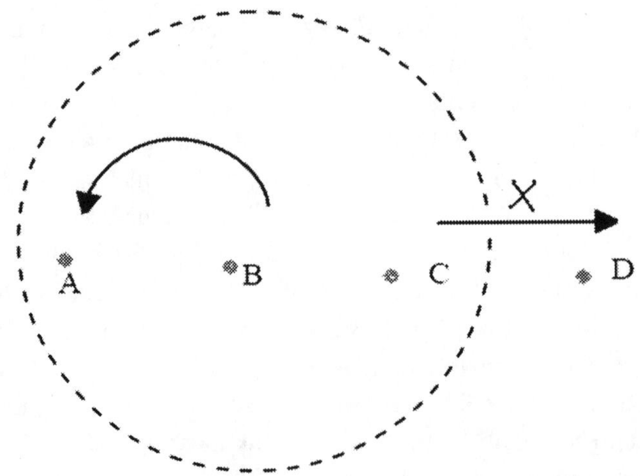

Figure 6. Example of network partition

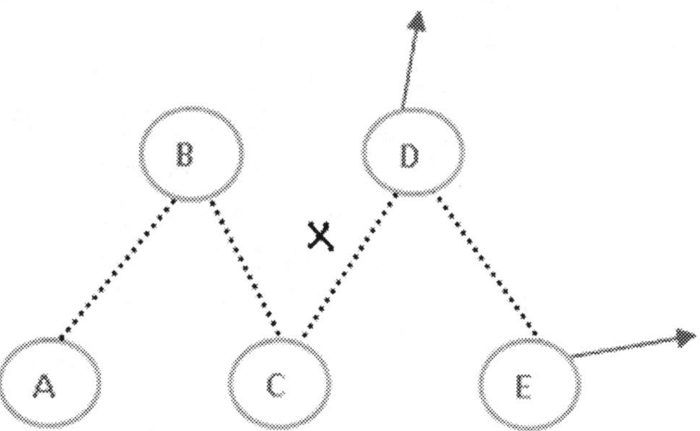

in SANETs. The route reestablishment duration after route failure in Ad hoc networks depends on the underlying routing protocol, mobility pattern of mobile nodes, and traffic characteristics. As already discussed in Section II-D, if TCP sender's does not have indications on the route re-establishment event, the throughput and session delay will degrade because of the large idle time. Also, if the new route established is longer or shorter, in term of hops, than the old route TCP will face a brutal fluctuation in Round Trip Time (RTT).

7.6 Power Constraints

Because batteries carried by each mobile node have limited power supply, processing power is limited. This is a major issue in Ad hoc networks, as each node is acting as an end system and as a router at the same time, with the implication that additional energy is required to forward and relay packets. TCP must use this scarce power resource in an "efficient" manner. Here, efficiency means minimizing the number of unnecessary retransmissions at the transport layer as well as at the link layer2. In general, in Ad hoc networks there are two correlated power problems: the first one is "power saving" that aims at reducing the power consumption; the second one is "power control" that aims at adjusting the transmission power of mobile nodes. Power saving strategies has been investigated at several levels of a mobile device including the physical layer transmissions, the operation systems, and the applications (Jones,2001). Power control can be jointly used with routing or transport agents to improve the performance of Ad hoc networks (Kleem,2003;Chiang,2005) power constraints communications reveal also the problem of cooperation between nodes, as nodes may not participate in routing and forwarding procedures in order to save battery power.

The challenges for TCP in MANETs span all the layers below the transport layer in the OSI network stack (Zimmermann,1988). That is physical layer, MAC layer, network layer, transport layer.

A. Physical Layer

At the PHY layer, interference and fading may result in bit errors and lost packets. While wired links can now be regarded as so stable that one can ignore the probability of packet loss caused by bit errors, this is not the case with wireless links. For wireless links, the bit error rate is several orders of magnitude higher than wired links (Pentikousis,2000). The TCP protocol was originally designed for wired networks, and its congestion avoidance mechanism does not consider link errors as a possible reason for packet errors or losses. Instead, TCP interprets packet losses caused by bit errors as congestion. This can significantly degrade the performance of TCP over wireless networks, when TCP unnecessarily invokes congestion control, causing reduction in throughput and link utilization.

B. Mac Layer

At the MAC layer, the contention based medium access may induce delay and is not able to completely avoid collisions, potentially causing packet loss if retransmission mechanisms are unable to salvage the problem. All MANET nodes share the same wireless medium. The contention and risk of collisions is much higher in such wireless networks than in the wired environment. The IEEE 802.11 is a CSMA/CA protocol, and work on such protocols(Gerla,1999) has shown that the TCP performance decreases drastically as the hop count is increased. Retransmission mechanisms may also further increase the transmission delay, and create jitter as the number of needed retransmissions varies. A consequence of unsuccessful transmissions can also be a signal modulation change to improve the transmission success rate. This may result in a reduction of the bit rate. The IEEE 802.11 standard (2007) states that if a node does not receive a link layer acknowledgement after retransmitting a DATA message 7 times (dot11S-hortRetryLimit), the node must consider the link to be broken and should drop the DATA packet it tries to transmit. It should also be noted that any MAC retransmission timeout must be kept at a significantly lower time frame compared to the retransmission timeout of TCP. If the two timeouts are too close, there is a chance that a packet may be retransmitted by TCP and by MAC at the same time, meaning that there will be duplicate TCP packets in the network, wasting resources. Some MAC implementations, such as the IEEE 802.11, implements dynamic change of modulation to achieve the best performance in changing network conditions. For upper layer protocols, this may lead to a high degree of variation in the available capacity. Another type of MAC layer capacity variation is Demand Assigned Multiple Access (DAMA), common in satellite communications, where the allocated bandwidth depends on the measured traffic load9. The allocated bandwidth may increase several times, creating unnecessary delay in achieving the desired and available capacity. In both cases, the underlying available capacity may vary, requiring the TCP protocol to adapt quickly and correctly in order to take full advantage of the available network resources. Another problem with varying link technology over a path, both static and dynamic, is buffer bloat (Gettys,2011; Nichols,2012). Buffer bloat is the existence of excessively large and frequently full buffers inside the network, where they damage the fundamental congestion-avoidance algorithms of TCP. This problem is especially pronounced at bottleneck links.

C. Network Layer

At the network layer, the routing protocol's delay in detecting topology changes may lead to periods without connectivity and a risk of loops, both in case of mobility and fluctuating links. Also, the end-to-end transmission time/RTT10 will change as a result of changing paths between the source and destination. If the RTT is increased too much, timeouts will occur on the TCP sender, causing unnecessary retransmissions. If two neighboring nodes have different relative mobility, they will eventually become disconnected. Any routes using this link will fail, and it is the task of the routing protocol to detect the link break and discover an alternative route between the source and destination. In a MANET, this kind of topology change will happen on a fairly frequent basis, due to the limited communication range of radios. Route failures and route changes may impact TCP in several ways. Route failures can cause packet drops at the intermediate nodes. These will be interpreted as congestion loss, a timeout event happens and TCP enters the slow-start process as if congestion occurred. Even if the routing protocol is able to reroute the packets without packet loss, route changes can introduce frequent out-of-order packet delivery. The cumulative acknowledgement mechanism of TCP will generate duplicate ACKs before receiving the expected packet in sequence. If the sender receives three of such duplicate ACKs, TCP also presumes the network is congested and invokes fast retransmission.

D. Transport Layer

The TCP is an end-to-end protocol. It should be agnostic to the available performance and attributes of the lower layers. However, any solution that aims to improve TCP performance in MANETs by tuning the TCP protocol will have to deal with senders that may not be aware that the receiver, or part of the route, is in a MANET. As such, the end-to-end functionality of TCP is a challenge, since an interconnected MANET will enable connections between end-users that may have greatly differing versions of TCP implemented.

8. PERFORMANCE OF TCP OVER MANET

In MANET node movement is governed by kind of mobility model is implemented. The mobility model is designed to describe the movement pattern of mobile users, and how their location, velocity and acceleration change over time. Since mobility patterns may play a significant role in determining the protocol performance, it is desirable for mobility models to emulate the movement pattern of targeted real life applications in a reasonable way. Below figure gives category of mobility model based on their specific mobility characterstics (Bai,2006).

The mostly used mobility model is Random Way Point mobility model. In this a node moves one position to another with a maximum speed V. Then it stay for defined time called pause time (p) before moving into another point. Author (Bisoy,2013) studied the interaction between mobility model and unipath routing protocol in MANET and shows that the performance of routing protocol varies with different mobility model used and connection pattern. We observe that DSR and AODV achieve the highest throughput and least overhead with RPGM when compared to RWP mobility models. In (Holland,2002) author analyzed the impact of mobility model in TCP over MANET. Author in (Bisoy,2013) studied the interaction between TCP variants and routing protocol in MANET. Main objective of this paper is to find suitable routing protocols for TCP variants and analyze the performance differential variation in terms of throughput, packet loss rate and energy consumption. Simulations result using NS2 shows

Figure 7. The categories of mobility models in Mobile Ad hoc Network

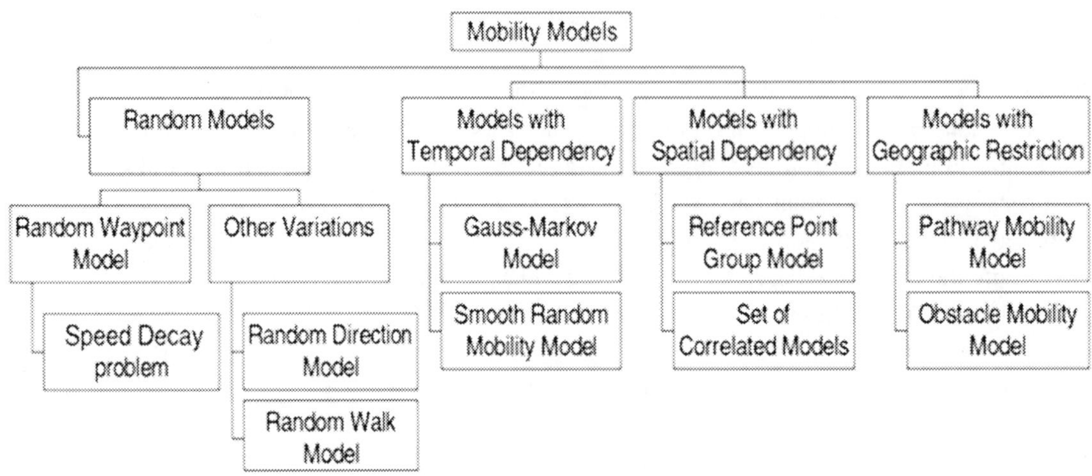

that, OLSR is best routing protocol with respect to throughput and packet loss ratio irrespective of TCP variants and it provides a lower packet loss rate (15% to 20%) than others in most situations. DSDV protocol consumes 15% to 25% less energy than AODV and 5 to 10% than OLSR.

Main objective of the paper(Biosy,2014) is to find suitable routing protocols for TCP variants and analyze the performance differential variation in static multi-hop ad hoc network in terms of throughput, packet delivery ratio, and packet loss. Result using NS2 shows that AODV is best routing protocol with respect to throughput and packet delivery ratio irrespective of TCP variants. Vegas is the best protocol among TCP variants due to its higher throughput and higher PDR and lower packet loss in most situations, and DSR has lower packet loss irrespective of TCP variants. Xu(2002) study the performance of TCP Tahoe, Reno, New Reno, Sack and Vegas4 over the multi-hop chain topology where the IEEE 802.11 protocol is used. It has shown that TCP Vegas delivers the better performance and does not suffer from instability.

Accuracy of routing protocol performance in mobile ad hoc network (MANET) depends on many parameters. Besides many parameters propagation model and node velocity are the two among them. Node mobility is responsible for network topology and propagation model for calculating signal strength at receiver. In wireless network MANET suffers a huge loss in performance due to obstacle between transmission and variation in signal strength at receiver. Many routing protocols are proposed based on which neglect the effect of fading and path loss. So it is important to find the effect of fading and node velocity for accurate estimation and analysis of performance of routing protocols in MANET. Bisoy(2014) investigate the effect of propagation model (both non-fading and fading) and mobility on the performance of the ad hoc routing protocol such as Ad hoc On Demand Distance Vector (AODV), Dynamic Manet On Demand (DYMO) and Dynamic Source Routing (DSR) and present the results gathered from simulation using NS2. The result shows that propagation model and mobility has strong impact on the performance of MANET routing protocol.

9. IMPROVEMENT OF TCP IN MANET

Several proposals to mend the many challenges encountered by TCP in MANETs have been generated through research. Some of these solutions are presented below. The intention is to give the reader an overview of the types of solutions that have been brought forward, for reference and for better understanding of the ways that TCP's challenges can be met. IETF has addressed TCP's challenges through several RFCs. Two of them are RFC3135 and RFC3449. RFC3135 (Border,2001) is a survey from 2001 of Performance Enhancing Proxys (PEPs) employed to improve degraded TCP performance caused by characteristics of specific link environments. RFC3449 (Balakrishnan,2002)presents best current practices (from 2002) with regards to network path asymmetry. There are a number of surveys delving into the challenges of TCP in MANETs and possible solutions. Wang and Zhang present a survey on TCP over MANETs, introducing three major challenges for TCP (Wang,2005). Two other publications that look at TCP and congestion control for MANETs are (Hanbali,2004;Lochert,2007). Hanbali et al(2004) present a survey of TCP alternatives for MANETs, classifying the alternatives in cross-layer and layered proposals. A very thorough survey of TCP and similar congestion control protocols for MANETs is presented in (Lochert,2007).

9.1 Split-TCP

Spilt-TCP(Kopparty,2002) is a solution for TCP seeking to resolve the unfairness suffered by connections with a large number of hops, compared to connections with a low number of hops. The scheme separates the functionalities of TCP congestion control and reliable packet delivery. For any TCP connection, certain nodes along the route take up the role of being proxies for that connection (Figure 4.2). The proxies buffer packets upon receipt and administer rate control. The buffering enables dropped packets to be recovered from the most recent proxy. The rate control helps in controlling congestion on inter-proxy segments. Thus, by introducing proxies, shorter TCP connections are emulated, and better parallelism in the network is achieved. The simulations show that the use of proxies abates the problems described as follows:

- It improves the total throughput by as much as 30% in typical scenarios.
- It reduces unfairness significantly. In terms of an unfairness metric that is introduced, the unfairness decreases from 0.8 to 0.2 (1.0 being the maximum unfairness). The authors conclude that incorporating TCP proxies is beneficial in terms of improving TCP performance in ad hoc networks.

9.2 Ad Hoc TCP(ADHOCTCP)

Mirhosseini and Torgheh (2011) propose to improve TCP for MANETs through a solution named ADHOCTCP, by identifying three packet loss inducing network states and have TCP act according to the packet loss reason. The three states are Congestion, Channel error and Disconnection. The congestion state is identified by use of two end-to-end measured metrics, Interpacket Delay Difference (IDD) and Short Term Throughput (STT), which complement each other. A situation where IDD is high and STT is low is defined as a congested state. The disconnection state is identified using Explicit Packet Loss Notification (EPLN) which is based on the Dynamic Source Routing (DSR) protocol and an Internet

Control Message Protocol (ICMP) "Host unreachable" message. Finally, the channel error state is assumed after Retransmission Timeout (RTO) if the network state is not detected as congestion by the end-to-end measurements.

9.3 Ad Hoc TCP (ADTCP)

ADTCP(Fu,2002) performs multi-metric joint identification for packet and connection behaviors based on end-to-end measurements, to robustly detect network states in the presence of measurement noise. The metrics, measured at the transport layer, are Inter-packet Delay Difference (IDD), Short Term Throughput (STT), Packet out-of-order delivery ratio (POR) and Packet loss ratio (PLR). The solution relies solely on end-to-end mechanisms. Using the technique, a network event is acted upon only if all the relevant metrics detect it.

9.4 TCP with Adaptive Pacing (TCP-AP)

In (ElRakabawy,2005), the authors introduce a novel congestion control algorithm for TCP over multi-hop IEEE 802.11 wireless networks implementing rate-based scheduling of transmissions within the TCP congestion window. It is shown how a TCP sender can adapt its transmission rate close to the optimum using an estimate of the current 4-hop propagation delay and the coefficient of variation of recently measured round-trip times. The novel TCP variant is denoted as TCP-AP. Opposed to previous proposals for improving TCP over multi-hop IEEE 802.11 networks, TCP-AP retains the end-to-end semantics of TCP and neither relies on modifications on the routing or the link layer nor requires cross-layer information from intermediate nodes along the path. A comprehensive simulation study using ns-2 shows that TCP-AP achieves up to 84% more goodput than TCP New-Reno, provides excellent fairness in almost all scenarios, and is highly responsive to changing traffic conditions.

9.5 TCP Detection of Out-of-Order and Response (TCP-DOOR)

TCP-DOOR(Wang,2002) is a new way to make TCP adapt to frequent route changes without relying on feedback from the network. It is based on TCP detecting out-of-order delivery events and inferring route changes from these events. Normal TCP performs poorly in ad hoc networks because of frequent route changes. In TCP-DOOR, the sender can distinguish route changes from network congestion by detecting out-of-order delivery, thereafter improve the performance of normal TCP by not invoking unnecessary congestion control. The simulation results showed that TCP-DOOR can improve the TCP throughput significantly, 50% on average. The approach does not rely on the feedback from lower layers or from the network. The feedback mechanism can be difficult to implement and expensive to deploy. The approach is purely end-to-end, where only the endpoints participate in the procedure to determine the network state. Another advantage is that this approach is also applicable in an environment having both ad hoc and fixed network. Assuming that sender S and receiver R are in two fixed networks interconnected by an ad-hoc network. The TCP connection between S and R faces the same problem of frequent route changes. As a pure end-to-end approach, TCP-DOOR will work well in this environment, but feedback-based approach will not. The obvious tradeoff is that a feedback-based approach is more accurate because the information is directly from the network. So the conclusion is, for improving TCP over ad hoc networks, the feedback-based approach should be used if available, otherwise, the approach can work on any environment and still deliver a significant improvement.

9.6 TCP-FIT

TCP-FIT(Wang,2010) is an improved TCP congestion control algorithm for wireless networks, and its performance is compared with existing state-of-the-art congestion control algorithms as well as an application layer Parallel TCP scheme. In TCP-FIT, N virtual TCP sessions are utilized in a single TCP connection. The algorithm uses both packet loss and queuing delay as inputs to the congestion window control algorithm. The congestion window of each sessions is controlled in an AIMD manner based on packet loss information, whereas the number N of virtual sessions is adjusted dynamically based on delay. Experimental results demonstrate significant performance improvements under various channel conditions. Compared with application layer Parallel TCP, the proposed algorithm has the additional advantage of not requiring changes to the application layer software.

9.7 TCP Veno

TCP Veno (Fu,2003) is a simple and effective end-to-end congestion control mechanism for dealing with random packet loss, which can be prominent in wireless access networks. Veno monitors the network congestion level and uses that information to decide whether packet losses are likely to be due to congestion or random bit errors. Specifically: (1) it refines the multiplicative decrease algorithm of TCP Reno by adjusting the slow-start threshold according to the perceived network congestion level rather than a fixed drop factor and (2) it refines the linear increase algorithm so that the connection can stay longer in an operating region in which the network bandwidth is fully utilized. Some results show that in typical wireless access networks with 1% random packet loss rate, throughput improvement of up to 80% can be demonstrated.

9.8 TCP Westwood and Westwood+

TCP Westwood (Mascolo,2001) proposed in 2001, is a sender-side modification of the TCP congestion window algorithm that is intended to improve upon the performance of TCP Reno and TCP New-Reno (WestwoodNR) in wired as well as wireless networks. The improvement is most significant in wireless networks with lossy links, since TCP Westwood relies on end-to-end bandwidth estimation to discriminate the cause of packet loss (congestion or wireless channel effect) which is a major problem in TCP Reno. TCP Westwood does not require inspection and/or interception of TCP packets at intermediate (proxy) nodes. Rather, it fully complies with the end-to-end TCP design principle. TCP Westwood relies on end-to-end bandwidth estimation to discriminate the cause of packet loss (congestion or wireless channel effect). The estimate is then used to compute congestion window and slow start threshold after a congestion episode, that is, after three duplicate acknowledgments or after a timeout. The rationale of this strategy is simple: in contrast with TCP Reno, which "blindly" halves the congestion window after three duplicate ACKs, TCP Westwood attempts to select a slow start threshold and a congestion window which are consistent with the effective bandwidth used at the time congestion is experienced. The mechanism is named "faster recovery". The proposed mechanism is particularly effective over wireless links where sporadic losses due to radio channel problems are often misinterpreted as a symptom of congestion by current TCP schemes and thus lead to an unnecessary window reduction. TCP Westwood+ (Mascolo,2001) is an evolution of TCP Westwood. The main novelty of Westwood+ is the algorithm used to estimate the available bandwidth end-to-end, since it was discovered that the Westwood bandwidth estimation algorithm did not work well in the presence of reverse traffic, due to ACK compression.

9.9 Ad hoc TCP (ATCP)

ATCP(Liu,2001)is a TCP adaptation for MANETs where TCP in addition to receiving information about route failures, takes into account high BER. Based on the information provided by ECN or ICMP "Destination Unreachable" packets, ATCP, a layer between IP and TCP, will put TCP in the proper state. The three states are persist, congestion control, and retransmit.

9.10 TCP Buffering capability and Sequence information (TCP-BuS)

TCP-BuS (Toh,1997) uses network layer feedback to detect route failure events and to take appropriate reaction to the event. The scheme introduces buffering capability in the mobile nodes. The scheme is based on the Associativity-Based Routing (ABR) protocol (Toh,1997). The node discovering a route failure is called the Pivoting Node (PN). Upon receiving notice of a disconnection, packets along the path from the source to the PN are buffered, and for these buffered packets, the retransmission timer is doubled. The lost packets along the path from the source to the PN are not retransmitted until the adjusted retransmission timer expires.

9.11 TCP Feedback (TCP-F)

TCP-F (Chandran,2001) is a TCP protocol based on feedback from the routing protocol to handle route failures in MANETs. A route failure notification is sent to the source by the routing agent on a node. The source freezes all variables for the TCP flow and puts the TCP flow on hold. The TCP flow is then resumed when a notification of the route reestablishment is given. To avoid blocking, the TCP protocol will timeout after a period without receiving a notification of re-establishment, invoking the normal congestion control algorithm.

9.12 TCP-Recomputation (TCP-RC)

TCP-RC (Zhou,2003) is a proposal for TCP in MANETs where the TCP source is notified through an Explicit Route Failure Notification (ERFN) message when a route fails. This freezes the retransmission timers and pauses the congestion control. Upon the reconstruction of the route, *cwnd* and *ssthresh* are re-computed for the TCP connection. Thus, it can adjust the TCP transmission rate adaptively according to the current capacity of the TCP connection. Consequently, TCP-RC lowers the possibility of bursty traffic and avoids invoking congestion control during a situation of high network load.

9.13 TCP Explicit Link Failure Notification (ELFN)

Holland et al. show in (Holland,2002) that the legacy TCP performs poorly under mobility, and propose ELFN as a solution to this problem. ELFN is similar to TCP Feedback (TCP-F), but with ELFN the TCP is more active in the pause period, probing the network to see if the route has been restored.

9.14 Link RED (LRED)/Adaptive Pacing

In (Fu,2003) authors study TCP performance over multi-hop wireless networks that use the IEEE 802.11 protocol as the access method. Concluding through analysis and simulations that TCP is poor at exploiting spatial reuse, the authors propose two techniques, LRED and Adaptive Pacing. These techniques yield improvement in TCP throughput by 5% to 30% in various simulated topologies. The authors also validate some simulation results through real hardware experiments. The LRED algorithm is motivated by the observation that TCP can potentially benefit from the built-in dropping mechanism of the 802.11 MAC. The main idea is to further tune up wireless link's drop probability, based on the perceived link drops. LRED is a simple mechanism that, by monitoring a single parameter, the average number of retries in the packet transmissions at the link-layer, accomplishes three goals: a) It helps to improve TCP throughput, b) It provides TCP an early sign of network overload, and c) It helps to improve inter-flow fairness. The goal of Adaptive Pacing is to improve spatial channel reuse, by distributing traffic among intermediate nodes in a more balanced way, while enhancing the coordination of forwarding nodes along the data path. The design is aimed at the IEEE 802.11 MAC, where a node is allowed to further backoff an additional packet transmission time when necessary, in addition to its current deferral period (i.e. the random backoff, plus one packet transmission time). The extra backoff interval helps in reducing contention drops caused by exposed receivers, and extends the range of the link-layer coordination from one hop to two hops, along the packet forwarding path. The LRED and Adaptive Pacing algorithm works together as follows: Adaptive pacing is enabled by LRED. When a node finds its average number of retries to be less than min_{th}, it calculates its backoff time as usual. When the average number of retries goes beyond min_{th}, Adaptive Pacing is enabled and the backoff period is increased by an interval equal to the transmission time of the previous data packet.

9.15 Loss Tolerant TCP (LT-TCP)

TCP performance suffers substantially when packet error rates increase beyond a value of about 1% - 5%. In (Tickoo,2005) the authors propose LT-TCP, an end-end mechanism to improve the TCP performance over networks comprised of lossy wireless link. The scheme separates the congestion indications from the wireless packet erasures by exploiting ECN. To overcome packet erasures, a dynamic and adaptive Forward Error Correction (FEC) scheme that includes adaptation of the MSS for TCP is employed. Redundancy is added in the form of proactive FEC which tunes itself to the measured error rate. The residual packet errors are handled by an enhanced retransmission scheme using reactive FEC repair packets to complement proactive FEC and SACK retransmission. Dynamically changing the MSS tailors the number of segments in the window for optimal performance. The scheme is built on top of TCP-SACK and depends on SACK and timeouts as a last resort.

9.16 Multipath-TCP

Lim et al. (2003) investigate the TCP performance over a multipath routing protocol. Multipath routing can improve the path availability in mobile environment. Thus, it has a great potential to improve TCP performance in ad hoc networks under mobility. Previous research on multipath routing has mostly used UDP traffic for performance evaluation. When TCP is used, the authors find that most times, using multiple paths simultaneously may actually degrade TCP performance. This is partly due to frequent out-of-order packet delivery via different paths. They then test another multipath routing strategy called backup path routing. Under the backup path routing scheme, TCP is able to gain improvements when challenged with mobility. Further, related issues of backup path routing which can affect TCP performance are studied.

9.17 TCP Proportional Rate Reduction

TCP Proportional Rate Reduction (PRR)(2013) is an algorithm designed to improve the accuracy of data sent during recovery. It is an alternative to the widely deployed Fast Recovery and Rate-Halving algorithms. These algorithms determine the amount of data sent by TCP during loss recovery. PRR minimizes excess window adjustments, and the actual window size at the end of recovery will be as close as possible to the *ssthresh*, as determined by the congestion control algorithm. The algorithm ensures that the window size after recovery is as close as possible to the Slow-start threshold.

10. CONCLUSION

We have presented the functionality of TCP in wired network and shown how congestion window mechanism was modified in the further course to cope in wireless network. Although TCP work in wireless and wired-cum-wireless network, the performance is not up to the mark. After this the challenges that TCP faces in ad hoc network is presented. At last different proposals to make TCP work better in MANETs was presented.

REFERENCES

Allman, M., Paxson, W., & Blanton, E. (2009). *RFC 5681: TCP Congestion Control*. IETF Standards Track.

Altman, E., & Jim'enez, T. (2003). *Novel delayed ACK techniques for improving TCP performance in multihop wireless networks*. Venice, Italy: Personal Wireless Communications. doi:10.1007/978-3-540-39867-7_26

Bai, F., & Helmy, A. (2006). *A Survey of Mobility Models in Wireless Adhoc Networks*. Wireless Ad Hoc Networks.

Bakre, A. V., & Badrinath, B. R. (1997). Implementation and performance evaluation of indirect TCP. *IEEE/ACM Transactions on Networking*, *46*(3), 260–278.

Balakrishnan, H., & Padmanabhan, V. (2001). How network asymmetry affects TCP. *IEEE Communications Magazine*, *39*(4), 60–67. doi:10.1109/35.917505

Balakrishnan, H., Padmanabhan, V., Seshan, S., & Katz, R. (1997). A comparison of mechanisms for improving TCP performance over wireless links. *IEEE/ACM Transactions on Networking*, *5*(6), 756–769. doi:10.1109/90.650137

Balakrishnan, H., Padmanabhan, V. N., Fairhurst, G., & Sooriyabandara, M. (2002). *RFC 3449: TCP Performance Implications of Network Path Asymmetry*. IETF Best Current Practice.

Balakrishnan, H., Seshan, S., Amir, E., & Katz, R. (1995). Improving TCP/IP performance over wireless networks. In ACM MOBIHOC (pp. 2-11). Berkeley, CA: ACM.

Balakrishnan, H., Seshan, S., & Katz, R. (1995). Improving reliable transport and handoff performance in cellular wireless networks. *ACM Wireless Networks*, *1*(4), 469–481. doi:10.1007/BF01985757

Bharghavan, V., Demers, A., Shneker, S., & Zhang, L. (1994). MACAW: a media access protocol for wireless LAN's. In ACM SIGCOMM (pp. 212–225). London, UK: ACM. doi:10.1145/190314.190334

Bisoy, S. K., Panda, M. R., Pallai, G. K., & Panda, D. (2013). Analysing the Interaction between Mobility Model and Unipath Routing Protocols in Mobile Ad Hoc Networks. *International Journal of Application or Innovation in Engineering & Management*, *2*(6), 449–455.

Bisoy, S. K., & Pattnaik, P. K. (2013). Interaction between Internet Based TCP Variants and Routing Protocols in MANET. In *International Conference on Frontiers of Intelligent Computing: Theory and Applications (FICTA) Springer Advances in Intelligent Systems and Computing* (vol. 247, pp. 423-433). Springer.

Bisoy, S. K., & Pattnaik, P. K. (2014). Analyzing the Interaction Between TCP Variants and Routing Protocols in Static Multi-hop Ad hoc Network. In *Intelligent Computing* (Vol. 308, pp. 717–724). Communication and Devices, Springer Advances in Intelligent Systems and Computing.

Bisoy, S. K., & Pattnaik, P. K. (2014). Impact of Radio Propagation Model and Mobility in On-Demand Routing Protocol of MANET. *Journal of Theoretical and Applied Information Technology*, *65*(1), 30–45.

Border, J., Kojo, M., Griner, J., Montenegro, G., & Shelby, Z. (2001). *RFC 3135: Performance Enhancing Proxies Intended to Mitigate Link-Related Degradations*. IETF Informational.

Braden, R. (Ed.). (1989). *RFC 1122: Requirements for Internet Hosts- - Communication Layers*. IETF Internet Standard.

Brakmo, L. S., O'Malley, S. W., & Peterson, L. L. (1994). TCP Vegas: new techniques for congestion detection and avoidance. *SIGCOMM Computer Communication Review*, *24*, 24-35. Retrieved October 1994, from http://doi.acm.org/10.1145/190809.190317

Brown, K., & Singh, S. (1997). M-TCP: TCP for mobile cellular networks. *Computer Communication Review*, *27*(5), 19–43. doi:10.1145/269790.269794

Cerf, V. G., & Kahn, R. E. (1974). A protocol for packet network intercommunication. *IEEE Transactions on Communications*, *22*(3), 637–648. doi:10.1109/TCOM.1974.1092259

Chandran, K., Raghunathan, S., Venkatesan, S., & Prakash, R. (2001). A Feedback Based Scheme for Improving TCP Performance in Ad-Hoc Wireless Networks. *IEEE Personal Communications*, *8*(1), 34–39. doi:10.1109/98.904897

Chiang, M. (2005). Balancing transport and physical layers in wireless ad hoc networks: Jointly optimal TCP congestion control and power control. *IEEE JSAC*, *23*(1), 104–116.

Deering, S., & Hinden, R. (1998). *RFC 2460: Internet Protocol, Version 6 (IPv6) Specification*. IETF Internet Standard.

Duke, M., Braden, R., Eddy, W., & Blanton, E. (2006). *RFC 4614: A Roadmap for Transmission Control Protocol (TCP) Specification Documents*. IETF Internet Standard.

Durst, R., Miller, G., & Travis, E. (1996). TCP extensions for space communications. In ACM MOBICOM (pp. 15-26). Rye, NY: ACM. doi:10.1145/236387.236398

ElRakabawy, S. M., Klemm, A., & Lindemann, C. (2005). TCP with adaptive pacing for multihop wireless networks. In *6th ACM international symposium on Mobile ad hoc networking and computing*, (pp. 288-299). New York, NY: ACM. doi:10.1145/1062689.1062726

Fu, C. P., & Liew, S. (2003). TCP Veno: TCP enhancement for transmission over wireless access networks. *IEEE Journal on Selected Areas in Communications*, *21*(2), 216–228. doi:10.1109/JSAC.2002.807336

Fu, Z., Greenstein, B., Meng, X., & Lu, S. (2002). Design and implementation of a TCP-friendly transport protocol for ad hoc wireless networks. In *10th IEEE International Conference on Network Protocol*, (pp. 216-225). IEEE Press.

Fu, Z., Zerfos, P., Luo, H., Lu, S., Zhang, L., & Gerla, M. (2003). The impact of multihop wireless channel on TCP throughput and loss. In IEEE INFOCOM, (pp.1744-1753). San Francisco, CA: IEEE. doi:10.1109/INFCOM.2003.1209197

Fu, Z., Zerfos, P., Luo, H., Lu, S., Zhang, L., & Gerla, M. (2003). The impact of multihop wireless channel on tcp throughput and loss. In *twenty-Second Annual Joint Conference of the IEEE Computer and Communications* (vol. 3, pp. 1744-1753). IEEE Societies. doi:10.1109/INFCOM.2003.1209197

Gerla, M., Tang, K., & Bagrodia, R. (1999). TCP Performance in Wireless Multi-hop Networks. In *Second IEEE Workshop on Mobile Computer Systems and Applications server* (pp.41-48). Washington, DC: IEEE Computer Society. doi:10.1109/MCSA.1999.749276

Gettys, J., & Nichols, K. (2011). Bufferbloat: Dark buffers in the internet. *Queue, 9*(11), 40-54. Retrieved from http://doi.acm.org/10.1145/2063166.2071893

Global Mobile Information Systems Simulation Library GloMoSim. (n.d.). Retrieved from http://pcl.cs.ucla.edu/projects/glomosim/

Ha, S., Rhee, I., & Xu, L. (2008). CUBIC: a new TCP-friendly high-speed TCP variant. *SIGOPS Oper. Syst. Rev.*, *42*, 64-74. Retrieved July, 2008, from http://doi.acm.org/10.1145/1400097.1400105

Hanbali, A., Altman, E., & Nain, P. (2004). *A Survey of TCP over Mobile Ad Hoc Networks*. INRIA, Research Report RR-5182. Retrieved 05 2004, from http://hal.inria.fr/inria-00071406/en

Henderson, T., Floyd, S., Gurtov, A., & Nishida, Y. (2012). *RFC 6582: The NewReno Modification to TCP's Fast Recovery Algorithm*. IETF Internet Standard.

Henderson, T., & Katz, R. (1999). Transport protocols for Internet-compatible satellite networks. *IEEE JSAC*, *17*(2), 345–359.

Holland, G., & Vaidya, N. (2002). Analysis of TCP performance over mobile ad hoc networks. *ACM Wireless Networks*, *8*(2), 275–288. doi:10.1023/A:1013798127590

Holland, G., & Vaidya, N. (2002). Analysis of TCP performance over mobile ad hoc networks. *Wireless Networks*, *8*(2/3), 275–288. doi:10.1023/A:1013798127590

IEEE 802.11 WLAN standard. (n.d.). Retrieved from http://standards.ieee.org/getieee802

Jacobson, V. (1988). Congestion avoidance and control. *SIGCOMM Comput. Commun. Rev.*, *18*, 314–329. Retrieved August 1988, from http://doi.acm.org/10.1145/52325.52356

Jacobson, V. (1990). Modified TCP Congestion Control Avoidance Algorithm. *end-2-end-interest mailing list*, 1-14.

Jacobson, V. (1990). *Compression TCP/IP headers for low speed serial links*. RFC 1144, Category: Proposed Standard.

Jones, C., Sivalingam, K., Agarwal, P., & Chen, J. (2001). A survey of energy efficient network protocols for wireless and mobile networks. *ACM Wireless Networks*, *7*(4), 343–358. doi:10.1023/A:1016627727877

Kamerman, A., & Monteban, L. (1997). WaveLAN-11: A high-performance wireless lan for the unlicensed band. *Bell Labs Technical Journal*, *2*(3), 118–133. doi:10.1002/bltj.2069

Karn, P., & Partridge, C. (1987). Improving round-trip time estimates in reliable transport protocols. *SIGCOMM Comput. Commun. Rev.*, *17*, 2–7. Retrieved August 1987, from http://doi.acm.org/10.1145/55483.55484

Kim, D., Toh, C.K., & Choi, Y. (2001). TCP-BuS: Improving TCP Performance in Wireless Ad Hoc Networks. *Journal of Communications And Networks*, *3*, 1707–1713.

Klemm, F., Krishnamurthy, S., & Tripathi, S. (2003). Alleviating effects of mobility on TCP performance in ad hoc networks using signal strength based link management. In Personal Wireless Communications (pp. 611-624). doi:10.1007/978-3-540-39867-7_59

Kopparty, S., Krishnamurthy, S., Faloutsos, M., & Tripathi, S. (2002). Split TCP for mobile ad hoc networks. In *Global Telecommunications Conference*, (pp. 138-142). IEEE Press. doi:10.1109/GLOCOM.2002.1188057

Lim, H., Xu, K., & Gerla, M. (2003). Tcp performance over multipath routing in mobile ad hoc networks. In *IEEE International Conference on Communications*, (vol. 2, pp. 1064-1068). doi:10.1109/ICC.2003.1204520

Liu, J., & Singh, S. (2001). ATCP: TCP for mobile ad hoc networks. *IEEE Journal on Selected Areas in Communications*, *19*(7), 1300–1315. doi:10.1109/49.932698

Lochert, C., Scheuermann, B., & Mauve, M. (2007). A survey on congestion control for mobile ad hoc networks: Research Articles. *Wireless Communication Mobile Computing*, *7*(5), 655–676. doi:10.1002/wcm.524

Mascolo, S., Casetti, C., Gerla, M., Sanadidi, M. Y., & Wang, R. (2001). TCP westwood: Bandwidth estimation for enhanced transport over wireless links. In *7th annual international conference on Mobile computing and networking, ser. MobiCom* (pp. 287-297). New York, NY: ACM.

Mathis, M., Dukkipati, N., & Cheng, Y. (2003). *RFC 6937: Proportional Rate Reduction for TCP*. IETF Standards Track.

Mathis, M., Mahdavi, J., Floyd, S., & Romanow, A. (1996). *RFC 2018: TCP Selective Acknowledgment Options*. IETF Internet Standard.

Mirhosseini, S. M., & Torgheh, F. (2011). ADHOCTCP: Improving TCP Performance in Ad Hoc Networks. Intech.

Nagle, J. (1984). *RFC 896: Congestion Control in IP/TCP Internetworks*. IETF Internet Standard.

Nichols, K., & Jacobson, V. (2012). Controlling queue delay. *Queue*, *10*(5), 20-34. Retrieved May 2012, from http://doi.acm.org/10.1145/2208917.2209336

Paxson, V., & Allman, M. (2000). *Computing TCP's retransmission timer*. RFC 2988, Category: Standard Track.

Paxson, V., Allman, M., Chu, J., & Sargent, M. (2011). *RFC 6298: Computing TCP's Retransmission Timer*. IETF Internet Standard.

Pentikousis, K. (2000). TCP in wired-cum-wireless environments. *IEEE Communications Surveys and Tutorials*, *3*(4), 2–14. doi:10.1109/COMST.2000.5340805

Postel, G. (1981, Sept.). RFC 793: Transmission Control Protocol. IETF Internet Standard.

Tan, K., Song, J., Zhang, Q., & Sridharan, M. (2005). *A Compound TCP Approach for High-speed and Long Distance Networks*. Microsoft Research, Tech. Rep.

The Network Simulator. (n.d.). *NS-2*. Retrieved from http://www.isi.edu/nsnam/ns/index.html

Tickoo, O., Subramanian, V., Kalyanaraman, S., & Ramakrishnan, K. K. (2005). Lttcp: End-to-end framework to improve TCP performance over networks with lossy channels. *Lecture Notes in Computer Science*, *3552*, 81–93. doi:10.1007/11499169_8

Tobagi, F., & Kleinrock, L. (1975). Packet switching in radio channels: Part ii - the hidden terminal problem in Carrier Sense Multiple-Access modes and the busy-tone solution. *IEEE/ACM Transactions on Networking*, *23*(12), 1417–1433.

Toh, C. K. (1997). Associativity-Based Routing For Ad-Hoc Mobile Networks. *Wireless Personal Communications Journal*, *4*(2), 103–139.

Tomlinson, R. S. (1975). Selecting sequence numbers. *SIGOPS Oper. Syst. Rev.*, *9*, 11-23. http://doi.acm.org/10.1145/563905.810894

Wang, F., & Zhang, Y. (2002). Improving TCP performance over mobile ad hoc networks with out-of-order detection and response. In ACM MOBIHOC (pp. 217-225). Lausanne, Switzerland: ACM. doi:10.1145/513800.513827

Wang, F., & Zhang, Y. (2002). Improving TCP performance over mobile ad-hoc networks with out-of-order detection and response. In *3rd ACM international symposium on Mobile ad hoc networking & computing*, (pp.217-225). New York, NY: ACM. doi:10.1145/513800.513827

Wang, F., & Zhang, Y. (2005). A Survey on TCP over Mobile Ad-Hoc Networks. In Y. Xiao & Y. Pan (Eds.), *Ad Hoc and Sensor Networks* (pp. 267–281). Nova Science Publishers.

Wang, J., Wen, J., Zhang, J., & Han, Y. (2010). TCP-FIT: A novel TCP congestion control algorithm for wireless networks. In *GLOBECOM Workshops (GC Wkshps),* (pp. 2065 –2069). IEEE Press.

Wireless LAN medium access control (MAC) and physical layer (PHY) specification. (2007, June). IEEE standard 802.11-2007.

Xiao, X., Hannan, A., Paxson, V., & Crabbe, E. (2000). *RFC 2873: TCP Processing of the IPv4 Precedence Field.* IETF Internet Standard.

Xiao, X., Hannan, A., Paxson, V., & Crabbe, E. (2000). *RFC 2873: TCP Processing of the IPv4 Precedence Field.* IETF Internet Standard.

Xu, L., Harfoush, K., & Rhee, I. (2004). Binary increase congestion control (BIC) for fast long distance networks. *IEEE Computer and Communications Societies, 4*, 2514-2524.

Xu, S., & Saadawi, T. (2002). Performance evaluation of TCP algorithms in multi-hop wireless packet networks. *Journal of Wireless Communications and Mobile Computing*, *2*(1), 85–100. doi:10.1002/wcm.35

Xu, K., Gerla, M., & Bae, s. (2003). Effectiveness of RTS/CTS handshake in IEEE 802.11 based ad hoc networks. *Ad Hoc Networks Journal, 1*(1), 107-123.

Zhou, J., Shi, B., & Zou, L. (2003). Improve TCP performance in ad-hoc network by TCP-RC. In *14th IEEE Int. Symposium on Personal, Indoor and Mobile Radio Communications* (pp.216-220). Beijing, China: IEEE.

Zimmermann, H. (1988). *OSI reference model—The ISO model of architecture for open systems interconnection.* Norwood, MA: Artech House, Inc.

Chapter 3
Efficient Classification Rule Mining for Breast Cancer Detection

Sufal Das
North-Eastern Hill University, India

Hemanta Kumar Kalita
North-Eastern Hill University, India

ABSTRACT

Breast cancer is the second largest cause of cancer deaths among women. Mainly, this disease is tumor related cause of death in women. Early detection of breast cancer may protect women from death. Various computational methods have been utilized to enhance the diagnoses procedures. In this paper, we have presented the genetic algorithm (GA) based association rule mining method which can be applied to detect breast cancer efficiently. In this work, we have represented each solution as chromosome and applied to genetic algorithm based rule mining. Association rules which imply classification rules are encoded with binary strings to represent chromosomes. Finally, optimal solutions are found out by develop GA-based approach utilizing a feedback linkage between feature selection and association rule.

3.1 INTRODUCTION

Cancer data classification and clustering (Kharya, S. 2012) have been the focus of critical research in the area of medical and artificial intelligence. Health care is now days very important for human being. Breast cancer is the most common cancer in women in many countries. It is a malignant tumor that starts in the cells of the breast. A malignant tumor is a group of cancer cells that can grow into surrounding tissues or spread to distant areas of the body (Gandhi, K. R., Karnan, M., & Kannan, S. 2010, February). Various data mining techniques have been used to improve the diagnoses procedures and to aid the physician's efforts (Safavi, A. A., Parandeh, N. M., & Salehi, M. 2010). Screening mammography is the best tool available for detecting cancerous lesions before clinical symptoms appear (Gandhi, K. R., Karnan, M., & Kannan, S. 2010). Early detection and treatment of breast cancer can significantly advance the

DOI: 10.4018/978-1-4666-8737-0.ch003

survival rate of patient. However, this is a challenging problem due to structure of cancer cells. Breast cancer detection, classification, scoring and grading of histopathological images is the standard clinical practice for the diagnosis and prognosis of breast cancer. It is a very complex and time-consuming duty for a pathologist to manually perform these tasks. Robust and efficient computer aided systems are therefore indispensible for automatic breast cancer detection.

In this chapter, we have considered classification problem as an association rule mining where antecedent part of a rule is considered as different conditions and consequent part of the rule is considered as class label. Data mining algorithms like association rule mining (Agrawal, R., & Srikant, R. 1994) perform an exhaustive search to find all rules satisfying some constraints. Hence, the number of discovered rules from database can be very large. Based on the earlier works, it is clear that it is difficult to identify the most effective rule. Therefore, in many applications, the size of the dataset is so large that learning might not work well before removing the unwanted features. To reduce the search space for large dataset, we have applied genetic algorithm over rule mining to make the learning efficient. Finally we have tried to find out best rules which can be applied for breast cancer detection (Anunciaçao, O., Gomes, B. C., Vinga, S., Gaspar, J., Oliveira, A. L., & Rueff, J. 2010).

3.2 BACKGROUND

A. Association Rule Mining

Association rule mining, one of the most important and well researched techniques of data mining, was first introduced in (Agrawal, R., & Srikant, R. 1994). It aims to extract interesting correlations, frequent patterns, associations or casual structures among sets of items in the transaction databases or other data repositories. Association rules are widely used in various areas such as telecommunication networks, market and risk management, inventory control etc. Various association mining techniques and algorithms will be briefly introduced and compared later. Association rule mining is to find out association rules that satisfy the predefined minimum support and confidence from a given database. The problem is usually decomposed into two sub-problems. One is to find those itemsets whose occurrences exceed a predefined threshold in the database; those itemsets are called frequent or large itemsets. The second problem is to generate association rules from those large itemsets with the constraints of minimal confidence.

Let $I = \{I_1, I_2, \ldots, I_m\}$ be a set of m distinct attributes, also called literals. $A_i = r$ is an item, where r is a domain value is attribute, Ai in a relation, R $(A_1, \ldots, A_n)$. A is an itemset if it is a subset of I. $D = \{t_i, t_{i+1}, \ldots\ldots, t_n)$ is a set of transactions, called the transaction (tid, t-itemset). A transaction t contains an itemset A if and only if for all items $i \in A$, i is in t-itemset.

An itemset A in a transaction database D has a support, denoted as Supp(A) (we also use p(A) to stand for Supp(A)), that is the ratio of transactions in D contain A.

$\text{Supp}(A) = |A(t)| / |D|$, where $A(t) = \{t \text{ in } D/t \text{ contains } A\}$. An itemset A in a transaction database D is called a large (frequent) itemset if its support is equal to, or greater than, a threshold of minimal support (minsupp), which is given by users or experts (Agrawal, R., & Srikant, R. 1994).

An association rule is an expression of the form IF A THEN C (or $A \Rightarrow C$), $A \cap C = \varphi$, where A and C are sets of items. The meaning of this expression is that transactions of the databases, which contain A, tend to contain C.

There are two important basic measures for association rules, support(s) and confidence(c). Since the database is large and users concern about only those frequently purchased items, usually thresholds of support and confidence are predefined by users to drop those rules that are not so interesting or useful. The two thresholds are called minimal support and minimal confidence respectively. Support(s) of an association rule is defined as the percentage/fraction of records that contain A∪B to the total number of records in the database. Suppose the support of an item is 0.1%, it means only 0.1 percent of the transaction contain purchasing of this item. Confidence of an association rule is defined as the percentage/fraction of the number of transactions that contain A∪B to the total number of records that contain A. Confidence is a measure of strength of the association rules, suppose the confidence of the association rule A⇒B is 80%, it means that 80% of the transactions that contain A also contain B together.

Each association rule has two quality measurements: support and confidence, defined as:

1. The support of a rule A⇒C is the support of A∪C, where A∪C means both A and C occur at the same time.
2. The confidence or predictive accuracy (Agrawal, R., & Srikant, R. 1994) of a rule A⇒C is conf (A->C) as the ratio: |(A∪C)(t)| / |A(t)| or Supp(A∪C) / Supp(A). That is, support = frequencies of occurring patterns; confidence = strength of implication.

In support-confidence framework (Agrawal, R., & Srikant, R. 1994), let I be the set of items in database D, A, C⊆ I be itemset, A∩C =φ, p(A) ≠0 and p(C) ≠0. Minimal support (minsupp) and minimal confidence (minconf) are given by users or experts. Then A⇒C is a valid rule if

1. Supp(A∪C) ≥ minsupp
2. Conf(A⇒C) ≥ minconf

Mining association rules can be broken down into the following two sub-problems:

1. Generating all itemsets that have support greater than, or equal to, the user specified minimal support. That is, generating all large itemsets.
2. Generating all the rules that have minimum confidence.

The first sub-problem can be further divided into two sub-problems: candidate large itemsets generation process and frequent itemsets generation process. We call those itemsets whose support exceed the support threshold as large or frequent item sets, those itemsets that are expected or have the hope to be large or frequent are called candidate itemsets. In many cases, the algorithms generate an extremely large number of association rules, often in thousands or even millions. Further, the association rules are some-times very large. It is nearly impossible for the end users to comprehend or validate such large number of complex association rules, thereby limiting the usefulness of the data mining results. Several strategies have been proposed to reduce the number of association rules, such as generating only "interesting" rules, generating only "non-redundant" rules, or generating only those rules satisfying certain other criteria such as coverage, leverage, lift or strength.

In general, a set of items (such as the antecedent or the consequent of a rule) is called an itemset. The number of items in an itemset is called the length of an itemset. Itemsets of some length k are referred to as k-itemsets. Generally, an association rules mining algorithm contains the following steps:

- The set of candidate k-itemsets is generated by 1-extensions of the large (k -1) itemsets generated in the previous iteration.
- Supports for the candidate k-itemsets are generated by a pass over the database.
- Itemsets that do not have the minimum support are discarded and the remaining itemsets are called large k-itemsets.

This process is repeated until no more large itemsets are found.

The AIS algorithm was the first algorithm proposed for mining association rule. In this algorithm only one item consequent association rules are generated, which means that the consequent of those rules only contain one item, for example we only generate rules like A∩B⇒C but not those rules as A⇒B∩C. The main drawback of the AIS algorithm is too many candidate itemsets that finally turned out to be small are generated, which requires more space and wastes much effort that turned out to be useless. At the same time this algorithm requires too many passes over the whole database. Apriori is more efficient during the candidate generation process (Agrawal, R., & Srikant, R. 1994). Apriori uses pruning techniques to avoid measuring certain itemsets, while guaranteeing completeness. These are the itemsets that the algorithm can prove will not turn out to be large. However there are two bottlenecks of the Apriori algorithm. One is the complex candidate generation process that uses most of the time, space and memory. Another bottleneck is the multiple scan of the database. Based on Apriori algorithm, many new algorithms were designed with some modifications or improvements.

Basic Algorithm:
Input:
I, D, s, α
Output:
Association rules satisfying s and α.
Algorithm:

Find all sets of items which occur with a frequency that is greater than or equal to the user-specified threshold support, s. Generate the desired rules using the large itemsets, which have user-specified threshold confidence, α.

The first step in Algorithm 1 finds *large* or *frequent itemsets.* Itemsets other than those are referred as *small itemsets.* Here an itemset is a subset of the total set of items of interest from the database. An interesting (and useful) observation about large itemsets is that:

If an itemset X is small, any superset of X is also small.

Of course the contrapositive of this statement (If X is a large itemset than so is any subset of X) is also important to remember. In the remainder of this paper we use L to designate the set of large itemsets. The second step in Algorithm 1 finds association rules using large itemsets obtained in the first step. Example 2 illustrates this basic process for finding association rules from large itemsets.

Example: Consider a small database with four items I={Bread, Butter, Eggs, Milk} and four transactions as shown in Table 1. Table 2 shows all itemsets for I. Suppose that the minimum support and minimum confidence of an association rule are 40% and 60%, respectively. There are several potential association rules. For discussion purposes we only look at those in Table 3. At first, we have to find out whether all sets of items in those rules are large. Secondly, we have to verify whether a rule has a confidence of at least 60%. If the above conditions are satisfied for a rule, we

Table 1. Transaction Database for the Example

Transaction ID	Items
i	Bread, Butter, Eggs
T2	Butter, Eggs, Milk
T3	Butter
T4	Bread, Butter

Table 2. Support for Itemsets in Table 1 and Large Itemsets with a support of 40%

Itemset	Support, s	Large/Small
Bread	50%	Large
Butter	100%	Large
Eggs	50%	Large
Milk	25%	Small
Bread, Butter	50%	Large
Bread, Eggs	25%	Small
Bread, Milk	0%	Small
Butter, Eggs	50%	Large
Butter, Milk	25%	Small
Eggs, Milk	25%	Small
Bread, Butter, Eggs	25%	Small
Bread, Butter, Milk	0%	Small
Bread, Eggs, Milk	0%	Small
Butter, Eggs, Milk	25%	Small
Bread, Butter Eggs, Milk	0%	Small

Table 3. Confidence of Some Association Rules for Example 1 where α=60%

Rule	Confidence	Rule Hold
Bread ⇒ Butter	100%	Yes
Butter ⇒ Bread	50%	No
Butter ⇒ Eggs	50%	No
Eggs ⇒ Butter	100%	Yes

can say that there is enough evidence to conclude that the rule holds with a confidence of 60%. Itemsets associated with the aforementioned rules are: {Bread, Butter}, and {Butter, Eggs}. The support of each individual itemset is at least 40% (see Table 2). Therefore, all of these itemsets are large. The confidence of each rule is presented in Table 3. It is evident that the first rule (Bread ⇒ Butter) holds. However, the second rule (Butter ⇒ Eggs) does not hold because its confidence is less than 60%.

For example, suppose we want to see whether the first rule {Bread ⇒ Butter) holds for Example 2. Here A= {Bread, Butter}, and B = {Bread}. Therefore, (A-B) = {Butter}. Now, the ratio of support(Bread, Butter) to support(Bread) is 100% which is greater than the minimum confidence. Therefore, the rule holds. For a better understanding, let us consider the third rule, Butter ⇒ Eggs, where x = {Butter}, and (l-x) = {Eggs}. The ratio of support(Butter, Eggs) to support(Butter) is 50% which is less than 60%. Therefore, we can say that there is not enough evidence to conclude {Butter} ⇒ {Eggs} with 60% confidence.

B. Classification

Classification consists of predicting a certain outcome based on a given input. In order to predict the outcome, the algorithm processes a training set containing a set of attributes and the respective outcome, usually called goal or prediction attribute. The algorithm tries to discover relationships between the attributes that would make it possible to predict the outcome. Next the algorithm is given a data set not seen before, called prediction set, which contains the same set of attributes, except for the prediction attribute – not yet known. The algorithm analyses the input and produces a prediction. The prediction accuracy defines how "good" the algorithm is. For example, in a medical database the training set would have relevant patient information recorded previously, where the prediction attribute is whether or not the patient had a heart problem. Table 4 below illustrates the training and prediction sets of such database.

Among several types of knowledge representation present in the literature, classification normally uses prediction rules to express knowledge. Prediction rules are expressed in the form of IF-THEN rules, where the antecedent (IF part) consists of a conjunction of conditions and the rule consequent (THEN part) predicts a certain predictions attribute value for an item that satisfies the antecedent. Using the example above, a rule predicting the first row in the training set may be represented as following:

IF (Age=65 AND Heart rate>70) OR (Age>60 AND Blood pressure>140/70) THEN Heart problem=yes

In most cases the prediction rule is immensely larger than the example above. Conjunction has a nice property for classification; each condition separated by OR's defines smaller rules that captures relations between attributes. Satisfying any of these smaller rules means that the consequent is the prediction.

Table 4. Training and Prediction Sets for Medical Database

Training set			
Age	**Heart rate**	**Blood pressure**	**Heart problem**
65	78	150/70	Yes
37	83	112/76	No
71	67	108/65	No
Prediction set			
Age	**Heart rate**	**Blood pressure**	**Heart problem**
43	98	147/89	?
65	58	106/63	?
84	77	150/65	?

Each smaller rule is formed with AND's which facilitates narrowing down relations between attributes. How well predictions are done is measured in percentage of predictions hit against the total number of predictions. A decent rule ought to have a hit rate greater than the occurrence of the prediction attribute. In other words, if the algorithm is trying to predict rain in Seattle and it rains 80% of the time, the algorithm could easily have a hit rate of 80% by just predicting rain all the time. Therefore, 80% is the base prediction rate that any algorithm should achieve in this case. The optimal solution is a rule with 100% prediction hit rate, which is very hard, when not impossible, to achieve. Therefore, except for some very specific problems, classification by definition can only be solved by approximation algorithms.

C. Genetic Algorithm

Genetic algorithms (GA) were first introduced by John Holland in the 1970s (Holland 1975) as a result of investigations into the possibility of computer programs undergoing evolution in the Darwinian sense.

GA are part of a broader soft computing paradigm known as evolutionary computation. They attempt to arrive at optimal solutions through a process similar to biological evolution. This involves following the principles of survival of the fittest, and crossbreeding and mutation to generate better solutions from a pool of existing solutions.

Genetic algorithms have been found to be capable of finding solutions for a wide variety of problems for which no acceptable algorithmic solutions exist. The GA methodology is particularly suited for *optimization*, a problem solving technique in which one or more very good solutions are searched for in a solution space consisting of a large number of possible solutions. GA reduce the search space by continually evaluating the current generation of candidate solutions, discarding the ones ranked as poor, and producing a new generation through crossbreeding and mutating those ranked as good. The ranking of candidate solutions is done using some pre-determined measure of goodness or fitness.

A genetic algorithm is a probabilistic search technique that computationally simulates the process of biological evolution. It mimics evolution in nature by repeatedly altering a population of candidate solutions until an optimal solution is found.

The GA evolutionary cycle starts with a randomly selected initial population. The changes to the population occur through the processes of selection based on fitness, and alteration using crossover and mutation. The application of selection and alteration leads to a population with a higher proportion of better solutions. The evolutionary cycle continues until an acceptable solution is found in the current generation of population, or some control parameter such as the number of generations is exceeded.

The smallest unit of a genetic algorithm is called a *gene*, which represents a unit of information in the problem domain. A series of genes, known as a *chromosome*, represents one possible solution to the problem. Each gene in the chromosome represents one component of the solution pattern.

The most common form of representing a solution as a chromosome is a string of binary digits. Each bit in this string is a gene. The process of converting the solution from its original form into the bit string is known as *coding*. The specific coding scheme used is application dependent. The solution bit strings are decoded to enable their evaluation using a fitness measure.

Selection

In biological evolution, only the fittest survive and their gene pool contributes to the creation of the next generation. Selection in GA is also based on a similar process. In a common form of selection, known as *fitness proportional selection*, each chromosome's likelihood of being selected as a good one is proportional to its fitness value.

Alteration to Improve Good Solutions

The alteration step in the genetic algorithm refines the good solution from the current generation to produce the next generation of candidate solutions. It is carried out by performing crossover and mutation.

Crossover may be regarded as artificial mating in which chromosomes from two individuals are combined to create the chromosome for the next generation. This is done by splicing two chromosomes from two different solutions at a crossover point and swapping the spliced parts. The idea is that some genes with good characteristics from one chromosome may as a result combine with some good genes in the other chromosome to create a better solution represented by the new chromosome (See Fig. 1).

Mutation is a random adjustment in the genetic composition. It is useful for introducing new characteristics in a population – something not achieved through crossover alone. Crossover only rearranges existing characteristics to give new combinations. For example, if the first bit in every chromosome of a generation happens to be a 1, any new chromosome created through crossover will also have 1 as the first bit.

The mutation operator changes the current value of a gene to a different one. For bit string chromosome this change amounts to flipping a 0 bit to a 1 or vice versa. Although useful for introducing new traits in the solution pool, mutations can be counterproductive, and applied only infrequently and randomly.

The steps in the typical genetic algorithm for finding a solution to a problem are listed below:

1. Create an initial solution population of a certain size randomly

Figure 1. Example for Crossover and Mutation

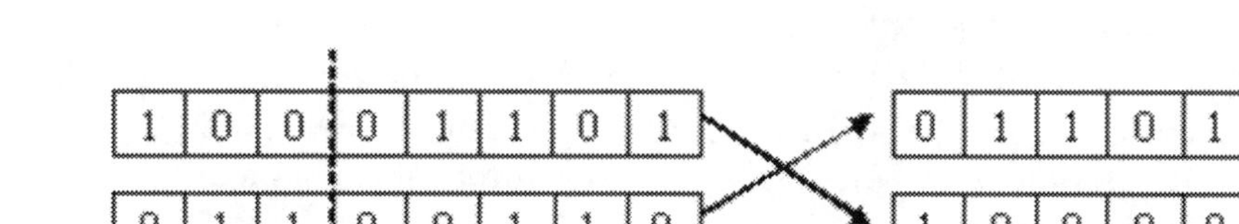

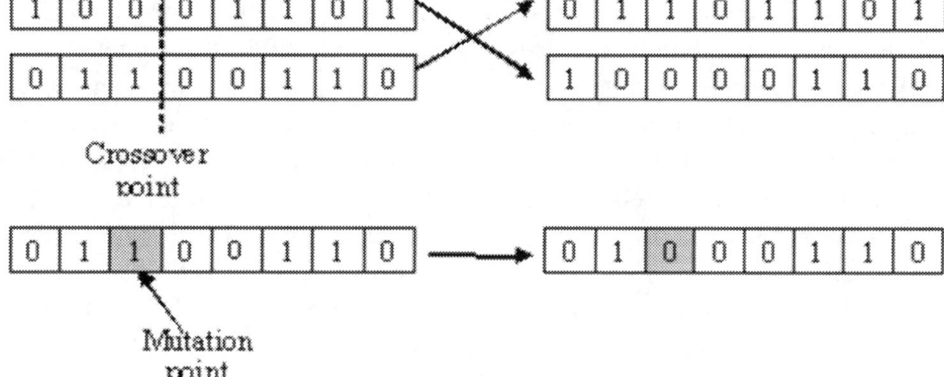

2. Evaluate each solution in the current generation and assign it a fitness value.
3. Select "good" solutions based on fitness value and discard the rest.
4. If acceptable solution(s) found in the current generation or maximum number of generations is exceeded then stop.
5. Alter the solution population using crossover and mutation to create a new generation of solutions.
6. Go to step 2.

GA can be used when no algorithms or heuristics are available for solving a problem. A GA based system can be built as long as a solution representation and an evaluation scheme can be worked out. Since it only requires the description of a good solution and not how to achieve it, the need for expert access is minimized. Even where rules are available for solving a problem, the number of rules may be too large or the nature of the knowledge base too dynamic. GA can act as alternative problem solving tools in such cases. Optimization problems in which the constraints and objective functions are non-linear and/or discontinuous are not amenable to solution by traditional methods such as linear programming. GA can solve such problems. GA do not guarantee optimal solutions, but produce near optimal solutions which are likely to be very good. Solution time with GA is highly predictable – it is determined by the size of the population, time taken to decode and evaluate a solution and the number of generations of population.

GA use simple operations, but are able to solve problems which are found to be computationally prohibitive by traditional algorithmic and numerical techniques. One example is the TSP problem (discussed earlier in this topic).

Because of their relative simplicity, GA software is reasonably sized and self-contained. Due to their compact nature, it is easier to embed them as a module in another system compared with rule based systems.

3.3 MAIN FOCUS OF THE CHAPTER

In the chapter, a cancer detection system is introduced using Pareto based genetic algorithm to find out an optimal set of classification rules. Here, each classification rule is resented as an association rule. Different the valid conditions are represented as antecedent part of the rule and class levels are represented as consequent part of the association rules. In the Pittsburgh approach (Das, S., & Saha, B. 2009), each chromosome represents a set of rules, and this approach is more suitable for classification rule mining. In this chapter, we consider each chromosome as set of different conditions with extra bits as class label. Basically, antecedent part of an association rule represents different conditions and consequent part represents the class label. We do not have a priori knowledge of the different conditions. So we take after another approach that is superior to this methodology from the purpose of capacity necessity. With each one attribute we relate one additional label bit. If this bit is 1, then the attribute next to this bit appears as a condition in the antecedent part and if it is 0, then the attribute do not appear as a condition in the antecedent part. Also we consider three bits after an attribute as the value of the attribute. So, a rule, A3B2E4F1->+ve will look like 1A011 1B010 0C110 0D010 1E100 1F001 1. Here, the last bit of a chromosome is considered as class label. If the bit is 0 then class label is –ve (negative) otherwise +ve (positive). The following step is to discover a suitable plan for encoding/decoding the association rules to/from binary chromosomes. Since the positions of attributes are fixed, we need not store the name of the attributes. We need to encode the values of different attribute in the chromosome only. Here the chromosomes are chosen (using standard selection scheme, e.g. roulette wheel selection) utilizing their fitness value.

Fitness value is calculated using confidence (accuracy) value and completeness value of a chromosome. It is very important that whatever rule will be selected for useful one this rule should represent all useful attributes or components. For that we have to select compact association rule with all useful features. So, we have to find out the frequent itemset with maximum length. The antecedent part and consequent for an association rule should cover all useful features as well as the two parts should be frequent. The following expression can be used to quantify the completeness of an association rule

Completeness Value = log ((1+ |A|) / |D|)

Here, |A| is the number of attributes involved in the antecedent part and |D| is the total number of records in the dataset.

Fitness value is calculated using their ranks, which are calculated from the non-dominance property of the chromosomes. A solution, say a, is said to be dominated by another solution, say b, if and only if the solution b is better or equal with respect to all the corresponding objectives of the solution a, and b is strictly better in at least one objective. Here the solution b is called a non-dominated solution. The ranking step tries to find the non-dominated solutions, and those solutions are ranked as one. Among the rest of the chromosomes, if pi individuals dominate a chromosome then its rank is assigned as 1 + pi. This process continues till all the chromosomes are ranked. Then fitness is assigned to the chromosomes such that the chromosomes having the smallest rank get the highest fitness and the chromosomes having the same rank gets the same fitness (Das, S., & Saha, B. 2009).

After assigning the fitness to the chromosomes, selection, replacement, crossover and mutation operators are applied to get a new set of chromosomes. (See Fig. 2)

Our method follows as:

Figure 2. Flowchart for the genetic method

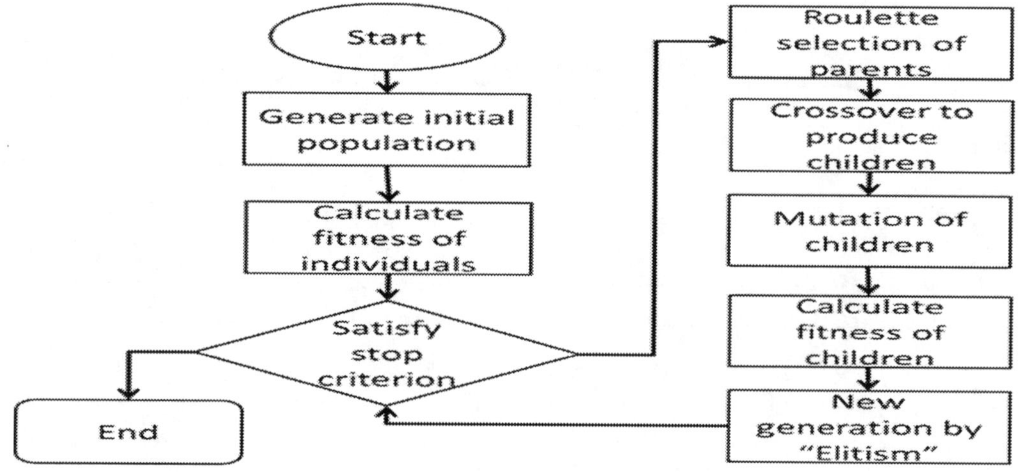

1. Load the dataset that fits in the memory.
2. Generate N chromosomes randomly.
3. Decode them to get the values of the different attributes.
4. Scan the loaded dataset to find the support of antecedent part, consequent part and the rule.
5. Find the confidence and completeness values for each chromosome.
6. Rank the chromosomes depending on the non- dominance property.
7. Assign fitness to the chromosomes using the ranks.
8. Select the chromosomes, for next generation, by roulette wheel selection scheme.
9. Bring a copy of the chromosomes ranked as 1 into an elite population, and store them if they are non-dominated in this population also. If some of the existing chromosomes of this population become dominated, due to this insertion, then remove the dominated chromosomes from this population.
10. Select the chromosomes, for next generation, by roulette wheel selection scheme using the fitness calculated in Step 7.
11. Replace all chromosomes of the old population by the chromosomes selected in Step 10.
12. Perform multi-point crossover and mutation on these new individuals.
13. If the desired number of generations is not completed, then go to Step 3.
14. Decode chromosomes from the final elite population.

3.4 EXPERIMENTATION AND RESULT ANALYSIS

The proposed method has been implemented on distinctive data sets with palatable results. Here we have considered the results on breast cancer data set having 9 attributes, 2 class label and 701 records. Crossover and mutation probabilities were taken respectively as 0.85 and 0.02; 4 point crossover operator was utilized and the population size and generation were kept fixed as 40 and 200 respectively. Performance analysis of the method as follow in

Table 5.

Data Attribute Names	Number of Instances	Efficiency of Our Method (%)
Clump Thickness	10	95.03
Cell Size Uniformity	10	92.13
Cell Shape Uniformity	10	95.42
Marginal Adhesion	10	93.71
Single Epi. Cell Size	10	94.16
Bare Nuclei	10	94.36
Bland Chromatin	10	93.62
Normal Nucleoli	10	95.43
Mitoses	10	95.07
Class	2 (Benign/Malignant)	Avg. 94.33

3.5 FUTURE RESEARCH DIRECTION

Health care is now days very important for human being. Breast cancer is the most common cancer in women in many countries. Various data mining techniques have been used to improve the diagnoses procedures and to aid the physician's efforts. Early detection and treatment of breast cancer can significantly advance the survival rate of patient. However, this is a challenging problem due to structure of cancer cells. Researchers are working with different machine learning techniques as well as self learning methods to increase the accuracy of cancer detection.

3.6 CONCLUSION

In this chapter, an automatic diagnosis system for detecting breast cancer based on association rules and genetic algorithm is introduced. Feature extraction is the key for pattern recognition and classification. The best classifier will perform poorly if the features are not chosen well. Normally association rule mining does not work well for large data set. It is required to select proper threshold values for different objectives which is also a challenging task. Our method is free from all these limitations as genetic algorithm gives an exhaustive search for large input spaces.

REFERENCES

Abdelaal, M. M. A., Farouq, M. W., Sena, H. A., & Salem, A. B. M. (2010, October). Using data mining for assessing diagnosis of breast cancer. In *Computer Science and Information Technology (IMCSIT), Proceedings of the 2010 International Multiconference on* (pp. 11-17). IEEE. doi:10.1109/IMCSIT.2010.5679647

Agrawal, R., Imieliński, T., & Swami, A. (1993, June). Mining association rules between sets of items in large databases. *SIGMOD Record*, *22*(2), 207–216. doi:10.1145/170036.170072

Agrawal, R., & Srikant, R. (1994, September). Fast algorithms for mining association rules. In *Proc. 20th int. conf. very large data bases, VLDB* (Vol. 1215, pp. 487-499). VLDB.

Anunciaçao, O., Gomes, B. C., Vinga, S., Gaspar, J., Oliveira, A. L., & Rueff, J. (2010). A data mining approach for the detection of high-risk breast cancer groups. In *Advances in Bioinformatics* (pp. 43–51). Springer Berlin Heidelberg. doi:10.1007/978-3-642-13214-8_6

Das, S., & Saha, B. (2009). Data quality mining using genetic algorithm. *International Journal of Computer Science and Security*, *3*(2), 105–112.

Fonseca, C. M., & Fleming, P. J. (1993, June). Genetic Algorithms for Multi-objective Optimization: Formulation Discussion and Generalization. In ICGA (Vol. 93, pp. 416-423). ICGA.

Fukuda, T., Morimoto, Y., Morishita, S., & Tokuyama, T. (1996). Data mining using two-dimensional optimized association rules: Scheme, algorithms, and visualization. *SIGMOD Record*, *25*(2), 13–23. doi:10.1145/235968.233313

Fukuda, T., Morimoto, Y., Morishita, S., & Tokuyama, T. (1996, June). Sonar: System for optimized numeric association rules. *SIGMOD Record*, *25*(2), 553. doi:10.1145/235968.280359

Fukuda, T., Morimoto, Y., Morishita, S., & Tokuyama, T. (1996, June). Mining optimized association rules for numeric attributes. In *Proceedings of the fifteenth ACM SIGACT-SIGMOD-SIGART symposium on Principles of database systems* (pp. 182-191). ACM. doi:10.1145/237661.237708

Gandhi, K. R., Karnan, M., & Kannan, S. (2010, February). Classification rule construction using particle swarm optimization algorithm for breast cancer data sets. In *Signal Acquisition and Processing, 2010. ICSAP'10. International Conference on* (pp. 233-237). IEEE. doi:10.1109/ICSAP.2010.58

Goebel, M., & Gruenwald, L. (1999). A survey of data mining and knowledge discovery software tools. *ACM SIGKDD Explorations Newsletter*, *1*(1), 20–33. doi:10.1145/846170.846172

Han, E. H., Karypis, G., & Kumar, V. (1997). Scalable parallel data mining for association rules. ACM.

Han, J., & Fu, Y. (1995, September). Discovery of multiple-level association rules from large databases. In VLDB (Vol. 95, pp. 420-431). VLDB.

Harada, L., Akaboshi, N., Ogihara, K., & Take, R. (1998, November). Dynamic skew handling in parallel mining of association rules. In *Proceedings of the seventh international conference on Information and knowledge management* (pp. 76-85). ACM. doi:10.1145/288627.288634

Hidber, C. (1999). Online association rule mining. ACM.

Houtsma, M., & Swami, A. (1995, March). Set-oriented mining for association rules in relational databases. In *Data Engineering, 1995. Proceedings of the Eleventh International Conference on* (pp. 25-33). IEEE. doi:10.1109/ICDE.1995.380413

Kharya, S. (2012). *Using data mining techniques for diagnosis and prognosis of cancer disease*. arXiv preprint arXiv:1205.1923.

Murthy, S. K. (1998). Automatic construction of decision trees from data: A multi-disciplinary survey. *Data Mining and Knowledge Discovery*, *2*(4), 345–389. doi:10.1023/A:1009744630224

Pei, M., Goodman, E. D., & Punch, W. F. (1998, October). Feature extraction using genetic algorithms. In *Proceedings of the 1st International Symposium on Intelligent Data Engineering and Learning, IDEAL* (Vol. 98, pp. 371-384). IDEAL.

Pitangui, C., & Zaverucha, G. (2006, December). Genetic based machine learning: merging Pittsburgh and Michigan, an implicit feature selection mechanism and a new crossover operator. In *Hybrid Intelligent Systems, 2006. HIS'06. Sixth International Conference on* (pp. 58-58). IEEE. doi:10.1109/HIS.2006.264941

Safavi, A. A., Parandeh, N. M., & Salehi, M. (2010, October). Predicting Breast Cancer Survivability using data mining techniques. In *Software Technology and Engineering (ICSTE), 2010 2nd International Conference on* (Vol. 2, pp. V2-227). IEEE.

KEY TERMS AND DEFINITIONS

Association Rule Mining: Association rule mining, an example of data mining methods, performs a comprehensive pursuit to discover association rules satisfying some constraints.

Cancer Detection: Cancer detection, classification, scoring and grading of histopathological images is the standard clinical practice for the diagnosis and prognosis of cancer.

Classification: Classification is a supervised pattern recognition method which is used to assign a class label to given input sets based on a training sample.

Evolutionary Algorithm: This incorporates Darwinian evolutionary theory with sexual reproduction. Genetic algorithm, an example of this method, is stochastic search algorithm modeled on the process of natural selection, which underlines biological evolution.

Genetic Algorithm: Genetic Algorithm is a stochastic search algorithm modeled on the process of natural selection, which underlines biological evolution. It has been successfully applied in many search, optimization, and machine learning problems. It process in an iteration manner by generating new populations of strings from old ones.

Chapter 4
Restoration Technique to Optimize Recovery Time for Efficient OSPF Network

Pertik Garg
Punjab Technical University, India

Ashu Gupta
Punjab Technical University, India

ABSTRACT

Some high speed IP networks, which involve interior gateway protocols, such as OSPF, are not capable of finding the new routes to bypass the effect like failure in time. At the point when the failure occurs the network must converge it before the traffic has the capacity to go to and from the network segment that caused a connection disconnect. The duration of the convergence period of these protocols vary from hundred of milliseconds to 10 seconds, which creates unsteadiness and results high packet loss rate. This issue may be determined by proposing an algorithm that can rapidly react to the topology change and reduce the convergence time by providing back up path which is already stored in routing table before the failover occurs.

INTRODUCTION

1. Routing Protocol

A routing protocol specifies how routers communicate with each other, disseminating information that enables them to select routes between any two nodes on a computer network. Routing algorithms determine the specific choice of route. Each router has a priori knowledge only of networks attached to it directly (Introduction IP Routing). A routing protocol shares this information first among immediate neighbors, and then throughout the network. This way, routers gain knowledge of the topology of the network. The term Routing Protocol refers specifically to one of the operating layers of the OSI model, which similarly disseminates topology information between routers. The specific characteristics (Wu,

DOI: 10.4018/978-1-4666-8737-0.ch004

n.d.) of routing protocols include: Routing path, Hop count, Convergence time, Scale up factor. There are three classes of Routing Protocols: Exterior gateway routing, Interior gateway routing by distance vector protocols, Interior gateway routing by link state routing protocols.

A. Exterior gateway routing: Border gateway protocol (BGP) is the routing protocol used on internet for exchange traffic between autonomous systems.
B. Interior gateway routing via distance vector routing protocols: It uses simple algorithm that calculates a cumulative distance value between routers based on hop count (Grang & Gupta, 2013).
C. Interior Gateway Routing via link state routing protocols: The basic concept of link-state routing is that every node constructs a map of the connectivity to the network, in the form of a graph, showing which nodes are connected to which other nodes. Each node then independently calculates the next best logical path from it to every possible destination in the network. The collection of best paths will then form the node's routing table. Through link state routing protocol(Introduction IP Routing):
    i. Routers broadcast and receive link state packets to and from other routers via the network.
    ii. Link state packets contain the status of a router's links or network interfaces.
    iii. The router builds a topology database of the network.
    iv. The router runs the Shortest Path First (SPF) algorithm against the database and generates a SPF tree of the network with itself as the root of the tree.
    v. The router populates it route table with optimal paths and ports to transmit data through to reach each network.

Examples of link state routing protocols are:

1. Open Shortest Path First (OSPF) for IP
2. The ISO's Intermediate System to Intermediate System (IS-IS) for CLNS and IP
3. DEC's DNA Phase V
4. Novell's NetWare Link Services Protocol (NLSP)

2. Open Shortest Path First (OSPF)

OSPF protocol was developed due to a need in the internet community to introduce a high functionality non-proprietary Internal Gateway Protocol (IGP) for the TCP/IP protocol family. OSPF (Moy, 1998; Coltun, Ferguson, Moy & Lindem, 2008) is a popular interior gateway routing protocol. Such protocols provide routing functionality within a domain, which is generally, although not necessarily, contained within an autonomous system (AS) (Hawkinson & Bates, 1996). OSPF belongs to the category of link state routing protocols that generally require each router in the network to know about the complete network topology. In 1989, the first version of OSPF was defined as OSPFv1, which was published in RFC 1131. The second version of OSPFv2 was introduced in 1998, which was defined in RFC 2328. In 1999, the third version of OSPFv3 for IPv6 was released in RFC 2740 (Islam & Ashique, 2010). OSPF has introduced new concepts such as authentication of routing updates, Variable Length Subnet Masks (VLSM), route summarization, and so forth.

Figure 1. Shows distance between the cities A, B, C, F and M.

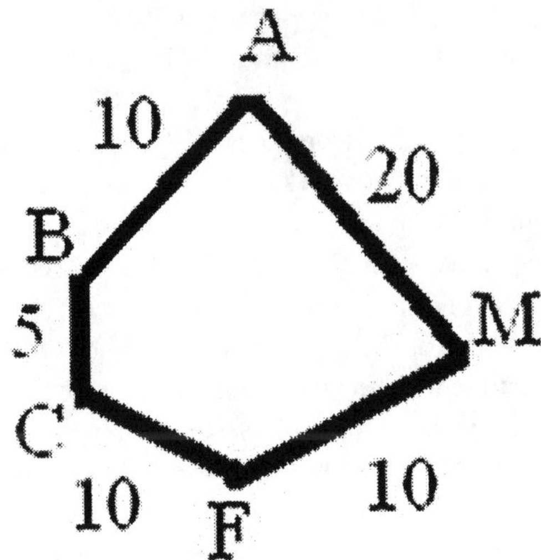

The path cost of an interface in OSPF is called metric that indicates standard value such as speed. The cost of an interface is calculated on the basis of bandwidth. Cost is inversely proportional to the bandwidth. Higher bandwidth is attained with a lower cost.

Cost $=10^8$/Bandwidth in bps

Where the value of 108 is 100000000 in bps is called reference bandwidth based on by default.

Open Shortest Path First (OSPF) is a link state routing protocol (LSRP) that uses the Shortest Path First (SPF) network communication algorithm (Dijkstra's algorithm) to calculate the shortest connection path between known devices (Hawkinson & Bates, 1996).

For example, as shown in figure 1 a person in city A wants to travel to city M and is given two options:

A. Travel via cities B and C. The route would be ABCM. And the distance (or bandwidth cost in the networking case) for A-B is 10 miles, B-C is 5 miles and C-M is 10 miles.
B. Travel via city F. The route would be AFM. And the distance for A-F is 20 miles and F-M is 10 miles.

The shortest route is always the one with least amount of distance covered in total. Thus, the ABCM route is the better option (10+5+10=25), even though the person has to travel to two cities as the associated total cost to travel to the destination is less than the second option with a single city (20+10=30). OSPF performs a similar algorithm by first calculating the shortest path between the source and destination based on link bandwidth cost and then allows the network to send and receive IP packets via the shortest route.

The OSPF routing policies to construct a route table are governed by link cost factors (external metrics) associated with each routing interface. Cost factors may be the distance of a router (round-trip time), network throughput of a link, or link availability and reliability, expressed as simple unit less numbers. This provides a dynamic process of traffic load balancing between routes of equal cost.

OSPF selects the best routes by finding the lowest cost paths to a destination. All router interfaces (links) are given a cost. The cost of a route is equal to the sum of all the costs configured on all the outbound links between the router and the destination network, plus the cost configured on the interface that OSPF received the Link State Advertisement on.

OSPF supports the following types of physical networks:

A. Point-to-point: A network of two routers, one at either end of a single connection. The point-to-point interfaces can be set up as numbered or unnumbered interfaces.
B. Broadcast: A network with potentially more than two routers, and capable of sending a single physical message to all the routers. An example of this type of network is an Ethernet network.
C. Non-broadcast: A network with potentially more than two routers, but without a mechanism to send a single physical message to all the routers. Examples of these types of network are frame relay or X.25 networks.

3. OSPF Convergence

Consider the network in figure 2 running OSPF (Islam & Ashique, 2010). Assume the link between R3 and R5 fails. R3 detects link failure and sends LSA to R2 and R4. Since a change in the network is detected traffic forwarding is suspended. R2and R4 updates their topology database, copies the LSA and flood their neighbors.

By flooding LSA all devices in the network have topological awareness. A new routing table is generated by all routers by running Dijkstra algorithm. The traffic is now forwarded via R4.

Figure 2. OSPF network

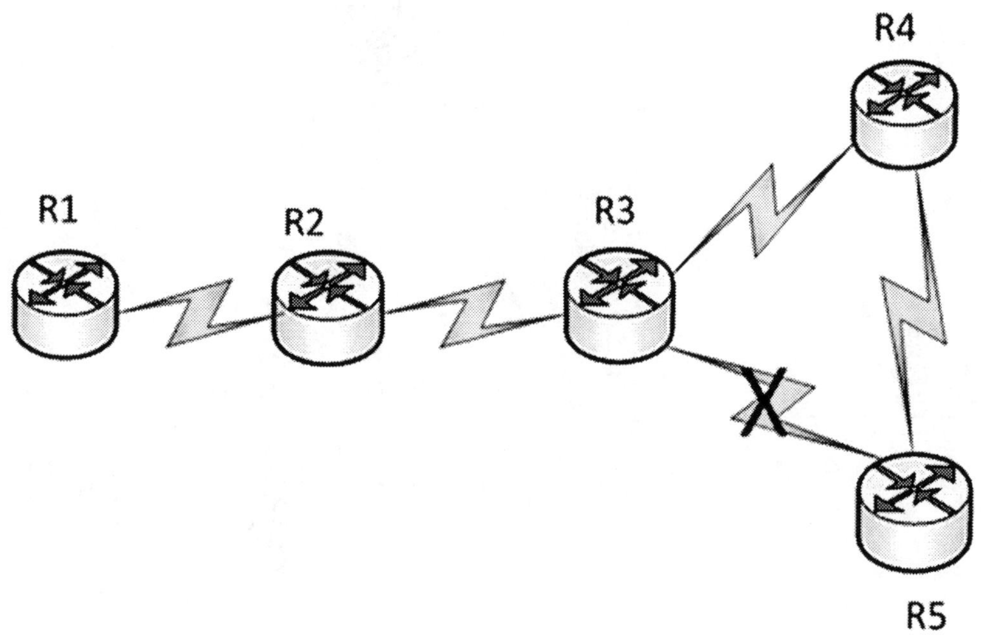

4. How OSPF Works

A. Routers in exchange link-state data start the process.
B. Each router stores the link-state information in memory using a structure named the topology table or topology database.
C. The router processes all data in the topology table and makes use of the Dijkstra algorithm to determine all routes to all networks, as well as the least-cost routes.
D. All this information is stored in the SFP tree, identifying preferred and secondary routes.
E. The routing information is propagated to the routing table as shown in figure 3.

When designing our OSPF network, the two main factors we have to work with are areas and how they fit within an AS. Areas are functional areas of our network, perhaps a building or the floor of a building, and Autonomous Systems (as shown in figure 4) are collections of areas, which typically are our entire network.

OSPF routers can be classified into four overlapping types:

A. Internal Router: Internal Routers route packets within a single area. The internal router can also be a backbone router if that router has no interfaces to other areas.
B. Area Border Router: Area border routers have interfaces in multiple areas, and route packets between these areas. Area border routers condense topological information before passing it to the backbone. This reduces the amount of routing information passed across the backbone.

Figure 3. SPF tree generate from topology table

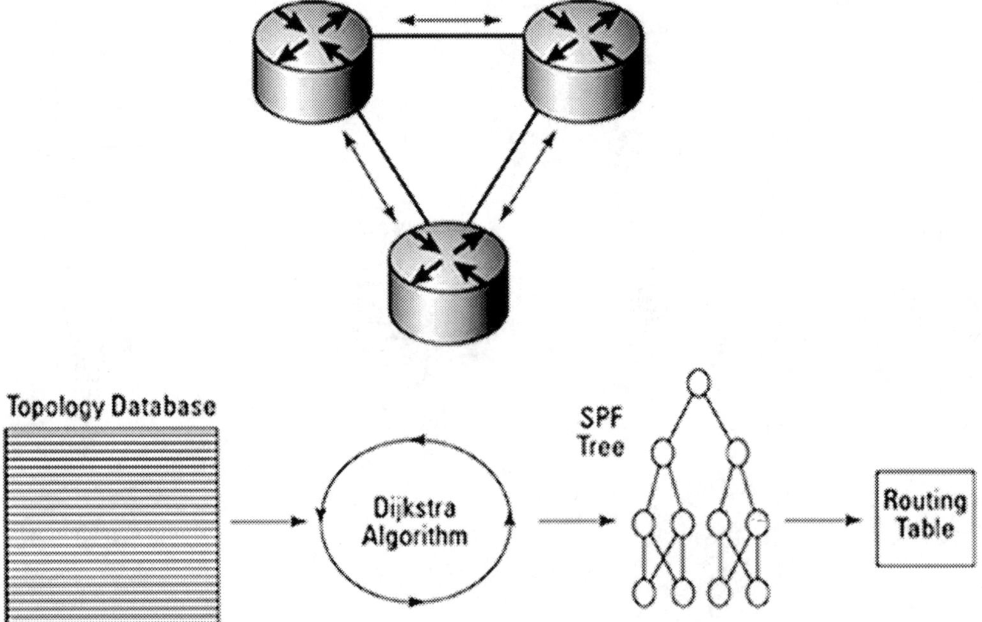

Figure 4. Link State Routing Protocol

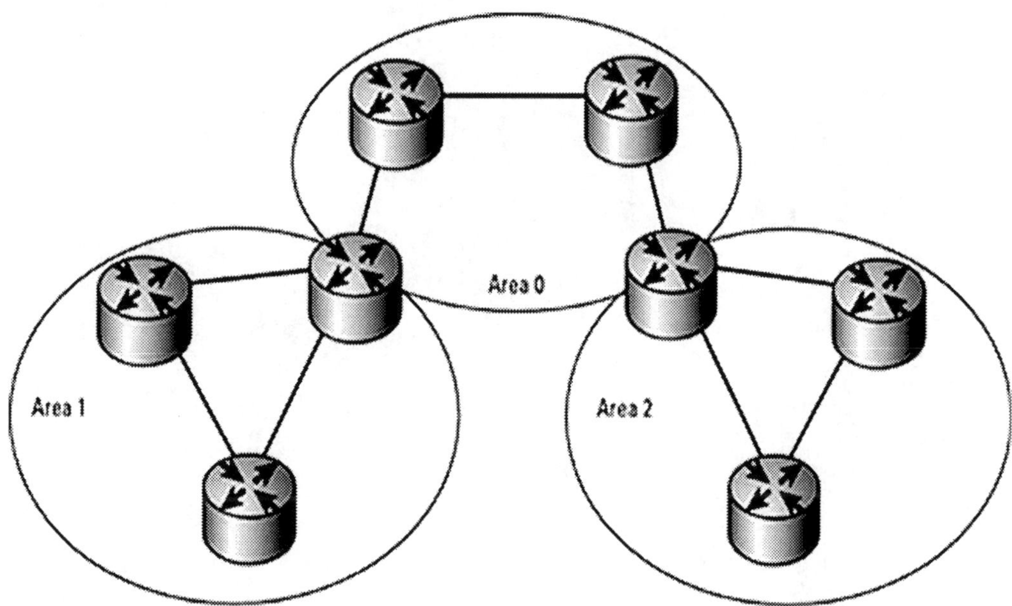

C. Backbone router: A backbone router has an interface on the backbone area.
D. AS boundary router: AS boundary routers exchange routing information with other autonomous systems.

The overall OSPF network is divided into groups called areas, whereas all routers in an organization are probably part of a single AS. The area is defined as a logical division of the AS, broken up into contiguous sections of the IP network.

In other words, we break the area along groups of subnets that can be grouped together with a single routing entry. In a typical large network, an area may consist of 30 to 40 routers.

OSPF does not use UDP or TCP, but is encapsulated directly in IP datagrams as protocol 89. This is in contrast to RIP, or BGP. OSPF handles its own error detection and correction functions.

The OSPF protocol, when running on IPv4, can operate securely between routers, optionally using a variety of authentication methods to allow only trusted routers to participate in routing. OSPFv3, running on IPv6, no longer supports protocol-internal authentication. Instead, it relies on IPv6 protocol security (IPsec).

As shown in figure 5 all the topology information is kept in a database separate from the routing table. It maintains 3 tables to collect routing information.

A. Neighbor Table: List of all recognized neighboring router to whom routing information will be interchanged.
B. Topology Table: Also called LSDB which maintain list of routers and their link information i.e. network destination, prefix length, link cost etc.
C. Routing table: Also called forwarding table contain only the best path to forward data traffic.

Figure 5. Link state Routing

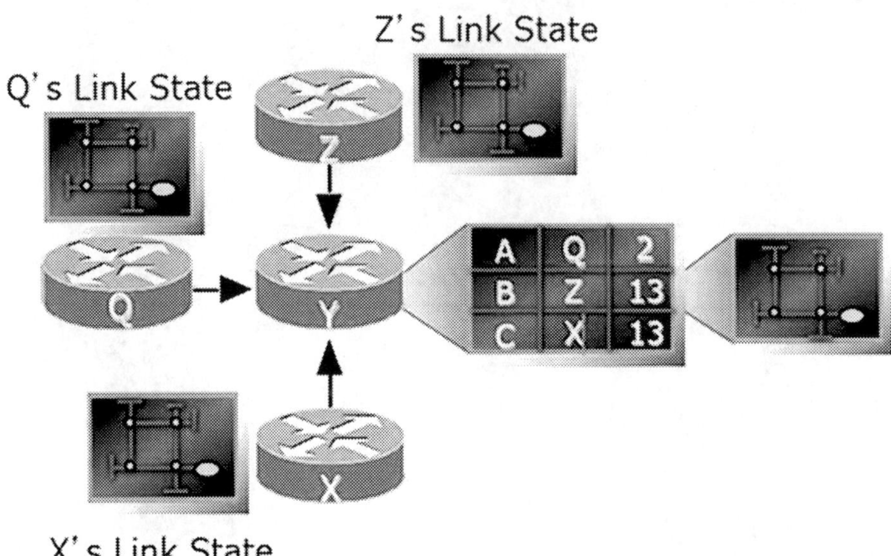

Every OSPF packet starts with a standard 24-byte header, and another 24 bytes of information or more. The header contains all the information necessary to determine whether the packet should be accepted for further processing. The OSPF protocol runs directly over IP, using the assigned number 89. The protocol uses five different packet types:

A. Hello: Used to discover and maintain neighbours.
B. Database Description: Used to form adjacencies. The router summarises all its link state advertisements and passes this information, via database description packets to the router it is forming an adjacency with.
C. Link State Request: After the database description packets have been exchanged with a neighbour, the router may detect link state advertisements it requires to update or complete the topological database. Link state request packets are sent to the neighbour requesting these link state advertisements.
D. Link State Update: Used for transmission of link state advertisements between routers. This could be in response to a link state request packet or to flood a new or more recent link state advertisement.
E. Link State Acknowledgment: Used to make the flooding of link state advertisements reliable. Each link state advertisement received is explicitly acknowledged,

5. Advantages and Disadvantages of OSPF

The advantages of OSPF are (Islam & Ashique, 2010):

A. OSPF is not a Cisco proprietary protocol.
B. OSPF always determine the loop free routes.
C. If any changes occur in the network it updates fast.
D. OSPF minimizes the routes and reduces the size of routing table by configuring area.

E. Low bandwidth utilization.
F. Multiple routes are supported.
G. Support variable length subnet masking.
H. It is suitable for large network.

Disadvantages of OSPF are:

A. Difficult to configure.
B. Link state scaling problem.
C. More memory requirements.

6. Performance Comparison between OSPF And EIGRP

When OSPF and EIGRP routers are compared it is the OSPF routing protocol which demands a lot of resources from the router, since OSPF has to undergo a lot of background processes such as electing a DR(Designated router) and a BDRBDR(Backup designated router).Also the router ID has to be computed on each router. This induces a lot of delay when compared to EIGRP routing protocol. Therefore total delay will be equal to average delay * no of routers. OSPF causes massive CPU utilization therefore more heat is produced; more amount of cooling is required. EIGRP being a hybrid protocol uses fewer amounts of CPU resources.

Since OSPF uses server-client relationship the DR router should be a powerful router to process a lot of incoming traffic otherwise it will crash bringing the entire router area down. The use of a server client model jams the bandwidth since the routing updates from all the routers have to go to the path connected to the DR after which the DR will forward them to the other routers. In case of EIGRP there will be no election of DR or BDR and hence there is less time delay and less consumption of router resources. Since EIGRP doesn't use the server client model therefore there will be no jamming of bandwidth.

7. The Hello Protocol

The hello protocol provides the default failure detection mechanism in OSPF. An OSPF router maintains an inactivity timer for each neighbor it has established full adjacency with. When a router receives a Hello from a neighbor, it resets the inactivity timer associated with the neighbor, scheduling it to fire after the Router Dead Interval. The Router Dead Interval is typically four times the Hello Interval. When the neighbor, or the link between the router and the neighbor, is no longer functional, the router will no longer receive the periodic hello from the neighbor and consequently the inactivity timer will fire Router Dead Interval after receipt of the last hello from the neighbor. The firing of the inactivity timer causes the router to terminate its adjacency with the neighbor and generate a new router LSA to this effect. Depending on when the failure takes place after the receipt of the last Hello from the neighbor, a router may take anywhere between three to four Hello Intervals to break the adjacency and thus detect the failure. With default value of 10 seconds for the Hello Interval, the Router Dead Interval would be 40 seconds and it would take anywhere between 30 and 40 seconds for a router to detect a failure. This time period typically constitutes the biggest chunk in the overall convergence delay.

Some hardware technologies, e.g., packet over sonnet (Eramo, Listanti & Cianfrani, 2008), allow the detection of a link failure within few tens of milliseconds by sending the routers at two ends of the link a loss of signal message. On receiving such a signal, the router waits for carrier delay duration (few hundred milliseconds too few seconds) before letting OSPF act on it. The carrier delay allows the router to avoid false alarms and identify link flapping. However, the hardware-based failure detection is not always possible. For example, if a failure involves the central route processor but the router's line cards are functional, hardware detection of such a failure may not be possible.

There have been several proposals to reduce the Hello Interval and hence the Router Dead Interval to reduce the failure detection time. Alaettinoglu et al. (Fujita & Iwata, 2001) proposed reducing the Hello Interval to millisecond range to achieve sub-second failure detection. There are multiple concerns with arbitrarily reducing the Hello Interval to very small values. One concern is that the need to send and receive the Hellos after every few milliseconds would cause the router CPU loads to shoot up. Another concern is that very small Router Dead Interval may result in frequent false alarms, i.e., false adjacency breakdowns. As the Hello Interval becomes smaller, there are more chances that the network congestion will lead to loss or delayed processing of several consecutive Hello messages and thereby cause false breakdown of adjacency between routers even though the routers and the link between them are functioning perfectly well. The LSAs generated because of a false alarm lead to new routing table calculations, avoiding the supposedly down link, by all the routers in the network. A false alarm is soon corrected by successful Hello exchanges between the affected routers, which cause these routers to re-establish adjacency and generate new LSAs. These new LSAs force all the routers in the area to perform routing table calculations again. Thus, the false alarms cause temporary changes in the network traffic paths as well as unnecessary processing load on the routers. The changes in the traffic paths may have a serious impact on the traffic QoS since the changed paths may have significantly worse delay and loss characteristics, possibly due to congestion induced by the changes themselves, than the original paths.

BACKGROUND

Fujita & Iwata (2001) discussed that Quality of Service (QoS) routing plays a key role in satisfying the QoS requirements of incoming traffic and increasing network resource utilization. They had proposed the overall IP-QoS routing system architecture, in which a QoS-enabled Open Shortest Path First (QOSPF) protocol is utilized as a key component. QoS routing protocols such as QOSPF often use a computation technique called "pre-computation", which is an effective method to expedite the response to a QoS path computation request. In pre-computation, candidate QoS paths are pre-computed and stored in advance, so it is important to select the candidate paths so that they provide good call-blocking performance, i.e. the rate of finding paths satisfying QoS requirements upon setup requests of a switched path such as Multi-Protocol Label Switching (MPLS). However, approaches in which the current network resources are reflected to the dynamic link metric have large computational overhead due to frequent pre-computation. Thus, they proposed pre-computing multiple candidate paths to each destination for diverse routing based on static configured link metrics instead of dynamic link metrics. The performance evaluation of the proposed scheme showed that it (i) reduces the computational overhead by re-computing candidate paths only upon detection of topology changes and (ii) obtains a call-blocking probability equivalent to that of the dynamic link metric based approach. They also showed that selecting multiple node disjoint paths as candidate paths provides good call-blocking performance. Node disjoint paths generally improve both network reliability and throughput. To find the multiple disjoint paths, the k-shortest path (KSP) algorithm has been proposed. Although the KSP algorithm does not calculate optimal disjoint paths, it provides a low processing cost with little optimality loss. However, it is computationally much more complex than a single Dijkstra calculation as used for regular OSPF, particularly in large-scale networks. This causes a longer convergence time for first bootstrapping due to frequent update calculations. Furthermore, the KSP algorithm requires a long time to update a pre-computed path table (i.e., a candidate path table that is created by pre-computation) upon detection of topology changes such as network failures. They suggested two schemes for efficient pre-computation of multiple paths: (i) adaptive pre-computation based on the current CPU load to reduce the convergence time for the first bootstrapping, and (ii) a virtual area partitioning (VAP) algorithm to reduce the update time of the multiple candidate paths. Simulation of the proposed schemes showed that the adaptive pre-computation significantly reduces the convergence time without degrading the optimality of routing entries. It also showed that VAP reduces the processing delay of the multiple path calculation to half that of the conventional k-shortest path (KSP) algorithm.

Basu & Riecke (2001) presented the stability of the OSPF protocol under steady state and perturbed conditions. They look at three indicators of stability, namely, (a) network convergence times, (b) routing load on processors, and (c) the number of route flaps. They study these statistics under three different scenarios: (a) on networks that deploy OSPF with TE extensions, (b) on networks that use sub second HELLO timers, and (c) on networks that use alternative strategies for refreshing link-state information. Their findings include the following. First, the OSPF-TE protocol does converge to steady state after (multiple) failure(s), despite the added complexities (and overheads) of rerouting traffic-engineered paths. On the other hand, multiple concurrent failures may result in high processor loads and increased number of route flaps for short time periods. In general, OSPF-TE appears to be quite robust.

Second, current proposals for subsecond HELLO timers do result in significant improvements in convergence times — at the same time, the processor loads stay within reasonable ranges. Finally, they suggest a way of avoiding LSA refresh synchronization using randomization and show its effectiveness using simulations.

In order to ensure the transferability of their results to real life networks, they use an implementation that duplicates the specifications in RFC 2328 and run their simulations over a real network topology consisting of 292 nodes and 765 links. While there have been simulation studies of a related nature in the past, they have typically used much smaller network topologies consisting of 10s of nodes. Finally, as mentioned earlier, they incorporate a very detailed processor model based on a real life commercial router. This provides very accurate estimates of queuing and processor delays related to scheduling as well as processor utilization times. Thus, they can assert with reasonable confidence that their simulations are as true-to-life as possible. They believe that their results will provide adequate guidelines for network operators deploying OSPF with TE extensions in their networks.

Haijun et al.(2003) analyzed the local congestion issue of network owing to traffic aggregation and improved OSPF and brought forward cost adaptive OSPF (CA-OSPF). They discussed that it is effective to solve the local congestion in a network that some or all routers in the network run CA-OSPF routing algorithm. Network performance can be improved greatly when the load of the whole network is light and only some links are congested. When the load of the whole network is heavy, CA-OSPF cannot improve the network performance. Comparing with OSPF, CA-OSPF has more protocol expense: routers calculates the bandwidth utilization ratios of its interfaces at regular intervals; when some interface is in over-used state, adjusts the interface's cost and distribute Router-LSA; when some interface is in under-used state, decrease the interface's cost. CA-OSPF is compatible with OSPF. It is no problem that some routers run OSPF and the other routers run CA-OSPF in a network, furthermore, the network performance can be improved in a certain extent. CA-OSPF is adaptive. The router running CA-OSPF can adjust its interface's cost automatically according to the interface's bandwidth utilization ratio, don't need the network administrator do anything.

Goyal et al. (2007) discussed that fast convergence to topology changes is now a key requirement in routing infrastructures while reducing the routing protocol's processing overhead continues to be as important as before. In this paper, they examined the problem of scheduling routing table updates in link state routing protocols. Commercial routers typically use a hold time based scheme to limit the number of routing table updates as new LSAs arrive at the router. The hold time schemes limit the number of routing table updates at the expense of increased delay in convergence to the new topology, which is clearly not acceptable any more. They analyze the performance of different hold time schemes and propose a new approach to schedule routing table updates, called LSA Correlation. Rather than using individual LSAs as triggers for routing table updates, LSA Correlation scheme correlates the information in the LSAs to identify the topology change that led to their generation. A routing table update is performed when a topology change has been identified. The analysis and simulation results presented in this paper suggest that the LSA Correlation scheme performs much better than the hold time based schemes for both isolated and large scale topology change scenarios.

Levchenko et al.(2008) had presented the XL routing algorithm, a new link-state routing algorithm specifically designed to minimize network communication. XL works by propagating only some of the link-state updates it receives, thereby reducing the frequency of routing updates in the network. They also formally proved the correctness of XL and validated our performance claims in simulation. In particular, our simulation showed that with a small penalty in stretch, our algorithm dramatically reduced the number of updates needing to be communicated and processed. However, in allowing the routing algorithm to choose slightly sub-optimal routes, the network operator also cedes some degree of control. In particular, traffic engineering via link costs is harder since current traffic forwarding will be determined, in part, by past link costs. Fortunately, it is easy to augment their algorithm to "flush" all suppressed updates periodically, causing it to propagate and use exact routing information. In fact, the approximation parameter can be adjusted dynamically in response to load. Finally, they also believed that there may be significant opportunities to improve the efficiency of link state routing even further. In particular, recall that the XL routing algorithm propagates all link cost increase updates, meaning that, on average, it will propagate half of all updates that affect it. It is natural to ask whether this is strictly necessary, or whether a superior algorithm—one that selectively suppresses link failures—can scale sub-linearly for typical networks.

Barreto et al. (2008) proposes a proactive approach of Fast Recovery Paths to aid OSPF bypass failures. FRP-S is a distributed approach to generate failure recovery paths identified as FRPs. The FRP-S conducts its calculations considering the number of routers and the OSPF metric: the shortest path from the source router to any destination router considering the sum of link weights. The use of OSPF metric allows a reuse of the already installed OSPF routes, which reduce the calculation complexity. This approach supports SRLG failures, asymmetric link weights, can reach 100% single-failure recovery and do not use encapsulation technique. All FRPs used by a router is previously generated by itself and are directly stored at the FIB, which allows an immediate failure recovery as soon as an adjacent failure is detected. For a 100% single-failure recovery, there must be a physical topology still able to have all its routers connected in the presence of a single failure or SRLG failure. Besides, in order to enable a successful recovery, a network traffic distribution that occupies, at most, 50% link capacity is also necessary.

This network traffic distribution is already been planned in real networks aiming to accommodate the deviated traffic during a failure occurrence. These restrictions can be adopted by any IPFRR approach; otherwise, neither recovery approaches can reach up to 100% failure recovery in a network topology.

According to their evaluation paths are shorter than other similar approaches and they significantly reduce the packet loss rate during the OSPF convergence period caused by a failure. This proactive approach generates failure recovery paths, each one identified as a Fast Recovery Path (FRP), which are added as small extensions in the Forwarding Information Base (FIB). The FRPs can be obtained without encapsulation process and can reach 100% failure recovery (single link, router or Shared Risk Link Group (SRLG) failure type). When a FRP is used, the deviated packets almost always follow the same shortest path that would be used by the packets after the OSPF reaction from the router adjacent to the failure. This feature can be considered a great advantage compared to other 100% single-failure recovery IPFRR (IP Fast Rerouting) approaches.

Goyal et al. (2009) discussed that OSPF is a popular interior gateway routing protocol. Commercial OSPF routers limit their processing load by using a hold time between successive routing table calculations as new link state advertisements (LSAs) arrive following a topology change. A large hold time value limits the frequency of routing table calculations but also causes large delays in convergence to the topology change. Hence, commercial routers now use an exponential back off scheme, where the hold time is initially set to a small value that is expected to rapidly increase, and hence limit the frequency of routing table calculations, in face of continuous LSA arrivals. In this paper, they analyzed the ability of different hold time schemes to limit the frequency of routing table calculations under continuous LSA arrivals starting with a small value for the hold time. This analysis is performed using

Markov Regenerative Process based stochastic models as well as simulations using an extensively modified ospfd simulator.

Eramo et al.(2008) analyzes intra-domain routing protocols improvements to support new features required by real time services. They propose a new multi-path dynamic algorithm which uses multipath information to make a fast determination about the new shortest paths when a link failure occurs, reducing this way the network re-convergence time. To evaluate the proposed algorithm performance they had implemented it in the OSPF code of the Quagga open-source routing software. They compare their own algorithm with three different dynamic algorithms, like the one implemented in Cisco routers and the two others, well known in literature, proposed by Narvaez and Ramalingam-Reps. They show how, by exploiting multi-path information, their algorithm performs, in many case studies, better than the above algorithms, especially in a link failure scenario. Their algorithm is a dynamic version of Dijkstra static algorithm which reacts to single link deletion and insertion; its relevant characteristic is the way it makes use of multi-path information to speed up SP computation.

Jiang et al. (2009) giving method for improving IGP Convergence through Distributed OSPF in Scalable Router; they propose a distributed OSPF (DOSPF) scheme to schedule routing computation through self-adaptively adjusting SPT waiting time. They analyze the convergence performance with DOSPF with Petri net. They then build a simulation tool to with routing trace in China Education and Research NETwork 2(CERNET2) to evaluate our DOSPF scheme. Their simulations show that DOSPF can effectively improve the IGP convergence performance.

SPT calculation is non-preemptable in the sense that router completes the calculation before doing any other OSPF processing. Router does not flood LSPs before it finished SPT computation and thus routers downstream do not receive updated LSPs and compute incorrect SPTs and FIBs. To overcome the problem and effectively utilize computing resources in scalable router, they divide OSPF protocol into three modules: signal module, routing computation module (SPT) and routing table management module (RTM). They are distributed in different CEs. Signal module is in charge of processing hello packets, establishing and maintaining neighbor relationship, flooding and synchronizing the LSDB. SPT module calculates routing table when it received a LSA reporting the topology change. The RTM module generates Routing Information Base (RIB) and updates the FIB on all line cards. In DOSPF, two SPT modules are running in parallel. In general, compared with the time of SPT computing with iSPF algorithm in current network size, if SPT initial-waiting delay is 10~25ms, two SPT modules can guarantee computing routing table in time by self-adaptively adjusting two consecutive SPT interval-time.

To improve the reliability of DOSPF, multiple CEs can backup different OSPF protocol functions each other in a redundance way.

Islam & Ashique (2010) discussed that Routing protocol is taking a vital role in the modern communication networks. The performance of each routing protocol is different from each other. In the context of routing protocol performance, each of them has different architecture, adaptability, route processing delays and convergence capabilities. Among different routing protocols, Enhanced Interior Gateway Routing Protocol (EIGRP) and Open Shortest Path First (OSPF) have been considered as the pre-eminent routing protocols for the real-time application. EIGRP and OSPF are dynamic routing protocols used in practical networks to disseminate network topology towards the adjacent routers. There are various numbers of static and dynamic routing protocols available but it is very important to select a right protocol among them. This selection depends on several parameters such as network convergence time, network scalability and bandwidth requirements. This paper reports a simulation based comparative performance analysis between EIGRP and OSPF for real time applications such as video streaming and voice conferencing by using OPNET. In order to evaluate the performance of EIGRP and OSPF, they designed two network models that are configured with EIGRP and OSPF, respectively. The evaluation of the routing protocols is performed based on quantitative metrics such as convergence time, packet delay variation, end-to-end delay, throughput and packet loss through the simulated network models. The evaluation results show that EIGRP routing protocol provides a better performance than OSPF routing protocol for real time applications.

Kang et al. (2010) proposed an Adaptive Link Establishment (ALE) scheme in wireless ad-hoc networks. The ALE scheme dynamically changes the latency of link creation by controlling the acceptance of incoming Hello messages based on the link stability without changing the HelloInterval. The ALE scheme consists of two main components: one for controlling the latency of link creation and the other for quantifying the degree of link stability. These components are implemented by incrementally modifying the OSPF Hello mechanism. The new Hello mechanism enabled by this scheme is compatible with the legacy OSPF Hello mechanism and can be applied to the either point-to-point or broadcast wireless medium. In addition, the ALE scheme behaves like the legacy OSPF when the network is topologically static (i.e low mobility) and the channel condition is stables (i.e. no intermittent connectivity). The ALE scheme has been implemented in the real OSPF routing protocol. They measure the performance of the ALE scheme in terms of flooding overhead, convergence time, packet drop rate and throughput. The proposed Adaptive Link Establishment (ALE) scheme has the following characteristics:

1. The Hello Interval and Router Dead Interval are not changed, which avoids configuration inconsistency in the point-to-point or broadcast based OSPF network.
2. The link creation latency is adaptively controlled per each neighbor node and each interface based on the link stability.

3. The degree of link stability is monitored in real time and quantified only based on the incoming Hello messages while allowing the use of link-layer or physical-layer information or user-supplied inputs.
4. The topology information, which is locally available from the LSDB, is used not to apply the ALE scheme when the link to be created is a bridge link.
5. To be compatible with the standard OSPF Hello mechanism, a link is removed from the LSDB based on the existing Hello mechanism (i.e. after not hearing from the neighbor node for the Router Dead Interval time).
6. The whole ALE scheme can be enabled or disabled dynamically at run-time.

Their experiment results show that the ALE scheme effectively suppresses the unnecessary link establishment caused by intermittent connectivity while having no impact on the convergence time when the network topology is stable. They also show that the end-to-end application throughput is improved by up to 66%.

Wei & Wang (2011) discussed that in order to enhance the reliability of the Internet, more and more ASes use multi-homing technology to provide redundant connection. When one of the connections fails or is in maintenance, the AS can still connect to the Internet via other connections. Multi-homing configuration can be achieved through multiple connections to different upstream providers or the same ISP. Multi-homing to a single provider is referred to as multi-attaching. For example, AT&T's Access Redundancy Options (MARO) allows its customers (single-homed ASes) to connect to AT&T network at multiple backbone routers. However, redundant connectivity does not necessarily enable 100% network uptime. Previous work has shown that continuous connectivity via redundant connections is hinged on how long it takes for BGP to failover to backup routes. Therefore, the reliability of the Internet depends on the reaction time necessary for the underlying routing protocols finding the backup paths in case of failures. Recently, several approaches have been extended to interdomain routing protocol to improve the reliability. Those approaches disseminate multiple paths to provide fast recovery from transient link failures. However, those approaches need to modify BGP implementation. In this paper, they proposed a simple and practical solution, called Fast Failover Configuration (FFC), which can provide fast failover upon inter-domain link failures. In particular, in order to increase route visibility, FFC uses route distribution among BGP and Interior Gateway Protocol (IGP) to propagate BGP routing information, which is called route redistribution. Recent work has shown that route redistribution is widely used in operational networks, such as corporate mergers or acquisitions. Their study extends the existing to inter-domain routing, and complements its results by showing that route redistribution is not only used to interconnect routing protocols and achieve design objectives, but also as a powerful tool to strengthen the reliability of inter-domain routing. Different from the existing solutions, their method is based on real-world and basic BGP implementations, and does not need using IP tunneling or MPLS to forwarding packets. That means, FFC is a pure IP-based fast failover technique. Most important, their method does not require any modification to BGP. Transit providers can immediately implement FFC to provide fast IP reroute. Their analysis and experimental result show that FFC can provide failover time in milliseconds. Furthermore, FFC can provide transparent failover, and will not translate the link failure into the fluctuations in BGP. Their experimental result shows that this method can reduce packet loss during link failures significantly.

M. Haider et al. (2011) presented a new routing table calculation scheme for OSPF routing protocol to better serve real-time applications. The proposed scheme focus on speeding up OSPF networks convergence time by optimizing the scheduling of routing table calculations using computational intelligence technique. There are two routing table calculation scheduling schemes in OSPF: 1) hold-time based scheme and 2) LSA Correlation. The hold-time based scheme uses values of delay parameters pre-configured by network operators. This scheme does not guarantee quick convergence time for all possible topology change scenarios. The LSA Correlation scheme schedules routing table calculation upon identification of a topology change. This scheme topology identification was complicated and not straightforward. Both schemes have not used computational intelligence (CI) technique. Their research explores the effectiveness of scheduling OSPF RTC based on CI. The computational intelligence technique that they use in the scheme is Feed Forward Back Propagation (BP) Neural Network. The scheme determines the suitable hold time based on three parameters: LSA-inter arrival time, the number of important control message in queue, and the computing utilization of the routers. They created training data sets for BP model and present the results in this paper. Based from this three parameters or inputs, the proposed model will determine the suitable hold time value as an output.They also provide performance comparison between their proposed scheme and another scheme which uses Generalized Regression Neural Network (GRNN). The result shows that the GRNN has higher accuracy and faster training speed compared to the BP neural network.

Sharma & Padda (2012) discussed that the term routing is used for taking a packet from one device and sending it through the network to another device on a different network. Routers don't really care about hosts they only care about networks and the best path to each network. Due to the major role that routing protocol play in computer network infrastructures, special cares have been given to routing protocols with built –in security constraints. In this paper they had shown how they can do routing with an EIGRP based routing protocol. Enhanced IGRP (EIGRP) is a classless, enhanced distance vector protocol that gives us a real edge over another Cisco proprietary protocol, Interior Gateway Routing Protocol (IGRP). That's basically why it's called Enhanced IGRP. Like IGRP, EIGRP uses the concept of an autonomous system. EIGRP is sometimes referred to as a hybrid routing protocol because it has characteristics of both distance-vector and link state protocols. For example, EIGRP doesn't send link-state packets as OSPF does; instead, it sends traditional distance vector updates containing information about networks plus the cost of reaching them from the perspective of the advertising router. And EIGRP has link-state characteristics as well—it synchronizes routing tables between neighbors at startup and then sends specific updates only when topology changes occur. This makes EIGRP suitable for very large networks. EIGRP has a maximum hop count of 255 (the default is set to 100). There are a number of powerful features that make EIGRP a real standout from IGRP and other protocols. The main ones are listed here:

1. Support for IP and IPv6 (and some other useless routed protocols) via protocol dependent modules.
2. Considered classless (same as RIPv2 and OSPF).
3. Support for VLSM/CIDR.
4. Support for summaries and discontiguous networks.
5. Efficient neighbor discovery.
6. Communication via Reliable Transport Protocol (RTP).
7. Best path selection via Diffusing Update Algorithm (DUAL).

It has shown that EIGRP choose best routing path on the basis of four metrics bandwidth, delay, load, reliability. EIGRP is the first internet routing protocol that provides loop freedom at every instant and convergence times comparable to those obtained with standard link state protocols. Furthermore, EIGRP provides multiple paths to every destination that may have different weights. A network model of Cisco routers has been employed in a network simulation software 'packet tracer'. Eventually an EIGRP routing protocol has been configured and run on a network model. Among all the routing protocols available EIGRP protocol has been mostly used for routing a complex network.

Dwyer & Jasani (2012) discussed that with internal networks growing larger, dynamic routing protocols are becoming more prevalent in autonomous systems. Due to the importance of computers and network resources, many organizations implement redundant links to allow failover in the event of a link failure. When this failover occurs, the network must converge before traffic will be able to pass to and from the network segment that incurred a link failure. The time that is required for the network to converge is referred to as convergence delay. This paper tests the scenario of a link failure and quantifies the convergence delay caused by the link failure event. As security is also a major concern for large enterprises, this paper also implemented key pair authentication with each protocol and quantified the convergence delay added by the addition of authentication. This paper compared the convergence delay caused by link failures in both EIGRP and OSPF. When comparing the results of the tests of EIGRP and OSPF without key authentication, the first conclusion is that EIGRP vastly outperforms OSPF. This should be self evident as the average convergence delay for OSPF is 542ms and the average convergence delay for EIGRP is 63ms. While this is true, it is important to remember that OSPF relies on the DR and BDR heavily during convergence. During this test, the link between the DR and BDR is disconnected. This causes OSPF to perform a DR election even though neither router truly went offline. The OSPF standard requires that after a DR election, there is a wait period of no less than 100ms before LSAs are sent out from the routers. The default wait period set by Cisco on all routers they distribute is 500ms. The fact that EIGRP is Cisco proprietary is likely the reason that it is not favored over OSPF in large enterprise environments. The comparison of EIGRP with and without key pair authentication brought about rather surprising results. The results showed no or very little quantifiable difference between the two over a period of 10 tests. This same trend can also be seen in the comparison of OSPF with and without the addition of key pair authentication. The results also showed no or very little difference between the two series of tests. It should be noted that with key pair authentication for both OSPF and EIGRP, it took longer for the network to initially converge at router startup, but convergence after a link failure did not appear to be affected. This is likely due to the fact that no new interfaces were being added and thus no new interfaced needed to be authenticated into the autonomous system.

Malik et al.(2012) proposed a novel method to compute the intra-area convergence time of open shortest path first (OSPF) based networks in the presence of designated routers (DRs) on Ethernet and non-broadcast multi-access segments. The capacity of the proposed method is demonstrated by evaluating the convergence time performance of OSFP on internet scale networks (having a thousand autonomous system level routers).The method had also been used to analyse the effects of: (a) the number of DRs, (b) cascading failures, and (c) topological changes on the convergence time of the routers within an area. Furthermore, the time the network takes from a cold state to reach a stable (steady) state in an area is also analysed. For their experiments, they simulated the detailed implementation of the OSPF protocol. To get realistic measurements they generate topologies from BRITE, using Otter that represents the exact same characteristics as those of the internet. The results and analysis provided in this Letter will be extremely useful for network administrators seeking to deploy OSPF. Moreover, the results are also useful in the behavioural analysis of OSPF and can provide the basis to re-evaluate the design of the protocol to achieve performance optimisation.

Spasov & Gushev (2012) gave an overview of distance vector routing protocols. They focus on the convergence mechanisms in two widely known distance vector routing protocols: EIGRP and RIP. With this proposal they are proposing a new protocol that is not backward compatible with previous RIP protocols. Their work is based on the implementation of the RIP protocol in the open-source Qugga routing software. The first upgrade that was done was to improve RIP's metric. Their solution is to introduce additional field in RIP entries. It would be simpler and more efficient if they use OSPF's metric instead of EIGRP's. The second step in building a better routing protocol is to eliminate the dependence on periodic broadcast updates and route aging timers. These mechanisms provide reliable but slow convergence. In order to achieve faster and reliable convergence, they had to use the TCP protocol for the RIP packets. If a route becomes unreachable neighbor routers will be queried for alternative routes. This implies that stuck in active timers must be implemented. In TCP usage requires periodic UDP broadcast to router's neighbors to establish associatively. They proposed these messages to include the number of entries in the routing table. If two neighbors disagree on this number will prompt routers to exchange their routing tables. The final step will be to implement a system for finding and keeping backup routes. With their proposal more backup routes will be found. Thus they increase the number of backup routes in a computer network. With the aim to provide open source protocol, they propose a solution that inherits the simplicity of the RIP protocol and the fast convergence of the EIGRP protocol. They believed that their proposal will provide faster convergence and better scalability in large networks.

NavaneethKrishnan et al. (2013) presented a paper that they have explored two eminent protocols namely, Enhanced Interior Gateway Routing Protocol (EIGRP) and Open Shortest Path First (OSPF) protocols. When OSPF and EIGRP routers are compared it is the OSPF routing protocol which demands a lot of resources from the router, since OSPF has to undergo a lot of background processes such as electing a DR and a BDR. Also the router ID has to be computed on each router. This induces a lot of delay when compared to EIGRP routing protocol. Therefore total delay will be equal to average delay * no of routers. OSPF causes massive CPU utilization therefore more heat is produced; more amount of cooling is required. EIGRP being a hybrid protocol uses fewer amounts of CPU resources. Since OSPF uses server-client relationship the DR router should be a powerful router to process a lot of incoming traffic otherwise it will crash bringing the entire router area down. The use of a server client model jams the bandwidth since the routing updates from all the routers have to go to the path connected to the DR after which the DR will forward them to the other routers. In case of EIGRP there will be no election of DR or BDR and hence there is less time delay and less consumption of router resources. Since EIGRP doesn't use the server client model therefore there will be no jamming of bandwidth. Supposing in a network, a path goes down then OSPF will have to use LSA hello packets again causing the finding neighbor process to start all over again therefore OSPF will fail to act fast in high speed networks and also a lot of energy is consumed due to high overhead of router. In case of EIGRP the router carries an alternative route known as the feasible successor router which will be used once the successor router goes down. Therefore EIGRP doesn't have to send hello packets once again or find its neighbors again. OSPF uses a backbone router to route between different areas, which increases equipment cost; EIGRP uses BGP protocol to route between different autonomous systems. This saves the cost of the extra router required in OSPF. Evaluation of these routing protocols was performed on a live network. Factors such the such as Convergence Time, Jitter, End-to-End delay, Throughput and Packet Loss were measured .The evaluation results show that EIGRP routing protocol provides a better performance than OSPF routing protocol for real time applications. Through experiments they had obtained the clock cycles of the router's CPU when it is running on EIGRP and OSPF. By expressing the power consumed by the router as a function of frequency and voltage they are able to state that the router consumes lesser power when running on EIGRP than when it runs on OSPF. Hence EIGRP is a greener routing protocol when compared to OSPF.

Hinds et al. (2013) discussed that IPv4 addressing space has almost been exhausted; many organisations will soon be required to perform the changeover to IPv6. Traditional IPv4 routing protocols must be replaced with new IPv6 compatible protocols to ensure systems continue to operate effectively; however these protocols have undergone significant changes in order to support IPv6. Understanding these changes is important when selecting a routing protocol for a system, in order to facilitate this, a study and comparison of two popular routing protocols; OSPF and EIGRP has been undertaken. The major changes between the IPv4 and IPv6 editions have been identified and discussed and the two protocols have been compared against a number of criteria, the criteria include desirable features as well as critical goals for administrators wishing to deploy networks. From the strengths and weaknesses, it can be argued that OSPFv3 will be most appropriate deployed in large networks which can make best use of its hierarchical nature and benefit from the scalability of the protocol, as well as networks which face budgetary constraints due to the flexibility of the hardware which the protocol can be deployed upon. EIGRPv6 will be most appropriate deployed in networks with very specific routing metric requirements due to its wide range of available metrics; it will also be a good choice in flat network topologies or networks which require very fast convergence times, however the requirements of Cisco hardware and associated costs may be a problem.

RESEARCH GAP

Following are the research gaps that need to fulfill in the present study.

1. In high speed IP networks, interior gateway protocol like OSPF have no facility to obtain a new route to bypass failure in time
2. In OSPF lots of packets lost during the OSPF convergence period caused by failure
3. Lack of backup rotes for destination so that it can quickly adapt to alternate routes
4. On link failure or topology change recompilation of SPF tree and route table.
5. Real time application like voice and video received qualities has been effected due to packet lost in convergence.

PROBLEM FORMULATION

1. **Need and Significance of Proposed work:** Fast convergence in OSPF is very important for widespread deployment of real time applications. The present study improve the OSPF performance convergence by providing back up path, improving OSPF routing algorithm in case of failure and make it a preferred choice for today's network designers. The proposed work will improve the functionalities of OSPF. Improved algorithm can quickly respond to the topology change and reduce the convergence time by providing back up path which is already stored in routing table before the failover occurs. This algorithm reduces the convergence delay caused by link failures in OSPF.

2. **Research Problem:** Quick convergence time is necessary to meet network based application requests and quality of service (QoS) prerequisites of modern dynamic vast-scale routing domains, such as data centre's. Although OSPF send triggered updates when a network change or failure occurs but OSPF have lack of facility to obtain a new route to bypass failure in time, lots of packet lost during convergence delay, Lack of backup routes for destination so that it can quickly adapt to alternate routes. The convergence delay in case of failure makes this technology a non-preferred choice for use in today's network design.

Real time application like voice and video received qualities has been effected due to packet lost in convergence. Communication dependability is a highly required property in computer networks. The main technology to increase the dependability of a network is to providing a quick backup path. OSPF have lack of backup path in case of failure occurs in the network.

EXPERIMENTAL TEST BED

In order to transmit a packet data (message) from source to destination, the packet follows a shortest path which is identified by OSPF as shown in figure 6 the packet starts from 192.168.1.1 follows the path as 20.1.0.0, 30.1.1.0, 40.1.1.0 and finally reached the destination as 172.16.1.1.

OSPF works on the concept of cost so it selects the path to send the packet from one router to another or one network to another which have minimum cost. Figure 7 shows packet successfully reached at destination (172.16.1.1).

OSPF uses link state algorithm to find the shortest path for routing. OSPF dynamically learn route information from neighbor route and advertise this information from neighbor route and advertise this information to another neighbors so that all the network information broadcast in OSPF network .When the OSPF identifies breakage in the path of transmission. As shown in figure 11 OSPF router design the topology again and find the another possible shortest path by following the path as 192.168.1.0, 50.1.1.0, 60.1.1.0, 70.1.1.0, 80.1.1.0 and finally got the desired destination 172.16.1.

Figure 6. Shows data (message) transfers from 192.168.1.1 to 172.16.1.1

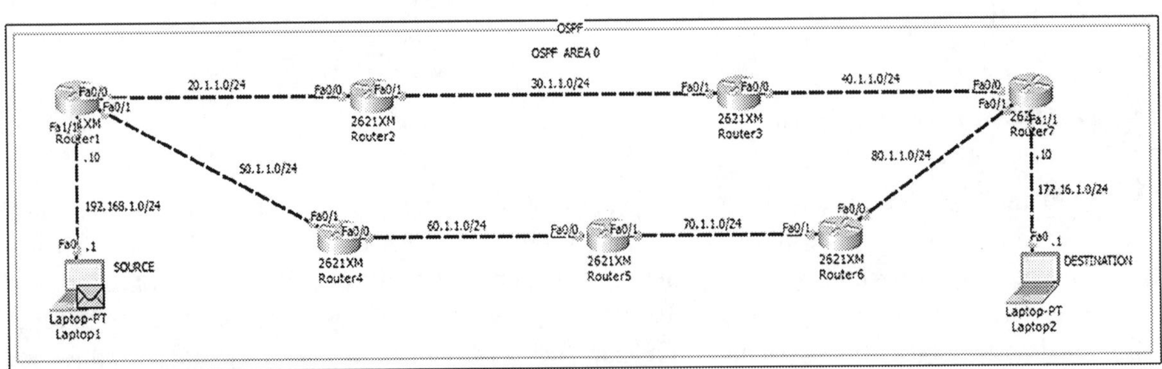

Figure 7. Successful arrivals of packets at Destination (172.16.1.1)

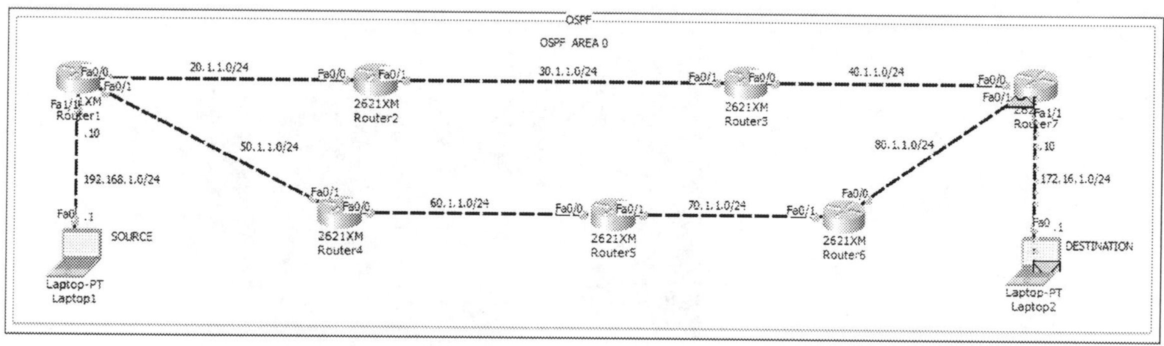

Figure 8. Shows after transmission of packet from source to destination not any packet lost, the entire 4 packet successfully reached

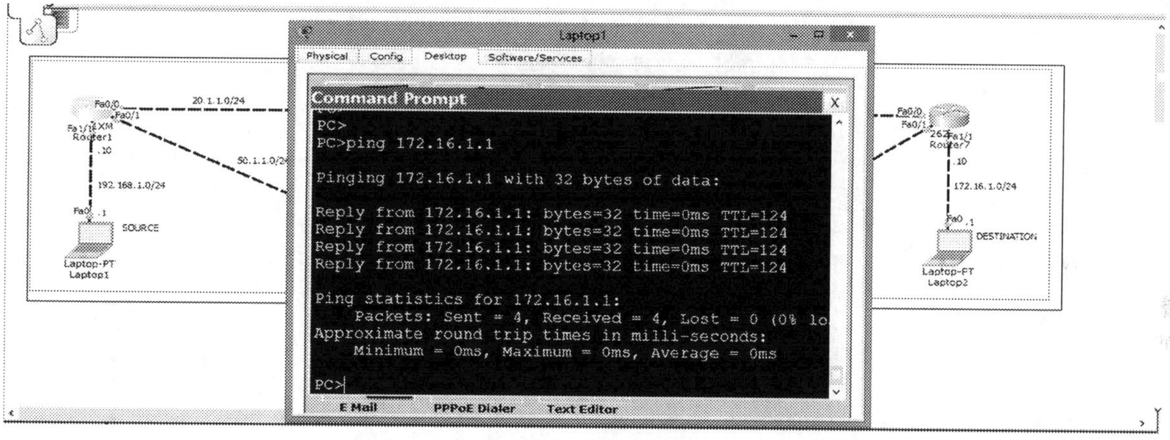

Figure 9. Shows the connection breakage at 20.1.1.0 due to this breakage there is loss of packets in the transmission

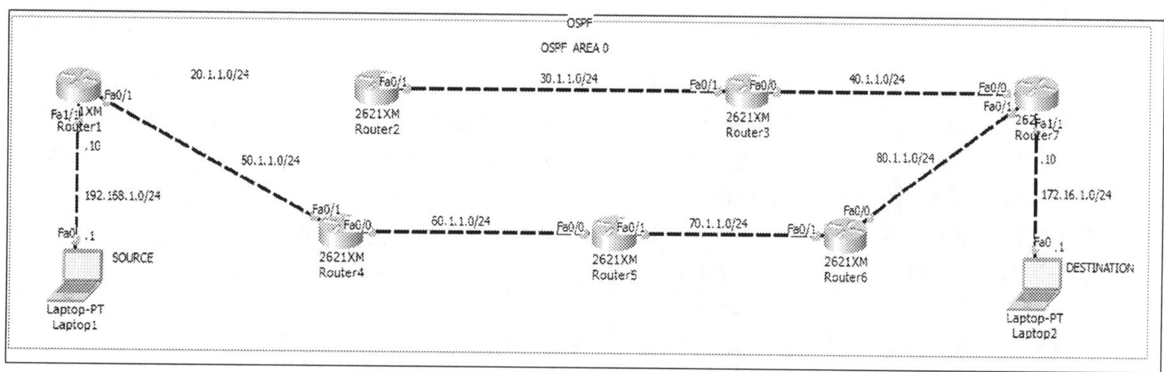

Figure 10. Shows packet lost in the transmission due to breakage in path

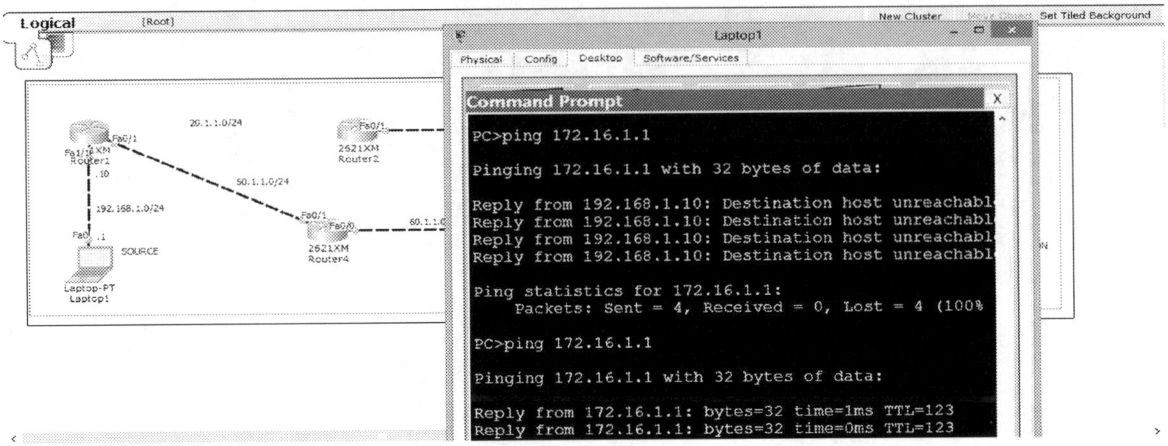

```
PC>ping 172.16.1.1

Pinging 172.16.1.1 with 32 bytes of data:

Reply from 192.168.1.10: Destination host unreachabl
Reply from 192.168.1.10: Destination host unreachabl
Reply from 192.168.1.10: Destination host unreachabl
Reply from 192.168.1.10: Destination host unreachabl

Ping statistics for 172.16.1.1:
    Packets: Sent = 4, Received = 0, Lost = 4 (100%

PC>ping 172.16.1.1

Pinging 172.16.1.1 with 32 bytes of data:

Reply from 172.16.1.1: bytes=32 time=1ms TTL=123
Reply from 172.16.1.1: bytes=32 time=0ms TTL=123
```

Figure 11. Shows message successfully reached by selecting the new route

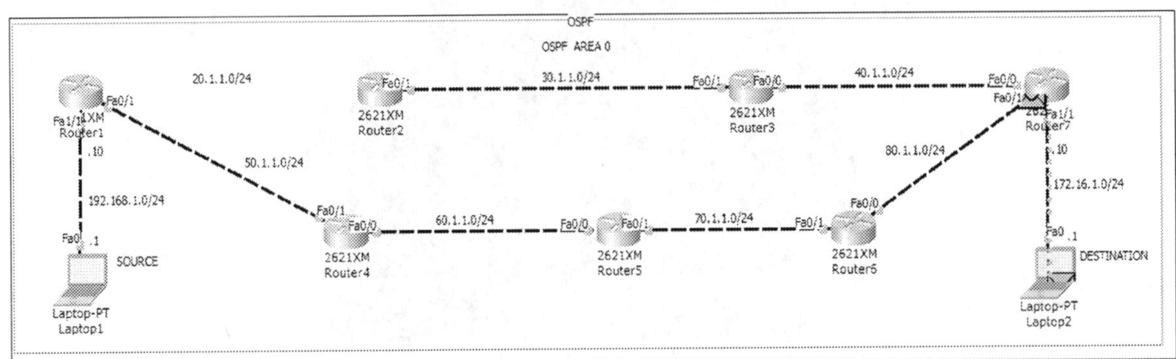

SOLUTIONS AND RECOMMENDATIONS

The main objectives of the study are:

1. Provides capability for obtain a new route to bypass failure in time
2. Reducing convergence delay because fast convergence time is required to meet network based application demands and quality of service (QoS) requirements of modern dynamic large-scale routing domains, such as data centres.
3. Developing an algorithm that can quickly respond to the topology change and reduce the convergence time by providing back up path which is already stored in routing table before the failover occurs
4. Design and develop the framework on the basis of backup routing algorithm
5. Rapid availability of backup path to improve the packet loss problem during convergence which produce negative effects on the received quality for both video and voice traffic.

FUTURE RESEARCH DIRECTIONS

Quick convergence in OSPF is imperative for widespread deployment of real time applications. The present study improve the OSPF performance convergence by providing back up path, improving OSPF routing algorithm in case of failure and make it a preferred choice for today's network designers. The proposed work will improve the functionalities of OSPF. Improved algorithm can quickly respond to the topology change and reduce the convergence time by providing back up path which is already stored in routing table before the failover occurs. This algorithm reduces the convergence delay caused by link failures in OSPF.

CONCLUSION

An analytical approach is presented in this paper, which focus on reduction in convergence delay and packet loss. In this paper we conclude that whenever the breakage or failure occurs in network, OSPF regenerate routing table and routing tree according to the topology by finding the path having minimum cost. The time that is required by OSPF for regeneration is referred to as convergence delay. The duration of the convergence period of these protocols vary from hundred of milliseconds to tens of seconds which results into instability, leads to high packet loss rate. Quick convergence time is necessary to meet network based application requests and quality of service (QoS) prerequisites of modern dynamic vast-scale routing domains, such as data centres.

REFERENCES

Barreto, F., Emílio, W. C. G., & Junior, L. N. (2008). Fast Recovery Paths: Reducing Packet Loss Rates during IP Routing Convergence. *The Fourth Advanced International Conference on Telecommunications*. doi:10.1109/AICT.2008.21

Basu, A., & Riecke, J. (2001, October). Stability issues in OSPF routing. *Computer Communication Review*, *31*(4), 225–236. doi:10.1145/964723.383077

Coltun, R., Ferguson, D., Moy, J., & Lindem, A. (2008, July). *OSPF for IPv6*. Internet Engineering Task Force, Request For Comments. (StandardsTrack) RFC 5340.

Dwyer, J., & Hetal, J. (2012). *An Analysis of Convergence Delay Caused by Link Failures in Autonomous Systems*. IEEE. doi:10.1109/SECon.2012.6196899

Eramo, V., Marco, L., & Antonio, C. (2008, December). Design and Evaluation of a New Multi-Path Incremental Routing Algorithm on Software Routers. *IEEE eTransactions on Network and Service Management*, *5*(4), 188–203. doi:10.1109/TNSM.2009.041101

Fujita, N., & Iwata, A. (2001). *Adaptive and Efficient Multiple Path Pre-computation for QoS Routing Protocols*. IEEE. doi:10.1109/GLOCOM.2001.966173

Goyal, M., Soperi, M., Hosseini, H., Trivedi, K. S., Shaikh, A., & Choudhury, G. (2009). *International Conference on Advanced Information Networking and Applications*. IEEE.

Goyal, M., Xie, W., Soperi, M, Hosseini, S.H. & Vairavan, K (2007, February). *Scheduling Routing Table Calculations to Achieve Fast Convergence in OSPF Protocol*. IEEE.

Grang, N., & Gupta, A. (2013). Compare OSPF Routing Protocol with other Interior Gateway Routing Protocols. *International Journal of Engineering Business and Enterprise Applications*, *4*(2), 166–170.

Haider, M. S., Mohd Zahid, M., & Bakar, K. A. (2011). Comparison of Intelligent Schemes for Scheduling OSPF Routing Table Calculation. IEEE.

Haijun, Z. H. O. U., Jin, P. A. N., & Pubing, S. H. E. N. (2003). Analyzes the local congestion issue of network owing to traffic aggregation and improved OSPF and brought forward cost adaptive OSPF (CA-OSPF). *Proceedings of the Fifth International Conference on Computational Intelligence and Multimedia Applications (ICCIMA'03)*.

Hawkinson, J. & Bates, T. (1996, March). *Guidelines for creation, selection and registration of an autonomous system (AS)*. Internet Engineering Task Force, Request For Comments (Best Current Practice) RFC 1930.

Hinds, Atojoko, & Zhu. (2013, August). Evaluation of OSPF and EIGRP Routing Protocols for IPv6. *International Journal of Future Computer and Communication, 2*(4).

Introduction IPRouting. (n.d.). Retrieved from http://www.cisco.com/en/US/tech/tk365/ts-d_technology_support_protocol_home.html

Islam, M. N., & Ashique, M. (2010). Simulation-Based Comparative Study Of EIGRP and OSPF for Real-Time Applications. Blekinge Institute of Technology, School of Computing, Karlskrona, Sweden.

Jiang, X., Xu, M., Li, Q., & Pan, L. (2009). Improving IGP Convergence through Distributed OSPF in Scalable Router. *11th IEEE International Conference on High Performance Computing and Communications*. doi:10.1109/HPCC.2009.21

Kang, J., Fecko, M. A., & Sunil, S. (2010). ALE: Adaptive Link Establishment in OSPF Wireless Ad-Hoc Networks. *IEEE The Military Communications Conference*. doi:10.1109/MILCOM.2010.5679573

Levchenko, Voelker, Paturi, & Savage. (2008, August). XL: An Efficient Network Routing Algorithm. *SIGCOMM'08*. ACM.

Malik, S. U., Srinivasan, S. K., & Khan, S. U. (2012, September). Convergence time analysis of open shortest path first routing protocol in internet scale networks. *Electronics Letters*, *48*(19), 1188. doi:10.1049/el.2012.2310

Moy, J. (1998, April). *OSPF version 2*. Internet Engineering Task Force, Request For Comments (Standards Track) RFC 2328.

NavaneethKrishnan, Y., Bhagwat, C. N., & Aparajit, U. (2013). Performance Analysis of OSPF and EIGRP Routing Protocols for Greener Internetworking. *International Conference in Distributed Computing & Internet Technology*.

Sharma, & Padda. (2012, February). Configuring an EIGRP based Routing Model. *International Journal of Scientific and Research Publications*, *2*(2).

Spasov, D., & Gushev, M. (2012). On the Convergence of Distance Vector Routing Protocols. *Proceedings of ICT Innovations 2012*.

Wei, Z.-Z., & Wang, F. (2011). Achieving Resilient Routing through Redistributing Routing Protocols. *Proceedings of the IEEE, ICC*, 2011.

Wu. (n.d.). *Simulation Based Performance Analyses on RIP, EIGRP and OSPF Using OPNET*. Academic Press.

KEY TERMS AND DEFINITIONS

Autonomous System: On the Internet, an autonomous system (AS) is the unit of router policy, either a single network or a group of networks that is controlled by a common network administrator (or group of administrators) on behalf of a single administrative entity (such as a university, a business enterprise, or a business division). An autonomous system is also sometimes referred to as a routing domain. An autonomous system is assigned a globally unique number, sometimes called an Autonomous System Number (ASN).

Convergence Process: When a routing protocol process is empowered, each participating router will attempt to exchange information about the topology of the network. The extent of this information exchange, the way it is sent and received, and the type of information required vary widely relying on the routing protocol in use e.g. RIP, OSPF and BGP4.

EIGRP: EIGRP (Enhanced Interior Gateway Routing Protocol) is a network protocol that lets routers exchange information more productively than with prior network protocols. EIGRP evolved from IGRP (Interior Gateway Routing Protocol) and routers using either EIGRP or IGRP can interoperate because the metric (criteria used for selecting a route) utilized with one protocol can be translated into the metrics of the other protocol.

Link-State Routing Protocols: Link-State routing protocols calculate their network routes by building a complete topology of the whole network area and then calculating the best path from this topology or map of all the interconnected networks.

Network Topology: Network topology refers to the physical or logical format of a network. It characterizes the way different nodes are placed and interconnected with one another. Alternately, network topology may describe how the information is exchanged between these nodes.

OSPF: OSPF is Interior Gateway Protocol (IGP) and conveys routing information just between routers fitting in with the same Autonomous System (AS). Like Routing Information Protocol (RIP), OSPF is assigned by the Internet Engineering Task Force (IETF) as one of several Interior Gateway Protocols (IGPs).

Packet Loss: The disposing of data packets in a network when a device (router, switch, and so forth.) is over-burden and can't acknowledge any approaching data at a given minute.

RIP: RIP (Routing Information Protocol) is one of the oldest distance-vector routing protocols, which utilizes the hop count as a routing metric. RIP prevents routing loops by executing an utmost on the quantity of hops permitted in a path from the source to a destination.

Router: A network device that forwards data packets from one network to another. Based on the address of the destination network in the incoming packet and an internal routing table, the router determines which port (line) to send out the packet (ports regularly connect to Ethernet cables).

Chapter 5
Cotton Leaf Disease Detection by Feature Extraction

Savita N. Ghaiwat
GHRCEM, India

Parul Arora
GHRCEM, India

ABSTRACT

Cotton leaf diseases have occurred all over the world, including India. They adversely affect cotton quality and yield. Technology can help in identifying disease in early stage so that effective treatment can be given immediately. Now, the control methods rely mainly on artificial means. This paper propose application of image processing and machine learning in identifying three cotton leaf diseases through feature extraction. Using image processing, 12 types of features are extracted from cotton leaf image then the pattern was learned using BP Neural Network method in machine learning process. Three diseases have been diagnosed, namely Powdery mildew, Downy mildew and leafminer. The Neural Network classification performs well and could successfully detect and classify the tested disease.

1. INTRODUCTION

Cotton is an important cash crop in India. Cotton plants suffer from various diseases that can prove detrimental to the quality and quantity of the yield. India was recognized as a place of origin of cotton industry. India thus the earliest country in the world to domesticate cotton and utilize its fiber to manufacture fabric. The textile industry in India, after agriculture, is the only industry that has generated huge employment for both skilled and unskilled labor in textiles. India is accounts for approximately 25 per cent of world's cotton area and 16 per cent of total cotton production. Maharashtra is the important cotton growing state in India with 31.33 lack hector area and production of 62.00 lack bales. India is the 2nd largest producer of cotton in the world. About 3 million farmers are engaged in cotton cultivation in the state mostly in backward region of Marathwada and Vidarbha .In Vidarbha region, cotton is the most important cash crop grown on an area of 13.00 lacks hectors with production of 27 lack bales of cotton.

DOI: 10.4018/978-1-4666-8737-0.ch005

Mainly the detection and identification of leaf diseases can be done by naked eye observation[1]. This in turn requires continuous monitoring which is practically not possible in large farms .Currently, the detection of crop diseases is mostly depend on manual recognition, but it can be erringly diagnosed by farmers because they usually judge the symptom by their experiences. The misidentification leads to some erroneous control measurements .Automatic detection of plant diseases is an essential research topic as it may prove benefits in monitoring and supervising large crop fields and early detection of the symptoms of diseases as soon as they appear on plant leaves [2;3]. Such systems include image enhancement, image segmentation, feature extraction and disease classification.

The main source for the disease is the leaf of the cotton plant. About 80 to 90% of disease on the cotton plant is on its leaves.

2. COTTON LEAF DISEASES

In this paper the leaf diseases considered are Powdery mildew, Downy mildew and leafminer. The symptoms of these diseases are as:

Powdery mildew is a fungal disease that affects a wide range of plants. As shown in fig 1.above infected plants display white powdery spots on the leaves and stems. The lower leaves are the most affected, but the mildew can appear on any above-ground part of the plant. Affected leaves eventually turn yellow, then brown. Although not fatal to plants, powdery mildew makes the leaves unattractive and will gradually weaken the plant.

Reproduction

Powdery mildew fungi reproduce both sexually and asexually. Sexual reproduction is via chasmothecia (formerly cleistothecium), a type of ascocarp. Within each ascocarp are several asci. Over time, ascospores mature and are released to initiate new infections. Conditions necessary for spore maturation differ among species

Vectors of Transmission

Wooly aphids (Eriosomatinae) and other sucking insects are often vectors of transmission for Powdery mildew, and other infectious diseases. Typically wooly aphids in sub temperate climates precede and are an indicator of various infections, including Powdery mildew. Aphids penetrate plant surfaces where they often reside and provide a host of potential inoculants through physical, digestive or fecal secretions. Aphids are often an indicator of other potential plant problems.

Management

In an agricultural setting, the pathogen can be controlled using chemical methods, genetic resistance, and careful farming methods.

Chemical control is possible with fungicides such as triadimefon and propiconazole.

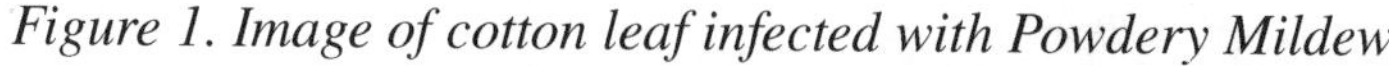

Figure 1. Image of cotton leaf infected with Powdery Mildew

Another chemical treatment involves treating with a silicon solution or calcium silicate slag. Silicon helps the plant cells defend against fungal attack by degrading haustoria and by producing callose and papilla. With silicon treatment, epidermal cells are less susceptible to powdery mildew of wheat.

Potassium bicarbonate is an effective fungicide against powdery mildew and apple scab, allowed for use in organic farming.

Milk has long been popular with home gardeners and small-scale organic growers as a treatment for powdery mildew. Milk is diluted with water (typically 1:10) and sprayed on susceptible plants at the first sign of infection, or as a preventative measure, with repeated weekly application often controlling or eliminating the disease. Studies have shown milk's effectiveness as comparable to some conventional fungicides,and better than benomyl and fenarimol at higher concentrations. Milk has proven effective in treating powdery mildew of summer squash, pumpkins, grapes, and roses.The exact mechanism of action is unknown, but one known effect is that ferroglobulin, a protein in whey, produces oxygen radicals when exposed to sunlight, and contact with these radicals is damaging to the fungus.

Downy mildew is a fungal disease that affects many plants and appears as yellow to white patches on the upper surfaces of older leaves as shown in fig.2 above. On the undersides, these areas are covered with white to grayish, cotton-like fungi. These "downy" masses are most often noticed after rain or heavy dew and disappear soon after sunny weather resumes. As the disease progresses leaves may eventually turn crisp and brown and fall off even though the plant has ample water.

In commercial agriculture, they are a particular problem for growers of crucifers, grapes and vegetables that grow on vines. The prime example is Peronospora farinosa featured in NCBI-Taxonomy and HYP3. This pathogen does not produce survival structures in the northern states of the USA, and overwinters as live mildew colonies in Gulf Coast states. It progresses northward with cucurbit production each spring. Yield loss associated with downy mildew is most likely related to soft rots that occur after plant canopies collapse and sunburn occurs on fruit. Cucurbit downy mildew only affects leaves of cucurbit plants

Figure 2. Image of cotton leaf infected with Downy Mildew

Symptoms

Initial symptoms include large, angular or blocky, yellow areas visible on the upper surface. As lesions mature, they expand rapidly and turn brown. The under surface of infected leaves appears watersoaked. Upon closer inspection, a purple-brown mold (see arrow) becomes apparent. Small spores shaped like footballs can be observed among the mold with a 10x hand lens. In disease-favorable conditions (cool nights with long dew periods), downy mildew will spread rapidly, destroying leaf tissue without affecting stems or petioles

Treatment and Management:

Cultural Options

Because the downy mildew pathogen does not overwinter in midwestern fields, crop rotations and tillage practices do not affect disease development. The pathogen tends to become established in late summer. Therefore, planting early season varieties may further reduce the already minor threat posed by downy mildew.

Chemical Control

Fungicides applied specifically for downy mildew control may be unnecessary. Broad spectrum protectant fungicides such as chlorothalonil, mancozeb, and fixed copper are at least somewhat effective in protecting against downy mildew infection. Systemic fungicides are labeled for use against cucurbit downy mildew, but are recommended only after diagnosis of this disease has been confirmed.

Organic Control

One way to control downy mildew is to eliminate moisture and humidity around the impacted plants. Watering from below, such as with a drip system, and improve air circulation through selective pruning. In enclosed environments, like in the house or in a greenhouse, reducing the humidity will help as well.

Plant Specific Mildews

Hop Downy Mildew (caused by *Pseudoperonospora humuli*) is specific to hops (*Humulus lupulus*). The disease is the single most devastating disease in Western United States hopyards, since the microbe thrives in moist climates. Infected young hop bines become stunted with thickened clusters of pale curled leaves. These spikes have a silvery upper surface, while the undersides of leaves become blackened with spores. These dwarfed spikes are called "basal spikes". 'Lateral' or 'terminal' spikes occur further up the vine. An entire hop crop could be devastated in only a few days.

Similarly, cucurbit downy mildew (caused by *Pseudoperonospora cubensis*) is specific to cucurbits (e.g., cantaloupe (*Cucumis melo*), cucumber (*Cucumis sativus*), pumpkin,squash, watermelon (*Citrullus lanatus*) and other members of the Cucurbitaceae/gourd family). The disease is one of the most significant diseases of cucurbits worldwide.

Plasmopara viticola is the causal agent of grapevine downy mildew.

A new and particularly aggressive form of impatiens downy mildew has recently emerged as a major threat to the cultivation of ornamental impatiens in the United States, where they are one of the most popular ornamental plants.

Downy mildew of basil caused by *Peronospora belbahrii* has been a huge problem for both commercial producers and home growers. The disease was first reported in Italy in 2004,[5] was reported in the U.S. in 2007 and 2008 and has been steadily increasing in prevalence, distribution, and economic importance since then.

Figure 3. Image of cotton leaf infected with Leaf miner

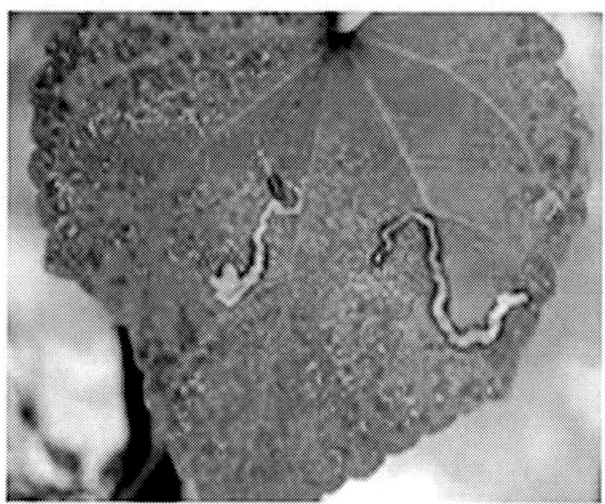

Leaf miner disease is caused by the larva of a tiny moth (Phyllocnistis citrella).The larva feeds just under the surface of the leaf. The thin line that appear on the leaves is the path where the larva has been and the poo it has left behind.

Like Woodboring beetles, leaf miners are protected from many predators and plant defenses by feeding within the tissues of the leaves themselves, selectively eating only the layers that have the least amount of cellulose. When attacking Quercus robur (English oak), they also selectively feed on tissues containing lower levels of tannin, a deterrent chemical produced in great abundance by the tree.

The precise pattern formed by the feeding tunnel is very often diagnostic for which kind of insect is responsible, sometimes even to genus level. The mine often contains frass, or droppings, and the pattern of frass deposition, mine shape and host plant identity are useful to determine the species of leaf miner. A few mining insects utilise other parts of a plant, such as the surface of a fruit.

Relationship with Humans

Leaf miners are regarded as pests by many farmers and gardeners as they can cause damage to agricultural crops and garden plants, and can be difficult to control with insecticide sprays as they are protected inside the plant's leaves. Spraying the infected plants withSpinosad, an organic insecticide, will control the leaf miner. Spinosad does not kill on contact but must be ingested by the leaf miner. Two or three applications may be needed in a season, being careful not to spray when bees are around.

Leaf miner infection can be reduced or prevented by planting trap crops near the plants to be protected. For example, lambsquarter,columbine, and velvetleaf will distract leaf miners, drawing them to those plants and therefore reducing the incidence of attack on nearby crops. This is a method of companion planting

4.REVIEW OF LITERATURE

In recent years, to identify plant leaves diseases there are many methods of image processing technology have been applied.

In [1] Yan-cheng zang et al. proposed the fuzzy feature selection approach –fuzzy curves (FC) and surfaces (FS) – for cotton leaves disease image feature selection. This research is done in two steps .Firstly to automatically and quickly isolate a small set of significant features from a set of original features according to their significance and to eliminate spurious features they make use of FC. Secondly to isolate the features dependent on the significant features, utilize FS. This approach is useful for practical classification applications which reduce the dimensionality of the feature space.

Ajay A. Gurjar and Viraj A. Gulhane [2] have developeda system by using Eigen feature regularization and extraction technique for detection of three cotton leaf diseases This system is having more accuracy, than that of the other feature detection techniques. With this method about 90% of detection of Red spot i.e. fungal disease is detected.

Dheeb Al Bashish & et al. [3] in paper titled Image Processing based software solution for automatic detection and classification of plant leaf disease proposed a system which involved the following main steps: In the first step the acquired images are segmented using the K-means techniques and then secondly the segmented images are passed through a pre-trained neural network .The images of leaves taken from Al-Ghor area in Jordan. Five diseases that are prevalent in leaves were selected for this research;

they are: Early scorch, Cottony mold, Ashen mold, late scorch, tiny whiteness. The experimental result indicates that the neural network classifier that is based on statistical classification support accurate and automatic detection of leaf diseases with a precision of around 93% .

A Meunkaewjinda & et al. [4] proposed a diagnosis system for grape leaf diseases This proposed system is composed of three main parts: Firstly grape leaf color extraction from complex background, secondly grape leaf disease color extraction and finally grape leaf disease classification.

In this analysis back-propagation neural network with a self-organizing feature map together is utilize to recognize colors of grape leaf. Further MSOFM and GA deployed for grape leaf disease segmentation and SVM for classification. Finally filtration of resulting segmented image is done by Gabor Wavelet and then SVM is again applied to classify the types of grape leaf diseases. This system can classify the grape leaf diseases into three classes: Scab disease, rust disease and no disease.The system demonstrates very promising performance for any agricultural product analysis.

Libo Liu & et al. [5] proposed a system for classifying the healthy and diseased part of rice leaves using BP neural network as classifier. In this study rice brown spot was select as a research object. The images of rice leaves were acquired from the northern part of Ningxia Hui autonomous region. Here the color features of diseases and healthy region were served as input values to BP neural network. The result shows that this method is also suitable to identify the other diseases.

3. THE BASIC APPROACH PROCEDURE

The overall concept that is the framework for any vision related algorithm of image classification is almost the same. First, the digital images are acquired from the environment using a digital camera. Then image-processing techniques are applied to the acquired images to extract useful features that are necessary for further analysis. After that, several analytical discriminating techniques are used to classify the images according to the specific problem at hand. Figure 4 show the basic procedure of the proposed detection algorithm in this paper.[6]

Figure 4. The basic procedure based disease detection solution

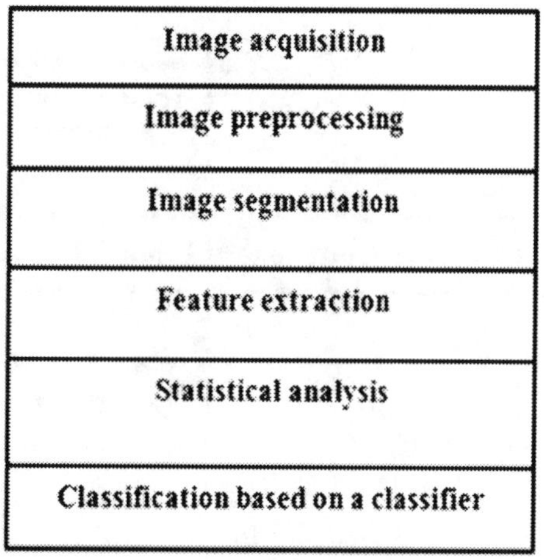

Image acquisition
Image preprocessing
Image segmentation
Feature extraction
Statistical analysis
Classification based on a classifier

4. PROPOSED APPROACH

The main functional module in this system are: image acquisition, color segmentation, Feature extraction, and classification by neural network .The block diagram in fig. 5shows the orientation of these modules.

Algorithm of Classification by Artificial Neural Network

1. Collection of database for different cotton diseased images.
2. Divide the available database into the training set and the testing set
3. In training phase (training done by six images):
    a. Read the input image
    b. Color image segmentation
    c. Feature extraction
    d. Trained the network by backpropogation algorithm
    e. Trained database
4. In testing phase (testing done by thirty eight images):
    a. Read the input image
    b. Color image segmentation
    c. Feature extraction

Figure 5. System block diagram

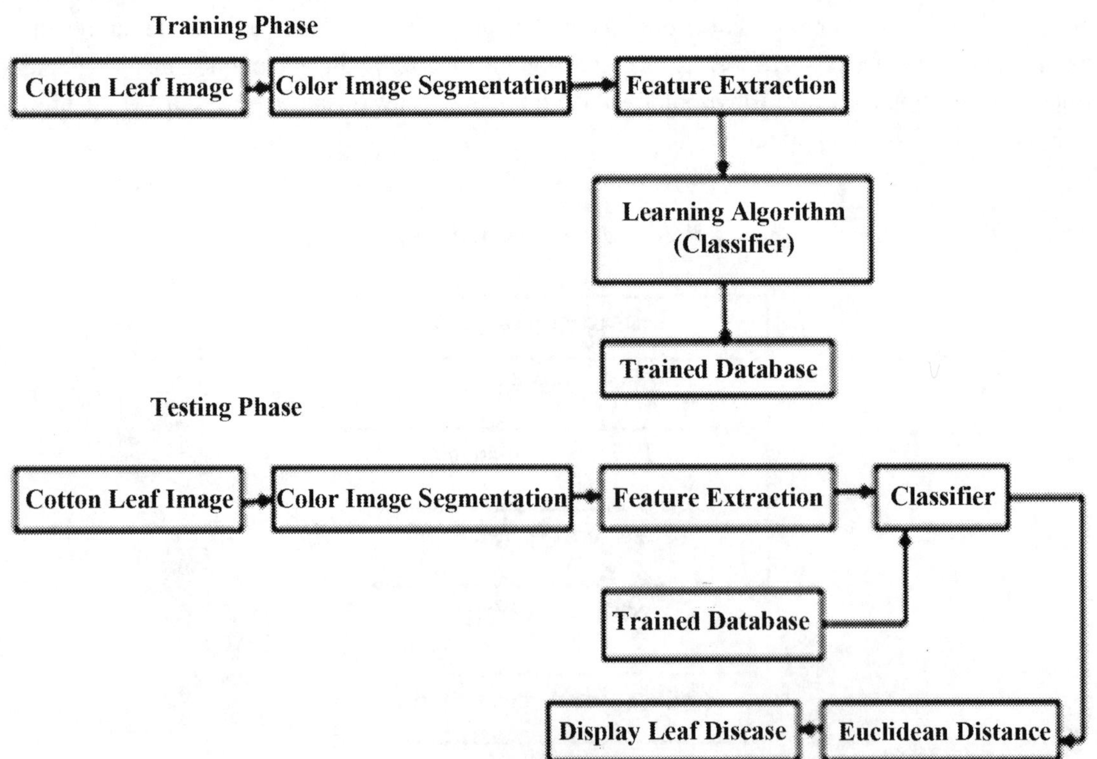

5. Send both features extracted from the test image and the trained database to the ANN
6. Classification done on the basis of minimum Euclidean distance between two vectors
7. Display the leaf disease

A. Image Acquisition

The first step phase is the image acquisition .In this phase the images of various cotton diseased leaves that are to be classified are taken from internet.Some samples of those diseases are shown in fig 6.The leaves belonging to three classes (Powdery mildew,Downey mildew and Leafminer) had minute differences as difficult to detect to the human eye,which may lead to misclassification.The available database of 44 images is divided into Training database (network is trained by 6 images) and Test database (network is tested by 38 images).

B. Color Image Segmentation

This is the second step, here we separated three planes R,G,B respectively before feature extraction step.In this case we decide one threshold value and separated three planes of the binary output image. (See Fig.7)

Result of color image segmentation:

C. Feature Extraction

When crops suffer from many diseases, spots often happen on leaves. Leaf spots are considered the important which indicates the existence of disease and regarded as indicator of crops disease. In order to classify leaf diseases, a set of spot features for classification and detection of the different disease leaves are investigated.

Figure 6. Sample images from database

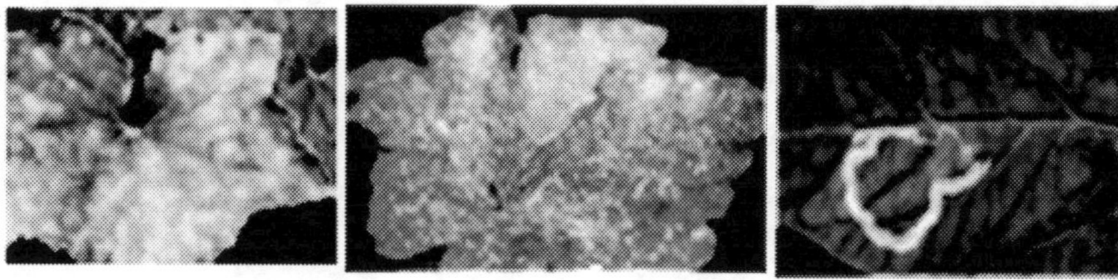

Figure 7. Seperation of RGB planes

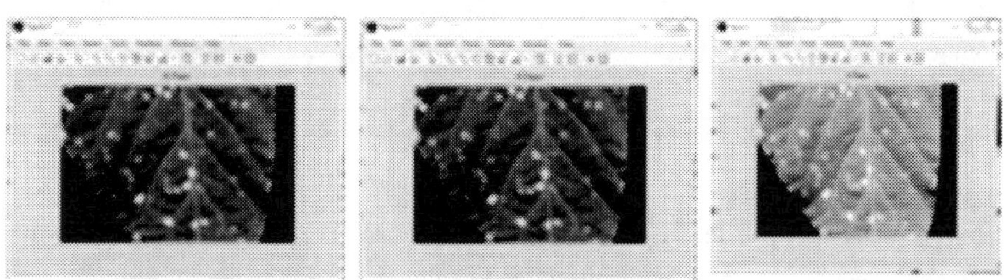

Spot features are extracted from image using the appropriate image processing method. These features are very important for the color and morphology of the leaf spots and they provide critical information about its visual representation. In the feature extraction, we have to classify our features in accordance with the various diseases presents on the leaf. As the diseases changes features are also changes.

The following morphological features are extracted from the preprocessed leaf images. These features are discussed below.

1. Area: Area is the actual number of pixels in the region.
2. Major Axis (L): The line segment connecting the base and the tip of the leaf is the major axis.
3. Minor Axis (W): The breadth between the two distant ends of the leaf.
4. Orientation: It is the angle of the Major Axis inclined with the X Axis itself. This depicts the nature of the leaf bending: whether the leaf is straight or slightly curved (Common nature of any leaf).

$$\theta = \frac{1}{2}\arctan\left[\frac{2^{*}\mu_{1,1}}{\mu_{2,0} - \mathrm{u}_{0,2}}\right]$$

5. Equivalent Diameter: Equivalent diameter specifies the diameter of a circle with the same area as the region.

$$\mathrm{sqrt}\left(4^{*}\mathrm{SpotArea} / \mathrm{pi}\right)$$

6. Eccentricity: The ratio of the distance between the foci and major axis length of the ellipse that has the same second –moments as the spot, also called circularity ratio. Its value is between 0 and 1, the spot whose eccentricity ratio is 1 is a line . The eccentricity ratio is calculated as:

$$2^{*}\mathrm{sqrt}(\left(\left(\mathrm{Major} / 2\right)\hat{}\, 2 - \left(\mathrm{Minor} / 2\right)\hat{}\, 2\right) / \mathrm{Major}$$

7. Solidity: also called compactness, has a value between 0 and 1, if the spot has a solidity value equal to 1, this means that it is fully compacted. It is the ratio the convex Area and the area of the spot, computed as:

$$\mathrm{SpotArea} / \mathrm{ConvexArea}$$

8. Extent: also called rectangularity ratio, the proportion of the pixels in the bounding box that are also in the spot. It has a value between 0 and 1, when this ratio of spot has the value one then its shape is perfectly rectangle. Computed as the spot area divided by the area of the bounding box:

$$\mathrm{SpotArea} / \mathrm{BoundingBoxArea}$$

9. Euler Number: It is an important measure for the topology of a binary image. It is measured as the total number of objects in the image minus the number of holes in those objects.

10. Perimeter: Perimeter of a leaf is the summation of the distances between each adjoining pair of pixels around the border of the leaf.
11. Filled Area: Scalar specifying the number of on pixels in Filled Image.[1]

D. Classification Based on Classifier

An artificial neural network, often just called as a neural network, is a mathematical model inspired by biological neural networks. A neural network consists of an interconnected group of artificial neurons, which are millions and millions in number.With the help of these interconnected neurons all the parallel processing is done in human body[7].

In most cases a neural network is an adaptive system changing its structure during a learning or training phase. For modeling complex relationships between inputs and outputs or to find patterns in data neural networks are used. The inspiration for neural networks came from examination of central nervous systems. In an artificial neural network, simple artificial nodes, called "neurons", "processing elements" or "units", are connected together to form a network which mimics a biological neural network.

Artificial neural networks are used with algorithms designed to adjust or change the strength of the connections in the network to produce a desired signal flow.

Neural networks are also similar to biological neural networks which perform parallel processing in human body. With the help of these interconnected neurons all the human body work is done with the help of neural network.

The backpropagation algorithm (Rumelhart and McClelland, 1986) is used in layered feed-forward Artificial Neural Networks. Back propagation algorithm is very popular and accurate for most classification problems. Backpropagation is a form of supervised training. The neural network is consists of three layers. These layers are input layer, hidden layer, and output layer. (See Fig. 8)

Figure 8. Schematic diagram of neural network

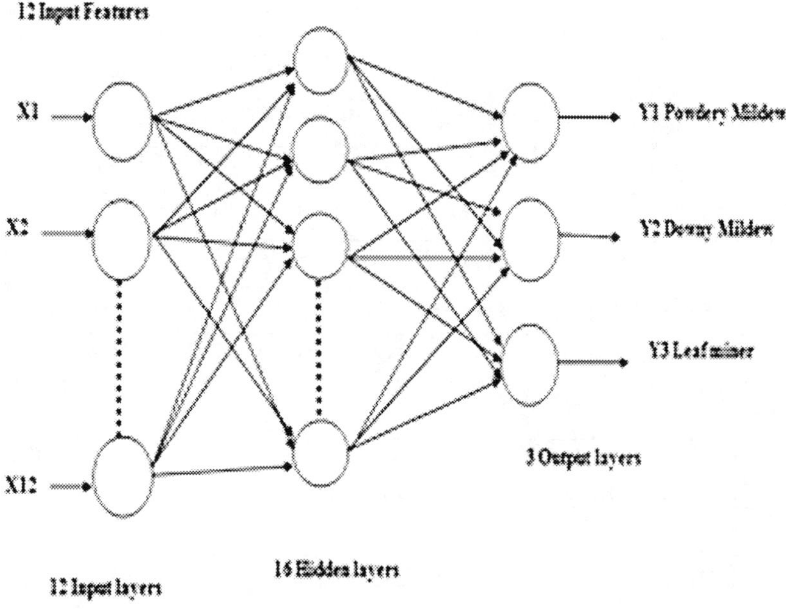

The architecture of the network used in this proposed system

1. The number of inputs to the neural network (i.e. the number of neurons) is equal to the number of features extracted from leaf.
2. Hidden layer consists of 16 neurons.
3. The number of output is 3 which is the number of classes representing the 3 diseases.

Experimental Results and Observations

Input Data Preparation and Experimental Settings

In this experiment, two main dataset were obtained they are: i) Training feature data and ii) Test feature data. The files have 6 columns representing 2 samples for each of the three classes of cotton diseases. Each column has 12 rows representing the 12 features extracted for a particular sample image. Then, a software program was written in MATLAB that would take in .mat files representing the training and testing data, train the classifier using the ―train dataset‖, and then use the ―test dataset to perform the classification task on the test data.

Experimental Results

Table 1 shows the twelve features values extracted from the leaf for the three diseases.

Table 2 shows the output matrix for training the network.

Table 1. Input features values

	Powdary Mildew		Downy Mildew		Leaf Miner	
Area	2683	8134	7716	857	96	7
Major Axis	65.1287005172629	151.259082849216	279.261258951770	108.365147476553	18.4021880145383	5.35956817499913
Minor Axis	54.7602002274219	108.409430248857	196.285622733553	54.9043718523050	9.33454775729058	2.92471204431520
Orientation	31.5614509752451	22.1792660084677	-7.06054005857763	58.3731032458635	-24.2817649021582	-14.5273020495386
Equivalent Diameter	58.4474267913006	101.767040130269	99.1176892748036	33.0328062664684	11.0558127830827	2.98541066072092
Eccentricity	0.541346144662250	0.697367711509354	0.711313863346641	0.862145485430079	0.861797742405998	0.837981137867449
Solidity	0.842386185243328	0.549817493578478	0.266179108596661	0.270688566013898	0.676056338028169	0.777777777777778
Extent	0.655189255189255	0.415021174549722	0.175236191860465	0.173904220779221	0.470588235294118	0.466666666666667
Euler Number	-38	-315	-48	1	0	1
Perimeter	393.102597104443	1532.16774773065	1473.08953724385	353.705627484772	55.1126983722081	10.8284271247462
Filled Area	2731	9426	7964	857	107	7
Density	65.8852258852259	47.9208122863411	17.9891896802326	18.3644480519481	47.0588235294118	46.6666666666667

Table 2. Output values

1	1	0	0	0	0
0	0	1	1	0	0
0	0	0	0	1	1

Figure 9. Brows Leaf Image from test database

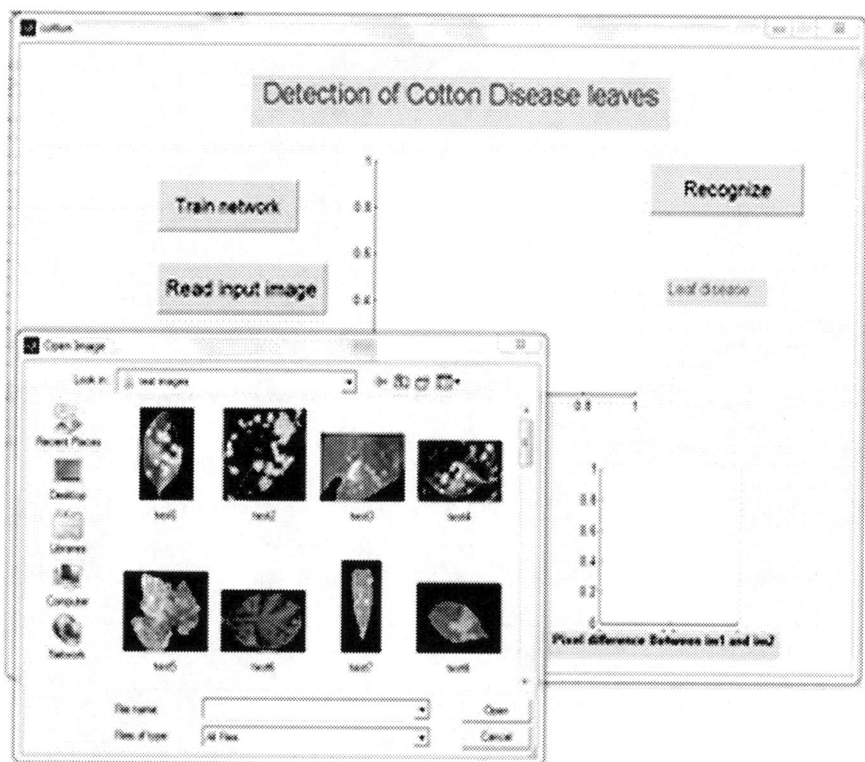

Detection and classification of diseases like Powdery mildew, Downy mildew and Leaf miner by ANN as classifier with the help of GUI.

Table 3 shows the result of classification by neural network.

5. CONCLUSION

In this proposed system we used ANN as a classifier. We tested this technique on three diseases they are Powdery mildew, Downy mildew and Leafminer. The experimental result indicates that by using ANN

Figure 10. Recognize the powdery mildew disease

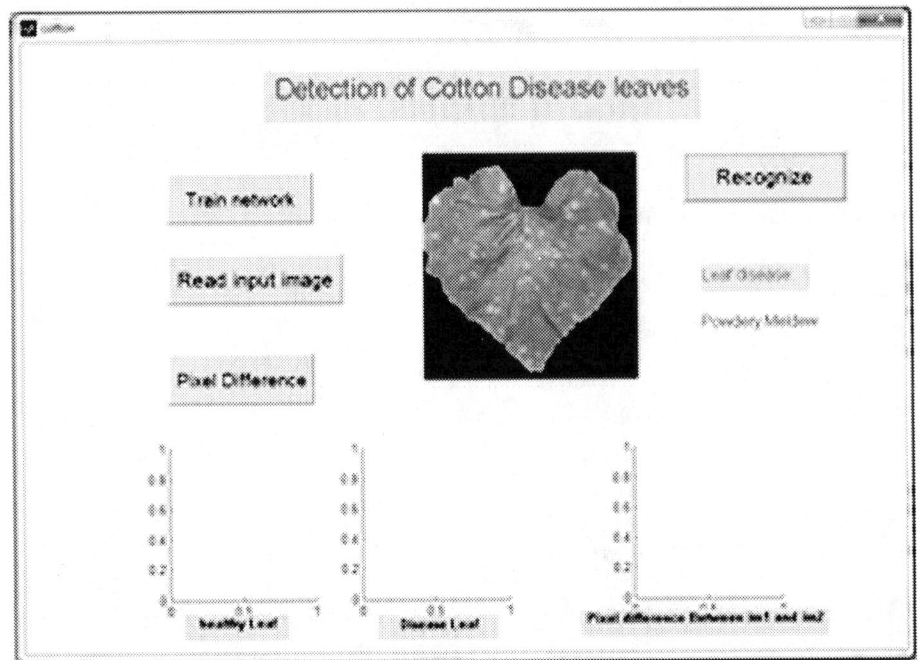

Table 3. Classification result for neural network

Sr. No.	Leaf Image	Diagnosis
1.	Test 3	Powdery mildew
2.	Test 5	Leaf miner
3.	Test 17	Downy mildew
4.	Test 27	Downy mildew
5.	Test 31	Leaf miner

as a classifier, the extracted features are used to train the network because of its adaptive learning characteristic i.e. an ability to learn how to do tasks based on the data given for training. The results shows that the Neural network classifier perform well, reliable and can successfully detect the tested disease.

REFERENCES

Al Bashish, D., Braik, M., & Bani-Ahmad, S. (2010). *A Framework for Detection and Classification of Plant Leaf and Stem Diseases.* International Conference on Signal and Image Processing.

Gurjar, & Gulhane. (n.d.). Disease Detection On Cotton Leaves by Eigenfeature Regularization and Extraction Technique. *International Journal of Electronics, Communication & Soft Computing Science and Engineering, 1*(1).

Image of cotton leaf infected with Leaf miner. (n.d.). Retrieved from http://en.wikipedia.org/wiki/Leaf_miner

Image of cotton leaf infected with Leaf miner. (n.d.). Retrieved from http://www.planetnatural.com/pest-problem-solver/plant-disease/downy-mildew/

Image of cotton leaf infected with Powdery Mildew. (n.d.). Retrieved from http://en.wikipedia.org/wiki/Powdery_mildew

Liu, L., & Zhou, G. (2009). Extraction of the Rice Leaf Disease Image Based on BP. *Neural Networks*, 2009.

Meunkaewjinda, Kumsawat, Attakitmongcol & Srikaew. (2008). Grape leaf disease detection from color imagery using hybrid intelligent system. *In Proceedings of ECTI-CON*.

The basic procedure based disease detection solution. (n.d.). Retrieved from http://www.planetnatural.com/pest-problem-solver/houseplant-pests/leafminer-control/

Zhang, Y. C., Mao, H. P., Hu, B., & Xili, M. (2007). Features selection of Cotton disease leaves image based on fuzzy feature selection techniques. In *Proceedings of the 2007 International Conference on Wavelet Analysis and Pattern Recognition*. Beijing, China: IEEE.

KEY TERMS AND DEFINITIONS

ANN: In machine learning, artificial neural networks (ANNs) are a family of statistical learning algorithms inspired by biological neural networks (the central nervous systems of animals, in particular the brain) and are used to estimate or approximate functions that can depend on a large number of inputs and are generally unknown. Artificial neural networks are generally presented as systems of interconnected "neurons" which can compute values from inputs, and are capable of machine learning as well as pattern recognitionthanks to their adaptive nature.

Backpropagation Neural Network: Backpropagation, an abbreviation for "backward propagation of errors", is a common method of training artificial neural networks used in conjunction with an optimization method such as gradient descent. The method calculates the gradient of a loss function with respects to all the weights in the network. The gradient is fed to the optimization method which in turn uses it to update the weights, in an attempt to minimize the loss function.

Leaf Miner: Leaf miner is the larva of an insect that lives in and eats the leaf tissue of plants. The vast majority of leaf-mining insects are moths (Lepidoptera), sawflies (Symphyta) and flies (Diptera), though beetles and wasps also exhibit this behavior.

Powdery Mildew: Powdery mildew is a fungal disease that affects a wide range of plants. Powdery mildew diseases are caused by many different species of fungi in the order Erysiphales, with Sphaerotheca fuliginea being the most commonly reported cause.

Downy Mildew: Downy mildew refers to any of several types of oomycete microbes that are obligate parasites of plants. Downy mildews exclusively belong to Peronosporaceae. In commercial agriculture, they are a particular problem for growers of crucifers, grapes and vegetables that grow on vines.

Image Segmentation: In computer vision, image segmentation is the process of partitioning a digital image into multiple segments (sets of pixels, also known as superpixels). The goal of segmentation is to simplify and/or change the representation of an image into something that is more meaningful and easier to analyze. Image segmentation is typically used to locate objects and boundaries (lines, curves, etc.) in images. More precisely, image segmentation is the process of assigning a label to every pixel in an image such that pixels with the same label share certain characteristics.

Chapter 6

The Pedagogy of English Teaching-Learning at Primary Level in Rural Government Schools:
A Data Mining View

P. Sunil Kumar
BPUT, India

Sateesh Kumar Pradhan
Utkal University, India

Sachidananda Panda
BPUT, India

ABSTRACT

English language is accepted as the global language in all walks of life today. Hence it becomes mandatory for everyone to learn English in order to be successful at the individual as well as social levels. Although Government has taken number of initiatives, it is necessary to mention that our rural schools at the primary level are adversely affected in this aspect, as the children are not properly taken care of in English teaching and learning skills. This paper is based on a survey work done amongst the students, parents and teachers by using data mining techniques like association rule mining measures and other interesting measures to reveal the facts for better implementation.

1. INTRODUCTION

Teaching of English at the primary level is a worldwide inevitability, however despite the utility and application and growing importance, its worth is meekly understood as a result of which it lacks its due importance as it requires. English, being one of the main communication languages in a multilingual country like India. NCERT-, an apex body for school education in the country was commissioned by

DOI: 10.4018/978-1-4666-8737-0.ch006

MHRD during 2009-10 for conducting a study on Teaching of English in Government Schools at the Primary Level in India. As state after state has been introducing teaching of English from class I, the pace at which the progresses are made as well as the materials prepared for the teachers for the class room preparation has raised many concerns as found by Usha(2012)

The outcome of the study has been that the state textbooks at level 1 (classes I & II) focus less on the listening and speaking skills and do not build familiarity with the language. The teaching pedagogy does not link the child's behavioural aspects both inside and outside the school environment. It is also found that Children do not get opportunity to listen to language or speak in English. They are unable to narrate experiences, exchange ideas and carry out brief conversations in English.

The level of speaking, understanding, and writing skills of a child in rural area in comparison to his or her counterpart in a CBSE or ICSE English mediums school is far from comparison and deplorably worse. Hence, it is required government needs to shift its focus on the qualitative enhancement of the aids to meet the short comings.

Data mining is finding hidden patterns in a large collection of data. Data Mining can be used in educational field to enhance our understanding of learning process to focus on identifying, extracting and evaluating Variables related to the learning process of students as described by Alaa el-Halees (2009).

In this paper it is tried to find out the association of various opinions on shortcomings affecting the pedagogy of English teaching and learning skills in rural areas.

2. BACKGROUND AND RELATED WORK

Educational data mining has emerged as an independent research area in recent years, culminating in 2008 with the establishment of the annual International Conference on Educational Data Mining, and the Journal of Educational Data Mining. Romero and Ventura (2007) provides a comprehensive study of EDM from 1995 to 2005. It describes the need for analyzing the student data which can be used by students, educators and administrators.

Z.N. Khan (2005) found Girls with high socio-economic status were relatively higher achievers in science stream and boys with low socio-economic status were relatively higher achievers in general.

Madhyastha and Tanimoto (2009) investigated the relationship between consistency and student performance with the aim to provide guidelines for scaffolding instruction.

Beck and Mostow (2008) and Pechenizkiy et al. (2008) discovered which types of pedagogical support are most effective, either overall or for different groups of students or in different situations. McQuiggan et al. (2008),found whether students are experiencing poor self-efficiency. Baker (2007) identified students who are off-task. D'Mello et al. (2008) studied on students who are bored or frustrated. Dekker et al. (2009), Romero et al. (2008) and Superby et al. (2006) found short comings that predict student shortcoming or non-retention in college courses.

Han and kamber describes data mining software that allows the users to analyze data from different dimensions and categorize it (2006).

Pandey and Pal (2011) conducted study on the student performance based by selecting 600 students from different colleges of Dr. R. M. L. Awadh University, Faizabad, India. By means of Bayes Classification on category, language and background qualification, it was found that whether new comer students will performer or not.

Hijazi and Naqvi (2006) conducted as study on the student performance by selecting a sample of 300 students (225 males, 75 females) from a group of colleges affiliated to Punjab university of Pakistan. The hypothesis that was stated as "Student's attitude towards attendance in class, hours spent in study on daily basis after college, students' family income, students' mother's age and mother's education are significantly related with student performance" was framed. By means of simple linear regression analysis, it was found that the factors like mother"s education and student"s family income were highly correlated with the student academic performance.

Khan (2005) conducted a performance study on 400 students comprising 200 boys and 200 girls selected from the senior secondary school of Aligarh Muslim University, Aligarh, India with a main objective to establish the prognostic value of different measures of cognition, personality and demographic variables for success at higher secondary level in science stream. The selection was based on cluster sampling technique in which the entire population of interest was divided into groups, or clusters, and a random sample of these clusters was selected for further analyses. It was found that girls with high socio-economic status had relatively higher academic achievement in science stream and boys with low socio-economic status had relatively higher academic achievement in general.

Galit (2007) gave a case study that use students data to analyze their learning behavior to predict the results and to warn students at risk before their final exams.

Al-Radaideh, et al. (2006) applied a decision tree model to predict the final grade of students who studied the C++ course in Yarmouk University, Jordan in the year 2005. Three different classification methods namely ID3, C4.5, and the NaïveBayes were used. The outcome of their results indicated that Decision Tree model had better prediction than other models.

Ayesha et al. (2010)] describe the use of k-means clustering algorithm to predict student"s learning activities. The information generated after the implementation of data mining technique may be helpful for instructor as well as for students.

Bray (2007) in his study on private tutoring and its implications, observed that the percentage of students receiving private tutoring in India was relatively higher than in Malaysia, Singapore, Japan, China and Sri Lanka. It was also observed that there was an enhancement of academic performance with the intensity of private tutoring and this variation of intensity of private tutoring depends on the collective factor namely socio-economic conditions.

Bhardwaj and Pal (2011) conducted study on the student performance based by selecting 300 students from 5 different degree college conducting BCA (Bachelor of Computer Application) course of Dr. R. M. L. Awadh University, Faizabad, India. By means of Bayesian classification method on 17 attributes, it was found that the factors like students" grade in senior secondary exam, living location, medium of teaching, mother"s qualification, students other habit, family annual income and student's family status were highly correlated with the student academic performance.

The rules discovered by a data mining method must be of interest for end-users in order to be considered useful. Measuring the interest in the rules discovered is an active and important area of data mining research as discussed by Geng and Hamilton (2006) Its main objective is to reduce the number of mined rules by evaluating and post-pruning the rules obtained in order to locate only the most interesting rules for a specific problem. This is very important for a non-expert user in data mining, like a teacher.

Minaei-Bidgoli et al. (2004) discover interesting contrast rules using different evaluation measures.

3. DATA MINING DEFINITION AND TECHNIQUES:

Data mining, also popularly known as Knowledge Discovery in Database, refers to extracting or "mining" knowledge from large amounts of data. Data mining techniques are used to operate on large volumes of data to discover hidden patterns and relationships helpful in decision making. While data mining and knowledge discovery in database are frequently treated as synonyms, data mining is actually part of the knowledge discovery process.

Various algorithms and techniques like Classification, Clustering, Regression, Artificial Intelligence, Neural Networks, Association Rules, Decision Trees, Genetic Algorithm, Nearest Neighbour method etc., are used for knowledge discovery from databases. These techniques and methods in data mining need brief mention to have better understanding.

A. Classification

Classification is the most commonly applied data mining technique, which employs a set of pre-classified examples to develop a model that can classify the population of records at large. This approach frequently employs decision tree or neural network-based classification algorithms. The data classification process involves learning and classification. In Learning the training data are analyzed by classification algorithm. In classification test data are used to estimate the accuracy of the classification rules. If the accuracy is acceptable the rules can be applied to the new data tuples. The classifier-training algorithm uses these pre-classified examples to determine the set of parameters required for proper discrimination. The algorithm then encodes these parameters into a model called a classifier.

B. Clustering

Clustering can be said as identification of similar classes of objects. By using clustering techniques we can further identify dense and sparse regions in object space and can discover overall distribution pattern and correlations among data attributes. Classification approach can also be used for effective means of distinguishing groups or classes of object but it becomes costly so clustering can be used as pre-processing approach for attribute subset selection and classification.

C. Predication

Regression technique can be adapted for predication. Regression analysis can be used to model the relationship between one or more independent variables and dependent variables. In data mining independent variables are attributes already known and response variables are what we want to predict. Unfortunately, many real-world problems are not simply prediction. Therefore, more complex techniques (e.g., logistic regression, decision trees, or neural nets) may be necessary to forecast future values. The same model types can often be used for both regression and classification. For example, the CART (Classification and Regression Trees) decision tree algorithm can be used to build both classification trees (to classify categorical response variables) and regression trees (to forecast continuous response variables). Neural networks too can create both classification and regression models.

D. Association Rule

Association and correlation is usually to find frequent item set findings among large data sets. This type of finding helps businesses to make certain decisions, such as catalogue design, cross marketing and customer shopping behavior analysis. Association Rule algorithms need to be able to generate rules with confidence values less than one. However the number of possible Association Rules for a given dataset is generally very large and a high proportion of the rules are usually of little (if any) value.

E. Neural Networks

Neural network is a set of connected input/output units and each connection has a weight present with it. During the learning phase, network learns by adjusting weights so as to be able to predict the correct class labels of the input tuples. Neural networks have the remarkable ability to derive meaning from complicated or imprecise data and can be used to extract patterns and detect trends that are too complex to be noticed by either humans or other computer techniques. These are well suited for continuous valued inputs and outputs. Neural networks are best at identifying patterns or trends in data and well suited for prediction or forecasting needs.

F. Decision Trees

Decision tree is tree-shaped structures that represent sets of decisions. These decisions generate rules for the classification of a dataset. Specific decision tree methods include Classification and Regression Trees (CART) and Chi Square Automatic Interaction Detection (CHAID).

G. Nearest Neighbour Method

A technique that classifies each record in a dataset based on a combination of the classes of the k record(s) most similar to it in a historical dataset (where k is greater than or equal to 1). Sometimes called the k-nearest neighbour technique.

4. ASSOCIATION RULE MINING

Data Mining is the discovery of hidden information found in databases as narrated by (chen, Jiawei and Philip, 1996) and (Usama, Piatetsky, Smyth,1996). Dunham (2006) categorized various models and tasks of data mining into two groups: predictive and descriptive. One of the most significant descriptive data mining applications is that of mining association rules. (Agrawal, Imielinski, Swami,1993) introduced mining of large databases extensively in marketing and retail communities in addition to many other diverse fields as discussed by Umarani and Punithavalli (2010). Association rule mining is one of the important technique which aims at extracting, interesting correlation, frequent patterns, associations or casual structures among set of items in the transaction databases or other data mining repositories as discussed by Umarani and Punithavalli (2010).

A formal statement of the association rule problem is as follows:

Definition: As given by Umarani and Punithavalli (2010) and (Cheung,Vincent,Wai-Chee,Yongjian,1996) Let $I = (i_{1.}i_{2}i_{3}\cdots i_{m})$ be a set of m distinct attributes. Let D be a database, where each record (tuple) T has a unique identifier, and contains a set of items such that $(T \subseteq I)$.An association rule is an implication of the form of $(X \Rightarrow Y), (X, Y \subseteq I)$ where are sets of items called item sets, and. $(X \cap Y = \phi)$ Here, X is called antecedent while Y is called consequent; the rule mean $(X \Rightarrow Y)$. Association rules can be classified based on the type of vales, dimensions of data, and levels of abstractions involved in the rule. If a rule concerns associations between the presence and absence of items, it is called Boolean association rule. And the dataset consisting of attributes which can assume only binary (0-absent, 1-present) values is called Boolean database.

5. APRIORI ALGORITHM

Apriori is a seminal algorithm proposed by R. Agrawal and R. Srikant in 1994 for mining frequent itemsets for Boolean association rules. The algorithm uses prior knowledge of frequent item set properties. Apriori employs an iterative approach known as a level-wise search, where k-itemsets are used to explore (k+1)-itemsets. First, the set of frequent 1-itemsets is found by scanning the database to accumulate the count for each item, and collecting those items that satisfy minimum support. The resulting set is denoted L1.Next, L1 is used to find L2, the set of frequent 2-itemsets, which is used to find L3, and so on, until no more frequent k-itemsets can be found. The finding of each Lk requires one full scan of the database.Lk-1 is used to find Lk. A two-step process is followed, consisting of join and prune actions.

5.1. The Join Step

To find Lk, a set of candidate k-itemsets is generated by joining Lk-1 with itself. This set of candidates is denoted Ck.

Let l1 and l2 be item sets in Lk-1.The notation li[j] refers to the jth item in li (e.g., l1[k-2] refers to the second to the last item in l1). By convention, Apriori assumes that items within a transaction or item set are sorted in lexicographic order. For the (k-1)-item set, li, this means that the items are sorted such that li[1] < li[2] <::: < li[k-1]. The join, Lk-1 Lk-1, is performed, where members of Lk-1 are joinable if their first (k-2) items are in common. That is, members l1 and l2 of Lk-1 are joined if (l1[1] = l2[1]) ^ (l1[2] = l2[2]) ^:::^(l1[k-2] = l2[k-2]) ^(l1[k-1] < l2[k-1]). The condition l1 [k-1] < l2 [k-1] simply ensures that no duplicates are generated. The resulting item set formed by joining l1 and l2 is l1[1], l1[2],:::, l1[k-2], l1[k-1], l2[k-1].

5.2. The Prune Step

Ck is a superset of Lk, that is, its members may or may not be frequent, but all of the frequent k-itemsets are included in Ck. As can of the database to determine the count of each candidate in Ck would result in the determination of Lk (i.e., all candidates having a count no less than the minimum support count are frequent by definition, and therefore belong to Lk). Ck, however, can be huge, and so this could involve heavy computation. To reduce the size of Ck, the Apriori property is used as follows. Any (k-1)-item set that is not frequent cannot be a subset of a frequent k-item set. Hence, if any (k-1)-subset of a candidate k-item set is not in Lk-1, then the candidate cannot be frequent either and so can be removed from Ck.

6. INTERESTING MEASURES

Support(X)=P(X)

Confidence $\left(X \Rightarrow Y\right) = \dfrac{P(X,Y)}{P(X)}$

Cosine $\left(X \Rightarrow Y\right) = \dfrac{P(X,Y)}{\sqrt{P(X)*P(Y)}}$

Added Value$\left(X \Rightarrow Y\right) = Confidnce(X \Rightarrow Y) - P(Y)$

Lift$\left(X \Rightarrow Y\right) = \dfrac{Confidence(X \Rightarrow Y)}{P(Y)}$

Correlation($\left(X \Rightarrow Y\right)$)= $\dfrac{P(X,Y) - P(X)*P(Y)}{\sqrt{P(X)*P(Y)(1-P(X))(1-P(Y))}}$

Conviction($\left(X \Rightarrow Y\right)$)= $\dfrac{Confidence(X \Rightarrow Y)}{P(Y)}$

7. INTERESTING MEASURES USED IN THIS PAPER

Support: The support (s) for an association rule $\left(X \Rightarrow Y\right)$ is the percentage of transaction that contains $\left(X \cup Y\right)$as defined by Dunham (2006). (See Table 1)

Table 1. Data Set

Variable	Description	Possible values
Sex	Boy or Girl	{boy, girl}
Late Learning(LL)	Course design not up to the mark, books high or low standard, comparison to private English medium school, slow learning	{Yes, No}
Teaching Competency (TC)	Teacher's Training, Qualification, use of Teaching Learning Material(TLM) grants	{Yes, No}
Environmental conditions (EC)	Presence of educated person at home	{Yes, No}

The size of the data set is 160.

Confidence: The confidence or strength (α) for an association rule $(X \Rightarrow Y)$ is the ratio of the number of transactions that contain X as defined by Dunham (2006).

Cosine: Consider two vectors X and Y and the angle they form when they are placed so that their tails coincide. When this angle nears 0°, then cosine nears 1, i.e. the two vectors are very similar: all their coordinates are pair wise the same. When this angle is 90 degree the vector are perpendicular, the most dissimilar, and the cosine is 0.The usual form that is given for cosine of an association rule is X, Y. The closer cosine$(X \Rightarrow Y)$ is to 1, the more transactions containing item X also contain item Y, and vice versa. On the contrary, the closer cosine$(X \Rightarrow Y)$ is to 0, the more transactions contain item X without containing item Y, and vice versa. This equality shows that transactions not containing neither item X nor item Y have no influence on the result of Cosine*GHRCEM, India*. This is known as the null-invariant property. Note also that cosine is a symmetric measure as defined by Merceron and Yacef(2007).

Added value: The added value of the rule $(X \Rightarrow Y)$ is denoted by AV $(X \Rightarrow Y)$ and measures whether the proportions of transactions containing Y among the transactions containing X is greater than the proportion of transactions containing Y among all transactions. Then, only if the probability of finding item Y when item X has been found is greater than the probability of finding item Y at all can we say that X and Y are associated and that X implies Y.A positive number indicates that X and Y are related, while a negative number means that the occurrence of X prevents Y from occurring. Added Value is closely related to another well-known measure of interest, the lift as revealed by Merceron and Yacef(2007).

Lift: Lift symmetric measure. A lift well above 1 indicates a strong correlation between X and Y. A lift around 1 says that P(X, Y) = P(X)*P(Y). In terms of probability, this means that the occurrence of X and the occurrence of Y in the same transaction are independent events, hence X and Y not correlated. It is easy to show that the lift is 1 exactly when added value is 0; the lift is greater than 1 exactly when added value is positive and the lift is below 1 exactly when added value is negative as defined by Merceron and Yacef(2007).

Correlation: Correlation is a symmetric measure. A correlation around 0 indicates that X and Y are not correlated a negative figure indicates that X and Y are negatively correlated, and a positive figure indicates that they are positively related. Note that the denominator of the division is positive and smaller than 1.In other words, if the lift is around 1, correlation can still be significantly different from 0 as defiened by Merceron and Yacef(2007).

Conviction: Conviction is not a symmetric measure. A conviction around 1 says that X and Y are independent; while conviction is infinite as conf $(X \Rightarrow Y)$ is tending to1.Note that if P(Y) is high then 1-P(Y) is small. In that case even if conf(X,Y) is strong conviction may be small as defined by Merceron and Yacef(2007). These measures are calculated on the test data.

8. APPLICATION OF THE MEASURES

In this study data was collected from the senior students, parents and teachers of Balianta Block, District Khorda. These data are analyzed using Association rules to find the interestingness measures and the various means to overcome the shortcomings in English Teaching and Learning (ETL).

In order to apply this following steps are performed in sequence:

6.1 Data set: The data set consisted of the following variables related to English Teaching and Learning (ETL) methodologies. All the attributes are listed as follows:

8.1 Data Selection and Transformation

The preprocessed data set in weka is shown in figure 1

The short comings basically fall into three categories irrespective of community enquired about the current scenario i.e. LL, EC and TC.

It has been seen that among the opinions given by the three communities there exist some similarities which is depicted by the Venn diagram (fig. 2) which shows the complete shortcomings opinion picture.

So, in this study it has been tried to find out the similar opinions about the shortcomings in teaching pedagogy, using the association rule mining technique.

On the basis of available data, it was decided to calculate the support of each shortcoming causing the poor performance of the students.

Figure 1. Preprocessed data in weka

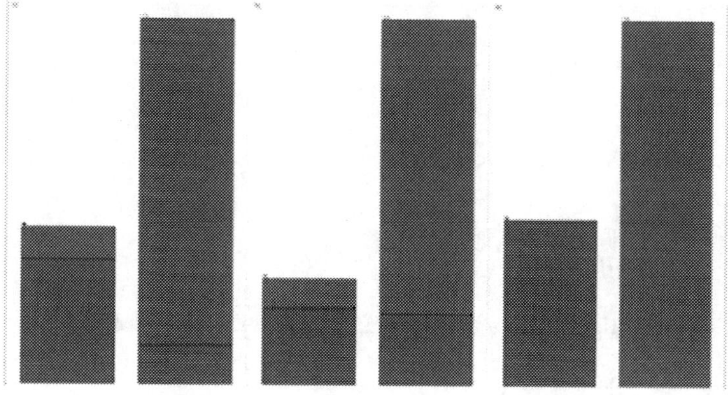

Figure 2. Survey Data as Venn diagram

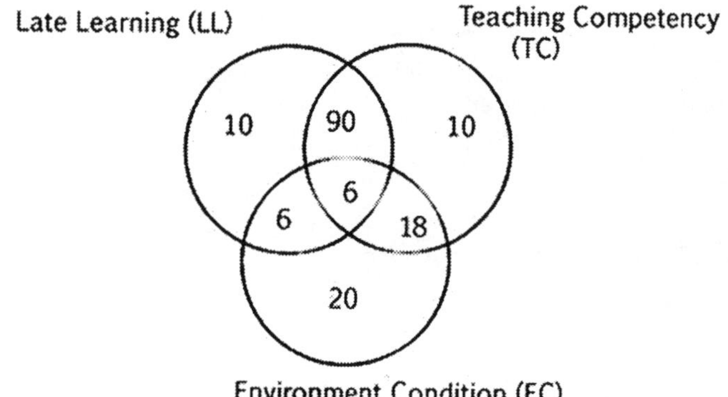

Following table 2 shows the support level for each shortcoming. It describes that higher percentage of ETL shortcoming is because of incompetent teachers whose support value is 0.77.

8.2. Measures and Their Analysis

The Apriori algorithm is implemented on the data set using weka as shown in figure 3. The results obtained like confidence, lift and conviction along with other interesting measures are analyzed one by one.

Table 3 describes that the most of the opinions i.e. 85% who said that the ETL is affected due to late learning are also of the opinion that that it is due to teacher incompetency because it has highest confidence.

Table 2. Support analysis

Shortcoming	Support
LL	0.7
EC	0.31
TC	0.77
(LL, TC)	0.6
(LL, EC)	0.07
(EC, TC)	0.15
(LL, TC,EC)	0.03

Table 3. Confidence Analysis

Shortcoming	Confidence
$LL \Rightarrow TC$	0.85
$TC \Rightarrow LL$	0.78
$EC \Rightarrow TC$	0.48
$TC \Rightarrow EC$	0.25

Figure 3. The Apriori Application in Weka

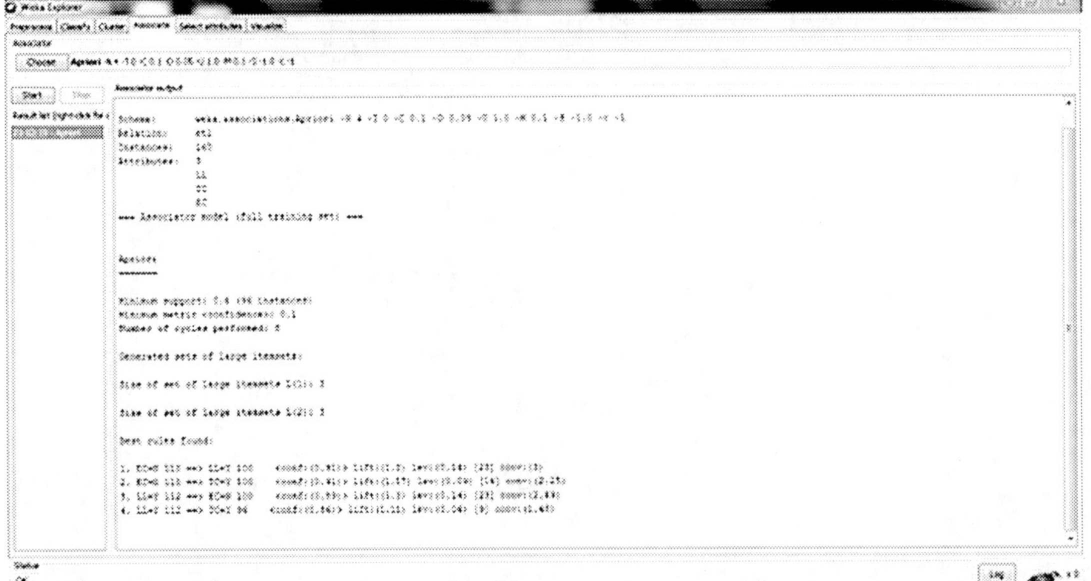

It is also found that 78% of the populations who are not satisfied with the teaching are also not happy with the slow process of learning in comparison to the pedagogy followed in CBSE or ICSE English medium schools.

Table 4 describes cosine analysis value. It is a symmetric analysis. It means two sets give same results in either direction. In this research paper it shows the angular value between two different shortcomings affecting the ETL shortcoming. Table 4 shows that LL and TC has lower angle (37.72) in comparison to EC and TC. It can be concluded that students failing due to Social Environment and TC have more similarity than the EC and TC

Table 5 shows the added value analysis.

In this table $LL \Rightarrow TC$ and $TC \Rightarrow LL$ has positive number which shows that they are related to each other. The presence of people with these dual opinions cannot prevent one another. $EC \Rightarrow TC$ and $TC \Rightarrow EC$ have negative number which shows that the occurrence of EC prevents occurring of TC. Similarly occurrence of TC prevents occurrence of EC.

Table 6 contains lift analysis. It is a symmetric analysis. It shows the occurrence of one item to another item.

In this table the first two rules have values greater than 1 which shows that occurrence of first is strongly correlated with the other. In the case of third and fourth rules, it has also same positive value but less than 1 which shows that they are negatively correlated.

Table 7 contains correlation value. In this table the first two rules have similar positive value indicating that they are positively correlated to each other. On the other hand third and fourth rules have similar negative value showing that they are negatively correlated to each other.

Table 8 shows conviction analysis. It shows that highest conviction is found in the association of $LL \Rightarrow TC$ with value 1.53. Lowest conviction is found in association of $EC \Rightarrow TC$ with value 0.47.

Table 4. Cosine Analysis

Shortcoming	Cosine	Angle
$LL \Rightarrow TC$	0.821	37.72
$TC \Rightarrow LL$	0.821	37.72
$EC \Rightarrow TC$	0.312	71.79
$TC \Rightarrow EC$	0.312	71.79

Table 5. Added value Analysis

Shortcoming	Added Value
$LL \Rightarrow TC$	0.01
$TC \Rightarrow LL$	0.15
$EC \Rightarrow TC$	-0.29
$TC \Rightarrow EC$	-0.06

Table 6. Lift Analysis

Shortcoming	Lift
$LL \Rightarrow TC$	1.08
$TC \Rightarrow LL$	1.1
$EC \Rightarrow TC$	0.62
$TC \Rightarrow EC$	0.80

Table 7. Correlation Analysis

Shortcoming	Correlation
$LL \Rightarrow TC$	0.36
$TC \Rightarrow LL$	0.36
$EC \Rightarrow TC$	-0.42
$TC \Rightarrow EC$	-0.42

Table 8. Conviction Analysis

Shortcoming	Conviction
$LL \Rightarrow TC$	1.53
$TC \Rightarrow LL$	1.36
$EC \Rightarrow TC$	0.47
$TC \Rightarrow EC$	0.92

9. FURTHER RESEARCH DIRECTION

EDM being an emerging research area a lot of work can be done to extend this current chapter. With the inclusion of Big Data similar work can be replicated at a larger scale. Research work can be carried out on various teaching-learning methods which in turn can give a shape to administrative policy decisions at the state as well as national level in the greater interest of the budding generations. The different domains of work may include the following

- The Teacher's problems viz. financial constraints, language constraints, and family constraints
- The student's problems viz. classroom, toilets, teaching aids etc.
- The Government issues viz. Mid-day meal, free education, Use of TLM, Recruitment of qualified teachers, Infrastructure of schools etc.

10. CONCLUSION

Association rules are used for finding the association between two elements and shows relationship between them. The conclusion is extracted from confidence, cosine, AV analysis, lift, correlation and conviction analysis is that most of the people commented on teaching competency as well as the course designed.

From the above analysis it can be concluded that the pedagogy of English teaching learning is affected more due to teaching incompetency and late learning at primary level in rural government schools. It can also be said that the environment at home of the pupil has less to do with the classroom teaching hence it is of less concern.

So as depicted by NCERT on ETL, Government of Odisha has to take necessary steps to enhance the pedagogy by recruiting teachers with higher qualifications and making suitable changes in the course to enable our rural pupil to read, write and speak English without fear and shyness.

REFERENCES

Agrawal, R., Imielinski, T., & Swami, A. (1993). Mining Associations between Sets of Items in massive Databases. In *Proc. of the ACM-SIGMOD Int'l Conference on Management of data*. Washington, DC: ACM.

Al-Radaideh, Al-Shawakfa, & Al-Najjar. (2006). Mining student data using decision trees. In *Proceedings of International Arab Conference on Information Technology (ACIT'2006)*. Yarmouk University.

Alaa. (2009). *Mining Students Data to Analyze e- Learning Behavior: A Case Study*. Academic Press.

Ayesha, , Mustafa, Sattar, & Khan. (2010). Data mining model for higher education system. *Europen Journal of Scientific Research*, *43*(1), 24–29.

Baker, R. S. J. D. (2007). Modeling and Understanding Students' Off-Task Behavior in Intelligent Tutoring Systems. In *Proceedings of the ACM Computer- Human Interaction Conference*, (pp. 1059-1068). ACM.

Beck, J. E., & Mostow, J. (2008). How who should practice: Using learning decomposition to evaluate the efficacy of different types of practice for different types of students. In *Proceedings of the 9th International Conference on Intelligent Tutoring Systems*, (pp. 353-362). doi:10.1007/978-3-540-69132-7_39

Bharadwaj, B. K., & Pal, S. (2011). Data Mining: A prediction for performance improvement using classification. *International Journal of Computer Science and Information Security*, *9*(4), 136–140.

Bray. (n.d.). *The shadow education system: private tutoring and its implications for planners* (2nd ed.). UNESCO.

D'mello, S. K., Craig, S. D., Witherspoon, A. W., McDaniel, B. T., & Graesser, A. C. (2008). Automatic Detection of Learner's Affect from Conversational Cues. *User Modeling and User-Adapted Interaction*, *18*(1-2), 45–80. doi:10.1007/s11257-007-9037-6

Dekker, G., Pechenizkiy, M., & Vleeshouwers, J. (2009). Predicting Students Drop Out: A Case Study. In *Proceedings of the International Conference on Educational Data Mining*.

Dunham. (2006). Data Mining Introductory and Advanced Topics. Pearson Education.

Cheung, Ng, Fu, & Fu. (1996). Efficient Mining of Association Rules in Distributedatabases. *IEEE Transactions on Knowledge and Data Engineering*, *8*(6), 866–883.

Fayyad, Shapiro, & Smyth. (1996). From Data Mining to knowledge Discovery: An Overview. AAAI Press.

Galit, et al. (2007). *Examining online learning processes based on log files analysis: a case study*. Research, Reflection and Innovations in Integrating ICT in Education.

Geng, L., & Hamilton, H. J. (2006). Interestingness Measures for Data MiningA Survey. *ACM Computing Surveys*, *38*(3), 1–32. doi:10.1145/1132960.1132963

Han, J., & Kamber, M. (2006). Data Mining: concepts and techniques (2nd ed.). Morgan Kaufmann.

Hijazi, S. T., & Naqvi, R. S. M. M. (2006). Factors affecting student"s performance: A Case of Private Colleges. *Bangladesh e- Journal of Sociology (Melbourne, Vic.)*, *3*(1).

Khan, Z. N. (2005). Scholastic Achievement of Higher Secondary Students in Science Stream. *Journal of Social Sciences*, *1*(2), 84–87. doi:10.3844/jssp.2005.84.87

Khan, Z. N. (2005). Scholastic achievement of higher secondary students in science stream. *Journal of Social Sciences*, *1*(2), 84–87. doi:10.3844/jssp.2005.84.87

Madhyastha, T., & Tanimoto, S. (2009). Student Consistency and Implications for Feedback in Online Assessment Systems. In *Proceedings of the 2nd International Conference on Educational Data Mining*, (pp. 81-90).

Mcquiggan, S., Mott, B., & Lester, J. (2008). Modeling Self-Efficacy in Intelligent Tutoring Systems: An Inductive Approach. *User Modeling and User-Adapted Interaction, 18*(1-2), 81–123. doi:10.1007/s11257-007-9040-y

Merceron, A., & Yacef, K. (2007a). *Interestingness Measures for Association Rules in Educational Data*. Academic Press.

Merceron, A., & Yacef, K. (2007b). Revisiting interestingness of strong symmetric association rules in educational data. In *Proceedings of the International Workshop on Applying Data Mining in e-Learning*.

Minaei-Bidgoli, B., Tan, P.-N., & Punch, W. F. (2004). Mining Interesting Contrast Rules for a Web-based Educational System. In *Proc. Int. Conf. on Machine Learning Applications*. doi:10.1109/ICMLA.2004.1383530

Ming-Syan Chen, , Jiawei Han, , & Yu, P. S. (1996). Data Mining-An Overview from a Database Perspective. *IEEE Transactions on Knowledge and Data Engineering, 8*(6), 866–883. doi:10.1109/69.553155

Pandey, U. K., & Pal. (2011). Data Mining: A prediction of performer or underperformer using classification. *International Journal of Computer Science and Information Technology, 2*(2), 686-690.

Pechenizkiy, M., Calders, T., Vasilyeva, E., & Debra, P. (2008). Mining the Student Assessment Data: Lessons Drawn from a Small Scale Case Study. In *Proceedings of the 1st International Conference on Educational Data mining*, (pp. 187-191).

Romera, C., & Ventura, S. (2007). A Survey from 1995 to 2005. *Expert Systems with Applications, 33*, 125–146.

Romero, C., Ventura, S., Eapejo, P. G., & Hervas, C. (2008). Data Mining Algorithms to Classify Students. In *Proceedings of the 1st International Conference on Educational Data Mining*.

Superby, J. F., Vandamme, J.-P., & Meskens, N. (2006). Determination of short comings influencing the achievement of thefirst-year university students using data mining methods. In *Proceedings of the Workshop on Educational Data Mining at the 8th International Conference on Intelligent Tutoring Systems (ITS)*.

Umarani & Punithavalli. (2010a). Sampling based Association Rules Mining- A Recent Overview. *International Journal on Computer Science and Engineering, 2*(2), 314-318.

Umarani & Punithavalli. (2010b). A study on effective mining of association rules from huge databases. *International Journal of Computer Science and Research, 1*(1).

Usha, D. & Neeru, B. (2012). *Teaching of English in Primary level in Government schools EdCIL*. Retrieved from http://www.ncert.nic.in/departments/nie/del/publication/pdf/English_Primary_level.pdf

KEY TERMS AND DEFINITIONS

CBSE: Central Board of Secondary Education.
EDM: Educational Data Mining.
ETL: English Teaching and Learning.
ICSE: Indian Certificate of Secondary Education.
MHRD: Ministry of Human Resource Development.
NCERT: National Council of Educational Research and Training.
TLM: Teaching and Learning Material.

Chapter 7
Indic Language:
Kannada to Braille Conversion Tool Using Client Server Architecture Model

Shaila H. Koppad
Bangalore University, India

T. M. Shwetha
Bangalore University, India

ABSTRACT

The aim of this research paper is to convert Kannada script to Braille, to enable the visually-impaired lead a better life by means of providing better learning aides. It proposes a possibility of facilitating the regional teachers to teach Kannada through Braille. "Braille Lipi" is instrumental in providing an able platform for the visually-impaired to habituate studying. This paper addresses the various aspects of "Braille Lipi", it throws light on the origin and various levels, which depends on user-type (either simple, moderate or expert) explained with architecture of Braille system. Kannada to Braille Conversion Tool mainly focuses on elaborating the conversion of Kannada script to Braille script. An attempt to better understand, by a brief insight to Kannada script, Kannada alphabets is made and the whole intention of the contribution is a humble gesture to humanity. The main advantage of the model is visually-impaired can also have access to e-governance.

INTRODUCTION

All over the world, persons who are visually impaired have used Braille as the primary means of accessing information. Also, the concept of Braille has been accepted as a universal approach that works across the boundaries of the world. Different countries of the world have adapted the system of Braille to suit their languages. Irrespective of these changes or modifications, visually disabled persons understand standard Braille for the English language making it possible to exchange information in a consistent fashion across different countries. Standard Braille is an approach for creating documents which could be sensed through touch. This is accomplished through the concept of a Braille cell consisting of raised

DOI: 10.4018/978-1-4666-8737-0.ch007

dots on thick sheet of paper. Also there are several communication methods that involve tactile sensation, such as Braille-Based typewriter (Baulblenkhorn,1997) a system for converting print to Braille (Basu & Lachikawa,2004), Braille text on a finger using Braille pin textile method (Blenkhorn,2010) and various Braille emulator method (Lee,2010;Gill,1992) available. However, some problems arise in such conversion, like lack of privacy for slow learners, complexity operation and mismatch for computer environment. Also person having problem like long term diabetics often have a condition known as "diabetic neuropathy a circulatory problem causing many of the complications that the diabetics might encounter. Neuropathy causes not only insensitivity in the fingertips and toes; it causes more blindness, kidney failure, heart attacks and other related medical problems. The continuous readings in Braille produces swelling in the ankles which cause reading times are very slow. So this proposed system gives easy conversion of Kannada text to Braille.

A man named Charles Barbier who served in Napoleon Bonaparte's French army developed a unique system known as "night writing" so soldiers could communicate safely during the night. Being a military veteran, Barbier had seen several soldiers killed because they used lamps after dark to read combat messages. The light shining from the lamps told enemy combatants where the French soldiers were and inevitably led to the loss of many men. Barbier based his "night writing" system on a raised 12-dot cell; two dots wide and six dots tall. Each dot or combination of dots within the cell represented a letter or a phonetic sound. The problem with the military code was that the human fingertip could not feel all the dots with one touch.

The Braille script was created in 1821 by the Frenchman Louis Braille who was born in the village of Coupvray, France on January 4, 1809. He was blinded at a very young age after he accidentally stabbed himself in the eye with his father's awl. Braille's father was a leather-worker and used the awl to poke holes in the leather goods he produced.At eleven years old, Braille was inspired to modify Charles Barbier's "night writing" code in an effort to create an efficient written communication system for fellow blind individuals. One year earlier he was enrolled at the National Institute of the Blind in Paris and spent the better part of the next nine years developing and refining the system of raised dots that has come to be known by his name, Braille.After all of Braille's work, the code was now based on cells with only 6-dots instead of 12 (like the example shown below). This improvement was crucial because it meant that a fingertip could encompass the entire cell unit with one impression and move rapidly from one cell to the next. Over time, braille gradually came to be accepted throughout the world as the fundamental form of written communication for blind individuals, and today it remains basically as he invented it.

The system is based on a code called night writing, which had been developed by Charles Barbier to enable soldiers to communicate silently and without the need for a light. Barbier's system used letters comprised of up to twelve raised dots, and proved too complex to be useful to the military. Louis Braille modified this concept to produce a script which used letters comprised of six dots. A dot may be raised at any or all of six positions called "cell". Braille is usually written using larger letters than standard printed text, to enable the reader to more easily make the distinction between letters. The figure1 represents a cell which is made up of six dots that fit under the fingertips, arranged in two columns of three dots each. Each cell represents a letter, a word, a combination of letters, a numeral or a punctuation mark. Counting a space in which there is no dot raised, there are 2 to the 6th power (2x2x2x2x2x2 = 64) possible combinations.

However, there have been some small modifications to the braille system, particularly the addition of contractions representing groups of letters or whole words that appear frequently in a language. The use of contractions permits faster braille reading and helps reduce the size of braille books, making them

Figure 1. The Braille Cell

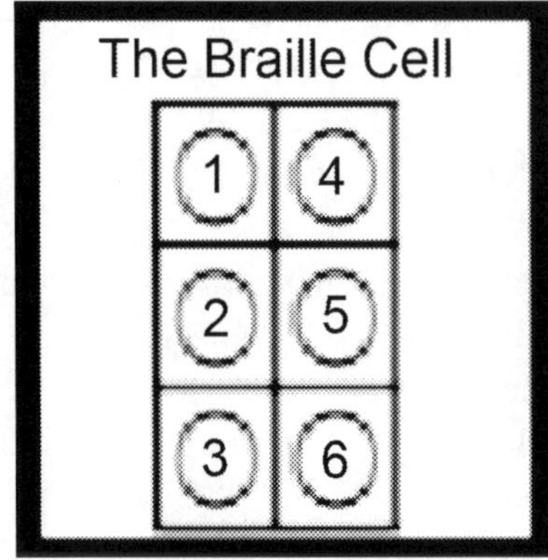

much less cumbersome. Braille passed away in 1853 at the age of 43, a year before his home country of France adopted braille as its' official communication system for blind individuals. A few years later in 1860, braille made its way "across the pond" to America where it was adopted by The Missouri School for the Blind in St. Louis.

People who have both sight and hearing impairments are known as blind and deaf. Because of their impairments they face many problems in their normal daily life. It is particularly difficult for totally deaf and visually impaired to acquire vital and sufficient information necessary for daily living, compared with sighted hearing people. In standard Braille, the concept of a Braille cell consisting of raised dots on thick sheet of paper as mentioned in figure 2.The protrusion of the dot is achieved through a process of embossing. A visually impaired person is taught Braille by training him or her in discerning the cells by touch, accomplished through his or her fingertips. The image below shows how this is done.

Kannada

The origin of Kannada language, also known as kannarese, can be traced to the early Christian era. Kannada is one of the most well-known Dravidian languages of India. It is as old as Tamil, the truest language

Figure 2. Braille Sheet

of the Dravidian family. It is spoken predominantly in the state of Karnataka in India (one of the four southern states in India), though a significant number of Kannada speaking people can also be found in the other states. A good number of people speaking this language who have migrated from India live in other parts of the world such as USA, UAE, Singapore, Australia, UK, etc. It stands in the 27th place of the most spoken language in the world and there are about 35 million Kannadigas (Kanadda speaking people) in the world. It is one of the official languages of the Republic of India and the official and administrative language of the Indian state, Karnataka. The earliest inscriptional records in Kannada are from the 6th century. Kannada script which is closely similar to Telugu script in origin. Kannada has a number of regional and social dialects and has marked distinctions between formal and informal usage.

Kannada script originated from southern Bramhilipi of Ashoka period. With time, it underwent so many changes in the reign of Sathavahanas, Kadambas, Gangas, Rastrakutas, and Hoysalas. A mixture of Telugu-Kannada scripts has been used in Kadambas of Banavasi and the early Chalukya of Badami inscriptions in the west even before the Seventh Century. In the middle of the seventh century a new variety of the Telugu-Kannada scripts was developed. Only in the 13th century, the modern Kannada and Telugu scripts were developed. Other languages like Konkani, Kodava and Tulu use only Kannada script. The early development of the Kannada language was independent of the Sanskrit influence. However during later centuries, Kannada, like the other Dravidian languages was greatly influenced by Sanskrit in terms of vocabulary, grammar and literary style. As such, Kannada shares a large number of structural features with other Indian language scripts. The writing system of Kannada script includes the principles that governs the phonetics and is a system of syllabic and phonemic writing.

The earliest inscriptional records in Kannada are from the 6th century. We cannot determine the origin of Kannada literature from early (pre 800 AD) pieces of work available now. The oldest extant book is king Nripatunga's literary critique Kavi Raja Marga (around 840AD). Jainism was a popular religion at that time and there were some Jaina poets like Srivijaya and GunaVarman. During the 10th century, a new tradition by mixing prose and verse with the campu (an Indian verse form) style was introduced. The poets Pampa, Ponna and Ranna, known as the "Three Gems of Kannada literature", extensively wrote on episodes from the Ramayana and Mahabharata and Jain legends and biographies. Then Chavunda Raya wrote the history of all the 24 Jainatirthankaras (saintly teachers).

Around the 11th century, Kannada literature experienced a setback due to invasion from Tamil kings and only a few literary works could be seen done in this period. The inscriptions of this period illustrate many variations of meters and structural variety. These inscriptions are a wealth of information for historical data, cultural life and study of Kannada language and literature of early times.

In the second half of the 12th century, Jainism was on decline and puranicVeerashaivism was gaining grounds. In the wake of veerashaiva theosophy, a very distinct phase of writing began to gain importance. A spate of literary works in praise of Lord Shiva from famous writers like Harihara, Raghavanka and KereyaPadmarasa, emerged during the 12th and 13th centuries. The Poetess Akkamahadevi is known for her bhakti poetries. However she has advocated strongly against the religious rituals. In the meantime the Jains, too came out with legendary histories of various tirthankaras (propagators). A comparative study of contemporary religions has been done by Samayaparikshe of Brahmasiva(c. 1150 A.D.) with his emphasis on the superiority of Jainism, the religion he followed. He is a bitter critic of all the other sects and their beliefs. The development of poems, literary criticism, grammar, natural science and translations from Sanskrit literary works is the highlight of the 13th century.

Eminent poets like BhimaKavi, Padmanaka, Mallanarya, Singiraja and Chamarasa lived in the realm of Vijayanagara kings and have made invaluable contribution to the Kannada literature with their bhakti poetries. The Bhakti movement lasted till the 16th century. The Ramayana, Mahabharata and Puranas were translated afresh using the folk meters, satpadi and regale. DasaSahithya, devotional songs of dasas (slaves of the Lord) sung in praise of God, were compiled, which formed an important part of popular literature. The renowned saints Sripadaraya (c. 1500 A.D.), Purandaradasa(c 1540 A.D.) and Kanakadasa form the great trinity of Vaishnava composers from Karnataka. Ramadhanyacharite written by Kanakadasa (1509-1600 A.D.) is the story of a quarrel between two cereals, paddy and ragi to establish their superiority. The verbal duel is fought before Lord Rama. Lord Rama orders for their imprisonment. After some time paddy degenerates while ragi emerges strong and sound, thus proving his superiority. The theme is unique and this concept is different.

The next two centuries witnessed much literary activities. Some of the famous works during this period are:

- Bhattakalanka Deva's Karnataka Shabdaushasana (1604AD) on grammar
- Sakdakshara Deva's the RajshekharaVilasa (1657AD), romantic campu, the historical compositions of the Wodeyar period (1650-1713AD)
- Nijaguna Yogi's VivekaChintamani of Shaiva lore (mid 17th century)
- Nanja Raja's Puranic works the Shiva Bhakti Mahatmya and HariVamsa (around 1760AD)

Dramatization of Puranic tales named Yakshagana in musical form, was a novel tradition of late 18th century and this tradition paved way for a number of celebrated creations of folk poetry.

Till late 19th century there was a lull in Kannada literature. Works based on Sanskrit models, like Shakuntala of BasavappaShastri continued till the late 19th century. The Christian missionaries put in some efforts with which the Academy of Kannada Literature was set up in Bangalore in 1914. Gradually, so many translations were made from English, Bengali and Marathi literature. Apart from the pioneers of novel writing, Kerur and Galaganatha, ShivaramaKaranta, K. V. Puttapa, G P Rajaratnam, BasavarajaKattimani and NanjanaguduTirumalamba (the first major woman writer in modern Kannada) are some more eminent novelists worth mentioning

NanjanaguduTirumalamba is the first major woman writer in modern Kannada. Short story writers such as PanjeMangeshaRao and MastiVenkateshaAyyangar made entry in this period. Kannada poetry soared to a new height with innovative poets like B. M. Shrikanthayya. Institutions like University of Mysore, Kannada SahityaParishad, etc. are doing a commendable job in pushing the Kannada literature further.

Kannada is one of the widely spoken languages in India especially in the state of Karnataka. The Kannada language has a classification of Dravidian, Southern, Tamil-Kannada, and Kannada. Regions Spoken: Kannada is also spoken in Karnataka, Andhra Pradesh, Tamil Nadu, and Maharashtra. Population: The total population of people who speak Kannada is 35,346,000, as of 1997. Alternate Name: Other names for Kannada are Kanarese, Canarese, Banglori, and Madrassi. Dialects: Some dialects of Kannada are Bijapur, JeinuKuruba, and AineKuruba. There are about 20 dialects and Badaga may be one. Kannada is the state language of Karnataka. About 9,000,000 people speak Kannada as a second language. The literacy rate for people who speak Kannada as a first language is about 60%, which is the same for those who speak Kannada as a second language (in India). Kannada was used in the Bible from 1831-2000("International Conference on Computer Science & Engineering, Pune",2013).

Kannada Alphabets

The Kannada script (aksharamale or varnamale) is a phonemic abugida of forty-nine letters, and is written from left to right (see Fig. 3). The character set is almost identical to that of other Brahmic scripts. Consonantal letters imply an inherent vowel. Letters representing consonants are combined to form digraphs(ottaksharas) when there is no intervening vowel. Otherwise, each letter corresponds to a syllable. The letters are classified into three categories: swara (vowels), vyanjana (consonants), and yogavaahaka (part vowel, part consonant). The Kannada words for a letter of the script are *akshara*, *akkara*, and *varna*. Each letter has its own form (*ākāra*) and sound (*shabda*), providing the visible and audible representations, respectively. Kannada is written from left to right("The Karnataka Official Language Act",2007).

Figure 3. Kannada Alphabets

Kannada Vowels (SwaragaLu)					
Kannada	Corresponding Caption	Callout Caption	Kannada	Corresponding Caption	Callout Caption
ಅ	a	Kannada Letter A	ಏ	E	Kannada Letter AE
ಆ	A	Kannada Letter AA	ಐ	Y	Kannada Letter AI
ಇ	i	Kannada Letter E	ಒ	o	Kannada Letter O
ಈ	I	Kannada Letter EE	ಓ	O	Kannada Letter OO
ಉ	u	Kannada Letter U	ಔ	V	Kannada Letter AU
ಊ	U	Kannada Letter UU	ಅಂ	aM	Kannada Letter AM
ಋ	Ru	Kannada Letter Vocalic Ru	ಅಃ	aH	Kannada Letter AH
ಎ	e	Kannada Letter e			
Kannada Consonants (VyanjangaLu)					
Kannada	Corresponding Caption	Callout Caption	Kannada	Corresponding Caption	Callout Caption
ಕ	k	Kannada Letter ka	ಧ	D	Kannada Letter dha
ಖ	K	Kannada Letter kha	ನ	n	Kannada Letter na
ಗ	g	Kannada Letter ga	ಪ	p	Kannada Letter pa
ಘ	G	Kannada Letter gha	ಫ	P	Kannada Letter pha
ಙ	Z	Kannada Letter nga	ಬ	b	Kannada Letter ba
ಚ	c	Kannada Letter cha	ಭ	B	Kannada Letter bha
ಛ	C	Kannada Letter chha	ಮ	m	Kannada Letter ma
ಜ	j	Kannada Letter ja	ಯ	y	Kannada Letter ya
ಝ	J	Kannada Letter jha	ರ	r	Kannada Letter ra
ಞ	z	Kannada Letter nya	ಲ	l	Kannada Letter la
ಟ	q	Kannada Letter tta	ವ	v	Kannada Letter va
ಠ	Q	Kannada Letter ttha	ಶ	S	Kannada Letter sha
ಡ	w	Kannada Letter dda	ಸ	s	Kannada Letter sa
ಢ	W	Kannada Letter ddha	ಷ	x	Kannada Letter ssa
ಣ	N	Kannada Letter nna	ಹ	h	Kannada Letter ha
ತ	t	Kannada Letter ta	ಳ	L	Kannada Letter lla
ಥ	T	Kannada Letter tha			

Kannada Braille

Bharati braille or Bhartiya Braille ("Indian braille"), is a largely unified braille script for writing the languages of India. When India gained independence, eleven braille scripts were in use, in different parts of the country and for different languages. By 1951 a single national standard had been settled on, Bharati braille, which has since been adopted by Sri Lanka,Nepal, and Bangladesh.There are slight differences in the orthographies for Nepali in India and Nepal, and for Tamil in India and Sri Lanka. There are significant differences in Bengali Braille between India and Bangladesh, with several letters differing. Pakistan has not adopted Bharati braille, so the Urdu Braille of Pakistan is an entirely different alphabet than the Urdu Braille of India, with their commonalities largely due to their common inheritance from English or International Braille. Sinhalese Braille largely conforms to other Bharati, but differs significantly toward the end of the alphabet, and is covered in its own article. Bharati braille alphabets use a 6-dot cell with values based largely on English Braille. Letters are assigned as consistently as possible across the various regional scripts of India as they are transliterated in the Latin script, so that, for example, Hindi, Urdu, Bengali, and English are rendered largely the same in braille.

Braille is adopted for most of the languages of the world.Kannada Braille is one of the Bharati braille alphabets, and it largely conforms to the letter values of the other Bharati alphabets. It is easy to adopt for those languages having less than 64 basic characters set as in the case of English language. Kannada, an official language of state of Karnataka in South India, has 49 basic characters. The basic character set is extended by the consonant – vowel combinations. This number crosses 500 and hence Braille cannot be adopted on one to one basis.

Conversion of Braille writing into normal language version manually is time consuming, laborious and requires a Braille literate. To overcome this problem, many researchers have tried to develop a Braille reading machine. Lot of constraints like quality of paper, lighting condition etc. are involved in conversion. We also observed that languages like Kannada add more constraints because of the combinational characters. In our previous work we have developed an algorithm which automatically converts the basic characters (not including combinational characters) of Kannada Braille into the normal version of it. This paper presents an algorithm to recognize the Braille character as to, whether it is a consonant, vowel or consonant- vowel combination and then convert it into its equivalent normal Kannada (Anoore & Murray, 2001).

For Example

1. If a dot 1 describes a cell with one dots raised, those dots being at the top and at the left column as in figure 4 then it denotes the letter "ಅ" in Kannada.

Figure 4. "ಅ" Kannada alphabet in Braille

Figure 5. "ಕ" Kannada alphabet in Braille

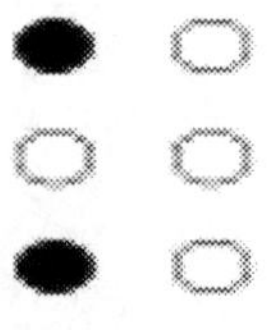

2. If a combination of dots 1-2 describes a cell with two dots raised, and first dot is at the top and at the left column and second raised dot is third row and left column as in figure 5 then it denotes the letter "ಕ" in Kannada.

GRADES OF BRAILLE

- **Grade 1:** Grade 1 is called the starting version of Braille. This is called letter by letter translation of Braille as shown in figure 6(Xuan, Cesar, & Fain, 2006; Kenneth, 2010). This is the Braille which is read by starting people. Like normal students learn a, b, c in nursery. For e.g. If we want to write "ಗದಗ" in grade 1 then it can be represented as shown in figure 4.
- **Grade 2:** Grade 2 is next version of grade 1, this is for those people who know about the letters or little bit about the Braille .This is the translation of combination words like "CH", "SH" as in figure 7. The contractions are used to save space because a Braille page cannot fit as much text as a standard printed page. Books, signs in public places, menus, and most other Braille materials are written in Grade 2 Braille (Xuan, Cesar, & Fain, 2006; Kenneth, 2010).
- **Grade 3:**Grade 3 is next version of grade 2. It is for those people who knows Braille very well and have good command in Braille. In this grade visually impaired use short cuts means which is used mainly in personal letters, diaries, and notes, and also in literature to some extent. It is a kind of shorthand, with entire words shortened to a few letters.

PROPOSED ARCHITECTURE OF KANNADA TO BRAILLE CONVERSION

Architecture is the conceptual design and fundamental operational structure of a system or model. It is the technical drawings and functional description of all design requirements,it is how to design and implement various parts of a computer.This is the Kannada to Braille conversion system in figure 8, which converts Kannada Script to Braille code through computer because today is the trend of computer.[5,6] Every work has done through the computer. This proposed system is very helpful for theteachers who teaches the visually impaired.

Figure 6. Grade 1 representation

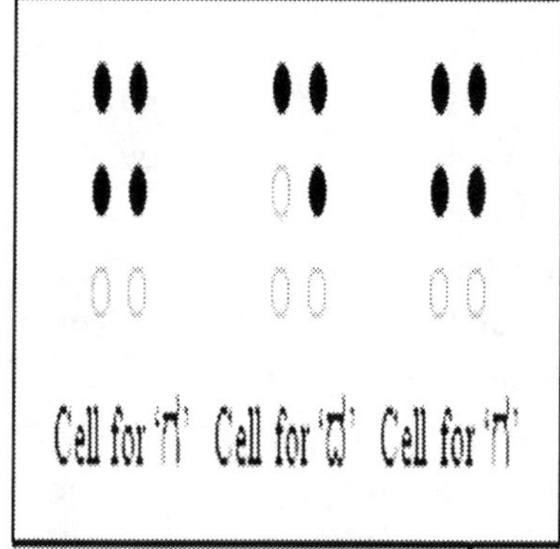

Figure 7. Grade 2 representation

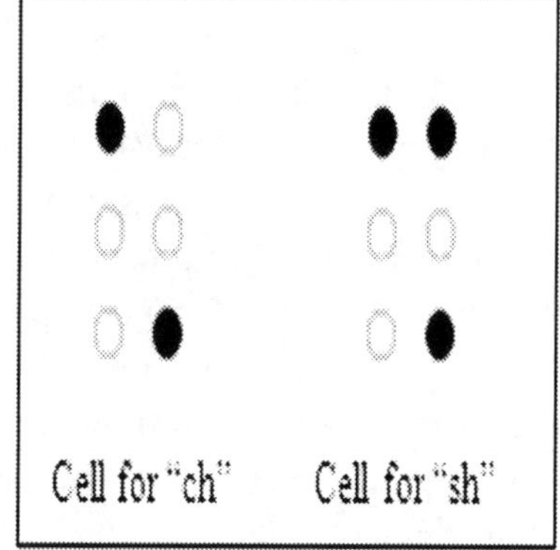

Figure 8. Kannada to Braille conversion system

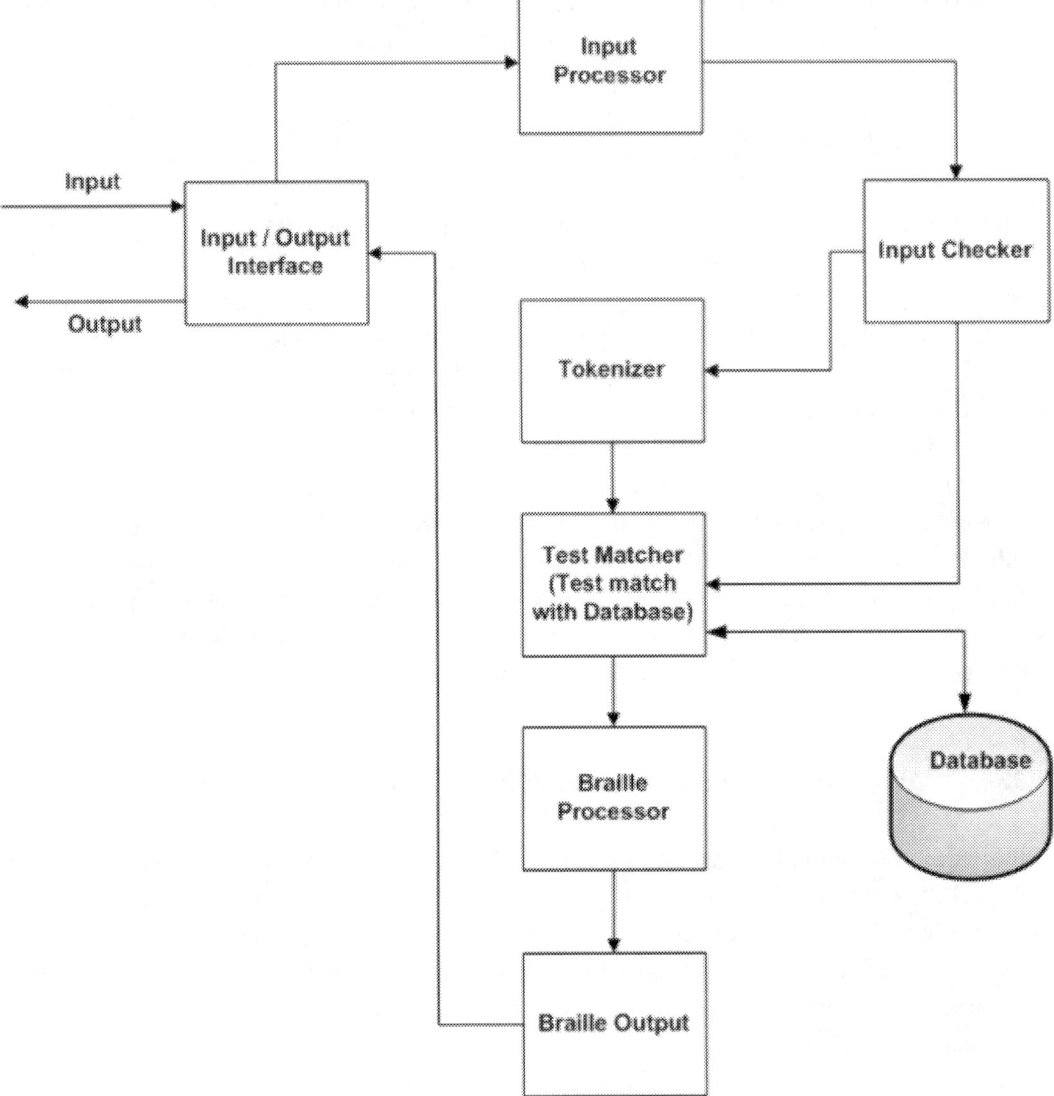

1. **Input Interface(II):**Input is the communication between an information processing system and the outside world, possibly a human or another information processing system. Inputs are the signals or data received by the system. Interface is a shared boundary across which two separate components of a computer system exchange information. The exchange can be between software, computer hardware, peripheral devices, humans and combinations of these.It refers to the communication between an information processing system (such as a computer), and the outside world, possibly a human, or another information processing system. Inputs are the signals or data received by the system, whenever you enter data into your computer, it is referred to as input as in Figure 9. This can be text typed in a word processing document, keywords entered in a search engine's search box, or data entered into a spreadsheet. Input can be something as simple as moving the mouse or clicking the mouse button or it can be as complex as scanning a document or downloading photos from a digital camera.

Figure 9. Input through user

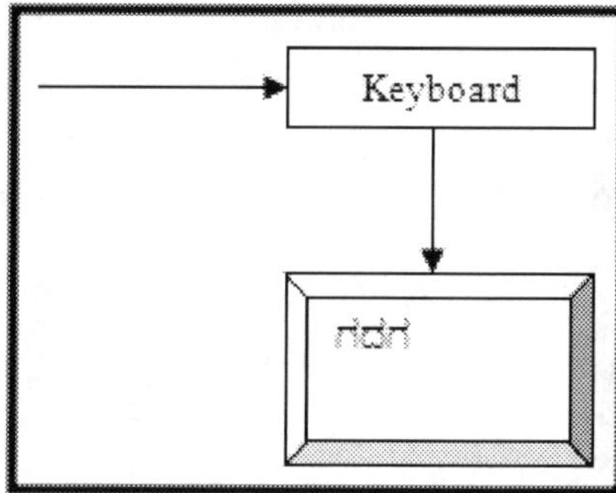

2. **Input Processor(IP):**A processor is the logic circuitry that responds to and processes the basic instructions that drive a computer.Input processor is a hardware device or software processor whose sole function is to handle input.
3. **Input Checker(IC):** Input processors give their problem to input checker. The main purpose of input checker is to find whether the input is string or character. If the input is a character it directly gives to the text matcher. If input is string, it gives their output to Tokenizer as shown in figure 10.
4. **Tokenzier(T):** The main purpose of tokenizer is to break the string and convert it into characters. The process of forming tokens from an input stream of characters is called tokenization.
5. **Text Matcher(TM):** Text matcher matches the input with the database. Whether the input character is present in the database or not.
6. **Database(D):** The term "database" may be narrowed to specify particular aspects of organized collection of data and may refer to the logical database, to physical database as data content in computer data storage or to many other database sub-definitions. A collection of information organized in such a way that a computer program can quickly select desired pieces of data. Text matcher matches the input data in the database. If the database contains that input. Then it gives the output to Braille processor, otherwise shows item is not in the database. Because the database stores all Kannada alphabets and corresponding mapping of Braille alphabets.
7. **Braille Processor(BP):** Braille Processor converts the inputted Kannada character into the Braille code or Braille cell which is used by visually impaired people.

Figure 10. Input Checking

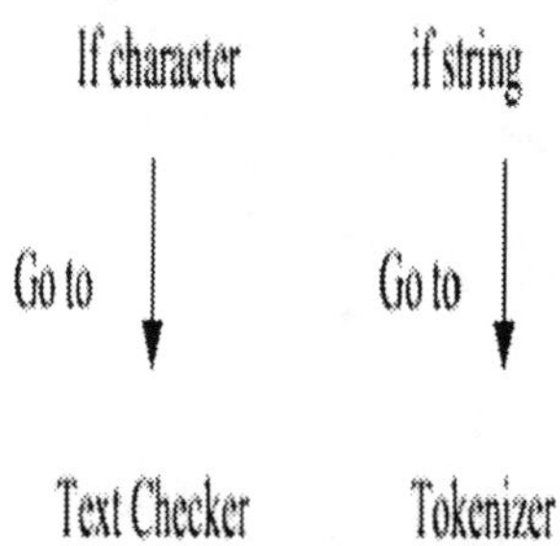

Figure 11. Proposed output

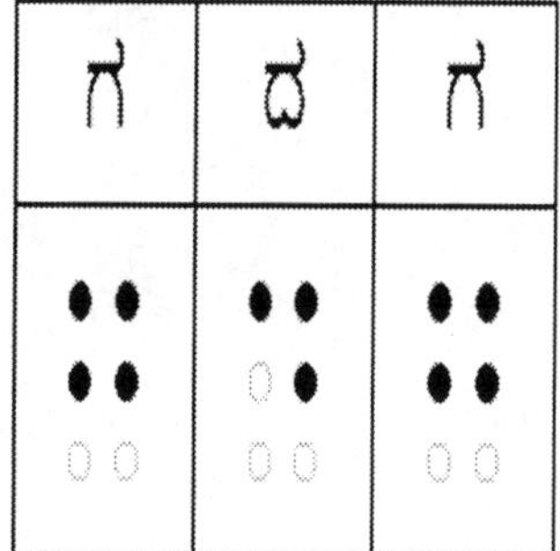

8. **Braille Output(BO):**Braille Processor gives their final output to Braille output Part. Braille output checks whether the output is according to the input or not, and then it finalizes output to output interface so that user can see it through output device.
9. **Output Interface(OI):** Output is the result produced by computer based on input provided by user. The expected output of the proposed system is as shown in figure 11.

EXPERIMENTAL RESULTS

In figure 12, the input value is "ಅ", after clicking the translate button, the corresponding Braille code is displayed in the output box.

In figure 13, the input value is "ನಡನ", after clicking the translate button, the corresponding Braille code is displayed in the output box. Here initially 3 character word are broken up into characters, then total number of input characters is found out with the software tool. The input characters are moved to Braille conversion software engine from the first letter to NULL value. The software will check all 64 combinations of Braille matching value for all the input character values. If a character match occurs, and then it will send the matched input value to the database and produces the corresponding Braille code as output. If no match occurs then the appropriate error message is generated in error box window.

Figure 12. Eperimental result 1

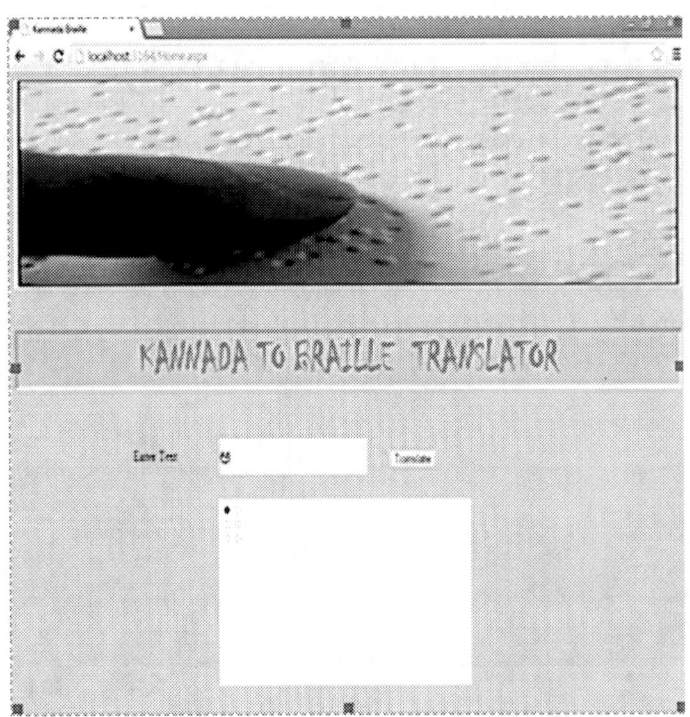

Figure 13. Eperimental result 2

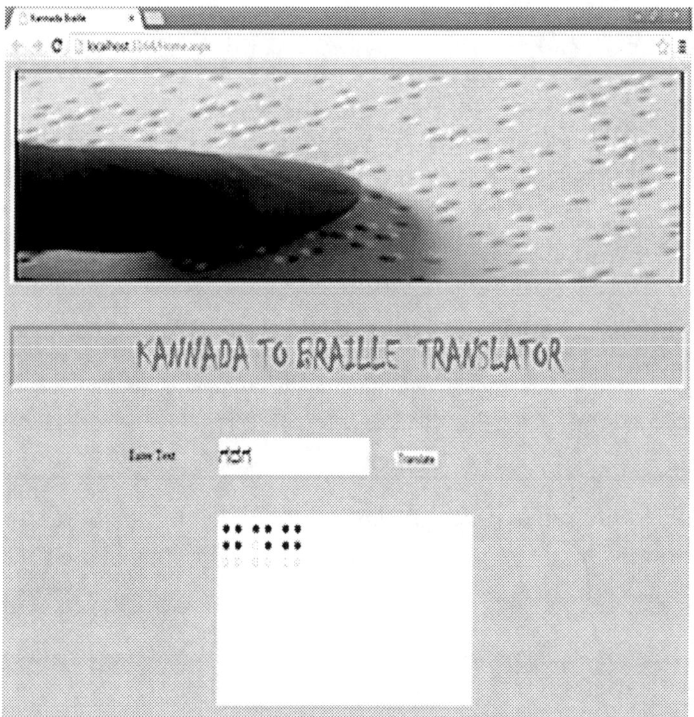

CONCLUSION

The development of low cost Kannada text to Braille is necessary for Braille teaching people and help to visually impaired community in Karnataka. It will show the new way of conversion method for people working in computer environment. The software algorithm which is coded reads the sentence from the Input box of the Braille software tool and breaks them into characters and are counted up to the value of the enter key. The Braille code equivalent of each character is generated in the output box of the tool. The same technique can be used in various languages like Bengali, Hindi, Tamil, etc., The Braille code conversion process is a single step and the data transfer rate is normal and it is controllable. It is one of the best tool for visually impaired people and Braille learning people using computer technology.

ACKNOWLEDGMENT

Every successful work is the result of cooperation and support of many people. This paper is no exception. We would like to thank each and every one who helped and encouraged us directly or indirectly on our successful work.

We express our deep fathomable feeling or gratitude to Dr.Mallamma. V. Reddy, Assistant Professor, Department of Computer Science, Rani Chennamma University, Karnataka, for her valuable suggestions, guidance and critical comments during discussion of this work.

We owe our parents above all for the successful completion of this paper. Thanks for their encouragement, patience and perpetual support.

REFERENCES

Abualkishik & Omar. (2008). *Quranic Braille System*. World Academy of Science, Engineering and Technology.

Anoore & Murray. (2001). An electronic design of a low cost Braille typewriter. In *Proceedings of Seventh Australian and new Zealand intelligent information system conference*. Perth, Australia.

Basu, B., & Lachikawa, A. (2004). Dialogue Languages and Persons with Disabilities. *IEICE Transactions, 8*(6), 31-43.

Baulblenkhorn. (1997). A system for conveting print into Braille. *IEEE Transactions on Rehabilitation Engineering, 5*(2), 23-30.

Blenkhorn. (n.d.). A system for converting Braille into print. *IEEE Transactions on Rehabilitation Engineering, 3*(2), 215-221.

Fritz, F. P., & Barner, P. (1999, August). Design of a Hepatic Visualization System for People with Visual Impairments. *IEEE Transactions on Rehabilitation Engineering*, *7*(3), 372–384. doi:10.1109/86.788473 PMID:10498382

Gill. (1992). *Priorities for technical research and development for visually disabled persons*. World Blind Union Res Committee.

Ingham. (2010). Braille, the language, its machine translation and display. *IEEE Transactions on Man-Machine Systems, 10*(4).

King. (2001). *Text and Braille Computer Translation*. Department of Computation.

Lee, C. (2010). Tactile Display as Braille Display for the Visually Disabled. In *Proceedings of IEEE/RSJ International Conference on Intelligent Robotics and Systems*.

Singh & Bhatia. (2010). Automated Conversion of English and Hindi Text to Braille. *International Journal of Computers and Applications*, *4*(6).

Slaby. (2010). Computerized Braille translation. *Microcomputer Applications*, *1*(13), 107-113.

Sleng & Lau, Y. (1999). Regular feature extraction for recognition of Braille. In *Proceedings of Third International Conference on Computational Intelligence and Multimedia Applications*.

Srinath, S., & RaviKumar, C. N. (2013). A Novel Method for Recognizing Kannada Braille: Consonant-Vowels. *International Journal of Emerging Technology and Advanced Engineering, 3*(1).

Zhang, X., Ortega-Sanchez, & Murray. (2006). *Text-to-braille translator in a chip*. Paper presented at the 4th International Conference on Electrical and Computer Engineering ICECE, Dhaka, Bangladesh.

KEY TERMS AND DEFINITIONS

Architecture of Kannada to Braille Conversion System: Converts Kannada Script to Kannada Braille cells.

Braille Cell: Braille cell is made up of six dots that fit under the fingertips, arranged in two columns of three dots each.

Braille System: Braille is the primary means of accessing information for the visually impaired people.

Charles Barbier: Charles Barbier developed the system called night writing, to enable soldiers to communicate silently and without the need for a light.

Grades in Braille: The different stages of learning the Braille system are called as grades in Braille.

Kannada Alphabets: The Kannada script (aksharamale or varnamale) consists forty-nine letters.

Kannada: Kannada is the state language of Karnataka.

Karnataka: Karnataka is the Southern state of India.

Louis Braille: The Braille script was created in 1821 by the Frenchman Louis Braille.

Tokenization: The process of forming tokens from an input stream of characters is called tokenization.

Chapter 8
Baseline Drift Removal of ECG Signal:
Comparative Analysis of Filtering Techniques

Akash Kumar Bhoi
Sikkim Manipal Institute of Technology (SMIT), India

Karma Sonam Sherpa
Sikkim Manipal Institute of Technology (SMIT), India

Bidita Khandelwal
Central Referral Hospital and SMIMS, India

ABSTRACT

The filtering techniques are primarily used for preprocessing of the signal and have been implemented in a wide variety of systems for Electrocardiogram (ECG) analysis. It should be remembered that filtering of the ECG is contextual and should be performed only when the desired information remains undistorted. Removal of baseline drift is required in order to minimize changes in beat morphology that do not have cardiac origin, which is especially important when subtle changes in the ''low-frequency'' ST segment are analyzed for the diagnosis of ischemia. Here, for baseline drift removal different filters such as Median, Low Pass Butter Worth, Finite Impulse Response (FIR), Weighted Moving Average and Stationary Wavelet Transform (SWT) are implemented. The fundamental properties of signal before and after baseline drift removal are statistically analyzed.

INTRODUCTION

ECG measures electrical potentials on the body surface *via* contact electrodes. Conditions such as movement of the patient, breathing, and interaction between the electrodes and skin cause baseline wandering of the ECG signal. Baseline drift may sometimes be caused by variations in temperature and bias in the instrumentation and amplifiers as well. Baseline wandering noise can mask some important features of the ECG signal; hence it is desirable to remove this noise for proper analysis of the ECG signal. The

DOI: 10.4018/978-1-4666-8737-0.ch008

frequency range of the ECG signal is 0 - 150 Hz and the frequency range of the baseline noise based on respiration frequency is 0 - 0.3 Hz and it is altering with the movement of the patient. The American Heart Association states that the filter's cut-off frequency should be in the order of 0.67 Hz, since it is generally thought that the slowest heart rate is 40 bpm, implying the lowest frequency to be 0.67 Hz. But when the heart rate increases, this frequency also changes. Thus, an adaptive cut-off frequency selection is required. Lisette et al. (2004) has designed a heart rate adaptive real-time bidirectional baseline drift suppression filter for multiple lead ECG. The filter is optimized for minimal delay, minimal non-linear phase shift, minimal calculation power and maximal signal-to-noise ratio and minimal ECG signal. Lisheng et al. (2002); Rangayyan (2002) discusses in their research that clinicians measure slopes and time intervals in ST, RR and QT segments to predict any abnormalities in the cardiac activity. Therefore, the slope of the baseline should be zero for clean ECG data. When there is baseline wandering noise in the ECG signal, the slope deviates from zero, and this causes difficulties in the evaluation of ECG recordings. For example, baseline drift makes analysis of isoelectric part of the ST segment difficult especially when there is an ST segment elevation or depression, where the slope of the interval is significant. If there is baseline wandering noise, it would be hard to differentiate noise related slope from the slope of the ST segment. Also, a large baseline drift may cause the positive or negative parts in the ECG to be clipped or badly detected by the analog to digital converter (ADC) or the other hardware. Jane, R. & Laguna, P. (1992) describes the most basic techniques for removing baseline wandering noise, which is known as the cubic spline method. This method is used as a reference method in many studies and performances of other filters are compared with cubic spline. In this method, first the QRS complexes are detected. Then the baseline wander is estimated with a third order polynomial using various points on the ECG such as Q, R and S points or isoelectric baseline locations as the knots of the splines. Finally, the estimated noise is subtracted from the ECG signal. Cubic spline method has a number of disadvantages; for example, in the presence of high amplitude noise, QRS detector may not operate correctly. Also, baseline wander with sharp transitions may not be accurately described by a cubic polynomial so the order of filter should be increased.

Pottala, E. W. & Gradwohl, J. R. (1992) have employed a good method of correcting baseline distortion implementing high pass filtering technique. One such filtering technique is to employ Finite Impulse Response (FIR) filters where the output of the FIR filter is combined with a group delay. As the filter order increases, the complexity of the filter increases. However, if the filter order is selected to be low, then the noise suppression performance of the filter will decrease. Infinite Impulse Response (IIR) filters, on the other hand, can achieve a sharp transition region with a small number of coefficients. However, an IIR filter that has a cut-off frequency high enough to remove baseline wander has a non-linear phase response which distorts meaningful components of the ECG waveform. To avoid this distortion, bidirectional filters are used that filter the signal in a forward direction over a selected window and then the same window is filtered in a reverse direction. Pottala, E. W. (1989) has designed a filter having a non-linear phase response using bilinearly transform to filter baseline from an ECG waveform. In this approach, the data are filtered both forward and backward in time, thereby, removing nonlinearities injected by the IIR filter. A short window was selected so that the filter could be used for real time purposes. Avionics, D.M. (1993); Patricia, A., & Tim. L. (1992) describes bidirectional IIR filters and methods for removing baseline from ECG signal for online and offline cases and these filters are licensed by US Patents.

Laguna, P. & Jane, R. (1992) have implemented an adaptive filter that consists of two adaptive stages. One stage is the 0 Hz adaptive filter. Second stage is an adaptive impulse correlated Least Mean Square

(LMS) filter cascaded with a QRS detector. This method is used for online filtering but high mathematical complexity of this filter causes problems in implementation. Rossi, R. (1992) has implemented a fast FIR filter for online filtering. He performed binomial filters like (1, 2, 1) and (1, 2, 4, 1) using moving averages. He tested the results and observed that the filters were fast but suppression performance of the filter was not adequate. Pandit, S. (1997) has discussed a time frequency analysis such as Short Time Fourier Transform (STFT) but he showed that it is not adequate when the online filtering window is shorter than four seconds. To have a good frequency resolution, the window time should be wider. Frau, D. & Novak, D. (2000) have also implemented an offline baseline removal method using wavelet approximations. This approximation is based on the signal decomposition in two parts; high frequency components, and the low frequency components. They reported that the results were quite accurate with much less effort than the frequency selective filters.

Shusterman, V. (2000) performed a wavelet based cascade adaptive filter to remove the baseline wander. This cascade adaptive filter worked in two stages. The first stage was a discrete Meyer wavelet filter and the second stage was the cubic spline estimation. But the wavelet filter's edge influence needed to be improved. While removing line interference, Mitov, I.P. (2004) has used the sampling rate integer multiple of the nominal power line frequency, his method is suitable for off line use than that of the real time because of the computational complexity. The efficiency of notch filters and a subtraction procedure for power-line interference cancellation in electrocardiogram (ECG) signals is assessed by the Dotsinsky, I. & Stoyanov, T. (2005). Kumaravel, N. et.al (1995) demonstrated a novel method of integrating rule-based system approach with linear FIR filter and also with wave digital filter has investigated. Different digital filter structures are available to eliminate these diverse forms of noise sources, described in Friesen,M. & Gary (1990). Mahesh, S. et al (2008) have design FIR filters using rectangular window for noise reduction in ECG signal. Chouhan,V.S. &Mehta,S.S. (2007) have developed an algorithm for total removal of baseline drift from ECG signal & deploy least square error correction & median based correction. Zahoor-uddin (1995) has presented Baseline Wandering Removal from Human Electrocardiogram Signal using Projection Pursuit Gradient Ascent Algorithm & shows the comparative study of the results of different algorithms like Kalman filter, cubic spline and moving average algorithms. Chavan, M.S. et al. (2008) have also presented the Comparative Study of Chebyshev I and Chebyshev II Filter for noise reduction in ECG Signal. As baseline noises occur due to low frequencies normally 0.05 to 0.5Hz described by Singh, G.K. et al. (2009), so high pass filtering technique can be a good method to eliminate baseline noises.

Hamilton, P.S. (1996) in his article compared adaptive and non adaptive filters for reduction of power line interference in the ECG. Ider, Y.Z. et al. (1995) have developed a method for line interference reduction to be used in signal averaged electrocardiography. Cramer, E. et al. (1987) have introduced a global filtering approach. In this method two types of the digital filters are used. One is using least square method and other is using special summation method. Different scientists i.e. McManus, C.D. et al. (1993);Sun, Y. et al. (2002); Levkov, C. et al.(2005);Wu, Y. & Yang, Y. (1999);Ferdjallah, M. & Barr, R.E. (1990); Kulkarni, P.K. et al. (1997); Ahlstrom, M.L. & Tomkins, W.J. (1885); Lynn,P.A. (1977); Challis, R.E. & Kitney R.I. (1983); Robertson, D.G. & Dowling, J.J. (2003) have tried for removing the power line interference and base line wonder specifically from the ECG signal. Zschorlich, V.R. (1989); Furno,G.S. & Tompkins,W.J. (1983) have also designed digital filters to cope with EMG signals. Webster, J. G., & Clark, J. W. (1978) have explained the instrumentation requirements for the ECG. McManus, C.D. et al. (1985) have developed estimation procedures for baseline drift using cubic spline, polynomial, and rational functions. In a test set of 50 electrocardiograms (ECGs), each of 2.5-sec duration, baseline stability was significantly improved by application of any of these methods, except rational function approximation. Amplitude histograms of clinical ECGs after subtraction of estimated baseline distortions showed only small baseline variations over the recording period. For a quantitative validation of the estimation procedures, 10 ECGs with artificial baseline drift were constructed and analyzed by correlation and mean square error calculations. Van Alste, J. A., Schilder, T. S. (1985) have proposed the linear phase filtering for the removal of baseline wander and power-line frequency components in electrocardiograms. Making use of the property that the spectrum period was 50 Hz, the spectrum can be realized with a considerably reduced number of impulse response coefficients. A suitable impulse response is designed with a pass band ripple of less than 0.5 dB and high stop-band attenuation. The applicability was demonstrated by applying the filtering to exercise electrocardiograms. Gradwohl, J.R. et al. (1988) have performed a study to compare the cubic spline methodwith a multi-pole, null-phased digital filter in their ability to correct for baseline wander on 69 ECG segments with both normal and abnormal rhythms. A signal-pole 0.05Hz filter as recommended by the 1975 AHA report was also included in their study for comparison. A null-phase, 6-pole filters with a cut-off between 0.75 and 1.0 Hz can attenuate low frequency noise (*i.e.*, correct baseline) as well as the cubic spline. The cubic spline was very dependent upon an accurate determination of QRS on set. The single-pole, 0.05 Hz filter does very little to attenuate low frequency noise. Sornmo, L. (1993) has applied the time-varying filtering techniques to the problem of baseline correction by letting the cut-off frequency of a linear filter be controlled by the low-frequency properties of the ECG signal. Sampling rate decimation and interpolation are employed because the design of a filter forbaseline reduction can be treated as a narrow band filtering problem. All filters have a linear phase response to reduce, for example, ST segment distortion. The performance of the technique presented was studied on ECG signals with different types of simulated baseline wander. The results were compared with the performance of time-invariant linear filtering and cubic spline interpolation. A method of removing low frequency interference froman ECG signal was presented by Allen, J. et al. (1994) have a simple alternative to some of the more computationally intensive techniques. The performance of the method was evaluated by examining changes in body surface iso-potential map feature locations, due to baseline wander. The results show that although baseline wander can seriously interfere with iso-potential map features, integrity can be restored by relatively simple methods. Choy T.T. & Leung P.M. (1988) have used 50 Hz notch filters for the real time application on the ECG signal it is found that filter was capable of filtering noise by 40 dB with bandwidth of 4 Hz and causes the attenuation in the QRS complex. The method used by Zhi-Dong, Z. & Yu-Quan, C. (2006) to remove baseline wander and power line interference in ECG signal was based on Empirical Mode Decomposition and notch filter. Principles and characteristics of Empirical Mode Decomposition are presented; ECG signal was decomposed into a series of Intrinsic Mode Functions (IMFs). Then 50Hz notch filter was designed, by which the IMF of ECG signal containing 50 Hz power line inference was filtered. The "clean" ECG signal was reconstructed by properly selecting IMFs. To evaluate the performance of the filter, Clinic ECG signals were used. Barati, Z. & Ayatollahi, A. (2006) show the ability of Independent Component Analysis (ICA) technique in removing baseline wandering from ECG by utilizing Single-Channel data. For applying ICA to single channel data, multi-channel signals were constructed by adding some delay to original data. For validation the effectiveness of the method, they applied ICA to constructed channels derived from each Frank lead in HRECG (High-Resolution Electrocardiogram) data as a pre-processing step in order to detect Ventricular Late Potentials (VLPs) by *Simson's* method. Results derived by this approach were compared with those obtained from traditional high-pass filtering for removing baseline wandering. The removal of baseline wander (BW) was a very important step in the preprocessing stage of electrocardiogram (ECG). In Pan, N. et al. (2007), proposed a method called Empirical Mode Decomposition (EMD), was used for accurate removal of the baseline wander (BW) in ECG. They briefly described the principles and characteristics of the EMD. To validate the proposed method, the recording from MIT/BIH database was used. They also applied the traditional median filter to remove BW in ECG for comparison with their EMD method. Markovsky, I.A. et al. (2008) have used band-pass, kalman and adaptive filters for removal of resuscitation artifacts from human ECG signals. A database of separately recorded human ECG wasused for evaluation of this method. The considered performance criterion is the signal-to-noise ratio (SNR) improvement, defined as the ratio of the SNRs of the filtered signal and the given ECG signal. The empirical results show that for low SNR of the given signal, a band-pass filter yields the good performance, while for high SNR; an adaptive filter yields the good performance. Hargittai, S. (2008) has presented multi rate architecture with linear phase low-pass filter working at low sampling rate for removal of the baseline wanders. Design trade-off between transition band width and filter delay was considered. The optimal decimation factor with respect to complexity and filter delay was determined. The traditional method which was based on moving average filter can remove the baseline wander in electrocardiogram signals, but also causes the loss of motive ECG signals, which makes distortions of filtered ECG signals. Min Dai & Shi-Liu Liana (2009) have proposed a modified moving average filter to selectively capture the low-frequency baseline wander noise and removeit from the detected signals in order to recover true ECG. The interval sampling data was taken into consideration when calculate the moving average in order to reduce the loss of useful ECG signals and distortions. The algorithm was developed for computer implementation using MATLAB. To validate the proposed methods, the recordings from MIT/BIH database were used. One of the drawbacks of this filter approach is that it does not accommodate for quick baseline changes [52].

Every type of filter has its strong point & weaknesses. In this paper, the main focus is to remove baseline noises by comparing five different filter's performances. Baseline noise elimination is often one of the first steps required in the processing of the electrocardiogram (ECG). Baseline noises make manual and automatic analysis of ECG records difficult, especially in the detection of ST-segment deviations. This segment is very important and has the information related to heart attack, described in, Zahoor-uddin (1995). It is necessary that the filter allow removing the baseline noises while preserving the useful clinical information.

FILTERS IMPLEMENTATION

The performances of five different filters (*i.e.* Median, Low-Pass Butter Worth, FIR, Weighted Moving Average and Stationary Wavelet Transform (SWT)) for removal of baseline drift is analyzed. Filtering operationsare performed for the selected initial waveform (*i.e.* 4 sec data) of the full length noisy ECG signal (Fig. 1) for better visualization of baseline drift removed results (Fig. 2-6).

Median Filter

The median filter is a non-linear digital filtering technique, often used to remove noise. Such noise reduction is a typical pre-processing step to improve the results of later processing.The main idea of the median filter is to run through the signal entry by entry, replacing each entry with the median of

Figure 1. Input ECG signal having baseline drift

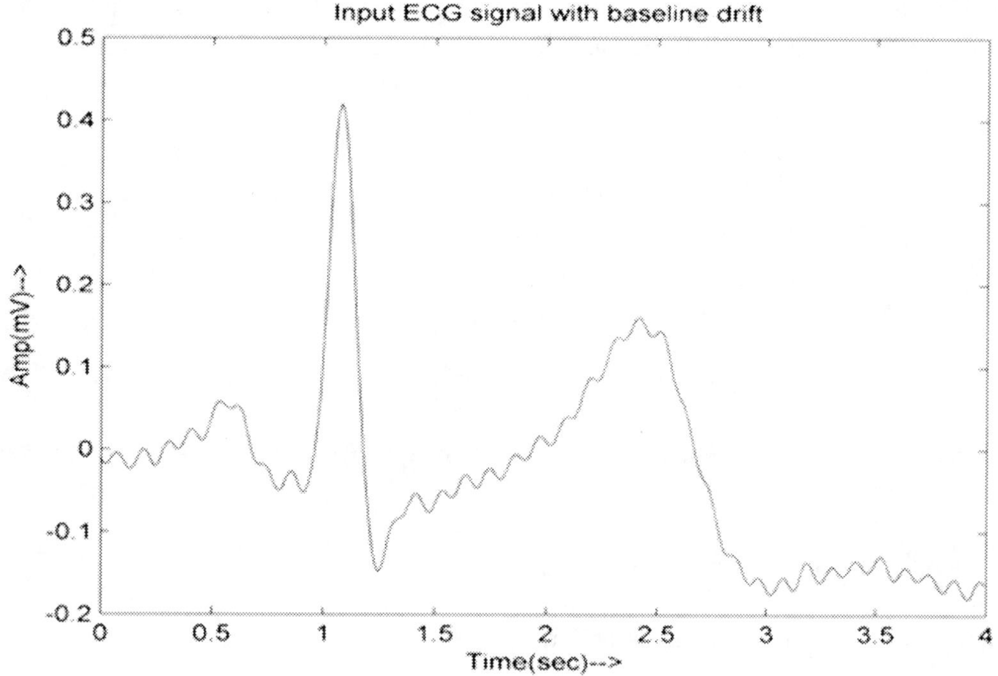

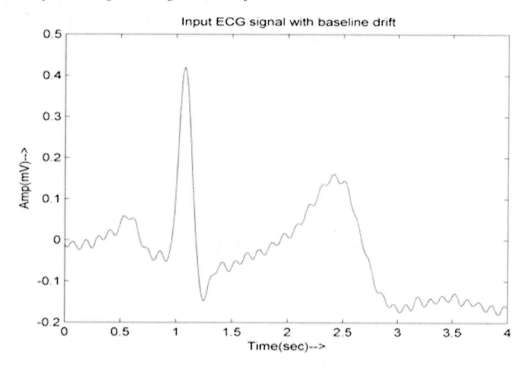

Figure 2. Baseline drift removed by Median filter

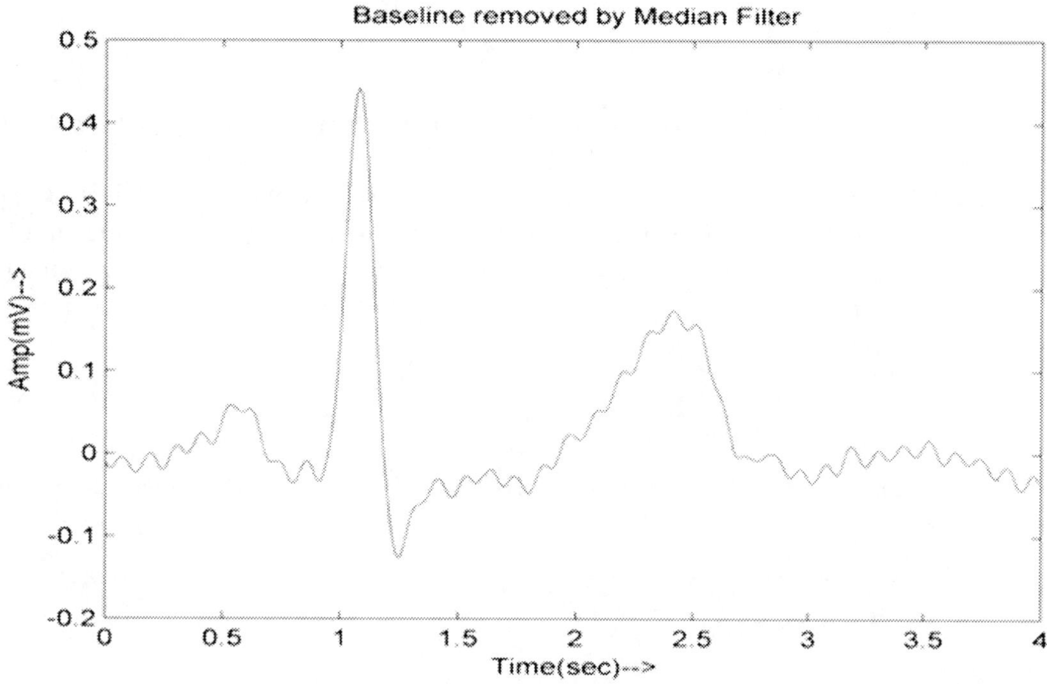

neighboring entries. The pattern of neighbors is called the "window", which slides, entry by entry, over the entire signal. The function considers the signal to be 0 beyond the endpoints. The output has the same length as *x*.For odd n, *y(k)* is the median of

$$x\left(k-(n-1)/2:k+(n-1)/2\right).$$

For even n, *y(k)* is the median of

$$x\left(k-n/2\right),x\left(k-\left(n/2\right)+1\right),\\ \dots,x\left(k+\left(n/2\right)-1\right).$$

In this case, medfilt1 sorts the numbers, then takes the average of the n/2 and *(n/2)+1* elements with window=150.

Butter Worth Filter

The generalized equation representing an "n^{th}" order Butterworth filter, the frequency response is given as:

$$H\left(jw\right)=\frac{1}{\sqrt{1+\varepsilon^{2}\left(\frac{w}{w_{p}}\right)^{2n}}} \tag{1}$$

where, *n* represents the filter order = 1, Omega 'ω' is equal to $2\pi f$, Epsilon 'ε' is the maximum pass-band gain, (Amax).

If Amax is defined at a frequency equal to the cut-off -3dB corner point (fc), ε will then be equal to one and therefore ε2 will also be one. However, if you now wish to define Amax at a different voltage gain value, for example 1dB, or 1.1220 (1dB = 20logAmax) then the new value of epsilon, ε is found by:

$$H_{1}=\frac{H_{0}}{\sqrt{1+\varepsilon^{2}}} \tag{2}$$

where, H0 = the Maximum Pass-band Gain, Amax, H1 = the Minimum Pass-band Gain, Transpose the equation to give:

$$\frac{H_0}{H_1} = 1.1220 = \sqrt{\left(1+\varepsilon^2\right)} \tag{3}$$

gives $\varepsilon = 0.5088$

The Frequency Response of a filter can be defined mathematically by its Transfer Function with the standard Voltage Transfer Function $H(j\omega)$ written as:

$$H\left(jw\right) = \left[\frac{V_{out}\left(jw\right)}{V_{in}\left(jw\right)}\right] \tag{4}$$

where, V_{out} = the output signal voltage, V_{in} = the input signal voltage, ω = the radian frequency ($2\pi f$)

Note: ($j\omega$) can also be written as (s) to denote the s-domain and the resultant transfer function for a second-order low-pass filter is given as:

$$H\left(s\right) = \frac{V_{out}}{V_{in}} = \frac{1}{s^2 + s + 1} \tag{5}$$

Figure 3. Baseline drift removed by Low-pass Butterworth filter

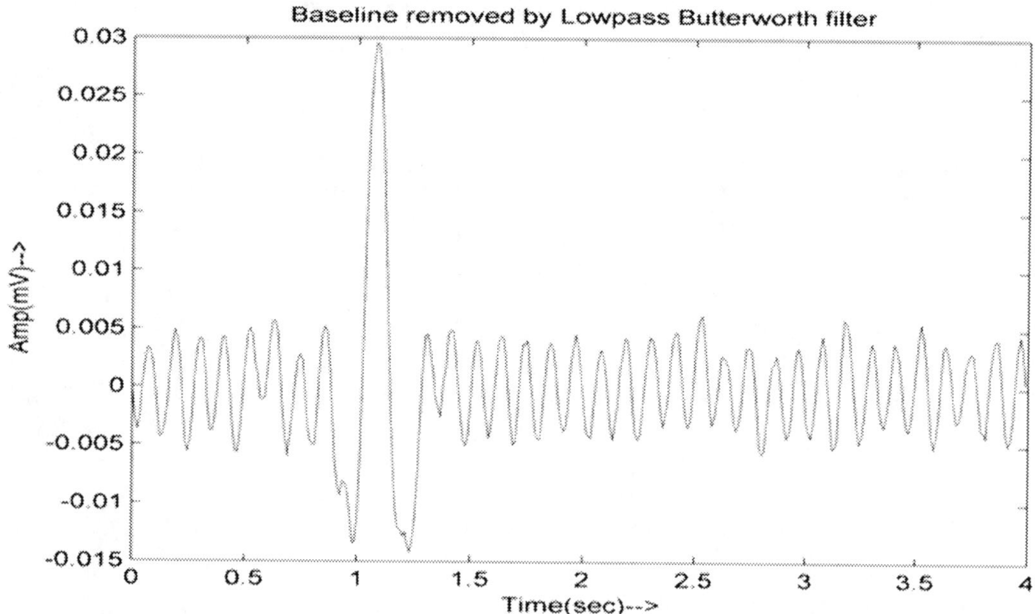

Finite Impulse Response(FIR) Filter

fir1 implements the classical method of windowed linear-phase FIR digital filter design. It designs filters in standard low pass, band pass, high pass, and band pass configurations. Here the output of filtered signal contains the n + 1 coefficients of an order *n* low pass FIR filter. This is a Hamming-windowed, linear-phase filter with cut-off frequency *Wn*. The output filter coefficients, b, are ordered in descending powers of z.

$$b(z) = b(1) + b(2)z^{-1} + \ldots. + b(n+1)z^{-n} \quad (6)$$

Wn, the cut-off frequency, is a number between 0 and 1, where 1 corresponds to half the sampling frequency (the Nyquist frequency).

If *Wn* is a two-element vector, *Wn = [w1 w2]*, fir1 returns a band pass filter with pass band w1 << w2.

fir1 uses the window method of FIR filter design. If w(n) denotes a window and the impulse response of the ideal filter is h(n), where h(n) is the invse Fourier transform of the ideal frequency response, then the windowed digital filter coefficients are given by $b(n) = w(n)h(n), 1 \le n \le N$. The window size applied for baseline drift removal is 150.

Figure 4. Baseline drift removed by FIR-1 filter

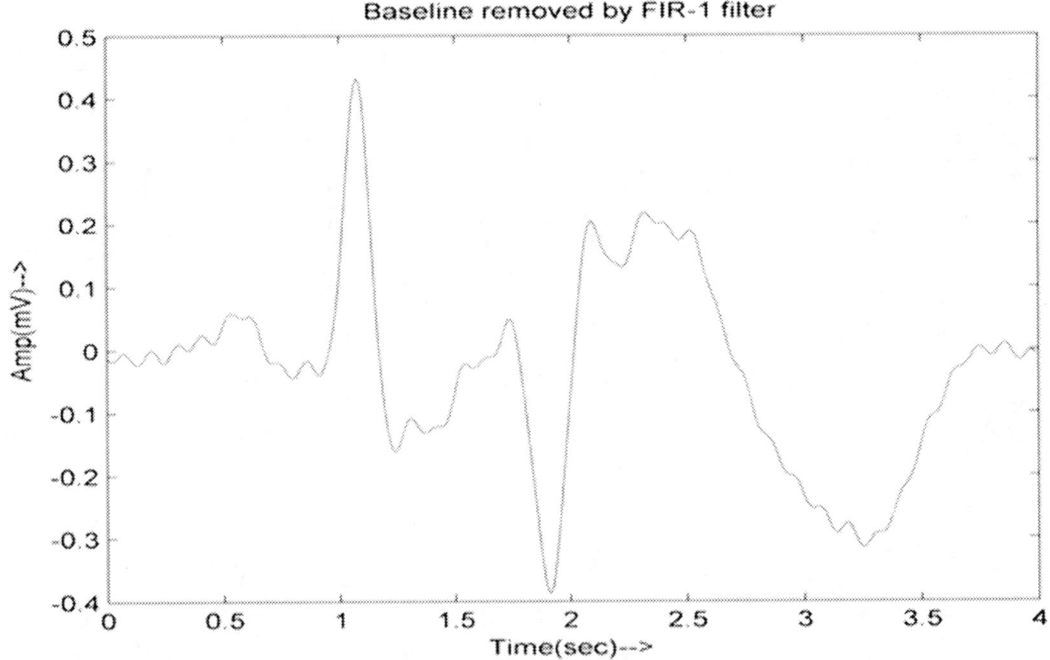

Weighted Moving Average

A weighted average is any average that has multiplying factors to give different weights to data at different positions in the sample window. Mathematically, the moving average is the convolution of the datum points with a fixed weighting function.

$$WMA_M = \frac{n_{p_M} + (n-1)_{p_{M-1}} + \ldots + 2p_{(M-n+2)} + p_{(M-n+1)}}{\mathrm{n} + (\mathrm{n}-1) + \ldots + 2 + 1} \tag{7}$$

e denominator is a triangle number equal to $\frac{n(n+1)}{2}$. In the more general case the denominator will always be the sum of the individual weights.

When calculating the WMA across successive values, the difference between the numerators of WMA_{M+1} and $\mathrm{WMA}_{\mathrm{M}}$ is $np_{M+1} - p_M - \cdots - p_M - n + 1$. If we denote the sum $p_M + \cdots + p_M - n + 1$. by $\mathrm{Total}_{\mathrm{M}}$, then

$$Total_M + p_{M+1} - p_{M-n+1} \tag{8}$$

Figure 5. Weighted Moving Average (WMA weightn = 15)

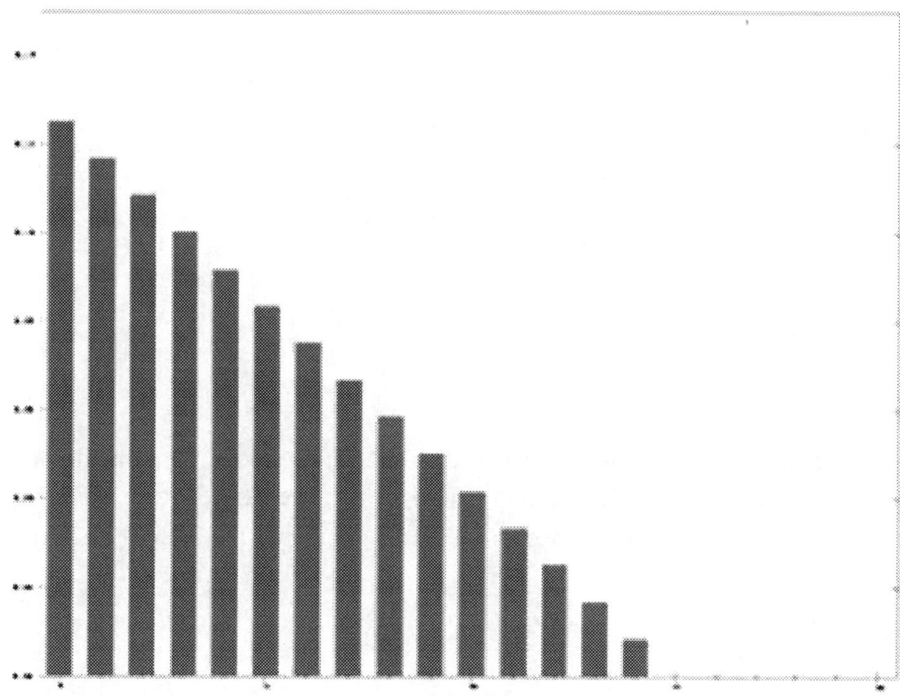

$$Numerator_{M+1} = Numerator_{M} + np_{M} + 1 - p_{M} - n + 1 \quad (9)$$

$$WMA_{M+1} = \frac{Numerator_{M+1}}{n+(n-1)+\ldots+2+1} \quad (10)$$

The graph shows how the weights decrease, from highest weight for the most recent datum points, down to zero. It can be compared to the weights in the exponential moving average which follows. The window length for this operation is 150.

Stationary Wavelet Transform (SWT)

The Stationary Wavelet Transform (SWT) is a wavelet transform algorithm designed to overcome the lack of translation-invariance of the discrete wavelet transform (DWT). Translation-invariance is achieved by removing the down samplers and up samplers in the DWT and up sampling the filter coefficients by a factor of $2^{(j-1)}$ in the jth level of the algorithm.

The following block diagram depicts the digital implementation of SWT; whereas Fig.9 shows the filtering performance of SWT.

In the above diagram, filters in each level are up-sampled versions of the previous (see figure 8).

DISCUSSION

The power spectral density (PSD) of a wide sense stationary random process *X* (*t*) is computed from the Fourier transform of the autocorrelation function *R* (τ);

$$2^{(j-1)} \quad (11)$$

where, the autocorrelation function

$$R(\tau) = E\left[X(t+\tau)X(t)\right] \quad (12)$$

The non-parametric methods are methods in which the estimate of PSD is made directly from a signal itself. One type of such methods is called periodogram. The periodogram estimate for PSD for discrete time sequence $x_1, x_2, x_3, \ldots x_k$ is defined as square magnitude of the Fourier transform of data:

$$s^{\%}(f) = \frac{1}{k} \cdot \left| \sum_{m=1}^{m=k} x_m . e^{-j2\pi fm} \right|^2 \quad (13)$$

Figure 6. Baseline drift removed by WMA filter

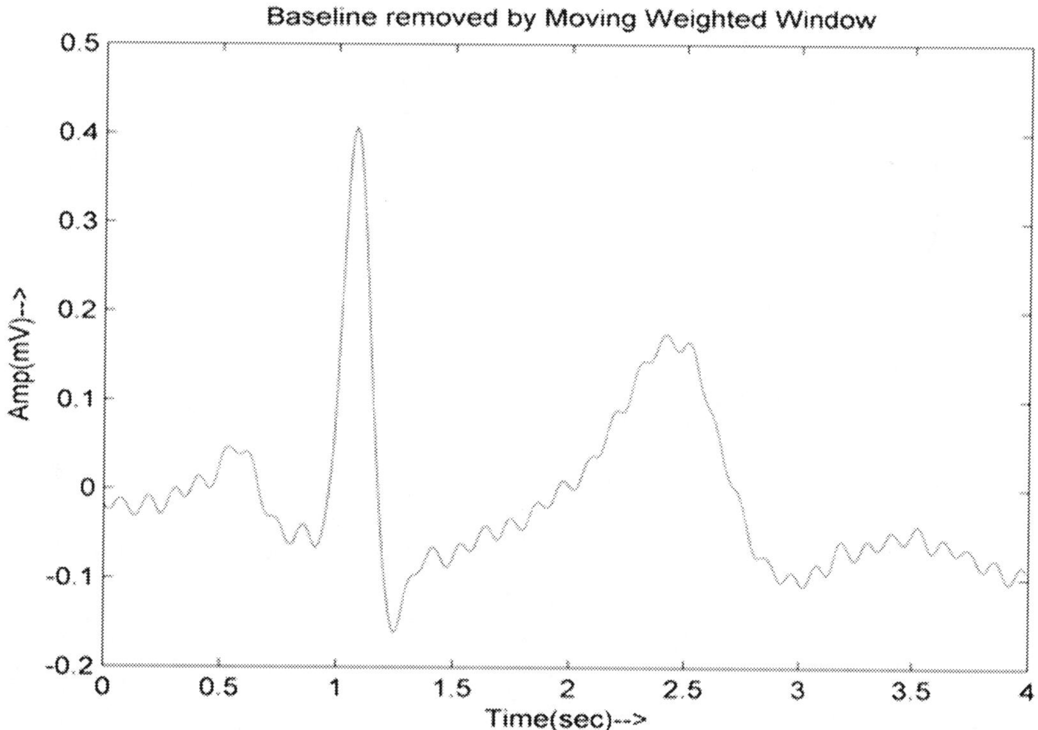

Figure 7. Block Diagram

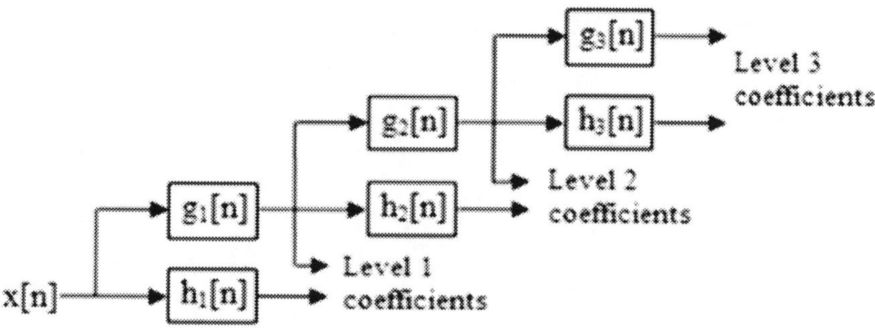

Figure 8.

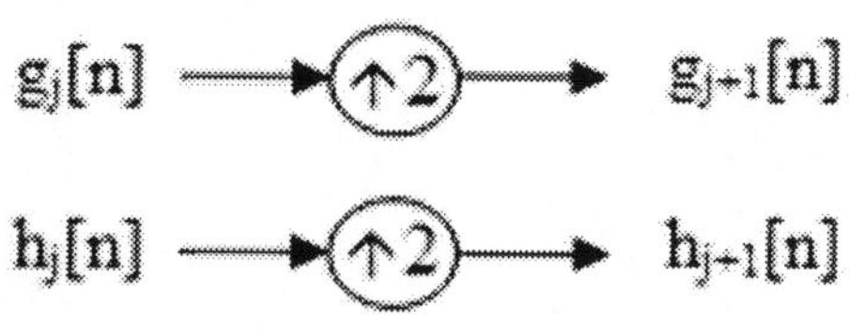

$g_j[n] \rightarrow (\uparrow 2) \rightarrow g_{j+1}[n]$

$h_j[n] \rightarrow (\uparrow 2) \rightarrow h_{j+1}[n]$

Figure 9. Baseline drift removed by SWT filter

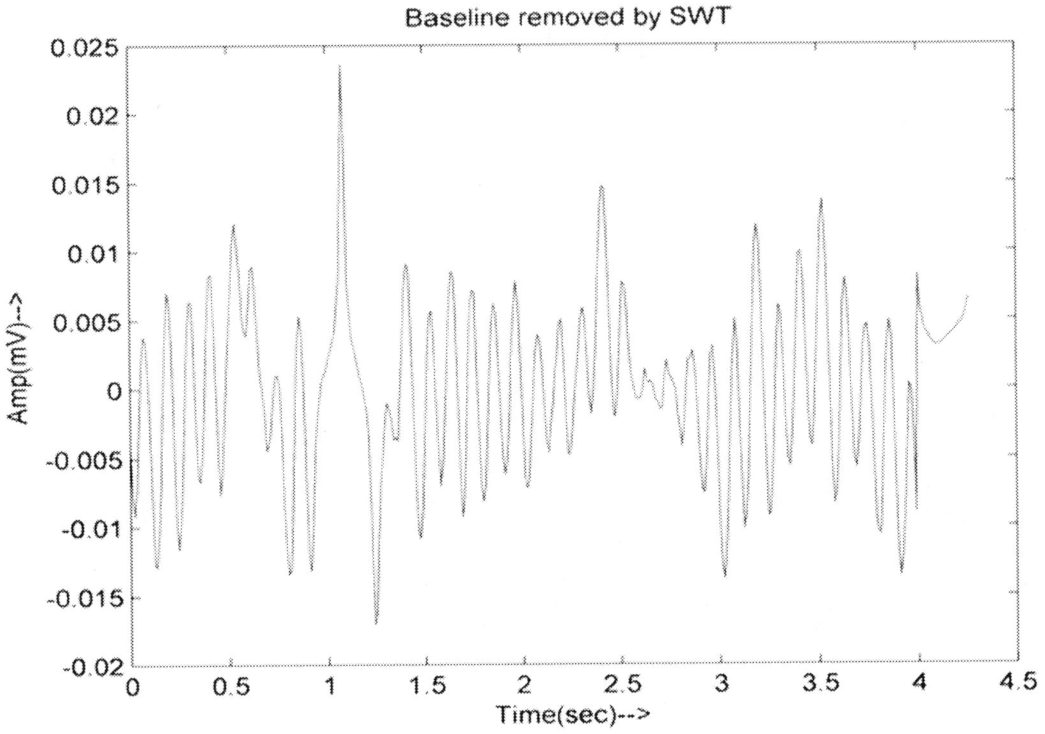

Figure 10. Amplitude changes after filtering

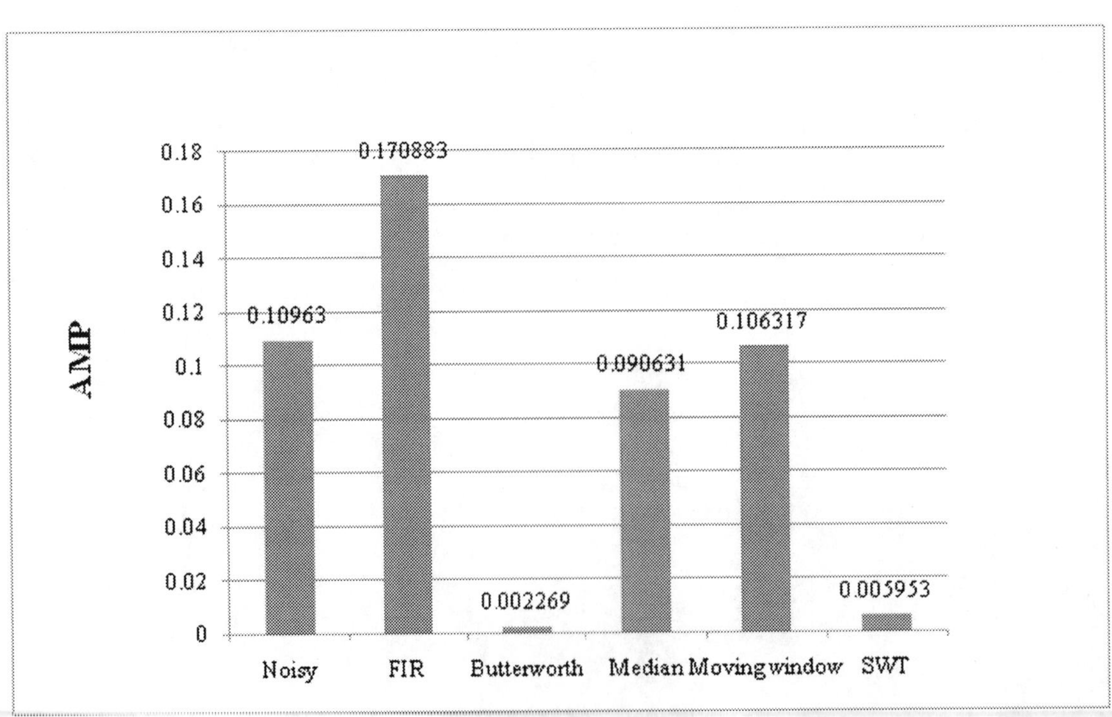

Figure 11. Frequency changes after filtering

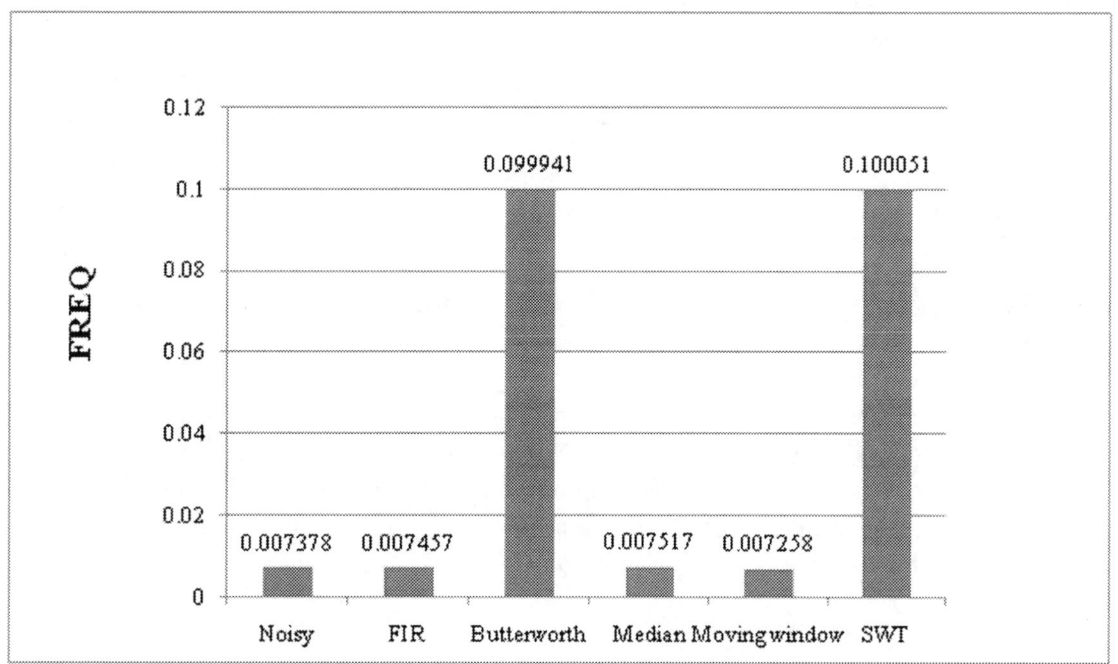

Figure 12. Power spectral density changes after filtering

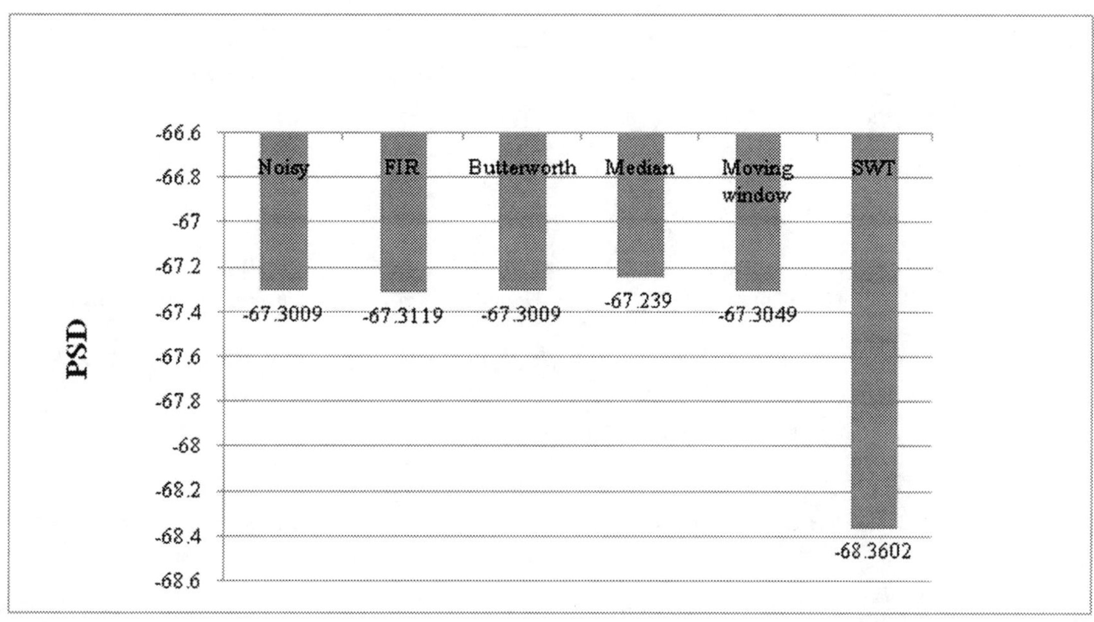

Baseline drift is removed by all the applied five filters, where as there are morphological changes (Fig. 10-12) in the filtered ECG waveforms of FIR, SWT and Low-Pass Butterworth filter, but there are no certain changes in case of Median and WMA filters. Moreover, the amplitude, frequency and PSD values for Median and WMA filter's output is quite similar with the input ECG signal having baseline drift between median and WMA, the filtering performance is comparatively better in case of WMA.

CONCLUSION

The electrocardiogram is a non-invasive and the record of variation of the bio-potential signal of the human heart beats. The ECG detection which shows the information of the heart and cardiovascular condition is essential to enhance the patient living quality and appropriate treatment. Filtering of ECG signal to remove this baseline wander while preserving the low frequency ECG clinical information is necessary. The future work primarily focus on designing filter for accurate removal of baseline wander and power line interference from ECG using digital filters. In the present paper effort has been made to perform the comparative analysis of five different filters that were statistically analyzed and WMA filter performance is found to be sought for removal of baseline drift.

REFERENCES

Ahlstrom, M.L. & Tomkins, W.J. (1885). Digital filter for ECG real time processing using microprocessors. *IEEE Transactions on BME*, *32*, 708-713.

Allen, J., Anderson, J., Mc, C., Dempsey, G. J., & Adgey, A. A. J. (1994). Efficient Baseline Wander Removal for Feature Analysis of Electrocardiographic Body Surface Maps. *IEEE Proceedings of Engineering in Medicine and Biology Society*, *2*, 1316 - 1317.

Avionics, D. M. (1993). *Electrocardiographic baseline filtering and estimation system with bidirectional filter.* US Patent, US5402795.

Barati, Z., & Ayatollahi, A. (2006). Baseline Wandering Removal by Using Independent Component Analysis to Single-Channel ECG Data. *IEEE Conference on Biomedical and Pharmaceutical Engineering*.

Challis, R. E., & Kitney, R. I. (1983). The design of digital filters for biomedical signal processing. Part 3: The design of Butterworth and Chebychev filters. *Journal of Biomedical Engineering*, *5*(2), 91–102. doi:10.1016/0141-5425(83)90026-2 PMID:6855219

Chavan, M. S., Agarwala, R. A., & Uplane, M. D. (2008). Comparative Study of Chebyshev I and Chebyshev II Filter used For Noise Reduction in ECG Signal. *International Journal Of Circuits, Systems Signal Processing*, *2*(1), 1–17.

Chouhan, V. S., & Mehta, S. S. (2007). Total Removal of Baseline Drift from ECG Signal. *International Conference on Computing: Theory and Applications-ICCTA*. doi:10.1109/ICCTA.2007.126

Choy, T. T., & Leung, P. M. (1988). Real Time Microprocessor-Based 50 Hz Notch Filter for ECG. *Journal of Biomedical Engineering*, *10*(3), 285–288. doi:10.1016/0141-5425(88)90013-1 PMID:3392981

Cramer, E., McManus, C. D., & Neubert, D. (1987). Estimation and removal of power line interference in the electrocardiogram: A comparison of digital approaches. *Computers and Biomedical Research, an International Journal*, *20*(1), 12–28. doi:10.1016/0010-4809(87)90014-0 PMID:3829639

Dai, M., & Liana, S.-L. (2009). Removal of Baseline Wander from Dynamic Electrocardiogram Signals. *IEEE Conference on Image and Signal Processing*. doi:10.1109/CISP.2009.5304473

Dotsinsky, I., & Stoyanov, T. (2005). Power-line interference cancellation in ECG signals. *Biomedical Instrumentation & Technology*, *39*(2), 155–162. PMID:15810791

Ferdjallah, M., & Barr, R. E. (1990). Frequency-domain digital filtering techniques for the removal of powerline noise with application to the electrocardiogram. *Computers and Biomedical Research, an International Journal*, *23*(5), 473–489. doi:10.1016/0010-4809(90)90035-B PMID:2225791

Frau, D., & Novak, D. (2000). Electrocardiogram Baseline Removal Using Wavelet Approximations. *Proceeding of the 15th Biennial Eurasip Conference Biosignal*.

Friesen, M., Jannett, T. C., Jadallah, M. A., Yates, S. L., Quint, S. R., & Nagle, H. T. (1990). Comparison of noise sensitivity of QRS Detection Algorithms. *IEEE Transactions on Bio-Medical Engineering*, *37*(1), 85–98. doi:10.1109/10.43620 PMID:2303275

Furno, G. S., & Tompkins, W. J. (1983). A learning filter for reducing noise interference. *IEEE Transactions on Bio-Medical Engineering*, *BME-30*(4), 234–235. doi:10.1109/TBME.1983.325225 PMID:6862503

Gradwohl, J. R., Pottala, E. W., Horton, M. R., & Bailey, J. J. (1988). Comparison of Two Methods for Removing Baseline Wander in the ECG. *IEEE Proceedings on Computers in Cardiology*.

Hamilton, P. S. (1996). A comparison of adaptive and non-adaptive filters for reduction of power line interference in the ECG. *IEEE Transactions on Bio-Medical Engineering*, *43*(1), 105–109. doi:10.1109/10.477707 PMID:8567001

Hargittai, S. (2008). Efficient and Fast ECG Baseline Wander Reduction without Distortion of Important Clinical Information. *IEEE Conferences on Computers in Cardiology*.

Ider, Y. Z., Saki, M. C., & Gcer, H. A. (1995). Removal of power line interference in signal-averaged electrocardiography systems. *IEEE Transactions on Bio-Medical Engineering*, *42*(7), 731–735. doi:10.1109/10.391173 PMID:7622157

Jane, R., & Laguna, P. (1992). Adaptive Baseline Wander Removal in the ECG: Comparative Analysis with Cubic Spline Technique. IEEE.

Kulkarni, P. K., Kumar, V., & Verma, H. K. (1997). Removal of powerline interference and baseline wonder using real time digital filter. *Proceedings of international conference on computer applications in electrical engineering, recent advances*.

Kumaravel, N., Senthil, A., Sridhar, K. S., & Nithiyanandam, N. (1995). Integrating the ECG power-line interference removal methods with rule-based system. *Biomedical Sciences Instrumentation*, *31*, 115–120. PMID:7654947

Laguna, P., & Jane, R. (1992). Adaptive Filtering of ECG Baseline Wander. IEEE.

Levkov, C., Mihov, G., Ivanov, R., Daskalov, I., Christov, I., & Dotsinsky, I. (2005). Removal of power-line interference from the ECG: A review of the subtraction procedure. *Biomedical Engineering Online*, *50*(4). PMID:16117827

Lisette, P., Harting, N. M., & Fedotov, C. H. S. (2004).On Baseline drift Suppressing in ECG-Recordings. *Proceedings of SPS (the 2004 IEEE Benelux Signal Processing Symposium).*

Lisheng, X., & Kuanquan, W. (2002). Adaptive Baseline Wander Removal in the Pulse Waveform. IEEE.

Lynn, P. A. (1977). *On* line digital filter for biological filters: Some fast designs for small computers. *Medical & Biological Engineering & Computing*, *15*(5), 91–101. doi:10.1007/BF02442281

Mahesh, S., Chavan, R. A., & Uplane, M. D. (2008). Interference Reduction in ECG using Digital FIR Filters based on rectangular window. *WSEAS Transactions on Signal Processing, 4*(5), 340-49.

Markovsky, I. A., & Anton, V. H. & Sabine (2008). Application of Filtering Methods for Removal of Resuscitation Artifacts from Human ECG Signals. *IEEE Conference of Engineering in Medicine and Biology Society*. doi:10.1109/IEMBS.2008.4649079

McManus, C. D., Neubert, K. D., & Cramer, E. (1993). Characterization and elimination of AC noise in electrocardiograms: A comparison of digital filtering methods. *Computers and Biomedical Research, an International Journal*, *26*(1), 48–67. doi:10.1006/cbmr.1993.1003 PMID:8444027

McManus, C. D., Teppner, U., Neubert, D., & Lobodzinski, S. M. (1985). Estimation and Removal of Baseline Drift in the Electrocardiogram. *Computers and Biomedical Research, an International Journal*, *18*(1), 1–9. doi:10.1016/0010-4809(85)90002-3 PMID:3971702

Mitov, I. P. (2004). A method for reduction of power line interference in the ECG. *Medical Engineering & Physics*, *26*(10), 879–887. doi:10.1016/j.medengphy.2004.08.014 PMID:15567704

Pan, N., Vai Mang, I., Mai, P. U., & Pun, S. H. (2007). Accurate Removal of Baseline Wander in ECG Using Empirical Mode Decomposition. *IEEE International Conference on Functional Biomedical Imaging*. doi:10.1109/NFSI-ICFBI.2007.4387719

Pandit, S. (1997). ECG Baseline Drift Removal through STFT. IEEE.

Patricia, A., & Tim, L. (1992). *Method and apparatus for removing baseline wander from an ECG signal.* US Patent, Hewlett Packard. US5318036.

Pottala, E. W. (1989). Suppression of Baseline Wander in the ECG Using a Bilinearly Transform, Null-Phase Filter. *Journal of E.cardiology*, 22.

Pottala, E. W., & Gradwohl, J. R. (1992). Comparison of Two Methods for Removing Baseline Wander. In *The ECG*. Pub Med National Library of Medicine.

Rangayyan, R. M. (2002). *Biomedical Signal Analysis*. John Wiley and Sons Publishing Company.

Robertson, D. G., & Dowling, J. J. (2003). Design and responses of Butterworth and critically damped digital filters. *Journal of Electromyography and Kinesiology*, *13*(6), 569–573. doi:10.1016/S1050-6411(03)00080-4 PMID:14573371

Rossi, R. (1992). *Fast FIR Filters for a Stres Test System*. IEEE.

Shusterman, V. (2000). Enhancing the Precision of ECG Baseline Correction. *Computers and Biomedical Research, an International Journal*, 33. PMID:10854121

Singh, G. K., Sharma, A., & Velusami, S. (2009). A Research Review on Analysis and Interpretation of Arrhythmias using ECG Signals. *IJMST*, *2*(3), 37-55.

Sornmo, L. (1993). Time-Varying Digital Filtering of ECG Baseline Wander. *Medical & Biological Engineering & Computing*, *31*(5), 503–508. doi:10.1007/BF02441986 PMID:8295440

Sun, Y., Chan, K., & Krishnan, S. M. (2002). ECG signal conditioning by morphological filtering. *Computers in Biology and Medicine*, *32*(6), 465–479. doi:10.1016/S0010-4825(02)00034-3 PMID:12356496

Van Alste, J. A., & Schilder, T. S. (1985). Removal of Baseline Wander and Power-Line Interference from the ECG by an Efficient FIR Filter with a Reduced Number of Taps. *IEEE Transactions on Bio-Medical Engineering*, *BME-32*(12), 1052–1060. doi:10.1109/TBME.1985.325514 PMID:4077083

Webster, J. G., & Clark, J. W. (1978). *Medical Instrumentation-Application and Design*. Houghton Mifflin.

Wu, Y., & Yang, Y. (1999). A new digital filter method for eliminating 50Hz interference from the ECG. *Zhongguo Yi Liao Qi Xie Za Zhi*, *23*(3), 145–148. PMID:12583053

Zahoor-uddin (1995). Baseline Wandering Removal from Human Electrocardiogram Signal using Projection Pursuit Gradient Ascent Algorithm. *International Journal of Electrical &Computer Sciences*, *9*(9), 11-13.

Zhi-Dong, Z., & Yu-Quan, C. (2006). A New Method for Removal of Baseline Wander and Power Line Interference in ECG Signals. *IEEE Conferences on Machine Learning and Cybernetics*.

Zschorlich, V. R. (1989). Digital filtering of EMG-signals. *Electromyography and Clinical Neurophysiology*, *29*(2), 81–86. PMID:2707144

KEY TERMS AND DEFINITIONS

Baseline Drift: Baseline drift in ECG signal is the biggest hurdle in visualization of correct waveform and computerized detection of wave complexes based on threshold decision. The baseline drift may be linear, static, non-linear or wavering. Reducing the baseline drift to a near zero value greatly helps in visually inspecting the morphology of the wave components as well as in computerized detection and delineation of the wave complexes.

ECG: Electrocardiography is the recording of the electrical activity of the heart. Traditionally this is in the form of a transthoracic (across the thorax or chest) interpretation of the electrical activity of the heart over a period of time, as detected by electrodes attached to the surface of the skin and recorded or displayed by a device external to the body.

FIR: In signal processing, a finite impulse response (FIR) filter is a filter whose impulse response (or response to any finite length input) is of finite duration, because it settles to zero in finite time.

Low Pass Butter Worth: The Butterworth filter is a type of signal processing filter designed to have as flat a frequency response as possible in the pass band. It is also referred to as a maximally flat magnitude filter.

Median: In statistics and probability theory, the median is the numerical value separating the higher half of a data sample, a population, or a probability distribution, from the lower half. The median of a finite list of numbers can be found by arranging all the observations from lowest value to highest value and picking the middle one.

Stationary Wavelet Transform: The Stationary wavelet transform (SWT) is a wavelet transform algorithm designed to overcome the lack of translation-invariance of the discrete wavelet transform (DWT).

Weighted Moving Average: A weighted average is any average that has multiplying factors to give different weights to data at different positions in the sample window. Mathematically, the moving average is the convolution of the datum points with a fixed weighting function.

Chapter 9
Signal Processing:
Iteration Bound and Loop Bound

Deepika Ghai
PEC University of Technology, India

Neelu Jain
PEC University of Technology, India

ABSTRACT

Digital signal processing algorithms are recursive in nature. These algorithms are explained by iterative data-flow graphs where nodes represent computations and edges represent communications. For all data-flow graphs, time taken to achieve output from the applied input is referred as iteration bound. In this chapter, two algorithms are used for computing the iteration bound i.e. Longest Path Matrix (LPM) and Minimum Cycle Mean (MCM). The iteration bound of single-rate data-flow graph (SRDFG) can be determined by considering the Multi-rate data-flow graph (MRDFG) equivalent of the SRDFG. SRDFG contain more nodes and edges as compared to MRDFG. Reduction of nodes and edges in MRDFG is used for faster determination of the iteration bound.

1. INTRODUCTION

Iteration bound means time taken to achieve output from the applied input (Parhi & Messerschmitt, 1987). Many Digital Signal Processing (DSP) algorithms like recursive and adaptive digital filters contain feedback loops which induce an inherent lower bound on iteration period (Gerez, Heemstra & Herrmann, 1992). This bound is called iteration bound. It is a fundamental limit of recursive Data Flow Graph (DFG) which tells how fast DSP program can be executed in hardware (Lee, Chan & Verbauwhede, 2007). It is used as a characteristic in representation of algorithm in the form of DFG (Ito & Parhi, 1995).

A graphical representation of a DSP based system $y(n) = ay(n-1) + x(n)$ is shown in Figure 1(a). DFG representation of this equation is shown in Figure 1(b). It consists of a set of nodes and edges. The nodes represent computations and has an execution time associated with it (Lee & Messerschmitt, 1987). Node A represents addition and node B corresponds to multiplication. The node A and node B have an

DOI: 10.4018/978-1-4666-8737-0.ch009

execution time of 4 u.t. (unit time) and 8 u.t. respectively. The edges represent communication between the nodes given by distinct direction. The edge A→B has zero delay and the edge B→A has one delay.

This chapter throws light on the following points:

1. Defines critical path, loop bound and iteration bound.
2. Algorithms such as Longest Path Matrix (LPM) and Minimum Cycle Mean (MCM) are defined to compute iteration bound.
3. The iteration bound of Single-rate DFG (SRDFG) from Multi-rate DFG (MRDFG) is addressed.

1.1 Critical Path

It is the path of DFG with longest computation time but should not contain any delay. The speed of DSP system depends on the critical path computation time and it decreases with increase in computation time. Figure 2 shows DFG of a DSP system consisting: (1) loop, (2) path - with delay, and (3) path - without delay.

1. **Loop**
   1→4→2→1
   1→5→3→2→1
   1→6→3→2→1
2. **Path - With Delay**
   1→4→2
   1→5→3→2
   1→6→3→2
3. **Path - Without Delay**
   4→2→1
   5→3→2→1
   6→3→2→1

The maximum computation time (6 u.t.) with zero delay among these paths is 6→3→2→1. This path is known as critical path.

Figure 1. (a) Graphical representation; (b) DFG of y(n)=ay(n-1)+x(n)

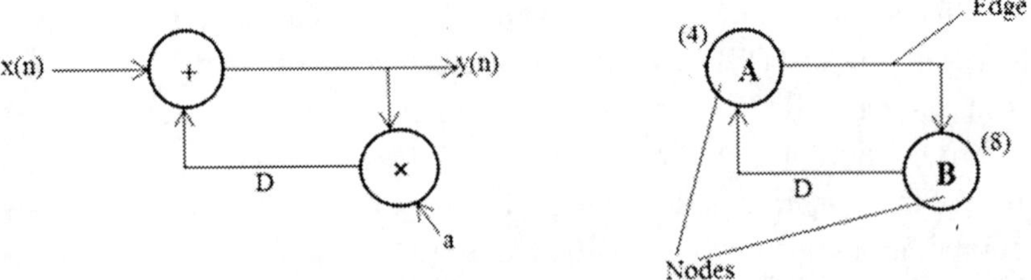

Figure 2. Critical path

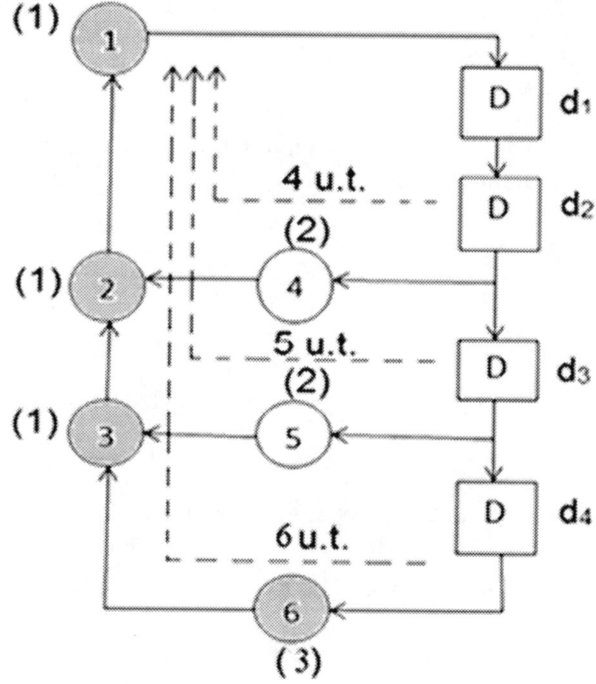

1.2 Loop Bound

It is a directed graph that begins and ends at the same node (Shatnawi, 2007) shown in Figure 3. It is represented by T_{loop} and is given as:

$$T_{loop} = \frac{t_l}{w_l}$$

where t_l= loop computation time and w_l= number of delays in the loop.

Three nodes DSP system is shown in Figure 3.

Figure 3. DFG has a loop bound of 8/2=4 u.t. and 13/1=13 u.t.

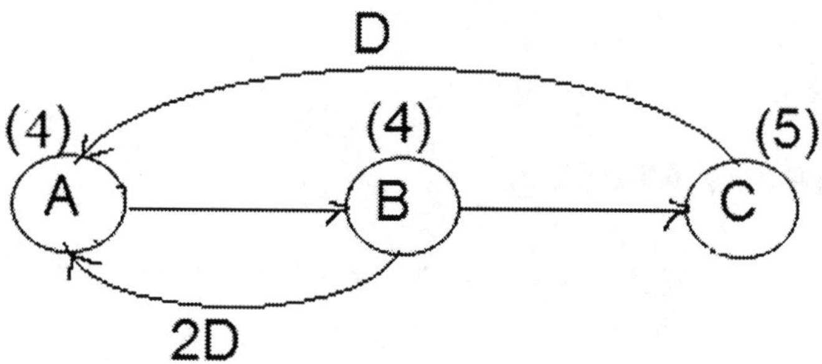

A→B→A: The loop has two delays requiring 8 u.t. to compute and has a loop bound of 8/2 = 4 u.t.
A→B→C→A: The loop has one delay requiring 13 u.t. to compute and has a loop bound of 13/1 = 13 u.t.

1.3 Iteration Bound

It is the critical loop (Ito & Parhi, 1995) with maximum loop bound for any DSP based system (Living & Al-Hashimi, 2012). It is represented by T_∞ and is given as:

$$T_\infty = \max_{l \in L} \left\{ \frac{t_l}{w_l} \right\}$$

where L is the set of loops in DFG; t_l is computation time of the loop; and w_l is number of delays in the loop.

A→B→A: The loop has two delays requiring 8 u.t. to compute and has a loop bound of 8/2 = 4 u.t. as shown in Figure 4 (a).
A→B→C→A: The loop has one delay requiring 13 u.t. to compute and has a loop bound of 13/1 = 13 u.t.

$$T_\infty = \max \left\{ \frac{8}{2}, \frac{13}{1} \right\} = \max \left\{ 4, 13 \right\} = 13 \text{ u.t.}$$

4→2→1: The loop has two delays requiring 4 u.t. to compute and has a loop bound of 4/2 = 2 u.t. as shown in Figure 4 (b).
5→3→2→1: The loop has three delays requiring 5 u.t. to compute and has a loop bound of 5/3 u.t.
6→3→2→1: The loop has four delays requiring 6 u.t. to compute and has a loop bound of 6/4 u.t.

$$T_\infty = \max \left\{ \frac{4}{2}, \frac{5}{3}, \frac{6}{4} \right\} = 2 \text{ u.t.}$$

2. ALGORITHM FOR COMPUTING ITERATION BOUND

The following algorithms are used to compute iteration bound:

2.1. Longest Path Matrix (LPM) algorithm
2.2. Minimum Cycle Mean (MCM) algorithm

2.1. Longest Path Matrix Algorithm

In this, diagonal elements of matrices are used to calculate iteration bound (Ito & Parhi, 1995).

Let d=number of delay elements in DFG.

Figure 4. (a) Iteration bound; (b) Iteration bound

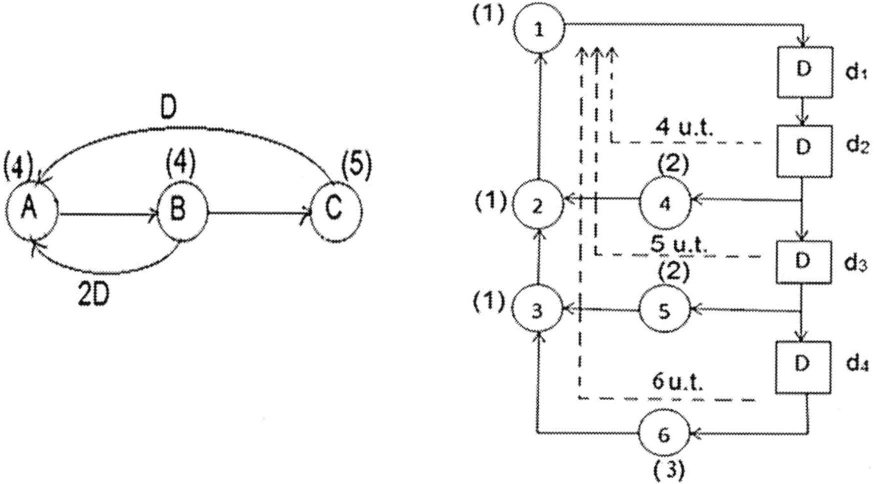

The delay matrices $L^{(m)}$, $m = 1, 2, 3, \ldots, d$ are constructed such that $l_{i,j}^{(m)}$ is the longest computation time of all paths from delay element d_i to d_j where i and j are row and column respectively. If no path exists between two delays elements then $l_{i,j}^{(m)} = -1$ (Kumar & Moorthy, 2012). Iteration can be recursively computed by the following equation:

$$l_{i,j}^{(m+1)} = \max_{k \in K}(-1,\ l_{(i,k)}^{(1)} + l_{(k,j)}^{(m)}) \tag{1}$$

where K is set of integers k in the interval $[1,d]$ such that neither $l_{(i,k)}^{(1)} = -1$ nor $l_{(k,j)}^{(m)} = -1$ holds.

T_∞ is calculated as:

$$T_\infty = \max_{(i,m)\in\{1,2,3,---,d\}} \left\{ \frac{l_{(i,i)}^{(m)}}{m} \right\} \tag{2}$$

Example 1: Find the iteration bound of DFG shown in Figure 5 using LPM algorithm.
Solution: As shown in Figure 5, For delay

d_1: It is connected to d_2; $K=\{2\}$
d_2: It is connected to d_1 and d_3; $K=\{1,3\}$
d_3: It is connected to d_1 and d_4; $K=\{1,4\}$
d_4: It is connected to d_1; $K=\{1\}$.

Computation of $L^{(1)}$ is given as follows:

Figure 5. Iteration bound T_∞=2

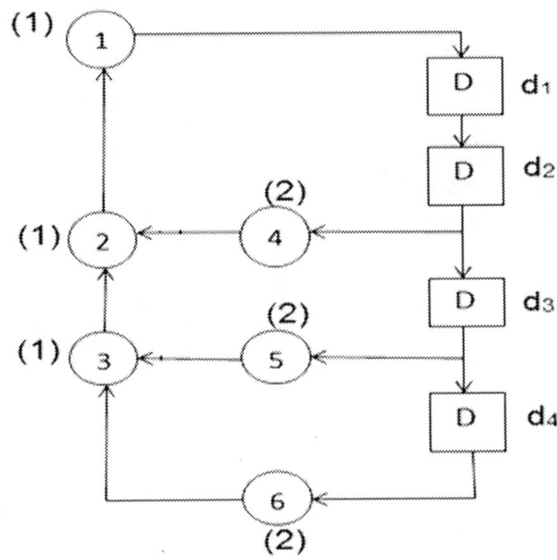

Elements		Computation Time
l_{12}	$\rightarrow$	0
l_{21}	$\rightarrow$	4
l_{24}	$\rightarrow$	no connection
l_{31}	$\rightarrow$	5
l_{43}	$\rightarrow$	no connection

$$, L^{(1)} = \begin{bmatrix} l_{11} & l_{12} & l_{13} & l_{14} \\ l_{21} & l_{22} & l_{23} & l_{24} \\ l_{31} & l_{32} & l_{33} & l_{34} \\ l_{41} & l_{42} & l_{43} & l_{44} \end{bmatrix} = \begin{bmatrix} -1 & 0 & -1 & -1 \\ 4 & -1 & 0 & -1 \\ 5 & -1 & -1 & 0 \\ 5 & -1 & -1 & -1 \end{bmatrix}$$

$L^{(2)}$ is computed with the help of $L^{(1)}$ as follows:

$$l_{i.j}^{(m+1)} = \max_{k\in K}(-1, l_{i.k}^{(1)} + l_{k.j}^{(m)}),\ l_{i.j}^{(1+1)} = \max_{k\in K}(-1, l_{i,k}^{(1)} + l_{k.j}^{(m)})$$

Computing $L^{(2)}$ from $L^{(1)}$, we get

$$\begin{aligned} l_{1.1}^{(1+1)} &= \max_{k\in\{2\}}(-1, l_{1.k}^{(1)} + l_{k.1}^{(1)}) \\ &= \max(-1, l_{1.2}^{(1)} + l_{2.1}^{(1)}) \\ &= \max(-1, 0+4) = 4 \end{aligned} \quad , \quad \begin{aligned} l_{1.2}^{(1+1)} &= \max_{k\in\{2\}}(-1, l_{1.k}^{(1)} + l_{k.2}^{(1)}) \\ &= \max(-1, l_{1.2}^{(1)} + l_{2.2}^{(1)}) \\ &= \max(-1,\ 0-1) = -1 \end{aligned}$$

[$\because$neither $l_{i.k}^{(1)} = -1$ nor $l_{k.j}^{(m)} = -1$ exist]

$$l_{1,3}^{(1+1)} = \max_{k\in\{2\}}(-1, l_{1,k}^{(1)} + l_{k,3}^{(1)}) = \max(-1, l_{1,2}^{(1)} + l_{2,3}^{(1)}) = \max(-1,\ 0+0) = 0 \quad , \quad l_{1,4}^{(1+1)} = \max_{k\in\{2\}}(-1, l_{1,k}^{(1)} + l_{k,4}^{(1)}) = \max(-1, l_{1,2}^{(1)} + l_{2,4}^{(1)}) = \max(-1,\ 0-1) = -1$$

$[\because$neither $l_{i,k}^{(1)} = -1$ nor $l_{k,j}^{(m)} = -1$ exist$]$

$$\begin{aligned} l_{2,1}^{(1+1)} &= \max_{k\in\{1,3\}}(-1, l_{2,k}^{(1)} + l_{k,1}^{(1)}) \\ &= \max(-1, l_{2,1}^{(1)} + l_{1,1}^{(1)}, l_{2,3}^{(1)} + l_{3,1}^{(1)}) [\because \text{neither } l_{i,k}^{(1)} = -1 \text{ nor } l_{k,j}^{(m)} = -1 \text{ exist}] \\ &= \max(-1,\ 4-1, 0+5) = 5 \end{aligned}$$

$$\begin{aligned} l_{2,2}^{(1+1)} &= \max_{k\in\{1,3\}}(-1, l_{2,k}^{(1)} + l_{k,2}^{(1)}) \\ &= \max(-1, l_{2,1}^{(1)} + l_{1,2}^{(1)}, l_{2,3}^{(1)} + l_{3,2}^{(1)}) [\because \text{neither } l_{i,k}^{(1)} = -1 \text{ nor } l_{k,j}^{(m)} = -1 \text{ exist}] \\ &= \max(-1,\ 4+0, 0-1) = 4 \end{aligned}$$

$$\begin{aligned} l_{2,3}^{(1+1)} &= \max_{k\in\{1,3\}}(-1, l_{2,k}^{(1)} + l_{k,3}^{(1)}) \\ &= \max(-1, l_{2,1}^{(1)} + l_{1,3}^{(1)}, l_{2,3}^{(1)} + l_{3,3}^{(1)}) [\because \text{neither } l_{i,k}^{(1)} = -1 \text{ nor } l_{k,j}^{(m)} = -1 \text{ exist}] \\ &= \max(-1,\ 4-1, 0-1) = -1 \end{aligned}$$

$$\begin{aligned} l_{2,4}^{(1+1)} &= \max_{k\in\{1,3\}}(-1, l_{2,k}^{(1)} + l_{k,4}^{(1)}) \\ &= \max(-1, l_{2,1}^{(1)} + l_{1,4}^{(1)}, l_{2,3}^{(1)} + l_{3,4}^{(1)}) [\because \text{neither } l_{i,k}^{(1)} = -1 \text{ nor } l_{k,j}^{(m)} = -1 \text{ exist}] \\ &= \max(-1,\ 4-1, 0+0) = 0 \end{aligned}$$

$$\begin{aligned} l_{3,1}^{(1+1)} &= \max_{k\in\{1,4\}}(-1, l_{3,k}^{(1)} + l_{k,1}^{(1)}) \\ &= \max(-1, l_{3,1}^{(1)} + l_{1,1}^{(1)}, l_{3,4}^{(1)} + l_{4,1}^{(1)}) [\because \text{neither } l_{i,k}^{(1)} = -1 \text{ nor } l_{k,j}^{(m)} = -1 \text{ exist}] \\ &= \max(-1,\ 5-1, 0+5) = 5 \end{aligned}$$

$$\begin{aligned} l_{3,2}^{(1+1)} &= \max_{k\in\{1,4\}}(-1, l_{3,k}^{(1)} + l_{k,2}^{(1)}) \\ &= \max(-1, l_{3,1}^{(1)} + l_{1,2}^{(1)}, l_{3,4}^{(1)} + l_{4,2}^{(1)}) [\because \text{neither } l_{i,k}^{(1)} = -1 \text{ nor } l_{k,j}^{(m)} = -1 \text{ exist}] \\ &= \max(-1,\ 5+0, 0-1) = 5 \end{aligned}$$

$$\begin{aligned} l_{3,3}^{(1+1)} &= \max_{k\in\{1,4\}}(-1, l_{3,k}^{(1)} + l_{k,3}^{(1)}) \\ &= \max(-1, l_{3,1}^{(1)} + l_{1,3}^{(1)}, l_{3,4}^{(1)} + l_{4,3}^{(1)}) [\because \text{neither } l_{i,k}^{(1)} = -1 \text{ nor } l_{k,j}^{(m)} = -1 \text{ exist}] \\ &= \max(-1,\ 5-1, 0-1) = -1 \end{aligned}$$

$$
\begin{aligned}
l_{3.4}^{(1+1)} &= \max_{k\in\{1.4\}}(-1, l_{3.k}^{(1)} + l_{k.4}^{(1)}) \\
&= \max(-1, l_{3.1}^{(1)} + l_{1.4}^{(1)}, l_{3.4}^{(1)} + l_{4.4}^{(1)})\ [\because \text{neither } l_{i.k}^{(1)} = -1 \text{ nor } l_{k.j}^{(m)} = -1 \text{ exist}] \\
&= \max(-1,\ 5-1,\ 0-1) = -1
\end{aligned}
$$

$$
\begin{aligned}
l_{4.1}^{(1+1)} &= \max_{k\in\{1\}}(-1, l_{4.k}^{(1)} + l_{k.1}^{(1)}) \\
&= \max(-1, l_{4.1}^{(1)} + l_{1.1}^{(1)}) \quad [\because \text{neither } l_{i.k}^{(1)} = -1 \text{ nor } l_{k.j}^{(m)} = -1 \text{ exist}] \\
&= \max(-1,\ 5-1) = -1
\end{aligned}
$$

$$
\begin{aligned}
l_{4.2}^{(1+1)} &= \max_{k\in\{1\}}(-1, l_{4.k}^{(1)} + l_{k.2}^{(1)}) \\
&= \max(-1, l_{4.1}^{(1)} + l_{1.2}^{(1)}) \\
&= \max(-1,\ 5+0) = 5
\end{aligned}
\quad , \quad
\begin{aligned}
l_{4.3}^{(1+1)} &= \max_{k\in\{1\}}(-1, l_{4.k}^{(1)} + l_{k.3}^{(1)}) \\
&= \max(-1, l_{4.1}^{(1)} + l_{1.3}^{(1)}) \\
&= \max(-1,\ 5-1) = -1
\end{aligned}
$$

$[\because \text{neither } l_{i.k}^{(1)} = -1 \text{ nor } l_{k.j}^{(m)} = -1 \text{ exist}]$

$$
\begin{aligned}
l_{4.4}^{(1+1)} &= \max_{k\in\{1\}}(-1, l_{4.k}^{(1)} + l_{k.4}^{(1)}) \\
&= \max(-1, l_{4.1}^{(1)} + l_{1.4}^{(1)}) \quad [\because \text{neither } l_{i.k}^{(1)} = -1 \text{ nor } l_{k.j}^{(m)} = -1 \text{ exist}] \\
&= \max(-1,\ 5-1) = -1
\end{aligned}
$$

$$
L^{(2)} = \begin{bmatrix} 4 & -1 & 0 & -1 \\ 5 & 4 & -1 & 0 \\ 5 & 5 & -1 & -1 \\ -1 & 5 & -1 & -1 \end{bmatrix}
$$

Similarly compute $L^{(3)}$ from $L^{(1)}$ and $L^{(2)}$

$$
l_{i.j}^{(m+1)} = \max_{k\in K}(-1, l_{i.k}^{(1)} + l_{k.j}^{(m)}),\ l_{i.j}^{(2+1)} = \max_{k\in K}(-1, l_{i.k}^{(1)} + l_{k.j}^{(2)})
$$

From the matrix $L^{(1)}$ and $L^{(2)}$, we get

$$
L^{(3)} = \begin{bmatrix} 5 & 4 & -1 & 0 \\ 8 & 5 & 4 & -1 \\ 9 & 5 & 5 & -1 \\ 9 & -1 & 5 & -1 \end{bmatrix}
$$

Similarly compute $L^{(4)}$ from $L^{(1)}$and $L^{(3)}$

$$l_{i,j}^{(m+1)} = \max_{k \in K}(-1, l_{i,k}^{(1)} + l_{k,j}^{(m)}),\ l_{i,j}^{(3+1)} = \max_{k \in K}(-1, l_{i,k}^{(1)} + l_{k,j}^{(3)})$$

From the matrix $L^{(1)}$ and $L^{(3)}$, we get

$$L^{(4)} = \begin{bmatrix} 8 & 5 & 4 & -1 \\ 9 & 8 & 5 & 4 \\ 10 & 9 & 5 & 5 \\ 10 & 9 & -1 & 5 \end{bmatrix}$$

T_∞ is given by:

$$T_\infty = \max_{i,m \in \{1,2,3,---,d\}} \left\{ \frac{l_{i,i}^{(m)}}{m} \right\},\ T_\infty = \max\left\{ \frac{4}{2}, \frac{4}{2}, \frac{5}{3}, \frac{5}{3}, \frac{5}{3}, \frac{8}{4}, \frac{8}{4}, \frac{5}{4}, \frac{5}{4} \right\} = 2 \text{ u.t.}$$

Example 2: Find the iteration bound of DFG shown in Figure 6 using LPM algorithm.

Solution: Two delay elements are present in DFG as shown in Figure 6. So, $L^{(1)}$ and $L^{(2)}$ have to be computed.

Computation of $L^{(1)}$ is given as follows, also shown in Figure 7.

Elements		Computation Time
l_{11}	$\rightarrow$	7
l_{12}	$\rightarrow$	4
l_{21}	$\rightarrow$	13
l_{22}	$\rightarrow$	10

$$, L^{(1)} = \begin{bmatrix} l_{11} & l_{12} \\ l_{21} & l_{22} \end{bmatrix} = \begin{bmatrix} 7 & 4 \\ 13 & 10 \end{bmatrix}$$

Figure 6. Iteration bound T_∞=10

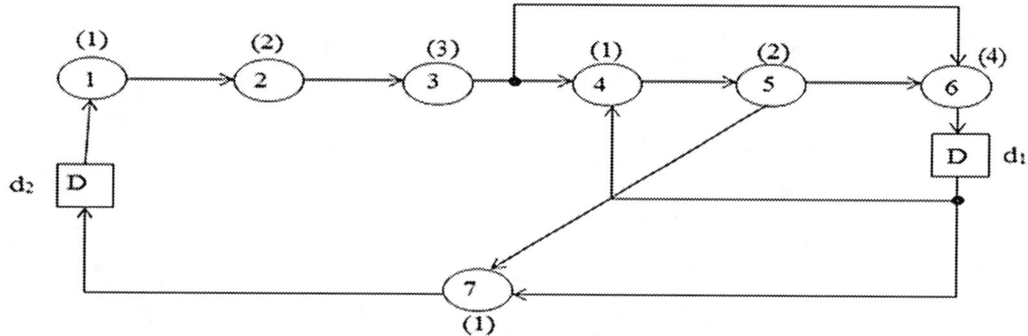

Figure 7. Calculation of $L^{(1)}$

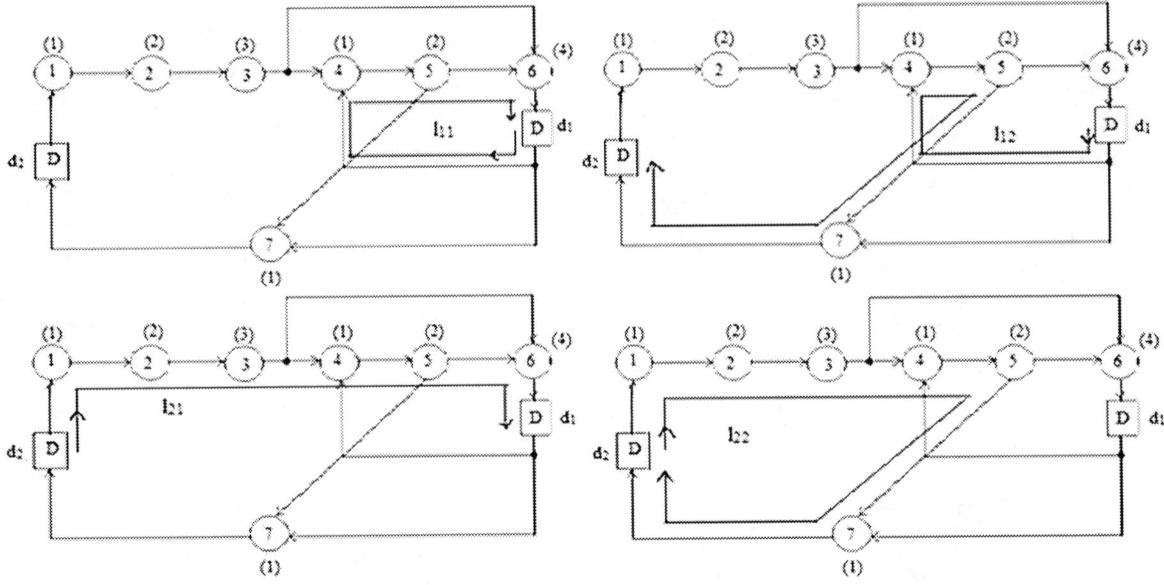

$L^{(2)}$ is computed with the help of $L^{(1)}$ as follows:

$$l_{i,j}^{(m+1)} = \max_{k \in K}(-1, l_{i,k}^{(1)} + l_{k,j}^{(m)}),\ l_{1,1}^{(1+1)} = \max_{k \in \{1,2\}}(-1, l_{1,k}^{(1)} + l_{k,1}^{(1)})$$

$$l_{1,1}^{(1+1)} = \max(-1, l_{1,1}^{(1)} + l_{1,1}^{(1)}, l_{1,2}^{(1)} + l_{2,1}^{(1)}),\ l_{1,1}^{(2)} = \max(-1, 7+7, 4+13) = 17$$

$$l_{1,2}^{(1+1)} = \max_{k \in \{1,2\}}(-1, l_{1,k}^{(1)} + l_{k,2}^{(1)}),\ l_{1,2}^{(1+1)} = \max(-1, l_{1,1}^{(1)} + l_{1,2}^{(1)}, l_{1,2}^{(1)} + l_{2,2}^{(1)})$$

$$l_{1,2}^{(2)} = \max(-1, 7+4, 4+10) = 14$$

$$l_{2,1}^{(1+1)} = \max_{k \in \{1,2\}}(-1, l_{2,k}^{(1)} + l_{k,1}^{(1)}),\ l_{2,1}^{(1+1)} = \max(-1, l_{2,1}^{(1)} + l_{1,1}^{(1)}, l_{2,2}^{(1)} + l_{2,1}^{(1)})$$

$$l_{2,1}^{(2)} = \max(-1, 13+7, 10+13) = 23$$

$$l_{2,2}^{(1+1)} = \max_{k \in \{1,2\}}(-1, l_{2,k}^{(1)} + l_{k,2}^{(1)}),\ l_{2,2}^{(1+1)} = \max(-1, l_{2,1}^{(1)} + l_{1,2}^{(1)}, l_{2,2}^{(1)} + l_{2,2}^{(1)})$$

$$l_{2,1}^{(2)} = \max(-1, 13+4, 10+10) = 20$$

$$L^{(2)} = \begin{bmatrix} 17 & 14 \\ 23 & 20 \end{bmatrix}$$

T_∞ is given by:

$$T_\infty = \max_{i,m \in \{1,2,3,\ldots,d\}} \left\{ \frac{l_{i,i}^{(m)}}{m} \right\},\ T_\infty = \max \left\{ \frac{7}{1}, \frac{10}{1}, \frac{17}{2}, \frac{20}{2} \right\} = 10\,\text{u.t.}$$

2.2. Minimum Cycle Mean Algorithm

The cycle mean [$m(c)$] of cycle (c) is the average length of the edges in c (Ito & Parhi, 1995). It is computed as the sum of edge length and dividing by the number of edges in a cycle (Karp, 1978).

The MCM λ_{min} is

$$\lambda_{\min} = \min_c m(c)$$

The MCM λ_{max} is

$$\lambda_{\min} = \max_c m(c)$$

Following steps are required for computing MCM:

1. Construct new graphs G_d and $\overline{G_d}$ from DFG. The Graph $\overline{G_d}$ is constructed from G_d by multiplying the weight of edges by -1 i.e. [$w(i,j)$ in G_d=-$w(i,j)$ in $\overline{G_d}$]
2. Compute maximum cycle mean:
   a. Construct the series of (d+1) vectors, $f^{(m)}$.
   b. Find the maximum cycle mean.
3. Compute the minimum cycle mean between each cycle.

The cycle mean $m(c)$ of new graph G_d constructed from DFG is shown in Figure 8. It is used for computing the iteration bound (Kumar & Moorthy, 2012). As shown in Figure 8 and Figure 9 from delay

d_1 to d_2: computation time is 0 u.t., therefore edge 1→2 exist with 0 u.t.
d_2 to d_1: computation time is 4 u.t., therefore edge 2→1 exist with 4 u.t.
d_2 to d_3: computation time is 0 u.t., therefore edge 2→3 exist with 0 u.t.
d_3 to d_1: computation time is 5 u.t., therefore edge 3→1 exist with 5 u.t.
d_4 to d_1: computation time is 5 u.t., therefore edge 4→1 exist with 5 u.t.
d_3 to d_4: computation time is 0 u.t., therefore edge 3→4 exist with 0 u.t.

Figure 8. Iteration bound

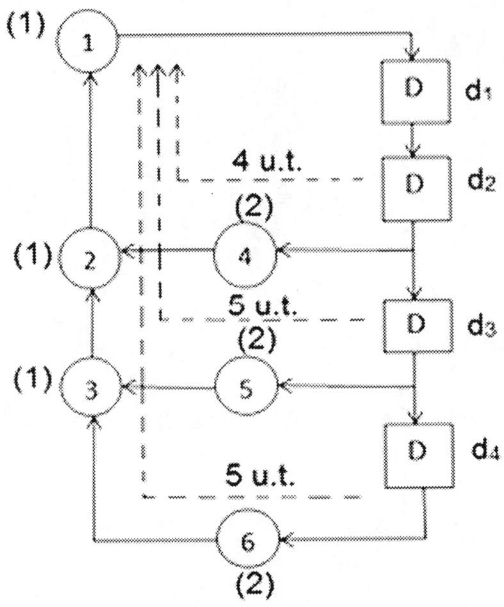

Figure 9. Graph (a) G_d and (b) $\overline{G_d}$

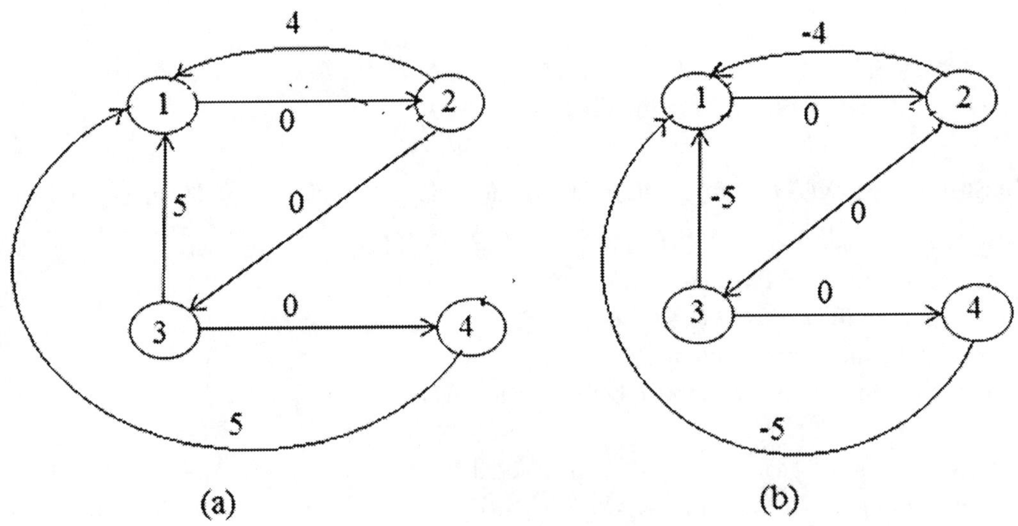

$$\text{Cycle mean } [m(c)] \text{ in } G_d = \frac{\text{maximum computation time of all cycles in } G \text{ having delays in } c}{\text{Number of delays in cycle in } G}$$

The MCM of $\overline{G_d}$ is formed by constructing $(d+1)$ vectors, $f^{(m)}$ where $m = 0, 1, 2, \ldots, d$ which are each of dimensions $d \times 1$ where d is number of delay elements. As shown in Figure 8, there are four delay elements therefore, matrix is 4×1 and vectors are 5 i.e. $f(0), f(1), f(2), f(3), f(4)$. If there is no connection between node, then $f^{(m)}(j)=\infty$.

The remaining vectors $f^{(m)}$, $m = 0, 1, 2, \ldots, d$ are recursively computing.

$$f^{(m)}(j) = \min_{i \in I} \left(f^{(m-1)}(i) + \overline{w}(i, j)\right) \tag{3}$$

where $\overline{w}(i, j)$ is the weight of the edge $i \rightarrow j$ in graph $\overline{G_d}$ and I is the number of delay elements.

T_∞ is given by:

$$T_\infty = - \min_{i \in \{1,2,3,---,d\}} \left(\max_{m \in \{0,1,2,---,(d-1)\}} \left(\frac{f^{(d)}(i) - f^{(m)}(i)}{d - m} \right) \right) \tag{4}$$

Node 1 is chosen as the reference node in graph $\overline{G_d}$ as shown in Figure 9(b).

$$f^{(0)} = \begin{bmatrix} f^{(0)}(1) \\ f^{(0)}(2) \\ f^{(0)}(3) \\ f^{(0)}(4) \end{bmatrix} = \begin{bmatrix} 0 \\ \infty \\ \infty \\ \infty \end{bmatrix}$$

$f^{(1)}$ is computed with the help of $f^{(0)}$ as follows:

$$f^{(1)}(j) = \min_{i \in \{1,2,3,4\}} \left(f^{(1-1)}(i) + \overline{w}(i, j)\right)$$

$$\begin{aligned} f^{(1)}(1) &= \min_{i \in \{1,2,3,4\}} \left(f^{(1-1)}(i) + \overline{w}(i, 1)\right) \\ &= \min\left(f^0(1) + \overline{w}(1,1), f^0(2) + \overline{w}(2,1), f^0(3) + \overline{w}(3,1), f^0(4) + \overline{w}(4,1)\right) \\ &= \min(0 + \infty, \infty - 4, \infty - 5, \infty - 5) = \infty \end{aligned}$$

$$\begin{aligned} f^{(1)}(2) &= \min_{i \in \{1,2,3,4\}} \left(f^{(1-1)}(i) + \overline{w}(i, 2)\right) \\ &= \min\left(f^0(1) + \overline{w}(1,2), f^0(2) + \overline{w}(2,2), f^0(3) + \overline{w}(3,2), f^0(4) + \overline{w}(4,2)\right) \\ &= \min(0 + 0, \infty + \infty, \infty + \infty, \infty + \infty) = 0 \end{aligned}$$

$$\begin{aligned} f^{(1)}(3) &= \min_{i \in \{1,2,3,4\}} \left(f^{(1-1)}(i) + \overline{w}(i, 3)\right) \\ &= \min\left(f^0(1) + \overline{w}(1,3), f^0(2) + \overline{w}(2,3), f^0(3) + \overline{w}(3,3), f^0(4) + \overline{w}(4,3)\right) \\ &= \min(0 + \infty, \infty + 0, \infty + \infty, \infty + \infty) = \infty \end{aligned}$$

$$f^{(1)}(4) = \min_{i \in \{1,2,3,4\}} (f^{(1-1)}(i) + \overline{w}(i,4))$$
$$= \min(f^0(1) + \overline{w}(1,4), f^0(2) + \overline{w}(2,4), f^0(3) + \overline{w}(3,4), f^0(4) + \overline{w}(4,4))$$
$$= \min(0 + \infty, \infty + \infty, \infty + 0, \infty + \infty) = \infty$$

$$f^{(1)} = \begin{bmatrix} f^1(1) \\ f^1(2) \\ f^1(3) \\ f^1(4) \end{bmatrix} = \begin{bmatrix} \infty \\ 0 \\ \infty \\ \infty \end{bmatrix}$$

$f^{2)}$ is computed with the help of $f^{1)}$ as follows:

$$f^{(2)}(1) = \min_{i \in \{1,2,3,4\}} (f^{(2-1)}(i) + \overline{w}(i,1))$$
$$= \min(f^1(1) + \overline{w}(1,1), f^1(2) + \overline{w}(2,1), f^1(3) + \overline{w}(3,1), f^1(4) + \overline{w}(4,1))$$
$$= \min(\infty + \infty, 0 - 4, \infty - 5, \infty - 5) = -4$$

$$f^{(2)}(2) = \min_{i \in \{1,2,3,4\}} (f^{(2-1)}(i) + \overline{w}(i,2))$$
$$= \min(f^1(1) + \overline{w}(1,2), f^1(2) + \overline{w}(2,2), f^1(3) + \overline{w}(3,2), f^1(4) + \overline{w}(4,2))$$
$$= \min(\infty + 0, 0 + \infty, \infty + \infty, \infty + \infty) = \infty$$

$$f^{(2)}(3) = \min_{i \in \{1,2,3,4\}} (f^{(2-1)}(i) + \overline{w}(i,3))$$
$$= \min(f^1(1) + \overline{w}(1,3), f^1(2) + \overline{w}(2,3), f^1(3) + \overline{w}(3,3), f^1(4) + \overline{w}(4,3))$$
$$= \min(\infty + \infty, 0 + 0, \infty + \infty, \infty + \infty) = 0$$

$$f^{(2)}(4) = \min_{i \in \{1,2,3,4\}} (f^{(2-1)}(i) + \overline{w}(i,4))$$
$$= \min(f^1(1) + \overline{w}(1,4), f^1(2) + \overline{w}(2,4), f^1(3) + \overline{w}(3,4), f^1(4) + \overline{w}(4,4))$$
$$= \min(\infty + \infty, 0 + \infty, \infty + 0, \infty + \infty) = \infty$$

$$f^{(2)} = \begin{bmatrix} f^2(1) \\ f^2(2) \\ f^2(3) \\ f^2(4) \end{bmatrix} = \begin{bmatrix} -4 \\ \infty \\ 0 \\ \infty \end{bmatrix}$$

$f^{(3)}$ is computed with the help of $f^{(2)}$ as follows:

$$\begin{aligned} f^{(3)}(1) &= \min_{i\in\{1,2,3,4\}} \left(f^{(3-1)}(i) + \overline{w}(i,1)\right) \\ &= \min\left(f^2(1) + \overline{w}(1,1), f^2(2) + \overline{w}(2,1), f^2(3) + \overline{w}(3,1), f^2(4) + \overline{w}(4,1)\right) \\ &= \min(-4+\infty, \infty-4, 0-5, \infty-5) = -5 \end{aligned}$$

$$\begin{aligned} f^{(3)}(2) &= \min_{i\in\{1,2,3,4\}} \left(f^{(3-1)}(i) + \overline{w}(i,2)\right) \\ &= \min\left(f^2(1) + \overline{w}(1,2), f^2(2) + \overline{w}(2,2), f^2(3) + \overline{w}(3,2), f^2(4) + \overline{w}(4,2)\right) \\ &= \min(-4+0, \infty+\infty, 0+\infty, \infty+\infty) = -4 \end{aligned}$$

$$\begin{aligned} f^{(3)}(3) &= \min_{i\in\{1,2,3,4\}} \left(f^{(3-1)}(i) + \overline{w}(i,3)\right) \\ &= \min\left(f^2(1) + \overline{w}(1,3), f^2(2) + \overline{w}(2,3), f^2(3) + \overline{w}(3,3), f^2(4) + \overline{w}(4,3)\right) \\ &= \min(-4+\infty, \infty+0, 0+\infty, \infty+\infty) = \infty \end{aligned}$$

$$\begin{aligned} f^{(3)}(4) &= \min_{i\in\{1,2,3,4\}} \left(f^{(3-1)}(i) + \overline{w}(i,4)\right) \\ &= \min\left(f^2(1) + \overline{w}(1,4), f^2(2) + \overline{w}(2,4), f^2(3) + \overline{w}(3,4), f^2(4) + \overline{w}(4,4)\right) \\ &= \min(-4+\infty, \infty+\infty, 0+0, \infty+\infty) = 0 \end{aligned}$$

$$f^{(3)} = \begin{bmatrix} f^3(1) \\ f^3(2) \\ f^3(3) \\ f^3(4) \end{bmatrix} = \begin{bmatrix} -5 \\ -4 \\ \infty \\ 0 \end{bmatrix}$$

$f^{(4)}$ is computed with the help of $f^{(3)}$ as follows:

$$\begin{aligned} f^{(4)}(1) &= \min_{i\in\{1,2,3,4\}} \left(f^{(4-1)}(i) + \overline{w}(i,1)\right) \\ &= \min\left(f^3(1) + \overline{w}(1,1), f^3(2) + \overline{w}(2,1), f^3(3) + \overline{w}(3,1), f^3(4) + \overline{w}(4,1)\right) \\ &= \min(-5+\infty, -4-4, \infty-5, 0-5) = -8 \end{aligned}$$

$$\begin{aligned} f^{(4)}(2) &= \min_{i\in\{1,2,3,4\}} \left(f^{(4-1)}(i) + \overline{w}(i,2)\right) \\ &= \min\left(f^3(1) + \overline{w}(1,2), f^3(2) + \overline{w}(2,2), f^3(3) + \overline{w}(3,2), f^3(4) + \overline{w}(4,2)\right) \\ &= \min(-5+0, -4+\infty, \infty+\infty, 0+\infty) = -5 \end{aligned}$$

$$f^{(4)}(3) = \min_{i\in\{1,2,3,4\}} (f^{(4-1)}(i) + \overline{w}(i,3))$$
$$= \min(f^3(1) + \overline{w}(1,3), f^3(2) + \overline{w}(2,3), f^3(3) + \overline{w}(3,3), f^3(4) + \overline{w}(4,3))$$
$$= \min(-5+\infty, -4+0, \infty+\infty, 0+\infty) = -4$$

$$f^{(4)}(4) = \min_{i\in\{1,2,3,4\}} (f^{(4-1)}(i) + \overline{w}(i,4))$$
$$= \min(f^3(1) + \overline{w}(1,4), f^3(2) + \overline{w}(2,4), f^3(3) + \overline{w}(3,4), f^3(4) + \overline{w}(4,4))$$
$$= \min(-5+\infty, -4+\infty, \infty+0, 0+\infty) = \infty$$

$$f^{(4)} = \begin{bmatrix} f^4(1) \\ f^4(2) \\ f^4(3) \\ f^4(4) \end{bmatrix} = \begin{bmatrix} -8 \\ -5 \\ -4 \\ \infty \end{bmatrix}$$

T_∞ is shown in Table 1 and calculated as:

$$T_\infty = -\min_{i\in\{1,2,3,---,d\}} \left(\max_{m\in\{0,1,2,---,d-1\}} \left(\frac{f^{(d)}(i) - f^{(m)}(i)}{d-m} \right) \right), \; T_\infty = -\min_{i\in\{1,2,3,4\}} \left(\max_{m\in\{0,1,2,3\}} \left(\frac{f^{(4)}(i) - f^{(m)}(i)}{4-m} \right) \right)$$

T_∞ = -min(-2, -1, -2, ∞) = 2u.t.

Example 3: Find the iteration bound of DFG shown in Figure 10 using MCM Algorithm.
Solution: As shown in Figure 10, there are two delay elements. So, matrix is 2×1 and vectors (d+1) are 3 i.e. $f(0)$, $f(1)$, $f(2)$. Node 1 is chosen as the reference node in graph $\overline{G}_d$ as shown in Figure 11(b).

Table 1. Iteration bound

No. of Delay Elements	m=0	m=1	m=2	m=3	$\max_{m\in\{0,1,2,3\}} \left(\frac{f^{(4)}(i) - f^{(m)}(i)}{4-m} \right)$
1	-2	-∞	-2	-3	-2
2	-∞	-5/3	-∞	-1	-1
3	-∞	-∞	-2	-∞	-2
4	∞	∞	∞	∞	∞

Figure 10. Iteration bound of DFG

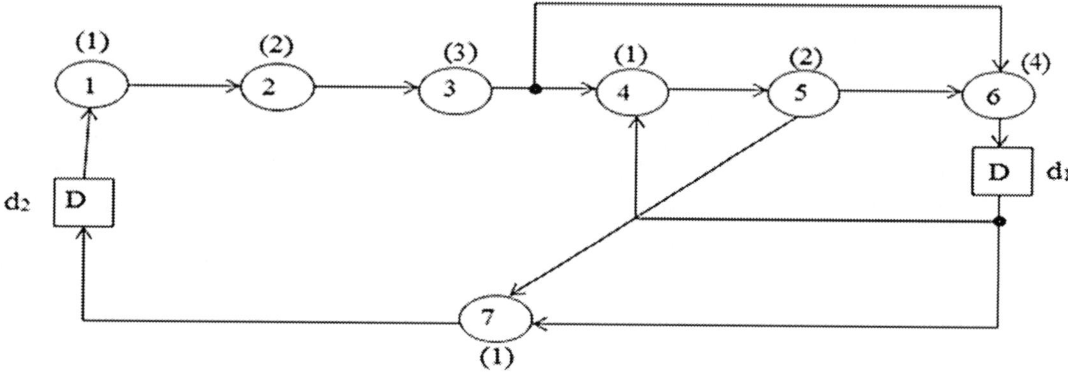

Figure 11. Graph (a) G_d and (b) $\overline{G_d}$

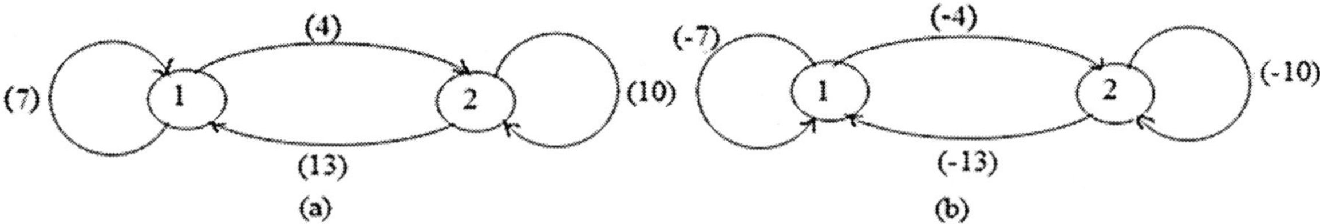

$$f^{(0)} = \begin{bmatrix} f^0(1) \\ f^0(2) \end{bmatrix} = \begin{bmatrix} 0 \\ \infty \end{bmatrix}$$

$f^{1)}$ is computed with the help of $f^{0)}$ as follows:

$$f^{(1)}(j) = \min_{i \in \{1,2\}} (f^{(1-1)}(i) + \overline{w}(i,j)),$$

$$f^{(1)}(1) = \min_{i \in \{1,2\}} (f^{(1-1)}(i) + \overline{w}(i,1))$$
$$= \min(f^0(1) + \overline{w}(1,1), f^0(2) + \overline{w}(2,1)),$$
$$= \min(0-7, \infty - 13) = -7$$

$$f^{(1)}(2) = \min_{i \in \{1,2\}} (f^{(1-1)}(i) + \overline{w}(i,2))$$
$$= \min(f^0(1) + \overline{w}(1,2), f^0(2) + \overline{w}(2,2)),$$
$$= \min(0-4, \infty - 10) = -4$$

$$f^{(1)} = \begin{bmatrix} f^1(1) \\ f^1(2) \end{bmatrix} = \begin{bmatrix} -7 \\ -4 \end{bmatrix}$$

$f^{2)}$ is computed with the help of $f^{1)}$ as follows:

$$f^{(2)}(j) = \min_{i\in\{1,2\}} (f^{(2-1)}(i) + \overline{w}(i,j)),$$

$$f^{(2)}(1) = \min_{i\in\{1,2\}} (f^{(2-1)}(i) + \overline{w}(i,1)) \qquad f^{(2)}(2) = \min_{i\in\{1,2\}} (f^{(2-1)}(i) + \overline{w}(i,2))$$

$$= \min(f^{1}(1) + \overline{w}(1,1), f^{1}(2) + \overline{w}(2,1)), \qquad = \min(f^{1}(1) + \overline{w}(1,2), f^{1}(2) + \overline{w}(2,2)),$$

$$= \min(-7-7, -4-13) = -17 \qquad = \min(-7-4, -4-10) = -14$$

$$f^{(2)} = \begin{bmatrix} f^{2}(1) \\ f^{2}(2) \end{bmatrix} = \begin{bmatrix} -17 \\ -14 \end{bmatrix}$$

T_∞ is shown in Table 2 and calculated as:

$$T_\infty = -\min_{i\in\{1,2,3,---,d\}} \left(\max_{m\in\{0,1,2,---,d-1\}} \left(\frac{f^{(d)}(i) - f^{(m)}(i)}{d-m} \right) \right), \; T_\infty = -\min_{i\in\{1,2\}} \left(\max_{m\in\{0,1\}} \left(\frac{f^{(2)}(i) - f^{(m)}(i)}{2-m} \right) \right)$$

T_∞ = -min(-8, 5, -10) = 10u.t.

3. ITERATION BOUND OF MULTI-RATE DFG

Multi rate DFG (MRDFG) uses lesser number of nodes and edges in comparison to Single rate DFG (SRDFG) (Chao & Wang, 1993). In SRDFG [Figure 12(a)] the node is executed once per iteration whereas the node is executed more than once in MRDFG [Figure 12(b)]. SRDFG contains 9 nodes and 26 edges as compared to 3 nodes and 4 edges in MRDFG (Chao, 1998). The iteration bound of SRDFG is same as in case of MRDFG.

O_{MN} corresponds to the number of samples produced by node M and I_{MN} is the number of samples consumed by node N. i_{MN} represents the number of delay elements (D) (Ito & Parhi, 1994-95) as shown in Figure 13.

If K_M and K_N determines the number of times node M and N executed in an iteration, then

$$K_M O_{MN} = K_N I_{MN} \tag{5}$$

Table 2. Iteration bound

No. of Delay Elements	m=0	m=1	$\max_{m\in\{0,1\}} \left(\frac{f^{(2)}(i) - f^{(m)}(i)}{2-m} \right)$
1	-8.5	-10	-8.5
2	-∞	-10	-10

Figure 12. (a) Single rate DFG (b) Multi rate DFG

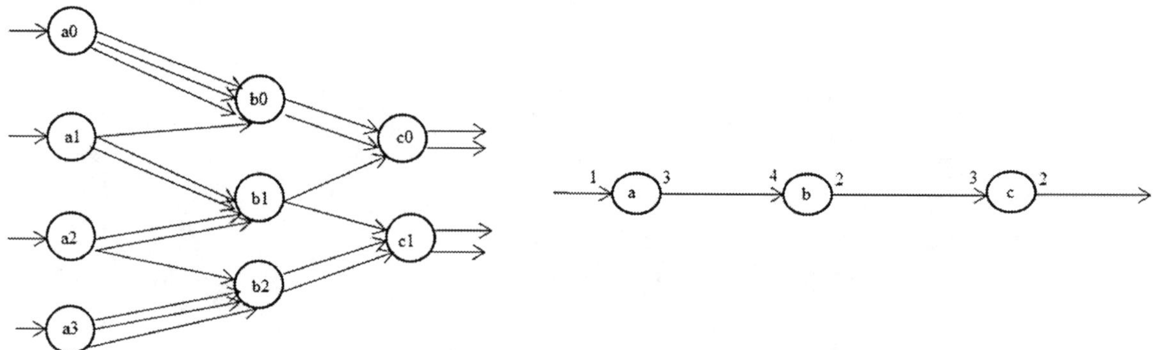

Figure 13. An edge M→N in multi-rate DFG

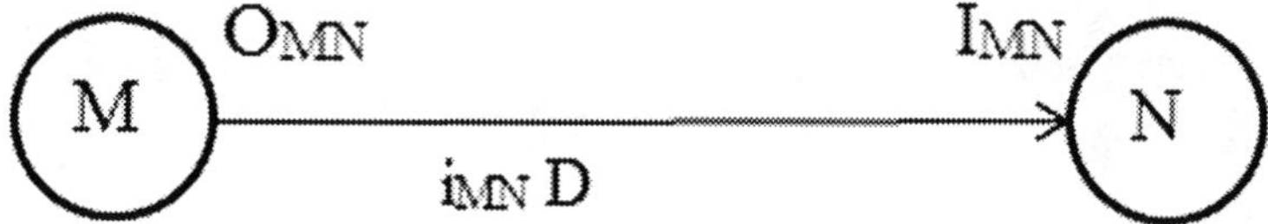

The following steps are required to convert SRDFG from MRDFG:

1. For each edge $M \xrightarrow{i_{MN}} N$ in MRDFG, and for j=0 to $O_{MN}K_M$ - 1
2. Draw an edge $M^{j/O_{MN}} \rightarrow N^{\left(\left(j+i_{MN}\right)/I_{MN}\right)\%K_N}$ in SRDFG with $(j+i_{MN})/(I_{MN}K_N)$ delays, where % and / is the remainder and quotient respectively.

Example 4: Calculate the iteration bound for Multi-rate DFG Shown in Figure 14.
Solution: Using equation (5), we get the following equations for MRDFG (shown in Figure 14)

$4K_A=3K_B$, $K_B = 2K_C$, $3K_C = 2K_A$, $K_C=K_C$

To determine how many times each node must be executed in iteration:

Figure 14. Multi-rate DFG

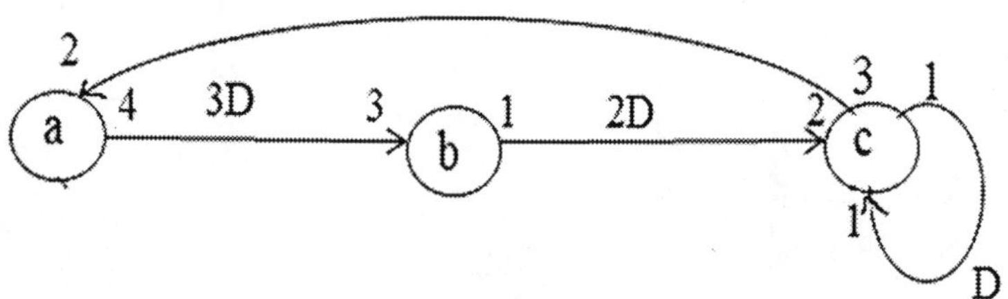

Put $K_C=K,\ K_A = \frac{3K}{2}$, $K_B=2K$

The solution is $K_A=3$, $K_B=4$, $K_C=2$.

There are three nodes and four edges. So for each edge, following steps are required to convert SRDFG from MRDFG.

(a) From state a to b

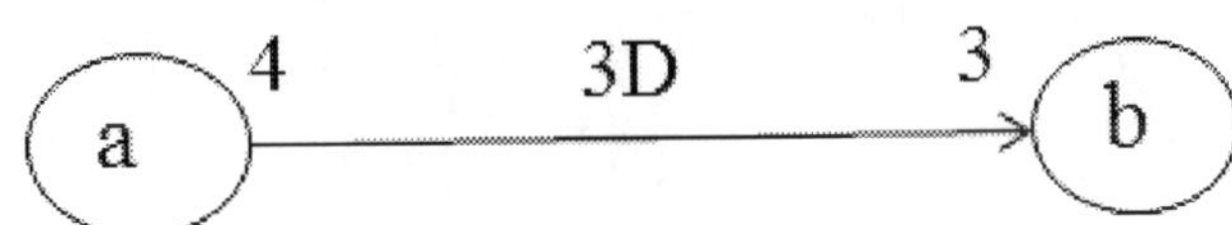

$K_A=3$, $K_B=4$, $O_{AB}=4$, $I_{AB}=3$, $i_{AB}=3$

$j=0$ to $O_{AB}K_A-1$, $j=0$ to 11

Edge from $A^0 \rightarrow B^{\left(\left(0+3\right)/3\right)\%4}$ $\Rightarrow A^0 \rightarrow B^1$
Delay = $(j+i_{AB})/(I_{AB}K_B) = (9+3)/(3\times4) = 1$

Therefore, no delays exist before 9.

(b) From state b to c

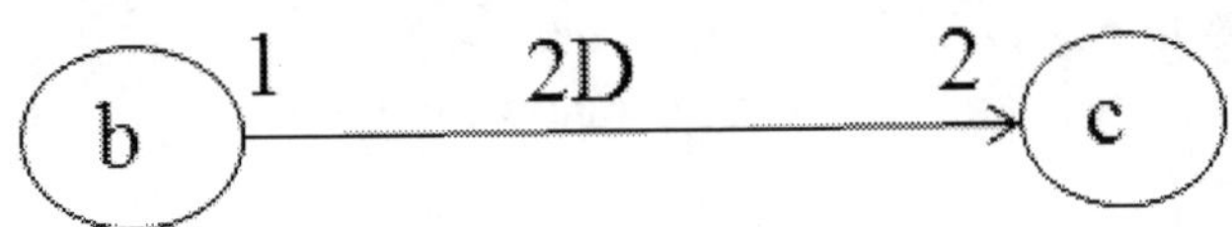

$K_A=4$, $K_B=2$, $O_{AB}=1$, $I_{AB}=2$, $i_{AB}=2$

$j=0$ to $O_{AB}K_A-1$, $j=0$ to 3

Edge from $B^0 \rightarrow C^{\left(\left(0+2\right)/2\right)\%2}$ $\Rightarrow B^0 \rightarrow C^1$
Delay = $(j+i_{AB})/(I_{AB}K_B) = (2+2)/(2\times2) = 1$

Therefore, no delays exist before 2.

(c) From state c to a

K_A=2, K_B=3, O_{AB}=3, I_{AB}=2, i_{AB}=0

j=0 to $O_{AB}K_A$-1, j=0 to5

Edge from $C^0 \rightarrow A^{\left(\left(0+0\right)/2\right)\%3}$ =>$C^0 \rightarrow A^0$
Delay = $(j+i_{AB})/(I_{AB}K_B)$ = (6+0)/(2×3) = 1

Therefore, no delays exist before 6.
Single-rate DFG obtained from Multi-rate DFG is given in Figure 15.

Example 5: Calculate the iteration bound for Multi-rate DFG Shown in Figure 16.
Solution: Using equation (5), we get the following equations for MRDFG (shown in Figure 16)

K_A=2K_B, 2K_B=K_A

To determine how many times each node must be executed in iteration: The solution is $K_A = 2$, $K_B = 1$.

Figure 15. SRDFG from MRDFG (Shown in Figure 14)

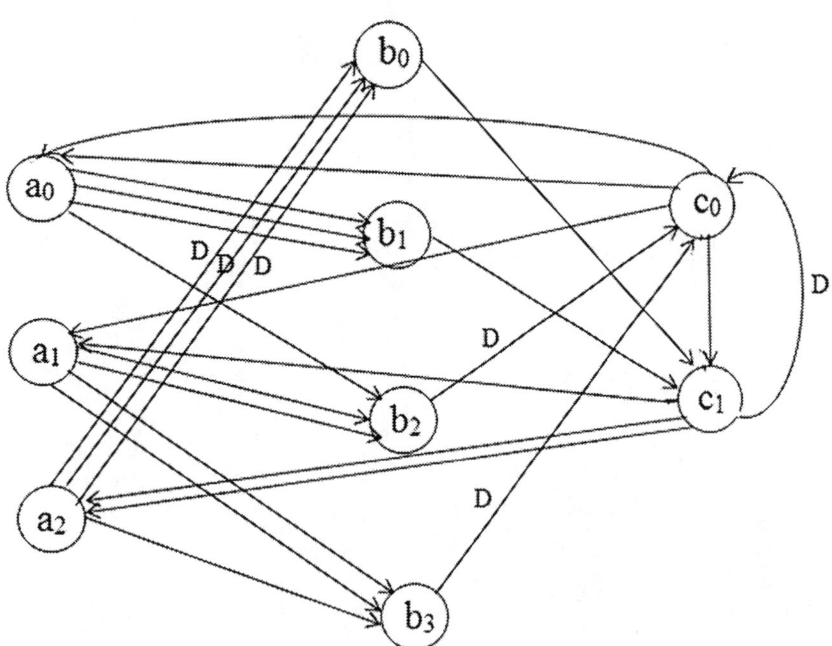

Figure 16. Multi-rate DFG

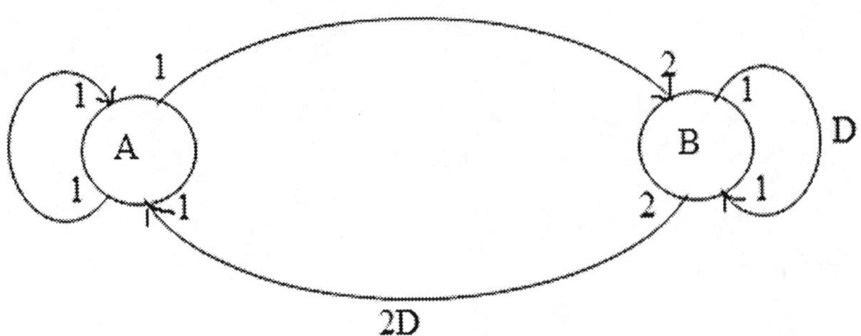

There are two nodes and four edges. So for each edge, following steps are required to convert SRDFG from MRDFG.

(a) From state a to b

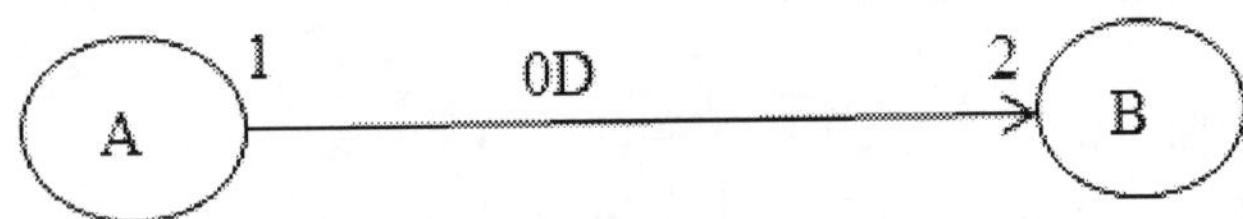

$K_A=2$, $K_B=1$, $O_{AB}=1$, $I_{AB}=2$, $i_{AB}=0$

$j=0$ to $O_{AB}K_A-1$, $j=0$ to 1

Edge from $A^0 \to B^0$
Delay $= (j+i_{AB})/(I_{AB}K_B) = 0$

Therefore, no delays exist.

(b) From state b to a

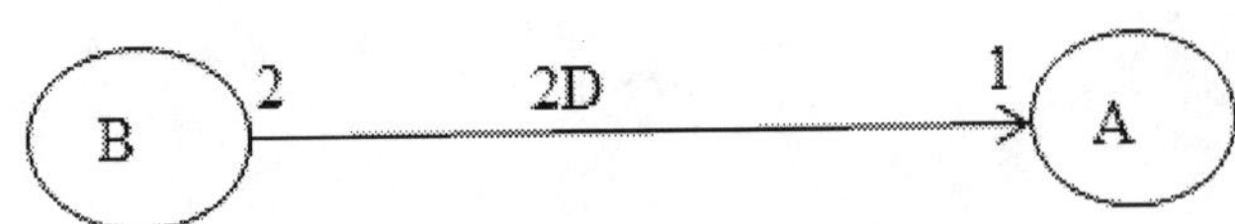

$K_A=1$, $K_B=2$, $O_{AB}=2$, $I_{AB}=1$, $i_{AB}=2$

$j=0$ to $O_{AB}K_A-1$, $j=0$ to 1

Edge from $B^0 \to A^{\left|{(0+2)}/{1}\right|\%2}$ $\Rightarrow B^0 \to A^0$
Delay $= (j+i_{AB})/(I_{AB}K_B) = (0+2)/(1\times2) = 1$

Therefore, no delays exist before 0.
Single-rate DFG obtained from Multi-rate DFG is given in Figure 17

4. SUMMARY

Many DSP algorithms are recursive in nature and represented by DFG's. In these, the maximum sampling frequency is dependent on the topology of the DFG. Iteration bound is the reciprocal of the maximum sampling frequency, which tells how fast DSP program can be implemented in hardware. Two algorithms (Longest Path Matrix and Minimum Cycle Mean) are used for computing iteration bound. The Minimum Cycle Mean algorithm is usually faster than the Longest Path Matrix algorithm. The iteration bound of Single Rate DFG is same as that of Multi Rate DFG. The Single Rate DFG contains more nodes and edges as compared to Multi Rate DFG.

Figure 17. SRDFG from MRDFG (shown in Figure 16)

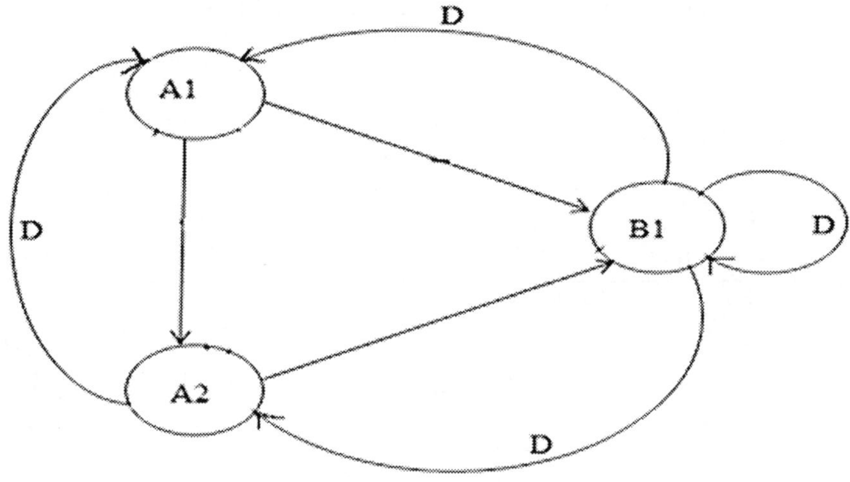

Figure 18. DFG used in Problem 1

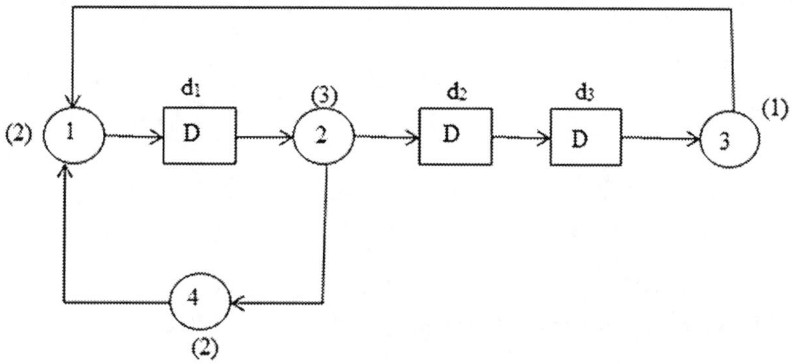

Figure 19. DFG used in Problem 2

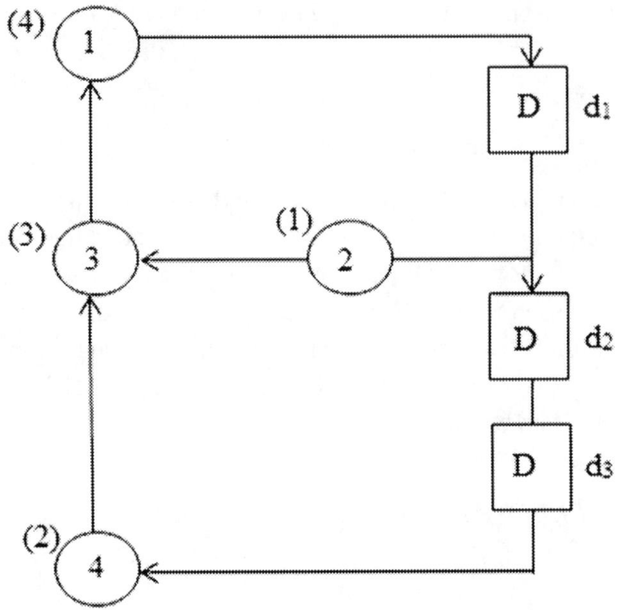

Figure 20. DFG used in Problem 3

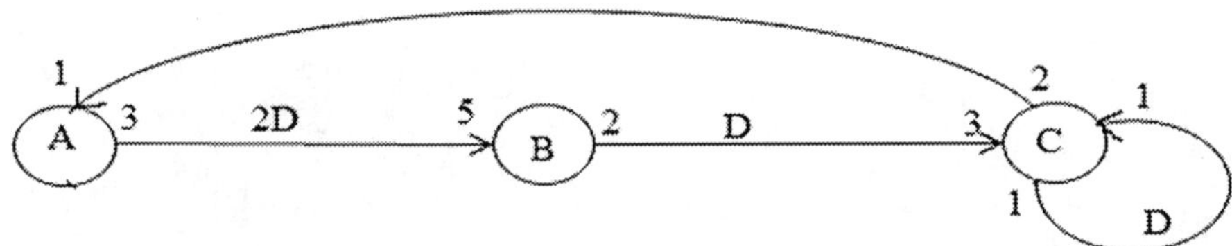

Problems

Problem 1: Find the iteration bound of DFG as shown in Figure 18 using LPM and MCM Algorithm.
Problem 2: Find iteration bound of DFG as shown in Figure 19 using LPM and MCM Algorithm.
Problem 3: Calculate the iteration bound for Multi-rate DFG as shown in Figure 20.

REFERENCES

Chao, D. Y. (1998). Conversion, Iteration Bound and X-Window Implementation for Multi –Rate Data Flow Graphs. *Proceedings of Natl. Sci. Council ROC (A)*, *22*, 362–371.

Chao, D. Y., & Wang, D. Y. (1993). Iteration Bounds of Single-Rate Data Flow Graphs for Concurrent Processing. *IEEE Transactions on Circuits System-I*, *40*(9), 629–634. doi:10.1109/81.244917

Gerez, S. H., Heemstra de Groot, S. M., & Herrmann, O. E. (1992). A Polynomial-Time Algorithm for the Computation of the Iteration-Period Bound in Recursive Data-Flow Graphs. *IEEE Transactions on Circuits System-I*, *39*(1), 49–52. doi:10.1109/81.109243

Ito, K., & Parhi, K. K. (1994). Determining the Iteration Bounds of Single-Rate and Multi-Rate Data-Flow Graphs. *Proceedings of IEEE Asia-Pacific Conference on Circuits and Systems*. doi:10.1109/APCCAS.1994.514543

Ito, K., & Parhi, K. K. (1995). Determining the Minimum Iteration Period of an Algorithm. *The Journal of VLSI Signal Processing*, *11*(3), 229–244. doi:10.1007/BF02107055

Karp, R. M. (1978). A Characterization of the Minimum Cycle Mean in a Digraph. *Discrete Mathematics*, *23*(3), 309–311. doi:10.1016/0012-365X(78)90011-0

Kumar, G. S. S., & Moorthy, H. K. (2012). Highly Efficient Design of DSP Systems Using Electronic Design Automation Tool to Find Iteration Bound. *International Journal of Advanced Networking and Applications*, *4*, 1560–1567.

Lee, E. A., & Messerschmitt, D. G. (1987). Static scheduling of Synchronous Data-flow Programs for Digital Signal Processing. *IEEE Transactions on Computers*, *36*(1), 24–35. doi:10.1109/TC.1987.5009446

Lee, Y. K., Chan, H., & Verbauwhede, I. (2007). Iteration Bound Analysis and Throughput Optimum Architecture of SHA-256 (384,512) for Hardware Implementations. *8th International Conference on Information Security Applications*, *4867*, 102-114. doi:10.1007/978-3-540-77535-5_8

Living, J., & Al-Hashimi, B. M. (2012). Mixed arithmetic architecture: a solution to the iteration bound for resources FPGA and CPLD recursive digital filters. *IEEE International Symposium on Circuits and Systems*, *1*, 478-481.

Parhi, K., & Messerschmitt, D. G. (1987). Look-ahead computation: Improving iteration bound in linear recursions. *IEEE International Conference on Acoustics, Speech and signal processing*, *12*, 1855-1858. doi:10.1109/ICASSP.1987.1169698

Shatnawi, A. (2007). Computing the Loop Bound in Iterative Data Flow Graphs Using Natural Token Flow. *International Journal of Computer Information Science and Engineering*, *1*, 819–824.

KEY TERMS AND DEFINITIONS

Algorithm: It is a step-by-step procedure for calculations.

Delay: It specifies how long it takes to travel across the network from one node to another.

Digital Filter: It is a system that performs mathematical operations on a sampled, discrete-time signal to reduce or enhance certain aspects of that signal.

Execution: It is the process by which a computer performs the instructions of a computer program.

Inherent: Existing in something as a permanent and inseparable element.

Iteration: It is the act of repeating a process with the aim of approaching a desired goal, target or result.

Recursive: It is the process of repeating items in a self-similar way.

Chapter 10
Application of Big Data in Economic Policy

Brojo Kishore Mishra
C.V. Raman College of Engineering, India

Abhaya Kumar Sahoo
C.V. Raman College of Engineering, India

ABSTRACT

Now-a-days main factor of any information in different fields is data. Different database like relational, object-oriented database is very different from traditional database in case of data retrieval, data management and data updation. So, Data mining is a process of extracting hidden knowledge or useful pattern from huge amount of data in case of efficient databases. As amount of data increases day by day, so it is very difficult to manage related data to different fields. Big data analysis takes a major role for accessing, managing and manipulating of both structured and unstructured data. It is possible to transform business, government and other aspects of the economy by big data. In this chapter, we discuss how big data analytics can be applied in economic policy of government and private sector for making better decision. Here we can use map-reduce programming model provided by Hadoop for analysis of big data in economic policy management.

1.1 INTRODUCTION

In every moment data is generated from different sources like social networking sites, search and retrieval engines, media sharing sites, stock trading sites and news sources etc. Now-a-days all people use face book in every time. So large amount of data is generated from this type of social networking site[3]. Like Face book, Twitter, Google, YouTube are producing large amount of data in every day. If we consider different sources of collection of data related to human like hospital monitoring system, climate system and insurance policy system etc, then management of data is very necessary for these different systems. In old days, traditional database system was used for data storage, data manipulation and data retrieval. To solve problems of traditional database, different databases like relational, object-oriented, network, object-relational came to the market.

DOI: 10.4018/978-1-4666-8737-0.ch010

The traditional method of managing structured data includes a relational database and schema to manage the storage and retrieval of the dataset. For managing large datasets in a structured fashion, the primary approaches are data warehouses and data marts[7].

A data warehouse is a relational database system used for storing, analyzing, and reporting functions. The data mart is the layer used to access the data warehouse. A data warehouse focuses on data storage. The main source of the data is cleaned, transformed, catalogued, and made available for data mining and online analytical functions[7]. The data warehouse and marts are Relational databases systems. The two main approaches to storing data in a data warehouse are dimensional and normalization of data.

There are several challenges that the enterprises are faced today owing to the limitations posed by relational databases. Some of these are: a) unstructured data that could provide a real-time business decision support remains unused as they cannot be stored, processed or analyzed. b) Several data islands are created and it becomes difficult to generate meaningful information from those. c) Data models are non-scalable and data becomes unmanageable. D) The cost of managing the data increases exponentially with the growth of data [1].

Data mining consists of five major elements [9]:

- Extract, transform, and load transaction data onto the data warehouse system.
- Store and manage the data in a multidimensional database system.
- Provide data access to business analysts and information technology professionals.
- Analyze the data by application software.
- Present the data in a useful format, such as a graph or table.

As now-a-days amount of data is increased, so it is very difficult to manage data in large data producing sources. Big data analytics takes a major role in handling huge amount of data. Now India is currently one of the world's most attractive investment destinations. With the opening up of foreign direct investment (FDI) in several sectors, the country is an eye-catching destination for overseas investors[10]. The relaxation of norms by the government has also created a vast opportunity for foreign players, who are competing for a greater role in the Indian market. Sectors projected to do well in the coming years include automotive, technology, life sciences and consumer products. So we can use big data concepts in economic policy related to government and private sector for making strong decisions. This chapter includes different sections. Section 2 explains details about big data and its working principle. Section 3 provides idea about economic policy. Section 4 explains how big data technique can be applied in economic policy.

1.2 BACKGROUND

A. Evolution of Big Data

A.1 Traditional Data Management System

Traditional data management system contains structured and unstructured data depending on various data models.

Figure 1. Traditional Data Management

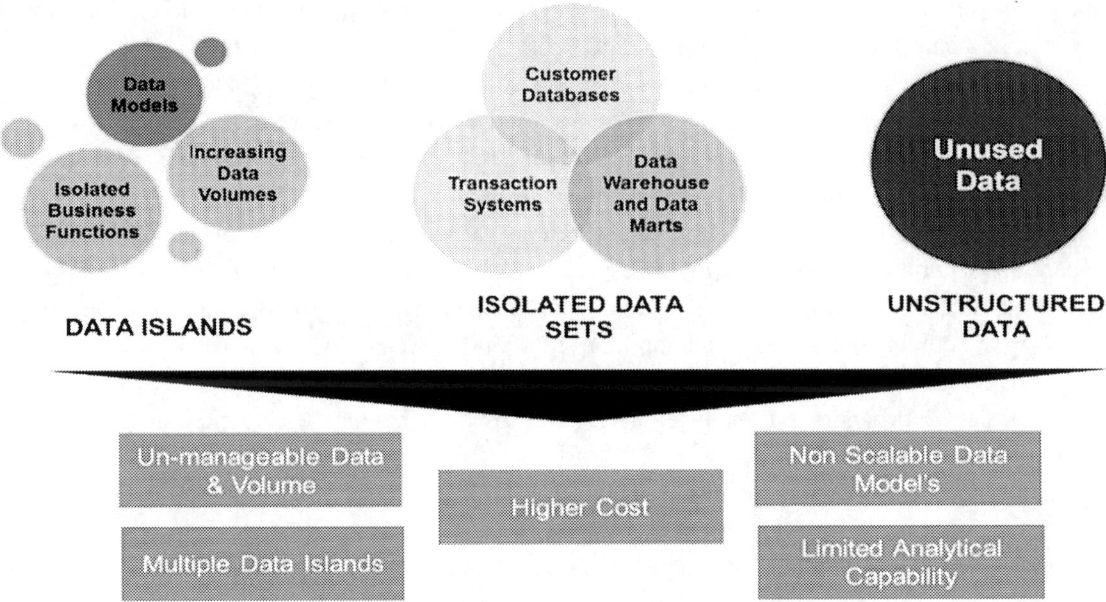

B. Introduction to Big Data

Big Data is a notion covering several aspects by one term, ranging from a technology base to a set of economic models. "Big Data" is a term encompassing the use of techniques to capture, process, analyze and visualize potentially large datasets in a reasonable timeframe not accessible to standard IT technologies[1]. By extension, the platform, tools and software used for this purpose are collectively called "Big Data technologies".

Big Data is not a new concept, but it can be seen as a moving target linked to a technology context. The new aspect of Big Data lies within the economic cost of storing and processing different datasets like the unit cost of storage has decreased by many orders of magnitude, amplified by the Cloud business model, significantly lowering the upfront IT investment costs for all businesses. As a consequence, the "Big Data concerns" have moved from big businesses and state research centers, to a mainstream status.

To analyze different types of data efficiently, big data concept came to the market. Big data is where the data volume, acquisition velocity, or data representation limits the ability to perform effective analysis using traditional relational approaches or requires the use of significant horizontal scaling for efficient Processing.

Big Data is a catch phrase that describes aspects of the data itself. IBM, a major player in this field, has four descriptors that are used to determine if data are classified as Big Data [2].

- **Volume:** The sheer size of the data set is enormous, making traditional data processing methods impossible.
- **Variety:** The data can be represented in a wide range of types, structured or unstructured, including text, sensor, streaming audio or video, or user-click streams, to name a few.

- **Velocity:** Many data need to be processed and analyzed in near real-time. For example, consider analyzing stock trades for a sudden move, or catching server attacks.
- **Veracity:** The resulting information for the analyses needs to be accurate and trustworthy. This is a huge problem considering the wide range of sources that data comes from. Multiply this to the enormous number of methods that continue to be introduced for data mining purposes, and you have a real challenge in earning the trust of any resulting analysis.

C. Big Data Management System

Many researchers have suggested that commercial DBMSs are not suitable for processing extremely large scale data. Classic architecture's potential bottleneck is the database server while faced with peak workloads. One database server has restriction of scalability and cost, which are two important goals of big data processing. Google seems to be more interested in small applications with light workloads whereas Azure is currently the most affordable service for medium to large services.

Most of recent cloud service providers are utilizing hybrid architecture that is capable of satisfying their actual service requirements. In this section, we mainly discuss big data architecture from three key aspects: distributed file system, non-structural and semi-structured data storage and open source cloud platform.

1. Distributed File System

Google File System (GFS)[4] is a chunk-based distributed file system that supports fault-tolerance by data partitioning and replication. As an underlying storage layer of Google's cloud computing platform, it is used to read input and store output of MapReduce[5]. Similarly, Hadoop also has a distributed file system as its data storage layer called Hadoop Distributed File System (HDFS)[6], which is an open-source counterpart of GFS. GFS and HDFS are user- level file systems that do not implement POSIX semantics and heavily optimized for the case of large files (measured in gigabytes)[7]. Amazon Simple Storage Service (S3)[8] is an online public storage web service offered by Amazon Web Services. This

Figure 2. Four V's of Big Data

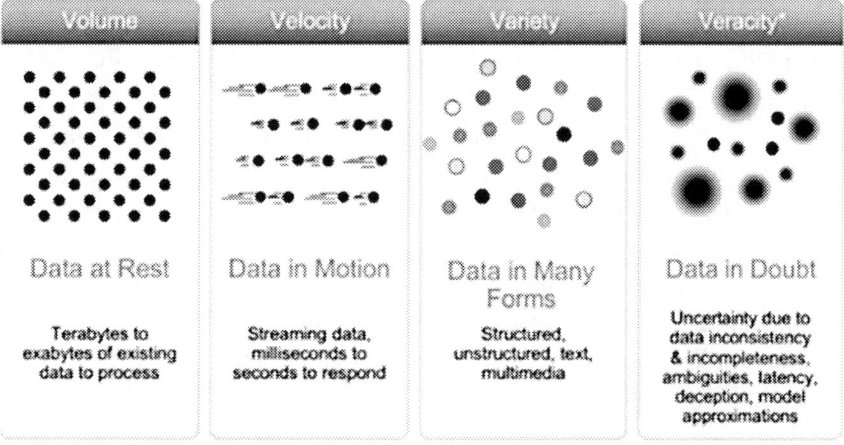

file system is targeted at clusters hosted on the Amazon Elastic Compute Cloud server-on-demand infrastructure. S3 aims to provide scalability, high availability, and low latency at commodity costs. The system provides efficient data loading from different sources, flexible data partitioning scheme, index and parallel sequential scan.

2. Non-Structural and Semi-Structured Data Storage

With the success of the Web 2.0, more and more IT companies have increasing needs to store and analyze the ever growing data, such as search logs, crawled web content, and click streams, usually in the range of petabytes, collected from a variety of web services. However, web data sets are usually non-relational or less structured and processing such semi-structured data sets at scale poses another challenge. Moreover, simple distributed file systems mentioned above cannot satisfy service providers like Google, Yahoo!, Microsoft and Amazon. All providers have their purpose to serve potential users and own their relevant state-of-the-art of big data management systems in the cloud environments. Bigtable[10] is a distributed storage system of Google for managing structured data that is designed to scale to a very large size (petabytes of data) across thousands of commodity servers. Big table does not support a full relational data model. However, it provides clients with a simple data model that supports dynamic control over data layout and format. PNUTS[11] is a massive-scale hosted database system designed to support Yahoo!'s web applications. The main focus of the system is on data serving for web applications, rather than complex queries.

Upon PNUTS, new applications can be built very easily and the overhead of creating and maintaining these applications is nothing much. The Dynamo[12] is a highly available and scalable distributed key/value based data store built for supporting internal Amazon's applications. It provides a simple primary-key only interface to meet the requirements of these applications. However, it differs from key-value storage system. Facebook proposed the design of a new cluster-based data warehouse system, Llama[13], a hybrid data management system which combines the features of row-wise and column-wise database systems. They also describe a new column-wise file format for Hadoop called CFile, which provides better performance than other file formats in data analysis .

3. Open Source Cloud Platform

The main idea behind data center is to leverage the virtualization technology to maximize the utilization of computing resources. Therefore, it provides the basic ingredients such as storage, CPUs, and network bandwidth as a commodity by specialized service providers at low unit cost. For reaching the goals of big data management, most of the research institutions and enterprises bring virtualization into cloud architectures. Amazon Web Services (AWS), Eucalptus, Opennebula, Cloudstack and Openstack are the most popular cloud management platforms for infrastructure as a service (IaaS). AWS9 is not free but it has huge usage in elastic platform. It is very easy to use and only pay-as-you-go. The Eucalyptus[14] works in IaaS as an open source. It uses virtual machine in controlling and managing resources. Since Eucalyptus is the earliest cloud management platform for IaaS, it signs API compatible agreement with AWS. It has a leading position in the private cloud market for the AWS ecological environment. OpenNebula[15] has integration with various environments. It can offer the richest features, flexible ways and better interoperability to build private, public or hybrid clouds.

OpenNebula is not a Service Oriented Architecture (SOA) design and has weak decoupling for computing, storage and network independent components. CloudStack10 is an open source cloud operating system which delivers public cloud computing similar to Amazon EC2 but using users' own hardware. CloudStack users can take full advantage of cloud computing to deliver higher efficiency, limitless scale and faster deployment of new services and systems to the end user. At present, CloudStack is one of the Apache open source projects. It already has mature functions. However, it needs to further strengthen the loosely coupling and component design. OpenStack11 is a collection of open source software projects aiming to build an open-source community with researchers, developers and enterprises. People in this community share a common goal to create a cloud that is simple to deploy, massively scalable and full of rich features. The architecture and components of OpenStack are straight forward and stable, so it is a good choice to provide specific applications for enterprises. In current situation, OpenStack has good community and ecological environment. However, it still have some shortcomings like incomplete functions and lack of commercial supports. Hadoop is a software framework introduced by Google for processing large datasets on certain kinds of problems on a distributed system. In the MapReduce [15] framework, a distributed file system (DFS) initially partitions data in multiple machines and data is represented as (key, value) pairs. The computation is carried out using two user defined functions: *map* and *reduce* functions. Both map and reduce functions take a key-value pair as input and may output key-value pairs. The map function defined by a user is first called in different partitions of input data in parallel. The key-value pairs output by each map function are next grouped and merged by each distinct key. Finally, a reduce function is invoked for each distinct key with the list of all values sharing the equations key. The output of each reduce function is written to a distributed file in the DFS.

1.3 WORKING PRINCIPLE OF BIG DATA ANALYTICS

Big Data Technologies

Indeed, researchers continue to develop new techniques and improve on existing ones, particularly in response to the need to analyze new combinations of data. However, all of the techniques we list here can be applied to big data and, in general, larger and more diverse datasets can be used to generate more numerous and insightful results than smaller, less diverse ones.

- **Data Fusion and Data Integration:** A set of techniques that integrate and analyze data from multiple sources in order to develop insights in ways that are more efficient and potentially more accurate than if they were developed by analyzing a single source of data. Signal processing techniques can be used to implement some types of data fusion. One example of an application is sensor data from the Internet of Things being combined to develop an integrated perspective on the performance of a complex distributed system such as an oil refinery. Data from social media, analyzed by natural language processing, can be combined with real-time sales data, in order to determine what effect a marketing campaign is having on customer sentiment and purchasing behavior.
- **Data Mining:** A set of techniques to extract patterns from large datasets by combining methods from statistics and machine learning with database management. These techniques include association rule learning, cluster analysis, classification, and regression. Applications include mining customer data to determine segments most likely to respond to an offer, mining human resources

data to identify characteristics of most successful employees, or market basket analysis to model the purchase behavior of customers. There are a growing number of technologies used to aggregate, manipulate, manage, and analyze big data. We have detailed some of the more prominent technologies but this list is not exhaustive, especially as more technologies continue to be developed to support big data techniques, some of which we have listed.

- **Big Table:** Proprietary distributed database system built on the Google File System.
- **Cassandra:** An open source (free) database management system designed to handle huge amounts of data on a distributed system. This system was originally developed at Face book and is now managed as a project of the Apache Software foundation.
- **Cloud Computing:** A computing paradigm in which highly scalable computing resources, often configured as a distributed system, are provided as a service through a network.
- **Data Mart:** Subset of a data warehouse, used to provide data to users usually through business intelligence tools.
- **Data Warehouse:** Specialized database optimized for reporting, often used for storing large amounts of structured data. Data is uploaded using ETL (extract, transform, and load) tools from operational data stores, and reports are often generated using business intelligence tools.
- **Distributed System:** Multiple computers, communicating through a network, used to solve a common computational problem. The problem is divided into multiple tasks, each of which is solved by one or more computers working in parallel. Benefits of distributed systems include higher performance at a lower cost (i.e., because a cluster of lower-end computers can be less expensive than a single higher-end computer), higher reliability (i.e., because of a lack of a single point of failure), and more scalability (i.e., because increasing the power of a distributed system can be accomplished by simply adding more nodes rather than completely replacing a central computer).

Figure 3 explains about analytical working flow of Big Data in Big Data Management System.

Figure 3. Overview of the analytics workflow for Big Data

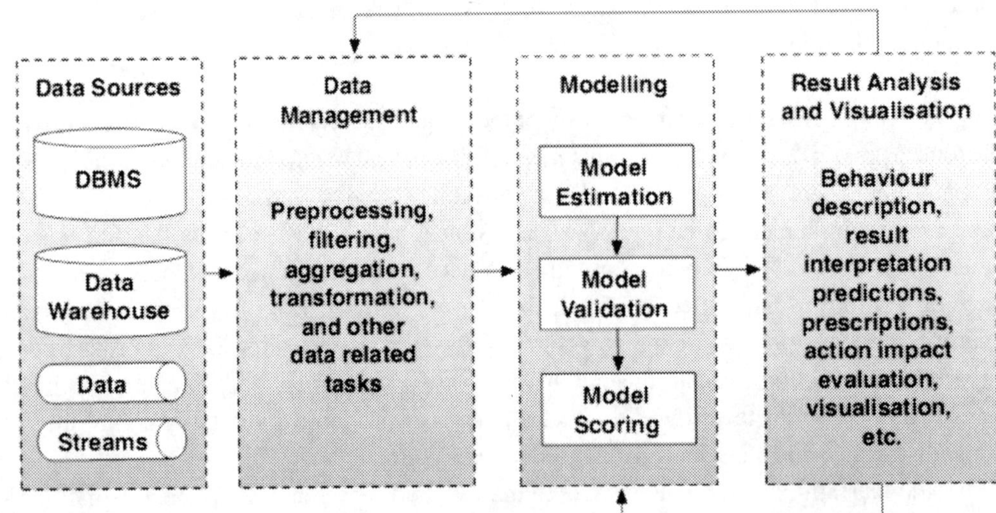

- **Extract, transform, and load (ETL):** Software tools used to extract data from outside sources, transform them to fit operational needs, and load them into a database or data warehouse.
- **Hadoop:** An open source (free) software framework for processing huge datasets on certain kinds of problems on a distributed system. Its development was inspired by Google's Map Reduce and Google File System. It was originally developed at Yahoo! and is now managed as a project of the Apache Software Foundation.
- **HBase:** An open source (free), distributed, non-relational database modeled on Google's Big Table. It was originally developed by Power set and is now managed as a project of the Apache Software foundation as part of the Hadoop.
- **Map Reduce:** A software framework introduced by Google for processing huge datasets on certain kinds of problems on a distributed system. Also implemented in Hadoop.
- **Metadata:** Data that describes the content and context of data files, e.g., means of creation, purpose, time and date of creation, and author.
- **Non-Relational Database:** A database that does not store data in tables (rows and columns) in contrast to relational database.
- **Relational Database:** A database made up of a collection of tables (relations), i.e., data is stored in rows and columns. Relational database management systems (RDBMS) store a type of structured data. SQL is the most widely used language for managing relational databases.
- **Semi-Structured Data:** Data that do not conform to fixed fields but contain tags and other markers to separate data elements. Examples of semi-structured data include XML or HTML-tagged text. Contrast with structured data and unstructured data.
- **SQL:** Originally an acronym for structured query language, SQL is a computer language designed for managing data in relational databases. This technique includes the ability to insert, query, update, and delete data, as well as manage data schema (database structures) and control access to data in the database.

Figure 4. Working Principle of Big Data Analytics

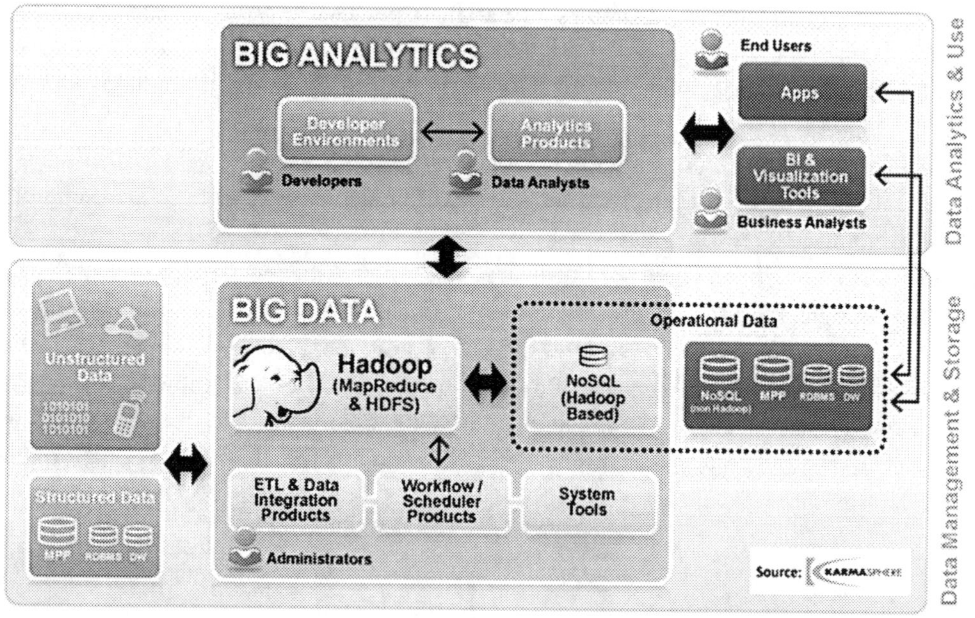

- **Structured Data:** Data that reside in fixed fields. Examples of structured data include relational databases or data in spreadsheets. Contrast with semi-structured data and unstructured data.
- **Unstructured Data:** Data that do not reside in fixed fields. Examples include free-form text (e.g., books, articles, body of e-mail messages), untagged audio, image and video data. Contrast with structured data and semi-structured data.
- **Visualization:** Technologies used for creating images, diagrams, or animations to communicate a message that are often used to synthesize the results of big data analyses.

1.4 BIG DATA APPLICATION AND ITS CHALLENGES

Most of the technology required for big-data computing is developing at a satisfactory rate due to market forces and technological evolution. For example, disk drive capacity is increasing and prices are dropping due to the ongoing progress of magnetic storage technology and the large economies of scale provided by both personal computers and large data centers. Other aspects require more focused attention, including[16]:

- **High-Speed Networking:** Although one terabyte can be stored on disk for just $100, transferring that much data requires an hour or more within a cluster and roughly a day over a typical "high-speed" Internet connection. (Curiously, the most practical method for transferring bulk data from one site to another is to ship a disk drive via Federal Express.) These bandwidth limitations increase the challenge of making efficient use of the computing and storage resources in a cluster. They also limit the ability to link geographically dispersed clusters and to transfer data between a cluster and an end user. This disparity between the amount of data that is practical to store, vs. the amount that is practical to communicate will continue to increase. We need a "Moore's Law" technology for networking, where declining costs for networking infrastructure combine with increasing bandwidth.
- **Cluster Computer Programming:** Programming large-scale, distributed computer systems is a longstanding challenge that becomes essential to process very large data sets in reasonable amounts of time. The software must distribute the data and computation across the nodes in a cluster, and detect and remediate the inevitable hardware and software errors that occur in systems of this scale. Major innovations have been made in methods to organize and program such systems, including the MapReduce programming framework introduced by Google. Much more powerful and general techniques must be developed to fully realize the power of big-data computing across multiple domains.
- **Extending the Reach of Cloud Computing:** Although Amazon is making good money with AWS, technological limitations, especially communication bandwidth, make AWS unsuitable for tasks that require extensive computation over large amounts of data. In addition, the bandwidth limitations of getting data in and out of a cloud facility incur considerable time and expense. In an ideal world, the cloud systems should be geographically dispersed to reduce their vulnerability due to earthquakes and other catastrophes. But, this requires much greater levels of interoperability and data mobility. For example, government contracts to universities do not charge overhead

for capital costs (e.g., buying a large machine) but they do for operating costs (e.g., renting from AWS). Over time, we can envision an entire ecology of cloud facilities, some providing generic computing capabilities and others targeted toward specific services or holding specialized data sets.

- **Machine Learning and Other Data Analysis Techniques:** As a scientific discipline, machine learning is still in its early stages of development. Many algorithms do not scale beyond data sets of a few million elements or cannot tolerate the statistical noise and gaps found in real-world data. Further research is required to develop algorithms that apply in real-world situations and on data sets of trillions of elements. The automated or semi-automated analysis of enormous volumes of data lies at the heart of big-data computing for all application domains.
- **Widespread Deployment:** Until recently, the main innovators in this domain have been companies with Internet-enabled businesses, such as search engines, online retailers, and social networking sites. Only now are technologists in other organizations (including universities) becoming familiar with the capabilities and tools. Although many organizations are collecting large amounts of data, only a handful are making full use of the insights that this data can provide. We expect "big-data science" – often referred to as eScience – to be pervasive, with far broader reach and impact even than previous-generation computational science.
- **Security and Privacy:** Data sets consisting of so much, possibly sensitive data, and the tools to extract and make use of this information give rise to many possibilities for unauthorized access and use. Much of our preservation of privacy in society relies on current inefficiencies. For example, people are monitored by video cameras in many locations – ATMs, convenience stores, airport security lines, and urban intersections.

We examine the current trends and characteristics of Big Data, its analysis and how these are presenting challenges in data collection, storage and management and security.

- **Collection:** One of the major problems with big data is its sheer size. The world's data is growing at an exponential rate. Cloud computing provides a solution that meets some scalability needs. The major problem with this system would be getting the data into the cloud to begin processing. Using standard Internet connections to upload the data to the cloud would be a significant bottleneck in the process. New techniques need to be investigated and developed to increase the efficiency of data movement into the cloud as well as across clouds [14].
- **Storage:** A significant problem with handling big data is the type of storage. Using a cloud approach, the traditional database is not currently suited to take advantage of the cloud's horizontal scalability. Current systems that exist handle scalability but do so at the expense of many of the advantages the relational model provides. New systems need to carefully take into account the need for these features while also providing a scalable model[13].
- **Analysis:** The major reason behind the need for handling big data is to be able to gain value from data analysis. Analytic techniques and methods need to be further researched to develop techniques that can be able to process large and growing data sets. Simplification of the analysis process of big data towards an automated approach is a major goal behind big data [14].
- **Security:** With the advent of knowledge discovery on big data there can be new information derived. There is much focus on two main problems when securing these large data systems. The first is to secure these systems such that there is a limited amount of overhead introduced so that

performance will be greatly unaffected. More research and development needs to be conducted on securing data in the new types of big data systems and throughout the data analysis pipeline. For instance, a potential attack on the MapReduce paradigm could be a malicious mapper that accesses sensitive data and modifies the result. Unlike most RDBMS, NoSQL security is largely relied on outside of the database system. Research into the types of attacks that are possible on these new systems would be beneficial[15].

1.5 MAPREDUCE PROGRAMMING MODEL USING HADOOP

Hadoop is basically a distributed file system (HDFS) which is used to store large amount of file data on a cloud of machines, handling data redundancy etc.

A. Hadoop Distributed File System (HDFS) [8]

The Hadoop Distributed File System (HDFS) is a distributed file system designed to run on commodity hardware. It has many similarities with the existing distributed file systems such as GFS whereas it also has a lot differences between other distributed file systems. HDFS is very efficient in fault-tolerant and is designed to be implemented on low cost systems or hardware. Throughput provision of HDFS for applications is very high and is suitable for such applications that have very large data sets. It uses a few POSIX requirements to enable high end streaming access to file system data. HDFS was originally built as infrastructure for the Apache Nutch web search engine project. A computation request given by an application to process data is very much efficient if it is executed near the data where it is stored or on that node, where the data resides.

The efficiency and performance of that computation increases to a very high extent when the size of the data set is huge as compared to the performance or when the data is brought to some other processing unit for the computation. This also has a number of effects on the network; it minimizes the network traffic congestion and finally increases the overall throughput of the system. Many a times it removes the bottleneck of network bandwidth for those computations which involves transfer of data. Therefore it is concluded that it is often better to move the computation closer to where the data is located rather than moving the data to where the processing place. HDFS gives a very efficient platform for applications so that they can move themselves closer to where the data is located.

On top of that distributed file system, Hadoop provides an API for processing all the stored data using Map-Reduce. The basic idea is that since the data is stored in many nodes, then it is used for processing in a distributed manner where each node can process the data stored on it rather than spend a lot of time moving it over the network.

B. Difference between RDBMS and Hadoop[7]

Unlike RDMS that you can query in real time, the map-reduce process takes time and does not produce immediate results. Now we can take difference between RDBMS and Hadoop from the following table.

Figure 5. Architecture of Hadoop Distributed File System

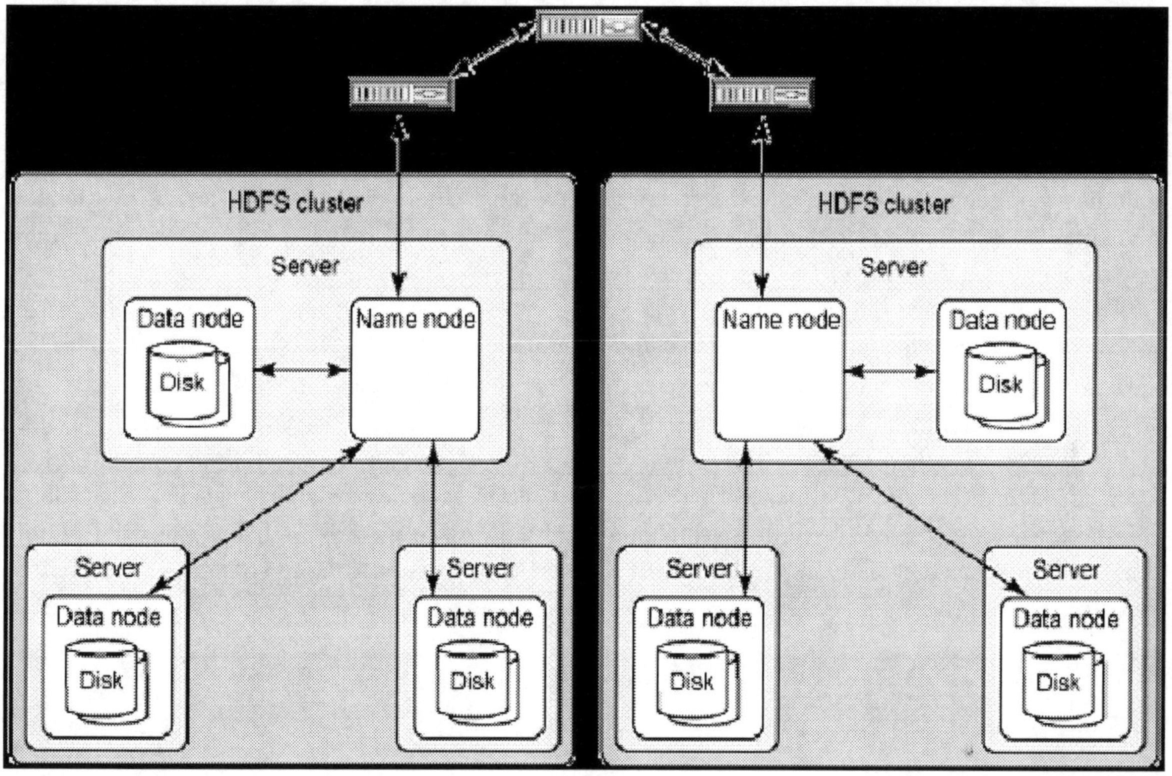

Table 1. Difference between RDBMS and HADOOP

	RDBMS	Hadoop
Description	Traditional row-column databases used for transactional systems, reporting, and archiving.	Distributed file system that stores large amount of file data on a cloud of machines, handles data redundancy etc. On top of that distributed file system, Hadoop provides an API for processing all that stored data - Map-Reduce. On top of this basic schema a Column Database, like hBase can be built.
Type of data supported	Works with structured data only	Works with structured, semi-structured, and unstructured data
Max data size	Terabytes	Hundreds of Petabytes
Limitations	Databases must slowly import data into a native representation before they can be queried, limiting their ability to handle streaming data.	Works well with streaming data
Read / write throughput limits	1000s queries/second	Millions of queries per second
Data layout	Row-oriented	Column family oriented

C. MapReduce Programming Model[8]

MapReduce is a programming model for processing large data sets with a parallel, distributed algorithm on a cluster of computers. Usually programming with map-reduce approach involves calling of two main functions i.e. a mapper and a reducer. The map function takes a key, value pair as arguments and outputs a list of intermediate values with the key. The map function is written in a specific way such that multiple map functions can run at once, so it's the part of the program that divides up tasks. The reduce function then takes the output of the map functions, and does some process on them, usually combining values, to generate the desired result in an output file.

When a map-reduce program runs through Hadoop, main job is assigned to name node or master node or job tracker. Then job tracker divides the main job into sub jobs which are run in parallel and sends to different slave nodes or task trackers. Also, the job tracker keeps track failed works, so that these tasks are again distributed to other task trackers, only causing a slight increase in execution time. In case of slower workers, any task still running once, there are no more new jobs which are left, given to machines that have already finished their tasks. Every process nodes which have small piece of large file, these files are accessed by utilizing high bandwidth of use of more hard disks in parallel. In this way, the performance of Hadoop may be able to be improved by working the I/O of nodes concurrently, providing more throughput.

Figure 6. Map Reduce Approach

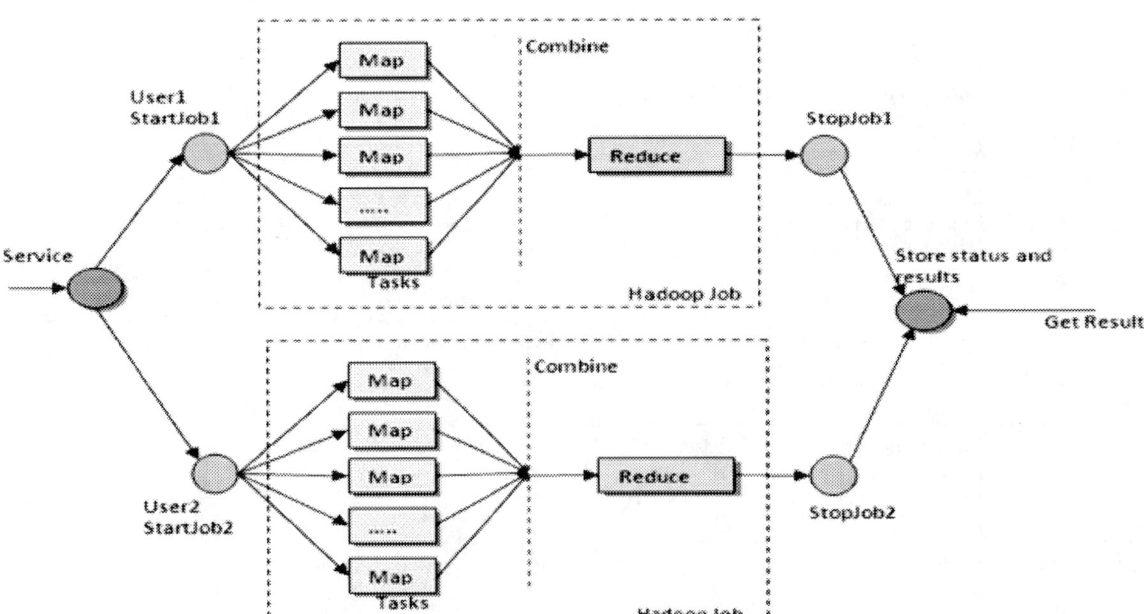

1.6 ECONOMIC POLICY IN INDIA

A. Economic Policy[12]

Economic policy refers to the actions that governments take in the economic field. It covers the systems for setting levels of taxation, government budgets, the money supply and interest rates as well as the labor market, national ownership, and many other areas of government interventions into the economy. Twenty years ago, data on economic activity were relatively scarce. Economists of our generation were trained to work with small datasets and econometric methods that may turn out to be quite different from those that current graduate students will use. Nowadays, an Internet retailer records far more than a customer's purchases: they track their search queries, the items they viewed and discarded, the recommendations or promotions they saw and the reviews they might leave subsequently. In principle, these data can be linked to other online activity, such as browsing activity, advertising exposure or social media consumption.

Improved data can also facilitate and enhance the type of empirical research that economists have been doing for decades: documenting and explaining historical patterns of economic activity and finding research designs that make it possible to trace out the causal effects of different policies. In fact, more granular and comprehensive data are likely to allow a range of clever and novel research designs: for example, by matching individuals more finely to create plausible control groups; or by taking advantage of discrete policy changes that create discontinuities in a cross-sectional or time-series dataset with many closely spaced observations. India is currently one of the world's most attractive investment destinations. With the opening up of foreign direct investment (FDI) in several sectors, the country is an eye-catching destination for overseas investors. The relaxation of norms by the government has also created a vast opportunity for foreign players, who are competing for a greater role in the Indian market. Sectors projected to do well in the coming years include automotive, technology, life sciences and consumer products.

B. Economic Policy in Government and Private Sector

On 14 August 1947, Nehru had declared: "Long years ago we made a tryst with destiny, and now the time comes when we shall redeem our pledge. The achievement we celebrate today is but a step, an opening of opportunity, to the great triumph and achievements that await us." He reminded the country that the tasks ahead included "the ending of poverty and ignorance and disease and inequality of opportunity". These were the basic foundations on which India embarked upon its path of development since gaining independence in 1947[11].

The private sector of Indian economy is the past few years have delineated significant development in terms of investment and in terms of its share in the gross domestic product. The key areas in private sector of Indian economy that have surpassed the public sector are transport, financial services etc. Indian government has considered plans to take concrete steps to bring affect poverty alleviation through the creation of more job opportunities in the private sector of Indian economy, increase in the number of financial institutions in the private sector, to provide loans for purchase of houses, equipments, education, and for infrastructural development also.

The private sector of Indian economy is recently showing its inclination to serve the society through women empowerment programs, aiding the people affected by natural calamities, extending help to the street children and so on. The government of India is being assisted by a number of agencies to identify the areas that are blocking the entry of the private sector of Indian economy in the arena of infrastructural development, like regulatory policies, legal procedures etc. The most interesting fact about the private sector of India economy is that though the overall pace of its development is comparatively slower than the public sector.

1.7 USE OF BIG DATA ANALYTICS IN ECONOMIC POLICY

The potential uses of big data for economic policy roughly parallel the uses in the private sector. In this section, we start by describing the data resources available to the government, and also how private sector data might be used to better track and forecast economic activity. We then describe how big data might be used to inform policy decisions or to improve government services, along the lines of some of the information products and services described in the prior section.

A. Making Use of Government Administrative Data[3]

Through its role in administering the tax system, social programs, and regulation, the federal government collects enormous amounts of granular administrative data. Examples include the rich micro level data sets maintained by the Social Security Administration, the Internal Revenue Service, and the Centers for Medicare and Medicaid. Although there is less uniformity, state and local governments similarly generate large amounts of administrative data, particularly in areas such as education, social insurance, and local government spending.

Government administrative data are almost certainly underutilized, both by government agencies and, because of limited and restricted access, by researchers and private data vendors who might use this data to uncover new facts. The major data sets also tend to be maintained separately, unlike in many European countries, which may have data sets that merge individual demographic, employment, and in some cases health data, for the entire population.

Administrative data is a powerful resource. It typically covers individuals or entities over time, creating a panel structure, and data quality is high. Moreover, because the coverage is "universal," administrative data sets can be linked to other, potentially more selective data.

In cases where the government has allowed access to administrative data sets, there often have been profound consequences for economic policy discussions. In many cases, this has not come from any clever research design or statistics, but simply from describing basic patterns.

B. New Measures of Private Sector Economic Activity [3]

Government agencies also play an important role in tracking and monitoring private sector economic activity. Traditionally, much of this has been done using survey methods. For example, the Bureau of Labour Statistics measures price inflation by sending surveyors out to stores to manually collect information on the posted prices and availability of approximately 80,000 appropriately selected items. These data are aggregated into various inflation indices such as the Consumer Price Index. Measures of employment, housing, consumer expenditure, and wages rely on similar survey based methodologies.

Alternative approaches to collecting large-scale, and even real- time, data on prices, employment, and spending are rapidly becoming available. It relies on data from hundreds of online retail websites in more than fifty countries. The data are used to construct price indices that can be updated in real time.

In countries such as the United States, the BPP index seems to track the CPI relatively closely. In other countries where government survey measures may be less reliable or nonexistent, the automatically gathered online data already may be preferable.

Similar possibilities also exist for augmenting the measurement of consumer spending and employment. MasterCard markets a product called "Spending Pulse" that provides real- time consumer spending data in different retail categories, and Visa generates periodic reports that successfully predict survey- based outcomes ahead of time. These approaches still have some disadvantages relative to government survey measures. Although the underlying data samples are large, they are essentially "convenience samples" and may not be entirely representative. They depend on who has a Visa or MasterCard and decides to use it, or on which firms are using ADP to manage their payroll records. On the other hand, the data are available at high frequency and granularity, and their representativeness could be assessed empirically. Plus, it is worth pointing out that many representative surveys are not immune to similar concerns due to selective responses and heterogeneous response quality.

Another intriguing idea is to use indirect measures such as search queries or social media posts to provide contemporaneous forecasts of economic statistics.

C. Improving Government Operations and Services [4]

One of the big changes in modern business is that debates and decisions are routinely informed by large amounts of data analytics, and in at least some companies, by extensive experimentation (Varian 2010). Many government agencies are increasingly smart about using data analytics to improve their operations and services. However, most agencies almost surely lag behind the best private sector firms, and face challenges of both infrastructure and personnel needs. In some cases, the government collects a great deal of data that would be useful for guiding policy decisions but has not been utilized very effectively. For example, the Center for Medicare and Medicaid Services has a record of every Medicare health claim over the last few decades, and eventually will have enormous amounts of clinical information from electronic health records. It also is routinely criticized for spending money ineffectively. The data it collects almost certainly would allow for detailed cost benefit analyses of different treatments and procedures, but it is proscribed from using this data intensive approach by Congress.

One opportunity that some government agencies seem to be exploring is to make data sets accessible and hope that researchers or other individuals will utilize these data sets in ways that end up improving agency functions. The repository includes geolocation data on schools, subways, Wi-Fi hotspots, information on metropolitan transit and electricity consumption, crime statistics, and hundreds of other types of data. One goal appears to be to encourage not just researchers but software developers to develop tools or applications that would be built on the underlying data, although it does not appear that many have been built so far.

D. Information Products or Services [4]

The most exciting private sector application of big data that we discussed above was using predictive modeling to automate business processes, or to improve or develop new products or services. While some government agencies probably are engaging in this type of activity, we are not aware of very many salient examples. However, it is easy to think of many examples where government data sets might be used to create the types of information products that are commonly seen in the private sector.

One area of government activity where we could imagine such products is consumer protection. The key challenge in consumer protection is to keep individuals from making decisions they will (predictably) come to regret without proscribing individual choice. Behavioral economics has emphasized that one way to strike this balance is through the framing of decisions (e.g., well- chosen defaults), and another way is through the careful presentation of information. For instance, people can end up making major financial decisions buying a house, saving for retirement, planning health care spending without good information about the financial consequences. The types of predictive models discussed above are particularly good for creating personalized summary information. How many consumers who take this type of loan with this type of financial situation ultimately default? What is the range of fees paid by a similar consumer for a particular financial product or service? What is the eventual cost for patients who choose this line of medical treatment? While the government might not be the right entity to create these tools, the information it collects surely would be a useful input.

A far more controversial idea would be to use predictive modeling to improve the targeting of government services. For instance, it is possible to imagine a utilitarian argument that Medicare should score individuals based on their likely response to a treatment and cover the treatment only if the score exceeded a particular level. Similarly, a tax rebate program that aimed to provide economic "stimulus" might be most effective if it were targeted specifically to those households who were predicted to have a particularly high marginal propensity to consume.

These examples are useful because they correspond roughly to the sorts of things that private sector companies are now doing all the time targeting discounts or rebates to particular consumers, or approving individuals for insurance or credit only if they meet certain scoring criteria. Of course, we tolerate this in the private sector, but many people's reaction to parallel approaches taken by the government would be horror. In this sense, it seems clear that there are constraints on the way that the government can target services that probably would rule out a range of "private sector- like" uses of predictive modeling.

1.8 MAPREDUCE PROGRAMMING MODEL FOR ANALYSIS OF ECONOMIC DATA

MapReduce allows for distributed processing of the map and reduction operations. Provided that each mapping operation is independent of the others, all maps can be performed in parallel – though in practice this is limited by the number of independent data sources and/or the number of CPUs near each source. Similarly, a set of 'reducers' can perform the reduction phase, provided that all outputs of the map operation that share the same key are presented to the same reducer at the same time, or that the reduction function is associative. While this process can often appear inefficient compared to algorithms that are more sequential, MapReduce can be applied to significantly larger datasets than "commodity" servers can handle – a large server farm can use MapReduce to sort a petabyte of data in only a few hours. The parallelism also offers some possibility of recovering from partial failure of servers or storage during the operation: if one mapper or reducer fails, the work can be rescheduled – assuming the input data is still available.

Another way to look at MapReduce is as a 5-step parallel and distributed computation[5]:

1. **Prepare the Map() input:** – the "MapReduce system" designates Map processors, assigns the input key value *K1* that each processor would work on, and provides that processor with all the input data associated with that key value.
2. **Run the user-provided Map () code:** – Map() is run exactly once for each *K1* key value, generating output organized by key values *K2*.
3. **"Shuffle" the Map output to the Reduce processors:** – the MapReduce system designates Reduce processors, assigns the *K2* key value each processor should work on, and provides that processor with all the Map-generated data associated with that key value.
4. **Run the user-provided Reduce() code:** – Reduce() is run exactly once for each *K2* key value produced by the Map step.
5. **Produce the final output:** – the MapReduce system collects all the Reduce output, and sorts it by *K2* to produce the final outcome.

These five steps can be logically thought of as running in sequence – each step starts only after the previous step is completed – although in practice they can be interleaved as long as the final result is not affected.

In many situations, the input data might already be distributed ("shared") among many different servers, in which case step 1 could sometimes be greatly simplified by assigning Map servers that would process the locally present input data. Similarly, step 3 could sometimes be sped up by assigning Reduce processors that are as close as possible to the Map-generated data they need to process.

1.9 CONCLUSION

Through Big Data analytics, many technical challenges as well as economic issues can be analyzed and solved efficiently. We must support and encourage fundamental research towards addressing current technical challenges if we achieve the promised benefits of Big Data. Big Data will change the landscape of economic policy and economic research using Hadoop. As no of economic policy to be implemented by Government, it will be easy to handle e-Governance system by use of recent advances in Big Data. Big Data analysis tools like Map Reduce over Hadoop and HDFS, promise to help organizations better understand their customers and the marketplace, hopefully leading to better business decisions, economic policy and competitive advantages.

REFERENCES

Ahuja, . (2013). *State of Big Data Analysis in the Cloud*. Network and Communication Technologies.

Bansal, . (2014). Transitioning from Relational Databases to Big Data. *International Journal of Advanced Research in Computer Science and Software Engineering*, *4*(1), 626–630.

Borkar, V. (2012). Inside Big Data Management: Ogres, Onions, or Parfaits. EDBT/ICDT 2012 Joint Conference, Berlin, Germany.

Bryant, et al. (2008). *Big-Data Computing: Creating revolutionary breakthroughs in commerce, science, and society*. Academic Press.

Bryant, R. E., Katz, R. H., & Lazowska, E. D. (2008). Big-data computing: Creating revolutionary breakthroughs in commerce, science, and society. In *Computing Research Initiatives for the 21st Century*. Computing Research Association. Retrieved from http://www.cra.org/ccc/docs/init/Big_Data.pdf

Chavan, . (2014). Opportunities and Challenges of Big Data in Economics Research and Enterprises. *International Journal of Computer Science and Mobile Computing*, *3*(4), 1155–1161.

Einav, . (2014). *The Data Revolution and Economic Analysis*. National Bureau of Economic Research.

Han, J., & Kamber, M. (2005). *Data Mining: Concepts and Techniques* (2nd ed.). Morgan Kaufmann Publishers.

McKinsey Global Institute, (2011). *Big data: The next frontier for innovation, competition, and productivity*. Author.

NESSI. (2012). *Big Data White Paper*. NESSI.

Rajan. 2012). *Top Ten Big Data Security and Privacy Challenges*. Retrieved from https://downloads.cloudsecurityalliance.org/initiatives/bdwg/Big_Data_Top_Ten_v1.pdf

Sahoo, A. K., Sahoo, K. S., & Tiwary, M. (2014). Signature based Malware detection for unstructured data in HADOOP. *IEEE International Conference on Advances in Electronics, Computers and Communications (ICAECC)*. doi:10.1109/ICAECC.2014.7002394

KEY TERMS AND DEFINITIONS

Big Data: Big data is a term that represents vast volumes of high speed, complex and variable data that require advanced procedures and technologies to enable the capture, storage, management, and analysis of the data.

Data Mining: Data mining is a process of extracting hidden pattern or knowledge from large amount of data.

Economic Policy: Economic policy refers to the actions that governments take in the economic field. It covers the systems for setting levels of taxation, government budgets, the money supply and interest rates as well as the labor market, national ownership, and many other areas of government interventions into the economy.

Hadoop: Apache Hadoop is an open-source software framework for distributed storage and distributed processing of Big Data on clusters of commodity hardware.

HDFS: The Hadoop Distributed File System (HDFS) is a distributed file system designed to run on commodity hardware. This gives a very efficient platform for applications so that they can move themselves closer to where the data is located.

MapReduce: In the MapReduce framework, a distributed file system (DFS) initially partitions data in multiple machines and data is represented as (key, value) pairs. The computation is carried out using two user defined functions: map and reduce functions. Both map and reduce functions take a key-value pair as input and may output key-value pairs.

RDBMS: Relational database management system is a database management system that is based on the relational model. Relational model represents data in the form a table. A table is a two dimensional array containing rows and columns. Each row contains data related to an entity. Each column contains the data related to a single attribute of the entity.

Chapter 11
Advanced Dimensionality Reduction Method for Big Data

Sufal Das
North-Eastern Hill University, India

Hemanta Kumar Kalita
North-Eastern Hill University, India

ABSTRACT

The growing glut of data in the worlds of science, business and government create an urgent need for consideration of big data. Big data is a term that describes large volumes of high velocity, complex and variable data that require advanced techniques and technologies to enable the capture, storage, distribution, management, and analysis of the information. Big data challenge is becoming one of the most exciting opportunities for the next years. Data mining algorithms like association rule mining perform an exhaustive search to find all rules satisfying some constraints. it is clear that it is difficult to identify the most effective rule from big data. A novel method for feature selection and extraction has been introduced for big data using genetic algorithm. Dimensionality reduction can be considered a problem of global combinatorial optimization in machine learning, which reduces the number of features, removes irrelevant, noisy and redundant data, to obtain the accuracy and saves the computation time and simplifies the result. A genetic algorithm was developed based approach utilizing a feedback linkage between feature selection and association rule using MapReduce for big data.

11.1 INTRODUCTION

Information is gathered almost everywhere in our everyday lives. Industries are generating huge amount of digital data as they go about their business and interactions with individuals. Big data is being presented through social media sites, smart phones, and other consumer devices including PCs and laptops which are being used by billons of individuals around the world.

Big data refers to very large datasets whose size is beyond the ability of typical software tools to gather, store, process, manage, and analyze (Gopalkrishnan, V., Steier, D., Lewis, H., & Guszcza, J. 2012). Big dataset needs to be in order to be considered big data i.e., we don't define big data in terms

DOI: 10.4018/978-1-4666-8737-0.ch011

of being larger than a certain number of terabytes (thousands of gigabytes) only. It is assumed that, as technology advances over time, the size of datasets that qualify as big data will also increase. Also the definition can vary by different fields, depending on what kinds of software tools are commonly available and what sizes of datasets are common in a particular company. Big data in many sectors today will range from a few dozen terabytes to multiple petabytes (thousands of terabytes).

For increasing of the amount of data in the field of medicals, management, genomics, communication, biology, environmental research and many others, it has become difficult to built, study patterns, relations within such large data.

Big data can be deliberated using the 4 V's: Volume, Velocity, Variety, and Veracity (Boyd, D., & Crawford, K. 2012).

- **Volume:** Everyday large volume of data is being collected from social media sites, smart phones, and other consumer devices. Too much volume is a storage issue, as well as too much data is also a massive analysis issue as traditional database system fails.
- **Velocity:** Velocity means both how fast data is being produced and how fast the data must be processed to meet demand. as large volume of data is being generated, it is very important to process with synchronization for a system.
- **Veracity:** Industry leaders don't want to share the information which they use to make decisions. Establishing trust in big data presents a huge challenge as the variety and number of sources grows.
- **Variety:** Translating large volumes of transactional information into decisions is a major concern while big data is considered. Now there are many types of information to analyze, mainly coming from social media and communication devices. Variety includes structured data like tabular data (databases), transactions etc. and unstructured and semi-structured data like hierarchical data, documents, e-mail, video, images, audio etc.

It would be difficult and time consuming for handling big data and we have to follow certain algorithm and method to analyze the data, find an appropriate classification among them. The standard data analysis method such as probing, clustering, factorial, analysis needs to be extended to get the information and extract new knowledge.

Feature selection is broad and spread across many fields, including document classification, data mining, object recognition, biometrics, remote sensing and computer vision. It is relevant to any job where the number of features or attributes is bigger than the number of training examples, or excessively huge to be computationally attainable. Feature selection is likewise identified with four different areas of exploration: dimensionality reduction, space partitioning, and feature extraction and decision tree. Most of the data includes irrelevant, redundant, or noisy features. Feature selection reduces the number of features, removes irrelevant, redundant, or noisy features, and brings about palpable effects on applications by speeding up a data mining algorithm, improving learning accuracy, and leading to better model comprehensibility.

Data mining algorithms like association rule mining (ARM) (Agrawal, R., Imieliński, T., & Swami, A. 1993) perform a comprehensive pursuit to discover rules satisfying some constraints. Hence, the number of discovered rules from database can be very large. Taking into account the prior works, it is clear that to identify the most effective rule is difficult. Therefore, in many applications, learning may not work well before removing the unwanted features as the size of the dataset is so large.

This chapter describes the methodology associated with genetic algorithm and association rule mining in MapReduce platform to find out features from big data that helps organizations to make better decisions.

11.2 BACKGROUND

A. Dimensionality Reduction

Dimensionality Reduction is about converting data of very high dimensionality into data of much lower dimensionality such that each of the lower dimensions conveys much more information. This is typically done while solving machine learning problems to get better features for a classification or regression task. Dimensionality reduction or dimension reduction is the process of reducing the number of random variables under consideration, and can be divided into feature selection and feature extraction. Dimensionality reduction is typically choosing a basis or mathematical representation within which can be described most but not all of the variance within data, thereby retaining the relevant information, while reducing the amount of information necessary to represent it. There are a variety of techniques for doing this including but not limited to Principal component analysis (PCA), Independent Component Analysis (ICA), and Matrix Feature Factorization. These will take existing data and reduce it to the most discriminative components. These all allow representing most of the information in your dataset with fewer, more discriminative features.

Feature selection is a term commonly used in data mining to describe the tools and techniques available for reducing inputs to a manageable size for processing and analysis. Feature selection implies not only cardinality reduction, which means imposing an arbitrary or predefined cutoff on the number of attributes that can be considered when building a model, but also the choice of attributes, meaning that either the analyst or the modeling tool actively selects or discards attributes based on their usefulness for analysis.

The ability to apply feature selection is critical for effective analysis, because datasets frequently contain far more information than is needed to build the model. For example, a dataset might contain 500 columns that describe the characteristics of customers, but if the data in some of the columns is very sparse you would gain very little benefit from adding them to the model. If you keep the unneeded columns while building the model, more CPU and memory are required during the training process, and more storage space is required for the completed model. Even if resources are not an issue, you typically want to remove unneeded columns because they might degrade the quality of discovered patterns, for the following reasons:

1. Some columns are noisy or redundant. This noise makes it more difficult to discover meaningful patterns from the data;
2. To discover quality patterns, most data mining algorithms require much larger training data set on high-dimensional data set. But the training data is very small in some data mining applications.

If only 50 of the 500 columns in the data source have information that is useful in building a model, you could just leave them out of the model, or you could use feature selection techniques to automatically discover the best features and to exclude values that are statistically insignificant. Feature selection helps solve the twin problems of having too much data that is of little value, or having too little data that is of high value.

Feature Selection is hand selecting features which are highly discriminative. This has a lot more to do with feature engineering than analysis, and requires significantly more work on the part of the data scientist. It requires an understanding of what aspects of your dataset are important in whatever predictions you're making, and which aren't. Feature extraction usually involves generating new features which are composites of existing features. Both of these techniques fall into the category of feature engineering. Generally feature engineering is important if you want to obtain the best results, as it involves creating information that may not exist in your dataset, and increasing your signal to noise ratio.

B. Association Rule Mining

Association rules are if/then statements that help uncover relationships between seemingly unrelated data in a transactional database, relational database or other information repository. Association rules are if/then statements that help uncover relationships between seemingly unrelated data in a relational database or other information repository. An example of an association rule would be "If a customer buys a dozen eggs, he is 80% likely to also purchase milk." An association rule has two parts, an antecedent (if) and a consequent (then). An antecedent is an item found in the data. A consequent is an item that is found in combination with the antecedent.

Association rules are created by analyzing data for frequent if/then patterns and using the criteria support and confidence to identify the most important relationships. Support is an indication of how frequently the items appear in the database. Confidence indicates the number of times the if/then statements have been found to be true. In data mining, association rules are useful for analyzing and predicting customer behavior. They play an important part in shopping basket data analysis, product clustering, and catalog design and store layout.

Market basket data sets are natural formats for generating association rules. However different data sets can be tailored to fit to the definition of transactional databases, so that association rules mining algorithms can be applied to them. For example text document can be seen as transaction data. Each document is a transaction and each distinctive word is an item. Mining can also be performed on relational tables. It is straightforward to convert a table data set to a transaction data set if each attributes in table takes categorical values. We simply change each value to an attribute-value pair.

Let I = $\{I_1, I_2 \ldots\ldots, I_m\}$ be a set of m distinct attributes, also called literals. A_i = r is an item, where r is a domain value is attribute, Ai in a relation, R $(A_1, \ldots, A_n)$. A is an itemset if it is a subset of I. D = $\{t_i, t_{i+1}, \ldots\ldots\ldots\ldots, t_n)$ is a set of transactions, called the transaction (tid, t-itemset). A transaction t contains an itemset A if and only if for all items $i \in A$, i is in t-itemset.

An itemset A in a transaction database D has a support, denoted as Supp(A) (we also use p(A) to stand for Supp(A)), that is the ratio of transactions in D contain A.

Supp(A) = |A(t)| / |D|, where A(t) = {t in D/t contains A}. An itemset A in a transaction database D is called a large (frequent) itemset if its support is equal to, or greater than, a threshold of minimal support (minsupp), which is given by users or experts (Agrawal, R., Imieliński, T., & Swami, A. 1993).

An association rule is an expression of the form IF A THEN C (or A -> C), $A \cap C = \varphi$, where A and C are sets of items. The meaning of this expression is that transactions of the databases, which contain A, tend to contain C.

Each association rule has two quality measurements: support and confidence, defined as:

1. The support of a rule A->C is the support of A∪C, where A∪C means both A and C occur at the same time.
2. The confidence or predictive accuracy of a rule A->C is conf (A->C) as the ratio: |(AUC)(t)| / |A(t)| or Supp(A∪C) / Supp(A). That is, support = frequencies of occurring patterns; confidence = strength of implication.

In support-confidence framework (Agrawal, R., Imieliński, T., & Swami, A. 1993), let I be the set of items in database D, A, $C \subseteq I$ be itemset, $A \cap C = \varphi$, $p(A) \neq 0$ and $p(C) \neq 0$. Minimal support (minsupp) and minimal confidence (minconf) are given by users or experts. Then A->C is a valid rule if

1. Supp(AUC) ≥ minsupp
2. Conf(A->C) ≥ minconf

Mining association rules can be broken down into the following two sub-problems:

1. Generating all itemsets that have support greater than, or equal to, the user specified minimal support. That is, generating all large itemsets.
2. Generating all the rules that have minimum confidence.

The key element that makes association rule mining practical is the minsup threshold. It is used to prune the search space and to limit the number of frequent itemsets and rules generated. However, using only a single minsup implicitly assumes that all items in the data are of the same nature and/or have similar frequencies in the database. This is often not the case in real-life applications. In many applications, some items appear very frequently in the data, while some other items rarely appear. If the frequencies of items vary a great deal, we can encounter two problems:

1. If the minsup is set too high, we will not find rules that involve infrequent items or rare items in the data.
2. In order to find rules that involve both frequent and rare items, we have to set the minsup very low.

However, this may cause combinatorial explosion and make mining impossible because those frequent items will be associated with one another in all possible ways.

C. Genetic Algorithm

Genetic Algorithm (GA) (Pitangui, C., & Zaverucha, G. 2006) was developed by Holland in 1970. This incorporates Darwinian evolutionary theory with sexual reproduction. GA is stochastic search algorithm modeled on the process of natural selection, which underlines biological evolution.

GA is a model of machine learning which derives its behavior from a metaphor of the processes of evolution in nature. This is done by the creation within a machine of a population of individuals represented by chromosomes, in essence a set of character strings that are analogous to the base-4 chromosomes that we see in our own DNA. The individuals in the population then go through a process of evolution.

GA has been successfully applied in many search, optimization, and machine learning problems. GA process in an iteration manner by generating new populations of strings from old ones. Every string is the encoded binary, real etc., version of a candidate solution. An evaluation function associates a fitness measure to every string indicating its fitness for the problem. Standard GA apply genetic operators such as selection, crossover and mutation on an initially random population in order to compute a whole generation of new strings.

Selection deals with the probabilistic survival of the fittest, in those more fit chromosomes are chosen to survive. Where fitness is a comparable measure of how well a chromosome solves the problem at hand.

Crossover takes individual chromosomes from P combines them to form new ones.

Mutation alters the new solutions so as to add stochasticity in the search for better solutions.

In general the main motivation for using GAs in the discovery of high-level prediction rules is that they perform a global search and cope better with attribute interaction than the greedy rule induction algorithms often used in data mining. This section of the paper discusses several aspects of GAs for rule discovery. This process has the advantage of progressing through the possible search space of the problem in an efficient, although somewhat random manner, and often leads to high-quality solutions in a relatively short space of time.

D. Hadoop MapReduce

Hadoop is a software framework introduced by Google for processing large datasets on certain kinds of problems on a distributed system. Hadoop MapReduce (Hadoop Map/Reduce) is a software framework for distributed processing of large data sets on compute clusters of commodity hardware. It is a subproject of the Apache Hadoop project. The framework takes care of scheduling tasks, monitoring them and re-executing any failed tasks. According to The Apache Software Foundation, the primary objective of Map/Reduce is to split the input data set into independent chunks that are processed in a completely parallel manner. The Hadoop MapReduce framework sorts the outputs of the maps, which are then input to the reduce tasks. Typically, both the input and the output of the job are stored in a file system.

Hadoop Distributed File System (HDFS) stores file in multiple equal large size block e.g. 64 MB, 128 MB etc. and MapReduce framework access and process these files in distributed environment. The MapReduce framework works on key-value pairs, it has two key parts Mapper and Reducer. Map Reducers read file and split and pass to Mapper. Mapper set the input as key-value pairs and pass to the intermediate for sorting and shuffling. Reducer takes the key and list of value, process and writes to the disk.

Job Client submit job to Job Tracker and simultaneously copy the Mapper, Reducer and config package to HDFS. Job Tracker lookup to NameNode to identify the data information. Job Tracker create execution plan and executes TaskTracker. JobTracker also coordinate the Task Tracker and keep maintain the status of TaskTracker. Task Tracker, which is placed locally to data node, identifies the available slots in the local node if it is not available in local it goes to rack or cross racks. Task Tracker report progress to Job Tracker via heartbeats. Job Tracker first allowed executing the entire Mapper task once all the mapper get complete it will start executing Reducer task. Job Tracker also reschedule the task if fails. Once TaskTracker finish it will update the status to Job Tracker. Map Reduce process keep the TaskTracker locally and it execute the job where data reside which optimize the network latency. TaskTracker split the file and pass to mapper and mapper converts it into <Key, Value> map. As per above example it uses TextInputFormat to split input file into lines. Mapper split the line into word and uses Text to store word as key and IntWritable to store 1 as count value. Mapper passes map to OutputCollector, which intern shuffle and sort the map. Combiner is optional which optimize the reducer on node level.

Mapper: A list of data elements are provided, one at a time, to a function called the mapper, which transform each element individually to an output data element.

Figure 1: Mapping of input to output

Reducer: A reducer function receives an integrator of input values from an input list. It then combines these values together, returning a single output value.

Figure 2: Reducing the input values to a single output value

Figure 1. Block Diagram of genetic Algorithm

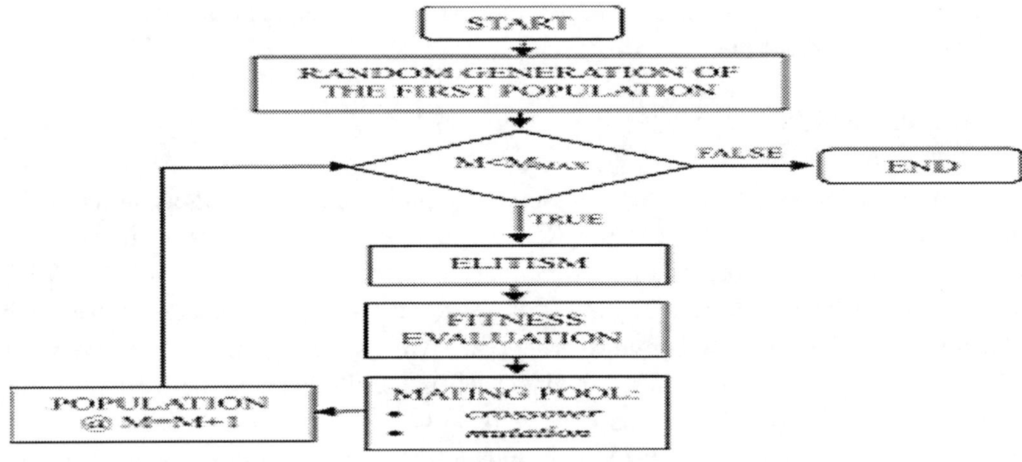

Figure 2. Example of MapReduce Process

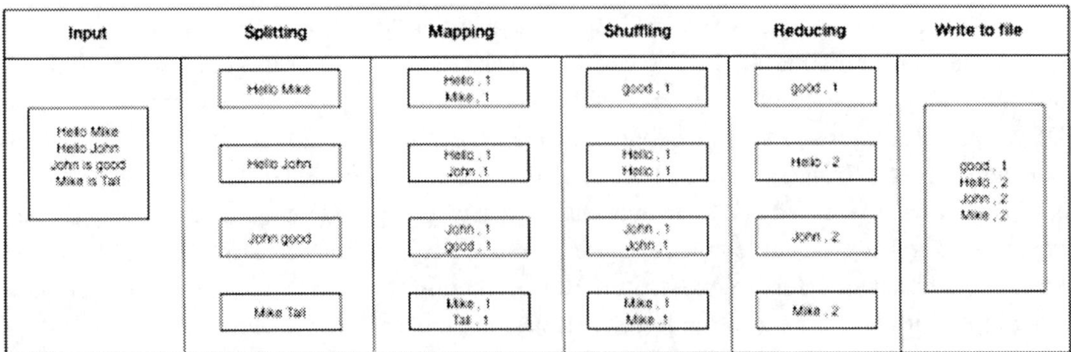

11.3 MAIN FOCUS OF THE CHAPTER

An association rule mining problem is introduced for big data with a Pareto based hereditary calculation in MapReduce platform. In the Michigan approach (Pitangui, C., & Zaverucha, G. 2006), where every chromosome speaks to a different rule. In the first Michigan approach we need to encode the antecedent and consequent parts independently; and subsequently this may be a productive route from the purpose of space usage since we need to store the void conditions as we don't know a priori which qualities will show up in which part. So we will take after another approach that is superior to this methodology from the purpose of capacity necessity. With each one attribute we relate two additional label bits. If these two bits are 00, then the attribute next to these two bits appears in the antecedent part and if it is 11, then the attribute appears in the consequent part. And the other two combinations, 01 and 10 will indicate the absence of the attribute in either of these parts. So the rule AEF->BC will look like 00A 11B 11C 01D 00E 00F.

The following step is to discover a suitable plan for encoding/decoding the association rules to/from binary chromosomes. Since the positions of attributes are fixed, we need not store the name of the attributes. We need to encode the values of different attribute in the chromosome only. Here the chromosomes are chosen (using standard selection scheme, e.g. roulette wheel selection) utilizing their fitness value.

Fitness value is calculated using confidence (accuracy) value and completeness value of a chromosome. It is very important that whatever rule will be selected for useful one this rule should represent all useful attributes or components. For that we have to select compact association rule with all useful features. So, we have to find out the frequent itemsets with maximum length. The antecedent part and consequent for an association rule should cover all useful features as well as the two parts should be frequent. The following expression can be used to quantify the completeness of an association rule

$$\text{Completeness Value} = \log\left(\left(|C| + |A|\right) / |D|\right) * \text{Supp}(A) * \text{Supp}(C)$$

Here, $|C|$ and $|A|$ are the number of attributes involved in the consequent part and the antecedent part respectively and $|D|$ is the total number of records in the dataset.

Fitness value is calculated using their ranks, which are calculated from the non-dominance property of the chromosomes. A solution, say a, is said to be dominated by another solution, say b, if and only if the solution b is better or equal with respect to all the corresponding objectives of the solution a, and b is strictly better in at least one objective. Here the solution b is called a non-dominated solution. The ranking step tries to find the non-dominated solutions, and those solutions are ranked as one. Among the rest of the chromosomes, if p_i individuals dominate a chromosome then its rank is assigned as $1 + p_i$. This process continues till all the chromosomes are ranked. Then fitness is assigned to the chromosomes such that the chromosomes having the smallest rank get the highest fitness and the chromosomes having the same rank gets the same fitness (Fonseca, C. M., & Fleming, P. J. 1993).

After assigning the fitness to the chromosomes, selection, replacement, crossover and mutation operators are applied to get a new set of chromosomes.

Then we use MapReduce framework, a distributed file system (DFS) initially partitions big data in multiple nodes and data is represented as (key, value) pairs. The computation is carried out using two user defined functions: map and reduce. Both map and reduce functions take a key-value pair as input and may output key-value pairs.

Mapper

1. Load the dataset that fits in the memory.
2. Generate N chromosomes randomly.
3. Decode them to get the values of the different attributes.
4. Scan the loaded dataset to find the support of antecedent part, consequent part and the rule.
5. Find the confidence and completeness values for each chromosome.
6. Rank the chromosomes depending on the non- dominance property.
7. Assign fitness to the chromosomes using the ranks.
8. Select the chromosomes, for next generation, by roulette wheel selection scheme.
9. Bring a copy of the chromosomes ranked as 1 into an elite population, and store them if they are non-dominated in this population also. If some of the existing chromosomes of this population become dominated, due to this insertion, then remove the dominated chromosomes from this population.
10. Select the chromosomes, for next generation, by roulette wheel selection scheme using the fitness calculated in Step 7.
11. Replace all chromosomes of the old population by the chromosomes selected in Step 10.
12. Perform multi-point crossover and mutation on these new individuals.
13. If the desired number of generations is not completed, then go to Step 3.
14. Decode chromosomes of the final elite population.
15. The output of the Mapper is a <key, value> pair, the union of antecedent and consequent parts of a rule being the key and the number of occurrences of the rule in the elite population being the value.

Reducer

1. Takes the output of all mappers from different data nodes.
2. For each union of antecedent and consequent parts of a rule, it combines all as total occurrences for the big data.

11.4 EXPERIMENTATION AND RESULT ANALYSIS

The proposed method has been implemented on distinctive data sets with palatable results. Here we have introduced the results on Musk (Version 2) Data Set having 52 attributes and 893563432 records having size 24.8 MB. Crossover and mutation probabilities were taken respectively as 0.85 and 0.02; 4 point crossover operator was utilized and the population size was kept fixed as 75. The following table shows the results with different parameters.

From the feature sets created from different nodes and for different number of generations it is observed that after 200 generations it stops to create more sets; in other words after that number of generations the GA converges (See Table 1). If the confidence of the rule is used as one measure, sometimes some rules with SUP (A) = 1, SUP(C) = 1, and SUP (AUC) = 1 may be generated. That govern will have a certainty 100%. So there is a risk that the standard may be pronounced as a non-dominated rule. However the records fulfilling that lead may be noise also. Current algorithms do not confront this issue, because the user predefined parameter called minimum support eliminates the probability of generation of such rules. Rather than the accuracy, we utilized the backing of the guideline as one measure to assess the standard subsequently beating this issue.

11.5 FUTURE RESEARCH DIRECTION

Big Data is going to continue growing during the next years, and each data scientist will have to manage much more amount of data every year. There is a great interest both in the commercial and in the research communities around big data. It has been predicted that analyzing big data will become a key basis of competition, underpinning new waves of productivity growth, innovation, and consumer surplus. Heterogeneity, scale, timeliness, security, and privacy problems with big data delay progress at all phases of the pipeline that can create value from data. Data analysis, association, retrieval, and modeling are other foundational challenges. As every sector continue to collect more data at this scale, formalizing the process of big data analysis will become vital.

11.6 CONCLUSION

Big data is going to keep developing amid the following years, and every information researcher will need to oversee a great deal more measure of information consistently. There is an incredible investment both in the business and in the research groups around enormous information. Since its introduction, association rule mining has become an important research area in data mining. It is troublesome to users or even specialists to suitably point out minimum support as a threshold. The utilization of a multi-objective evolutionary structure for association rule mining offers an enormous adaptability to endeavor in further work. In this chapter, a Pareto based genetic algorithm has been utilized to illuminate the multi-objective rule mining issue utilizing two measures - accuracy and comprehensibility. Using MapReduce platform, distributed parallel processing has been achieved for big data to find out the optimal association rules which can be as a role of dimensionality reduction method for big data.

Table 1.

Number of Data Nodes	Number of Generations	Number of Feature Sets Generated	Time (sec)
2	100	18	235
	200	27	239
	300	30	245
4	100	25	124
	200	32	129
	300	36	133
6	100	21	78
	200	29	83
	300	31	90
8	100	27	51
	200	30	57
	300	34	61

REFERENCES

Agrawal, R., Imieliński, T., & Swami, A. (1993, June). Mining association rules between sets of items in large databases. *SIGMOD Record*, *22*(2), 207–216.

Agrawal, R., & Srikant, R. (1994, September). Fast algorithms for mining association rules. In *Proc. 20th int. conf. very large data bases, VLDB* (Vol. 1215, pp. 487-499). VLDB.

Begoli, E., & Horey, J. (2012, August). Design principles for effective knowledge discovery from big data. *In Software Architecture (WICSA) and European Conference on Software Architecture (ECSA), 2012 Joint Working IEEE/IFIP Conference on* (pp. 215-218). IEEE. doi:10.1109/WICSA-ECSA.212.32

Boyd, D., & Crawford, K. (2012). Critical questions for big data: Provocations for a cultural, technological, and scholarly phenomenon. *Information Communication and Society*, *15*(5), 662–679.

Das, S., & Saha, B. (2009). Data quality mining using genetic algorithm. *International Journal of Computer Science and Security*, *3*(2), 105–112.

Devaney, M., & Ram, A. (1997, July). Efficient feature selection in conceptual clustering. In ICML (Vol. 97, pp. 92-97). ICML.

Dy, J. G., & Brodley, C. E. (2004). Feature selection for unsupervised learning. *Journal of Machine Learning Research*, *5*, 845–889.

Fan, W., & Bifet, A. (2013). Mining big data: current status, and forecast to the future. *ACM sIGKDD Explorations Newsletter, 14*(2), 1-5.

Fonseca, C. M., & Fleming, P. J. (1993, June). Genetic Algorithms for Multiobjective Optimization: FormulationDiscussion and Generalization. In ICGA (Vol. 93, pp. 416-423). ICGA.

Goebel, M., & Gruenwald, L. (1999). A survey of data mining and knowledge discovery software tools. *ACM SIGKDD Explorations Newsletter*, *1*(1), 20–33.

Gopalkrishnan, V., Steier, D., Lewis, H., & Guszcza, J. (2012, August). Big data, big business: bridging the gap. In *Proceedings of the 1st International Workshop on Big Data, Streams and Heterogeneous Source Mining: Algorithms, Systems, Programming Models and Applications* (pp. 7-11). ACM.

Han, E. H., Karypis, G., & Kumar, V. (1997). Scalable parallel data mining for association rules. ACM.

Han, J., & Fu, Y. (1995, September). Discovery of multiple-level association rules from large databases. In VLDB (Vol. 95, pp. 420-431). VLDB.

Ivanka Valova, I. C. S. R. Processing Of Large Data Sets: Evolution, Opportunities And Challenges. *Proceedings of PCaPAC08*.

Marz, N., & Warren, J. (2015). *Big Data: Principles and best practices of scalable realtime data systems*. Manning Publications Co.

Morimoto, Y., Ishii, H., & Morishita, S. (1997). Efficient construction of regression trees with range and region splitting. In *Proceedings of the 23rd VLDB Conference*.

Parker, C. (2012, August). Unexpected challenges in large scale machine learning. In *Proceedings of the 1st International Workshop on Big Data, Streams and Heterogeneous Source Mining: Algorithms, Systems, Programming Models and Applications* (pp. 1-6). ACM.

Pei, M., Goodman, E. D., & Punch, W. F. (1998, October). Feature extraction using genetic algorithms. In *Proceedings of the 1st International Symposium on Intelligent Data Engineering and Learning, IDEAL* (Vol. 98, pp. 371-384). IDEAL.

Pei, M., Goodman, E. D., & Punch, W. F. (1998, October). Feature extraction using genetic algorithms. In *Proceedings of the 1st International Symposium on Intelligent Data Engineering and Learning, IDEAL* (Vol. 98, pp. 371-384). IDEAL.

Pitangui, C., & Zaverucha, G. (2006, December). Genetic based machine learning: merging Pittsburgh and Michigan, an implicit feature selection mechanism and a new crossover operator. In *Hybrid Intelligent Systems, 2006. HIS'06. Sixth International Conference on* (pp. 58-58). IEEE.

Spitters, M. (2000). *Comparing feature sets for learning text categorization*. Academic Press.

Tenenbaum, J. B., De Silva, V., & Langford, J. C. (2000). A global geometric framework for nonlinear dimensionality reduction. *Science*, *290*(5500), 2319–2323. PMID:11125149

Vaccaro, R. J. (1991). *SVD and Signal Processing II: Algorithms, analysis and applications*. Elsevier Science Inc.

Wallis, N. (2012). Big Data in Canada: Challenging Complacency for Competitive Advantage. *IDC*.

Webb, A. R. (2003). *Statistical pattern recognition*. John Wiley & Sons.

Weng, J., Zhang, Y., & Hwang, W. S. (2003). Candid covariance-free incremental principal component analysis. *Pattern Analysis and Machine Intelligence. IEEE Transactions on*, *25*(8), 1034–1040.

Yadav, C., Wang, S., & Kumar, M. (2013). *Algorithm and approaches to handle large Data-A Survey*. arXiv preprint arXiv:1307.5437.

Yan, X., Zhang, C., & Zhang, S. (2005). ARMGA: Identifying interesting association rules with genetic algorithms. *Applied Artificial Intelligence*, *19*(7), 677–689.

Zikopoulos, P., & Eaton, C. (2011). *Understanding big data: Analytics for enterprise class hadoop and streaming data*. McGraw-Hill Osborne Media.

KEY TERMS AND DEFINITIONS

Association Rule Mining: Association rule mining, an example of data mining methods, performs a comprehensive pursuit to discover association rules satisfying some constraints.

Big Data: Big data is a term that represents vast volumes of high speed, complex and variable data that require advanced procedures and technologies to enable the capture, storage, management, and analysis of the data.

Feature Selection: The feature selection process can be considered a problem of global combinatorial optimization in machine learning, which reduces the number of features, removes irrelevant, noisy and redundant data, to obtain the accuracy and saves the computation time and simplifies the result.

Genetic Algorithm: Genetic Algorithm is a stochastic search algorithm modeled on the process of natural selection, which underlines biological evolution. It has been successfully applied in many search, optimization, and machine learning problems. It process in an iteration manner by generating new populations of strings from old ones.

MapReduce: In the MapReduce framework, a distributed file system (DFS) initially partitions data in multiple machines and data is represented as (key, value) pairs. The computation is carried out using two user defined functions: map and reduce functions. Both map and reduce functions take a key-value pair as input and may output key-value pairs.

Chapter 12
HTLS Conductors:
A Novel Aspect for Energy Conservation in Transmission System

Abhilash Netake
Dr. Babasaheb Ambedkar Technological University, India

P. K. Katti
Dr. Babasaheb Ambedkar Technological University, India

ABSTRACT

The power system has undergone multifold growth in its generation, transmission and distribution in past few decades. The types of conductors used for transmission system in India are ACSR / AAAC. These conductors have several constraints. The Ampacity of these conductors is less and hence they cannot be operated at high temperature also the losses in these type of conductors are more. To overcome the drawbacks of ACSR / AAAC conductors, this paper proposes a new approach of using High Tension Low Sag (HTLS) conductors, also a comparison is made between ACSR, AAAC and HTLS conductors on the basis of voltage drop and power loss for benefit evaluation of HTLS conductor over traditionally used conductors.

1. INTRODUCTION

The basic function of transmission system is to transfer electrical power from one location to another location. A transmission system include terminal substation, transmission line and intermediate substation associated control, protection, auxiliaries etc.

The Modern civilization depends heavily on the consumption of electrical energy for industrial, commercial, agricultural, domestic and social purpose. Electrical power is generated in large thermal hydro nuclear power station. The energy is transfer from this generating station to distant distribution network via transmission system.

DOI: 10.4018/978-1-4666-8737-0.ch012

The modern electrical power system is in form of large interconnected three phase AC network. The generating station, transmission system, and distribution system are interconnected to form three phase AC system operating synchronously at a common frequency of 50 Hz.

The electrical power system mainly aims at following:

- To supply required amount of power continuously over the entire geographical area.
- To provide maximum security of supply and minimum fault duration.
- To supply electrical power within targeted limit of frequency within a specified limit of voltage.
- To supply electrical energy economically.

Nowadays, power systems are extensively interconnected requiring the huge transfer of electric power. Considering that a typical transmission line with a certain voltage level, can only carry a limited capacity, to carry an enormous power it is required to construct extra high voltage (EHV) transmission lines.

Industrial-minded countries of the world require a vast amount of energy of which electrical energy forms a major fraction. This requires very high voltages for transmission. The very rapid strides taken by development of dc transmission since 1950 are playing a major role in extra-long-distance transmission, complementing or supplementing EHVAC transmission. They have their roles to play and a country must make intelligent assessment of both in order to decide which is best suited for the country's economy.

The demand for electricity has been increased due to vast industrialisation and also due to the increased domestic consumers. To fulfil this increased demand for electricity, the transmission network must be robust and have enough capacity to carry the maximum amount of power generated to the load area. The power handling capacity of 400 kV is falling short of and is not sufficient to fulfil the increased demand. To fulfil the increased demand for electricity and to carry the maximum power generated at the power station to load centre it has become necessary to find out the best possible solution. For this it is necessary to study drawbacks of the existing system and to go for new technologies which can fulfil the requirement.

This paper has proposed one of the technique i.e. reconductoring of the existing transmission network to overcome the problems of the existing system. The reconductoring of the system can be done with the help of HTLS (High Tension Low Sag) conductors which has been described in the paper. By using the new HTLS conductors the loss minimization throughout the transmission network can be achieved also the voltage drop can also be reduced so improvement in voltage regulation can be achieved. This paper proposes this technique for the energy conservation purpose throughout the transmission network.

2. TECHNICAL REQUIREMENT FOR DESIGN OF TRANSMISSION NETWORK

For capacity enhancement of transmission line different option available are:

A. Improvement of Transmission System

This part of the transmission network design requires various calculation to be completed for efficient transmission of power. This part is important to understand the level of safety required during the operation of the network and various clearances to be considered after selection of the voltage level for transmission.

In this paper this part of the design of the transmission system is not discussed whether, the other important part of design section is discussed thoroughly.

The important calculations required while designing a new transmission system are listed below:

1. Short circuit calculation
2. Crossection for fitting two parts together
3. Geometrical Mean Radius
4. Geometrical Mean Distance
5. No of insulators in the string
6. Voltage gradient calculation
7. Critical voltage
8. Amount of corona losses
9. Corona ring design
10. Voltage regulation calculation

B. Design and Selection of Conductor

There are various types of conductors used for the transmission of electric power. The foremost important task of the transmission system is transfer bulk amount of power from the generating station to the load centers. This transmission of the power must take place with minimum amount of losses in the transmission, by this the goal of energy conservation can be fulfilled up to a certain level.

Conductor design and selection for transmission and distribution lines has become a science. The selection of the optimum conductor type and size for a given transmission or distribution line design, requires a complete understanding of the characteristics of all the available conductor types. This understanding must encompass more than just the current carrying capability or thermal performance of a conductor. It must include a systems approach to conductor selection: line stability versus current loading; economic operation versus thermal loading; conductor creep and resultant sag under high temperature and adverse mechanical loading; conductor strength as determined by component metal stress-strain performance and metal fatigue characteristics are just a few of the system design parameters to be evaluated.

3. TYPES OF CONDUCTORS USED IN TRANSMISSION SYSTEM

There is no unique process by which all transmission and/or distribution lines are designed. It is clear, however, that all major cost components of line design depend upon the conductor's electrical and mechanical parameters.

There are various types of overhead conductors used for electrical transmission and distribution. Some of them are listed below:

A. ACSR - Aluminium Conductor Steel Reinforced
B. AAAC - All Aluminium Alloy Conductor
C. TACSR - Thermal Alloy Conductor Steel Reinforce
D. ACSS - Aluminium Conductor Steel Supported

E. STACIR - Super Thermal Alloy Conductor, Invar Reinforced
F. ACCC - Aluminium Conductor Composite Core
G. AL 59 - Alloy conductor (of Aluminium, Magnesium and Silicon)

A. ACSR (Aluminium Conductor Steel Reinforced)

Aluminium Conductor Steel Reinforced, a standard of the electrical utility industry since the early 1900's, consists of a solid or stranded steel core surrounded by one or more layers of strands of 1350 aluminium (See Fig. 1). Historically, the amount of steel used to obtain higher strength soon increased to a substantial portion of the cross-section of the ACSR, but more recently, as conductors have become larger, the trend has been to less steel content. To meet varying requirements, ACSR is available in a wide range of steel content - from 7% by weight for the 36/1 stranding to 40% for the 30/7 stranding. Early designs of ACSR such as 6/1, 30/7, 30/19, 54/19 and 54/7 stranding featured high steel content, 26% to 40%, with emphasis on strength perhaps due to fears of vibration fatigue problems.

B. "AAAC" (All Aluminium Alloy Conductor)

A high strength Aluminium-Magnesium-Silicon Alloy Cable was developed to replace the high strength 6/1 ACSR conductors. Originally called AAAC, this alloy conductor offers excellent electrical characteristics with a conductivity of 52.5% IACS, excellent sag-tension characteristics and superior corrosion resistance to that of ACSR. The temper of 6201 is normally T81.

6201 Aluminium alloy conductors are typically sold as O.D. equivalents for 6/1 and 26/7 ACSR constructions. The O.D. equivalent 6201 conductors have approximately the same amplicity and strength as their ACSR counterparts with a much improved strength-to-weight ratio. 6201 conductors also exhibit substantially better electrical loss characteristics than their equivalent single layer ACSR constructions. However, the thermal coefficient of expansion is greater than that of ACSR. As with AAC conductors, the maximum short circuit temperature of 6201 must be kept below 340°C to prevent dangerous conductor annealing.

Figure 1. ACSR Conductor

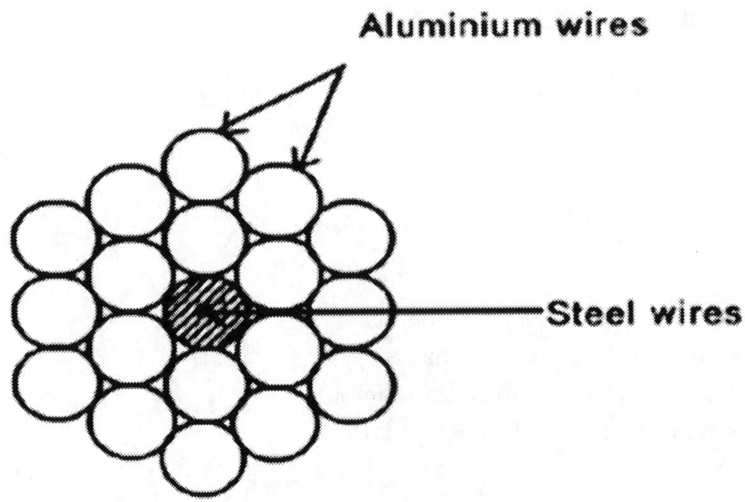

As compared to ACSR, AAAC's lighter weight, comparable strength and current carrying capacity, lower electrical losses and superior corrosion resistance have given this conductor wide acceptance as a distribution conductor. It has found limited use, however, as a transmission conductor. (See Fig. 2)

C. TACSR (Thermal Alloy Conductor Steel Reinforce)

TACSR conductors are the conductors wherein the inner core is composed of galvanised steel and outer layers are composed of thermal – resistant aluminium alloy (See Fig. 3).

Benefits

- Ampacity is almost 50% more- Higher Power Transfer Capacity.
- Higher capacities line built can cater to future increased demand of power.
- Can be used with existing tower designs.
- Can be used up to 150 °C.

D. ACSS (Aluminium Conductor Steel Supported)

ACSS conductors are manufactured from annealed Aluminium 1350 wires and an inner high tensile strength core of Galfan (Zn 5% Al Mischmetal) coated steel wire.

Figure 2. AAAC conductor

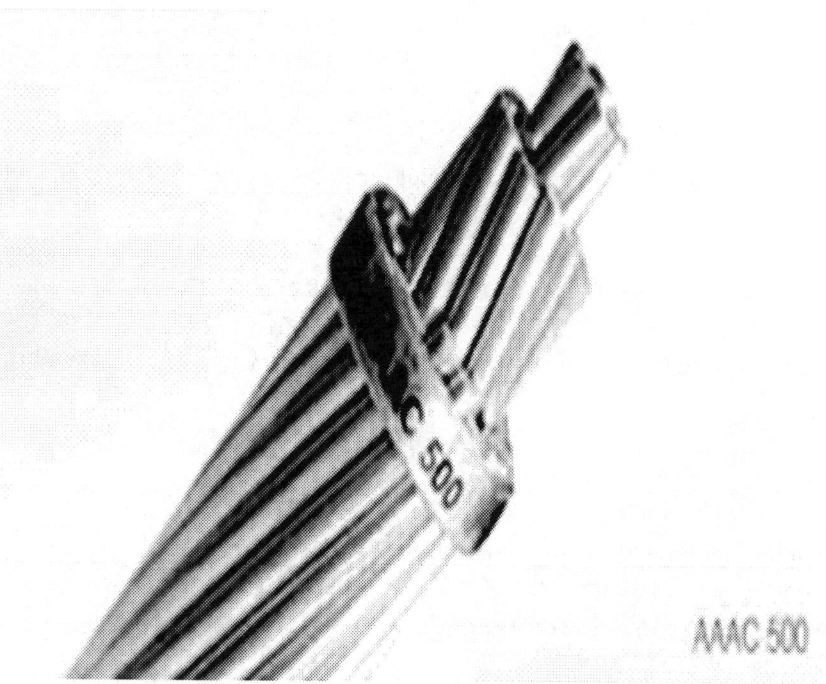

Figure 3. TACSR conductor

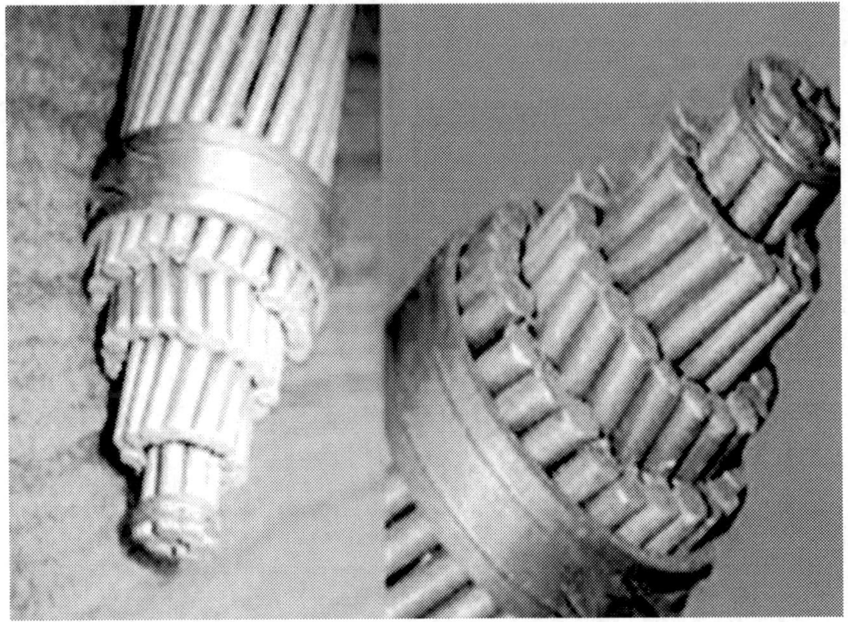

Benefits

- Preferred for Reconductoring as well as new line applications.
- Offers low sag, even when operating at up to 200°*C*.
- Aluminium wires of ACSS have an increased conductivity of 63% IACS.

Performance

- With the same tower loading, an ACSS conductor can carry up to two times the rating of conductor with the same diameter it would replace (See Fig. 4).

E. STACIR (Super Thermal Alloy Conductor, Invar Reinforced)

This low sag conductor is manufactured from Al-Zr (Aluminium Zirconium) alloy rods.

Benefits

- Preferred for re-conductoring applications.
- No modification/reinforcement is required to the existing towers.
- Can carry 100% more current as that of ACSR of the same size, while maximum sag and maximum working tension remains the same as that of ACSR.
- Can be used up to 200 °C

Figure 4. ACSS conductor

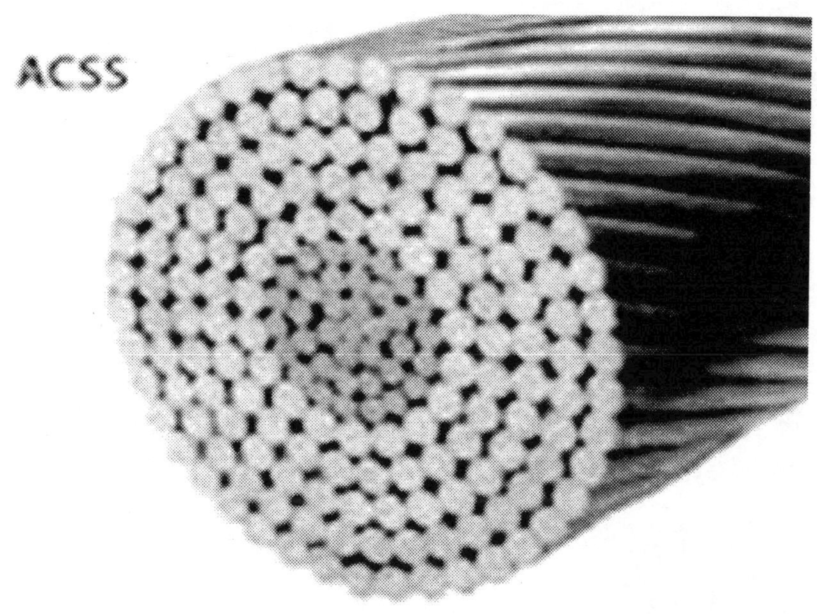

Performance

- With the same tower loadings a STACIR conductor can *carry up to two times the rating* of a conductor with the same diameter it would replace (See Fig. 5).

F. ACCC (Aluminium Conductor Composite Core)

These are high Ampacity, low loss hybrid conductors. These are made up of Carbon, glass fibre and trapezoidal shaped aluminium, that are resistant to environmental degradation. These conductors can reduce line losses up to 40% compared with conventional conductors of the same diameter and weight (See Fig. 6).

Benefits

- 28% More Aluminium = Greater Capacity, Reduced Losses, and Cooler Temperatures.
- 25% stronger and 60% lighter vs. traditional steel core = fewer or lower structures.
- Lower Coefficient of thermal expansion = less sag at higher temperatures.
- It can be used up to 175 °C.

G. AL59(Alloy conductor of Aluminium, Magnesium and Silicon)

This has 26% to 31% more current carrying capacity as that of ACSR Conductor of same size while maximum sag remains the same and working tension is lesser than that of ACSR. Also its resistivity is substantially lesser that of ACSR /AAAC conductor resulting in lower I^2R losses. It has higher corrosion resistance than that of 6201 series (AAAC).

Figure 5. STACIR Conductor

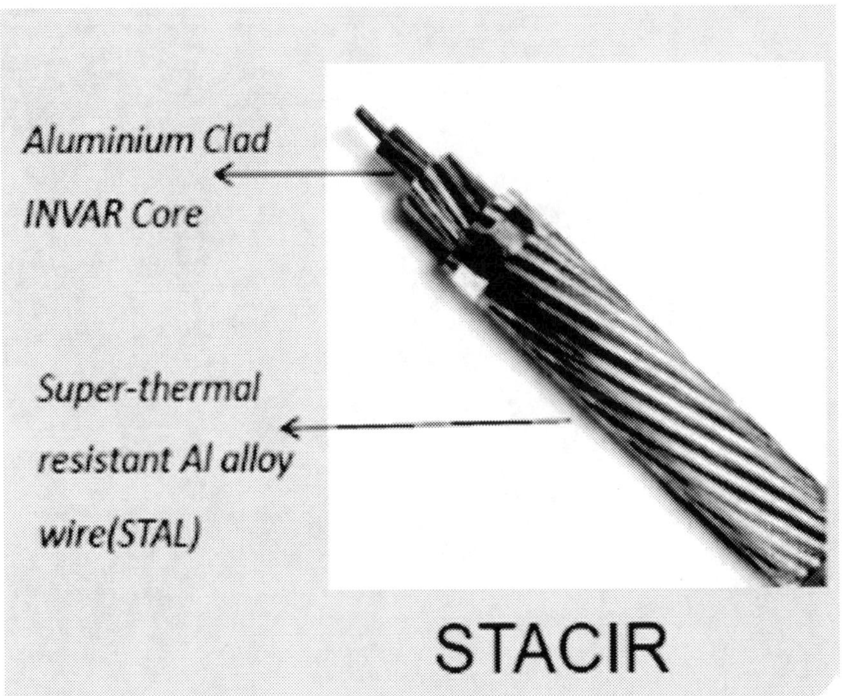

Figure 6. ACCC conductor

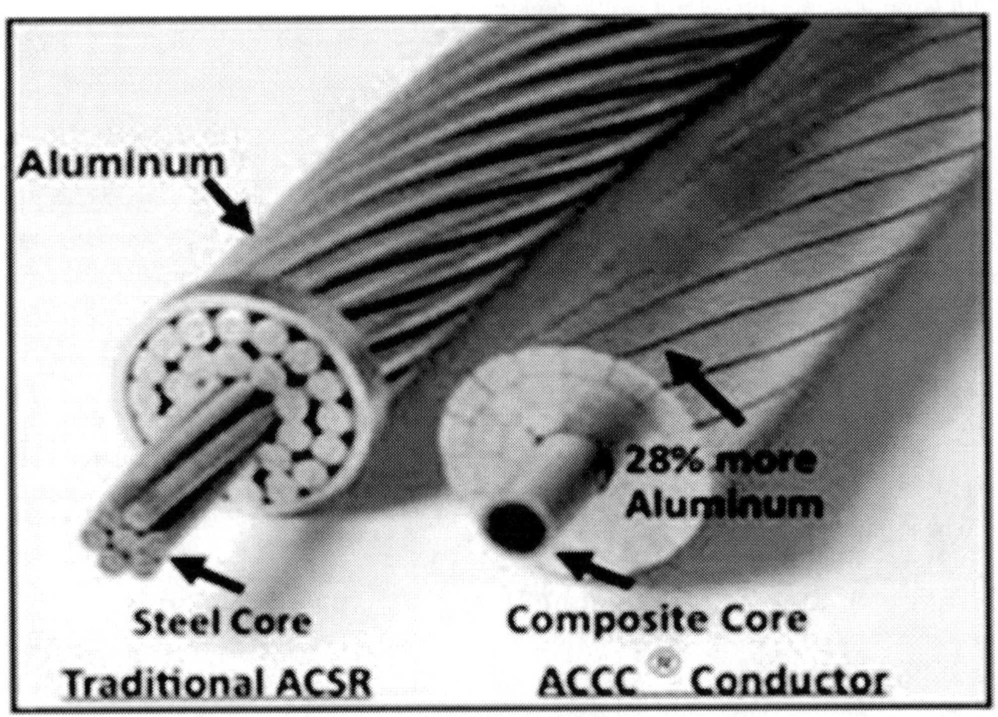

4. TECHNICAL ASPECTS OF VARIOUS CONDUCTORS

To study technical aspects of the transmission network; a three phase, 50Hz, transmission line having 5000 MVA power to be transfer along the distance of 800 km with 50% Compensation has been typically considered.

$$\text{Power handling capacity per circuit} = \left(\frac{E^2 * \sin'}{L*X} + \sim 10\%overlading\right)\text{MW} \quad (1)$$

$$\text{Total Current } I_t = \frac{S}{\sqrt{3}V}\text{kA} \quad (2)$$

$$\text{No. of circuits required} = \frac{\textit{total power to be transferred}}{\textit{power handling capacity per circuit}} \quad (3)$$

$$\text{Current per Circuit, } I = \frac{\text{Total Current}}{\text{No. of Circuits}}\text{kA} \quad (4)$$

$$\text{Voltage Drop} = I * R * L \text{ kV} \quad (5)$$

$$\%\text{ Voltage Regulation} = \frac{V_{s-}V_r}{V_s} * 100 \quad (6)$$

Where,

P = Power in MW
E_s, E_r = Sending and receiving end voltage in kV
δ= Phase difference between E_s and E_r
X = positive sequence reactance, /km
= 0.327/km
R = Resistance of transmission line in Ω/km
L= Line length, km

For consideration of stability, δ is limited to about 30°· for a preliminary estimate of power, consider $E_r = E_s = E$

Resistances considered for benefit evaluation.

5. RESULT AND DISCUSSION

From the following graphs and tables the following inferences can be drawn;

- The traditionally used conductors in the transmission system have more resistance than some of the HTLS conductors.
- Though the HTLS conductors have high resistances but they can be operated at high temperatures such as STACIR, ACSS can be operated up to 200°C whereas the existing system conductors ACSR and AAAC conductors can be operated up to 95 °C.
- The voltage drop through the HTLS conductor is found to be very less compared to traditionally used conductors.
- As the resistance of HTLS conductors are less, so the power loss through HTLS conductors is also less compared to ACSR / AAAC Conductor.
- The voltage regulation is found to be 10-12% for a typical 765kV system considered in this paper.
- So the judicatory selection of conductor is to be done according to technical specification and atmospheric conditions.

Table 1. Resistances at different temperature for MOOSE equivalent conductor (Source: CEA)

Name of Conductor	DC-Resistance	AC Resistance values at different temperatures (in Ω/km)			
	20 °C	20 °C	75 °C	85 °C	95 °C
ACSR	0.05552	0.05699	0.069	0.07112	NA
AAAC	0.05980	0.06116	0.074	0.07646	0.07882
TACSR	0.05460	0.05609	0.068	0.07001	0.07213
AL59	0.05070	0.05231	0.063	0.06518	0.06714
ACSS	0.05210	0.05368	0.065	0.06691	0.06896
STACIR	0.06820	0.06941	0.084	0.08689	0.08960
ACCC	0.04340	0.04527	0.055	0.05618	0.05788

Table 2. Comparison of parameters for 400kV and 765kV

Parameters Calculated	400kV	765kV
Power handling capacity	680MW	2980MW
No. of Circuit	8 Single Circuits 4 Double circuits	2 Single Circuits 1 Double Circuit
Total current	7.2169kA	3.7735kA
Current per circuit	0.91kA	1.89kA

Table 3. Voltage drop at different temperature

Name of Conductor	Voltage Drop in kV				% Voltage Regulation at 20° C
	20 °C	75 °C	85 °C	95 °C	
ACSR	86.16	104.33	107.53	NA	11.26
AAAC	92.47	111.88	115.61	119.17	12.09
TACSR	84.81	102.81	105.86	109.06	11.08
AL59	79.10	95.26	98.55	101.52	10.34
ACSS	81.164	98.28	101.17	104.27	10.61
STACIR	104.95	127.01	131.38	135.48	13.72
ACCC	68.45	83.16	84.95	87.52	8.95

Figure 7. Voltage Drop through various conductor at 20° C

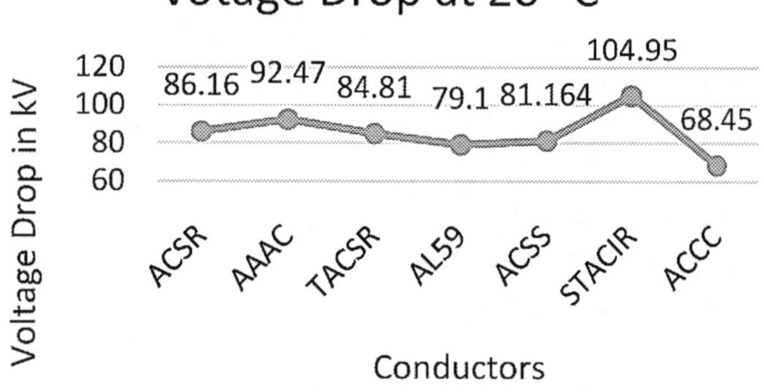

Table 4. Power Loss at different temperature

Name of Conductor	Power Loss			
	20 °C	75 °C	85 °C	95 °C
ACSR	162.86	197.17	203.24	NA
AAAC	174.77	211.46	218.50	225.24
TACSR	160.28	194.32	200.07	206.12
AL59	149.49	180.03	186.26	191.86
ACSS	153.40	185.75	189.15	197.07
STACIR	198.35	240.05	248.31	256.05
ACCC	129.37	157.17	160.54	165.40

Figure 8. Power Loss through various conductors at 20° C

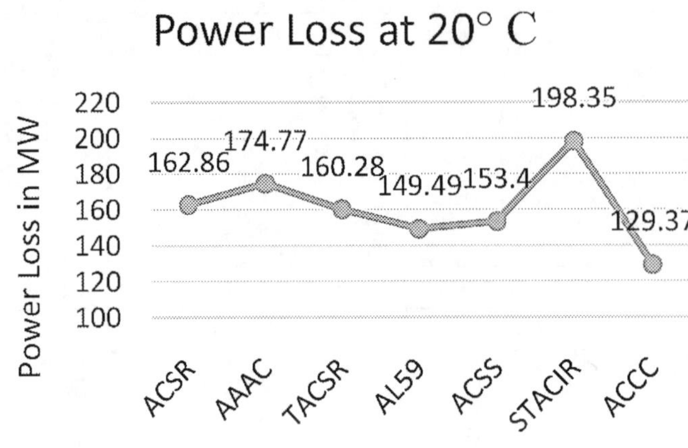

5. CONCLUSION

From above result and discussion it can conclude that:

- Though the resistance of some of the HTLS conductors are more but it is evident to say that it will be beneficial to go for HTLS conductors as they can be operated up to higher temperature compared to traditionally used conductors.
- The voltage drop for various HTLS conductor is less than ACSR/AAAC conductor and is minimum for ACCC.
- Also the power loss for HTLS conductor is minimum compared to traditionally used conductors
- It can be concluded that, judiciary selection of the conductor will lead to save energy in the transmission system as reduction of loss is nothing but saving of energy. Also saving of 1 MW of energy leads to save 800 tons of coal and 2000 tons of CO_2 emission reduction. So reconductoring the existing system with new HTLS conductor will lead to save energy with minimum impact on environment.

FUTURE SCOPE

- Technical aspects other than discussed in this paper can be further studied.
- Economic impact of using HTLS conductor can be studied.

REFERENCES

Central Electrical Authority. (2013). *Manual on Transmission Planning Criteria*. Author.

Rao. (n.d.). *EHV-AC, HVDC Transmission & Distribution* (3rd ed.). Khanna Publication. Begumudre. (2011). *Extra High Voltage AC Transmission Engineering* (4th ed.). New Age International Publishers.

Abhilash, A., & Netake, P. K. (2014). 765kV Transmission Line for Capacity Enhancement. *International Journal on Research and Scientific Innovation, 1*(7), 200–204.

Geary, R., Condon, T., Kavanagh, T., Armstrong, O., & Doyle, J. (2012). *Introduction of high temperature low sag conductors to the Irish Transmission grid.* B2-104, CIGRE 2012 ESB International Ireland.

Chapter 13
A Study on Different Facial Features Extraction Technique

Arnab Kumar Maji
North Eastern Hill University, India

Bandariakor Rymbai
North Eastern Hill University, India

Debdatta Kandar
North Eastern Hill University, India

ABSTRACT

Facial recognition is the most natural means of biometric identification as it deals with the measurement of a biological relevance. Since, faces varies from each and every person, therefore, it can be used for security purpose. Face recognition is a very challenging problem, where the human face changes over time, as it depends on the pose, expression, occlusion, aging, etc. It can be used in many areas such as for surveillance purposes, security, general identity verification, criminal justice system, smart cards, etc. The most important part of the face recognition is the evaluation of facial features. With the help of facial feature, the system usually looks for the position of eyes, nose and mouth and distances between them can be detected and computed. This chapter will discuss some of the techniques that can be used to extract important facial features.

1. INTRODUCTION

Face recognition involves an evaluation of facial features. The system usually look for some fiducially for the positioning of eyes, nose and mouth and distances between these features. Face plays an important role in our social interactions, validating the identity of a person. The skin color of a face can change depending on the exposure while it imaged, that is the different of the same face when exposed to sunlight or in the dark room, etc. It can also depend on the emotion of a person. It may change when there are any cuts, scrapes bandages from injuries, beard, mustache, etc. and also wrinkles, weight loss, weight gain caused by aging.

DOI: 10.4018/978-1-4666-8737-0.ch013

1. 1 Various Factors Affecting Face Recognition

Face recognition is susceptible to a variety of factors, such as pose and lighting variations, expression variations, age variations.

1. **Pose Variation:** While capturing a face image of different pose, images taken at two different viewpoints of the same person (intra-user variation) may appear more different than two images taken from the same view point for two different people (inter-user variation).
2. **Lighting Variation:** The difference in face images of the same person due to severe lighting variation. The skin color of a face can change depending on the exposure while it imaged, that is the different of the same face when exposed to sunlight or in the dark room, etc.
3. **Expression:** Facial expression is an internal variation that causes large intra-class variation. The recognition of facial expressions is an active research area in human computer interaction and communications.
4. **Age Variation:** Aging related changes on the face appear in a number of different ways such as:
   - Wrinkles
   - Weight loss and gain, and
   - Change in shape of face primitives
5. **Occlusion:** Face images often appear occluded by other objects or by the face itself (i.e., self-occlusion). It may depend on the emotion of a person and also it may change when there is any cuts, scrapes bandages from injuries, beard, mustache, etc.

2. BACKGROUND

Face plays an important role in our social interactions, especially in conveying people's identity. Face recognition have applicability in the following areas:

1. It can be used as a security for accessing controls as in airports, ATM machines, email authentication, system authentication, etc.
2. It can also be used as an identity of a person in electoral registration, passports, driver license, student's identity, etc.
3. It can also be used in police department as criminal investigation, etc.

Therefore the needs of a face recognition system are important, where each and every organization is used for security, as each and every people want to protect their own identities.

There are three stages of face recognition. The three stages are shown in the block diagram shown in figure 1.

1. **Face Detection:** At first, face will be captured using camera. Then face will be detected from the captured photography.
2. **Feature Extraction:** Features are required to extract for reducing the dimension and also removing the noise and distortion for better computation.

Figure 1. Block diagram of a face recognition technique

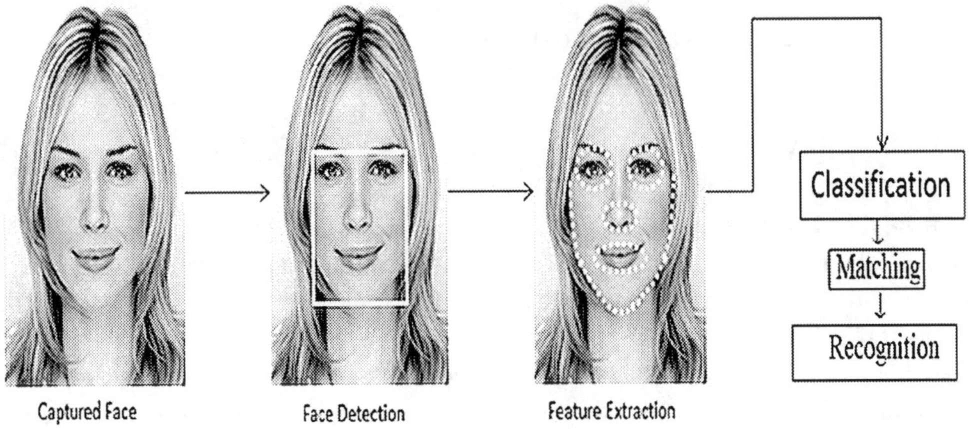

3. **Face Recognition:** The extracted features are classified for matching procedure in order to recognize a face.

From all the three stages, the most important stage is feature extraction which extract the important feature that will result into a best recognition system, as human faces changes from time to time, it may depends on the emotions of a person, an image of a person captured while laughing is different from an image captured at the times of depression. It also affect in the variations of pose, expression, illumination, occlusion, etc. Therefore analyzing and comparing of all the existing feature extraction techniques are required.

Facial features needed to be extracted. It can be global features or local features, Yu Su et al. (2007):

- Global features are the features which contains the information of the whole face, which is used for rough representation. Therefore it correspond *Holistic approach.*
- Local features represent the specific local region of a face, such as eyes, nose and mouth, which correspond to *Analytical approach.*
- A combination of Global and Local feature is correspond to *Hybrid Approach.*

Feature Extraction is the most important part of face recognition. We will discuss different approaches of facial feature extraction that are:

- Holistic Approach (Saini et al., 2014)
- Analytical Approach (Gursimarpreet et al., 2014)
- Hybrid Approach (Riddhi et al., 2013)

3. HOLISTIC APPROACH

Holistic approach (Saini et al., 2014) is also called appearance-based approach, which uses the whole information of a face and performs some transformation to get a compact representation for recognition.

It uses the global feature. Global feature means the overall structural configuration of the facial organs, as well as the face contour. Global features should correspond to the lower frequencies. There are different kind of holistic approaches are there. They are briefly categorized as

- **Principal Component Analysis:** Also called an *Eigenfaces*, which is widely used for dimensionality reduction.
- **Linear Discriminant Analysis:** Also known as *Fisherfaces* method, which is a dimension reduction based on discrimination purposes as well as to find bases for projection that minimize the intra-class variation but preserve the inter-class variation.
- **Independent Component Analysis:** It is a generalization of PCA. It is a technique for extracting statistically independent variables from a mixture of them. It helps in recognizing faces when changes in expression.

3.1 Principal Component Analysis

Principal Component Analysis (Kumar et al., 2011) is also known as Karhunen-Loeve transformation or eigenspace projection. It is usually a statistical technique for optimizing data compression by reducing the dimensionality of face images called Eigenfaces. The eigenspace are the subspace of an image gathered by a set of eigenvectors of the covariance matrix which is of the trained images. These eigenvectors are also called eigenfaces. Here faces are normalized in order to hold the most important features of a face to make an easy comparison. By applying eigenfaces, two main approaches are required for recognition. In the appearance model each face in the database is represented as a linear combination of eigenfaces. Here, the recognition process is done by projecting a test image to be identified with the same eigenspace. The resulting vector will be a point in eigenspace, then by measuring the distance between these points, it will be able to compare with the training images. The other approach is called a discriminative model. Two datasets are obtained by measuring the intrapersonal and interpersonal differences that is matching two different images of the same individual in the dataset and matching the different individual in the dataset respectively. Two datasets of eigenfaces are projected by performing Principal Component Analysis on each class and a similarity between the two is derived by calculating a Bayesian Probability measure.

The PCA algorithms are as follows:

1. Compute the mean vector φ where $\varphi = \frac{1}{N}\sum_{i=1}^{N} x_i$
2. Subtract each x_i by φ and get Φ_i as the variation matrix, $\Phi_i = x_i - \varphi$, where, $S = |\Phi_1, \Phi_2, \ldots . \Phi_N|$, represent how images varies form mean image.
3. The covariance matrix of all the s is calculated as

$$C = \frac{1}{N}\sum_{i=1}^{N} {}_{i}^{T} = SS^T \text{ and } \Omega_{test} = W^T x_{test}$$

4. Calculating the eigenvectors and eigenvalues for an image is a very large task, as the covariance matrix C has dimension $(N^2 \times N^2)$, therefore to find the eigenvectors for SS^T ,
   a. Consider an eigenvectors z_i of $S^T S$, such that, $S^T Sz_i = \mu_i z_i$
   b. Multiplying both sides by S, we have, $S(S^T S)z_i = S\left(\mu_i z_i\right)$

$\left(SS^T\right)\left(Sz_i\right) = \mu_i\left(Sz_i\right)$, Where z_i are the eigenvector and μ_i are the eigenvalues of $C = SS^T$.

5. The eigenvectors and eigenvalues are sorted in descending order of eigenvalues.

$$U_i = Sz_i = \sum_{k=1}^{N} z_k^i \Phi_k$$

6. $W_i = \dfrac{U_k^T\left(x_i - \varphi\right)}{\mu_k}$, k=1,2...N Where W_i denotes a weight vector is the eigenfaces representation.

3.1.1 Experimental Results

Figure 2, 3 and 4 shows the experimental results of the said algorithm.

3.2 Fisherfaces or Linear Discriminant Analysis

Linear Discriminant Analysis (LDA) is also called Fisher Discriminant Analysis, which can be used for dimension reduction based on discrimination purpose which helps to find the lines that best separates the point. In other words, it means grouping the same image of the same class and separate mages of different class. This method also creates an optimal projection of the dataset that maximizes the ratio of the determinant of the between class scatter matrix of the projected samples and minimize the determinant of the within-class scatter matrix of the projected samples.

Figure 2. The z org are the six faces in the database and an average face is shown

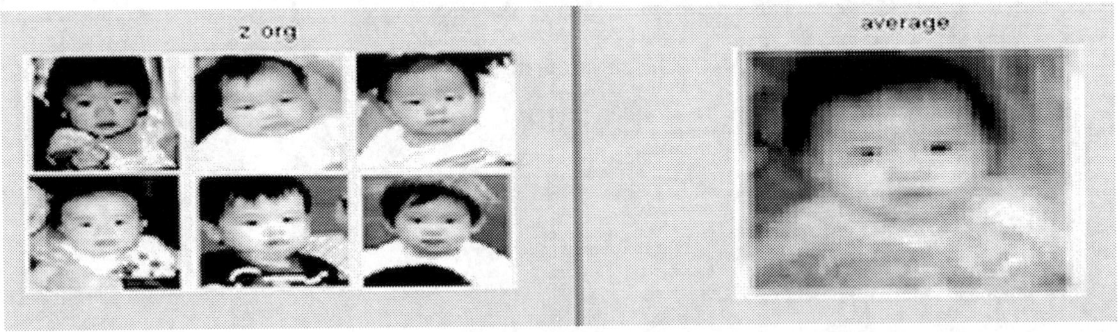

Figure 3. The average of all the six faces and the covariance matrix

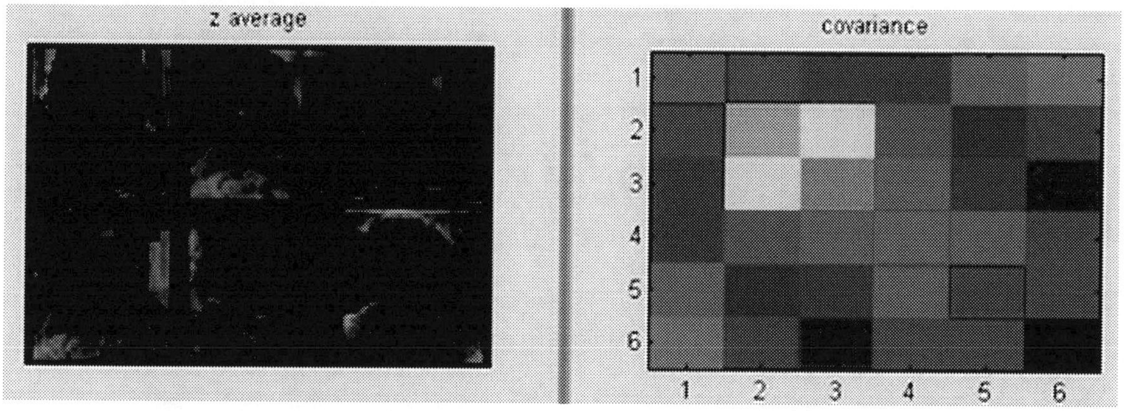

Figure 4. Five Eigenfaces are displayed, arranging in descending order from right to left and top to bottom

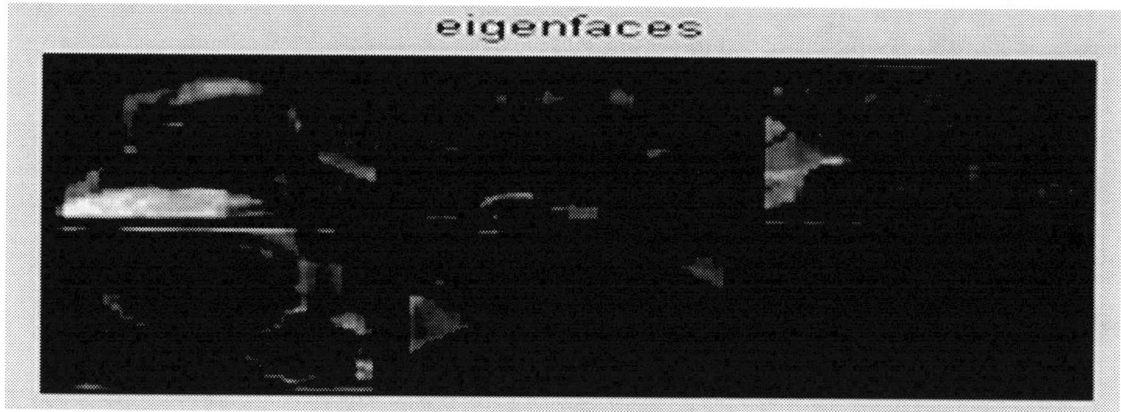

The within-class which is the intra-personal, that is, the variation in appearance due to exposure and expression of the same individual. The between-class scatter is an interpersonal which represents the variation of the appearance due to difference in identity.

3.2.1 Methods for Computing Fisher Linear Discriminant Analysis

Assume a dataset of D-dimensional samples {} , N_1 belongs to class, ω_1, and N_2 to class ω_2, Project the samples v onto a line $z = w^T v$ to obtain a scalar v. From all the possible lines, select the one that maximizes the difference of the scalars. In order to find a good projection vector, a measurable of separation is required to be defined. The mean vector of each class in v-space and z-space is

$$\mu_i = \frac{1}{N_i}\sum_{v \in \omega_i} v, \text{ and } \mu_i = \frac{1}{N_i}\sum_{z \in \omega_i} z = \frac{1}{N_i}\sum_{v \in \omega_i} w^T v = w^T \mu_i$$

Then choose the distance between the projected means as the objective function

$$J(w) = |\tilde{\mu}_1 - \tilde{\mu}_2| = |w^T(\mu_1 - \mu_2)|$$

However, the distance between projected means is not good measure since it does not account for the standard deviation within classes.

Fisher suggested maximizing the difference between the means, normalized by a measure of the within-class scatter.

For each class, the scatter, an equivalent of the variance is defined as

$$\tilde{s}_i^2 = \sum_{z \in \omega_i} (z - \tilde{\mu}_1)^2$$

where the quantity $(\tilde{s}_1^2 + \tilde{s}_2^2)$ is called the within-class scatter of the projected examples.

The Fisher linear discriminant is defined as the linear function $w^T x$ that maximizes the criterion function

$$J(w) = \frac{|\tilde{\mu}_1 - \tilde{\mu}_2|^2}{\tilde{s}_1^2 + \tilde{s}_2^2}$$

To find the optimum $w^*, J(w)$ is expressed as a function of w:

First, a measure of the scatter in feature space x is defined as:

$$s_i \sum_{v \in \omega_i} (v - \mu_i)(v - \mu_i)^T$$

$s_1 + s_2 = s_w$, where s_w is called the within-class scatter matrix.

The scatter of the projection y can be expressed as a function of the scatter matrix in feature space x

$$\tilde{s}_i^2 = \sum_{z \in \omega_i} \left(z - \tilde{\mu}_i\right)^2 = \sum_{v \in \omega_i} (w^T v - w^T \mu_i)^2 = \sum_{v \in \omega_i} w^T (v - \mu_i)(v - \mu_i)^T w = w^T s_i w$$

$$\tilde{s}_1^2 + \tilde{s}_2^2 = w^T s_w w$$

Similarly, the difference between the projected means can be expressed in terms of the means in the original feature space

$$\left(\tilde{\mu}_1 - \tilde{\mu}_2\right)^2 = (w^T\mu_1 - w^T\mu_2)^2 == w^T\left(\mu_1 - \mu_2\right)(\mu_1 - \mu_2)^T w == w^T s_B w$$

where $s_B = \left(\mu_1 - \mu_2\right)(\mu_1 - \mu_2)^T$

The matrix s_B is called the between class scatter. Since s_B is the outer product of two vectors, its rank is at most one. The Fisher criterion in terms of s_w and s_B can be expressed as

$$J(w) = (w^T s_B w)\ /\ (w^T s_w w)$$

To find the maximum of J(w),

$$\frac{d}{dw}\left[J\left(w\right)\right] = \frac{d}{dw}\left[\frac{w^T s_B w}{w^T s_w w}\right] = 0$$

$$=> \left[w^T s_w w\right]\frac{d\left[w^T s_B w\right]}{dw} - w^T s_B w \frac{d\left[w^T s_w w\right]}{dw} = 0$$

$$=> \left[w \hat{}\ T s\_ww\right]2s_B w - \left[w^T s_B w\right]2s_w w = 0$$

Dividing by $w^T s_w w$

$$\left[\frac{w^T s_B w}{w^T s_w w}\right]s_B w - \left[\frac{w^T s_B w}{w^T s_w w}\right]s_w w = 0$$

$$=> s_B w - J s_w w = 0$$

$$=> s_w^{-1} s_B w - J w = 0$$

Solving the generalized eigenvalue problem $(s_w^{-1} s_B w - Jw = 0)$ yields

$$w* = arg\,max\left[\frac{w^T s_B w}{w^T s_w w}\right] = s_w^{-1}\left(\mu_1 - \mu_2\right)$$

3.3 Independent Component Analysis

The Independent Component Analysis (ICA) is a generalization of the PCA, which is sensitive to higher order statistics. It is a technique for extracting statistically independent variables from a mixture of them. The goal is to provide an independent rather than an uncorrelated image decomposition and representation. (Barlett et al., 2002) derived the ICA bases from the principle of optimal information transfer through sigmoidal neurons. In addition, they proposed two architectures for dimension-reduction decomposition. One of the architectures considers the image as random variables and the pixels as outcomes, whereas another architectures considers the pixels as random variables and the image as outcomes. The first architectures finds a set of statistically independent basis images and each of them captures the features such as eyes, eyebrows and mouth. The second architectures finds the basis images which have similar appearances as the PCA does and has the decomposition. This architecture uses the ICA to find representation where the coefficients used to code images are statistically independent. Therefore, the first architecture projects spatially local basis images for the face, while the second architecture projects a factorial code. Therefore ICA helps in recognizing faces when changes in expression.

3.4 Analytical Approach

It is also called a Feature-based method or component based method, which uses the geometric relationship among the facial features like mouth, nose and eyes as distances and angles between these features points, shapes of facial features or local features. It is a process that uses image processing, computer vision and domain knowledge from human.

The difference feature-based methods are discussed below:

3.4.1 Gabor Wavelet

Wavelets are mathematical function that extract both the time and spatial frequency information from a given signal, and then performs multi-resolution analysis. Thus it is suitable for application such as image compression, edge detection, etc. Kumar et al. Gabor Wavelets was named after Dennis Gabor, Hungarian physicist in 1946. Gabor wavelet is an optimal basis for extracting local features due to its biological relevance. It also yields distortion tolerance space for pattern recognition task. Its representation is optimal and gives better performance in classification of facial actions.

Gabor wavelet is based on topographical ordered spatially localized feature points to represent pattern in the image. Gabor wavelet or filters are exploited to extract local variations features with varying scales and orientations.

Images can be represented by placing the wavelets at each pixel. Examples, supposed at each point, 60 Gabor wavelets (6 scales and 10 orientation) are used. If the size of image is 100 * 100, the dimension of the feature vector will be 600,000, therefore it will lead to an expensive computational and storage cost.

Another method, a face graph is placed, where the nodes of the graph lie on facial features. It requires a fine localization of facial feature points. This method also has some disadvantages as only the areas which can be reliably located are used for recognition purposes.

In between these two methods, another method is by placing a rectangular grid over the face region.

3.4.1.2 Representations of Gabor Wavelets

A set of frequencies and angles at each feature points of the wavelet net are chosen to represent the image.

Now, the Lower Bound and the Upper Bound frequencies are defined:

$$f_{LB} = \frac{1}{x_1\sqrt{2}}, and\, f_{UB} = \frac{1}{x_2\sqrt{2}}$$

The values of x_1 and x_2 are chosen such that $x_1 > x_2$. A set of frequencies to be used at each feature point is obtained by starting at f_{LB} and multiplying by 2 until f_{UB} is reached. The number of frequencies is given by P.

For each frequency, a set of orientations is chosen ranging from to $-\pi$ to π

The step size between any two θ is $\frac{2À}{n}$, where n is chosen appropriately. The number of orientations is given by Q.

The wavelet points are denoted by (c_x, c_y) as per the Cartesian co-ordinates. The number of these points is given by R.

A set of frequencies and orientations are obtained at each feature point (c_x, c_y).

The number of wavelets $N = P * Q * R.I(x, y)$ represents the input image, $'x' and\ 'y'$ represent the coordinates of each pixel in the Cartesian system.

Hence $'x' and\ 'y'$ ranges from $0 to\ 'h' and 0 to\ 'w'$ respectively where $'h'$ is the height of the image and $'w'$ is the width of the image.

A family of N Gabor $_{\text{wavelet}}$ functions $\{\partial = \partial_{1,1,1} \ldots\ldots$.K, $\partial_{P,Q,R}\}$, of the form

$$\partial_{i,j,k}(x, y)\, f_i$$

$$= \frac{f_i^2}{2\pi} \exp\left\{-0.5 f_i^2 \left[\left(x - c_{yk}\right)^2 + \left(y - c_{yk}\right)^2\right]\right\} * \sin\{2\pi f_i [\left(x - c_{x_k}\right) cos\theta_j + \left(y - c_{y_k}\right) sin\theta_j]\}$$

denotes the frequency, θ_j denotes orientation and c_{x_k}, c_{y_k} denotes wavelet position.

The wavelet function $\partial_{i,j,k}$ (x, y) is normalized by scaling the reciprocal of its length $\|\, \partial i, j, k(x, y)\, \|$ to obtain a unit vector

$$\partial_{i,j,k} = \frac{\partial_{i,j,k}}{\partial_{i,j,k}}$$

The first weight w_1 associated with wavelet ∂_1 is given by the dot product of as $I\, and\ (\partial_{i,j,k})_1$

$w_1 = I.\ (\partial_{i,j,k})_1$

The subsequent weights $w_u \left(2 \le u \le N\right)$ associated with wavelets ∂_u are determined by calculating the dot product of I_{diff_u} and $(\partial_{i,j,k})_u$ as

$w_u = I_{diff_u} \cdot (\partial_{i,j,k})_u$, where I_{diff_u} represent the intermediate difference image:

$$I_{diff_u} = I_{diff_{(u-1)}} - I_{u-1}\, with\, I_{diff_1} = I\left(x, y\right) for \left(2 \le u \le N\right),$$

where $\hat{I}_u$ is the intermediate reconstructed image for each wavelet given by

$$I_u = w_u.(\partial_{i,j,k})_u, for\ (2 \le u < -N)$$

The final reconstructed image is given by

$$I_u = \sum_{u=0}^{N-1} I_u$$

Thus, from the reconstruction process above, a set of weights are obtained, the $'n'$ highest weights are selected. These 'n' weights along with the corresponding set of $'n'$ frequencies and orientations are the features.

3.4.1.3 Merits and Demerits of Gabor wavelets

- Merits
  - Modeling local patch which is beyond the isolated pixels.
  - Robust to noise, local distortion (due to mis-alignment, little pose variation, lighting changing).
  - Extract high-order correlation between neighborhood pixels.
  - Dense sampling no need to find points of interest (or landmarks, such as eye corners, nose tips, mouth corners).
- Demerits
  - High dimensionality.

3.4.1.4 Experimental Results

Figure 5, 6, 7, 8 show the experimental results of Gabor wavelet.

Figure 5. A grayscale image is taken as input.

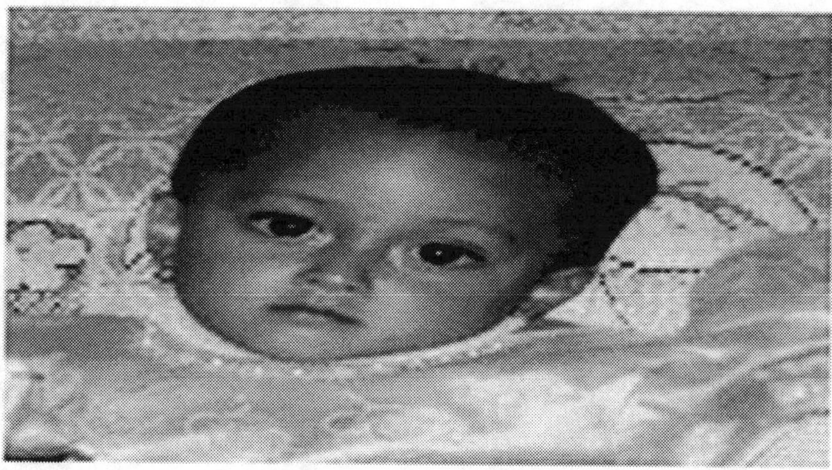

Figure 6. The magnitudes of the grey scale image shown in figure 5.

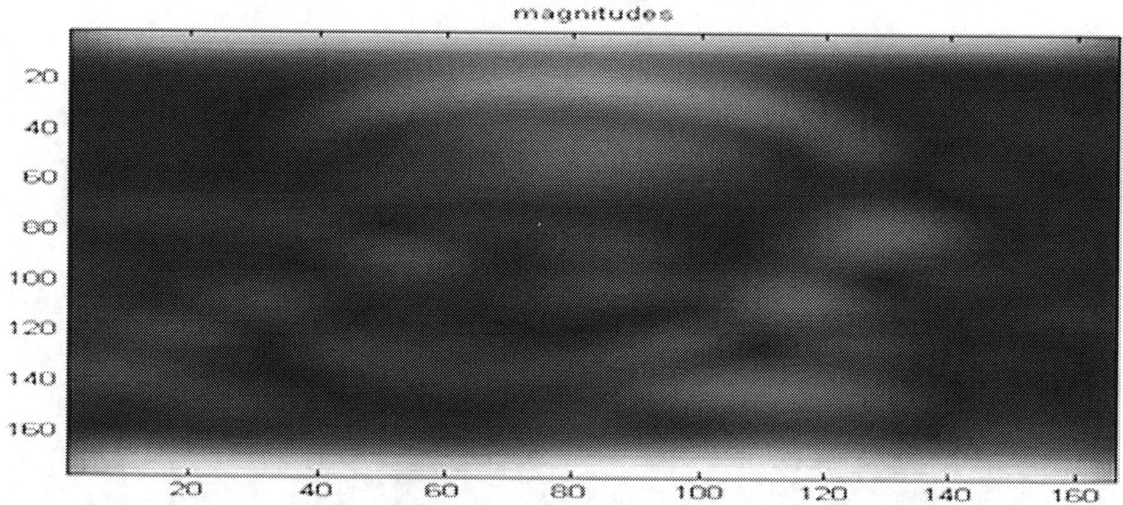

4. ELASTIC BUNCH GRAPH MATCHING

Lades et al. (1993) pioneered the application of Gabor wavelet for face recognition by using the elastic graph matching framework for finding feature points and executing distance measurement based on the face model, whereas the Gabor wavelets are used to extract local feature at these feature points, and a set of complex Gabor wavelet coefficients for each points is called a jet.

The two phases to build the graph g^I for face image I and compute the similarity with a model graph g^M.

Figure 7. After applying different filters on face shown in figure 5.

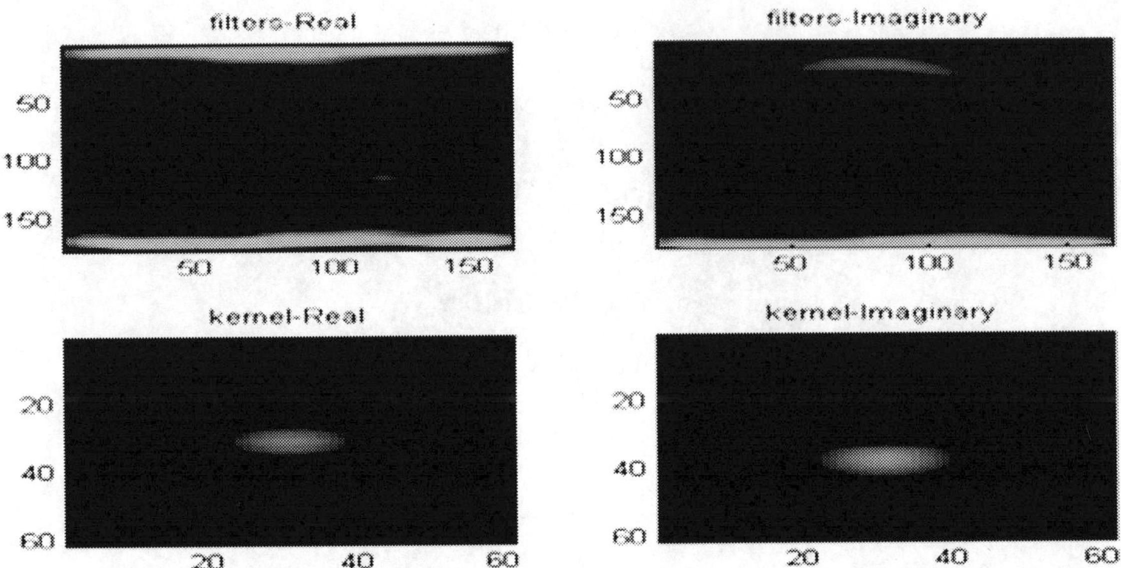

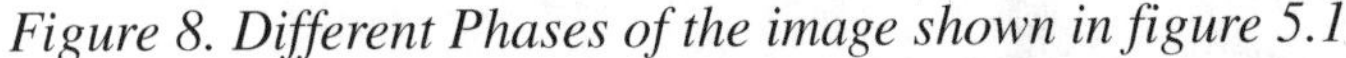
Figure 8. Different Phases of the image shown in figure 5.1

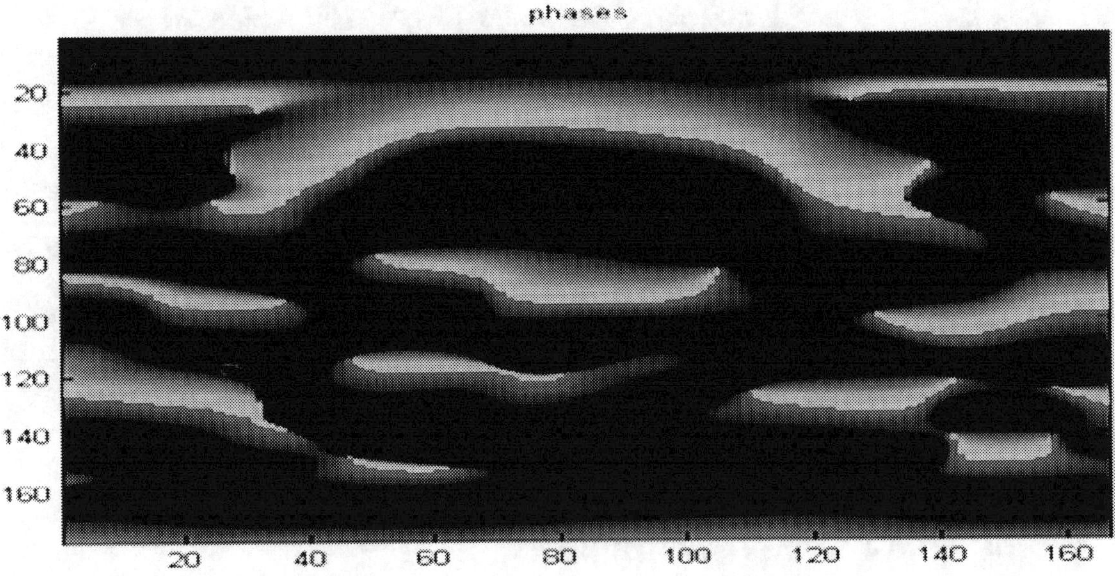

Phase One: g^M is moved with the input image for finding the perfect global offsets of g^I and retaining its shape inelastic.

Phase Two: each vertex in g^I is moved in a topological order to compensate the local alterations due to rotations in expression variations.

It is the deformation of the vertices that make the graph matching procedure elastic.

Therefore, to achieve these two stages, the cost measure function

$$S\left(g^{M},g^{I}\right)=\sum_{n}S_{m}S_{m\left(J_{n}^{I}-J_{n}^{M}\right)}=\lambda\sum_{e}\left(\Delta\vec{x}_{e}^{I}-\Delta\vec{x}_{e}^{M}\right)^{2}$$

is required, so that these two stages will terminate till the function reaches its extreme value, where λ is the relative importance of jet similarity and the topography term, $\Delta\vec{x}_{e}$ is the distance vector of the labeled edge e between two vertices, J_{n} is the set of jets vertex at vertex n, and S_{m} is the distance measure function between two jets based on magnitude of jets.

Lades et al.'s (1993) used a simple rectangular graph to model faces in the database, while each vertex is without a direct object meaning on faces. The rectangular graph is manually placed on each face and the features are extracted at the individual vertices, as there is no deformation process in the database building phase. Therefore, when we input a new face I, the distance between it and all the faces in the database are required to compute, which is very expensive for large database.

5. FACE BUNCH GRAPH

Wiskott et al. (1999) proposed an enhanced elastic graph matching framework to deal with the computational expensive of elastic bunch graph matching and also enriched the performance. They employed object-adaptive graph to model faces in the database, where the vertices of a graph refer to special facial landmarks and enhance the alteration tolerant capability. The distance measure function counts the magnitude information and also takes in the phase's information from the features jets. The used of Face bunch graph is the most important improvement, composed of several face models to cover a wide range of possible variations in the appearance of faces, such as differently shaped eyes, mouth, or noses, different types of beard, variations due to sex, age, race, etc. where a bunch is a set of jets taken from the same landmark, for examples, an eye bunch may include jets from closed, open, female and male eyes, etc. The cost function of a face bunch graph is defined as

$$s\left(B,g^{I}\right)=\frac{1}{N}\sum_{n}max_{m}\,s_{p}\left(J_{n}^{I}-J_{n}^{B_{m}}\right)-\frac{\lambda}{E}\sum_{e}\frac{\left(\partial\vec{x}_{e}^{I}-\partial\vec{x}_{e}^{B}\right)^{2}}{\left(\partial\vec{x}_{e}^{B}\right)^{2}},$$

where B is the Face Bunch Graph representation, N and E are the total amounts of vertices and edges in the $Face\,Bunch\,Graph$.

$B_{m}, them^{th}$ model graph of $B and S_{p}$ is the new defined distance measure function which take the phase jets into account.

To build the database, a Face Bunch Graph is first produced and models for individual faces which are made by elastic graph matching procedure based on Face Bunch Graph. When there is a new input face, the same elastic matching process based on Face Bunch Graph is executed to create a new face model in the database without re-modeling. Thus Face Bunch Graph reduces the computation of face models.

5.1 Steps for Matching Process

Assume that the faces of known pose and estimated the standard size, so that only one Face Bunch Graph is required.

Step 1: Find the approximate position

Summarize the Face Bunch Graph into an average graph by taking the average magnitudes of the jets in each bunch of Face Bunch Graph. Use this as a grid model ($\lambda = 8$) and evaluate its similarity at each location of a square lattice with a spacing of 4 pixels. At this step the similarity function S_a without phase is used instead of S_b. Repeat the scanning around the best fitting position with spacing of pixel. The best fitting position finally serves as the starting point of the step.

Step 2: Refine position and size

Now the Face Bunch Graph is used without averaging, varying it in the position and size. Check the four different position ($\pm 3, \pm 3$) pixels displaced from the position found in Step 1, and at each position check two different sizes which have the same center position smaller or larger than the Face Bunch Graph average size. This is without effect on the metric similarity. Since the vectors $\vec{x}_e^B$ are transformed accordingly. For each of these eight variations, the best fitting jet for each node is selected and its displacement is computed as in Wiskott et al. (1999) the displacement can be of magnitude up to eight pixels. The grid are then rescaled and repositioned to minimize the square sum over the displacements. The best of the eight variations can be taken as the starting point of the next step.

Step 3: Refine size and find aspect ratio

A similar relaxation process as described in Step 2 is used, but reducing the $x\, and\, y$ dimension independently.

Step 4: Local distortion

In pseudo-random arrange the position of each individual image node is varied to further increase the similarity to the Face Bunch Graph. Now the metric similarity is taken into account by setting $\lambda = 2$ and using vectors $\vec{x}_e^B$ as obtained in Step 3. In this step only those positions for which the estimated displacement vector is small Wiskott et al. (1999) are considered.

The subsequent graph is called the image graph, where it can be used as a representation of the individual face of the image.

To minimize the computing cost, a face representation can be extracted into two stages, that is, the first stage called the normalization stage, which helps in assessing the position and size of the face in the original image, for scaling and cutting the image into a standard size. The second stage uses the normalized image as input and extracts an accurate image graph which can be applied for face recognition purposes. The first stage has to deal with larger vagueness about size and position of the head and has to enhance the consistency with which it finds the face, but it is not essential to find fiducially points with any accuracy or extracting significant data for face recognition. The second stage can start with slight vagueness about position and size of the head, but has to extract a complete face graph with higher accuracy.

6. HYBRID APPROACH

Hybrid Approach is the combination of any of the techniques discussed above, i.e., the mixture of Analytic approach and Holistic approach, which means both global and local feature are extracted to recognize a face. Liu et al. (2002) have applied the Enhanced Fisher Linear Discriminant Model (EFM) to the feature vector of a Gabor Wavelet representation of face images, for obtaining the discrimination low dimensional feature. They have derived a Gabor feature vector by down sampling the Gabor wavelet representation of a face images, and using the Principal Component Analysis for dimensional reduction of the vector, finally, the Independent Gabor feature is defined based on the Independent Component Analysis. Arindam Kar et al. (2011) defined a technique that combine the Independent Component Analysis with the high intensity feature vectors extracted from the Gabor wavelet representation of a face. Cevikalp et al. (2005) proposed a method, called Discriminant Common Vector (DCV) by applying the within-class scatter matrix of the sample from all the methods. Wavelet transform is widely used as a subspace method where it can extract the localized time frequency information.

7. DISCRIMINATIVE COMMON VECTOR

A discriminant feature is created from the Gabor and wavelet coefficient by applying the within-class scatter matrix method. A common vector, called the Discriminative Common Vectors Thangairulappan et al's (2012) is formed by eliminating all the features of the eigenvectors corresponds to the nonzero eigenvalues of the within-class scatter matrix.

7.1 Methods to Compute Discriminant Common Vector

Let the classes C be the training set, where each class contains N samples. Let x_m^i be the sample from the ith class. Then construct the within-class matrix of a samples to form the feature vectors,

$$S_w = AA^T,$$

where the matrix A is given by

$$A = \left[x_1^1 - \mu_1, \ldots.., x_N^1 - \mu_1, x_1^2 - \mu_2, \ldots.., x_N^C - \mu_C\right],$$

where $x_i^j\ is\ the\, i^{th}$ sample of the class $j\, and\, \mu_j$ is the mean of the samples in the jth class.

Let $Q = \left[\alpha_1 \ldots \alpha_r\right]$, be the set of orthonormal eigenvectors corresponds to the nonzero eigenvalues of the within-class scatter matrix and r be the dimension of S_w.

Then, the projection matrix can be expressed as $P = Q\bar{Q}$

Choose the input sample and project it on the null space of the within-class scatter matrix, to get a common vectors as

$$x^i_{com} = x^i_m + Q\bar{Q}\,x^i_m,$$

where $m = 1\ldots..N$ samples and $i = 1\ldots\ldots C$ classes.

Compute the principal components, where the eigenvectors w_k of S_{com} correspond to the non-zero eigenvalues as

$$J\left(W_{opt}\right) = arg\,max\left[W^T S_{com} W\right],$$

where S_{com} is computed as

$$S_{com} = A_{com} A^T_{com},$$

where A_{com} is given by

$$A_{com} = \left[x^1_{com} - \mu_{com} \ldots x^C_{com} - \mu_{com}\right]$$

The feature vector of the training set is calculated as

$$\Omega_i = W^T x^i_m$$

Similarly, to recognize a test image x_{test}, the feature vector of this test is found by

$$\Omega_{test} = W^T x_{test}$$

The features extracted can be used for face recognition with any suitable classification process, such as, Neural network, K- mean clustering, etc.

8. CLASSIFICATION USING NEURAL NETWORK

Neural networks have been employed for a number of classification problem, its accuracy is equivalent to, or slightly better than other methods. Also due to its simplicity, generality and good learning ability of the neural network, classifier is more efficient. An artificial neural network (ANN), is an interconnected group of artificial neurons that uses a mathematical or computational model for information processing based on the connection approach for computation. It is an adaptive system that changes its structure based on external and internal information that owes through the network. They are non-linear statistical data modeling tools, which can be used to model complex relationship between inputs and outputs or to find patterns in data.

8.1 Multilayer Perceptron

This is a type of neural network which consists of multi layers of computational units, usually interconnected in a feed forward way. Each neuron in one layer has directed connections to the neurons of the subsequent layer. In many applications the units of these networks apply a sigmoid function as an activation function. Multi-layer uses a variety of learning techniques, the most popular method is back-propagation. The output values are compared with the answer to compute the value of some predefines error-function. By various techniques the error is then fed back through the network. Then the weight of each connection can be adjusted in order to reduce the value of the error function by some small amount. After repeating this process for a sufficiently large number of training cycles the network will usually converge to some state where the error of the calculations is small.

8.2 Gabor Wavelet with Neural Network

The Multi-layer feed forward architecture, Mathukannan et al. (2013) with the input layer, hidden layer and output layer. Various factors should be considered for selecting and designing the structure, which is calculation volume, responding time, and generalization capability. Generalization capability is the limited number with small training data trained by the network, such as face and non-face vectors so that the network can provide a sufficient responses against the observed vectors. The training data and the extracted characteristics are very important for improving the network. After extracting the characteristics from windows referred to network, data will be transformed into the form vector. The histogram of the image will be justified for better contrast. Then the image will be convolved with the Gabor filters in frequency domain. The input layer of this network has N units for an N dimensional input vector. The input vectors I are connected to the hidden layers H, which are then connected to the output layers J, where j is the number of output classes. The technique is discussed in figure 9.

Figure 9. Neural Network Structure

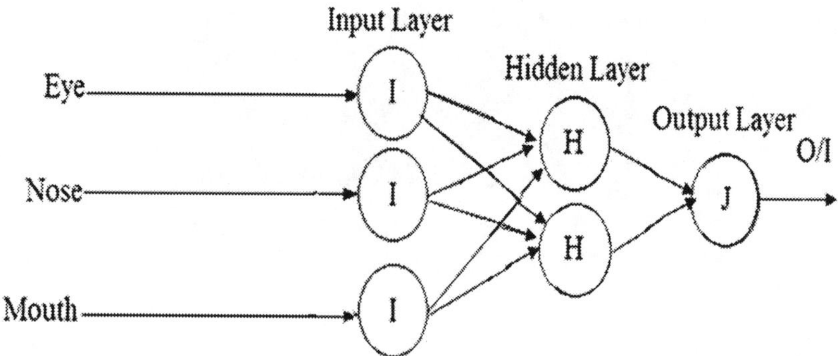

9. FACE DETECTION USING GABOR WAVELET AND NEURAL NETWORK

With the use of Gabor wavelet and feed forward neural network, a face detection can be done. This method helps in finding both the features points and also feature vectors. A set of a face and a non-face is created to train in the neural network. The dimension of the images given to the database is taken as 27 x 18, for reducing the training time.

9.1 Experimental Results

9.1.1 Test Case 1

Here, an image with the dimension of 163*139 is tested to detect a face and non-face. We can see in the figure 10, all the four faces are tested and features are extracted from them. The colored points are the features extracted from the faces.

In figure 11 we can see that all grey points are detected as features of the captured face.

9.1.2 Test Case 2

Here, an image with the dimension of 267*113 is tested to detect a face and non-face. We can see in figure 11 that all nine faces are tested and features are extracted from them.

In figure 12, we can see the features are extracted. The grey points shown in the figure are the extracted features.

But after extracting all the features, we can see clearly that, out of nine faces only seven faces are detected. Rest two are detected as non face.

Figure 10. There are four faces tested and features are extracted

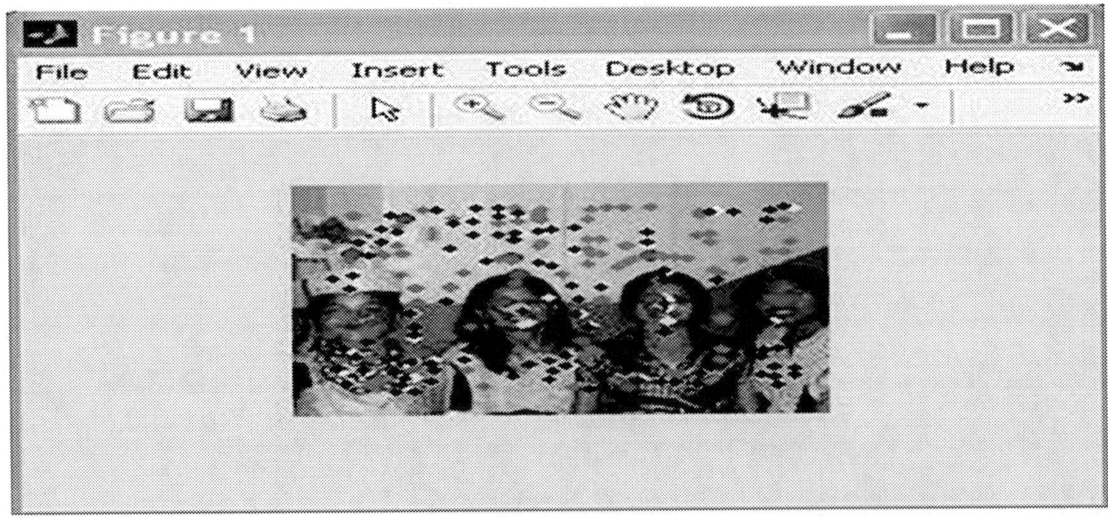

Figure 11. All nine faces tested and features are extracted

Figure 12. The grey point are shown as the extracted features

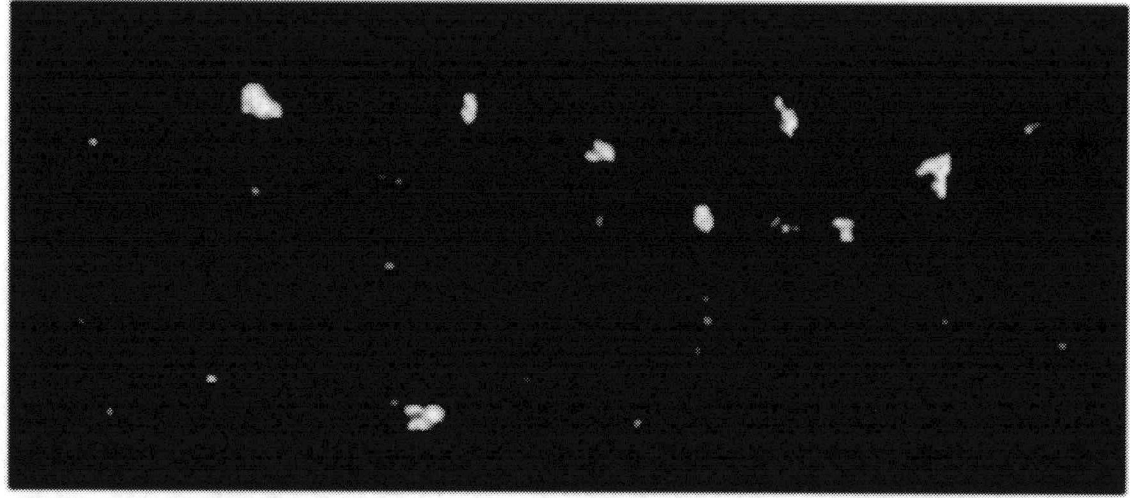

9.1.3 Test Case 3

Here, an image with the dimension of 200*104 is tested to detect a face and non-face.

We can see clearly from figure 13, 14 and 15 that, although from all the six faces features are extracted, but only four faces out six are detected.

From the example of the entire given image test, a simple comparison of performance analysis of the detection rate is shown in the given Table 1 below.

Figure 13. Seven faces are detected, some detection of a non-face occur due to the non-face database, since it is very difficult to select non-face that can be stored in a database.

Figure 14. Six faces are tested and features are extracted.

Figure 15. Grey points are shown as extracted features.

Table 1. Performance analysis of the detection rate.

Image dimension	Detected faces	Undetected faces
Image 1 (163 * 139)	All four faces are detected	None
Image 2 (267 * 113)	Only seven faces are detected	There are two faces which cannot be detected
Image 3 (200 * 104)	Only four faces detected	There are two faces which cannot be detected
Average in percentage	81.43%	14.8%

10. RESULTS AND RELATIVE COMPARISON AMONGST DIFFERENT METHODOLOGIES

Here, a comparison of the various techniques for feature extraction is done based on the method used, the features that can be extracted and their performance based on their illumination, expression, occlusion, posing and computational cost has also been compared. Comparison is shown in table 2.

11. SOME OF THE FACE DATABASES

In this section, we are going to discuss about the various databases which can be used for face recognition, some of them can be mentioned, such as FERET, ESSEX, YALE, ORL, FRGC, JAFFE, etc.

FERET: The Facial Recognition Technology (FERET) program was sponsored by The US Department of Defense (DoD) Counterdrug Technology Development Program Office. The goal of the FERET program was to develop automatic face recognition capabilities that could be employed to assist security, intelligence, and law enforcement personnel in the performance of their duties.

ESSEX: The database consists of images of 153 individual of resolution 180 by 200 pixels (in portrait format) of female and male (20 images each). It has plain green background with no head scale but with very minor variation in Head turn, tilt and slant. It does not have Image lighting and individual hairstyle variation.

Figure 16. Amongst six faces, only four faces are detected.

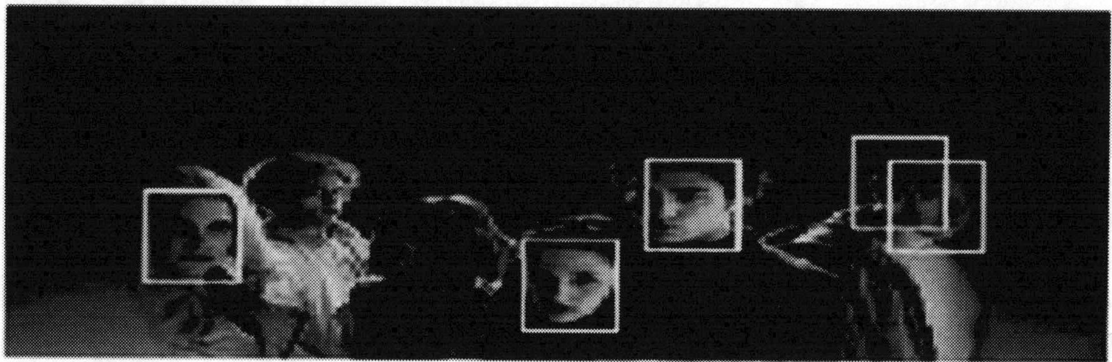

Table 2. Comparison of different feature extraction techniques

Category	Techniques	Feature Extraction	Performance
Holistic based	Principal Component Analysis, Eigenfaces	Global	Robust to low resolution images as it can extract necessary feature for normalization, but it cannot used for variation in scale, orientation and also illumination, it also need good quality images and large database requirement. Computational cost is less
Holistic based	Linear Discriminant Analysis, Fisherface	Global	Lower error rate, classify different people with different facial expression and more complex computational, it also need good quality images and large database requirement.
Holistic based	Independent Component Analysis, Higher- order statistical dependencies	Global	Independent Component Analysis basis vector are specially more localized than Principal Component Analysis, but it may produce different results as it extract more localized feature, it also need good quality images and large database requirement.
Analytic based	Gabor wavelets	Local	It is sensitive to large facial expression variation, homogenous illumination changes, robust against beard, glasses, etc., but a large number of features are used.
Analytic based	Elastic Bunch Graph Matching	Local	Computationally expensive especially for large database
Analytic based	Face Bunch Graph	Local	Reduces cost computation and also it can tolerate local distortion.
Hybrid based	Discriminant Common Vector	Both Global and Local	Computational complexity is lower as it obtain low dimensional with enhanced discrimination power.

YALE: The Yale face database consists of monochrome images, only frontal images, facial expressions, and facial details, different light conditions, center-light, w/glasses, happy, left-light, w/no glasses, normal, right-light, sad, sleepy, surprised, wink. The image size is of 320 * 243. Number of feces of different person are 15, and the number of face expression of each person are 11.

ORL: The ORL database of Faces consists of monochrome images, different times, varying the lighting, facial expressions (open / closed eyes, smiling /not smiling and facial details (glasses / no glasses). All the images were taken against a dark homogeneous background. Read Olivetti ORL face database (now ATT). Image size can be 92 * 112, the number of faces of different person are 40. And there are 10 different facial expression of each person.

FRGC: The primary goal of the FRGC was to promote and advance face recognition technology designed to support existing face recognition efforts in the U.S. Government. FRGC developed new face recognition techniques and prototype systems while increasing performance by an order of magnitude. The FRGC was open to face recognition researchers and developers in companies, academia, and research institutions. FRGC ran from May 2004 to March 2006. In the FRGC, high resolution images consist of facial images with 250 pixels between the centers of the eyes on average. The FRGC will facilitate the development of new algorithms that take advantage of the additional information inherent in high resolution images.

JAFFE: The Japanese Female Facial Expression, images may be used for non-commercial research. The database contains 213 images of 7 facial expressions (6 basic facial expressions + 1 neutral) posed by 10 Japanese female models. Each image has been rated on 6 emotion adjectives by 60 Japanese subjects. The images size is 256 * 256, and no color. The database was planned and assembled by Michael Lyons, Miyuki Kamachi, and Jiro Gyoba.

12. CONCLUSION

In this chapter, we have discussed about different facial feature extraction scheme. All of these schemes are implemented in MATLab. Based on the implementation, we have prepared a comparison table. After careful comparison of all of these approaches, we have found that the best performance can be achieved by using a hybrid approach, which is a combination of different techniques applied in the other approaches, as we can see that extraction of local and global features are both required for face recognition.

13. FUTURE RESEARCH DIRECTION

Here in this chapter, we have studied different methodologies of feature extraction scheme in facial recognition. Basically two types of features are there. First one is known as local features and second one is known as global features, we have studied different methodologies to extract the both local and global features. All the techniques extract the local and global features separately. Each feature has some advantages and limitations. But both of them complement each other. For computing the local and global feature separately the cost of computation is much higher. So in future, we will try to devise the algorithms, which will extract the local and global feature at the same time.

REFERENCES

Barlett, M. S., Movellan, J. R., & Sejnowski, T. J. (2002). Face recognition by Independent Component Analysis. *IEEE Transactions on Neural Networks*, *13*(6), 1450–1464. doi:10.1109/TNN.2002.804287 PMID:18244540

Cevikalp, H., Neamtu, M., Wilkes, M., & Barkma, A. (2005). Discriminative Common Vecctor for Face Recognition. *IEEE Transactions on Pattern Analysis and Machine Intelligence*, *27*(1), 44–53. doi:10.1109/TPAMI.2005.9 PMID:15628264

Gursimarpreet, K., & Chander Kant, V. (2014). Comparative Analysis of Biometric Modalities. *International Journal of Advanced Research in Computer Science and Software Engineering*, *4*(4), 603–613.

Kar, Battacharjee, Basu, Nasipuri, & Kundu. (2011). High Performance Human Face Recognition Using Independent High Intensity Gabor Wavelet Responses: A Statistical Approach. *International Journal of Computer Science and Emerging Technologies*, *2*(1), 178-187.

Kumar, V. B., & Shreyas, B. S. (2011). Face Recognition Using Gabor Wavelets. In *Conference Proceedings of the IEEE Asilomar Conference on Signals, Systems and Computers*. IEEE.

Lades, M., Vorbriggen, J. C., Buhmann, J., Lange, J., & Konen, W. (1993). Distortion invariant object recognition in the dynamic link architecture. *IEEE Transactions on Computers*, *2*(3), 300–311. doi:10.1109/12.210173

Liu, C. J., & Wechsler, H. (2002). Gabor Feature Based Classi_cation Using the Enhanced Fisher Linear Discriminant Model for Face Recognition. *IEEE Transactions on Image Processing*, *11*(4), 467–476. doi:10.1109/TIP.2002.999679 PMID:18244647

Mathukannan, K., Latha, P., & Manimaran, J. (2013). Implementation of Artificial Neural Network for Face Recognition Using Gabor Feature Extraction. *ICTACT Journal on Image and Video Processing*, *4*(2), 690–694.

Riddhi, & Shruti. (2013). A Literature Survey on Face Recognition Techniques. *International Journal of Computer Trends and Technology*, *5*(4), 189–195.

Saini, R., & Narinder, R. (2014). Comparison of various Biometric Methods. *International Journal of Advances in Science and Technology*, *2*(1), 24–30.

Su, Y., Shan, S., Chen, X., & Gao, W. (2007). Hierarchical Ensemble of Global and Local Classifiers for Face Recognition. *IEEE Transaction on Pattern Recognition*, *25*(7), 1885–1895. PMID:19556198

Thangairulappan, K., Beaulah, J., & Jeyasingh, V. (2012). Face Representation Using Combined Method of Gabor Filters,Wavelet Transformation and DCV and Recognition Using RBF. *Journal of Intelligent Learning and Applications*, *5*(7), 266–273. doi:10.4236/jilsa.2012.44027

Wiskott, L., Fellous, J.-M., Uger, N. K., & Malsburg, C. V. D. (1999). Face Recognition by Elastic Bunch Graph Matching. *Intelligent Biometric Techniques in Fingerprint and Face Recognition*, *11*(5), 355–396.

KEY TERMS AND DEFINITIONS

Arnab Kumar Maji: completed his B. Tech and M.Tech in the field of Information Technology in the year of 2003 and 2005 respectively. He is working as an Assistant Professor of North Eastern Hill University, Shillong, Meghalaya, India since 2006. He has published more than 25 numbers of research paper in the field of algorithm, image processing and e-commerce. He is a professional member of ACM India.

Bandariakor Rymbai: is M.Tech student in the department of Information Technology of North Eastern Hill University. She successfully published around 05 papers on face recognition in her own credit.

Debdatta Kandar: Born in 1977 at Deulia, Purba Medinipur, West Bengal, INDIA has received *PhD(Engg.)* from Department of Electronics and Telecommunication Engineering, Jadavpur University, Kolkata, in the year 2011. He has been awarded *'Young Scientist'* award from *URSI GA-2005* at Vigyan Bhaban, Delhi. He also worked on a DRDO sponsored project. Mobile Communication, Soft Computing and Radar Operation are the area of specializations. Currently, he is holding the post of Associate Professor in the Department of Information Technology, North-Eastern Hill University.

Discriminant Common Vector: It is a common vector, which can be used for feature extraction formed by removing all the features of the eigenvectors corresponds to the nonzero eigenvalues of the within-class scatter matrix.

Eigen Faces: Eigen Face is also called a Principal Component Analysis. It is widely used for dimensionality reduction.

Elastic Graph: Elastic graph is basically used to plot the graph based on different feature points. All the feature points are connected to plot the graph. They are elastic in nature, because based on the facial expression, the graph may distort.

Face Bunch Graph: Face bunch graph is similar to elastic graph only. The modification in the face bunch graph is that, here every node has some attribute that is known as jet.

Facial Recognition System: It is a computer application for automatically identifying or verifying a person from a digital image or a video frame from a video source. One of the ways to do this is by comparing selected facial features from the image and a facial database.

Fisher Faces: It is also known as Linear Discriminant Analysis. It is also used for dimension reduction based. It basically categorizes the faces in different classes.

Gabor Wavelets: Gabor wavelets are basically used to classify the faces based on different frequency values.

Global Feature: Global feature of face recognition system considers the overall patter of the face such as shape of the face, hair color, eye brow color, lip color, color of the faces etc.

Identification: It deals with identifying a person based on the image of a face. This face image has to be compared with all the registered person (one-to-many matching).

Independent Component Analysis: It is the generalization of Principal Component Analysis. It is a technique used for extracting statistically independent variables.

Jets: A Jet is a small area in an image which is of grey values in a pixel based on the wavelet transform.

Local Feature: Local feature in face recognition refers to the relative position of mouth, eye, lips of a face.

Multi-Layer Perceptron: It is a neural network which consists of multi layers of computational units, usually interconnected in a feed forward way. Each neuron in one layer gets inputs from the previous layer and feed their output to the subsequent layer.

Neural Network: It is an interconnected group of artificial neurons that uses a mathematical or computational model for information processing based on the connection approach for computation. It is an adaptive system that changes its structure based on external and internal information that flows through the network.

Recognition: It is a biometric identification by scanning a person's face and matching it against a library of known faces.

Verification: It is concerned with validating a claimed identity based on the image of a face, either accepting or rejecting the identity claim (one-to-one matching).

Chapter 14
Adoption of Dual Iris and Periocular Recognition for Human Identification

R. Deepika
East West Institute of Technology, India

Srinivas Chetana
East West Institute of Technology, India

M. R. Prasad
JSS Academy of Technical Education, India

T. C. Manjunath
HKBK College of Engineering, India

ABSTRACT

Personal identification from the iris images acquired under less-constrained imaging environment is highly challenging. Such environment requires the development of efficient iris segmentation approach and recognition strategy which can exploit multiple features available for the potential identification. So, along with the iris features periocular features have increasing attention in biometrics technology. For the recognition purpose iris and periocular information are collected from both the eyes of same person simultaneously. The term periocular refers to the facial region in the immediate vicinity of the eye. Acquisition of image for periocular biometric is expected to require less subject cooperation. In this chapter, a dual iris based multimodal biometric system that increases the performance and accuracy of the typical iris recognition system is proposed.

INTRODUCTION

1. Biometric System

Authentication plays a major role to defend against intruders. The three main types of authentication are: Something you know such as a password, something you have such as a card or token, something you are such as biometrics. Biometric identification utilizes physiological and behavioral characteristics to authenticate a person's identity as shown in Figure 1. Physical characteristics that may be used for identification include: Fingerprints, palm prints, hand geometry, retinal patterns and iris patterns. Behavioural characteristics include: Signature, voice pattern and keystroke dynamics. As in Figure 1

DOI: 10.4018/978-1-4666-8737-0.ch014

Figure 1. Biometric system

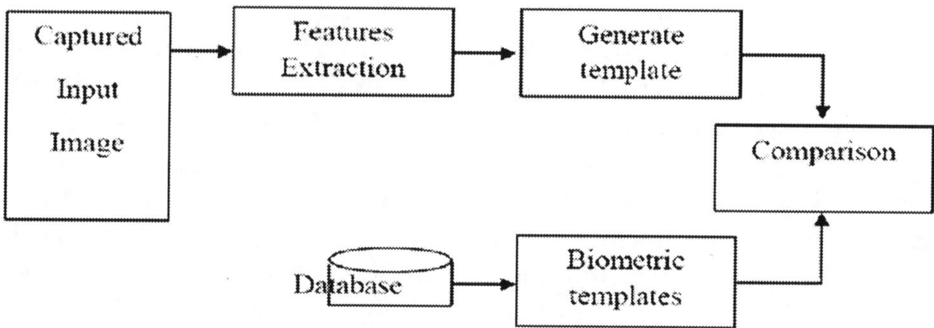

biometric system works by capturing and storing the biometric information and then comparing the scanned biometric with what is stored in the repository. A good biometric is characterized by use of a feature that is highly unique, stable, be easily captured.

Identity management refers to the challenge of providing authorized users with secure and easy access to information and services across a variety of networked systems. A reliable identity management system is a critical component in several applications that render their services only to legitimate users. Examples of such applications include physical access control to a secure facility, e-commerce, access to computer networks and welfare distribution. The primary task in an identity management system is the determination of an individual's identity.

Traditional methods of establishing a person's identity include knowledge-based (e.g., passwords) and token-based (e.g., ID cards) mechanisms. These surrogate representations of the identity can easily be lost, shared or stolen. Therefore, they are not sufficient for identity verification in the modern day world. Biometrics offers a natural and reliable solution to the problem of identity determination by recognizing individuals based on their physiological and/or behavioral characteristics that are inherent to the person. A biometric system can operate in two modes, verification and identification.

Verification: It is one to one comparison of a captured biometric with a stored template to verify that the individual is the one who he claims to be. If the two samples match well enough, the identity claim is verified, and if the two samples do not match well enough, the claim is rejected. Verification can be done accompanied with a smart card, username or ID number. In a verification decision context there are four possible outcomes normally called:

- False Accept Rate (FAR) or False Match Rate (FMR) or False Positive (FP): Occurs when the system accepts an identity claim, but the claim is not true. The proportion of impostor attempts whose Hamming Distance (HD) is below a given threshold.
- Correct Accept (CAR) or True Positive (TP) or True Accept (TA): Occurs when the system accepts, or verifies, an identity claim, and the claim is true.
- False Reject (FRR) or False Non Match Rate (FNMR) or False Negative (FN): Occurs when the system rejects an identity claim, but the claim is true. The proportion of genuine or authentic attempts whose HD exceeds a given threshold.
- Correct Reject (CRR) or True Negative (TN) or True Reject (TR): Occurs when the system rejects an identity claim and the claim is false.

Identification: It is one too many comparison of the captured biometric against a biometric database or gallery (The set of enrolled samples is often called a gallery) in attempt to identify an unknown individual. The identification only succeeds in identifying the individual if the comparison of the biometric sample with a template in the database falls within a previously set threshold. As verification mode, in identification decision context there are four possible outcomes normally called like verification:

- False Accept Rate (FAR) or False Match Rate (FMR) or False Positive (FP): Occurs when the system says that an unknown sample matches a particular person in the gallery and the match is not correct. The rate at which a matching algorithm incorrectly determines that an impostor's biometric sample matches an enrolled sample. The proportion of impostor attempts whose HD is below a given threshold.
- Correct Accept (CA) or True Positive (TP) or True Accept (TA): Occurs when the system says that an unknown sample matches a particular person in the gallery and the match is correct.
- False Reject (FR) or False Non Match Rate (FNMR) or False Negative (FN): Occurs when the system says that the sample does not match any of the entries in the gallery, but the sample in fact does belong to someone in the gallery. The proportion of genuine or authentic attempts who's HD exceeds a given threshold. The rate at which a matching algorithm incorrectly fails to determine that a genuine sample matches an enrolled sample.
- Correct Reject (CR) or True Negative (TN) or True Reject (TR): Occurs when the system says that the sample does not match any of the entries in the gallery, and the sample in fact does not.

Why Iris as Biometrics

The iris has many features that can be used to distinguish one iris from another as shown in Figure 2. One of the primary visible characteristic is the trabecular meshwork, a tissue which gives the appearance of dividing the iris in a radial fashion that is permanently formed by the eighth month of gestation. During the development of the iris, there is no genetic influence on it, a process known as chaotic morphogenesis that occurs during the seventh month of gestation, which means that even identical twins have differing irises. Formation of the unique patterns of the iris is random and not related to any genetic factors. Due to the epigenetic nature of iris patterns: The two eyes of an individual contain completely independent iris patterns and Identical twins possess uncorrelated iris patterns.

The human eye is composed by three layers or tunics: the external layer or fibrous tunic, constituted by the sclera, and, in its anterior part, by the cornea; the middle layer or uvea/vascular tunic, composed by the ciliary body and the iris; and the internal layer or the nervous tunic, where the retina is found. In a typical non-invasive image of the eye three anatomical features are visible: the sclera, the iris and the pupil.

The sclera is the external, firm, opaque and white posterior layer of the eye. It consists in conjunctive tissue, made of collagen and elastin fibers, and its main roles are the maintenance of the three-dimensional structure of the eye and the connection with the insertion points of the muscles responsible for eye movement. The iris is the colored part of the eye and its denomination comes from the fact that its color differs between individuals. Brown eyes possess a brown melanin pigment, absent in blue eyes, where the color derives from a light diffraction process similar to the one observed in the atmosphere and that confers the sky its color.

Figure 2. Typical eye image

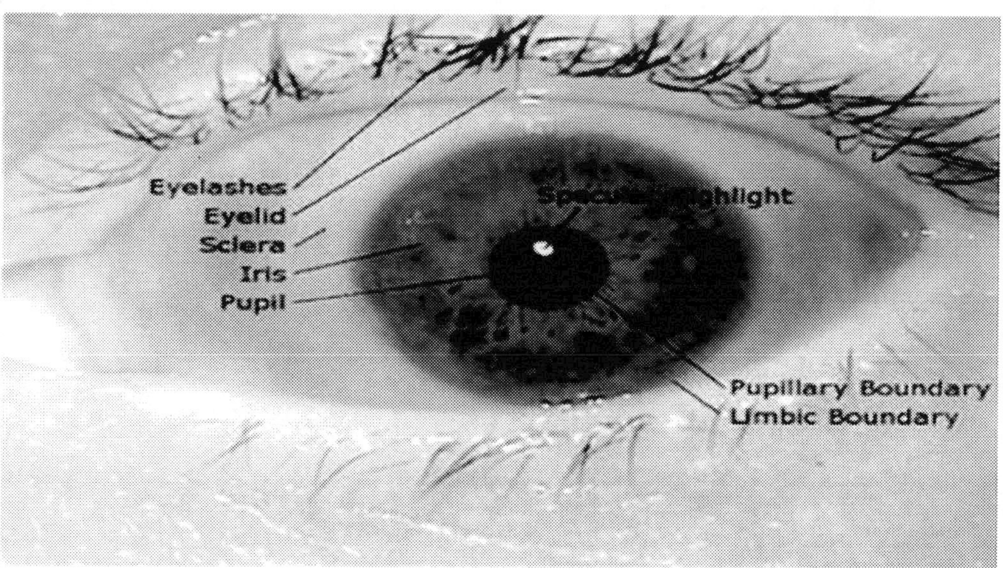

It's a contractile structure mainly composed of smooth muscle, surrounding an aperture, known as the pupil. Light penetrates the eye through the pupil and the iris regulates the quantity of light by adjusting the size of the pupil. The iris begins to form during the third month of gestation and the structure is complete by the eighth month, although pigmentation continues into the first year after birth. The visible features of the iris arise from a complex trabecular meshwork of connective tissues whose complex and unique patterns are seen under visible light illumination of the iris.

A high degree of uniqueness is however constrained by the acquisition condition: the quality of the iris image must be strictly monitored to ensure reasonable textural detail. To improve the quality of these images, near-infrared (NIR) light is typically chosen for illumination, as it is detectable by most cameras but not by the tested subject. It is almost impossible to surgically alter iris texture information and algorithms for artificial/fake iris detection are already developed and even blind people can use iris recognition systems. Early problems related with user collaboration and high associated costs are already being overcome with the development of user-friendly/cost-effective versions.

The fact that the iris is protected as in Figure 3 behind the eyelid, cornea and aqueous humour means that, unlike other biometrics such as fingerprints, the likelihood of damage is minimal. The iris is also not subject to the effects of aging which means it remains in a stable form from about the age of one until death. The use of glasses or contact lenses has little effect on the representation of the iris.

2. Iris Recognition System

The characteristics of the iris make it very attractive for use as a biometric for identifying individuals. Figure 4 shows general iris recognition system(J. Daugman, 2004)

A. Image processing techniques can be employed to extract the unique iris pattern from a digitized image of the eye, encode it into a biometric template, which can be stored in a database.

Figure 3. Eye Anatomy

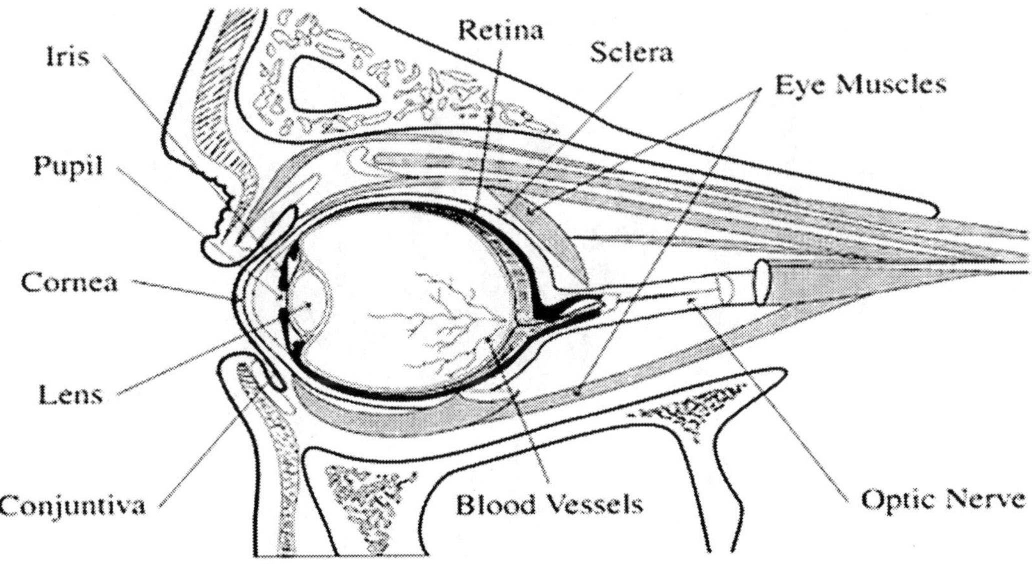

Figure 4. Iris Recognition System

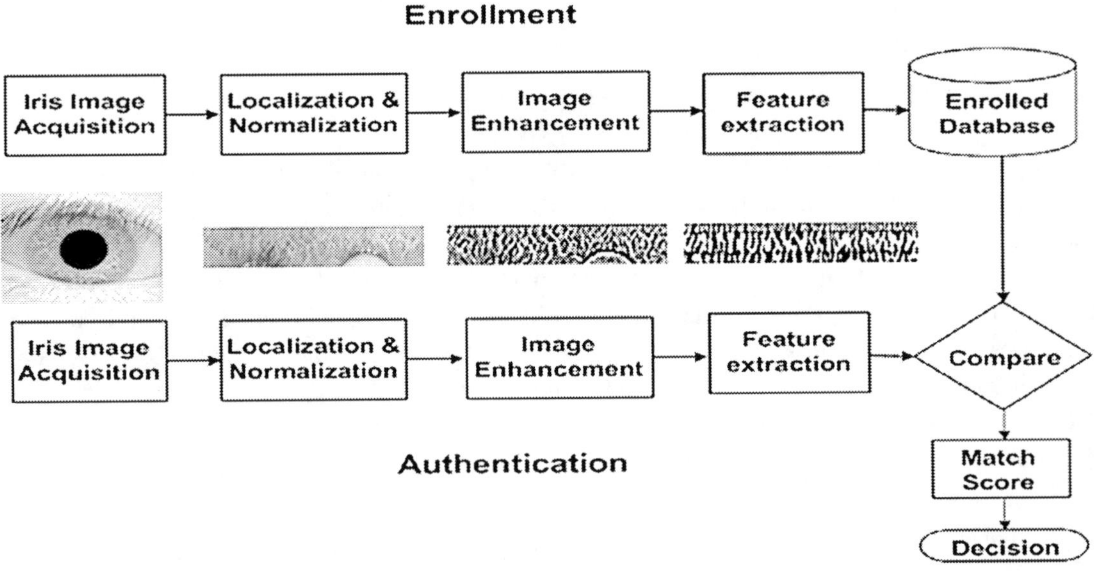

B. This biometric template contains an objective mathematical representation of the unique information stored in the iris, and allows comparisons to be made between templates.

C. When a subject wishes to be identified by iris recognition system, their eye is first photographed, and then a template created for their iris region.

D. This template is then compared with the other templates stored in a database until either a matching template is found and the subject is identified, or no match is found and the subject remains unidentified.

Iris scans analyze the features in the tissue surrounding the pupil which has more than 200 points that can be used for comparison, including rings, furrows and freckles. In computer vision, image segmentation is the process of partitioning a digital image into multiple segments sets of pixels, also known as super pixels. Segmentation involves detecting and isolating the iris structure from an image of the eye. The segmentation process has to accurately detect boundaries separating the iris from Sclera and pupil. Segmentation routine should detect occlusions due to eyelashes that can confound the extracted features. Errors in segmentation may result in inferior recognition performance due to inaccurate encoding of the textural content of the iris.

Normalization is a process that changes the range of pixel intensity values. Applications include photographs with poor contrast due to glare. In more general fields of data processing, such as digital signal processing, it is referred to as dynamic range expansion. The normalization process will produce iris regions, which have the same constant dimensions, so that two photographs of the same iris under different conditions will have characteristic features at the same spatial location.

Feature extraction is a special form of dimensionality reduction. When the input data to an algorithm is too large to be processed and it is suspected to be notoriously redundant then the input data will be transformed into a reduced representation set of features. Transforming the input data into the set of features is called feature extraction. If the features extracted are carefully chosen it is expected that the features set will extract the relevant information from the input data in order to perform the desired task using this reduced representation instead of the full size input. Matching For templates without strong features, or for when the bulk of the template image constitutes the matching image, a template-based approach may be effective.

As aforementioned, since template-based template matching may potentially require sampling of a large number of points, it is possible to reduce the number of sampling points by reducing the resolution of the search and template images by the same factor and performing the operation on the resultant downsized images, providing a search window of data points within the search image so that the template does not have to search every viable data point, or a combination of both.

3. Advantages of Iris Recognition System

The iris recognition system is being used for the human identification because of the following advantages:

A. Firstly, the physiological properties of irises are major advantages to using them as a method of authentication. The morphogenesis of the iris that occurs during the seventh month of gestation results in the uniqueness of the iris even between multi-birth children. These patterns remain stable throughout life and are protected by the body's own mechanisms. This randomness in irises makes them very difficult to forge and hence imitate the actual person.

B. Secondly, Iris-scanning technology is not very intrusive as there is no direct contact between the subject and the camera technology. It is non-invasive, as it does not use any laser technology, just simple video technology. The camera does not record an image unless the user actually engages it. It poses no difficulty in enrolling people that wear glasses or contact lenses. The accurateness of the scanning technology is a major benefit with error rates being very low, hence resulting in a highly reliable system for authentication.

C. Thirdly, scalability and speed of the technology. The technology is designed to be used with large-scale applications such as with ATMs. The speed of the database iris records are stored in is very important. Users do not like spending a lot of time being authenticated and the ability of the system to scan and compare the iris within a matter of minutes is a major benefit.

4. Overview of Traditional Biometrics

In the mid 1980s two ophthalmologists, Drs Leonard Flom and Aran Safir, proposed that no two irises are alike, even in twins, thus making them a good biometric. This belief was based on their clinical experience where they observed the distinctive features of irises including the "many collagenous fibres, contraction furrows, coronas, crypts, colour, serpentine vasculature, striations, freckles, rifts and pits". After researching and documenting the potential use of irises as a means of identifying people they were awarded a patent in 1987.

They then approached Dr John Daugman, a Harvard mathematician, in 1989 to assist with creating the mathematical algorithms required for digitally encoding an image of an iris to allow comparison with a real time image. By 1994 the algorithms had been developed and patented and are now used as "the basis for all iris recognition systems and products" currently being developed and sold.

Most of the existing system adopts NIR (near infrared) illumination with the wavelength between 700 and 900 nm. It is believed that with NIR illumination, the iris shows more detailed patterns. The NIR based acquisition setups operate in stop-and-stare mode which requires full cooperation from the subjects to provide images within close distance that is 1–3 feet in order to ensure the acquired images are in good quality. The constraints imposed in the conventional NIR-based iris recognition systems have limited the applicability of the iris recognition technology for forensic and surveillance applications, such as searching missing children and identifying terrorists from the crowd.

LITERATURE SURVEY

- **Efficient and Robust Segmentation of Noisy Iris Images For Non-Cooperative Iris Recognition:** It employs a constellation model to perform the iris segmentation task. The constellation model places multiple integro-differential operators at the current evaluating pixel in order to find the local minimum score. The pixel found to be at local minimum will be employed in the next iteration. The process is then iterated until it converges or the predefined maximum number of iterations is reached.Multiple integro-differential operators are repeated until the predefined maximum number of iterations is reached (T. Tan, Z. He, & Z. Sun, 2010). There are a few limitations observed in this method.
    - The segmentation model is still relying on the conventional segmentation approach which may not effectively segment the real-world acquired images.
    - The parameters for initial clustering pixels must be carefully chosen as it will affect the performance of the subsequent segmentation operations.
    - The constellation model may lead to a non-optimal iris center.
- **Iris Recognition: On the Segmentation of Degraded Images Acquired In the Visible Wavelength:** Two neutral network classifiers were trained by exploiting local color features to

classify image pixels into sclera/non-sclera and iris/non-iris categories. The trained classifiers operated in cascade order by firstly classifying sclera and then feeding the classified sclera pixels into the next classifier for iris pixels classification (H. Proenca,2010). Limitations of this work:

- There exists a strong dependency between the two classifiers.
- Any classification error from the first classifier will be propagated to the subsequent classifier. And it is not completely automated framework.

- **A unified framework for automated iris segmentation using distantly acquired face images:** Localized Zernike features were exploited for classifying image pixels into either iris or non-iris category using NN/SVM classifiers(Chun-Wei Tan and Ajay Kumar, 2012). Limitation of this work:
    - The Zernike features were computed for every single pixel which incurred heavily computational cost.
    - Did not suitable for time sensitive applications.
- **New Recognition Methods for Human Iris Patterns:** Two new methods are introduced to implement feature extraction. Method 1: mean thresholding, Method 2: mean-by-median thresholding. Both methods use a sliding-window technique and different mathematical operations on the pixels to produce feature vectors. Results of the methods produced relatively small feature vectors. Small templates improve the overall speed and reduce the amount of storage space required. The effect of light intensity was eliminated (Khalid A. Darabkh, Raed T. Al-Zubi, and Mariam T. Jaludi, 2014). Limitation of this work:
    - It does not concentrate on noise removal technique which may affect the accuracy of the segmentation.
- **Automated Segmentation of Iris Images Using Visible Wavelength Face Images:** Simultaneously exploits two set of the features for sclera and iris classification. Iris features are extracted by exploiting localized Zernike moments. Sclera features are extracted by using discriminant color features. Pixel based strategy is employed (C.-W. Tan and A. Kumar, 2011). Limitations of this work:
    - Heavy computational cost.
    - Require to undergo extensive training.
- **Efficient and Accurate at-a-distance Iris Recognition Using Geometric Key based Iris Encoding:** A set of coordinate-pairs, which is referred to as geometric key is randomly generated and exclusively assigned to each subject enrolled into the system. Geometric key uniquely defines the way how the iris features are encoded from the localized iris region pixels. Both the GeoKey encoded iris features and log-Gabor encoded iris features scores are fused (Chun-Wei Tan, Ajay Kumar, 2014). Limitation of this work:
    - Recognition accuracy for the distantly acquired iris images still not improved
    - Not incorporated the occlusion masks.
- **Challenging Ocular Image Recognition:** Ocular recognition is a new area of investigation targeted at overcoming the limitations of iris recognition performance in the presence of non-ideal data. The coir database of metadata was developed by collecting the ocular features from the images which is already present in the database. Scale-invariant feature transform was able to reliably match ocular features without the need for segmentation (V. P. Pauca, M. Forkin, X. Xu, R. Plemmons and A. Ross, 2011). Limitation of this work:

    - It cannot automatically collect the metadata
    - No fusioning is done.
- **Periocular biometrics when iris recognition fails:** The periocular biometrics, works as an alternative to iris recognition if the iris images are captured at a distance. Global features are obtained from the normalized iris image. From the input eye image local features are extracted. Scores are stored in the database. These two scores are normalized and fused for decision making (S. Bharadwaj, H.S. Bhatt, M. Vatsa, and R. Singh, 2010). Limitation of this work:
    - Only eyebrow region is included.
    - Effect of expression, wrinkles, makeup and spectacles on periocular biometrics is not studied.
- **Dual Iris Based Human Identification:** For the iris recognition at a distance capturing the good quality image of the same eye every time is a challenging task and the dual iris approach is beneficial. So, in system takes images from both eyes simultaneously. The hamming distance is chosen as the matching metric. The system matched both of the eyes of same person and if, for both eyes hamming distance less than the threshold then the person was identified as match (Iftakhar Hasan,Minnatul Fatema & M. Asharaful Amin, 2011). Limitation of this work:
    - Not concentrated on noise removal techniques which may affect the segmentation accuracy.
    - Works good for small number of images.
- **Half Iris Gabor iris recognition:** In proposed system (Ali M A M, MD Tahir N, 2014) iris having unique pattern, the segmentation proper then the high recognition rate, to segment and normalization use the conventional methods. In proposed system Gabor filter is used for feature extraction especially for half iris with support vector machine as classifier.
- **Long Distance iris Recognition:** In proposed system (Amandi R, Bayat M, Bazarghan, M, Minakhani K,& Mirloo H, 2013) image captured for long distance introduces algorithms to analyze and the software developed to identification efficiently .here Instead of finding the boundaries both inner and outer boundaries algorithm finds estimated pupil region for detection omitting other region for efficient search. Gaussian methods to mask which helpful for matching process. Feature extraction is done and matched through SIFT algorithm for CASIA.4 at distance.
- **Noise reduction in iris recognition using multiple thresholding:** In an iris recognition noise is considered as of the challenging issues. Where these noises having the different thresholds compare to normal regions, may cause improper detection of iris. In proposed system (Abu-Bakar S.A.R, Dehkordi A.B, 2013) noise detected using information obtained from histogram which is applied to CASIA V.3.
- **Optimizing 2D Gabor Filters for Iris Recognition:** In eye image iris structure are complex in nature, in our proposed system (Deravi F, Howells, W.G.J. Hoque S, Radu P & Sirlantzis K, 2013) 2D Gabor filter bank analysis technique is more accurate one to analyze these complex structures. Technique uses the multiple sets of parameters for analysis; these parameters gradually increase accuracy of recognition system. An advantage of the proposed system is suitable to apply on both near infrared visible spectrum iris images.
- **Novel iris segmentation and recognition system for human identification:** Segmentation is extraction required features from eye image. In iris recognition system it place important role, performance of segmentation affects to recognition. If iris features wrongly segmented hence lead to false identification. Some authors use Circular Hough Transform but it requires high processing

time and consumption of memory. It also fails to find the iris boundaries properly. In proposed method (Khurshid J, Zafar MF, Zaheer Z, 2013) canny edge technique is used for proper boundary detection. Feature extraction through curvelet Transform and SVM has used as classifier.

- **ORNL biometric eye model for iris recognition:** Non-ideal condition is unresolved problem which reduce recognition rate. Iris recognition system is reliable and accurate in order to prove that, in the proposed system (Barstow D.R, Boehnen C.B, Chaum E, Karakaya M, Santos-Villalobos H.J, 2012) using the Ray tracing Techniques, Which able to construct the transformation function for non refracted state. Linear elliptical unwrapping technique is proposed for normalization to improving the performance of the iris recognition system.
- **Iris recognition using 2-D elliptical support wavelet filter bank:** Iris recognition consists of four important steps. Iris segmentation, normalization, feature extraction and matching. In proposed system (Abdul-Jabbar.M, Abdulkader Z.N, 2012) segmentation, normalization uses the state of art method. For feature extraction new method that is 2-d elliptical wavelet and Haar filter bank for feature characteristics these are needed to form a reduced fixed length quantized feature vector. Using this method also improve recognition rate.

Disadvantages of Existing System

- In all the existing methodologies the iris and periocular biometrics are implemented separately.
- When one of the biometrics is degraded or missing cannot be further processed.
- Most of the existing system cannot operate simultaneously on visible and NIR illumination.
- It is not easy to capture good quality of same eye every time for iris recognition at a distance.

PROPOSED SYSTEM

Problem Statement: Iris recognition is well known to provide high recognition rates in controlled acquisition conditions. In instances where the iris is occluded or where segmentation fails due to harsh illumination, specular reflections, the performance of the iris recognition algorithms can degrade considerably. One potential solution is to use the ocular region of the face, sometimes referred to as periocular region. The term periocular refers to the facial region in the immediate vicinity of the eye. So the fusion of dual iris and periocular features increases the performance and accuracy of the typical iris recognition system.

Proposed Approach: An efficient iris segmentation approach and recognition strategy which can exploit multiple features available for the potential identification is proposed as shown in Figure 5. The iris segmentation approach applies random walker algorithm to efficiently estimate coarsely segmented iris images. The segmented iris images are post-processed using a sequence of operations which can effectively improve the segmentation accuracy. The joint strategy is employed in this chapter by combining the iris and extracted periocular features to achieve significant performance improvement. Dual iris approach is employed.

Advantages of Proposed System

- Multimodal biometric systems seek to alleviate some of the problems by providing multiple piece of evidence for the same identity.

Figure 5. Proposed system

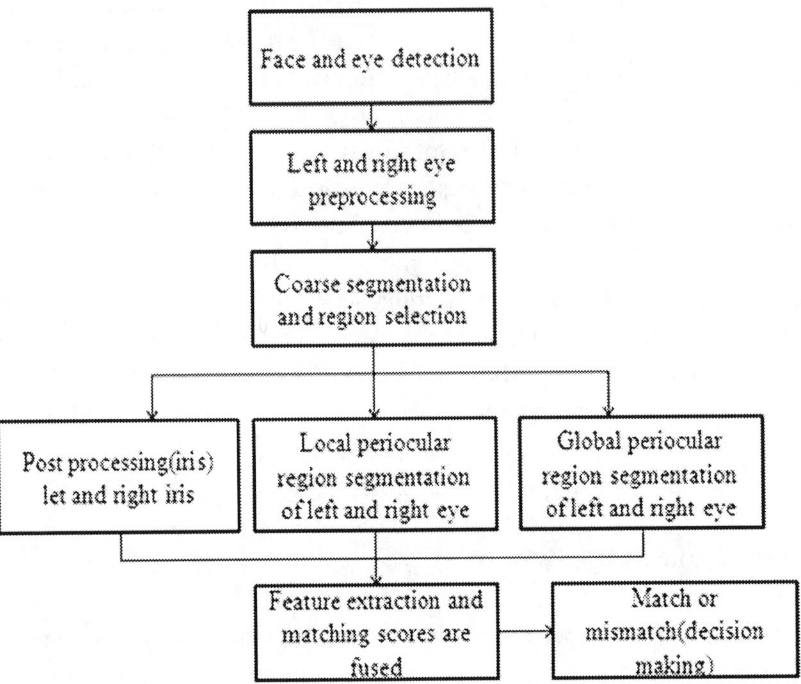

- Dual iris recognition approach is being used it improves the recognition accuracy compared to that of the single iris.
- Proposed segmentation approach does not require rigorous training hence it has less complexity compared to existing systems.

Applications of Iris Recognition Technology

- The most obvious use of iris recognition technology is within the computing environment: There is a lot of valuable data stored on a company's network and being able to access the network with a username and password is the most common method of authentication today. If a username and password is stolen then this gives the thief all of that person's access privileges and this can be detrimental to a company in today's competitive environment. Implementing an iris recognition system to authenticate users on the network means that there are no passwords to steal and no tokens to lose. Users are only able to access the systems they have privileges to access and it's very difficult for someone to replicate an iris for authentication.
- Another area iris recognition is useful with is physical security to data centers or computer rooms: Mounting a scanner by the access door and authenticating people via their iris is a good method of ensuring only those whose templates are in the database for computer room access are actually allowed in. This helps to alleviate problems associated with swipe card access where some systems have to be manually programmed with specific card numbers and robust processes need to be in place to ensure access lists are regularly reviewed. Swipe cards are also easily lost, stolen or borrowed.

- ATM is a major area where iris recognition is being trailed: The use of this technology with ATMs means that customers can discard their plastic cards and PINs thus eliminating the possibility of having cards and/or PINs stolen or lost.
- The banking industry is also involved in looking at implementing the technology in over the counter transactions with customers. This would reduce the requirement for customers to produce identification, bank books, account numbers etc and would result in faster transaction times that leave the bank teller with more time to concentrate on the level of service provided to the customer.
- Airport security: Airport security has seen a huge increase in focus after the recent events of September 11, 2001. Heathrow airport is already testing a system that scans a passenger's iris rather than the passenger needing to provide their passport. The aim behind the trial is to speed up processing of passengers and to detect illegal immigrants into the country.
- Adhaar India's unique id project for its one billion citizens uses iris scan as one of the identification features.

FUTURE RESEARCH DIRECTIONS

Future research could be conducted along the following directions to build a robust iris recognition system by developing more robust feature encoding schemes and also like to study the impact of cosmetics on the texture of the periocular region and the ensuing recognition capability.

CONCLUSION

The purpose of Iris recognition, a biometrical based technology for personal identification and verification, is to recognize a person from his/her iris prints. In this chapter, an attempt has been made to present of different iris and periocular recognition methods separately. The study of different techniques provides a development of new technique in this area as combining the iris and periocular features of both the eyes of same person and expected the more recognition accuracy than that of the existing approaches. The primary objective of this chapter is to improve the iris recognition accuracy by exploiting the iris and periocular information from both eyes simultaneously. Since this chapter provides idea of combining the iris and periocular features from both the eyes of same person works efficiently and expected better recognition accuracy compared to literature for the distantly acquired noisy iris images.

REFERENCES

Abdul-Jabbar, M., & Abdulkader, Z. N. (2012). Iris Recognition using 2-D elliptical-support wavelet filter bank. *IPTA*, 359-363.

Abu-Bakar, S. A. R., & Dehkordi, A. B. (2013). Noise reduction in iris recognition using multiple thresholding. *ICSIPA*, 140-144.

Ali, M. A. M., & Tahir, N. (2014). Half Iris Gabor iris recognition. *CSPA*, 282-287.

Amandi, R., Bayat, M., Minakhani, K., Mirloo, H., & Bazarghan, M. (2013). Long Distance Iris Recognition. *MVIP*, 164-168.

Barstow, D. R., Bohenen, C. B., Chaum, E., Barstow, D. R., Karakaya, M., Santos-Villalobos, H. J. (2012). ORNL biometric eye model for iris recognition. *BTAS*, 176-182.

Bharadwaj, S., Bhatt, H. S., Vatsa, M., & Singh, R. (2010). Periocular biometrics: When iris recognition fails. *Proc. BTAS 2010.*

Chinese Academy of Sciences CASIA iris image database. (2004). Institute of Automation. Retrieved from http://www.sinobiometrics.com

Daugman, J. (2004). How iris recognition works. *IEEE Transactions on Circuits and Systems for Video Technology*, *14*(1), 21–30. doi:10.1109/TCSVT.2003.818350

Deravi, F., Howells, W. G. J., Hoque, S., Radu, P., & Sirlantzis, K. (2013). Optimizing 2-D Gabor Filters for Iris Recognition. *EST*, 47-50.

Khalid, A. (2014). New Recognition Methods for Human Iris Patterns. Academic Press.

Khurshid, J., Zafar, M. F., & Zaheer, Z. (2013). Novel iris segmentation and recognition system for human identification. *IBCAST*, 128-131.

Park, U., Jillela, R. R., Ross, A., & Jain, A. K. (2011). Periocular biometrics in the visible spectrum. *IEEE Trans. Info. Forensics & Security*, *6*(1), 96–106. doi:10.1109/TIFS.2010.2096810

Pauca, V. P., Forkin, M., Xu, X., Plemmons, R., & Ross, A. (2011). Challenging Ocular Image Recognition. *Proc. of SPIE, 8029*.

Proenca, H. (2010). Iris recognition: On the segmentation of degraded images acquired in the visible Wavelength. *IEEE Transactions on Pattern Analysis and Machine Intelligence*, *32*(8), 1502–1516. doi:10.1109/TPAMI.2009.140 PMID:20558880

Radu, P., Srilantzis, K., Howells, V., Hoque, S., & Deravi, F. (2010). *Are Two Eyes Better Than One? An Experimental Investigation on Dual Iris Recognition*. University of Kent.

Tan, C.-W., & Kumar, A. (2011). Automated segmentation of iris images using visible wavelength face images. *Proc. CVPR*. doi:10.1109/CVPRW.2011.5981682

Tan, C.-W., & Kumar, A. (2012). A unified framework for automated iris segmentation using distantly acquired face images. *IEEE Transactions on Image Processing*, *21*(9), 4068–4079. doi:10.1109/TIP.2012.2199125 PMID:22614641

Tan, C.-W., & Kumar, A. (2014). *Efficient and Accurate at-a-distance Iris Recognition Using Geometric Key based Iris Encoding. IEEE Trans. Information Forensics and Security.*

Tan, T., He, Z., & Sun, Z. (2010). Efficient and robust segmentation of noisy iris images for non-cooperative iris recognition. *Image and Vision Computing*, *28*(2), 223–230. doi:10.1016/j.imavis.2009.05.008

KEY TERMS AND DEFINITIONS

Acceptability: Degree of approval of a technology.

Authentication: Authentication is the process of determining whether someone or something is, in fact, who or what is declared to be.

Biometrics: Biometrics refers to metrics related to human characteristics, it is used to identify the in a group under surveillance.

Circumvention: Ease of use of a substitute.

Collectability: Ease of acquisition for measurement.

Digitize: Converting picture or sound into digital form that can be processed by a computer.

Encode: The process of encoding the images and sensory information.

Iris recognition: Process of identifying individuals by recognizing the iris features.

Multimodal: More than one biometric feature is used for identification.

NIR: Light illumination that has the wavelength of 700nm-1mm.

Performance: Accuracy, speed, and robustness of technology used.

Periocular: The term periocular refers to the facial region in the immediate vicinity of the eye.

Permanence: Measures how well a biometric resists aging and other variance over time.

Pixel: Pixel is a physical point in an image. It is the basic unit of the programmable color on computer display.

Segmentation: It is the process of partitioning a digital image into multiple segments.

Template: It is a standardized non-executable file type used by computer software as pre formatted examples on which to base other files.

Uniqueness: Is how well the biometric separates individuals one from another.

Universality: Each person should have the characteristic.

Visible: Light rays having the illumination of 380nm-700nm wavelength.

APPENDIX

Abbreviations

HD: Hamming Distance
FAR: False Accept Rate
FRR: False Reject Rate
CAR: Correct Accept Rate
CRR: Correct Reject Rate
FMR: False Match Rate
FNMR: False Non Match Rate
CMC: Cumulative Match Characteristic
TP: True Positive
TN: True Negative
TA: True Accept
TR: True Reject
EER: Equal Error Rate
NIR: Near Infrared
CASIA: Chinese Academy of Sciences Institute of Automation

Additional Information

CASIA Iris

Db-CASIA.v1: It is an iris database provided by National Laboratory of Pattern Recognition, Institute of Automation, and Chinese Academy of Sciences freely for iris recognition researchers. Iris images of CASIA-IrisV1were captured with a homemade iris camera. Eight 850nm NIR illuminators are circularly arranged around the sensor to make sure that iris is uniformly and adequately illuminated. In order to protect our IPR in the design of iris camera especially the NIR illumination scheme before appropriate patents were granted, the pupil regions of all iris images in CASIA-IrisV1 were automatically detected and replaced with a circular region of constant intensity to mask out the specular reflections from the NIR illuminators before public release. Clearly, such processing may affect pupil detection but has no effects on other components of an iris recognition system such as iris feature extraction since iris feature extraction only uses the image data in the region between the pupil and the sclera, i.e. the ring-shaped iris region. The database includes 756 iris images from 108 eyes. For each eye, 7 images are captured in two sessions with our self-developed device CASIA close up iris camera, where three samples are collected in the first session and four in the second session. All images are stored as BMP format with resolution 320*280.

Db-CASIA.v2: It was used for the First Biometrics Verification Competition (BVC) on face, iris, and fingerprint recognition in the 5th Chinese Conference on Biometrics Recognition (Sinobiometrics, 2004), held in GuangZhou, Chinain 2004. CASIA-IrisV2 includes two subsets captured with two different devices: Irispass-H developed by OKI and they self-developed device CASIA-IrisCamV2. Each subset includes 1200 images from 60 classes.

Db-CASIA.v3: It was used in the experimental evaluation of the iris indexing techniques proposed by (Mukherjee and Ross, 2008). This database includes three subsets which are labeled as CASIA-Iris-Interval, CASIA-Iris-Lamp and CASIA-Iris-Twins. CASIA-Iris.v3 contains a total of 22,034 iris images from more than 700 subjects. All iris images are 8 bit gray-level JPEG files, collected under near infrared illumination. Almost all subjects are chinese except a few in casia-iris-intervals. Because the three data sets were collected in different times, only CASIA-Iris Interval and CASIA-Iris-Lamp have a small overlap in subjects.

DB-CASIA.v3-Interval: Iris images of CASIA-Iris-Interval were captured with a self developed close-up iris camera. The most compelling feature of this iris camera is that it has designed a circular NIR LED array, with suitable luminous flux for iris imaging. Because of this novel design, this iris camera can capture very clear iris images. CASIA Iris- Interval is well-suited to study the detailed texture features of iris images.

DB-CASIA.v3-Lamp: CASIA-Iris-Lamp was collected using a hand-held iris sensor produced by OKI. A lamp was turned on/off close to the subject to introduce more intraclass variations when we collected CASIA-Iris-Lamp. Elastic deformation of iris texture due to pupil expansion and contraction under different illumination conditions is one of the most common and challenging issues in iris recognition. So CASIA-Iris- Lamp is good for studying problems of non-linear iris normalization and robust iris feature representation.

DB-CASIA.v3-Twins: CASIA-Iris-Twins contains iris images of 100 pairs of twins, which were collected during Annual Twins Festival in Beijing using OKI's IRISPASS-h camera. Although iris is usually regarded as a kind of phenotypic biometric characteristics and even twins have their unique iris patterns, it is interesting to study the dissimilarity and similarity between iris images of twins.

Db-CASIA.v4: It is an extension of CASIA-IrisV3 and contains six subsets. The three subsets from CASIA-IrisV3 are CASIA.v3-Iris- Interval, CASIA.v3-Iris-Lamp and CASIA.v3-Iris-Twins respectively. The three new subsets are CASIA.v4-Iris-Distance, CASIA.v4-Iris-Thousand, and CASIA.v4-Iris-Syn. DB-CASIA.v4-Distance: CASIA-Iris-Distance contains iris images captured using a self developed Long-range Multi-modal Biometric image acquisition and recognition System (LMBS). The advanced biometric sensor can recognize users from 3 meters away by actively searching iris face or palm print patterns in the visual field via an intelligent multi-camera imaging system. The LMBS is human-oriented by fusing computer vision, human computer interaction and multi-camera coordination technologies and improves greatly the usability of current biometric systems. The iris images of CASIA-Iris-Distance were captured by a high resolution camera so both dual-eye iris and face patterns are included in the image region of interest. And detailed facial features such as skin pattern are also visible for multi-modal biometric information fusion.

DB-CASIA.v4-Thousand: CASIA-Iris-Thousand contains 20,000 iris images from 1,000 subjects, which were collected using IKEMB-100 camera produced by IrisKing. IKEMB-100 is a dual-eye iris camera with friendly visual feedback, realizing the effect of ——What You See Is What You Get||. The bounding boxes shown in the frontal LCD help users adjust their pose for high-quality iris image acquisition. The main sources of intra-class variations in CASIA-Iris-Thousand are eyeglasses and specular reflections. Since CASIA-Iris-Thousand is the first publicly available iris dataset with one thousand subjects, it is well-suited for studying the uniqueness of iris features and develops novel iris classification and indexing methods.

DB-CASIA.v4-Syn: CASIA-Iris-Syn contains 10,000 synthesized iris images of 1,000 classes. The iris textures of these images are synthesized automatically from a subset of CASIA-IrisV1 with the approach. Then the iris ring regions were embedded into the real iris images, which makes the artificial iris images more realistic. The intra-class variations introduced into the synthesized iris dataset include deformation, blurring, and rotation, which raise a challenge problem for iris feature representation and matching. Was demonstrated that the synthesized iris images are visually realistic and most subjects cannot distinguish genuine and artificial iris images. More importantly, the performance results tested on the synthesized iris image database have similar statistical characteristics to genuine iris database. So users of CASIA-IrisV4 are encouraged to use CASIA-Iris- Syn for iris recognition research.

Chapter 15
CUDA or OpenCL:
Which is Better? A Detailed Performance Analysis

Mayank Bhura
National Institute of Technology Karnataka, India

Pranav H. Deshpande
National Institute of Technology Karnataka, India

K. Chandrasekaran
National Institute of Technology Karnataka, India

ABSTRACT

Usage of General Purpose Graphics Processing Units (GPGPUs) in high-performance computing is increasing as heterogeneous systems continue to become dominant. CUDA had been the programming environment for nearly all such NVIDIA GPU based GPGPU applications. Still, the framework runs only on NVIDIA GPUs, for other frameworks it requires reimplementation to utilize additional computing devices that are available. OpenCL provides a vendor-neutral and open programming environment, with many implementations available on CPUs, GPUs, and other types of accelerators, OpenCL can thus be regarded as write once, run anywhere framework. Despite this, both frameworks have their own pros and cons. This chapter presents a comparison of the performance of CUDA and OpenCL frameworks, using an algorithm to find the sum of all possible triple products on a list of integers, implemented on GPUs.

INTRODUCTION

Of recent, multi-core and many-core processors have far surpassed the performance of the sequential processor. Since the advent of GPGPUs, their inherent parallel architecture coupled with the much higher amount of bandwidth and floating operations per second (FLOPS), there has been an increase in the use of high-end graphic processors over the past many years. High Definition graphics has led its way from the glory of gaming industry to the scientific realm of higher floating point calculations. Complex operations are executed in parallel in a multithreaded environment with enormous computa-

DOI: 10.4018/978-1-4666-8737-0.ch015

tional horsepower. Increasing parallelism rather than clock rate has been the motive ever since. Titan, a supercomputer built for use in science projects, is the first hybrid model consisting of both CPUs and GPUs to achieve 17.59 petaFLOPS in speed, its theoretical peak value being 27petaFLOPS. It consists of 18,688 AMD Opteron 6274 16-core CPUs and 18,688 Nvidia Tesla K20X GPUs.

Over the years, many frameworks have been developed to efficiently utilizethe parallelism and bandwidth of our modern day GPUs. CUDA (Compute Unified Device Architecture), developed by Nvidia, has eliminated the need of graphic API. Similarly, the APP (Advanced Parallel Processing) framework, developed by ATI, allows ATI's GPUs to work together with CPUs to achieve an even greater amount of scalability and parallelism. OpenCL (Open Computing Language) on the other hand, is a standard framework for parallel programming on Heterogeneous Systems. Its portability enables various platforms to be tested without the need to rebuild the programs from scratch.All these frameworks have been developed over a long time of research, starting from the high-level shading languages such as HLSL and GLSL, and research is bound to further reach new limits in the era of parallel computing.

But when it comes to decide which framework to choose, deep thought has to be given in to decide the parameters of comparison, along with proper implementations in the respective frameworks to have a fair comparison. There are all kinds of applications. Each of them can have their own domain of tasks. Thus, it may not be suitable to fix a framework for creating all types of applications. Each framework has its own pros and cons, which makes it mandatory that for a good performance utilization, we first decide which one to choose for our application. Thus,we need to be able to compare and decide as to which of the frameworks are suitable for a given computational task, on a given computational environment.

This is exactly what this chapter is for. This chapter investigates the portability vs performance feature of the two frameworks, CUDA and OpenCL, over various parameters, through a common problem: finding the sum of all triple products over an increasing list of real numbers.Though simple, this problem requires large amount of multiplication operations. Moreover, the list consists of floating point numbers, which requires precision in calculations. This enables us to easily move forward to the implementation issues. It also enables the readers to understand the problem and its complexity, with just a basic level of knowledge in algorithms, which in turn would make it possible for many beginners to understand the matter being presented in this chapter, with ease.

For the implementation hardware, the authors decided to go with NVIDIA GPUs as the best choice for comparison. The reason being, CUDA only supports NVIDIA hardware, while OpenCL can be run on many other GPUs, including that of NVIDIA. Moreover, it cannot be said that CUDA is at an advantage while running it on its own vendor's hardware. As the chapter will disclose, the performance readings have not been too different from each other.

Efforts are to further optimize the algorithm implementations in terms of parallel execution with minimum overheads, and compare the kernel runtime of the two frameworks for the same problem. This chapter also studies how the execution times of both frameworks change as load on GPU increases. In the upcoming sections we discuss some of the related work and later move on towards discussing the algorithm, optimization strategies and comparison of performance.

Background

There have been debates regarding the better and more suitable one between OpenCL and CUDA. CUDA currently has only one vendor, NVIDIA, while OpenCL is a vendor-neutral framework, making it possible to run OpenCL code on any hardware, since it is portable. On the other hand, CUDA has advantages of including a debugger and a profiler. The CUDA "runtime API" is easier to use than OpenCL. CUDA allows C++ constructs also whereas OpenCL is based on C99 implementation. The main advantage of OpenCL lies in its portability. OpenCL is open-standard, and all sorts of machines can be used in conjunction, called "contexts" in OpenCL terminology. This enables the powerful multicore CPUs to be used for computation as well. However, CUDA has more advanced and fine-grained API, allowing us to handle each and every detail down to the hardware.In this chapter the authors have compared performance versus portability trade-offs as seen in the sections below.

OPENCL VS. CUDA

Issues, Controversies, Problems

The authors personally feel that OpenCL is more likely to be used more often, in spite of the performances of both frameworks being nearly the same.The primary reason beingthat OpenCL supports more graphics processor vendors including the most used AMD and NVIDIA cards. CUDA, on the other hand, is only limited to NVIDIA processors.

OpenCL is interfaced from code used in production and is portable between different graphics hardware (context creation is possible in OpenCL). It has limited operations, but still a wide range of functions to do the complex tasks. Thanks to its open-standard nature, developers can have a single set of code, to be used in many programs, running on different types of devices, knowing that it can be compiled again each time, with ease. The devices on which it can be run include our normal use CPUs, servers and even mobile devices.

CUDA, on the other hand, is a separate language (CUDA C). It has been created by NVIDIA scientists and hence, is made to support only NVIDIA hardware (Eg. NVIDIA GPUs). It has almost full control over the programming aspect. It can thus be said to be like a language in itself. Apart from this, CUDA also has lots of code profiling and debugging tools.

As seen, there are quite a lot of differences between the two frameworks, and comparing both takes quite more than just observation. Some of the differences being: OpenCL is portable, while CUDA is NVIDIA-only.

In terms of ease of usage, OpenCL is easier to use out of the box. However, once the CUDA environment is set up, it is almost like programming in any other language, since it has its own set of libraries for all the complex and simple tasks to perform. In terms of community and documentation, both CUDA and OpenCL frameworks have an extensive documentation, as well as an extremely good range of examples.

If we take into account the performance measure, which the authors will be discussing in this chapter, we find that OpenCL and CUDA, both the frameworks perform nearly the same, if given the same running environments and coded properly, keeping in mind the minute differences in which OpenCL and CUDA operate. OpenCL also allows tasks to be run on groups of machines, called "contexts". This allows programs to be run on the faster CPUs in conjunction with our parallel GPUs. The programmer can choose which device is most suitable to execute a specific type of job. All of this can be done with a single programming API, which gives us a wide range of possibilities of how to efficiently be able to use the devices at hand.

There have been many debates and research papers published, throwing light upon various aspects of both frameworks, which shows that both have been heavily tested. While the OpenCL library is extensive with many added features, CUDA has advanced proprietary libraries which favor in mathematical tasks. Some have an opinion that OpenCL is still not as advanced, while others are of the belief that OpenCL is the future, being open-source, and not restricted to a particular hardware or vendor. Some, on the other hand, have found both the frameworks to be far too complex to use, making development costly and involving poor code maintainability. This makes projects undertaken become too costly to start with, due to which several approaches have been made to further simplify the development process.

The authors have detailed the minute performance differences and compared on varied GPU loads. The reasons behind the gaps are analyzed thoroughly and they can all be essentially related to various behaviors of programmers, compilers and users.

Categorization

The authors have divided their work based on as follows:

1. Related work done by researchers on the field.
2. Problem statement, Algorithm Description and Optimization.
3. Implementation of OpenCL and CUDA kernels.
4. Comparison and Evaluation of Performance in terms of various parameters.

Related Work

It was realised that the need to increase parallel computing is more than increasing clock rate. John Owens(2008) neatly describes the powerful, programmable and highly parallel GPUs in his description. In the Havok FX implementation, the GPU stores object details whereas CPU performs broad phase collision detection using sweep algorithms and sorting algorithms. It also discusses loop unrolling mechanisms. Importance is given to double-precision floating point architecture along-with the increasing bandwidth capacity of PCI (between CPU and GPU). The GPU usage has been staggering in terms of signalling sampling as pointed out byToral O.A (2014). David Maletz (2011) demonstrates high-quality rendering of dynamic scenes at 3 - 4 seconds per frame (evaluated at every pixel) for a 512 x 512 image on an NVIDIA 480 GTX. In the work of Jianbin Fang (2011), 16 benchmarks have been compared. Their findings show that under fair comparisons OpenCL performs equivalent to CUDA. Importance has been given on OpenCL's performance and portability under fair conditions. Algorithms such as BFS and FFT have been tested on GTX480, GTX280 and Radeon HD5870 clocking TP*FLOPS* equal to 933.12 GFlops/sec and 1344.96 GFlops/sec for GTX280 and GTX480 respectively. CUDA and OpenCL have also been implemented by J.W.S. Liu (1991) andG. F. Diamos (2008). In the work of J. W. S. Liu. (1991)we look forward at imprecise algorithms or approximate algorithms. G. F. Diamos (2008) dealt with choosing an algorithm from an existing number of algorithms to bring about the best performance. The process of choosing the algorithm happens at runtime where faster GPU computations take place.

Rick Weber (2011) ran Quantum Monte Carlo Algorithms, implemented in CUDA, OpenCL, Brook+, C++ and VHDL. This provided us with a clean comparison ground, of man application accelerators on performance, design, platform and architectures. The results obtained from them, show that OpenCL features portability between different types of hardware, of all sorts of vendors, but may suffer from performance issues, due to the ease in portability offered. Ping Du (2010) evaluated many aspects of OpenCL as a performance-portable method for GPGPU application development. The triangular solver (TRSM) and matrix multiplication (GEMM) problems have been selected for implementation in OpenCL. Their experimental results show that nearly 50% of peak performance could be obtained in GEMM on both NVIDIA Tesla C2050 and ATI Radeon 5870 in OpenCL. Their results also reveal that the performance can significantly improve if we get into the details of the architecture on which the algorithm is being implemented. Each machine has its own architecture, and if we take into account to get optimizations, they are bound to perform better under the latter case. Anthony Danalis (2010) presented a Scalable Heterogeneous Computing (SHOC) benchmark suite. SCHO is a collection of programs that are used to evaluate various performance parameters of these heterogeneous computing systems. Its initial focus was on systems containing GPUs and multi-core processors, and on the new OpenCL programming standard. SHOC uses micro-benchmarks to assess architectural features of the systems. At higher levels, SHOC uses application kernels to determine system-wide performance including many system features. It has programs written in both CUDA as well as OpenCL in order to provide a comparison for both of these programming models.

K. Komatsu1 (2010) quantitatively evaluated the performance of CUDA and OpenCL programs with almost the same computations. The main reasons behind these performance differences are found out for applications including matrix multiplication from the CUDA SDK and CP, MRI-Q, MRI-HD, from the Parboil benchmark suite. The results led to the conclusion that with certain optimizations and fine-tuning of kernels specific to the architecture, OpenCL and its counter-part, CUDA, can perform nearly the same.They also showed that the compiler options of the OpenCL C compiler and the execution configuration parameters have to be tuned for each GPU to obtain its best performance.

Rob van Nieuwpoort (2011) explained how to implement and optimize signal-processing applications on multi-core CPUs and many-core architectures. Correlation was used as a running example, throwing into light the aspects of performance, power efficient ability, along with programmability. This stud includes an interesting analysis of OpenCL: the problem of performance portability is not fully solved by OpenCL and thus programmers have to take prepare kernels such that they comply with the minute details and optimizations of the underlying processors. In the work of T. I. Vassilev (2010), the authors compare features of programming, platform, performance and device portability of GPU APIs for cloth modeling. Implementations in GLSL, CUDA and OpenCL are given. They arrive to the conclusion that OpenCL and CUDA are more advanced that GLSL, in terms of flexibility in programming options for general purpose computations. However, in the field of graphics, GLSL remains better for interoperability with graphics API. In the work of K. Karimi (2010), the author carried out a performance comparison of CUDA and OpenCL frameworks, using complex, almost identical kernels. Their results arrived to the conclusion that there are minimal modifications involved when converting a CUDA kernel to an OpenCL kernel, and vice-versa. Their experiments conducted regarding performance comparison, measure and compare data transfer time to and from the GPU, kernel execution time, and end-to-end application execution time for both CUDA as well as OpenCL. Only one application or algorithm is used in all the work mentioned above.

In the work ofR. Amorim (2009), a comparison between two GPGPU programming approaches (CUDA and OpenGL) is given, which uses a weighted Jacobi iterative solver for the bidomain equations. The conclusion arrived at was that the CUDA approach using a special texture memory in the GPU, proved to be faster than the OpenGL version.

In this chapter, the authors have tried to compare OpenCL and CUDA frameworks using a similar method used by the previous works as mentioned, but the only difference being that the problem chosen is simple, easy to understand, yet requires as many computations as any other complex question.

Problem Statement

This problem has been chosen by the authors so that its simplicity allows the readers to concentrate more on the implementation, rather than understanding the algorithm used to implement it. The problem is as follows:

Given a list of real numbers A[1..N], find the sum of products of all possible triplets (A[i], A[j], A[k]), such that $1 \leq i < j < k \leq N$.

Algorithm

This algorithm is implemented on both OpenCL and CUDA frameworks, separately. The programs have been run on the same platform, to ensure fair comparison. The results are then compared. The authors describe the implementation of algorithm in this section. Following are the hardware specifications of the machine which the authors used to implement the algorithm. The authorshave tried to keep the load on Host CPU as low as possible, so that calculations could be carried out in a fair manner. Any minor differences are manageable. However, to take care of that, individual programs were run multiple times and then the average values were calculated.

A. Compute Environment Specifications

1. Host CPU

Intel(R) Xeon(R) CPU X5660 @2.80 GHz.

2. Table 1 shows the GPU Specifications

Given a list of numbers A[1..N], we define triple product from a 3-tuple (i, j, k) such that $1 \leq i < j < k \leq N$, and the product will be A[i] x A[j] x A[k]. For N as the size of the list, N threads will be spawned. Each thread i (1<=i<=N) will calculate sum of all triple products whose first element is A[i], and store it in a global array "Output []" at index i. Thus the output for thread i can be summarized as:

$$Output[i] = A[i] \times \sum_{j=i+1}^{N-1} \sum_{k=j+1}^{N} (A[j] \times A[k]) \quad (1)$$

Table 1. GPU specifications

Manufacturer	NVIDIA
Series	Tesla
Model #	C2075
Memory	6GB GDDR5 384-bit
#Cores	448
Bandwidth	144GB/s
Interface	PCI Express 2.0 X16 Gen2

B. Load-Balancing and Optimization Details:

1. Since warp size was 32, to avoid wastage of compute power of the GPU the authors chose N as a multiple of 32. Thus threads can be divided into 'Groups' of 32 and fully mapped onto a Streaming Multiprocessor, where each group is executed.
2. To avoid unnecessary multiplications, the authors improved the calculation part for each thread from Eqn. (1) to:

$$Output[i] = A[i] \times \sum_{j=i+1}^{N-1} A[i] \sum_{k=j+1}^{N} A[k] \tag{2}$$

3. By doing this, the authors are reducing the number of global memory accesses by a significant amount, which improves the performance by a lot of margin.
4. To further minimize global memory access, Output[i] is only accessed once by each thread, i.e. when its required value is calculated (Eqn.2).Another much efficient way would be to stop redundant summations of the inner loop. This would reduce global memory accesses by a much greater margin.
5. For a fair comparison of kernel execution times in terms of FLOPS (Floating-point operations per sec), floating point numbers was chosen as the domain of elements in the list.
6. The authors also need fast loop operations. Scott Grauer-Gray (2012)discusses auto-tuning on a large optimization space on GPU kernels. It primarily focuses on loop permutation, tiling, and loop unrolling, and specifying which loop to parallelize, and show results on convolution kernels.

Computer Code

Below given is the author's code for both CUDA and OpenCL Kernels:

1. OpenCL Kernel Code:

```
//OpenCL KERNEL to find sum of all possible triple products
//under LIMIT.
__kernel void findTripleProd(__global double* arr, __global
     double* SUM, __global int LIMIT)
{
double localSum, tempSum;
int i, j, id;
//getting the global id of Thread
id = get_global_id(0);
//initializing localSum.
localSum = 0.0;
//Each thread with id='id' calculates sum of
```

```
//all triplets (id, i, j), id<i<j<=LIMIT.
for(i = id + 1; i <= LIMIT - 1; i++)
{
tempSum=0.0;
for(j = i + 1; j <= LIMIT; j++)
{
 tempSum += arr[j];
}
localSum += arr[i] * tempSum;
}
//Storing back the results.
SUM[id] = localSum * arr[id];
}
```

2. CUDA Kernel code:

```
//CUDA KERNEL to find sum of all possible triple
//products under LIMIT.
__global__ void findTripleProduct(double* arr,
     double* SUM, int LIMIT)
{
double localSum, tempSum;
int i, j, tid;
//calculating thread ID..
tid = blockIdx.x * blockDim.x + threadIdx.x;
//initializing localSum.
localSum = 0.0;
//Each thread with id='tid' calculates sum of
//all triplets (tid, i, j), tid<i<j<=LIMIT.
for(i = tid + 1; i <= LIMIT - 1; i++)
{
tempSum=0.0;
for(j = i + 1; j <= LIMIT; j++)
{
 tempSum += arr[j];
}
localSum += arr[i] * tempSum;
}
//Storing back the results.
SUM[tid] = localSum * arr[tid];
}
```

Explanation of the Kernel Code

The *SUM* array is accessed only once. The *tempSum* and *localSum* variables are used to store temporary values to build the required *SUM* array. The array elements are randomly assigned, and following steps follow:

1. Copy Data from CPU to GPU.
2. Execute kernel on GPU.
3. Copy back Data from GPU to CPU.

After the *SUM* array is read back from the GPU, the sum of all its elements gives the required answer.

Before discussing the CUDA kernel code for the algorithm, let us discuss similarities in the terminology of both frameworks, as shown in table 2 below:

We can see that the kernel codes are roughly the same, only difference being in keywords. In CUDA, a kernel function is declared as __global__, whereas in OpenCL it is declared as __kernel. Thread IDs are calculated in a different manner, as seen from the code snippets.

PERFORMANCE COMPARISON AND ANALYSIS

After executing the OpenCL and CUDA kernels on our GPU, the authors focus on the timing results. The kernels have been run 20 times each to obtain an average value with a standard deviation of less than 0.02ms. Apart from NVIDIA Tesla C2075, the authors also implemented the same kernels on NVIDIA Quadro 4000 GPU, to get a similar pattern of results for both the frameworks. Temperature changes of the GPU were also noted, and each time the kernel execution was started at a GPU temperature close to 60 degrees Celsius.For proper running and to avoid overheating, the GPU was kept in acooling chamber. Following are the kernel execution times obtained, for both CUDA and OpenCL:

From Fig. 1, we can say that CUDA performs slightly better than OpenCL for given environment and program code.The accurate values are given in Table III. The difference in the values is very small initially but increases as we increase the array size. For example, for an array size of 80,000 we get a significant difference of 1ms. If we continue increasing the array sizes, we note that the difference between both rises in the same fashion, and reaches a near constant value later on.

However, we can account the small difference in runtimes to the fact that CUDA is only oriented to NVIDIA CUDA architectures, whereas OpenCL is compatible to other architectures as well (Intel, AMD and NVIDIA being the main ones). Since the hardware being used is an NVIDIA Tesla, and since

Table 2. Similarities between CUDA and OpenCL Terminology

CUDA Framework	OpenCL Framework
Thread	Work-item
Thread-Blocks	Work-groups
Memory (Shared)	Memory (Local)
Memory (Local)	Memory (Private)

Table 3. Comparison of CUDA and OpenCL Kernel Running Times

Array Size	CUDAKernel Runtime (ms)	OpenCL Kernel Runtime (ms)
1,000	2.389	2.391
2,000	2.662	2.669
3,000	2.910	2.921
4,000	3.149	3.160
5,000	3.393	3.403
10,000	5.887	6.101
20,000	10.531	11.053
40,000	15.523	16.028
80,000	28.144	29.292

Figure 1. CUDA vs. OpenCL Kernel Runtimes

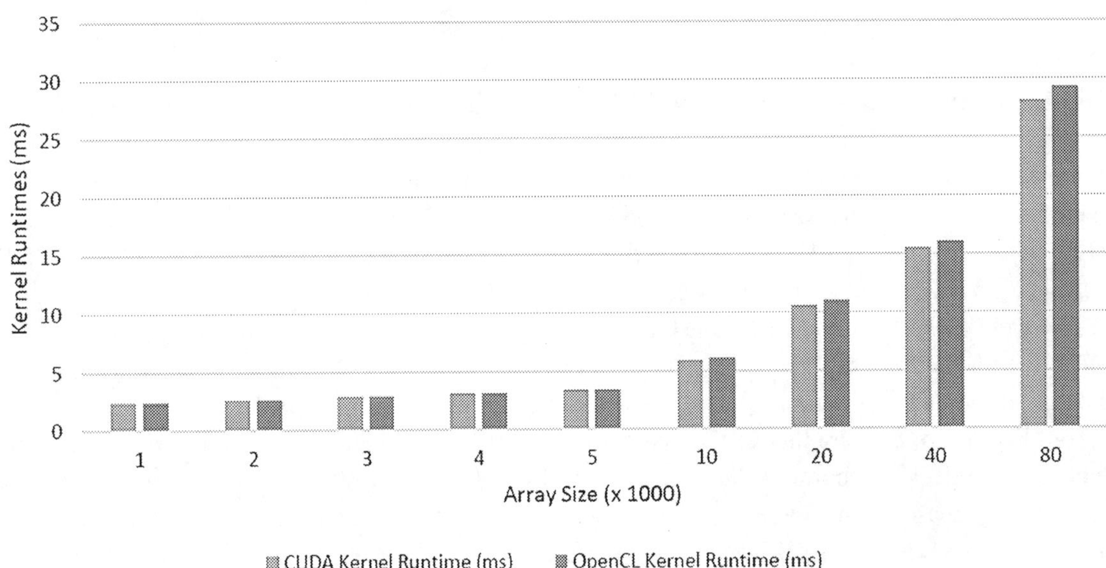

CUDA has more fine-grained API as compared to its counterpart, we can account for the difference in running times of both the frameworks. However, strictly speaking, since we cannot compare both in an environment exclusive of NVIDIA GPUs, this is the best we can get.

Since the difference in runtimes is nearly a constant, so we can say that one can interchangeably use CUDA or OpenCL frameworks while implementing on CUDA architectures.

Thus, the authors arrive at a conclusion that, under similar running environments, both OpenCL and CUDA can be used without worrying much about difference in performances. Most of the times, it actually depends on the problem at hand, and the environment we are supposed to use. But if we ignore those for a moment, both the frameworks perform nearly equal. Each has its own pros and cons, each is improving over time in its APIs and hardware optimizations, and each has its own preference in different fields of GPGPU applications.

FUTURE RESEARCH DIRECTIONS

Both the OpenCL and CUDA frameworks have a lot of scope in future. Even for their useful features already provided, there are certain features that can be added and/or improved in each of these. Presently it is quite difficult to ship binary OpenCL code. OpenCL is already working on creating OpenCL-SPIR, that takes care of this problem. Also, since OpenCL supports only C structs, CUDA would be more useful for complex tasks due to its support of C++ classes. These are only some of the many areas that these frameworks can work on.

Performance comparison will always be prevalent whenever any alternatives are present. Thus this chapter provides one of the many ways to compare OpenCL and CUDA, knowledge of which might be of use to other researchers who hope to make future comparisons.

CONCLUSION

We do see that OpenCL is in no way a bad choice compared to CUDA, given a fair comparison. The performance gaps initially noted are stated due to API implementations, native kernel optimizations and the efficient use of memory. OpenCL also has portability as its main benefits, while CUDA continues to be refined by developers at NVIDIA. We also observed that OpenCL model (14) does not support architecture of CPU in terms of parallel operating and (6) has a different memory model. We can also note that increasing cache utilization can optimize CPU performance.

REFERENCES

Amorim, R., Haase, G., Liebmann, M., & Weber dos Santos, R. (2009). *Comparing CUDA and OpenGL implementations for a Jacobi iteration*. doi:10.1109/HPCSIM.2009.5192847

Bhura, M., Deshpande, P. H., & Chandrasekaran, K. (2014). Comparison of OpenCL and CUDA frameworks on Heterogeneous Systems. *7th International Conference on Electrical, Electronics, Computing and Communication Systems (EECCS'15).*

Danalis, A., Marin, G., McCurdy, C., Meredith, J. S., Roth, P. C., Spafford, K., & Vetter, J. S. et al. (2010). The Scalable Heterogeneous Computing (SHOC) benchmark suite. In *Proceedings of the 3rd Workshop on General-Purpose Computation on Graphics Processing Units, GPGPU '10*. doi:10.1145/1735688.1735702

Diamos, G. F., & Yalamanchili, S. (2008). Harmony: an ExecutionModel and Runtime for Heterogeneous Many Core Systems. In *Proceedings of the 17th international symposium on High performance distributed computing,* (pp. 197–200). Academic Press.

Fang, J., Varbanescu, A. L., & Sips, H. (2011). A Comprehensive Performance Comparison of CUDA and OpenCL. *International Conference on Parallel Processing*. doi:10.1109/ICPP.2011.45

Grauer-Gray, S., Xu, L., Searles, R., Ayalasomayajula, S., & Cavazos, J. (2012). *Auto-tuning a High-Level Language Targeted to GPU Codes*. IEEE. doi:10.1109/InPar.2012.6339595

Houston, M. (2011). *General Purpose Computation on Graphics Processors (GPGPU)*. Stanford University Graphics Lab.

Karimi, Dickson, & Hamze. (2010). *A Performance Comparison of CUDA and OpenCL*. Academic Press.

Karimi, K., Dickson, N. G., & Hamze, F. (2010). *A Performance Comparison of CUDA and OpenCL*. Available at http://arxiv.org/abs/1005.2581

Komatsu1, Sato, Arai, Koyama, Takizawa, & Kobayashi. (2010). Evaluating Performance and Portability of OpenCL Programs. *5th international Workshop on Automatic Performance Tuning(iWAPT2010)*.

Komatsu, Sato, Arai, Koyama, Takizawa, & Kobayashi. (2010). Evaluating Performance and Portability of OpenCL Programs. In *Proceedings of the Fifth international Workshop on Automatic Performance Tuning(iWAPT2010)*.

Liu, J. W. S., Lin, K.-J., Shih, W.-K., Yu, A. C., Chung, J.-Y., & Zhao, W. (1991). Algorithms for Scheduling Imprecise Computations. *IEEE Comput.*, *24*(5), 58–68. doi:10.1109/2.76287

Liu, W., & Wang, C., Zeng, & Li. (2011). Scalable Multi-GPU Decoupled Parallel Rendering Approach in Shared Memory Architecture. International Conference on Virtual Reality and Visualization.

Maletz & Wang. (2011). Importance Point Projection for GPU-based Final Gathering. *Eurographics Symposium on Rendering*, *30*(4).

Owens, Houston, Luebke, Green, Stone, & Phillips. (2008).GPU Computing. IEEE, 96, 5.

Polok & Smrz. (2012). Fast Linear Algebra on GPU. *IEEE 14th International Conference on High Performance Computing and Communications*.

Sung, Liu, & Hwu. (2012). *DL: A Data Layout Transformation System for Heterogeneous Computing*. IEEE.

Toral, O. A., Ergun, S., Kurt, M., & Ozturk, A. (2014). Mobile GPU-based importance sampling. Signal Processing and Communications Applications Conference (SIU).

Trabzon, P., Du, R., Weber, P., Luszczek, S., & Tomov, G. Peterson, & Dongarra. (2010). From CUDA to OpenCL: Towards a Performance-portable Solution for Multi-platform GPU Programming. tech. rep., Department of Computer Science, UTK, Knoxville Tennessee.

van Nieuwpoort, R., & Romein, J. (2011). Correlating radio astronomy signals with Many-Core hardware. *International Journal of Parallel Programming*, *39*(1), 88–114. doi:10.1007/s10766-010-0144-3

Vassilev, T. I. (2010). Comparison of several parallel API for cloth modelling on modern GPUs. In *Proceedings of the 11th International Conference on Computer Systems and Technologies and Workshop for PhD Students in Computing on International Conference on Computer Systems and Technologies, CompSysTech '10*. ACM. doi:10.1145/1839379.1839403

Weber, Gothandaraman, Hinde, & Peterson. (2011). Comparing Hardware Accelerators in Scientific Applications: A Case Study. *IEEE, 22*.

Weber, R., Gothandaraman, A., Hinde, R. J., & Peterson, G. D. (2011). Comparing Hardware Accelerators in Scientific Applications: A Case Study. *IEEE Transactions on Parallel and Distributed Systems*, *22*(1), 58–68. doi:10.1109/TPDS.2010.125

KEY TERMS AND DEFINITIONS

API: Set of procedures and tools for building software.

Compiler: A computer program that transforms source code written in a programming language into machine level language.

CUDA (Computed Unified Device Architecture): A framework provided by NVIDIA, for writing programs for heterogeneous architectures, with parallel execution methods.

FLOPS (Floating Point Operations Per Second): Measure of performance of a processor. Denoted by number of floating point operations per second that can be performed by a processor. Useful mainly in scientific computing, where large floating point calculations are carried out.

GPGPU: (General Purpose Computing on Graphics Processing Units): Using GPUs to perform tasks generally performed by CPUs, that uses their inherently parallel architecture to perform general purpose tasks.

GPU (Graphics Processing Unit): A chip consisting of multiprocessors with parallel thread execution.

Heterogeneous Systems: Systems that consist of more than one kind of processor.

Kernel: It is a function written to run in parallel on processors while programming in CUDA or OpenCL.

OpenCL (Open Computing Language): Framework for writing programs for heterogeneous platforms consisting of various types of processors.

Parallel Computing: Solving a problem with multiple computers or computers made up of multiple processors.

Thread: Smallest unit of execution of a program.

Chapter 16
Speckle Noise Filtering Using Back-Propagation Multi-Layer Perceptron Network in Synthetic Aperture Radar Image

Khwairakpam Amitab
North-Eastern Hill University, India

Debdatta Kandar
North-Eastern Hill University, India

Arnab K. Maji
North-Eastern Hill University, India

ABSTRACT

Synthetic Aperture Radar (SAR) are imaging Radar, it uses electromagnetic radiation to illuminate the scanned surface and produce high resolution images in all-weather condition, day and night. Interference of signals causes noise and degrades the quality of the image, it causes serious difficulty in analyzing the images. Speckle is multiplicative noise that inherently exist in SAR images. Artificial Neural Network (ANN) have the capability of learning and is gaining popularity in SAR image processing. Multi-Layer Perceptron (MLP) is a feed forward artificial neural network model that consists of an input layer, several hidden layers, and an output layer. We have simulated MLP with two hidden layer in Matlab. Speckle noises were added to the target SAR image and applied MLP for speckle noise reduction. It is found that speckle noise in SAR images can be reduced by using MLP. We have considered Log-sigmoid, Tan-Sigmoid and Linear Transfer Function for the hidden layers. The MLP network are trained using Gradient descent with momentum back propagation, Resilient back propagation and Levenberg-Marquardt back propagation and comparatively evaluated the performance.

DOI: 10.4018/978-1-4666-8737-0.ch016

1. INTRODUCTION

Radar system was developed during World War II to track aircrafts and ships. Radar system measures distance to the target by precisely calculating the time delay between sent and received signal. Doppler shifts were used to measure target speed. In 1951, Carl Wiley from Goodyear Aerospace found that radar can be used to create images from target and earth surface. In 1970s applications of Remote Sensing was open for civilian use (Chan and Koo, 2008). It drew the attention of researchers and application grew rapidly.

SAR produces high resolution two dimensional images of mapped areas (Tomiyasu, 1978). It is mounted on moving platform such as aircraft or spacecraft. A SAR works by illuminating the scanned surface with a beam of coherent electromagnetic radiation in a side-looking direction, the returned echo form the illuminated are collected by SAR receiver and processed to reconstruct the image of the surface. SAR geometry is shown in Figure 1(Dastgir, 2007). The SAR platform flies along the azimuth direction at constant velocity. It is not feasible for a spacecraft to carry a very large antenna, which is required for producing high resolution image of the earth surface. SAR uses the forward motion of platform to

Figure 1. SAR Geometry

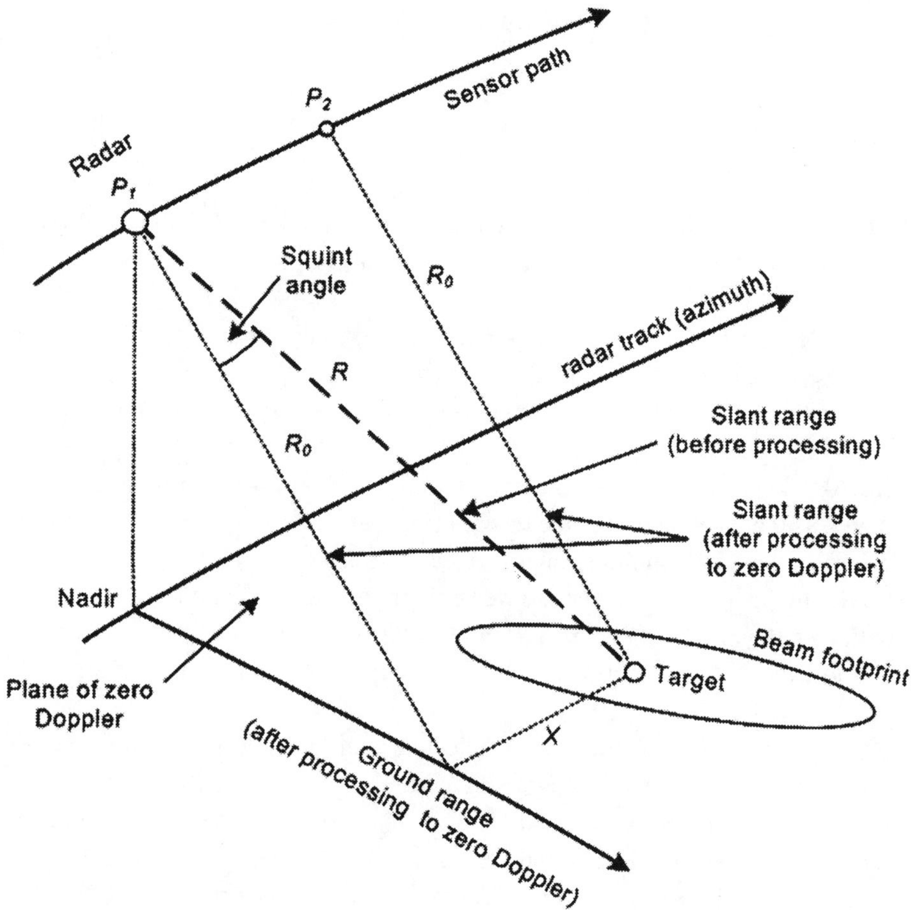

synthesize a very large antenna. Range is the direction perpendicular to flight path of the aircraft. By measuring the time difference between the transmitted pulse and received echo, the range of the reflecting object can be determined.

Range resolution is the ability to separate two object points in the range direction. Mathematically Range resolution(***R***) can be defined as:

$$R = \frac{ct}{2} \tag{1}$$

where ***t*** is the pulse width and ***c*** is the speed of light. From the equation shown above it can be observed that smaller value of ***t*** will give high (finer) resolution. However decreasing the value of ***t*** will also reduce Signal to Noise Ratio (SNR). To solve this problem SAR uses pulse compression techniques. In this technique long-duration Linear Frequency Modulated (LFM) pulse are transmitted, it allows the pulse energy to be transmitted with a lower peak power. The LFM pulse when filtered with a matched filter produces a narrow pulse in which all the pulse energy is collected to the peak value. Thus, when a matched filter is applied to the received echo signal, it is same as transmitting narrow pulse.

Azimuth is the direction parallel to the flight path of the aircraft. To obtain high azimuth resolution, a large antenna is needed to focus the transmitted and received echo into a sharp pencil like beam. The sharpness of the beam defines the Azimuth resolution (***A***).

$$A = \frac{R\lambda}{L} \tag{2}$$

where ***R*** is slant range, λ is the wave length of the transmitted signal and ***L*** is the length of the antenna.

SAR has different mode of operations based on their application. Following are the modes of operation:

- **Stripmap SAR:** In this mode, the antenna points to a fixed direction. The beam sweeps along the surface with a constant rate and a contiguous image is formed.
- **ScanSAR:** This mode collects several range samples while sweeping along the surface, it results a wider swath but less azimuth resolution.
- **Spotlight SAR:** This mode improves the resolution by gradually steering the radar beam toward the target area as the antenna passes the desired target area.
- **Inverse SAR:** In this mode illuminating sensor is stationary and the target moves.
- **Bistatic SAR:** In this mode, receiver and transmitter are not in one unit.
- **SAR Interferometry:** In this mode, two complex images are obtained from same position or slightly different positions. These images are conjugate multiplied and the result is an interferogram.

Reconstruction of image from continuously collected returned echo is two dimensional problems; echo signal of a point target is spread in range and azimuth. The collected returned echo is processed to reconstruct the image of the scanned surface. The most commonly used algorithm is the Range Doppler Processing algorithm (Cumming and Bennett, 1979; JCurlander 1991). It consists of Range Compression, Azimuth Fast Fourier transform, Range Cell Migration Correction (RCMC) and Azimuth Compression. The matched filtering of the received echo is called range compression. Range compression can be done efficiently by using Fast Fourier Transform (FFT). The range matched filter may use the replica of the transmitted pulse or computed form the received echo. FFT is performed in azimuth direction on each range line to transform the data into the range Doppler domain. As the SAR platform moves over the target the distance of platform from the target decreases and then increases as it move away, so the instantaneous slant range changes, this causes changing of phase in echo as a function of cross-range or azimuth this phenomenon is called as range cell migration, it must be corrected before azimuth compression. The RCMC can be implemented by using interpolation in the range direction. Azimuth compression is the matched filtering of signal in azimuth direction; it can be performed efficiently using FFT. Figure 2 illustrates the reconstruction of a point target form the received echo signals using Range Doppler Algorithm.

SAR works in all-weather condition, day and night. As SAR uses electromagnetic signal (microwave) that can penetrate cloud, it is able to acquire cloud-free images in all weather. This is useful in the tropical regions which are frequently covered by cloud. It is also capable of operating at night as it illuminates the scanned surface by signals emitted from the SAR.

There are wide ranges of application for SAR techniques. It includes satellite remote sensing of land and sea, target imaging for military purposes, geo-science and climate change research, urban planning, environmental monitoring and planetary exploration.

SAR images are formed by coherent interaction of the transmitted signals with the targets. Speckle noise arises due to coherent summation of the signals scattered from ground or nearby object and dis-

Figure 2. Range doppler processing

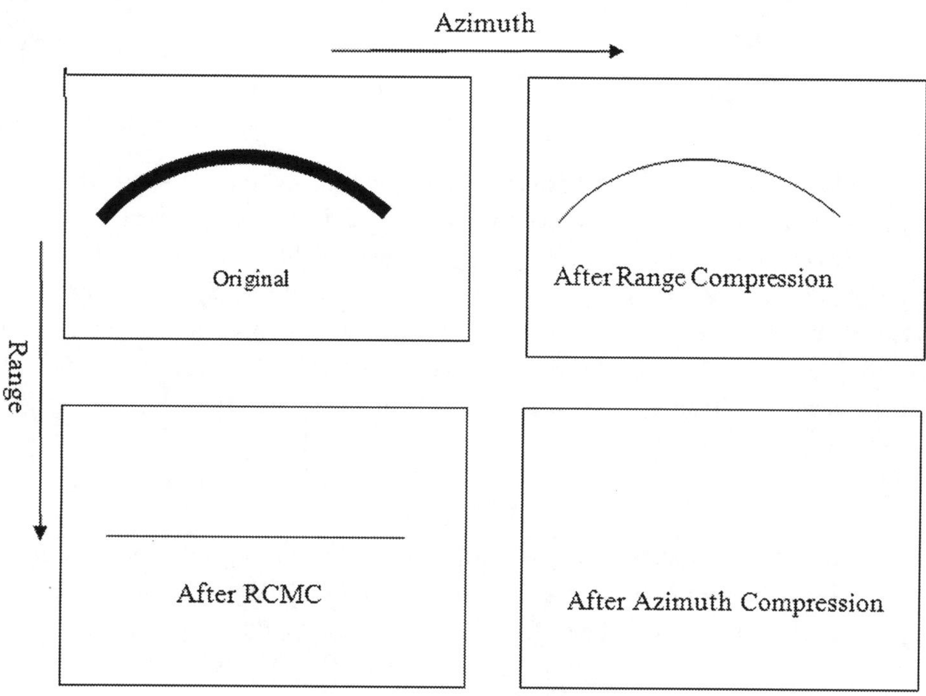

tributed randomly within each pixel. Speckle is a granular noise and inherently exists in all types of coherent imagery such as Radar image, acoustic, and laser illuminated imagery. It degrades the quality of the image and causes serious difficulty in analyzing the images. Speckle noise are multiplicative.

2. SPECKLE NOISE REDUCTION TECHNIQUES

Many speckle noise reduction techniques have been presented previously. Some of the commonly used speckle noise filters are discussed below.

2.1 Mean Filter

Mean Filter is also known as averaging filter it works by replacing each pixel value by mean value of the neighboring pixel value. It is based on kernel which defines the shape and size of the neighborhood that will be considered for calculating the mean value. This technique is easy to implement however it blurs the image and details are lost.

2.2 Median Filter

Median filter is nonlinear digital filter (Pitas and Venetsanopoulos, 2013). It is widely used for removing noise because under certain condition it can remove noise and preserve edges. This technique defines a window which slides over each pixel in the image and replace the central pixel by median of neighboring pixel value. Median can be found by sorting the pixel values in ascending order and choosing the middle value, if there is no middle value then median is defined as the mean of the two middle values.

2.3 Lee Filter

The work of Lee (1986) converts the multiplicative noise into an additive noise, thereby reducing the problem of dealing with speckle noise. The Lee filter filters the data based on local statistics calculated within a window. It is based on Minimum Mean Square Error (MMSE) design approach. Within each window, the local mean and variances are calculated. In the areas of low signal activity or flat regions the estimated pixel approaches the local mean, whereas in the areas of high signal activity or edge areas the estimated pixel favors the corrupted image pixel, thus retaining the edge information. The major drawback of the filter is that it leaves noise in the vicinity of edges and lines.

2.4 Frost Filter

Frost, Stiles, Shanmugan, and Holtzman, (1982) proposed the Frost filter. It replaces the pixel of interest with a weighted sum of the values within the moving window. The pixel being filtered is replaced with a value calculated based on the distance from filter center, damping factor and local variance. The weighting factors decrease with distance from the pixel of interest. The weighting factors increase for the central pixels as variance within the window increases. This filter assumes multiplicative noise and stationary noise statistics.

2.5 Kuan Filter

The work of Kuan, Sawchuk, Strand and Chavel (1985) converts the multiplicative noise into an additive noise. This filter is similar to the Lee filter but uses a different weighting function. It is a local linear Mean Square Error (MSE) filter. Kaun filter is comparatively better than the lee filter.

2.6 Wiener Filter

Wiener (1949) proposed Wiener filter, it can be implemented using Fourier transform or mean squared method. The former method is used for denoising and deblurring, whereas the later is used only for denoising. Fourier transform method normally requires a priori knowledge of the power spectra of noise and the original image. But in mean-squared method a priori knowledge is not is required. Wiener filter is based on the least-squared principle, it minimizes the mean-squared error (MSE) between the actual output and the desired output. Image statistics vary from a region to another even within the same image. Thus, both global statistics and local statistics are important and used in Wiener filtering.

2.7 Morphological Filters

Morphological filter rely on the relative ordering of pixel values not on pixel density (Maragos, 2005). Morphological filters probe an image with a structuring element or template, the structuring element is positioned at all possible locations in the image and compared with the corresponding neighborhood of pixels to reduce the noise locally (Mashaly, AbdElkawy and Mahmoud, 2010).

2.8 Wavelet Filters

Wavelets are mathematical functions which decomposed the data into different frequency components and analyze each component. Speckle noise appears as high-frequency component of image in wavelet coefficient. These high frequency components are removed by using thresholding approach to remove the speckle noise (Kaur and Singh, 2010).

Artificial Neural Network (ANN) is gaining importance in speckle noise reduction. ANN have the ability to learn from previous experience and uses this knowledge to improve the result. ANN based filter are robust, if it is trained properly they can even reduce unknown noise. Using ANN for reduction of noise produces better results compared to conventional statistical techniques (Khowaja and Shah, 2014). The work of Saikia and Sarma (2014), Park and Nishimura (2007), Blacknell, Oliver and Warner (1995), White (1991), Long and Cat (2009) have used ANN as a tool for reducing speckle noise.

3. ARTIFICIAL NEURAL NETWORK

An Artificial Neural Network (ANN) is information processing system inspired by biological neural network. It is consist of a large number of interconnected simple processing elements known as neurons, these neurons work together to solve specific problems. ANNs is an intelligent system capable of learning. ANN is configured based on specific application, such as optimization, function approximation, pattern recognition, data classification etc, through a learning process. The main advantages of using

ANN is the ability to learn based on the data given for training or pass experience. Other advantages includes Self-Organization of information receives during learning, ANN computations can be carried out in parallel, ANN is Fault Tolerant as partial destruction of a network does not stop the computation but it my leads to degradation of performance.

ANN follows a different approach to solve problem compared to conventional statistical techniques. Conventional techniques use an algorithmic approach and are unable to solve an unknown problem which limits the problem solving capability. Neural networks process information in a similar way the human brain does.

An artificial neuron usually has many inputs and one output. The neuron has training mode and testing mode. In the training mode, the neuron are trained to fire for particular input patterns. In the testing mode when a known input pattern is detected at the inputs the associated output is produced. If the input pattern does not belong in the known input patterns, the firing rule is used to determine whether to fire or not.

The main components of ANN are neurons or activation function, topology and training algorithm. Structure of a basic neuron is shown in Figure 3. It consists of inputs, which are multiplied by their respective weights, and then mathematically computed which determines the activation of the neuron. Large number of neurons is interconnected; the interconnectivity defines the topology of the ANN. The weights are adjusted using training algorithm.

Neural networks are typically organized in layers. A simple neural network is shown in Figure 4. Each layer consists of a number of interconnected nodes or neurons. Input patterns are presented to the network using the input layer, which communicates to hidden layers where the actual processing is done. The hidden layers are then link to an output layer, the output is produce through output layer.

3.1 Architecture of ANN

ANN can be viewed as weighted directed graphs in which artificial neurons are nodes and directed weighted edges are connections between neuron outputs and neuron inputs. Based on the connection pattern, ANNs can be grouped together into feed-forward and feedback (recurrent) network.

Figure 3. An Artificial neuron

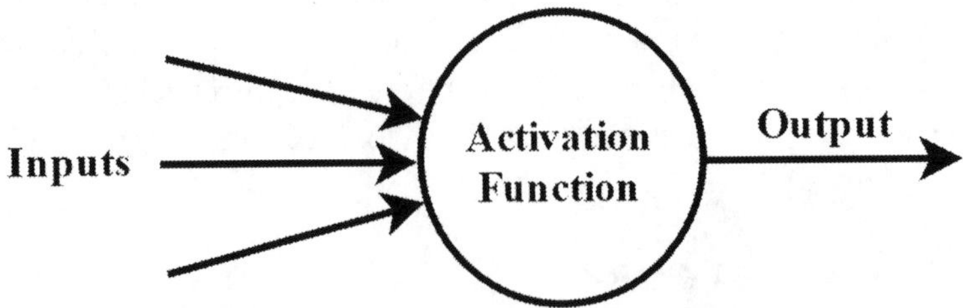

Figure 4. Neural network

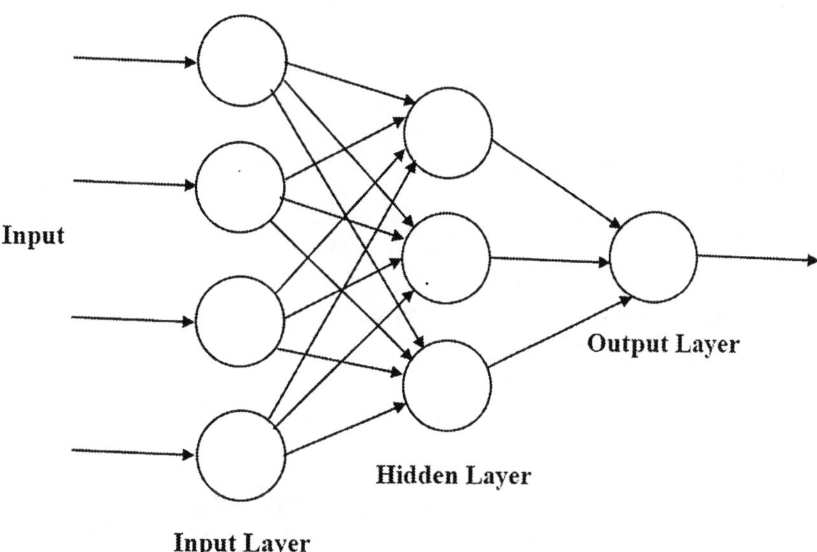

3.1.1 Feed Forward ANN

Feed-forward ANNs allow signals to travel from the input nodes, through the hidden nodes and to the output nodes, there are no feedback or loops. Every neuron in a layer is connected with all the neuron in the previous layer. Each connection may have a different strength or weight. They are extensively used in pattern recognition. This type of architecture is also known as top-down.

3.1.2 Feedback ANN

Feedback networks allow signals to travel in both directions by introducing loops. Feedback networks are dynamic; their state changes until they reach an equilibrium point. Feedback architectures are also referred to as interactive or recurrent neural network.

3.2 Training ANN

Learning in ANN is achieved through training. Learning process updates connection weights so that the network can efficiently perform a specific task. The network usually learns from available training patterns. Learning algorithms are used to train the network. Learning algorithms can be categorized into supervised, unsupervised, and hybrid.

3.2.1 Supervised Learning

In supervised learning, the network is provided with a correct output for every input pattern. The network processes the inputs and compares its resulting outputs against the desired outputs. Errors are computed and propagated back through the network, the system adjust the weights to minimize the error. This process repeats several times until the desire criteria are achieved.

3.2.2 Unsupervised Learning

It does not require a correct output associated with each input pattern in the training data set. Unsupervised learning is also known as self organizing. It explores the underlying structure in the data, or correlations between patterns in the data, and organizes patterns into categories from these correlations. Unsupervised learning is suitable for clustering or classification.

3.2.3 Hybrid Learning

Hybrid learning combines supervised and unsupervised learning. Parts of the weights are determined through supervised learning, while the others are determine through unsupervised learning.

4. MULTI-LAYER PERCEPTRON (MLP)

MLP is the most popular type of ANN in use today; it is a feed forward artificial neural network model that consists of an input layer, one or more hidden layers, and an output layer. MLP is a nonlinear function that maps input vector via several hidden layers to output vector, it uses a supervised learning technique called back propagation for training the network. MLPs are widely used for pattern classification, recognition, prediction and approximation (Santhanam and Radhika, 2011). Patino-Escarcina and Costa (2007) comparatively evaluated the performance of traditional filters such as mean and median, and MLP networks experimental result shows that overall efficiency of MLP networks is better.

4.1 Architecture of MLP

In MLP neurons are known as perceptron. In figure 5 all input $\boldsymbol{x_j}$ is multiplied by the corresponding scalar weight $\boldsymbol{w_{ji}}$ to form the product $\boldsymbol{w_{ji}x_j}$, and bias $\boldsymbol{\Theta_i}$ is added to form $\boldsymbol{n_i}$ in (3). n_i is given as input to the transfer function $\boldsymbol{g}$. The output $\boldsymbol{y_i}$ is shown in (4).

$$n_i = \sum_{j=1}^{k} w_{ji}x_j + \theta_i \tag{3}$$

$$y_i = g\left(\sum_{j=1}^{k} w_{ji}x_j + \theta_i\right) \tag{4}$$

The activation depends on the inputs and the weights. The most commonly used transfer functions for MLP are Log-sigmoid, Tan-Sigmoid and Linear Transfer Function.

Log-sigmoid function generates outputs between 0 and 1 as the neuron's net input goes from negative to positive infinity. The mathematical expression of Log-sigmoid is:

$$\log sig(n) = \frac{1}{1+e^{-n}} \tag{5}$$

Figure 5. A perceptron of MLP network.

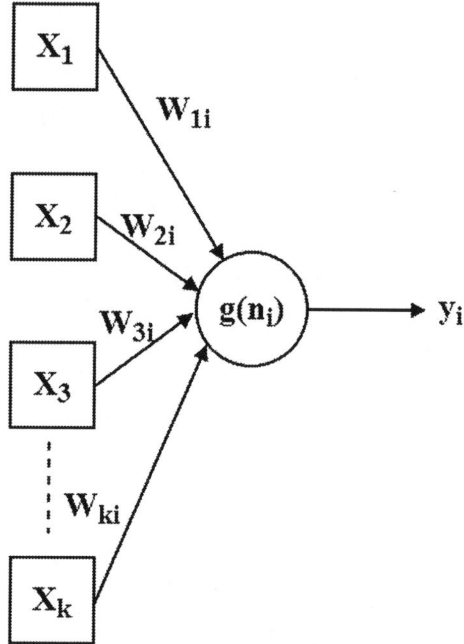

Tan-Sigmoid is mathematically equivalent to hyperbolic tangent:

$$\tan sig(n) = \frac{2}{1+e^{-2n}} \tag{6}$$

Linear Transfer Function gives same output as the input, Following equation shows the relation between input and output.

$$purelin(n) = n \tag{7}$$

The graph of Log-sigmoid, Tan-Sigmoid and Linear Transfer Function are shown in Figure 6(a), Figure 6(b) and Figure 6(c) respectively.

The architecture of MLP which has an input layer with $\boldsymbol{k}$ input, one hidden layer with three neurons and an output layer with two neurons is shown in Figure 7.The output of the MLP network $\boldsymbol{y_i}$, for $\boldsymbol{i}$=1,2 of can be defined as

$$y_i = g\left(\sum_{j=1}^{3} w^2{}_{ji} g\left(\sum_{k=1}^{K} w^1 x_k + \theta^1{}_j\right) + \theta^2{}_i\right) \tag{8}$$

Figure 6a. Log-Sigmoid

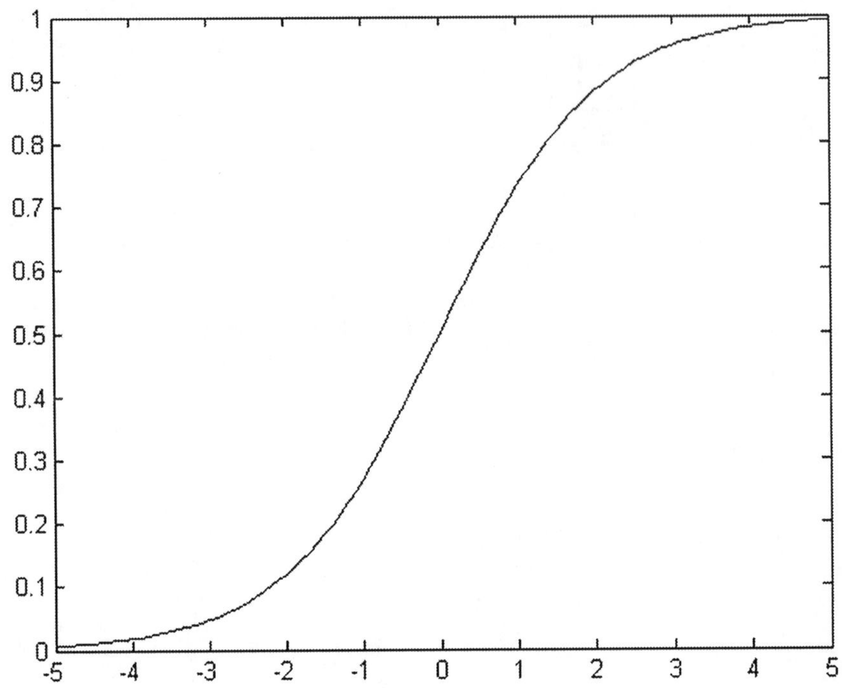

Figure 6b. Tan-Sigmoid

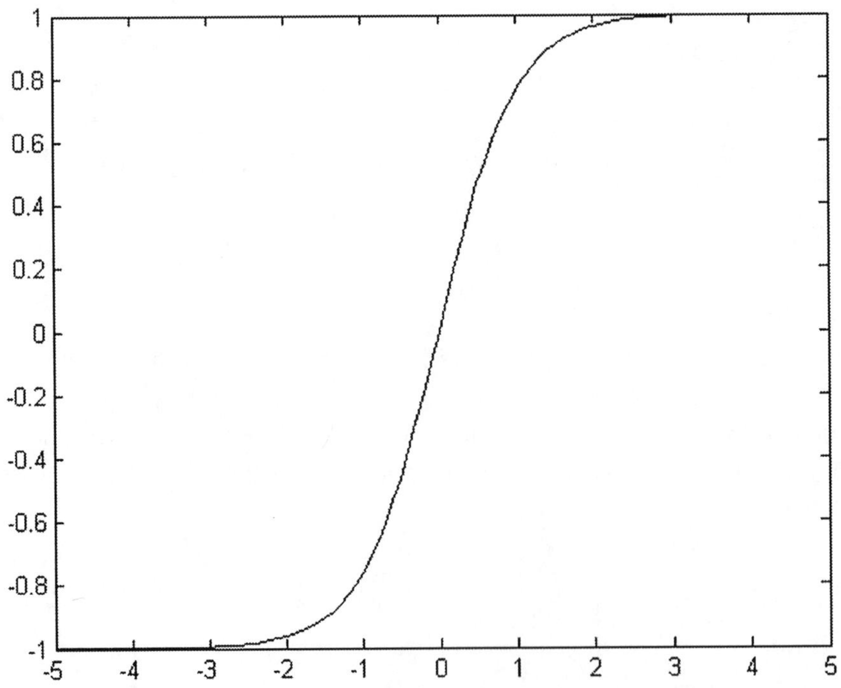

Figure 6c. Linear Transfer Function

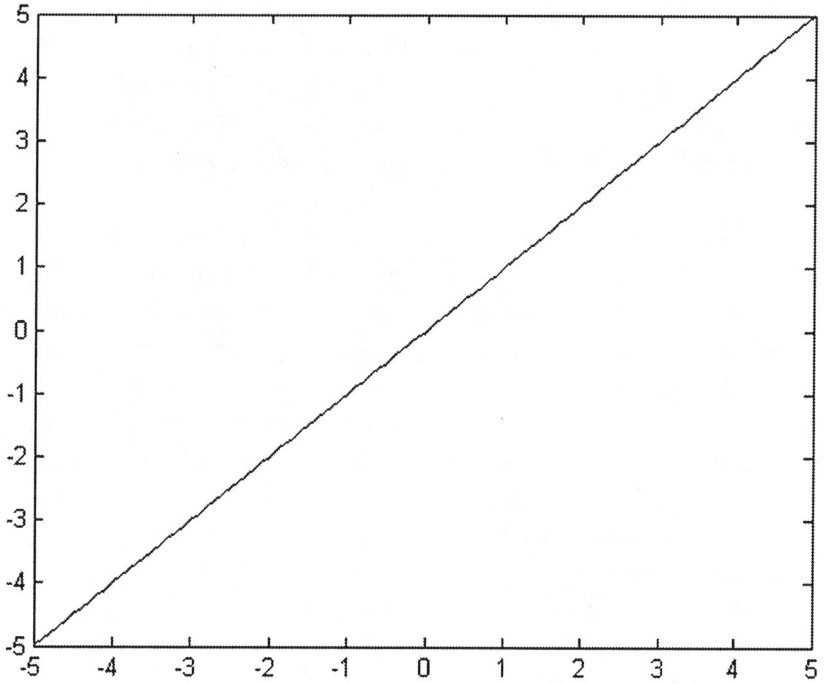

Figure 7. Architecture of MLP network

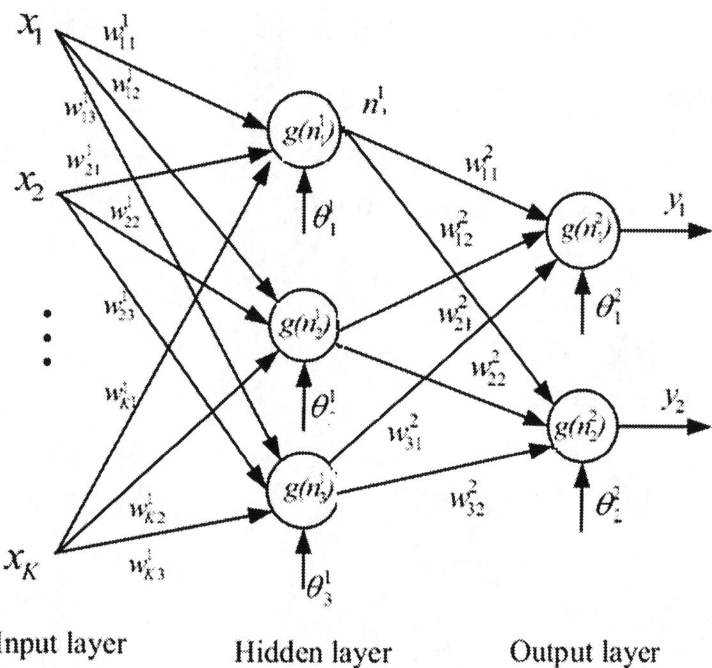

4.2. Training the MLP Using Back Propagation Algorithm

Learning takes place during training phase. The goal of the training process is to find the set of weight $w_{ij}(n)$ that will cause the output from the neural network to match target values as closely as possible. The most commonly used algorithm for adjusting weights in MLP during the training phase is back-propagation (Beale and Jackson, 1990; Rumelhart, McClelland and PDP, 1988). A Back Propagation network learns by example (Supervised Learning)

It consists of two passes forward and backward (Dao and Vemuri, 2002). In the forward pass, an input pattern is supplied to the network, and it propagates through the network from input layer to output layer and output response is produces. During the backward pass, the output response is compared to desired output and the error is calculated. This error signal propagates backward through the network. Based on this error weights are adjusted, the weight adjustment is done by using Mean Square Error (MSE). The weight adjustment is performed repeatedly until the error value is minimized.

Consider a multilayer back propagation neural network shown in figure 8. Let N_j represents the number of neurons in j^{th} layer, Y_{ji} be the output from the ith neuron in layer j for p^{th} pattern, W_{jik} be the connection weight from k^{th} neuron in layer $(j-1)$ to i^{th} neuron in layer j, and δ_{ji} be the error value associated with the ith neuron in layer j.

The following steps are performed in back propagation algorithm.

1. Iinitialize the network weights with random values.
2. Present the input vector of pattern $X_p = (X_{p1}, X_{p2,\ldots\ldots}, X_{pNo})$and the corresponding output $T_p=(T_{p1}, T_{p2,\ldots}, T_{pNM})$ to the network.
3. For every input node i in layer 0, perform: $Y_{0i} = X_{p.}$
4. For every neuron i in every layer $j=1,2,3,\ldots,M$, calculate the output from the neuron. Where $f(x)$ is the transfer function. $Y_{ji} = f\left(\sum_{k=1}^{N_{j-1}} Y_{(j-1)k} W_{jik}\right)$

Figure 8. Back propagation Neural Network with M Layer.

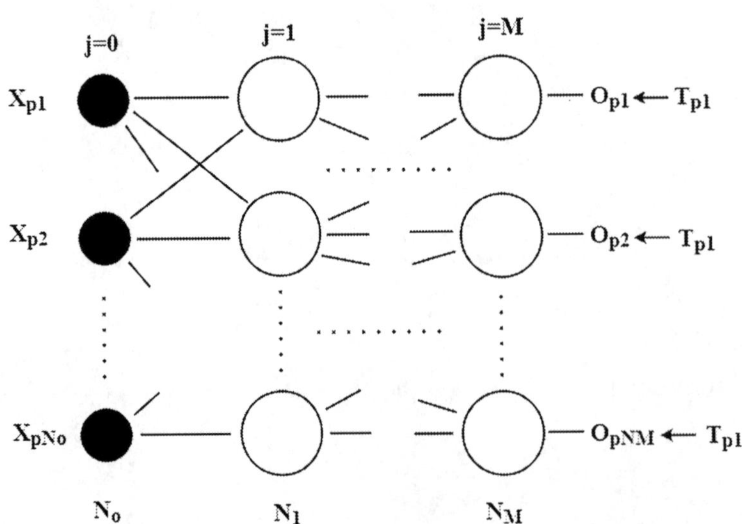

5. Determine the output for every node i in layer M, perform: $O_{pi} = Y_{Mi}$
6. Calculate error value δ_{ji} for every neuron i in every layer in backward direction $j=M, M\text{-}1,\ldots,1$, from output to input layer and adjust the weights. For the output layer, the error value is:

$$\delta_{Mi} = Y_{Mi}(1-Y_{Mi})(T_{pi}-Y_{Mi}) \text{, and for hidden layer } \delta_{ji} = Y_{ji}(1-Y_{ji})\sum_{k=1}^{N_{j+1}} \delta_{(j+1)k} W_{(j+1)ki}$$

The weight adjustments are performed for every connection from neuron k in layer $(i\text{-}1)$ to every neuron i in every layer j: $W_{jik} = W_{jik} + \beta\delta_{ji}Y_{ji}$, where β represents weight adjustment factor.

Steps 2 through 6 are repeated until the root mean square (RMS) of output errors is minimized.

Gradient descent with momentum back propagation, Resilient back propagation and Levenberg-Marquardt back propagation are commonly used back-propagation algorithm.

4.2.1 Gradient Descent with Momentum Back Propagation

In order to train neural networks using gradient descent, we have to compute the gradient with respect to each weight W_{ji} of the network. For each point p in the training data:

$$E_p = \frac{1}{2}\sum_{j=1}^{N_M}(T_{pj}-O_{pj})^2$$

Using chain rule compute partial derivatives of each parameter with respect to this error:

$$\nabla E(w) = \left(\frac{\partial E}{\partial w_1},\ldots,\frac{\partial E}{\partial w_M}\right)$$

The vector of partial derivatives is called the gradient of the error. The negative gradient points in the direction of steepest error descent in weight space. The steps in Gradient Descent Algorithm are:

1. Initialize all weights to small random values.
2. Repeat
   a. For each weight w_{ji} set $\Delta w_{ji}=0$
   b. For each data point p in (X, T)
      i. Set input to X
      ii. Compute the output.
      iii. For each weight W_{ji} set $\Delta w_{ji} = \Delta w_{ji} + (T_j - O_j)O_j$
   c. For each weight w_{ji} set $w_{ji} = w_{ji} + \mu\Delta w_{ji}$ where μ is the learning rate

The algorithm terminates when it reaches sufficiently near to the minimum of the error function, the algorithm converge when G = 0.

Gradient descent can be very slow if μ is small, and can oscillate widely if μ is large. The inclusion of a momentum term increases the rate of convergence dramatically (Rumelhartet al., 1986) and that reduces the risk of getting stuck in a local minimum.

Let ***E(w)*** be the error function, and ***w*** be the vector representing all the weights in the network, the gradient descent algorithm, modifies the weights at time step ***t*** according to: $\Delta w_t = -\mu \nabla_w E(w_t)$

With momentum the above equation become $\Delta w_t = -\mu \nabla_w E(w_t) + p\Delta w_{t-1}$

The modification of weight vector at the current time step depends on current gradient and the weight change of the previous step (Qian,1999).

4.2.2 Resilient Back Propagation

Resilient back-propagation (RPROP) is considered the best algorithm, measured in terms of convergence speed, accuracy and robustness (Riedmiller and Braun, 1993). In RPROP only the sign of the derivative is used to determine the direction of the weight update; the magnitude of the derivative has no effect on the weight update (KISI and Uncuoglu, 2005). For each weight, if there was a sign change in partial derivative of the total error function for two successive iteration, the update value for that weight is multiplied by a factor η^-, where $\eta^- < 1$. If two successive iteration produced the same sign, the update value is multiplied by a factor of η^+, where $\eta^+ > 1$. Complete description of the RPROP algorithm is available in the work of Riedmiller and Braun (1993).

4.2.3 Marquardt Back Propagation

Marquardt (1963) presented the Marquardt-Levenberg algorithm; it is an approximation to Newton's method. The Marquardt algorithm is very efficient when training networks which have up to a few hundred weights (Hagan and Menhaj, 1994). It was designed to approach second-order training speed without computing the Hessian matrix. The Hessian matrix is approximated as: $H = J^T J$, and the gradient can be computed as: $G = J^T E$ where ***J*** is the Jacobian matrix containing first derivatives of the network errors with respect to the weights and biases, and **E** is the error vector of network. The Jacobian matrix can be computed through a standard back propagation technique (Hagan and Menhaj, 1994).

The Levenberg-Marquardt algorithm uses approximation of Hessian matrix in the following equation:

$$X_{k+1} = X_k - \left[J^T J + \mu I\right]^{-1} J^T e$$

When the scalar μ is zero it is similar as Newton's method. When μ is large, it is similar to gradient descent with a small step size. Newton's method is faster and accurate near an error minimum, so the aim is to shift towards Newton's method as quickly as possible.

5. IMPLEMENTATION AND RESULT

MLP is implemented in MATLAB and ALOS-PALSAR image (ORNL DAAC) is used for testing. Implementation process can be divided into three phases namely designing the MLP network, training and testing. The designed architecture of the MLP network using neural network toolbox is shown in Fig. 9 (Demuth and Beale, 2000; Koivo, 2008). It consists of an input layer with a node and takes a single input, two hidden layer; the first layer has nine neurons and second layer has single neuron and an output layer with single node. We have used all the possible combination of Log-sigmoid, Tan-Sigmoid and Linear transfer function in hidden layer.

Gradient descent with momentum back propagation, Resilient back propagation and Levenberg-Marquardt back propagation are used for training the network. and comparatively evaluated the performance in terms of Peak Signal to Noise Ratio (PSNR). The parameters associated with the training algorithm are defined as Maximum epochs=600, Error goal = 0.0, Maximum validation failures=5, learning rate to 0.001 and Momentum constant=0.9.

PSNR is the ratio between the maximum possible power of a signal and the power of noise that affects the quality of the image. PSNR is defined using Mean Square Error (MSE):

$$MSE = \frac{1}{mn}\sum_{i=0}^{m-1}\sum_{j=0}^{n-1}[I(i,j) - K(i,j)]^2$$

Where $\boldsymbol{I}$ is an image of size $\boldsymbol{m \times n}$ and $\boldsymbol{K}$ is the noisy image. PSNR in decibel (db) is defined as:

$$PSNR = 10\log_{10}\left(\frac{MAX^2}{MSE}\right)$$

MAX is the maximum possible pixel value of the image. It is either specified by the user or taken from the range of the image data type.

The input image to the training algorithm is shown in Figure. 10 and the target image is shown in Fig. 11. Figure. 10 is the effect of speckle noise in Figure. 11. Speckle noise is usually modeled as purely multiplicative noise (Schulze and & Wu, 1995). The multiplicative speckle noise is created by using:

Figure 9. Architecture of Designed MLP

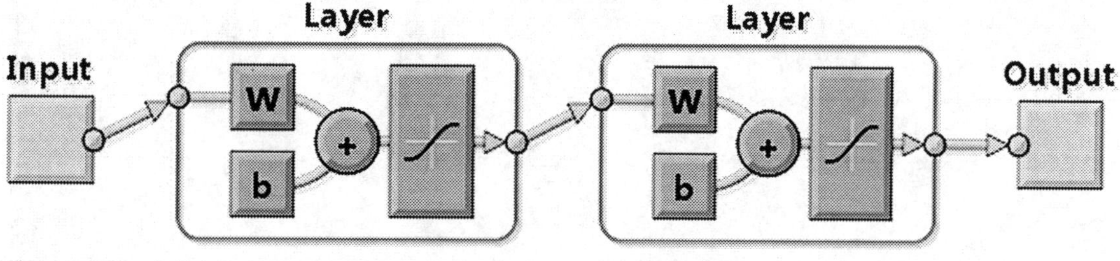

Figure 10. Speckle noise effected image

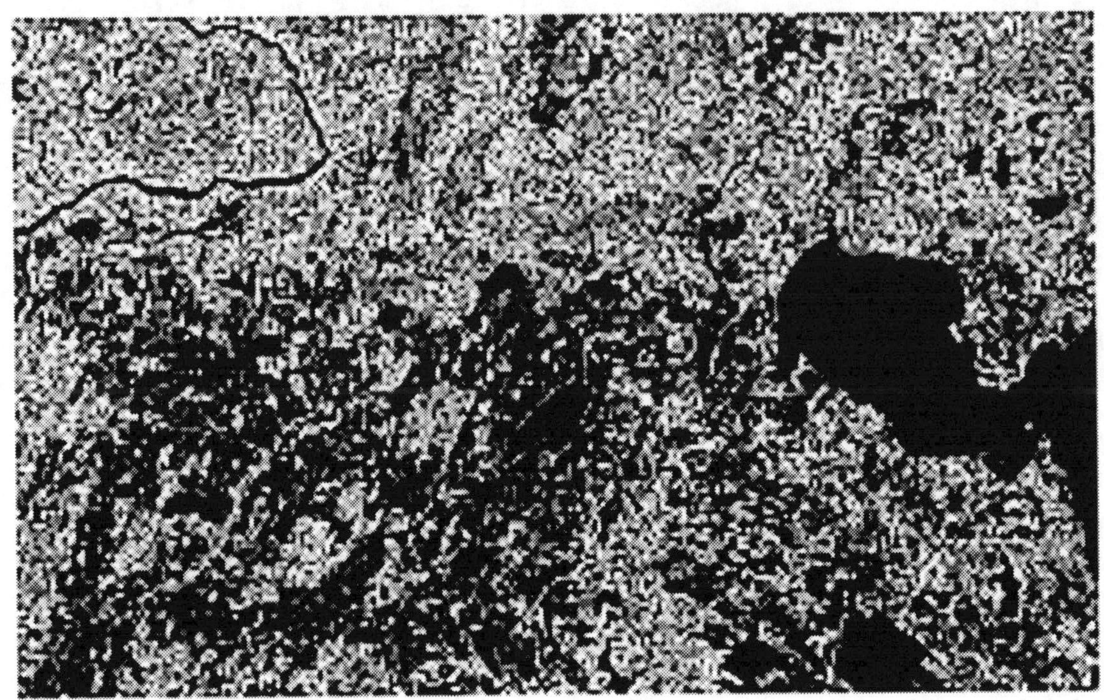

Figure 11. Target image

J = I + n * I

Where is ***J*** is the noisy image, ***I*** is the original image, ***n*** is uniformly distributed random noise.

The same training parameters are used for all the training algorithms. To evaluate the performance we have used the image in Figure 10 as the test image. The test result in decibel is presented in Table 1. Figure 12, Figure 13 and Figure 14 are the samples of denoised images using Levenberg-Marquardt, Resilient and Gradient descent with momentum back propagation training algorithm respectively.

Table 1. Simulation results of designed MLP network

Transfer Functions		**PSNR by using Levenberg-Marquardt, Resilient and Levenberg-Marquardt training algorithm**		
Layer 1	**Layer 2**	**Gradient descent with momentum back propagation**	**Resilient**	**Levenberg-Marquardt**
Log-sigmoid	Log-sigmoid	54.7989	70.7548	70.7799
Log-sigmoid	Tan-Sigmoid	59.8017	70.7470	70.7800
Log-sigmoid	Linear	62.1224	70.7381	70.7800
Tan-Sigmoid	Log-sigmoid	59.3987	70.7230	70.7799
Tan-Sigmoid	Tan-Sigmoid	63.5685	70.7266	70.7800
Tan-Sigmoid	Linear	65.5659	70.6755	70.7800
Linear	Log-sigmoid	58.5352	68.6869	68.6869
Linear	Tan-Sigmoid	66.8746	69.8703	69.8703
Linear	Linear	69.0680	69.0722	69.0722

Figure 12. Denoised image using Levenberg-Marquardt training algorithm

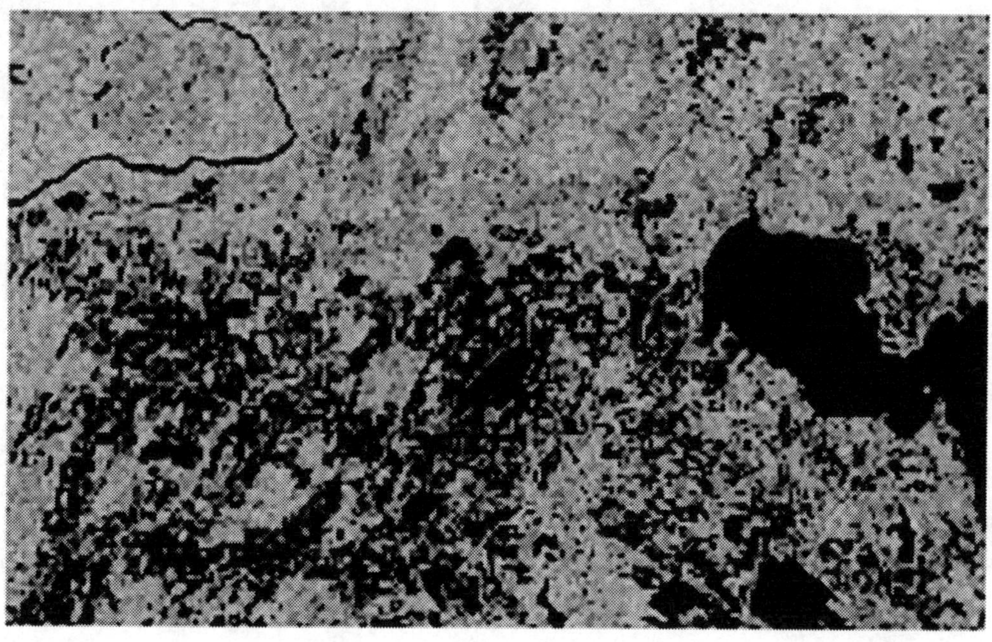

Figure 13. Denoised image using Resilient training algorithm

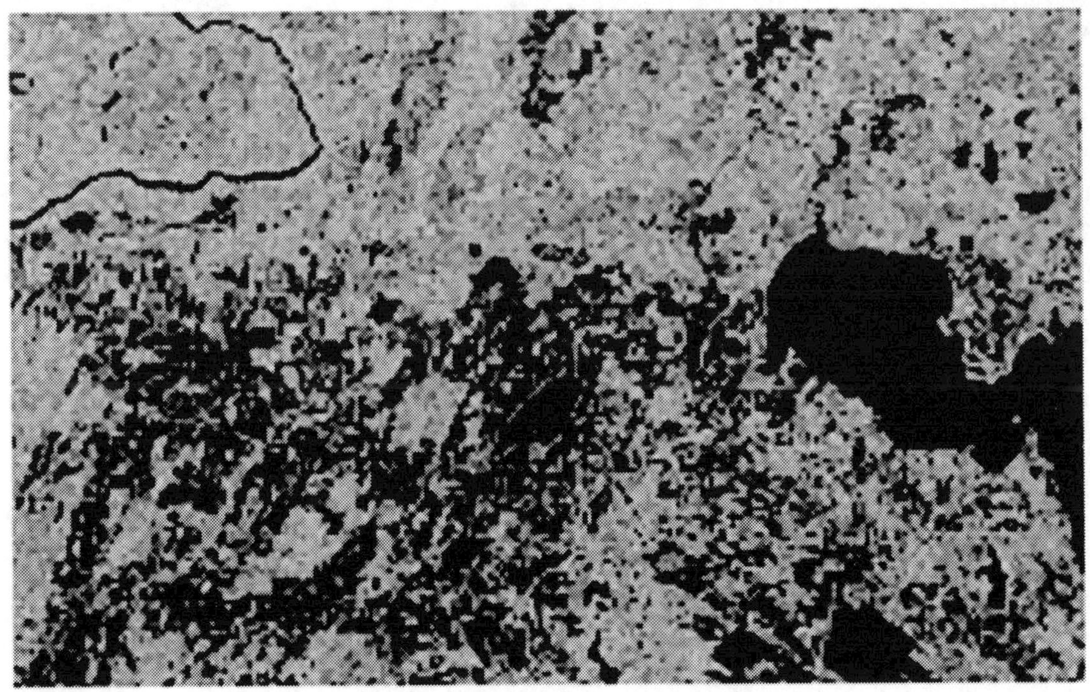

Figure 14. Denoised image using Gradient descent with momentum back propagation

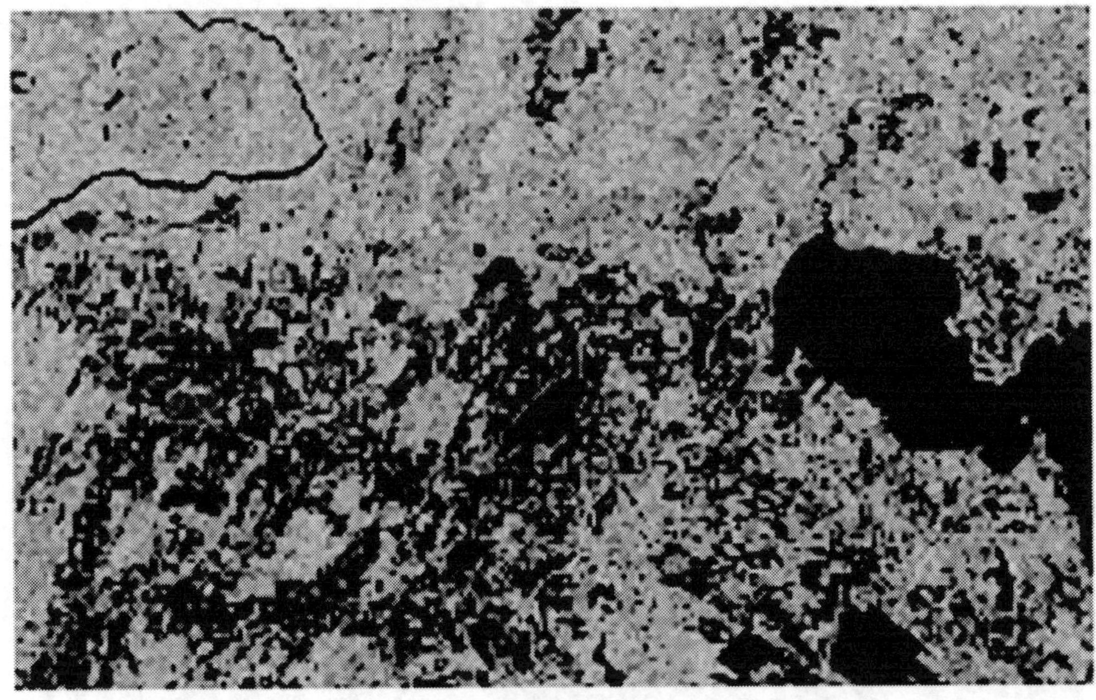

6. CONCLUSION

The concept of SAR is to produce high quality images in all weather condition, day and night. The quality of SAR image is affected by speckle noise. MLP is an ANN capable of reducing noise in images. We have presented MLP with two hidden layer, trained using Gradient descent with momentum back propagation, Resilient back propagation and Levenberg-Marquardt back propagation. It is found that MLP can reduce speckle noise in SAR image. The designed MLP network trained using Levenberg-Marquardt gives better result (evaluated using PSNR) amongst the chosen training algorithm. Due to unavailability of field experimental data, we performed offline SAR image processing.

In future work, performance of SAR using MLP is to be compared with other Soft Computing tools. We are also planning to implement radial basis function network for reducing speckle noise and comparatively evaluate the performance with MLP.

REFERENCES

Beale, R., & Jackson, T. (1990). *Neural Computing-an introduction*. CRC Press. doi:10.1887/0852742622

Blacknell, D., Oliver, C. J., & Warner, M. (1995, November). Speckle reduction of SAR images using neural networks. *Satellite Remote Sensing*, *2*, 179–187.

Chan, Y. K., & Koo, V. C. (2008). An introduction to synthetic aperture radar (SAR). *Progress In Electromagnetics Research B*, *2*, 27–60. doi:10.2528/PIERB07110101

Cumming, I. C., & Bennett, J. R. (1979, April). Digital processing of SEASAT SAR data. In *Acoustics, Speech, and Signal Processing, IEEE International Conference on ICASSP'79* (Vol. 4, pp. 710-718). IEEE. doi:10.1109/ICASSP.1979.1170630

Curlander, R. (1991). Synthetic Aperture Radar: Systems and Signal Processing. John Wiley and Sons.

Dao, V. N., & Vemuri, V. R. (2002). A performance comparison of different back propagation neural networks methods in computer network intrusion detection. *Differential Equations and Dynamical Systems, 10*(1&2), 201-214.

Dastgir, N. (2007). Processing SAR Data using Range Doppler and Chirp Scaling Algorithms. *Master's of Science Thesis in Geodesy Report*, (3096), 07-005.

Demuth, H., & Beale, M. (2000). *Neural network toolbox user's guide*. MathWorks.

Frost, V. S., Stiles, J. A., Shanmugan, K. S., & Holtzman, J. C. (1982). A model for radar images and its application to adaptive digital filtering of multiplicative noise. *Pattern Analysis and Machine Intelligence, IEEE Transactions on*, (2), 157-166.

Hagan, M. T., & Menhaj, M. B. (1994). Training feedforward networks with the Marquardt algorithm. *Neural Networks. IEEE Transactions on*, *5*(6), 989–993.

Kaur, A., & Singh, K. (2010, March). Speckle noise reduction by using wavelets. In *National Conference on Computational Instrumentation CSIO NCCI* (pp. 198-203).

Khowaja, S., & Shah, S. Z. S. (2014). Noise reduction technique for images using radial basis function neural networks. *Mehran University Research Journal of Engineering & Technology, 33*(3).

Kisi, Ö., & Uncuoglu, E. (2005). Comparison of three back-propagation training algorithms for two case studies. *Indian Journal of Engineering & Materials Sciences, 12*(5), 434-442.

Koivo, H. N. (2008). *Neural networks: Basics using matlab neural network toolbox*. MathWorks.

Kuan, D. T., Sawchuk, A., Strand, T. C., & Chavel, P. (1985). Adaptive noise smoothing filter for images with signal-dependent noise. *Pattern Analysis and Machine Intelligence, IEEE Transactions on*, (2), 165-177.

Lee, J. S. (1986). Speckle suppression and analysis for synthetic aperture radar images. *Optical Engineering (Redondo Beach, Calif.), 25*(5), 255636–255636. doi:10.1117/12.7973877

Long, P. D., & Cat, P. T. (2009, December). Real-time speckle reducing by Cellular Neural Network. In *Information, Communications and Signal Processing, 2009. ICICS 2009. 7th International Conference on* (pp. 1-4). IEEE. doi:10.1109/ICICS.2009.5397738

Maragos, P. (2005). *Morphological Filtering for Image Enhancement and Feature Detection. In The Image and Video Processing Handbook* (2nd ed.). Elsevier Academic Press.

Marquardt, D. W. (1963). An algorithm for least-squares estimation of nonlinear parameters. *Journal of the Society for Industrial and Applied Mathematics, 11*(2), 431–441. doi:10.1137/0111030

Mashaly, A. S., AbdElkawy, E. E. F., & Mahmoud, T. (2010, November). Speckle noise reduction in SAR images using adaptive morphological filter. In *Intelligent Systems Design and Applications (ISDA), 2010 10th International Conference on* (pp. 260-265). IEEE.

ORNL DAAC. (n.d.). *Alos-palsar image*. Retrieved from http://webmap.ornl.gov/wcsdown/dataset.jsp?ds_id=993

Park, H., & Nishimura, T. (2007, August). Reduced speckle noise on medical ultrasound images using cellular neural network. In *Engineering in Medicine and Biology Society, 2007. EMBS 2007. 29th Annual International Conference of the IEEE* (pp. 2138-2141). IEEE. doi:10.1109/IEMBS.2007.4352745

Patino-Escarcina, R. E., & Costa, J. A. F. (2007, October). An evaluation of MLP neural network efficiency for image filtering. In *Intelligent Systems Design and Applications, 2007. ISDA 2007. Seventh International Conference on* (pp. 335-340). IEEE. doi:10.1109/ISDA.2007.134

Pitas, I., & Venetsanopoulos, A. N. (2013). *Nonlinear digital filters: principles and applications* (Vol. 84). Springer Science & Business Media.

Qian, N. (1999). On the momentum term in gradient descent learning algorithms. *Neural Networks, 12*(1), 145–151. doi:10.1016/S0893-6080(98)00116-6 PMID:12662723

Riedmiller, M., & Braun, H. (1993). A direct adaptive method for faster backpropagation learning: The RPROP algorithm. In *Neural Networks, 1993., IEEE International Conference on* (pp. 586-591). IEEE.

Rumelhart, D. E., & McClelland, J. L.PDP Research Group. (1988). *Parallel distributed processing* (Vol. 1, pp. 354–362). IEEE.

Saikia, T., & Sarma, K. K. (2014, February). Multilevel-DWT based image de-noising using feed forward artificial neural network. In *Signal Processing and Integrated Networks (SPIN), 2014 International Conference on* (pp. 791-794). IEEE. doi:10.1109/SPIN.2014.6777062

Santhanam, T., & Radhika, S. (2011). Applicability of BPN and MLP neural networks for classification of noises present in different image formats. *International Journal of Computers and Applications*, *26*(5), 10–14. doi:10.5120/3101-4259

Schulze, M. A., & Wu, Q. X. (1995). *Noise reduction in synthetic aperture radar imagery using a morphology-based nonlinear filter*. Digital Image Computing and Applications.

Tomiyasu, K. (1978). Tutorial review of synthetic-aperture radar (SAR) with applications to imaging of the ocean surface. *Proceedings of the IEEE*, *66*(5), 563–583. doi:10.1109/PROC.1978.10961

White, R. G. (1991). Change detection in SAR imagery. *International Journal of Remote Sensing*, *12*(2), 339–360. doi:10.1080/01431169108929656

Wiener, N. (1949). *Extrapolation, interpolation, and smoothing of stationary time series* (Vol. 2). Cambridge, MA: MIT Press.

Chapter 17
Face Recognition using Fast Fourier Transform

Shivakumar Baragi
BVBCET, India

Nalini C. Iyer
BVBCET, India

ABSTRACT

Biometrics refers to metrics related to human characteristics and Traits. Face Recognition is the process of identification of a person by their facial image. It has been an active area of research for several decades, but still remains a challenging problem because of the complexity of the human face. The objective is to authenticate a person, to have a FAR and FRR very low. This project introduces a new approach for face recognition system using FFT algorithm. The database that contains the images is named as train database and the test image which is stored in test database is compared with the created train database. For further processing RGB data is converted into grayscale, thus reduces the matrix dimension. FFT is applied to the entire database and mean value of the images is computed and the same is repeated on test database also. Based on the threshold value of the test image, face recognition is done. Performance evaluation of Biometrics is done for normal image, skin color image, ageing image and blur image using False Acceptance Rate(FAR), False Rejection Rate(FRR), Equal Error Rate(EER) and also calculated the accuracy of different images.

1. INTRODUCTION

1.1 Biometrics

Biometrics is an emerging field of information technology which aims to identification of an individual. Biometric identifiers are the distinctive, measurable characteristics used to label and describe individuals (Jain, Hong, & Pankanti, 2000). Biometric identifiers are often categorized as physiological versus behavioral characteristics (Jain, & Ross, 2008).. It has been shown that information characteristics of each individual can be extracted in order to verify the identity of that individual in a population. Biometric

DOI: 10.4018/978-1-4666-8737-0.ch017

based identification is more reliable than token based system (card, key, and etc.), and face recognition among biometric identification systems are natural and does not have less negative responses in using from peoples, and thus much more research efforts have been pouring into this area among biometric areas (Zhao, Chellappa, Phillips, & Rosenfeld, 2003). (Li, & Jain, 2004)

Biometrics authentication (or realistic authentication) is used in computer science as a form of identification and access control (Jain, Ross, Nandakumar, 2009). It is also used to identify individuals in groups that are under surveillance. Biometric authentication requires comparing a registered or enrolled biometric sample (biometric template or identifier) against a newly captured biometric sample (for example, captured image during a login). During enrollment a sample of the biometric trait is captured, processed by a computer, and stored for later comparison.

Biometric recognition can be used in mode, where the biometric system identifies a person from the entire enrolled population by searching a database for a match based solely on the biometric. Sometime identification is called "one-to-many" matching. A system can also be used in mode, where the biometric system authenticates a person claimed identity from their previously enrolled pattern this is also called "one-to-one matching. In most computer access or network access environments, verification mode would be used. The main advantages of biometrics over other standard security systems are that biometric traits cannot be forgotten or lost. They are difficult to copy, share and distribute and they require the person to be present at the time of authentication.

1.2 Face as a Biometric

Facial images are the most common biometric characteristic used by humans to make a personal recognition, hence the idea to use this biometric in technology. Face verification involves extracting a feature set from a two-dimensional image of the user's face and one method to proceed by comparing selected facial features from the image and a facial database. Face recognition is a challenging task for the researchers, on one side its applications is used for verification and recognition on other side it is complicated to implement due to all different situation that a human face can be found. The most popular approaches to face recognition are based on either the location or shape of facial attributes such as eyes, eyebrows, nose, lips and chin. For best work of facial recognition system in practice, it should automatically

- Detect whether face is available in the acquired image.
- Locate the face if there is only one face and,
- Recognize the face.

Face recognition is a process does not require active co -operation of a person so without instructing the person can recognize the person, so face recognition is much more advantageous compared to the other biometrics. Face recognition has a high identification or recognition rate of greater than 90 percent for huge face databases with well-controlled pose and illumination conditions.

1.3 Face Recognition

Face recognition is one of the most common methods used for identifying or verifying a person due to its non-intrusive nature, as acquiring face images can be done at a distance. Recognizing faces and facial expressions is becoming very important in many practical applications, such as in border control and airport security. Therefore there are two types of approaches for face recognition. One is image based and another one is video- based. Face Recognition becomes one of the most biometrics authentication techniques from the past few years. Face recognition is an interesting and successful application of Pattern recognition and Image analysis.

Face recognition system has two main tasks: verification and identification. Face verification means a 1:1 match that compares a face images against a template face images whose identity being claimed. Face identification means a 1: N problem that compares a query face image against all image templates in a face database. Machine recognition of faces is gradually becoming very important due to its wide range of commercial and law enforcement applications, which include forensic identification, access control, border surveillance and human inter- actions and availability of low cost recording devices. Facial recognition system should be able to automatically detect a face in an image, extract its features and then recognize it from a general viewpoint (i.e., from any pose) which is a rather difficult task (Jain, Ross, & Prabhakar, 2004).

This paper introduces a new approach to face recognition systems using the FFT algorithm. The adapted methodology is: the color image is taken and stored in test database which is compared with train database after the images are preprocessed. FFT is applied on the entire database, as images are two dimensional, computation of mean value of the FFT images is done, and then the above steps are repeated for test database also. Lastly the difference between test and train database are computed. Based on the set threshold value comparison between mean values of test and train database is carried out. The performance estimation is done by calculating False Acceptance Rate (FAR) and False Rejection Rate (FRR) for different images.

The motivate behind the implementation was to authenticate a person, to create a database set of face images, to performing tests for accuracy, to have a FAR and FRR very low.

The Organization of the paper is section I describes the introduction of the biometrics, face recognition with the highlighted view of an objectives of the work which is to be carried out in this paper. Section II discusses the methodology adapted, the block diagram, FFT and the performance evaluation of Biometrics. Section III deals with the result and calculation of FAR and FRR for various images. Section IV gives the conclusions and possible directions for future work.

2. LITERATURE SURVEY

These section overviews the major human face recognition techniques that apply mostly to frontal faces. The methods considered are eigenface (eigen-feature), neural network, dynamic link architecture, hidden Markov model, geometrical feature matching, and template matching. The approaches are analyzed in terms of the facial representations they used. Automated face recognition is a relatively new concept, developed in the 1960s, the first semi-automated system for face recognition required the administrator to locate features (such as eyes, ears, nose, and mouth) on the photographs before it calculated distances and ratios to a common reference point, which were then compared to reference data.

Eigenface is one of the most thoroughly investigated approaches for face recognition. It is also known as Karhunen Loeave expansion, eigenpicture, eigenvector, and principal component.

2.1 Related Work

(Sirovich, & Kirby, 1987) and (Kirby et al., 1990) used principal component analysis to efficiently represent pictures of faces. They argued that any face images could be approximately reconstructed by a small collection of weights for each face and a standard face picture (eigenpicture). The weights describing each face are obtained by projecting the face image onto the eigenpicture.

(Turk, & Pentland, 1991), used eigenfaces, which was motivated by the technique of Kirby and Sirovich, for face detection and identification. In mathematical terms, eigenfaces are the principal components of the distribution of faces, or the eigenvectors of the covariance matrix of the set of face images. The eigenvectors are ordered to represent different amounts of the variation, respectively, among the faces. Each face can be represented exactly by a linear combination of the eigenfaces. It can also be approximated using only the best eigenvectors with the largest eigenvalues. The best M eigenfaces construct an M dimensional space, i.e., the face space. The authors reported 96 percent, 85 percent, and 64 percent correct classifications averaged over lighting, orientation, and size variations, respectively. Their database contained 2,500 images of 16 individuals. As the images include a large quantity of background area, the above results are influenced by back-ground. The authors explained the robust performance of the system under different lighting conditions by significant correlation between images with changes in illumination.

To compute the covariance matrix using three images each taken in different lighting conditions to account for arbitrary illumination effects, if the object is Lambertian was proposed by Zhao and Yang. (Zhao, & Yang, 1999).

(Pentland et al.,1994) extended their early work on eigenface to eigenfeatures corresponding to face components, such as eyes, nose, and mouth. They used a modular eigenspace which was composed of the above eigenfeatures (i.e. eigeneyes, eigennose, and eigenmouth). This method would be less sensitive to appearance changes than the standard eigenface method. The system achieved a recognition rate of 95 percent on the FERET database of 7,562 images of approximately 3,000 individuals. In summary, eigenface appears as a fast, simple, and practical method. However, in general, it does not provide invariance over changes in scale and lighting conditions.

The attractiveness of using neural network could be due to its nonlinearity in the network. Hence, the feature extraction step may be more efficient than the linear Karhunen-Loeve methods. One of the first artificial neural network (ANN) techniques used for face recognition is a single layer adaptive network called WISARD which contains a separate network for each stored individual (Stonham, 1984, pp. 426-441). The way in constructing a neural network structure is crucial for successful recognition.

(Lawrence et al., 1997) proposed a hybrid neural network which combined local image sampling, a self-organizing map (SOM) neural network, and a convolution neural network. The SOM provides a quantization of the image samples into a topological space where inputs that are nearby in the original space are also nearby in the output space, thereby providing dimension reduction and invariance to minor changes in the image sample. The convolution network extracts successively larger features in a hierarchical set of layers and provides partial invariance to translation, rotation, scale, and deformation. The authors reported 96.2 percent correct recognition on ORL database of 400 images of 40 individuals. The classification time is less than 0.5 second, but the training time is as long as 4 hours.

(Lin et al., 1997) used probabilistic decision-based neural network (PDBNN) which inherited the modular structure from its predecessor, a decision based neural network (DBNN). The PDBNN can be applied effectively to

- **Face Detector:** which finds the location of a human face in a cluttered image.
- **Eye Localizer:** determines the positions of both eyes in order to generate meaningful feature vectors.
- **Face Recognizer:** A hierarchical neural network structure with non-linear basis functions and a competitive credit -assignment scheme was adopted.

PDBNN-based biometric identification system has the merits of both neural networks and statistical approaches, and its distributed computing principle is relatively easy to implement on parallel computer.

In (Lin, Kung, & Lin, 1997) it was reported that PDBNN face recognizer had the capability of recognizing up to 200 people and could achieve up to 96 percent correct recognition rate in approximately 1 second. However, when the number of persons increases, the computing expense will become more demanding. In general, neural network approaches encounter problems when the number of classes increases. Moreover, they are not suitable for a single model image recognition task because multiple model images per person are necessary in order for training the systems to optimal parameter setting.

Graph matching is another approach to face recognition. (Lades et al., 1993) presented a dynamic link structure for distortion invariant object recognition which employed elastic graph matching to find the closest stored graph. Dynamic link architecture is an extension to classical artificial neural networks. Memorized objects are represented by sparse graphs, whose vertices are labeled with a multi-resolution description in terms of a local power spectrum and whose edges are labeled with geometrical distance vectors. Object recognition can be formulated as elastic graph matching which is performed by stochastic optimization of a matching cost function. They reported good results on a database of 87 people and a small set of office items comprising different expressions with a rotation of 15 degrees. The matching process is computationally expensive, taking about 25 seconds to compare with 87 stored objects on a parallel machine with 23 transporters.

Wiskott and Von der Malsburg (1996) extended the technique and matched human faces against a gallery of 112 neutral frontal view faces. Probe images were distorted due to rotation in depth and changing facial expression. Encouraging results on faces with large rotation angles were obtained. They reported recognition rates of 86.5 percent and 66.4 percent for the matching tests of 111 faces of 15 degree rotation and 110 faces of 30 degree rotation to a gallery of 112 neutral frontal views. In general, dynamic link architecture is superior to other face recognition techniques in terms of rotation invariant; however, the matching process is computationally expensive.

(Samaria & Fallside, 1993) applied this method to human face recognition. Faces were intuitively divided into regions such as the eyes, nose, mouth etc., which can be associated with the states of a hidden Markov model. Since HMMs require a one-dimensional observation sequence and images are two-dimensional, the images should be converted into either 1D temporal sequence or 1D spatial sequence.

In (Samaria & Fallside, 1993) a spatial observation sequence was extracted from a face image by using a band sampling technique. Each face image was represented by a 1D vector series of pixel observation. Each observation vector is a block of L lines and there is an M lines overlap between successive observations. An unknown test image is first sampled to an observation sequence. Then, it is matched against every HMM in the model face database. The match with the highest likelihood is considered the best match and the relevant model reveals the identity of the test face. The recognition rate of HMM approach is 87 percent using ORL database consisting of 400 images of 40 individuals.

A pseudo 2D HMM (Samaria, & Harter, 1994) was reported to achieve a 95 percent recognition rate in their preliminary experiments. Its classification time and training time were not given. The choice of parameters had been based on subjective intuition. Geometrical feature matching techniques are based on the computation of a set of geometrical features from the picture of a face. The fact that face recognition is possible even at coarse resolution as low as 8 pixels, when the single facial features are hardly revealed in detail, implies that the overall geometrical configuration of the face features is sufficient for recognition. The overall configuration can be described by a vector representing the position and size of the main facial features, such as eyes and eyebrows, nose, mouth, and the shape of face outline. One of the pioneering works on automated face recognition by using geometrical features was done by (Kanade, 1973). Their system achieved a peak performance of 75 percent recognition rate on a database of 20 people using two images per person, one as the model and the other as the test image.

(Bruneli & Poggio, 1993) automatically extracted a set of geometrical features from the picture of a face, such as nose width and length, mouth position, and chin shape. There were 35 features extracted to form a 35 dimensional vector. The recognition was then performed with a Bayes classifier. They reported a recognition rate of 90 percent on a database of 47 people.

(Cox et al., 1996) introduced a mixture-distance technique which achieved 95 percent recognition rate on a query database of 685 individuals. Each face was represented by 30 manually extracted distances.

(Manjunath et al., 1992) used Gabor wavelet decomposition to detect feature points for each face image which greatly reduced the storage requirement for the database. Typically, 35-45 feature points per face were generated. The matching process utilized the information presented in a topological graphic representation of the feature points. After compensating for different centroid location, two cost values, the topological cost, and similarity cost, were evaluated. The recognition accuracy in terms of the best match to the right person was 86 percent and 94 percent of the correct person's face was in the top three candidate matches. In summary, geometrical feature matching based on precisely measured distances between features may be most useful for finding possible matches in a large database such as a mug shot album. However, it will be dependent on the accuracy of the feature location algorithms. Current automated face feature location algorithms do not provide a high degree of accuracy and require considerable computational time.

In (Bruneli & Poggio, 1993) automatically selected a set of four features templates, i.e., the eyes, nose, mouth, and the whole face, for all of the available faces. They compared the performance of their geometrical matching algorithm and template matching algorithm on the same database of faces which contains 188 images of 47 individuals. The template matching was superior in recognition(100 percent recognition rate) to geometrical matching (90 percent recognition rate) and was also simpler. Since the principal components (also known as eigenfaces or eigenfeatures) are linear combinations of the templates in the databases, the technique cannot achieve better results than correlation (Takacs, 1998, pp. 1873-1881) but it may be less computationally expensive. One drawback of template matching is its computational complexity. Another problem lies in the description of these templates. Since the recognition system has to be tolerant to certain discrepancies between the template and the test image, this tolerance might average out the differences that make individual faces unique. In general, template-based approaches compared to feature matching are a more logical approach.

In summary, no existing technique is free from limitations. Further efforts are required to improve the performances of face recognition techniques, especially in the wide range of environments encountered in real world. Edge information is a useful object representation feature that is insensitive to illumination changes to certain extent. Though the edge map is widely used in various pattern recognition fields, it has been neglected in face recognition except in recent work reported in (Takacs, 1998, pp. 1873-1881). Face recognition employing the spatial information of edge map associated with local structural information remains an unexplored area Based on the summary, the gaps in the previous work were identified and a new methodology is proposed to fill that gap and enhanced face recognition technique for various kinds of images.

3. METHODOLOGY

The Fast Fourier Transform (FFT) is simply a fast way to calculate the Discrete Fourier Transform (DFT). FFT algorithm was first published by Cooley and Tukey in 1965. This is a clever algorithm which can be used to transform a signal from time domain to frequency domain. The FFT greatly reduces the amount of calculation and the noise of a signal that is present in the time domain.

Functionally, the FFT decomposes the set of data to be transformed into a series of smaller data sets to be transformed. Then, it decomposes those smaller sets into even smaller sets. At each stage of pre-processing, the results of previous stages are combined in special way. Finally, it calculates the DFT of each small data set. For example, an FFT of size 32 is broken into 2 FFTs of size16, which are broken into 4 FFTs of size 8,which are broken into 8 FFTs of size 4, which are broken into 16 FFTs of size 2 ("dspGuru by Lowegian International").

3.1 Proposed Block Diagram

Figure 1 shows the proposed block diagram. It consists of two database namely train database and test database. In this paper Cooley-Tukey algorithm is used to compute FFT. It re-expresses the Discrete Fourier Transform (DFT) of an arbitrary composite size N = N1N2 in terms of smaller DFTs of sizes N1 and N2, recursively, in order to reduce the computation time to O (NlogN) for highly composite N. The Cooley-Tukey algorithm can be combined arbitrarily with any other algorithm, as it breaks the DFT into smaller DFTs (Cooley James, & Tukey John, n.d.).

The various blocks are explainedi n the following subsections.

3.2 Databases

Two databases is created namely train database and test database. Train database consist of number of face images whereas test database consist of test image, which is compared with train database.

Figure 1. Block diagram of FFT based face recognition

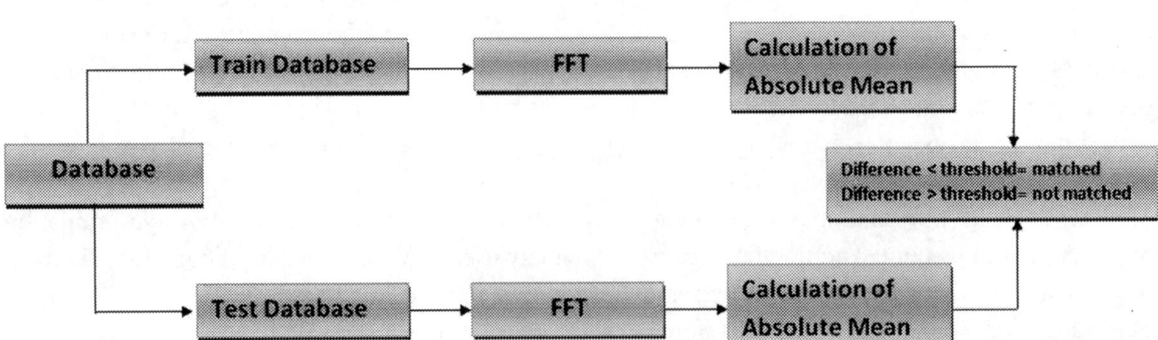

3.3 Fast Fourier Transform (FFT)

The Fast Fourier Transform (FFT) is simply a fast (computationally efficient) way to calculate the Discrete Fourier Transform (DFT). FFT algorithm was first published by Cooley and Tukey in 1965. This is a clever algorithm which can be used to transform a signal from time domain to frequency domain. The FFT greatly reduces the amount of calculation. It also reduces the noise of a signal that is present in the time domain.

Functionally, the FFT decomposes the set of data to be transformed into a series of smaller data sets to be transformed. Then, it decomposes those smaller sets into even smaller sets. At each stage of preprocessing, the results of previous stages are combined in special way. Finally, it calculates the DFT of each small data set. For example, an FFT of size 32 is broken into 2 FFTs of size16, which are broken into 4 FFTs of size 8,which are broken into 8 FFTs of size 4, which are broken into 16 FFTs of size 2 ("dspGuru by Lowegian International").

3.4 Fast Fourier Transform on an Image

FFT on image is a representation of the image in frequency domain. Its function on image is to decompose it into its real and imaginary components, taking an image as an input then the number of frequencies in the frequency domain is equal to the number of pixels in the original image (Muthyalam, n.p.).The FFT is given by the following equations:

$$F(X)=\sum_{n=0}^{N-1} f(n)e^{-j2\pi(x\frac{n}{N})}$$

The FFT of a 2D image is given by the following equations:

$$F(X,Y)=\sum_{m=0}^{M-1}\sum_{n=0}^{N-1} F(m,n)e^{-j2\pi(x\frac{m}{M}+y\frac{n}{N})}$$

Here f (m, n) is the pixel at f(m, n) coordinates, F(x, y) is the value of the image in the frequency domain at (x, y) coordinates. M and N are the dimensions of the image. Since image are two dimensional, so applied 2D FFT on it. The 2D transform can be done as two 1D transforms as shown in equations (shown only the horizontal direction) one in the horizontal direction followed by the other in the vertical direction on the result of the horizontal transform. The end result is equivalent to perform the 2D transform in the frequency space. The FFT implemented in this application requires that the dimensions of the image are power of two. An interesting property of FFT is that the transform of N points can be written as the sum of two N/2 transforms. This is important because some of the computations can be reused thus eliminating expensive operations (Muthyalam, n.p.).

The output of the Fourier Transform is a complex number and has a much greater range than the image in the spatial domain. Therefore, to accurately store these values are stored as floats. Furthermore, the dynamic range of the Fourier coefficient is too large to be displayed on the screen and these values are scaled to bring them within the range of values that can be displayed (Muthyalam, n.p.).

A modern interpretation of FFT states that, -any well-behaved function can be represented by a superposition (combination or sum) of sinusoidal waves. It can be said that, the frequency domain representation is just another way to store and reproduce the spatial domain image.

By taking a single row or column of the pixel from any image and graph it, it looks more like a wave (See Fig. 2).

If the fluctuations are more regular in spacing and amplitude, would get something more like a wave pattern (See Fig. 3).

The superposition of waves or addition of waves in much closer, but still does not match the image pattern. However it can continue in this manner, adding more waves and adjusting them until the resulting composite wave gets closer and closer to the actual profile of the original image. Eventually by adding enough waves it can exactly reproduce the original image. Therefore, it can be said that images are nothing but the summation of sine and cosine waves.

If more waves adding, it might get a pattern that is closer to the original image which can be shown as.

In other words, by adding together a sufficient number of sine waves of the right frequency and amplitude, any fluctuating pattern can be reproduced. Fourier Transform generally works out to find out the waves that comprise an image (Weinhaus, 2000).

The FFT is an important in image processing tool, which is used to decompose an image into its sine and cosine components or waves. Undoubtedly, the output of FFT represents the image in the frequency domain, while the input image is the spatial domain or time domain equivalent. In the Fourier domain image, each point represents a particular frequency contained the spatial domain image. Then to access the geometric characteristic of a spatial domain image, FFT can be used. Because the image in the Fourier domain is decomposed into its sinusoidal components, which is the easy way to examine or process certain frequencies of the image, that influences the geometric structure in the spatial domain (Weinhaus, 2000).

Figure 2. Graph of single row/column of pixel for an image

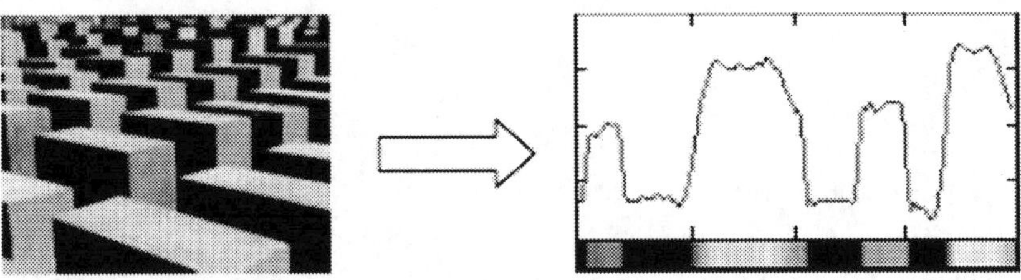

Figure 3. Graph of pixel for an image with regular fluctuations in spacing and amplitude

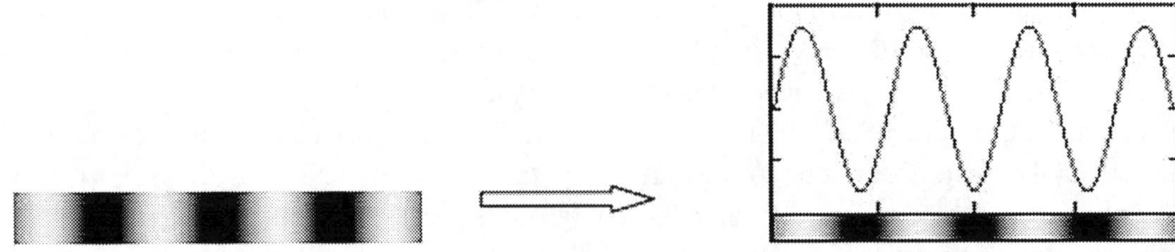

Figure 4. Addition of more waves to get pattern closer to original image

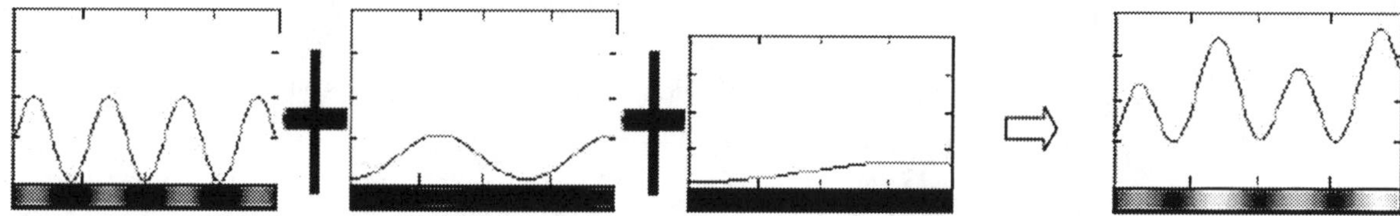

In most implementations the Fourier image is shifted in such a way that the DC-value or the image mean is displayed in the center of the image, center of an image point is nothing but the higher corresponding frequency (Gonzales, & Woods, 1992) &(Jain, 1989, pp 15-20). In general applying FFT on an image will get the complex result.

The magnitude calculated from the complex result is shown in Figure 5. It is seen that the DC value is by far the largest component of the image. However, the intensity values in the Fourier image or the dynamic ranges of the Fourier coefficients is too large to be displayed on the screen, therefore all other values appear as black. By applying logarithmic transformation to the image, it can be shown in Figure 6.

Figure 6 contains component of all frequencies, but their magnitude gets smaller for higher frequencies. Hence, low frequencies contain more image information than the higher ones. The transformed image tells that there are two dominating directions in the Fourier image, one passing vertically and another passing horizontally through the center. These originate from the regular patterns in the background of the original image. The value of each point determines the phase of the corresponding frequency. As in the magnitude image, it can identify the vertical and horizontal lines corresponding to patterns in the original image. The phase image does not contain much new information about the structures of the

Figure 5. The magnitude calculated from the complex result

Figure 6. Magnitude after logarithmic transform

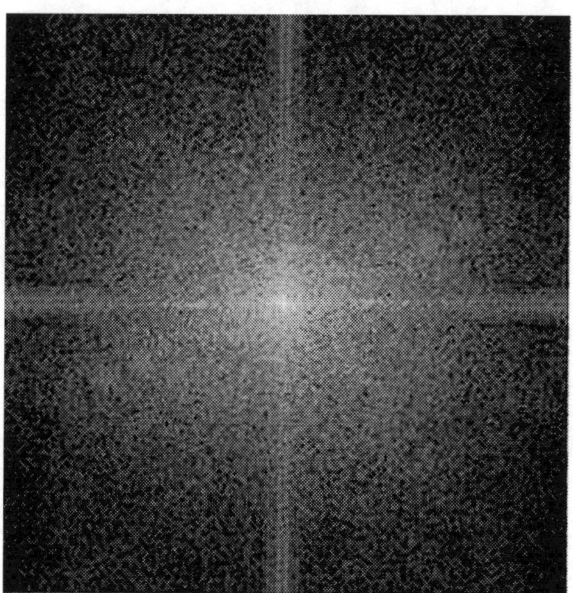

spatial domain image (Gonzales, & Woods, 1992) &(Jain, 1989, pp 15-20). Therefore, it will confine to displaying only the magnitude of the Fourier Transform unless our interest does not belong to reconstruct the image. Figure 7 shows the phase of the FFT.

On the other hand, do not separating the magnitude and phase part of an image, after applying FFT on the image. The FFT of an image is shown in Figure 8.

3.5 Performance Evaluation of Biometrics

Samples of the same biometric trait of a user obtained over a period of time can differ dramatically. The variability observed in the biometric feature set of an individual is known as Intra-user variations. For example, in the case of fingerprints, factors such as placement of finger on the sensor, applied finger pressure, skin condition and feature extraction errors lead to large Intra-user variations. On the other hand, features extracted from biometric traits of different individuals can be quite similar. For example, some pairs of individuals can have nearly identical facial appearance due to genetic factors (e.g. father and son, identical twins). Appearance-based facial features will exhibit a large similarity for these pairs of individuals and such a similarity is usually referred to as Inter-user similarity.

A biometric system can make two types of errors namely, False Acceptance Rate (FAR) and False Rejection Rate (FRR) ("Characteristics Of Biometric Systems").

- **The False Acceptance Rate (FAR):** is the probability that the system incorrectly authorizes a non-authorized person, due to incorrectly matching the biometric input with a database. The FAR is normally expressed as a percentage, which is the percentage of invalid inputs which are incorrectly accepted. False Accept Rate is also called False Match Rate.

Figure 7. The phase of FFT

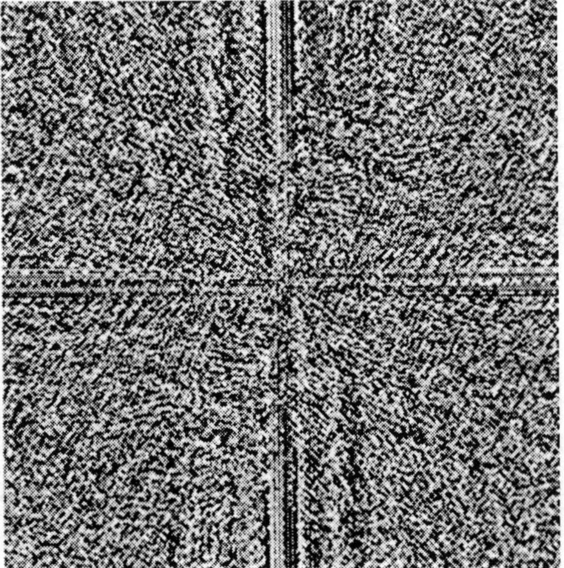

Figure 8. FFT

- **The False Rejection Rate (FRR):** is the probability that the system incorrectly rejects access to an authorized person, due to failing to match the biometric input with a database. The FRR is normally expressed as a percentage, which is the percentage of valid inputs which are incorrectly rejected. False Reject Rate is sometimes referred to as False Non-Match Rate.
- **Equal Error Rate (EER):** is defined as it is the value where both the FRR and FAR rates are equal.

Figure 9 shows the performance evaluation of Biometrics such as FAR, FRR and EER graph.

4. RESULT AND DISCUSSION

The result of the proposed algorithm is verified in Matlab. The creation of database is done and ten images were taken in train database which is shown in figure 10 and also twenty test images is taken which is combination of known and unknown face images.

Figure 9. Performance evaluation of biometrics

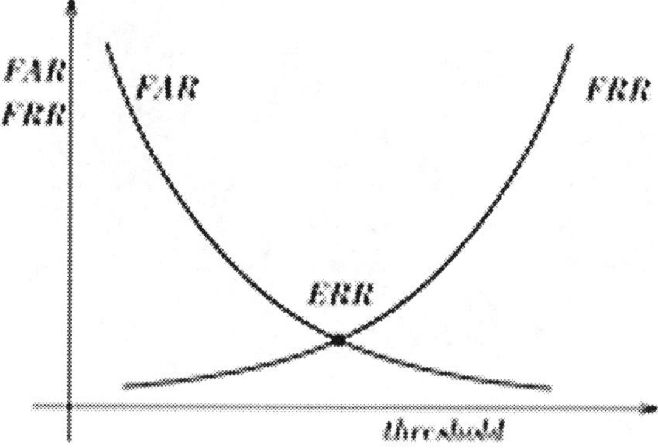

Figure 10. Train database

Test database is created using the same procedure used for creation of train database; the input image is stored in the test database and then compared with train database. The input image is shown in figure 11

As the input image is present in train database, the threshold value of the both images will match and the result is displayed in figure 12.

Another test image which is stored in the test database and compared with train database, the image is shown in figure 13.

As the input image is not present in the train database, the threshold value of the both images will not match and the result is displayed in figure 14.

The calculation of FAR, FRR and EER is done for various images namely Normal, Ageing, Skin color and Blur images and also find the accuracy for various images. Taken ten images in train database and twenty input images is tested which is combination of known and unknown face images and calculated FAR and FRR.

Figure 11. Test image

Figure 12. Matched image

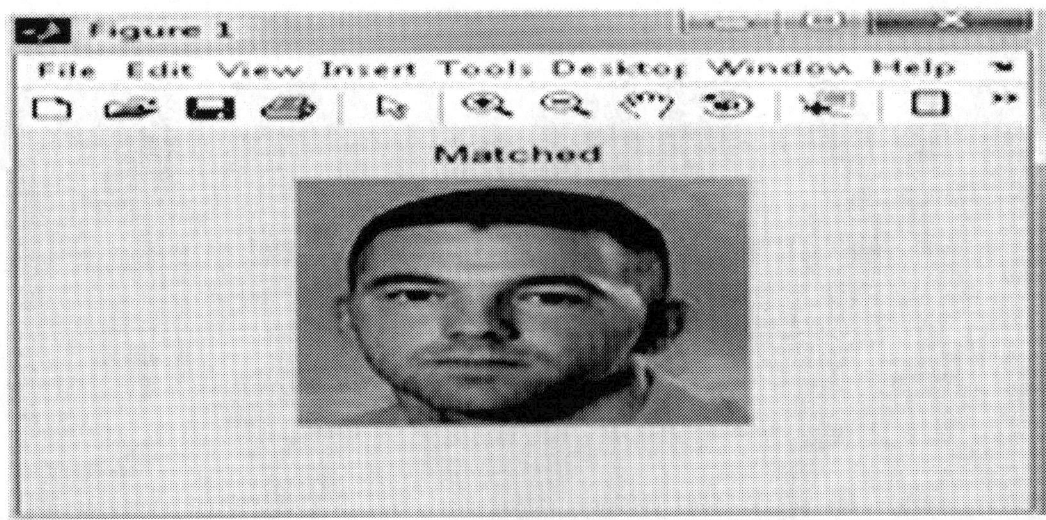

Figure 13. Test image

Figure 14. Not matched image

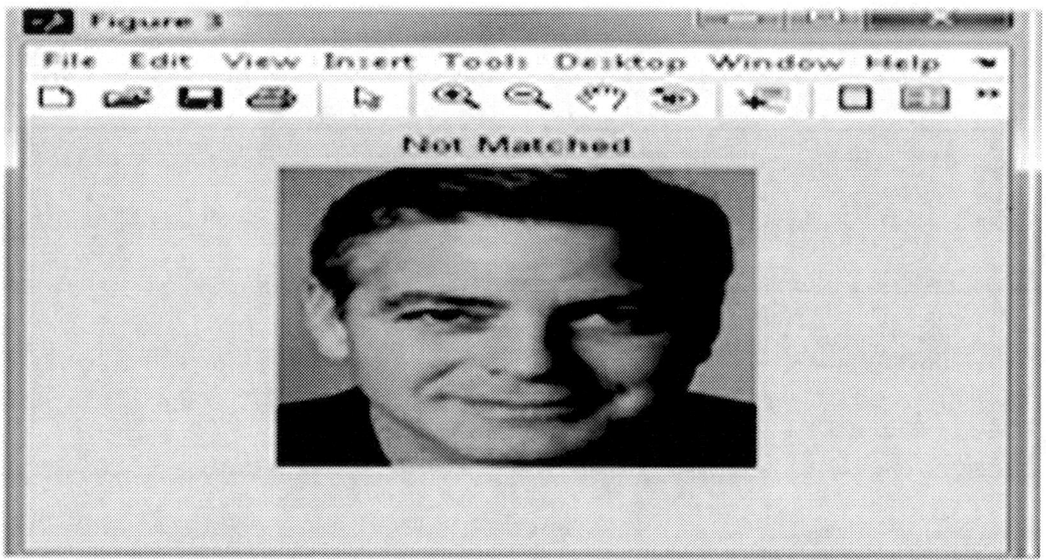

4.1 Normal Images

The databases were created which are considered to test the algorithm for performance analysis. Table 1 shows the variations of performance parameters such as FAR and FRR for different values of threshold.

In Table 1, as the value of threshold increases, the values of FAR increases and FRR are zero respectively for normal images.

Figure 15. shows the variations of FAR and FRR with threshold values for normal images. At the threshold value 1, FAR is equal to FRR that is 0 which is called Equal Error Rate (EER).

Table 1. FAR and FRR with Variation of Threshold Values

Threshold	FAR	FRR
1	0	0
5	0.1	0
10	0.1	0
15	0.1	0
20	0.3	0
25	0.6	0
30	0.8	0
35	0.8	0
40	1	0

Figure 15. Variations of FAR and FRR with threshold for normal images

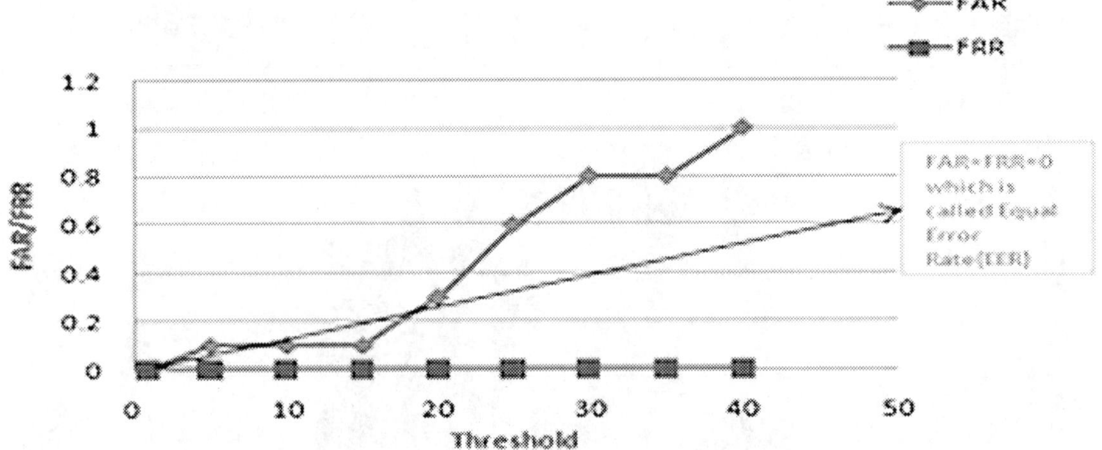

4.2 Skin Color Images

Skin color image depends on facial skin marks, mole and tattoos, such images were employed for the task of personal identification. Table 2 shows the calculation of FAR and FRR for skin color image.

As the value of threshold increases, the values of FAR increases and FRR decreases for skin color image. Figure 16 shows the variation of FAR and FRR with different threshold values, at the threshold value 23, FAR is equal to FRR which is called Equal Error Rate (EER) i.e. 0.5.

4.3 Ageing Images

Another important aspect is to be discussed is the ageing of human being. The databases used for testing are collected over a time of few months or years, face change gradually with time this may be due to ageing, illness or any other environmental factor. Table 3 shows the variations of performance parameters such as FAR and FRR for different values of threshold.

Table 2. FAR and FRR with Variation of Threshold Values

Threshold	FAR	FRR
1	0	1
5	0	1
10	0.2	0.6
15	0.3	0.5
20	0.4	0.5
23	0.5	0.5
25	0.5	0.4
30	0.5	0.2
35	0.6	0.2
40	0.6	0.1
50	0.7	0
60	0.9	0
70	0.9	0
80	1	0

Table 3. FAR and FRR with Variation of Threshold Values

Threshold	FAR	FRR
1	0	1
5	0	1
10	0.1	1
15	0.3	0.9
20	0.3	0.8
25	0.6	0.8
30	0.6	0.7
35	0.6	0.7
40	0.7	0.7
50	0.9	0.7
60	1	0.6

Figure 16. Variations of FAR and FRR with threshold for skin color images

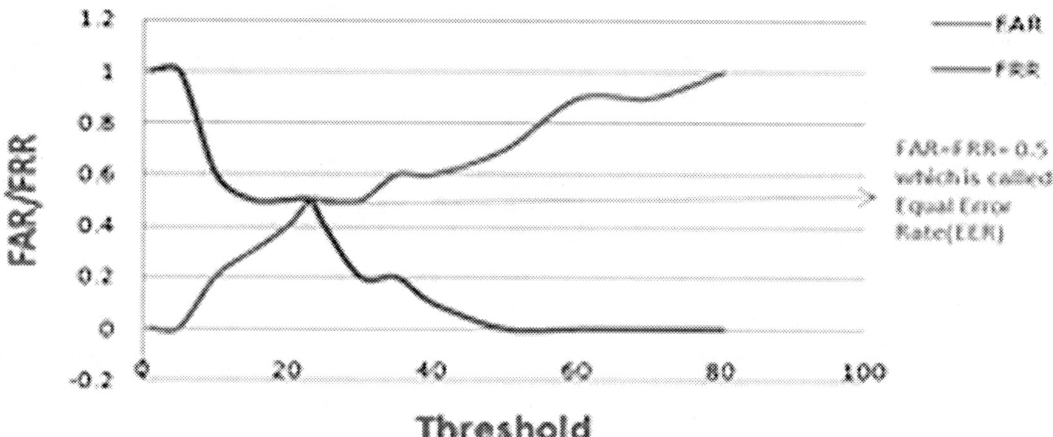

For ageing images when the threshold value is Minimum, the values of FRR are Maximum and FAR are minimum. Figure 17 shows the variation of FAR and FRR with different threshold values, at the threshold value 40, the EER is 0.7 where the FAR is equal to FRR.

4.4 Blur Images

The FAR and FRR is also calculated for blur images. Blur image depends on quality of image. The values of FRR and FAR with variable threshold for blur images are shown in Table 4.

Figure 17. Variations of FAR and FRR with threshold for ageing images

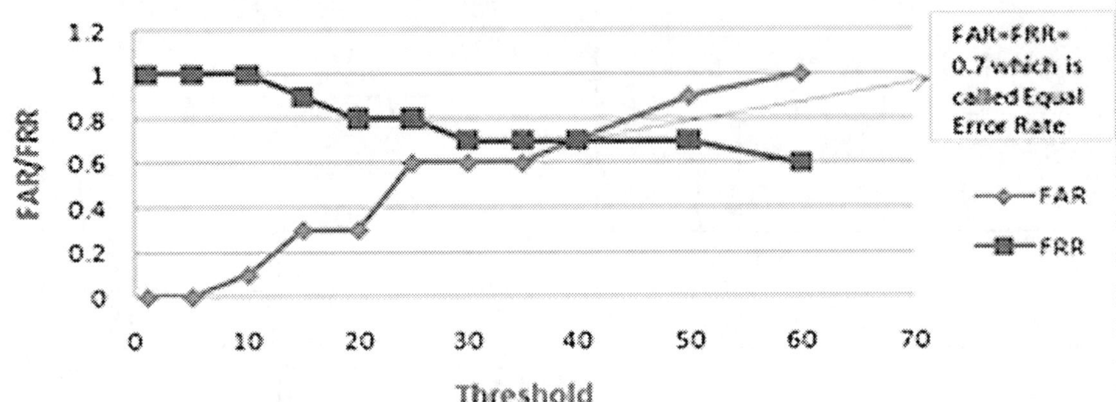

Table 4. FAR and FRR with Variation of Threshold Values

Threshold	FAR	FRR
1	0	1
5	0.1	1
10	0.5	0.9
15	0.5	0.9
20	0.6	0.9
25	0.8	0.9
30	0.8	0.9
35	0.8	0.9
40	0.8	0.9
50	0.8	0.8
60	0.9	0.8
70	1	0.8
80	1	0.8

When the threshold value is minimum then FAR is minimum (0) and FRR is maximum (1) for blur images.

The variations of FAR and FRR with threshold variations for blur images which shown in figure 18 at the threshold value 50, FAR is equal to FRR that is 0.8 which is known as Equal Error Rate(EER).

Recognition rate is calculated for different types of images for constant threshold value which is set to 15. Table 5 shows the FAR, FRR and recognition rate of different images at constant threshold. In Table 5, as the recognition rate decreases the values of FAR and FRR increases for different types of images.

Figure 18. Variations of FAR and FRR with threshold for Blur images

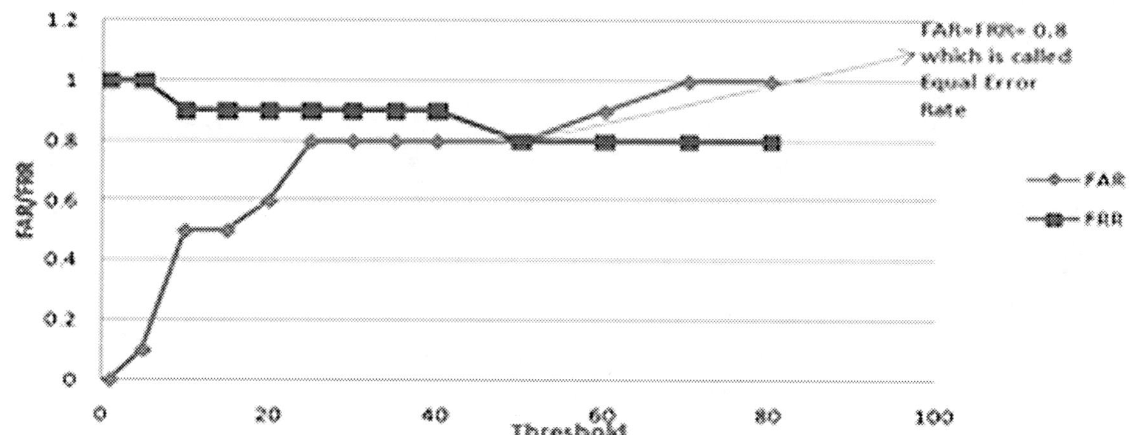

5. CONCLUSION

The face image is physiological trait and is a better biometric data as the samples can be obtained without the cooperation of a person as well as can also be captured with reasonable distance. The face recognition system is implemented using FFT algorithm. The databases namely train database and test database were created. All images were resized, then converted from RGB data to grayscale and stored in train database. Then the differences of means between test and train databases were calculated and the test image is compared with all the images present in the train database. Based on the threshold value of the test image the acceptance or rejection of the test image is decided. A software implementation of the algorithm is examined in MATLAB to verify its accuracy.

Performance estimation is done by calculating False Acceptance Rate (FAR) and False Rejection Rate (FRR) by keeping constant threshold value which is set to 15, the result analysis of different images and recognition rate is shown in table 6.

In Table 6, the normal images having greater recognition rate compare to other images. As in skin color images there will be lot of changes in face such as marks, tattoos and spects because of this reason recognition rate will be less compare to normal image which is 99.60%, then the ageing face changes

Table 5. FAR, FRR and Recognition Rate with Constant Threshold Values

Images	FAR	FRR	Recognition Rate
Normal Image	0.1	0	99.95%
Skin color image	0.3	0.5	99.60%
Ageing Images	0.3	0.9	99.40%
Blur Images	0.5	0.9	99.30%

Table 6. The result analysis of different images and recognition rate

Images	Recognition Rate
Normal Images	99.95%
Skin color Images	99.60%
Ageing Images	99.40%
Blur Images	99.30%

Figure 19. Recognition rate of the different images at constant threshold

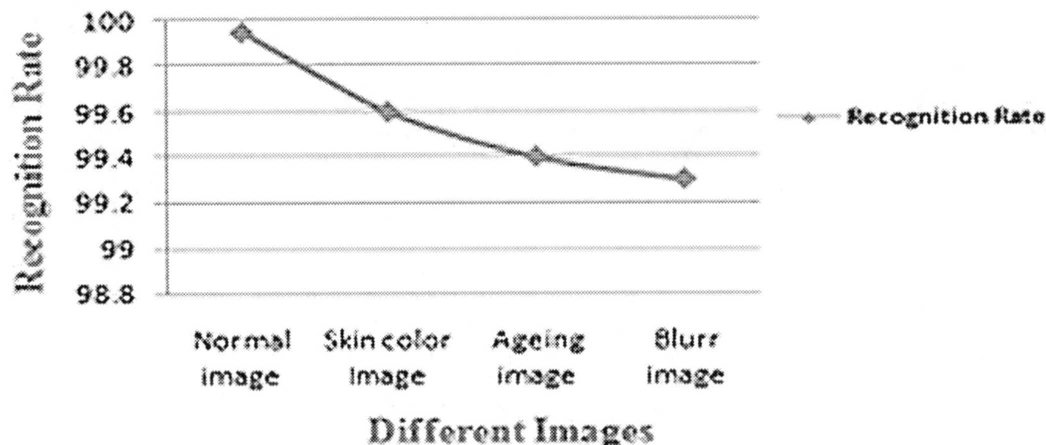

gradually with time this may be due to ageing, illness or any other environmental factor, so gives the less recognition rate which is 99.40%. Blur images are depends on quality of the image; if the quality of the image is low then the recognition rate is less which is 99.30%. Figure 19 shows the Recognition Rate of the different images at constant threshold.

6. FUTURE WORK

In future improvements this algorithm could be implemented on FPGA. This project focuses on developing a Face recognition system on FPGA. An advantage of developing this system on a FPGA is the ability to update the functionalities or correct any error by re-programming the FPGA with a systems new version. This system is targeted for access control, face databases, face identification, human computer interaction, law enforcement, smart cards, featuring important characteristics to achieve this goal. This algorithm can be implemented in DSP processor to speed up the process of face recognition techniques. This algorithm can be implement in real time application.

REFERENCES

Bruneli, R., & Poggio, T. (1993). Face Recognition: Features versus Templates. *IEEE Transactions on Pattern Analysis and Machine Intelligence*, *15*(10), 1042–1052. doi:10.1109/34.254061

Characteristics Of Biometric Systems. (n.d.). Retrieved from https://www.cccure.org/Documents/HISM/039-041.html

Cooley James, W., & Tukey John, W. (1965, May 1). An algorithm for the machine calculation of complex Fourier series. *Mathematics of Computation*, *19*(90), 297–301. doi:10.1090/S0025-5718-1965-0178586-1

Cox, I. J., Ghosn, J., & Yianios, P. N. (1996). *Feature Based Face Recognition Using Mixture Distance*. Computer Vision and Pattern Recognition. doi:10.1109/CVPR.1996.517076

Gonzales, R., & Woods, R. (1992). *Digital Image Processing*. Addison-Wesley Publishing Company.

Jain, A. K. (1989). *Fundamentals of Digital Image Processing*. Prentice Hall.

Jain, A. K., Hong, L., & Pankanti, S. (2000). *Biometric Identification*. Retrieved from http://helios.et.put.poznan.pl/~dgajew/download/PUT/SEMESTR_10/IO/FACE_RECOGNITION/BiometricsACM.pdf

Jain, A. K., Ross, A., & Prabhakar, S. (2004). An Introduction to Biometric Recognition. *IEEE Transactions on Circuits and Systems for Video Technology*, *14*(1), 4–19. doi:10.1109/TCSVT.2003.818349

Jain, A. K., & Ross, A. A. (2008). *Introduction to Biometrics*. Retrieved from http://www.springer.com/computer/image+processing/book/978-1-4419-4375-0

Jain, A. K., Ross, A. A., & Nandakumar, K. (2009). *Introduction to Biometrics*. Retrieved from http://biometrics.cse.msu.edu/

Kanade, T. (1973). *Picture Processing by Computer Complex and Recognition of Human Faces*. Kyoto Univ.

Kirby, M., & Sirovich, L. (1990). Application of the Karhunen-Loeave Proce-dure for the Characterisation of Human Faces. *IEEE Transactions on Pattern Analysis and Machine Intelligence*, *12*(1), 831–835. doi:10.1109/34.41390

Lades, M., Vorbrueggen, J. C., & Buhmann, J. (1993). Distortion Invariant Object Recognition in the Dynamic Link Architecture. *IEEE Transactions on Computers*, *42*(3), 300–311. doi:10.1109/12.210173

Lawrence, S., Giles, C. L., Tsoi, A. C., & Back, A. D. (1997). Face Recognition: A Convolution Neural Network Approach. *IEEE Transactions on Neural Networks*, *8*(1), 98–113. doi:10.1109/72.554195

Li, S. Z., & Jain, A. K. (2004). Handbook of Face Recognition. Academic Press.

Lin, S. H., Kung, S. Y., & Lin, L. J. (1997). Face Recognition/Detection by Probabilistic Decision Based Neural Network. *IEEE Transactions on Neural Networks*, *8*(1), 114–132. doi:10.1109/72.554196

Manjunath, B. S., Chellappa, R., & von der Malsburg, J. C. (1992). A Feature Based Approach to Face Recognition. *Proc. IEEE CS Conf. Computer Vision and Pattern Recognition*. doi:10.1109/CVPR.1992.223162

Pentland, A., Moghaddam, B., & Starner, T. (1994). View-Based and Modular Eigenspaces for Face Recognition. In *Proc. IEEE CS Conf. Computer Vision and Pattern Recognition*, (pp. 84-91). doi:10.1109/CVPR.1994.323814

Samaria, F., & Fallside, F. (1993). Face Identification and Feature Extraction Using Hidden Markov Models. In G. Vernazza (Ed.), *Image Processing: Theory and Application*. Elsevier.

Samaria, F., & Harter, A. C. (1994). Parameterization of a Stochastic Model for Human Face Identification. *Proc. Second IEEE Workshop Applications of Computer Vision*.

Sirovich, L., & Kirby, M. (1987). Low-Dimensional Procedure for the Characterisation of Human Faces. *Journal of the Optical Society of America*, *4*(3), 519–524. doi:10.1364/JOSAA.4.000519

Stonham, T. J. (1984). Practical Face Recognition and Verification with WISARD. Aspects of Face Processing.

Takacs, B. (1998). Comparing Face Images Using the Modified Hausdorff Distance. *Pattern Recognition*, *31*(12), 1873–1881. doi:10.1016/S0031-3203(98)00076-4

Turk, M., & Pentland, A. (1991). Eigenfaces for Recognition. *Journal of Cognitive Neuroscience*, *3*(1), 71–86. doi:10.1162/jocn.1991.3.1.71

Weinhaus, F. (2000). Retrieved from http://www.imagemagick.org/Usage/fourier/

Wiskott, L., & von der Malsburg, J. C. (1996). Recognizing Faces by Dynamic Link Matching. *NeuroImage*, *4*(3), S14–S18. doi:10.1006/nimg.1996.0043

Zhao, L., & Yang, Y. H. (1999). Theoretical Analysis of Illumination in PCA-Based Vision Systems. *Pattern Recognition*, *32*(4), 547–564. doi:10.1016/S0031-3203(98)00119-8

Zhao, W., Chellappa, R., Phillips, J., & Rosenfeld, A. (2003). Face Recognition: A Literature Survey. *ACM Computing Surveys*, *35*(4), 399–458. doi:10.1145/954339.954342

Chapter 18
White Patch Detection in Brain MRI Image Using Evolutionary Clustering Algorithm

Pradeep Kumar Mallick
St. Peter's University, India

Mihir Narayan Mohanty
SOA University, India

S. Saravana Kumar
Sree Vidyanikethan Engineering College, India

ABSTRACT

Though image segmentation is a fundamental task in image analysis; it plays a vital role in the area of image processing. Its value increases in case of medical diagnostics through medical images like X-ray, PET, CT and MRI. In this chapter, an attempt is taken to analyze an MRI brain image. It has been segmented for a particular patch in the brain MRI image that may be one of the tumors in the brain. The purpose of segmentation is to partition an image into meaningful regions with respect to a particular application. Image segmentation is a method of separating the image from the background, read the contents and isolating it. In this chapter both the concept of clustering and thresholding technique have been used. The standard methods such as Sobel, Prewitt edge detectors is applied initially. Then the result is optimized using GA for efficient minimization of the objective function and for improved classification of clusters. Further the segmented result is passed through a Gaussian filter to obtain a smoothed image.

1. INTRODUCTION

Over last two decades bio-image analysis and processing occupied an important position. Image segmentation is the process of distinguishing the objects and background in an image. It is an essential preprocessing task for many applications that depend on computer vision such as medical imaging, locating objects in satellite images, machine vision, fingerprint and face recognition, agricultural imaging

DOI: 10.4018/978-1-4666-8737-0.ch018

and other many applications. The accuracy of image segmentation stage would have a great impact on the effectiveness of subsequent stages of the image processing. Image segmentation problem has been studied by many researchers for several years; however, due to the characteristics of the images such as their different modal histograms, the problem of image segmentation is still an open research issue and so further investigation is needed.

Identifying specific organs or other features in medical images require a considerable amount of expertise concerning the shapes and locations of anatomical features. Such segmentation is typically performed manually by expert physicians as part of treatment planning and diagnosis. Due to the increasing amount of available data and the complexity of features of interest, it is becoming essential to develop automated segmentation methods to assist and speedup image-understanding tasks. Medical imaging is performed in various modalities, such as magnetic resonance imaging (MRI), computed tomography (CT), ultrasound, etc. Several automated methods have been developed to process the acquired images and identify features of interest, including intensity-based methods, region-growing methods and deformable contour models. Intensity-based methods identify local features such as edges and texture in order to extract regions of interest. Region-growing methods start from a seed-point (usually placed manually) on the image and perform the segmentation task by clustering neighboring pixels using a similarity criterion. Deformable contour models are shape-based feature search procedures in which a closed contour deforms until a balance is reached between its internal energy (smoothness of the curve) and external energy (local region statistics such as first and second order moments of pixel intensity). The genetic algorithm framework brings considerable flexibility into the segmentation procedure by incorporating both shape and texture information. In the following sections we describe our algorithm in depth and relate our methodology to previous work in this area.

W. Pratt, Rafael C *et.al*, and A.K Jain provide the fundamental of image segmentation. A.Haldar *et. al.* described automatic image segmentation using fuzzy c-means clustering algorithm. Similarly A. Jyoti *et.al.* has been described CT brain image segmentation using clustering methods for effective and accurate feature extraction even in the presence of noise. Manoj K *et. al.*, S.Lakshmi I et.al., S.Behera *et. al.,* V.Rani *et.al.* and Muthukrishnan.R *et. al.* have beeb proposed various edge detection techniques for image segmentation. S. K. Kar *et. al.* discussed a statistical approach for recognition of color of the object. Here threshold is determined based on basic statistical method that leads to color recognition of an object. Applying the method of thresholding iteratively over the ROI selected, the recognition of the color of the desired object is performed.

Woo-seok Jang *et.al* proposed Optimized Fuzzy Clustering By Predator Prey Particle Swarm Optimization .Here fuzzy clustering is optimised using predator prey particle swarm optimizations (PPPSO). In order to avoid local optimal solutions and find global optimal solution efficiently. The performance of fuzzy c-means (FCM), particle swarm fuzzy clustering (PSFC) and predator prey particle swarm fuzzy clustering (PPPSFC) are compared. P. K. Sahoo *et. al.,* Liu Jianzhuang Xidian Univ *et.al,* M. Cheriet *et.al* have been described various thresholding techniques of Image processing .

In this paper an attempt is made to segment an image using fuzzy c-means clustering algorithm with its modified objective function by considering the approach of genetic algorithm. This proposed method minimizes the objective function better than the conventional FCM and gives superior quality of segmented result.

1.1 Clustering

Cluster analysis or clustering is the task of grouping a set of objects in such a way that objects in the same group (called a cluster) are more similar (in some sense or another) to each other than to those in other groups (clusters). It is a main task of exploratory data mining, and a common technique for statistical data analysis, used in many fields, including machine learning, pattern recognition, image analysis, information retrieval, and bioinformatics.

According to Vladimir Estivill-Castro, the notion of a "cluster" cannot be precisely defined, which is one of the reasons why there are so many clustering algorithms.[4] There is a common denominator: a group of data objects. However, different researchers employ different cluster models, and for each of these cluster models again different algorithms can be given. The notion of a cluster, as found by different algorithms, varies significantly in its properties. Understanding these "cluster models" is key to understanding the differences between the various algorithms. Typical cluster models include:

- **Connectivity Models:** For example hierarchical clustering builds models based on distance connectivity.
- **Centroid Models:** For example the k-means algorithm represents each cluster by a single mean vector.
- **Distribution Models:** Clusters are modeled using statistical distributions, such as multivariate normal distributions used by the Expectation-maximization algorithm.
- **Density Models:** For example DBSCAN and OPTICS defines clusters as connected dense regions in the data space.
- **Subspace Models:** In Biclustering (also known as Co-clustering or two-mode-clustering), clusters are modeled with both cluster members and relevant attributes.
- **Group Models:** Some algorithms do not provide a refined model for their results and just provide the grouping information.
- **Graph-Based Models:** A clique, i.e., a subset of nodes in a graph such that every two nodes in the subset are connected by an edge can be considered as a prototypical form of cluster. Relaxations of the complete connectivity requirement (a fraction of the edges can be missing) are known as quasi-cliques.

A "clustering" is essentially a set of such clusters, usually containing all objects in the data set. Additionally, it may specify the relationship of the clusters to each other, for example a hierarchy of clusters embedded in each other. Clustering's can be roughly distinguished as:

- **Hard Clustering:** Each object belongs to a cluster or not.
- **Soft Clustering (also Fuzzy Clustering):** Each object belongs to each cluster to a certain degree (e.g. a likelihood of belonging to the cluster).

There are also finer distinctions possible, for example:

- **Strict Partitioning Clustering:** Here each object belongs to exactly one cluster.
- **Strict Partitioning Clustering with Outliers:** Objects can also belong to no cluster, and are considered outliers.

- **Overlapping Clustering (also Alternative Clustering, Multi-View Clustering):** While usually a hard clustering, objects may belong to more than one cluster.
- **Hierarchical Clustering:** Objects that belong to a child cluster also belong to the parent cluster.
- **Subspace Clustering:** While an overlapping clustering, within a uniquely defined subspace, clusters are not expected to overlap.

1.2 Types of Clustering Algorithm

Data clustering algorithms: Clustering algorithms can be categorized based on their cluster model, as listed above. The following overview will only list the most prominent examples of clustering algorithms, as there are possibly over 100 published clustering algorithms. Not all provide models for their clusters and can thus not easily be categorized. An overview of algorithms explained in Wikipedia can be found in the list of statistics algorithms.

There is no objectively "correct" clustering algorithm, but as it was noted, "clustering is in the eye of the beholder." The most appropriate clustering algorithm for a particular problem often needs to be chosen experimentally, unless there is a mathematical reason to prefer one cluster model over another. It should be noted that an algorithm that is designed for one kind of model has no chance on a data set that contains a radically different kind of model .For example, k-means cannot find non-convex clusters.

Hierarchical clustering: Connectivity based clustering, also known as hierarchical clustering, is based on the core idea of objects being more related to nearby objects than to objects farther away. These algorithms connect "objects" to form "clusters" based on their distance. A cluster can be described largely by the maximum distance needed to connect parts of the cluster. At different distances, different clusters will form, which can be represented using a dendrogram, which explains where the common name "hierarchical clustering" comes from: these algorithms do not provide a single partitioning of the data set, but instead provide an extensive hierarchy of clusters that merge with each other at certain distances. In a dendrogram, the y-axis marks the distance at which the clusters merge, while the objects are placed along the x-axis such that the clusters don't mix.

Connectivity based clustering is a whole family of methods that differ by the way distances are computed. Apart from the usual choice of distance functions, the user also needs to decide on the linkage criterion (since a cluster consists of multiple objects, there are multiple candidates to compute the distance to) to use. Popular choices are known as single-linkage clustering (the minimum of object distances), complete linkage clustering (the maximum of object distances) or UPGMA ("Unweighted Pair Group Method with Arithmetic Mean", also known as average linkage clustering). Furthermore, hierarchical clustering can be agglomerative (starting with single elements and aggregating them into clusters) or divisive (starting with the complete data set and dividing it into partitions).

K-means clustering: In centroid-based clustering, clusters are represented by a central vector, which may not necessarily be a member of the data set. When the number of clusters is fixed to k, k-means clustering gives a formal definition as an optimization problem: find the k cluster centers and assign the objects to the nearest cluster center, such that the squared distances from the cluster are minimized.

Distribution-based clustering: The clustering model most closely related to statistics is based on distribution models. Clusters can then easily be defined as objects belonging most likely to the same distribution. A convenient property of this approach is that this closely resembles the way artificial data sets are generated: by sampling random objects from a distribution.

Figure 1. K–mean clustering

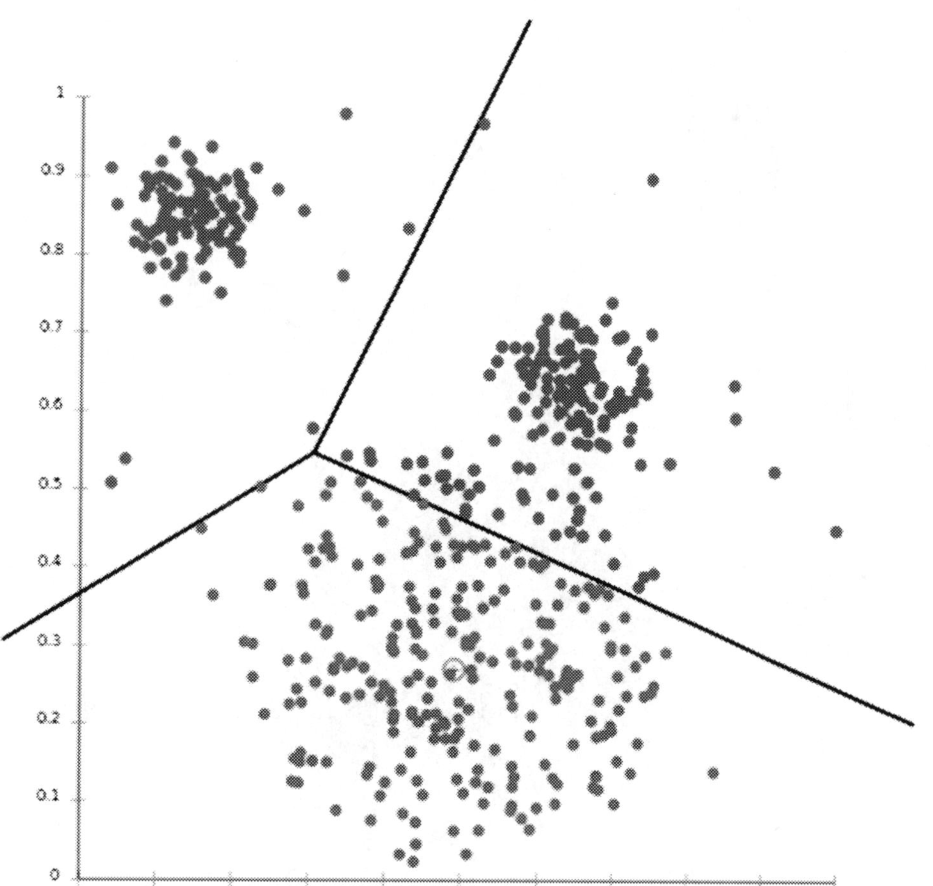

While the theoretical foundation of these methods is excellent, they suffer from one key problem known as overfitting, unless constraints are put on the model complexity. A more complex model will usually be able to explain the data better, which makes choosing the appropriate model complexity inherently difficult.

One prominent method is known as Gaussian mixture models (using the expectation-maximization algorithm). Here, the data set is usually modelled with a fixed (to avoid overfitting) number of Gaussian distributions that are initialized randomly and whose parameters are iteratively optimized to fit better to the data set. This will converge to a local optimum, so multiple runs may produce different results. In order to obtain a hard clustering, objects are often then assigned to the Gaussian distribution they most likely belong to; for soft clusterings, this is not necessary.

Distribution-based clustering produces complex models for clusters that can capture correlation and dependence between attributes. However, these algorithms put an extra burden on the user: for many real data sets, there may be no concisely defined mathematical model (e.g. Assuming Gaussian distributions is a rather strong assumption of the data).

This chapter is organized as follows. Section 2 depicts the methods for image segmentation. The result is discussed in section 3 and finally in section 4 concludes the work.

Figure 2. Distribution-based clustering

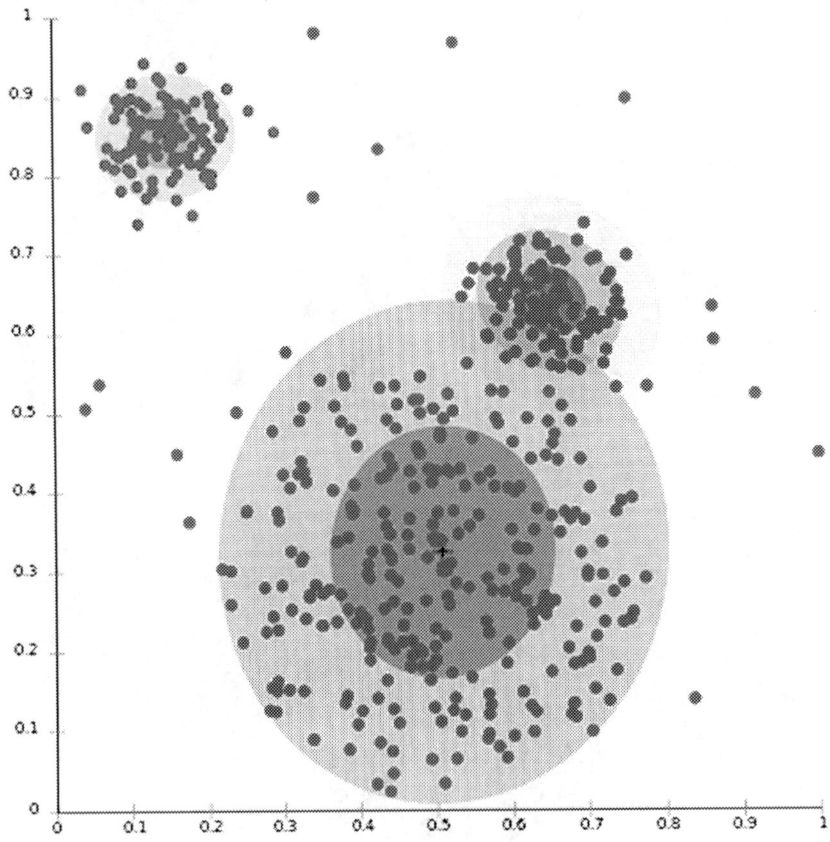

1.3 Evolutionary Method for Clustering

Evolutionary clustering is the problem of processing timestamped data to produce a sequence of clusterings; that is, a clustering for each timestep of the system. Each clustering in the sequence should be similar to the clustering at the previous timestep, and should accurately reflect the data arriving during that timestep. The primary setting for this problem is the following. Every day, new data arrives for the day, and must be incorporated into a clustering. If the data does not deviate from historical expectations, the clustering should be "close" to that from the previous day, providing the user with a familiar view of the new data. However, if the structure of the data changes significantly, the clustering must be modified to reflect the new structure. Thus, the clustering algorithm must trade off the benefit of maintaining a consistent clustering over time with the cost of deviating from an accurate representation of the current data. The benefits of evolutionary clustering compared to traditional clustering appear in situations in which the current (say, daily) clustering is being consumed regularly by a user or system. In such a setting, evolutionary clustering is useful for the following reasons:

1. **Consistency:** A user will find each day's clustering familiar, and so will not be required to learn a completely new way of segmenting data. Similarly, any insights derived from a study of previous clusters are more likely to apply to future clusters.

2. **Noise Removal:** Providing a high-quality and historically consistent clustering provides greater robustness against noise by taking previous data points into effect. As we describe later, our method subsumes standard approaches to windowing and moving averages.
3. **Smoothing:** If the true clusters shift over time, evolutionary clustering will naturally present the user with a smooth view of the transition.
4. **Cluster Correspondence:** As a side effect of our framework, it is generally possible to place today's clusters in correspondence with yesterday's clusters. Thus, even if the clustering has shifted, the user will still be situated within the historical context.

2. PROPOSED METHOD

The C-means clustering method is optimized using the evolutionary computing approach as GA approach and the procedure is given as follows:

2.1 Proposed Algorithm

1. The MRI brain image has been considered for the work as input image.
2. The point of interest is a particular area within the brain image, as it is of the patient case. For this reason, the ROI was extracted for analysis of the image. The ROI is evaluated by statistical method from the pixel by considering the boundary.
3. Then the image was de-noised using a Gaussian filter and the model is given as: [16]

$$H(u,v) = e^{-D^2}(u,v)/2D_0^2$$

4. The image matrix was then converted to intensity matrix with values ranging from 0 to 1 to prepare for the vital clustering stage.
5. It follows the cluster analysis algorithm as explained (Fuzzy C-means algorithm):
   a. The number of class c and *U (t)* were initialized. The fuzzification Parameter m with *(1<m< ∞)*, value, ∈ >0 and *t=0* were set.
   b. The class center matrix $W^{(t)}$ = *[w1,w2,….,wc]* was calculated, using U(t)

$$wi = \frac{1}{\sum_{x=1}^{n} (¼_{x,i})^{m}} \sum_{x=1}^{n} (¼_{x,i})^{m} z_x \text{ , for every } i;$$

   c. The linear membership function considered to calculate membership matrix, $U^{(t+1)} = [¼_{1,j}]$ using $W^{(t)}$ is:

$$[¼_{x,i}] = \left[\sum_{j=1}^{C} \left(\frac{|z_x - w_i|}{|z_x - w_j|} \right)^{2/(m-1)} \right]^{-1} \text{ , for every } x \text{ and } i;$$

d. Parameter = max[$|U^{(t+1)} - U^{(t)}|$] was calculated. If $\Delta > \varepsilon$, then $t = t+1$ was set and steps b-d were repeated till the condition got satisfied.

e. It can meet the objective function:

$$j_m(U,v)=\sum_{k=1}^{N}\sum_{i=1}^{c}(u_{ik})^m \, y_k - V_{iA}^2,$$

where,

$y = \{ y_1, y_2 \ldots\ldots y_N \} \subset R^n$ =the data;
c = number of clusters in Y; $2 \leq c < n$,
m = weighting exponent; $1 \leq m < \infty$,
U = fuzzy c-partition of Y; $U \in M_{fc}$
$v = (v_1, v_2 \ldots\ldots v_c)$ = vectors of centers,
$v_i = (v_{i1}, v_{i2}, \ldots, v_{in})$ = center of cluster i,
$\| \|_A$ = induced A-norm on R^n
A = positive-definite $(n \times n)$ weight matrix.

and can be optimized. The optimization is carried out as evolutionary computing method as genetic algorithm and is described in the following section.

6. The optimized value is used as an initial value for the initialization of FCM, and the process was carried out as described in step 5.
7. The image was binarized using a threshold value [16].
8. The unwanted boundary is removed.
9. Then the edge detection was performed using well-known "Sobel" operator to get the segmented image.
10. The final smoothed image was obtained by the following morphological operations:
    a. Suitable structuring elements (SE) were created. The shape of all structuring elements may be line based flat, linear or both. Different structuring elements were selected for the erosion and dilation operations. In order to have a basic link between both the operations a difference angle= 90^0 between the dilation angle and the erosion angle is considered.
    b. Dilate the image. Dilation of a grayscale image A (x, y) by a grayscale structuring element B (s, t) can be performed by:

$$A \oplus B = \max_{[i,j]\forall B}\{a[m-j,n-k]+b[j,k]\}$$

    c. Start from forming an array X0 of zeros which is same size as the array containing A, except at the locations in X0 corresponding to the given point in each hole, which is set to one. Then, the following procedure fills all the holes with ones: $X_k = (X_{k-1} \oplus B) \cap A$. The algorithm terminates at the iteration step k if Xk = Xk-1.

d. Erode the image. Erosion of image A (x, y) by a grayscale structuring element B (s, t) can be performed by: $A\Theta B = \min_{[i,j]\forall B}\{a[m-j,n-k]+b[j,k]\}$

e. Find the edges using morphological operator for different structuring elements.

$$\text{Edge}(A) = (A \oplus B) - (A\Theta B)$$

where 'A' represents the input image

f. Closing of grayscale image A (x, y) by grayscale structuring element B (s, t) is denoted by as follows:

$$A \bullet B = (A \oplus B)\Theta B$$

2.2 Optimization Using Genetic Algorithm

A population of individuals reproduces and transmits characteristics to other generations (inheritance). This concept determines that every individual, called chromosome carries a potential solution to the optimization problem in question. The solution represents the genetic trace of the individual, the chromosomes' components, the alleles, and it's encoded and structured in some way. These individuals are capable of reproduction, which is, a combination between two individuals and, after this process, future generation carry characteristics of previous ones.

Genetic variation: the individual reproduction mechanism generates modifications in the genetic trace of the next population's individuals. A process known as mutation allows the exploration of new solutions inside the search space.

Natural selection: the living environment for individuals is competitive, for only one of them will give a more adequate and useful solution to a given problem. So, it's necessary to define some way to verify how much an individual is able to participate in the process of generation of new individuals. The evaluation is realized through a performance evaluation function, known as fitness function, and is defined by:

The fitness computation of each individual in that population was calculated, considering the penalty for covered and uncovered points. A point x is called a covered point if $x \in S_j$, S_j is a region that contains connected points around the center C_j, and x is called is uncovered if $x \in S_j$, S_j [10].

$$\text{Fitness} = \pm\sum_{i=1}^{n}\sum_{j=1}^{k} C_j - R_j(X_i, y_i)^2 + NCR$$

where NCR is a penalty for uncover points.

The Euclidian distance term represents the shortest distances between the centroid c_j, j =1, 2...k, and all pixels p_i, i=1,2,...N, of a region R_j.

If $d_{ij}<d_{euclid}$, then it finalize the point x_j, as a covered value, else it is uncovered.

The minimum of the first term is obtained when all pixels fall in regions with the Center c_j. Some pixels which are uncovered by regions are represented by NCR and should be minimized for optimal value of fitness, which can be calculated as:

$$\mathrm{NCR} = \pm \sum_{i=1}^{m} \mathrm{Median} - R\left(x_i, y_i\right)^2$$

where m is the number of uncovered points.

The optimization technique of GA optimizes the fuzzy C-Means data and can be termed of GFCM algorithm. The major points for optimization are as follows:

1. Coding. It refers to how to encode the solution (the chromosome); one way of doing this is the string-of-group-numbers encoding where for Z coded solutions (partitions), represented by strings of length N, each element of each string (an allele) contains a cluster number.
2. Initialization. The initial population P0 is defined randomly: each allele is initialized to a cluster number. The next population Pi+1 is defined in terms of the selection, mutation and the C-means operator.
3. Selection. Chromosomes from a previous population are chosen randomly according to a distribution.
4. Crossover. It is a probabilistic process that exchanges information between two parent chromosomes for generating two new (descendant) chromosomes.
5. Mutation. The mutation operator changes an allele value depending on the distances of the cluster centroids from the corresponding pattern.
6. C-Means Operator (CMO). This operator is used to speed up the convergence process and is related to one step of the classical C-means algorithm. Given a chromosome, each allele is replaced in order to be closer to its centroid.

A Specified number of iterations with a required fitness value to bring this generation cycle to an end.

3. RESULT

In this work, we have considered the brain images for two different cases. In case I, the patch is located on the back side of the brain. The image is shown in Figure 3. As the patch is to be detected first, the region of interest has been found as described in the section 2 and shown in Figure 4. As the pre-processing job, it has been passed through the Gaussian filter and the result of filtered ROI is shown in Figure 5. For detection it was segmented and smoothed. The corresponding result is shown in Figure 6 and Figure 7 respectably. The fuzzy C-means based clustered image is shown in Figure 8 and the optimized result is shown in Figure 9.

Similarly, the result of case II is shown in Figure 10 through Figure 16 respectively.

From the result it has been distinguished clearly. Also the Table 1 (Case I) and Table 2 (Case II) are shown for comparison purpose. The relative parameters are calculated and compared.

Figure 3. Original image

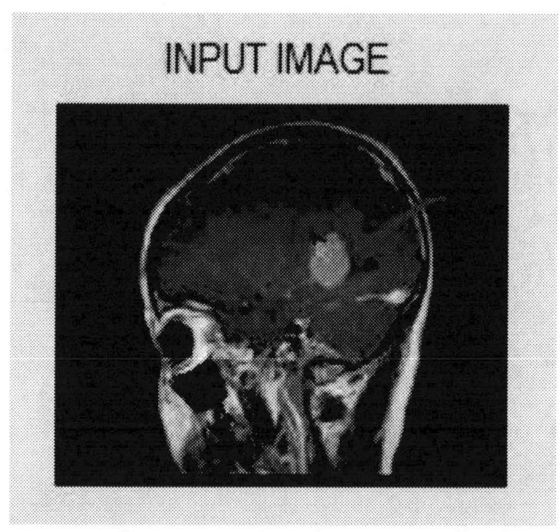

Figure 4. ROI of the original image

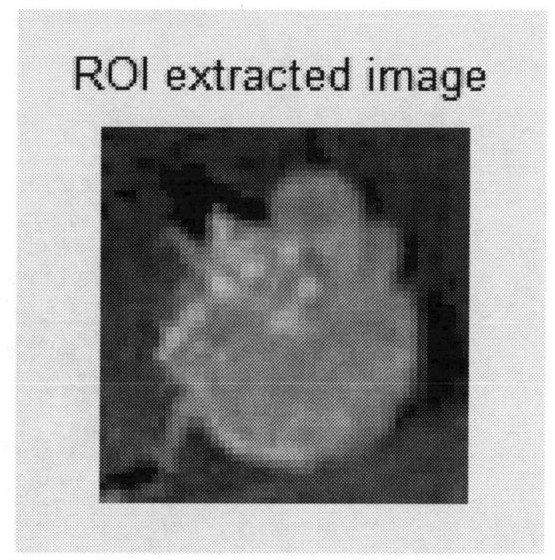

Figure 5. Pre-processed image using Gaussian Filter

Figure 6. Segmented image

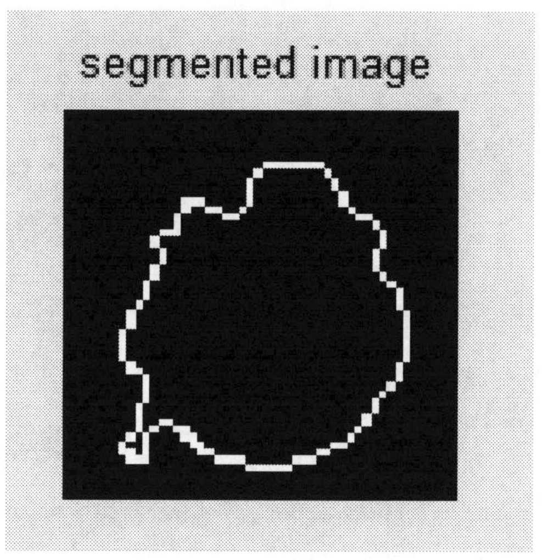

Table 1. Comparison among FCM and GFCM through different parameters for Case I

	MSE	PSNR	SSIM
FCM	0.0477	30.4239	0.9992
GFCM	0.0325	34.2687	0.9994

Table 2. Comparison among FCM and GFCM through different parameters for Case II

	MSE	PSNR	SSIM
FCM	0.0498	29.9940	0.9765
GFCM	0.046382	30.708	0.9984

Figure 7. Output after detection

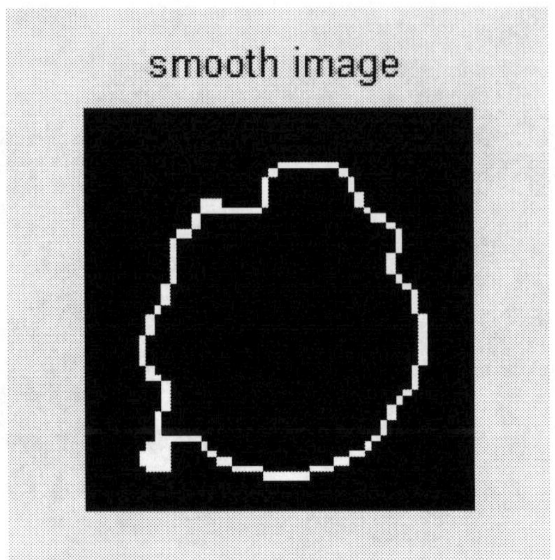

Figure 8. Clustering using FCM

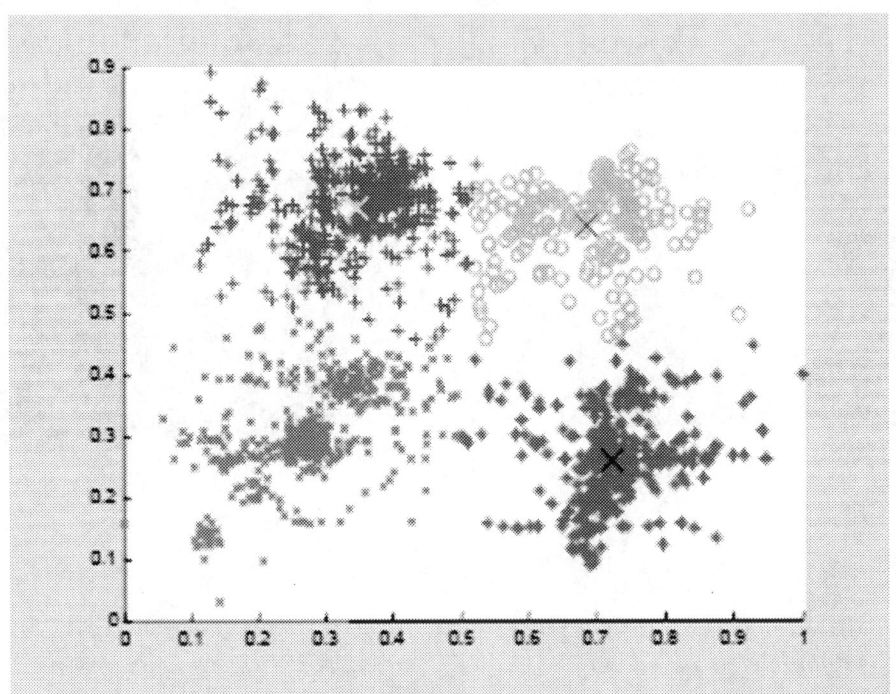

Figure 9. Clustering using GFCM

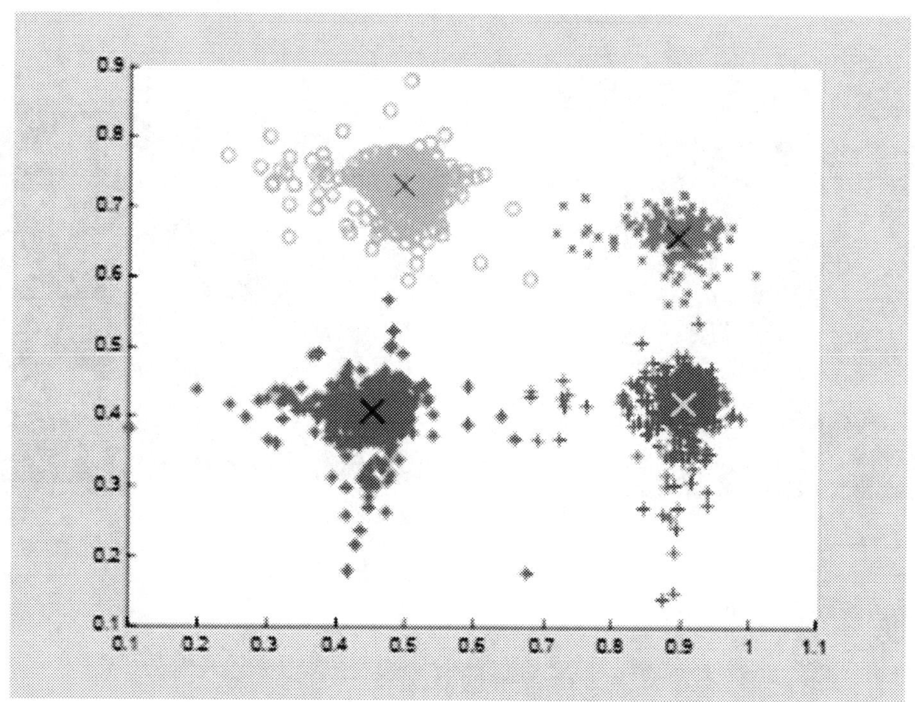

Figure 10. Original image

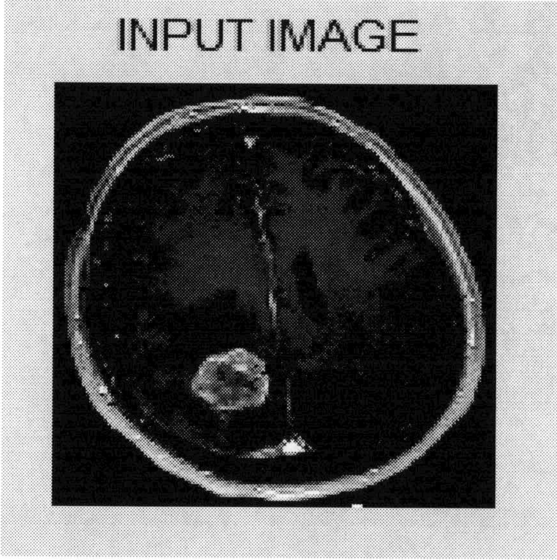

Figure 11. ROI of the original image

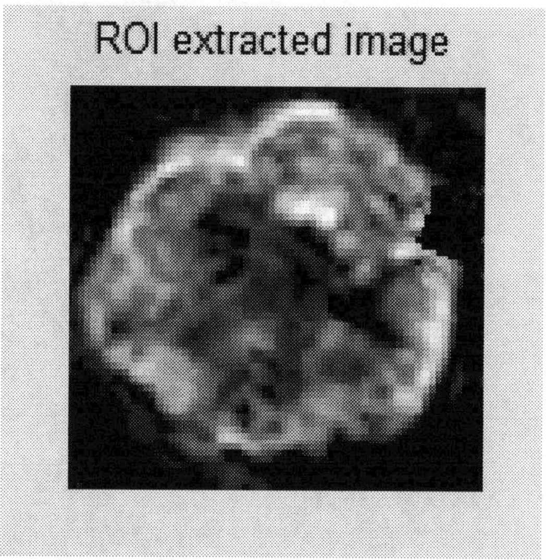

Figure 12. Pre-processed image using Gaussian Filter

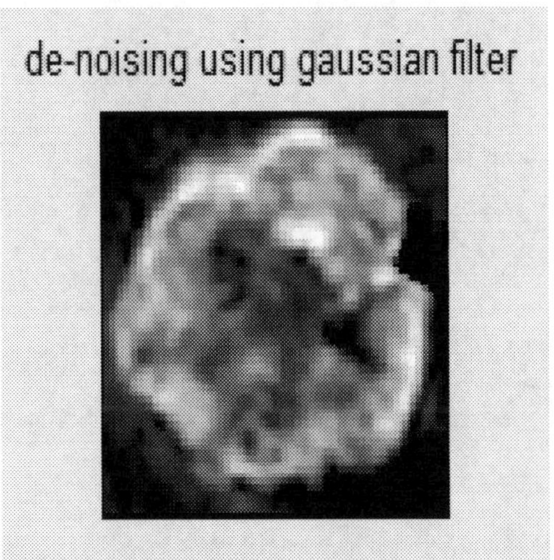

Figure 13. Segmented image

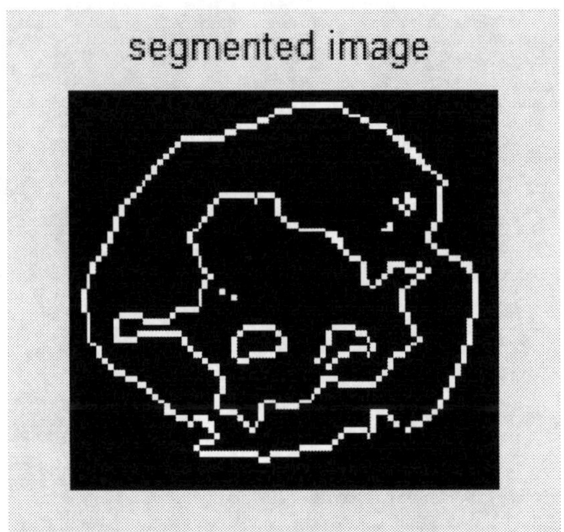

Figure 14. Output after detection

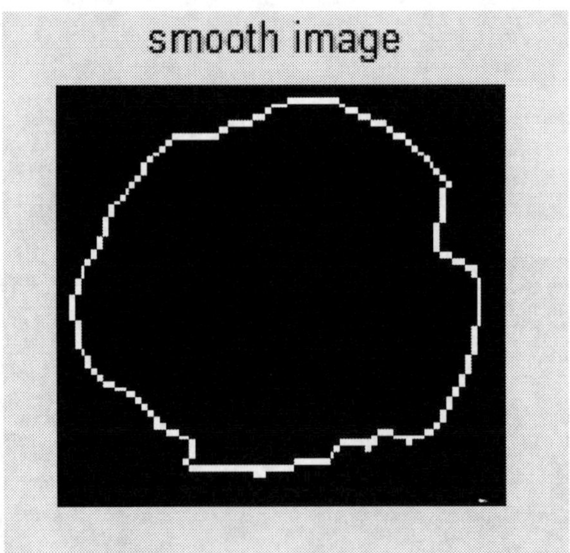

4. CONCLUSION

In this chapter, an optimized method for image segmentation using GFCM is described. The segmentation helps to detect the patch in the brain MRI. We have analyzed the fuzzy based clustering method. Further it has been optimized using evolutionary computing as genetic algorithm. The proposed segmentation scheme focuses on the clustering and optimized clustering approach. As shown in our experimental results, the algorithm generates visually meaningful segmentation results. It demonstrated that proposed method is efficient for medical image analysis. Finally, it is to mention that automated

Figure 15. Clustering using FCM

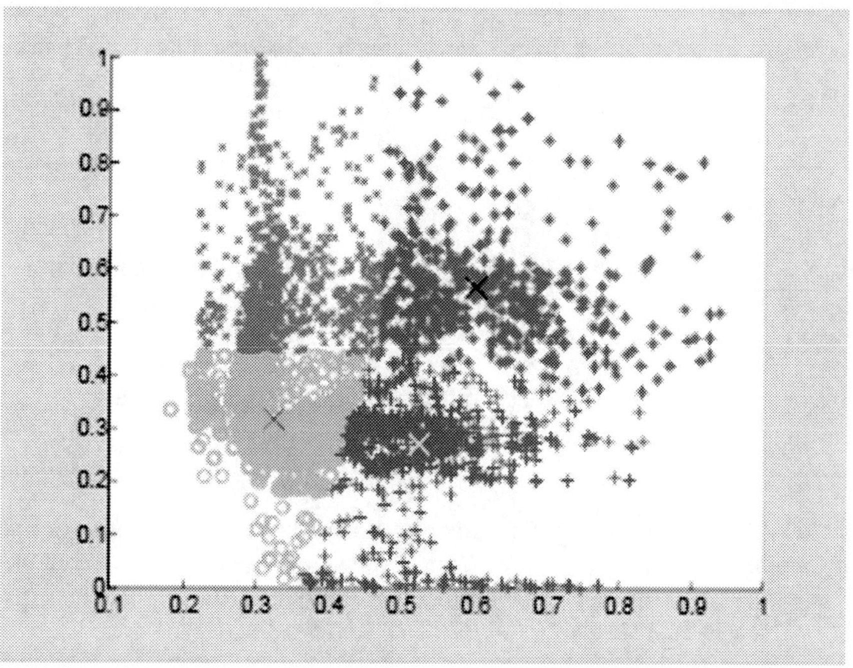

Figure 16. Clustering using GFCM

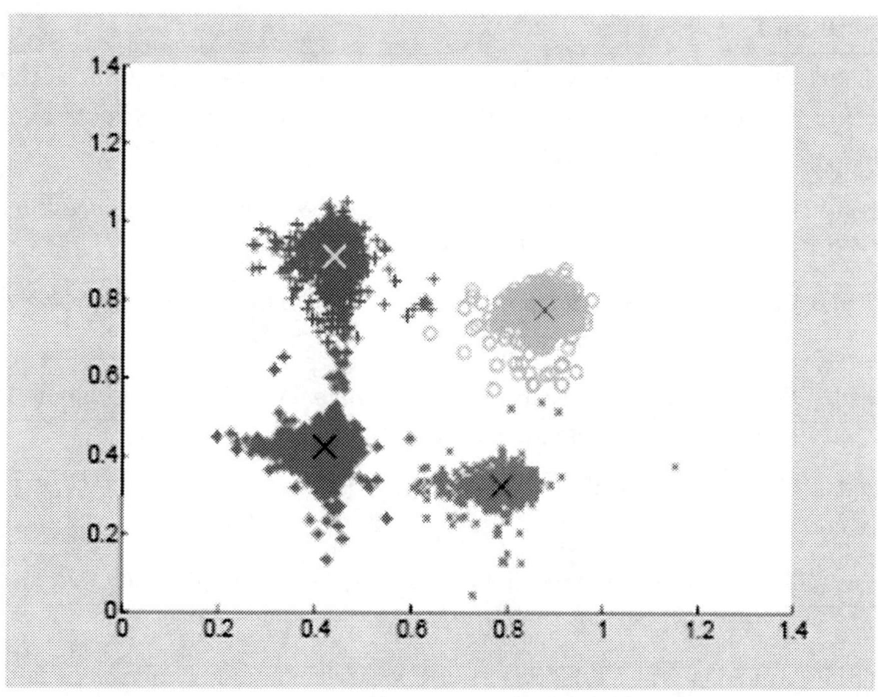

segmentation methods can never replace doctors but they will likely become vital elements of medical image interpretation. Thus, there are numerous challenges to improve clinical decision making based on automated processing for engineers, mathematicians, physicists and physicians working to advance the field of image segmentation and its analysis.

REFERENCES

Amlan, J., Mohanty, M. N., & Mallick, P. K. (2014). Morphological Based Segmentation of Brain Image for Tumor Detection. In *Proceedings of International Conference on Electronics and Communication Systems* (ICECS'14). IEEE.

Behera, S., Mohanty, M. N., & Patnaik, S. (2012). A Comparative Analysis on Edge Detection of Colloid Cyst: A Medical Image Approach. Int. Journ. of Image Processing, 6(6), 413-421. doi:10.1007/978-3-642-25507-6_7

Cheriet, M., Said, J. N., & Suen, C. Y. (1998). A Recursive Thresholding Technique For Image Segmentation. *IEEE Transactions on Image Processing*, *7*(6), 918–921. doi:10.1109/83.679444 PMID:18276308

Gonzalez, R. C., & Woods, R. E. (2008). *Digital Image Processing*. PHI.

Halder, Pramanik, & Kar. (2011). Dynamic Image Segmentation using Fuzzy C-Means based Genetic Algorithm. *International Journal of Computer Applications, 28*(6).

Jain, A. K. (1999). *Digital Image Processing*. Retrieved from http://www.yvonnefoong.com/2009/05/25/time-to-think-of-my-trigone-meningioma/

Jyoti, A., Mohanty, M. N., & Kar, S. K. (2014). Optimized Clustering Method for CT Brain Image Segmentation. In *Proceedings of the International Conference on Frontiers of Intelligent Computing: Theory and Applications* (FICTA). Springer.

Kalaivani, A. (2013). *SAutomatic Dominant Region Segmentation For Natural Images. In Iccsea, Sppr, Csia, WimoA – 2013* (pp. 273–280). CS & IT-CSCP.

Kar, S. K., & Mihir, N. (2013). Statistical Approach for Color Image Detection. In *Proceedings of IEEE Int. Conf. on Computer Communication and Informatics* (ICCCI). IEEE.

Kowar & Yadav. (2012). Brain Tumor Detection and Segmentation Using Histogram Thresholding. *International Journal of Engineering and Advanced Technology, 1*(4).

Lakshmi & Sankaranarayanan. (2010). A study of Edge Detection Techniques for Segmentation Computing Approaches. *IJCA* .

Liu, J., & Xian, L. (1991). Automatic thresholding of gray-level pictures using two-dimension Otsu method. *Circuits and Systems, 1*, 325-327.

Muthukrishnan, R., & Radha, M. (2011). Edge Detection Techniques For Image Segmentation. *International Journal of Computer Science & Information Technology, 3*(6).

Pratt, W. (2001). *Digital Image Processing* (3rd ed.). Wiley. doi:10.1002/0471221325

Rani, & Sharma. (2012). Edge Detection in Image Segmentation. *International Journal of Advanced Research in Electronics and Communication Engineering, 1*(6).

Sahoo, P. K., Soltani, S., & Wong, A. K. C. (1988). A Survey of Thresholding techniques. *Computer Vision Graphics and Image Processing, 41*(2), 233–260. doi:10.1016/0734-189X(88)90022-9

Woo-seok, J., Hwan-il, K., Byung-hee, L., Kim, Shin, & Kim. (2007). Optimized Fuzzy Clustering By Predator Prey Particle Swarm Optimization. In *Proceedings of IEEE Congress on Evolutionary Computation*. IEEE.

KEY TERMS AND DEFINITIONS

Clustering: Cluster analysis or clustering is the task of grouping a set of objects in such a way that objects in the same group (called a cluster) are more similar (in some sense or another) to each other than to those in other groups (clusters). It is a main task of exploratory data mining, and a common technique for statistical data analysis, used in many fields, including machine learning, pattern recognition, image analysis, information retrieval, and bioinformatics.

Genetic Algorithm: In the field of artificial intelligence, a genetic algorithm (GA) is a search heuristic that mimics the process of natural selection. This heuristic (also sometimes called a metaheuristic) is routinely used to generate useful solutions to optimization and search problems.[1] Genetic algorithms belong to the larger class of evolutionary algorithms (EA), which generate solutions to optimization problems using techniques inspired by natural evolution, such as inheritance, mutation, selection, and crossover

Morphological Operator for Edge Detection: Morphology is a branch of biology dealing with the study of the form and structure of organisms and their specific structural features.

Optimization: In mathematics, computer science, economics, or management science, mathematical optimization (alternatively, optimization or mathematical programming) is the selection of a best element (with regard to some criteria) from some set of available alternatives.

Thresholding: Thresholding is the simplest method of image segmentation. From a grayscale image, thresholding can be used to create binary images.

Compilation of References

Abdelaal, M. M. A., Farouq, M. W., Sena, H. A., & Salem, A. B. M. (2010, October). Using data mining for assessing diagnosis of breast cancer. In *Computer Science and Information Technology (IMCSIT),Proceedings of the 2010 International Multiconference on* (pp. 11-17). IEEE. doi:10.1109/IMCSIT.2010.5679647

Abdul-Jabbar, M., & Abdulkader, Z. N. (2012). Iris Recognition using 2-D elliptical-support wavelet filter bank. *IPTA*, 359-363.

Abhilash, A., & Netake, P. K. (2014). 765kV Transmission Line for Capacity Enhancement. *International Journal on Research and Scientific Innovation*, *1*(7), 200–204.

Abualkishik & Omar. (2008). *Quranic Braille System*. World Academy of Science, Engineering and Technology.

Abu-Bakar, S. A. R., & Dehkordi, A. B. (2013). Noise reduction in iris recognition using multiple thresholding. *ICSIPA*, 140-144.

Agrawal, R., Imielinski, T., & Swami, A. (1993). Mining Associations between Sets of Items in massive Databases. In *Proc. of the ACM-SIGMOD Int'l Conference on Management of data*. Washington, DC: ACM.

Agrawal, R., Imieliński, T., & Swami, A. (1993, June). Mining association rules between sets of items in large databases. *SIGMOD Record*, *22*(2), 207–216. doi:10.1145/170036.170072

Agrawal, R., & Srikant, R. (1994, September). Fast algorithms for mining association rules. In *Proc. 20th int. conf. very large data bases, VLDB* (Vol. 1215, pp. 487-499). VLDB.

Ahlstrom, M.L. & Tomkins, W.J. (1885). Digital filter for ECG real time processing using microprocessors. *IEEE Transactions on BME*, *32*, 708-713.

Ahuja, . (2013). *State of Big Data Analysis in the Cloud*. Network and Communication Technologies.

Al Bashish, D., Braik, M., & Bani-Ahmad, S. (2010). *A Framework for Detection and Classification of Plant Leaf and Stem Diseases*. International Conference on Signal and Image Processing.

Alaa. (2009). *Mining Students Data to Analyze e- Learning Behavior: A Case Study*. Academic Press.

Ali, M. A. M., & Tahir, N. (2014). Half Iris Gabor iris recognition. *CSPA*, 282-287.

Allen, J., Anderson, J., Mc, C., Dempsey, G. J., & Adgey, A. A. J. (1994). Efficient Baseline Wander Removal for Feature Analysis of Electrocardiographic Body Surface Maps. *IEEE Proceedings of Engineering in Medicine and Biology Society*, *2*, 1316 - 1317.

Allman, M., Paxson, W., & Blanton, E. (2009). *RFC 5681: TCP Congestion Control*. IETF Standards Track.

Al-Radaideh, Al-Shawakfa, & Al-Najjar. (2006). Mining student data using decision trees. In *Proceedings ofInternational Arab Conference on Information Technology (ACIT'2006)*. Yarmouk University.

Altman, E., & Jim'enez, T. (2003). *Novel delayed ACK techniques for improving TCP performance in multihop wireless networks*. Venice, Italy: Personal Wireless Communications. doi:10.1007/978-3-540-39867-7_26

Amandi, R., Bayat, M., Minakhani, K., Mirloo, H., & Bazarghan, M. (2013). Long Distance Iris Recognition. *MVIP*, 164-168.

Amlan, J., Mohanty, M. N., & Mallick, P. K. (2014). Morphological Based Segmentation of Brain Image for Tumor Detection. In *Proceedings of International Conference on Electronics and Communication Systems* (ICECS'14). IEEE.

Amorim, R., Haase, G., Liebmann, M., & Weber dos Santos, R. (2009). *Comparing CUDA and OpenGL implementations for a Jacobi iteration*. doi:10.1109/HPCSIM.2009.5192847

Anoore & Murray. (2001). An electronic design of a low cost Braille typewriter. In *Proceedings of Seventh Australian and new Zealand intelligent information system conference*. Perth, Australia.

Anunciaçao, O., Gomes, B. C., Vinga, S., Gaspar, J., Oliveira, A. L., & Rueff, J. (2010). A data mining approach for the detection of high-risk breast cancer groups. In *Advances in Bioinformatics* (pp. 43–51). Springer Berlin Heidelberg. doi:10.1007/978-3-642-13214-8_6

Avionics, D. M. (1993). *Electrocardiographic baseline filtering and estimation system with bidirectional filter.* US Patent, US5402795.

Ayesha, , Mustafa, Sattar, & Khan. (2010). Data mining model for higher education system. *Europen Journal of Scientific Research*, *43*(1), 24–29.

Bai, F., & Helmy, A. (2006). *A Survey of Mobility Models in Wireless Adhoc Networks*. Wireless Ad Hoc Networks.

Baker, R. S. J. D. (2007). Modeling and Understanding Students' Off-Task Behavior in Intelligent Tutoring Systems. In *Proceedings of the ACM Computer- Human Interaction Conference*, (pp. 1059-1068). ACM.

Bakre, A. V., & Badrinath, B. R. (1997). Implementation and performance evaluation of indirect TCP. *IEEE/ACM Transactions on Networking*, *46*(3), 260–278.

Balakrishnan, H., Seshan, S., Amir, E., & Katz, R. (1995). Improving TCP/IP performance over wireless networks. In ACM MOBIHOC (pp. 2-11). Berkeley, CA: ACM.

Balakrishnan, H., & Padmanabhan, V. (2001). How network asymmetry affects TCP. *IEEE Communications Magazine*, *39*(4), 60–67. doi:10.1109/35.917505

Balakrishnan, H., Padmanabhan, V. N., Fairhurst, G., & Sooriyabandara, M. (2002). *RFC 3449: TCP Performance Implications of Network Path Asymmetry*. IETF Best Current Practice.

Balakrishnan, H., Padmanabhan, V., Seshan, S., & Katz, R. (1997). A comparison of mechanisms for improving TCP performance over wireless links. *IEEE/ACM Transactions on Networking*, *5*(6), 756–769. doi:10.1109/90.650137

Balakrishnan, H., Seshan, S., & Katz, R. (1995). Improving reliable transport and handoff performance in cellular wireless networks. *ACM Wireless Networks*, *1*(4), 469–481. doi:10.1007/BF01985757

Bansal, . (2014). Transitioning from Relational Databases to Big Data. *International Journal of Advanced Research in Computer Science and Software Engineering*, *4*(1), 626–630.

Barati, Z., & Ayatollahi, A. (2006). Baseline Wandering Removal by Using Independent Component Analysis to Single-Channel ECG Data. *IEEE Conference on Biomedical and Pharmaceutical Engineering.*

Barlett, M. S., Movellan, J. R., & Sejnowski, T. J. (2002). Face recognition by Independent Component Analysis. *IEEE Transactions on Neural Networks, 13*(6), 1450–1464. doi:10.1109/TNN.2002.804287 PMID:18244540

Barreto, F., Emílio, W. C. G., & Junior, L. N. (2008). Fast Recovery Paths: Reducing Packet Loss Rates during IP Routing Convergence. *The Fourth Advanced International Conference on Telecommunications.* doi:10.1109/AICT.2008.21

Barstow, D. R., Bohenen, C. B., Chaum, E., Barstow, D. R., Karakaya, M., Santos-Villalobos, H. J. (2012). ORNL biometric eye model for iris recognition. *BTAS*, 176-182.

Basu, B., & Lachikawa, A. (2004). Dialogue Languages and Persons with Disabilities. *IEICE Transactions, 8*(6), 31-43.

Basu, A., & Riecke, J. (2001, October). Stability issues in OSPF routing. *Computer Communication Review, 31*(4), 225–236. doi:10.1145/964723.383077

Baulblenkhorn. (1997). A system for conveting print into Braille. *IEEE Transactions on Rehabilitation Engineering, 5*(2), 23-30.

Beale, R., & Jackson, T. (1990). *Neural Computing-an introduction.* CRC Press. doi:10.1887/0852742622

Beck, J. E., & Mostow, J. (2008). How who should practice: Using learning decomposition to evaluate the efficacy of different types of practice for different types of students. In *Proceedings of the 9th International Conference on Intelligent Tutoring Systems*, (pp. 353-362). doi:10.1007/978-3-540-69132-7_39

Begoli, E., & Horey, J. (2012, August). Design principles for effective knowledge discovery from big data. *In Software Architecture (WICSA) and European Conference on Software Architecture (ECSA), 2012 Joint Working IEEE/IFIP Conference on* (pp. 215-218). IEEE. doi:10.1109/WICSA-ECSA.212.32

Behera, S., Mohanty, M. N., & Patnaik, S. (2012). A Comparative Analysis on Edge Detection of Colloid Cyst: A Medical Image Approach. Int. Journ. of Image Processing, 6(6), 413-421. doi:10.1007/978-3-642-25507-6_7

Bharadwaj, B. K., & Pal, S. (2011). Data Mining: A prediction for performance improvement using classification. *International Journal of Computer Science and Information Security, 9*(4), 136–140.

Bharadwaj, S., Bhatt, H. S., Vatsa, M., & Singh, R. (2010). Periocular biometrics: When iris recognition fails. *Proc. BTAS 2010.*

Bharghavan, V., Demers, A., Shneker, S., & Zhang, L. (1994). MACAW: a media access protocol for wireless LAN's. In ACM SIGCOMM (pp. 212–225). London, UK: ACM. doi:10.1145/190314.190334

Bhura, M., Deshpande, P. H., & Chandrasekaran, K. (2014). Comparison of OpenCL and CUDA frameworks on Heterogeneous Systems.*7th International Conference on Electrical, Electronics, Computing and Communication Systems (EECCS'15).*

Bisoy, S. K., & Pattnaik, P. K. (2013). Interaction between Internet Based TCP Variants and Routing Protocols in MANET. In *International Conference on Frontiers of Intelligent Computing: Theory and Applications (FICTA) Springer Advances in Intelligent Systems and Computing* (vol. 247, pp. 423-433). Springer.

Bisoy, S. K., Panda, M. R., Pallai, G. K., & Panda, D. (2013). Analysing the Interaction between Mobility Model and Unipath Routing Protocols in Mobile Ad Hoc Networks. *International Journal of Application or Innovation in Engineering & Management, 2*(6), 449–455.

Bisoy, S. K., & Pattnaik, P. K. (2014). Analyzing the Interaction Between TCP Variants and Routing Protocols in Static Multi-hop Ad hoc Network. In *Intelligent Computing* (Vol. 308, pp. 717–724). Communication and Devices, Springer Advances in Intelligent Systems and Computing.

Bisoy, S. K., & Pattnaik, P. K. (2014). Impact of Radio Propagation Model and Mobility in On-Demand Routing Protocol of MANET. *Journal of Theoretical and Applied Information Technology*, *65*(1), 30–45.

Blacknell, D., Oliver, C. J., & Warner, M. (1995, November). Speckle reduction of SAR images using neural networks. *Satellite Remote Sensing*, *2*, 179–187.

Blenkhorn. (n.d.). A system for converting Braille into print. *IEEE Transactions on Rehabilitation Engineering, 3*(2), 215-221.

Border, J., Kojo, M., Griner, J., Montenegro, G., & Shelby, Z. (2001). *RFC 3135: Performance Enhancing Proxies Intended to Mitigate Link-Related Degradations*. IETF Informational.

Borkar, V. (2012). Inside Big Data Management: Ogres, Onions, or Parfaits. EDBT/ICDT 2012 Joint Conference, Berlin, Germany.

Boyd, D., & Crawford, K. (2012). Critical questions for big data: Provocations for a cultural, technological, and scholarly phenomenon. *Information Communication and Society*, *15*(5), 662–679.

Braden, R. (Ed.). (1989). *RFC 1122: Requirements for Internet Hosts- - Communication Layers*. IETF Internet Standard.

Brakmo, L. S., O'Malley, S. W., & Peterson, L. L. (1994). TCP Vegas: new techniques for congestion detection and avoidance. *SIGCOMM Computer Communication Review*, *24*, 24-35. Retrieved October 1994, from http://doi.acm.org/10.1145/190809.190317

Bray. (n.d.). *The shadow education system: private tutoring and its implications for planners* (2nd ed.). UNESCO.

Brown, K., & Singh, S. (1997). M-TCP: TCP for mobile cellular networks. *Computer Communication Review*, *27*(5), 19–43. doi:10.1145/269790.269794

Bruneli, R., & Poggio, T. (1993). Face Recognition: Features versus Templates. *IEEE Transactions on Pattern Analysis and Machine Intelligence*, *15*(10), 1042–1052. doi:10.1109/34.254061

Bryant, et al. (2008). *Big-Data Computing: Creating revolutionary breakthroughs in commerce, science, and society.* Academic Press.

Bryant, R. E., Katz, R. H., & Lazowska, E. D. (2008). Big-data computing: Creating revolutionary breakthroughs in commerce, science, and society. In *Computing Research Initiatives for the 21st Century*. Computing Research Association. Retrieved from http://www.cra.org/ccc/docs/init/Big_Data.pdf

Central Electrical Authority. (2013). *Manual on Transmission Planning Criteria*. Author.

Cerf, V. G., & Kahn, R. E. (1974). A protocol for packet network intercommunication. *IEEE Transactions on Communications*, *22*(3), 637–648. doi:10.1109/TCOM.1974.1092259

Cevikalp, H., Neamtu, M., Wilkes, M., & Barkma, A. (2005). Discriminative Common Vecctor for Face Recognition. *IEEE Transactions on Pattern Analysis and Machine Intelligence*, *27*(1), 44–53. doi:10.1109/TPAMI.2005.9 PMID:15628264

Challis, R. E., & Kitney, R. I. (1983). The design of digital filters for biomedical signal processing. Part 3: The design of Butterworth and Chebychev filters. *Journal of Biomedical Engineering*, *5*(2), 91–102. doi:10.1016/0141-5425(83)90026-2 PMID:6855219

Chandran, K., Raghunathan, S., Venkatesan, S., & Prakash, R. (2001). A Feedback Based Scheme for Improving TCP Performance in Ad-Hoc Wireless Networks. *IEEE Personal Communications*, *8*(1), 34–39. doi:10.1109/98.904897

Chan, Y. K., & Koo, V. C. (2008). An introduction to synthetic aperture radar (SAR). *Progress In Electromagnetics Research B*, *2*, 27–60. doi:10.2528/PIERB07110101

Chao, D. Y. (1998). Conversion, Iteration Bound and X-Window Implementation for Multi –Rate Data Flow Graphs. *Proceedings of Natl. Sci. Council ROC (A)*, *22*, 362–371.

Chao, D. Y., & Wang, D. Y. (1993). Iteration Bounds of Single-Rate Data Flow Graphs for Concurrent Processing. *IEEE Transactions on Circuits System-I*, *40*(9), 629–634. doi:10.1109/81.244917

Characteristics Of Biometric Systems. (n.d.). Retrieved from https://www.cccure.org/Documents/HISM/039-041.html

Chavan, . (2014). Opportunities and Challenges of Big Data in Economics Research and Enterprises. *International Journal of Computer Science and Mobile Computing*, *3*(4), 1155–1161.

Chavan, M. S., Agarwala, R. A., & Uplane, M. D. (2008). Comparative Study of Chebyshev I and Chebyshev II Filter used For Noise Reduction in ECG Signal. *International Journal Of Circuits, Systems Signal Processing*, *2*(1), 1–17.

Chen, Mao, & Liu. (2014). *Big Data: A Survey*. Springer.

Cheriet, M., Said, J. N., & Suen, C. Y. (1998). A Recursive Thresholding Technique For Image Segmentation. *IEEE Transactions on Image Processing*, *7*(6), 918–921. doi:10.1109/83.679444 PMID:18276308

Cheung, Ng, Fu, & Fu. (1996). Efficient Mining of Association Rules in Distributedatabases. *IEEE Transactions on Knowledge and Data Engineering*, *8*(6), 866–883.

Chiang, M. (2005). Balancing transport and physical layers in wireless ad hoc networks: Jointly optimal TCP congestion control and power control. *IEEE JSAC*, *23*(1), 104–116.

Chinese Academy of Sciences CASIA iris image database. (2004). Institute of Automation. Retrieved from http://www.sinobiometrics.com

Chouhan, V. S., & Mehta, S. S. (2007). Total Removal of Baseline Drift from ECG Signal. *International Conference on Computing: Theory and Applications-ICCTA*. doi:10.1109/ICCTA.2007.126

Choy, T. T., & Leung, P. M. (1988). Real Time Microprocessor-Based 50 Hz Notch Filter for ECG. *Journal of Biomedical Engineering*, *10*(3), 285–288. doi:10.1016/0141-5425(88)90013-1 PMID:3392981

Coltun, R., Ferguson, D., Moy, J., & Lindem, A. (2008, July). *OSPF for IPv6*. Internet Engineering Task Force, Request For Comments. (StandardsTrack) RFC 5340.

Cooley James, W., & Tukey John, W. (1965, May1). An algorithm for the machine calculation of complex Fourier series. *Mathematics of Computation*, *19*(90), 297–301. doi:10.1090/S0025-5718-1965-0178586-1

Cox, I. J., Ghosn, J., & Yianios, P. N. (1996). *Feature Based Face Recognition Using Mixture Distance*. Computer Vision and Pattern Recognition. doi:10.1109/CVPR.1996.517076

Cramer, E., McManus, C. D., & Neubert, D. (1987). Estimation and removal of power line interference in the electrocardiogram: A comparison of digital approaches. *Computers and Biomedical Research, an International Journal*, *20*(1), 12–28. doi:10.1016/0010-4809(87)90014-0 PMID:3829639

Cumming, I. C., & Bennett, J. R. (1979, April). Digital processing of SEASAT SAR data. In *Acoustics, Speech, and Signal Processing, IEEE International Conference on ICASSP'79* (Vol. 4, pp. 710-718). IEEE. doi:10.1109/ICASSP.1979.1170630

Curlander, R. (1991). Synthetic Aperture Radar: Systems and Signal Processing. John Wiley and Sons.

Dai, M., & Liana, S.-L. (2009). Removal of Baseline Wander from Dynamic Electrocardiogram Signals. *IEEE Conference on Image and Signal Processing*. doi:10.1109/CISP.2009.5304473

Danalis, A., Marin, G., McCurdy, C., Meredith, J. S., Roth, P. C., Spafford, K., & Vetter, J. S. et al. (2010). The Scalable Heterogeneous Computing (SHOC) benchmark suite. In *Proceedings of the 3rd Workshop on General-Purpose Computation on Graphics Processing Units, GPGPU '10*. doi:10.1145/1735688.1735702

Dao, V. N., & Vemuri, V. R. (2002). A performance comparison of different back propagation neural networks methods in computer network intrusion detection. *Differential Equations and Dynamical Systems, 10*(1&2), 201-214.

Das, S., & Saha, B. (2009). Data quality mining using genetic algorithm. *International Journal of Computer Science and Security, 3*(2), 105–112.

Dastgir, N. (2007). Processing SAR Data using Range Doppler and Chirp Scaling Algorithms. *Master's of Science Thesis in Geodesy Report*, (3096), 07-005.

Daugman, J. (2004). How iris recognition works. *IEEE Transactions on Circuits and Systems for Video Technology, 14*(1), 21–30. doi:10.1109/TCSVT.2003.818350

Deering, S., & Hinden, R. (1998). *RFC 2460: Internet Protocol, Version 6 (IPv6) Specification*. IETF Internet Standard.

Dekker, G., Pechenizkiy, M., & Vleeshouwers, J. (2009). Predicting Students Drop Out: A Case Study. In *Proceedings of the International Conference on Educational Data Mining*.

Demuth, H., & Beale, M. (2000). *Neural network toolbox user's guide*. MathWorks.

Deravi, F., Howells, W. G. J., Hoque, S., Radu, P., & Sirlantzis, K. (2013). Optimizing 2-D Gabor Filters for Iris Recognition. *EST*, 47-50.

Devaney, M., & Ram, A. (1997, July). Efficient feature selection in conceptual clustering. In ICML (Vol. 97, pp. 92-97). ICML.

Diamos, G. F., & Yalamanchili, S. (2008). Harmony: an ExecutionModel and Runtime for Heterogeneous Many Core Systems. In *Proceedings of the 17th international symposium on High performance distributed computing*, (pp. 197–200). Academic Press.

Divyakant & El Abbadi. (2011). *Big Data and Cloud Computing: Current State and Future Opportunities*. ACM.

D'mello, S. K., Craig, S. D., Witherspoon, A. W., McDaniel, B. T., & Graesser, A. C. (2008). Automatic Detection of Learner's Affect from Conversational Cues. *User Modeling and User-Adapted Interaction, 18*(1-2), 45–80. doi:10.1007/s11257-007-9037-6

Dotsinsky, I., & Stoyanov, T. (2005). Power-line interference cancellation in ECG signals. *Biomedical Instrumentation & Technology, 39*(2), 155–162. PMID:15810791

Duke, M., Braden, R., Eddy, W., & Blanton, E. (2006). *RFC 4614: A Roadmap for Transmission Control Protocol (TCP) Specification Documents*. IETF Internet Standard.

Dunham. (2006). Data Mining Introductory and Advanced Topics. Pearson Education.

Durst, R., Miller, G., & Travis, E. (1996). TCP extensions for space communications. In ACM MOBICOM (pp. 15-26). Rye, NY: ACM. doi:10.1145/236387.236398

Dwyer, J., & Hetal, J. (2012). *An Analysis of Convergence Delay Caused by Link Failures in Autonomous Systems*. IEEE. doi:10.1109/SECon.2012.6196899

Dy, J. G., & Brodley, C. E. (2004). Feature selection for unsupervised learning. *Journal of Machine Learning Research*, *5*, 845–889.

Einav, . (2014). *The Data Revolution and Economic Analysis*. National Bureau of Economic Research.

ElRakabawy, S. M., Klemm, A., & Lindemann, C. (2005). TCP with adaptive pacing for multihop wireless networks. In *6th ACM international symposium on Mobile ad hoc networking and computing*, (pp. 288-299). New York, NY: ACM. doi:10.1145/1062689.1062726

Eramo, V., Marco, L., & Antonio, C. (2008, December). Design and Evaluation of a New Multi-Path Incremental Routing Algorithm on Software Routers. *IEEE eTransactions on Network and Service Management*, *5*(4), 188–203. doi:10.1109/TNSM.2009.041101

Fan, W., & Bifet, A. (2013). Mining big data: current status, and forecast to the future. *ACM sIGKDD Explorations Newsletter, 14*(2), 1-5.

Fang, J., Varbanescu, A. L., & Sips, H. (2011). A Comprehensive Performance Comparison of CUDA and OpenCL. *International Conference on Parallel Processing*. doi:10.1109/ICPP.2011.45

Fayyad, Shapiro, & Smyth. (1996). From Data Mining to knowledge Discovery: An Overview. AAAI Press.

Ferdjallah, M., & Barr, R. E. (1990). Frequency-domain digital filtering techniques for the removal of powerline noise with application to the electrocardiogram. *Computers and Biomedical Research, an International Journal*, *23*(5), 473–489. doi:10.1016/0010-4809(90)90035-B PMID:2225791

Fonseca, C. M., & Fleming, P. J. (1993, June). Genetic Algorithms for Multi-objective Optimization: Formulation Discussion and Generalization. In ICGA (Vol. 93, pp. 416-423). ICGA.

Fonseca, C. M., & Fleming, P. J. (1993, June). Genetic Algorithms for Multiobjective Optimization: FormulationDiscussion and Generalization. In ICGA (Vol. 93, pp. 416-423). ICGA.

Frau, D., & Novak, D. (2000). Electrocardiogram Baseline Removal Using Wavelet Approximations. *Proceeding of the 15th Biennial Eurasip Conference Biosignal.*

Friesen, M., Jannett, T. C., Jadallah, M. A., Yates, S. L., Quint, S. R., & Nagle, H. T. (1990). Comparison of noise sensitivity of QRS Detection Algorithms. *IEEE Transactions on Bio-Medical Engineering*, *37*(1), 85–98. doi:10.1109/10.43620 PMID:2303275

Fritz, F. P., & Barner, P. (1999, August). Design of a Hepatic Visualization System for People with Visual Impairments. *IEEE Transactions on Rehabilitation Engineering*, *7*(3), 372–384. doi:10.1109/86.788473 PMID:10498382

Frost, V. S., Stiles, J. A., Shanmugan, K. S., & Holtzman, J. C. (1982). A model for radar images and its application to adaptive digital filtering of multiplicative noise. *Pattern Analysis and Machine Intelligence, IEEE Transactions on*, (2), 157-166.

Fu, Z., Zerfos, P., Luo, H., Lu, S., Zhang, L., & Gerla, M. (2003). The impact of multihop wireless channel on TCP throughput and loss. In IEEE INFOCOM, (pp. 1744-1753). San Francisco, CA: IEEE. doi:10.1109/INFCOM.2003.1209197

Fu, C. P., & Liew, S. (2003). TCP Veno: TCP enhancement for transmission over wireless access networks. *IEEE Journal on Selected Areas in Communications*, *21*(2), 216–228. doi:10.1109/JSAC.2002.807336

Fujita, N., & Iwata, A. (2001). *Adaptive and Efficient Multiple Path Pre-computation for QoS Routing Protocols*. IEEE. doi:10.1109/GLOCOM.2001.966173

Fukuda, T., Morimoto, Y., Morishita, S., & Tokuyama, T. (1996). Data mining using two-dimensional optimized association rules: Scheme, algorithms, and visualization. *SIGMOD Record*, *25*(2), 13–23. doi:10.1145/235968.233313

Fukuda, T., Morimoto, Y., Morishita, S., & Tokuyama, T. (1996, June). Mining optimized association rules for numeric attributes. In *Proceedings of the fifteenth ACM SIGACT-SIGMOD-SIGART symposium on Principles of database systems* (pp. 182-191). ACM. doi:10.1145/237661.237708

Fukuda, T., Morimoto, Y., Morishita, S., & Tokuyama, T. (1996, June). Sonar: System for optimized numeric association rules. *SIGMOD Record*, *25*(2), 553. doi:10.1145/235968.280359

Furno, G. S., & Tompkins, W. J. (1983). A learning filter for reducing noise interference. *IEEE Transactions on Bio-Medical Engineering*, *BME-30*(4), 234–235. doi:10.1109/TBME.1983.325225 PMID:6862503

Fu, Z., Greenstein, B., Meng, X., & Lu, S. (2002). Design and implementation of a TCP-friendly transport protocol for ad hoc wireless networks. In *10th IEEE International Conference on Network Protocol*, (pp. 216-225). IEEE Press.

Galit, et al. (2007). *Examining online learning processes based on log files analysis: a case study*. Research, Reflection and Innovations in Integrating ICT in Education.

Gandhi, K. R., Karnan, M., & Kannan, S. (2010, February). Classification rule construction using particle swarm optimization algorithm for breast cancer data sets. In *Signal Acquisition and Processing, 2010. ICSAP'10. International Conference on* (pp. 233-237). IEEE. doi:10.1109/ICSAP.2010.58

Geary, R., Condon, T., Kavanagh, T., Armstrong, O., & Doyle, J. (2012). *Introduction of high temperature low sag conductors to the Irish Transmission grid*. B2-104, CIGRE 2012 ESB International Ireland.

Geng, L., & Hamilton, H. J. (2006). Interestingness Measures for Data MiningA Survey. *ACM Computing Surveys*, *38*(3), 1–32. doi:10.1145/1132960.1132963

Gerez, S. H., Heemstra de Groot, S. M., & Herrmann, O. E. (1992). A Polynomial-Time Algorithm for the Computation of the Iteration-Period Bound in Recursive Data-Flow Graphs. *IEEE Transactions on Circuits System-I*, *39*(1), 49–52. doi:10.1109/81.109243

Gerla, M., Tang, K., & Bagrodia, R. (1999). TCP Performance in Wireless Multi-hop Networks. In *Second IEEE Workshop on Mobile Computer Systems and Applications server*(pp.41-48). Washington, DC: IEEE Computer Society. doi:10.1109/MCSA.1999.749276

Gettys, J., & Nichols, K. (2011). Bufferbloat: Dark buffers in the internet. *Queue*, *9*(11), 40-54. Retrieved from http://doi.acm.org/10.1145/2063166.2071893

Gill. (1992). *Priorities for technical research and development for visually disabled persons*. World Blind Union Res Committee.

Global Mobile Information Systems Simulation Library GloMoSim. (n.d.). Retrieved from http://pcl.cs.ucla.edu/projects/glomosim/

Goebel, M., & Gruenwald, L. (1999). A survey of data mining and knowledge discovery software tools. *ACM SIGKDD Explorations Newsletter*, *1*(1), 20–33. doi:10.1145/846170.846172

Gonzales, R., & Woods, R. (1992). *Digital Image Processing*. Addison-Wesley Publishing Company.

Gopalkrishnan, V., Steier, D., Lewis, H., & Guszcza, J. (2012, August). Big data, big business: bridging the gap. In *Proceedings of the 1st International Workshop on Big Data, Streams and Heterogeneous Source Mining: Algorithms, Systems, Programming Models and Applications* (pp. 7-11). ACM.

Goyal, M., Xie, W., Soperi, M, Hosseini, S.H. & Vairavan, K (2007, February). *Scheduling Routing Table Calculations to Achieve Fast Convergence in OSPF Protocol.* IEEE.

Goyal, M., Soperi, M., Hosseini, H., Trivedi, K. S., Shaikh, A., & Choudhury, G. (2009). *International Conference on Advanced Information Networking and Applications.*IEEE.

Gradwohl, J. R., Pottala, E. W., Horton, M. R., & Bailey, J. J. (1988). Comparison of Two Methods for Removing Baseline Wander in the ECG. *IEEE Proceedings on Computers in Cardiology.*

Grang, N., & Gupta, A. (2013). Compare OSPF Routing Protocol with other Interior Gateway Routing Protocols. *International Journal of Engineering Business and Enterprise Applications, 4*(2), 166–170.

Grauer-Gray, S., Xu, L., Searles, R., Ayalasomayajula, S., & Cavazos, J. (2012). *Auto-tuning a High-Level Language Targeted to GPU Codes.* IEEE. doi:10.1109/InPar.2012.6339595

Gurjar, & Gulhane. (n.d.). Disease Detection On Cotton Leaves by Eigenfeature Regularization and Extraction Technique. *International Journal of Electronics, Communication & Soft Computing Science and Engineering, 1*(1).

Gursimarpreet, K., & Chander Kant, V. (2014). Comparative Analysis of Biometric Modalities. *International Journal of Advanced Research in Computer Science and Software Engineering, 4*(4), 603–613.

Ha, S., Rhee, I., & Xu, L. (2008). CUBIC: a new TCP-friendly high-speed TCP variant. *SIGOPS Oper. Syst. Rev., 42*, 64-74. Retrieved July, 2008, from http://doi.acm.org/10.1145/1400097.1400105

Hagan, M. T., & Menhaj, M. B. (1994). Training feedforward networks with the Marquardt algorithm. *Neural Networks. IEEE Transactions on, 5*(6), 989–993.

Haider, M. S., Mohd Zahid, M., & Bakar, K. A. (2011). Comparison of Intelligent Schemes for Scheduling OSPF Routing Table Calculation. IEEE.

Haijun, Z. H. O. U., Jin, P. A. N., & Pubing, S. H. E. N. (2003). Analyzes the local congestion issue of network owing to traffic aggregation and improved OSPF and brought forward cost adaptive OSPF (CA-OSPF). *Proceedings of the Fifth International Conference on Computational Intelligence and Multimedia Applications (ICCIMA'03).*

Halder, Pramanik, & Kar. (2011). Dynamic Image Segmentation using Fuzzy C-Means based Genetic Algorithm. *International Journal of Computer Applications, 28*(6).

Hamilton, P. S. (1996). A comparison of adaptive and non-adaptive filters for reduction of power line interference in the ECG. *IEEE Transactions on Bio-Medical Engineering, 43*(1), 105–109. doi:10.1109/10.477707 PMID:8567001

Han, J., & Fu, Y. (1995, September). Discovery of multiple-level association rules from large databases. In VLDB (Vol. 95, pp. 420-431). VLDB.

Han, J., & Kamber, M. (2006). Data Mining: concepts and techniques (2nd ed.). Morgan Kaufmann.

Han, Tian, Yoon, & Lee. (2012). *A Big Data Model supporting Information Recommendation in Social Networks.* IEEE.

Hanbali, A., Altman, E., & Nain, P. (2004). *A Survey of TCP over Mobile Ad Hoc Networks.* INRIA, Research Report RR-5182. Retrieved 05 2004, from http://hal.inria.fr/inria-00071406/en

Han, E. H., Karypis, G., & Kumar, V. (1997). Scalable parallel data mining for association rules. ACM.

Han, J., & Kamber, M. (2005). *Data Mining: Concepts and Techniques* (2nd ed.). Morgan Kaufmann Publishers.

Harada, L., Akaboshi, N., Ogihara, K., & Take, R. (1998, November). Dynamic skew handling in parallel mining of association rules. In *Proceedings of the seventh international conference on Information and knowledge management* (pp. 76-85). ACM. doi:10.1145/288627.288634

Hargittai, S. (2008). Efficient and Fast ECG Baseline Wander Reduction without Distortion of Important Clinical Information. *IEEE Conferences on Computers in Cardiology.*

Hawkinson, J. & Bates, T. (1996, March). *Guidelines for creation, selection and registration of an autonomous system (AS).* Internet Engineering Task Force, Request For Comments (Best Current Practice) RFC 1930.

Henderson, T., Floyd, S., Gurtov, A., & Nishida, Y. (2012). *RFC 6582: The NewReno Modification to TCP's Fast Recovery Algorithm.* IETF Internet Standard.

Henderson, T., & Katz, R. (1999). Transport protocols for Internet-compatible satellite networks. *IEEE JSAC, 17*(2), 345–359.

Hidber, C. (1999). Online association rule mining. ACM.

Hijazi, S. T., & Naqvi, R. S. M. M. (2006). Factors affecting student"s performance: A Case of Private Colleges. *Bangladesh e- Journal of Sociology (Melbourne, Vic.), 3*(1).

Hinchcliffe, D. (2011). *How social media and big data will unleash what we know.* Retrieved from http://www.zdnet.com/blog/hinchcliffe/how-social-media-and-big-data-will-unleash-what-we-know/1533

Hinds, Atojoko, & Zhu. (2013, August). Evaluation of OSPF and EIGRP Routing Protocols for IPv6. *International Journal of Future Computer and Communication, 2*(4).

Ho, R. (2008). *How Hadoop Map/Reduce works.* Retrieved April 2013, from http://architects.dzone.com/articles/how-hadoopmapreduce-work

Holland, G., & Vaidya, N. (2002). Analysis of TCP performance over mobile ad hoc networks. *ACM Wireless Networks, 8*(2), 275–288. doi:10.1023/A:1013798127590

Houston, M. (2011). *General Purpose Computation on Graphics Processors (GPGPU).* Stanford University Graphics Lab.

Houtsma, M., & Swami, A. (1995, March). Set-oriented mining for association rules in relational databases. In *Data Engineering, 1995.Proceedings of the Eleventh International Conference on* (pp. 25-33). IEEE. doi:10.1109/ICDE.1995.380413

Ider, Y. Z., Saki, M. C., & Gcer, H. A. (1995). Removal of power line interference in signal-averaged electrocardiography systems. *IEEE Transactions on Bio-Medical Engineering, 42*(7), 731–735. doi:10.1109/10.391173 PMID:7622157

IEEE 802.11 WLAN standard. (n.d.). Retrieved from http://standards.ieee.org/getieee802

Image of cotton leaf infected with Leaf miner. (n.d.). Retrieved from http://en.wikipedia.org/wiki/Leaf_miner

Image of cotton leaf infected with Leaf miner. (n.d.). Retrieved from http://www.planetnatural.com/pest-problem-solver/plant-disease/downy-mildew/

Image of cotton leaf infected with Powdery Mildew. (n.d.). Retrieved from http://en.wikipedia.org/wiki/Powdery_mildew

Ingham. (2010). Braille, the language, its machine translation and display. *IEEE Transactions on Man-Machine Systems, 10*(4).

Introduction IPRouting. (n.d.). Retrieved from http://www.cisco.com/en/US/tech/tk365/ts-d_technology_support_protocol_home.html

Islam, M. N., & Ashique, M. (2010). Simulation-Based Comparative Study Of EIGRP and OSPF for Real-Time Applications. Blekinge Institute of Technology, School of Computing, Karlskrona, Sweden.

Ito, K., & Parhi, K. K. (1994). Determining the Iteration Bounds of Single-Rate and Multi-Rate Data-Flow Graphs. *Proceedings of IEEE Asia-Pacific Conference on Circuits and Systems*. doi:10.1109/APCCAS.1994.514543

Ito, K., & Parhi, K. K. (1995). Determining the Minimum Iteration Period of an Algorithm. *The Journal of VLSI Signal Processing*, *11*(3), 229–244. doi:10.1007/BF02107055

Ivanka Valova, I. C. S. R. Processing Of Large Data Sets: Evolution, Opportunities And Challenges. *Proceedings of PCaPAC08*.

Jacobson, V. (1988). Congestion avoidance and control. *SIGCOMM Comput. Commun. Rev.*, *18*, 314–329. Retrieved August 1988, from http://doi.acm.org/10.1145/52325.52356

Jacobson, V. (1990). *Compression TCP/IP headers for low speed serial links*. RFC 1144, Category: Proposed Standard.

Jacobson, V. (1990). Modified TCP Congestion Control Avoidance Algorithm. *end-2-end-interest mailing list*, 1-14.

Jain, A. K. (1999). *Digital Image Processing*. Retrieved from http://www.yvonnefoong.com/2009/05/25/time-to-think-of-my-trigone-meningioma/

Jain, A. K., & Ross, A. A. (2008). *Introduction to Biometrics*. Retrieved from http://www.springer.com/computer/image+processing/book/978-1-4419-4375-0

Jain, A. K., Hong, L., & Pankanti, S. (2000). *Biometric Identification*. Retrieved from http://helios.et.put.poznan.pl/~dgajew/download/PUT/SEMESTR_10/IO/FACE_RECOGNITION/BiometricsACM.pdf

Jain, A. K., Ross, A. A., & Nandakumar, K. (2009). *Introduction to Biometrics*. Retrieved from http://biometrics.cse.msu.edu/

Jain, A. K. (1989). *Fundamentals of Digital Image Processing*. Prentice Hall.

Jain, A. K., Ross, A., & Prabhakar, S. (2004). An Introduction to Biometric Recognition. *IEEE Transactions on Circuits and Systems for Video Technology*, *14*(1), 4–19. doi:10.1109/TCSVT.2003.818349

Jane, R., & Laguna, P. (1992). Adaptive Baseline Wander Removal in the ECG: Comparative Analysis with Cubic Spline Technique. IEEE.

Jiang, X., Xu, M., Li, Q., & Pan, L. (2009). Improving IGP Convergence through Distributed OSPF in Scalable Router. *11th IEEE International Conference on High Performance Computing and Communications*. doi:10.1109/HPCC.2009.21

Jones, C., Sivalingam, K., Agarwal, P., & Chen, J. (2001). A survey of energy efficient network protocols for wireless and mobile networks. *ACM Wireless Networks*, *7*(4), 343–358. doi:10.1023/A:1016627727877

June, L. G. (2014). *How Intel is using IoT and big data to improve food and water security*. Retrieved from www.techrepublic.com/article/how-intel-is-using-iot-and-big-data-to-improve-food-and-water-security/

Jyoti, A., Mohanty, M. N., & Kar, S. K. (2014). Optimized Clustering Method for CT Brain Image Segmentation. In *Proceedings of the International Conference on Frontiers of Intelligent Computing: Theory and Applications* (FICTA). Springer.

Kalaivani, A. (2013). *SAutomatic Dominant Region Segmentation For Natural Images. In Iccsea, Sppr, Csia, WimoA – 2013* (pp. 273–280). CS & IT-CSCP.

Kamerman, A., & Monteban, L. (1997). WaveLAN-11: A high-performance wireless lan for the unlicensed band. *Bell Labs Technical Journal*, *2*(3), 118–133. doi:10.1002/bltj.2069

Kanade, T. (1973). *Picture Processing by Computer Complex and Recognition of Human Faces*. Kyoto Univ.

Kang, J., Fecko, M. A., & Sunil, S. (2010). ALE: Adaptive Link Establishment in OSPF Wireless Ad-Hoc Networks. *IEEE The Military Communications Conference*. doi:10.1109/MILCOM.2010.5679573

Kar, Battacharjee, Basu, Nasipuri, & Kundu. (2011). High Performance Human Face Recognition Using Independent High Intensity Gabor Wavelet Responses: A Statistical Approach. *International Journal of Computer Science and Emerging Technologies*, *2*(1), 178-187.

Kar, S. K., & Mihir, N. (2013). Statistical Approach for Color Image Detection. In *Proceedings ofIEEE Int. Conf. on Computer Communication and Informatics* (ICCCI). IEEE.

Karimi, Dickson, & Hamze. (2010). *A Performance Comparison of CUDA and OpenCL*. Academic Press.

Karimi, K., Dickson, N. G., & Hamze, F. (2010). *A Performance Comparison of CUDA and OpenCL*. Available at http://arxiv.org/abs/1005.2581

Karn, P., & Partridge, C. (1987). Improving round-trip time estimates in reliable transport protocols. *SIGCOMM Comput. Commun. Rev.*, *17*, 2–7. Retrieved August 1987, from http://doi.acm.org/10.1145/55483.55484

Karp, R. M. (1978). A Characterization of the Minimum Cycle Mean in a Digraph. *Discrete Mathematics*, *23*(3), 309–311. doi:10.1016/0012-365X(78)90011-0

Katal, Wazid, & Goudar. (2013). *Big Data: Issues, Challenges, Tools and Good Practices*. IEEE.

Kaur, A., & Singh, K. (2010, March). Speckle noise reduction by using wavelets. In *National Conference on Computational Instrumentation CSIO NCCI*(pp. 198-203).

Keahey, R. (2012). *Cloud Computing and Big Data*. Retrieved from http://www.slideshare.net/rkeahey/cloud-computing-and-big-data

Khalid, A. (2014). New Recognition Methods for Human Iris Patterns. Academic Press.

Khan, Z. N. (2005). Scholastic Achievement of Higher Secondary Students in Science Stream. *Journal of Social Sciences*, *1*(2), 84–87. doi:10.3844/jssp.2005.84.87

Kharya, S. (2012). *Using data mining techniques for diagnosis and prognosis of cancer disease*. arXiv preprint arXiv:1205.1923.

Khowaja, S., & Shah, S. Z. S. (2014). Noise reduction technique for images using radial basis function neural networks. *Mehran University Research Journal of Engineering & Technology, 33*(3).

Khurshid, J., Zafar, M. F., & Zaheer, Z. (2013). Novel iris segmentation and recognition system for human identification. *IBCAST*, 128-131.

Kim, D., Toh, C.K., & Choi, Y. (2001). TCP-BuS: Improving TCP Performance in Wireless Ad Hoc Networks. *Journal of Communications And Networks*, *3*, 1707–1713.

King. (2001). *Text and Braille Computer Translation*. Department of Computation.

Kirby, M., & Sirovich, L. (1990). Application of the Karhunen-Loeave Proce-dure for the Characterisation of Human Faces. *IEEE Transactions on Pattern Analysis and Machine Intelligence*, *12*(1), 831–835. doi:10.1109/34.41390

Kisi, Ö., & Uncuoglu, E. (2005). Comparison of three back-propagation training algorithms for two case studies. *Indian Journal of Engineering & Materials Sciences, 12*(5), 434-442.

Klemm, F., Krishnamurthy, S., & Tripathi, S. (2003). Alleviating effects of mobility on TCP performance in ad hoc networks using signal strength based link management. In Personal Wireless Communications (pp. 611-624). doi:10.1007/978-3-540-39867-7_59

Koivo, H. N. (2008). *Neural networks: Basics using matlab neural network toolbox*. MathWorks.

Komatsu, Sato, Arai, Koyama, Takizawa, & Kobayashi. (2010). Evaluating Performance and Portability of OpenCL Programs. In *Proceedings of the Fifth international Workshop on Automatic Performance Tuning(iWAPT2010)*.

Komatsu1, Sato, Arai, Koyama, Takizawa, & Kobayashi. (2010). Evaluating Performance and Portability of OpenCL Programs. *5th international Workshop on Automatic Performance Tuning(iWAPT2010)*.

Kopparty, S., Krishnamurthy, S., Faloutsos, M., & Tripathi, S. (2002). Split TCP for mobile ad hoc networks. In *Global Telecommunications Conference*, (pp. 138-142). IEEE Press. doi:10.1109/GLOCOM.2002.1188057

Kowar & Yadav. (2012). Brain Tumor Detection and Segmentation Using Histogram Thresholding. *International Journal of Engineering and Advanced Technology, 1*(4).

Kuan, D. T., Sawchuk, A., Strand, T. C., & Chavel, P. (1985). Adaptive noise smoothing filter for images with signal-dependent noise. *Pattern Analysis and Machine Intelligence, IEEE Transactions on*, (2), 165-177.

Kulkarni, P. K., Kumar, V., & Verma, H. K. (1997). Removal of powerline interference and baseline wonder using real time digital filter. *Proceedings of international conference on computer applications in electrical engineering, recent advances*.

Kumaravel, N., Senthil, A., Sridhar, K. S., & Nithiyanandam, N. (1995). Integrating the ECG power-line interference removal methods with rule-based system. *Biomedical Sciences Instrumentation, 31*, 115–120. PMID:7654947

Kumar, G. S. S., & Moorthy, H. K. (2012). Highly Efficient Design of DSP Systems Using Electronic Design Automation Tool to Find Iteration Bound. *International Journal of Advanced Networking and Applications, 4*, 1560–1567.

Kumar, V. B., & Shreyas, B. S. (2011). Face Recognition Using Gabor Wavelets. In *Conference Proceedings of the IEEE Asilomar Conference on Signals, Systems and Computers*. IEEE.

Lades, M., Vorbriggen, J. C., Buhmann, J., Lange, J., & Konen, W. (1993). Distortion invariant object recognition in the dynamic link architecture. *IEEE Transactions on Computers, 2*(3), 300–311. doi:10.1109/12.210173

Laguna, P., & Jane, R. (1992). Adaptive Filtering of ECG Baseline Wander. IEEE.

Lakshmi & Sankaranarayanan. (2010). A study of Edge Detection Techniques for Segmentation Computing Approaches. *IJCA* .

Lawrence, S., Giles, C. L., Tsoi, A. C., & Back, A. D. (1997). Face Recognition: A Convolution Neural Network Approach. *IEEE Transactions on Neural Networks, 8*(1), 98–113. doi:10.1109/72.554195

Lee, C. (2010). Tactile Display as Braille Display for the Visually Disabled. In *Proceedings of IEEE/RSJ International Conference on Intelligent Robotics and Systems*.

Lee, E. A., & Messerschmitt, D. G. (1987). Static scheduling of Synchronous Data-flow Programs for Digital Signal Processing. *IEEE Transactions on Computers, 36*(1), 24–35. doi:10.1109/TC.1987.5009446

Lee, J. S. (1986). Speckle suppression and analysis for synthetic aperture radar images. *Optical Engineering (Redondo Beach, Calif.)*, *25*(5), 255636–255636. doi:10.1117/12.7973877

Lee, Y. K., Chan, H., & Verbauwhede, I. (2007). Iteration Bound Analysis and Throughput Optimum Architecture of SHA-256 (384,512) for Hardware Implementations.*8th International Conference on Information Security Applications*, *4867*, 102-114. doi:10.1007/978-3-540-77535-5_8

Levchenko, Voelker, Paturi, & Savage. (2008, August). XL: An Efficient Network Routing Algorithm. *SIGCOMM'08*. ACM.

Levkov, C., Mihov, G., Ivanov, R., Daskalov, I., Christov, I., & Dotsinsky, I. (2005). Removal of power-line interference from the ECG: A review of the subtraction procedure. *Biomedical Engineering Online*, *50*(4). PMID:16117827

Li, S. Z., & Jain, A. K. (2004). Handbook of Face Recognition. Academic Press.

Lim, H., Xu, K., & Gerla, M. (2003). Tcp performance over multipath routing in mobile ad hoc networks. In *IEEE International Conference on Communications*, (vol. 2, pp. 1064-1068). doi:10.1109/ICC.2003.1204520

Lin, S. H., Kung, S. Y., & Lin, L. J. (1997). Face Recognition/Detection by Probabilistic Decision Based Neural Network. *IEEE Transactions on Neural Networks*, *8*(1), 114–132. doi:10.1109/72.554196

Lin, W., Hu, C., Li, Y., & Cheng, X. (2013). Virtual Dataspace-A Service Oriented Model for Scientific Big Data. *IEEE Fourth International Conference on Emerging Intelligent Data and Web Technologies*. doi:10.1109/EIDWT.2013.5

Lisette, P., Harting, N. M., & Fedotov, C. H. S. (2004).On Baseline drift Suppressing in ECG-Recordings. *Proceedings of SPS (the 2004 IEEE Benelux Signal Processing Symposium).*

Lisheng, X., & Kuanquan, W. (2002). Adaptive Baseline Wander Removal in the Pulse Waveform. IEEE.

Liu, J., & Xian, L. (1991). Automatic thresholding of gray-level pictures using two-dimension Otsu method. *Circuits and Systems*, *1*, 325-327.

Liu, W., & Wang, C., Zeng, & Li. (2011). Scalable Multi-GPU Decoupled Parallel Rendering Approach in Shared Memory Architecture. International Conference on Virtual Reality and Visualization.

Liu, C. J., & Wechsler, H. (2002). Gabor Feature Based Classi_cation Using the Enhanced Fisher Linear Discriminant Model for Face Recognition. *IEEE Transactions on Image Processing*, *11*(4), 467–476. doi:10.1109/TIP.2002.999679 PMID:18244647

Liu, J. W. S., Lin, K.-J., Shih, W.-K., Yu, A. C., Chung, J.-Y., & Zhao, W. (1991). Algorithms for Scheduling Imprecise Computations. *IEEE Comput.*, *24*(5), 58–68. doi:10.1109/2.76287

Liu, J., & Singh, S. (2001). ATCP: TCP for mobile ad hoc networks. *IEEE Journal on Selected Areas in Communications*, *19*(7), 1300–1315. doi:10.1109/49.932698

Liu, L., & Zhou, G. (2009). Extraction of the Rice Leaf Disease Image Based on BP. *Neural Networks*, 2009.

Living, J., & Al-Hashimi, B. M. (2012). Mixed arithmetic architecture: a solution to the iteration bound for resources FPGA and CPLD recursive digital filters.*IEEE International Symposium on Circuits and Systems*, *1*, 478-481.

Lochert, C., Scheuermann, B., & Mauve, M. (2007). A survey on congestion control for mobile ad hoc networks: Research Articles. *Wireless Communication Mobile Computing*, *7*(5), 655–676. doi:10.1002/wcm.524

Long, P. D., & Cat, P. T. (2009, December). Real-time speckle reducing by Cellular Neural Network. In *Information, Communications and Signal Processing, 2009. ICICS 2009. 7th International Conference on* (pp. 1-4). IEEE. doi:10.1109/ICICS.2009.5397738

Lynn, P. A. (1977). *On* line digital filter for biological filters: Some fast designs for small computers. *Medical & Biological Engineering & Computing, 15*(5), 91–101. doi:10.1007/BF02442281

Madhyastha, T., & Tanimoto, S. (2009). Student Consistency and Implications for Feedback in Online Assessment Systems. In *Proceedings of the 2nd International Conference on Educational Data Mining*, (pp. 81-90).

Mahesh, S., Chavan, R. A., & Uplane, M. D. (2008). Interference Reduction in ECG using Digital FIR Filters based on rectangular window. *WSEAS Transactions on Signal Processing, 4*(5), 340-49.

Maletz & Wang. (2011). Importance Point Projection for GPU-based Final Gathering.*Eurographics Symposium on Rendering, 30*(4).

Malik, S. U., Srinivasan, S. K., & Khan, S. U. (2012, September). Convergence time analysis of open shortest path first routing protocol in internet scale networks. *Electronics Letters, 48*(19), 1188. doi:10.1049/el.2012.2310

Manjunath, B. S., Chellappa, R., & von der Malsburg, J. C. (1992). A Feature Based Approach to Face Recognition. *Proc. IEEE CS Conf. Computer Vision and Pattern Recognition.* doi:10.1109/CVPR.1992.223162

Maragos, P. (2005). *Morphological Filtering for Image Enhancement and Feature Detection. In The Image and Video Processing Handbook* (2nd ed.). Elsevier Academic Press.

Markovsky, I. A., & Anton, V. H. & Sabine (2008). Application of Filtering Methods for Removal of Resuscitation Artifacts from Human ECG Signals. *IEEE Conference of Engineering in Medicine and Biology Society.* doi:10.1109/IEMBS.2008.4649079

Marquardt, D. W. (1963). An algorithm for least-squares estimation of nonlinear parameters. *Journal of the Society for Industrial and Applied Mathematics, 11*(2), 431–441. doi:10.1137/0111030

Marz, N., & Warren, J. (2015). *Big Data: Principles and best practices of scalable realtime data systems.* Manning Publications Co.

Mascolo, S., Casetti, C., Gerla, M., Sanadidi, M. Y., & Wang, R. (2001). TCP westwood: Bandwidth estimation for enhanced transport over wireless links. In *7th annual international conference on Mobile computing and networking, ser. MobiCom* (pp. 287-297). New York, NY: ACM.

Mashaly, A. S., AbdElkawy, E. E. F., & Mahmoud, T. (2010, November). Speckle noise reduction in SAR images using adaptive morphological filter. In *Intelligent Systems Design and Applications (ISDA),201010th International Conference on* (pp. 260-265). IEEE.

Mathis, M., Dukkipati, N., & Cheng, Y. (2003). *RFC 6937: Proportional Rate Reduction for TCP.* IETF Standards Track.

Mathis, M., Mahdavi, J., Floyd, S., & Romanow, A. (1996). *RFC 2018: TCP Selective Acknowledgment Options.* IETF Internet Standard.

Mathukannan, K., Latha, P., & Manimaran, J. (2013). Implementation of Artificial Neural Network for Face Recognition Using Gabor Feature Extraction. *ICTACT Journal on Image and Video Processing, 4*(2), 690–694.

McKinsey Global Institute, (2011). *Big data: The next frontier for innovation, competition, and productivity.* Author.

McManus, C. D., Neubert, K. D., & Cramer, E. (1993). Characterization and elimination of AC noise in electrocardiograms: A comparison of digital filtering methods. *Computers and Biomedical Research, an International Journal*, *26*(1), 48–67. doi:10.1006/cbmr.1993.1003 PMID:8444027

McManus, C. D., Teppner, U., Neubert, D., & Lobodzinski, S. M. (1985). Estimation and Removal of Baseline Drift in the Electrocardiogram. *Computers and Biomedical Research, an International Journal*, *18*(1), 1–9. doi:10.1016/0010-4809(85)90002-3 PMID:3971702

Mcquiggan, S., Mott, B., & Lester, J. (2008). Modeling Self-Efficacy in Intelligent Tutoring Systems: An Inductive Approach. *User Modeling and User-Adapted Interaction*, *18*(1-2), 81–123. doi:10.1007/s11257-007-9040-y

Merceron, A., & Yacef, K. (2007a). *Interestingness Measures for Association Rules in Educational Data*. Academic Press.

Merceron, A., & Yacef, K. (2007b). Revisiting interestingness of strong symmetric association rules in educational data. In *Proceedings of the International Workshop on Applying Data Mining in e-Learning*.

Meunkaewjinda, Kumsawat, Attakitmongcol & Srikaew. (2008*)*. Grape leaf disease detection from color imagery using hybrid intelligent system. *In Proceedings of ECTI-CON.*

Minaei-Bidgoli, B., Tan, P.-N., & Punch, W. F. (2004). Mining Interesting Contrast Rules for a Web-based Educational System. In *Proc. Int. Conf. on Machine Learning Applications*. doi:10.1109/ICMLA.2004.1383530

Ming-Syan Chen, , Jiawei Han, , & Yu, P. S. (1996). Data Mining-An Overview from a Database Perspective. *IEEE Transactions on Knowledge and Data Engineering*, *8*(6), 866–883. doi:10.1109/69.553155

Mirhosseini, S. M., & Torgheh, F. (2011). ADHOCTCP: Improving TCP Performance in Ad Hoc Networks. Intech.

Mitov, I. P. (2004). A method for reduction of power line interference in the ECG. *Medical Engineering & Physics*, *26*(10), 879–887. doi:10.1016/j.medengphy.2004.08.014 PMID:15567704

Morimoto, Y., Ishii, H., & Morishita, S. (1997). Efficient construction of regression trees with range and region splitting. In *Proceedings of the 23rd VLDB Conference*.

Moy, J. (1998, April). *OSPF version 2*. Internet Engineering Task Force, Request For Comments (Standards Track) RFC 2328.

Murthy, S. K. (1998). Automatic construction of decision trees from data: A multi-disciplinary survey. *Data Mining and Knowledge Discovery*, *2*(4), 345–389. doi:10.1023/A:1009744630224

Muthukrishnan, R., & Radha, M. (2011). Edge Detection Techniques For Image Segmentation. *International Journal of Computer Science & Information Technology, 3*(6).

Nagle, J. (1984). *RFC 896: Congestion Control in IP/TCP Internetworks*. IETF Internet Standard.

NavaneethKrishnan, Y., Bhagwat, C. N., & Aparajit, U. (2013). Performance Analysis of OSPF and EIGRP Routing Protocols for Greener Internetworking. *International Conference in Distributed Computing & Internet Technology.*

NESSI. (2012). *Big Data White Paper*. NESSI.

Nichols, K., & Jacobson, V. (2012). Controlling queue delay. *Queue*, *10*(5), 20-34. Retrieved May 2012, from http://doi.acm.org/10.1145/2208917.2209336

ORNL DAAC. (n.d.). *Alos-palsar image*. Retrieved from http://webmap.ornl.gov/wcsdown/dataset.jsp?ds_id=993

Owens, Houston, Luebke, Green, Stone, & Phillips. (2008).GPU Computing. IEEE, 96, 5.

Pandey, U. K., & Pal. (2011). Data Mining: A prediction of performer or underperformer using classification. *International Journal of Computer Science and Information Technology, 2*(2), 686-690.

Pandit, S. (1997). ECG Baseline Drift Removal through STFT. IEEE.

Pan, N., Vai Mang, I., Mai, P. U., & Pun, S. H. (2007). Accurate Removal of Baseline Wander in ECG Using Empirical Mode Decomposition. *IEEE International Conference on Functional Biomedical Imaging*. doi:10.1109/NFSI-ICFBI.2007.4387719

Parhi, K., & Messerschmitt, D. G. (1987). Look-ahead computation: Improving iteration bound in linear recursions.*IEEE International Conference on Acoustics, Speech and signal processing, 12*, 1855-1858. doi:10.1109/ICASSP.1987.1169698

Park, H., & Nishimura, T. (2007, August). Reduced speckle noise on medical ultrasound images using cellular neural network. In *Engineering in Medicine and Biology Society, 2007. EMBS 2007. 29th Annual International Conference of the IEEE* (pp. 2138-2141). IEEE. doi:10.1109/IEMBS.2007.4352745

Parker, C. (2012, August). Unexpected challenges in large scale machine learning. In *Proceedings of the 1st International Workshop on Big Data, Streams and Heterogeneous Source Mining: Algorithms, Systems, Programming Models and Applications* (pp. 1-6). ACM.

Park, U., Jillela, R. R., Ross, A., & Jain, A. K. (2011). Periocular biometrics in the visible spectrum. *IEEE Trans. Info. Forensics & Security, 6*(1), 96–106. doi:10.1109/TIFS.2010.2096810

Patino-Escarcina, R. E., & Costa, J. A. F. (2007, October). An evaluation of MLP neural network efficiency for image filtering. In *Intelligent Systems Design and Applications, 2007. ISDA 2007. Seventh International Conference on* (pp. 335-340). IEEE. doi:10.1109/ISDA.2007.134

Patricia, A., & Tim, L. (1992). *Method and apparatus for removing baseline wander from an ECG signal.* US Patent, Hewlett Packard. US5318036.

Pauca, V. P., Forkin, M., Xu, X., Plemmons, R., & Ross, A. (2011). Challenging Ocular Image Recognition. *Proc. of SPIE, 8029.*

Paxson, V., & Allman, M. (2000). *Computing TCP's retransmission timer.* RFC 2988, Category: Standard Track.

Paxson, V., Allman, M., Chu, J., & Sargent, M. (2011). *RFC 6298: Computing TCP's Retransmission Timer.* IETF Internet Standard.

Pechenizkiy, M., Calders, T., Vasilyeva, E., & Debra, P. (2008). Mining the Student Assessment Data: Lessons Drawn from a Small Scale Case Study. In *Proceedings of the 1st International Conference on Educational Data mining*, (pp. 187-191).

Pei, M., Goodman, E. D., & Punch, W. F. (1998, October). Feature extraction using genetic algorithms. In *Proceedings of the 1st International Symposium on Intelligent Data Engineering and Learning, IDEAL* (Vol. 98, pp. 371-384). IDEAL.

Pentikousis, K. (2000). TCP in wired-cum-wireless environments. *IEEE Communications Surveys and Tutorials, 3*(4), 2–14. doi:10.1109/COMST.2000.5340805

Pentland, A., Moghaddam, B., & Starner, T. (1994). View-Based and Modular Eigenspaces for Face Recognition. In *Proc. IEEE CS Conf. Computer Vision and Pattern Recognition*, (pp. 84-91). doi:10.1109/CVPR.1994.323814

Pitangui, C., & Zaverucha, G. (2006, December). Genetic based machine learning: merging Pittsburgh and Michigan, an implicit feature selection mechanism and a new crossover operator. In *Hybrid Intelligent Systems, 2006. HIS'06. Sixth International Conference on* (pp. 58-58). IEEE.

Pitangui, C., & Zaverucha, G. (2006, December). Genetic based machine learning: merging Pittsburgh and Michigan, an implicit feature selection mechanism and a new crossover operator. In *Hybrid Intelligent Systems, 2006. HIS'06. Sixth International Conference on* (pp. 58-58). IEEE. doi:10.1109/HIS.2006.264941

Pitas, I., & Venetsanopoulos, A. N. (2013). *Nonlinear digital filters: principles and applications* (Vol. 84). Springer Science & Business Media.

Polok & Smrz. (2012). Fast Linear Algebra on GPU. *IEEE 14th International Conference on High Performance Computing and Communications.*

Postel, G. (1981, Sept.). RFC 793: Transmission Control Protocol. IETF Internet Standard.

Pottala, E. W. (1989). Suppression of Baseline Wander in the ECG Using a Bilinearly Transform, Null-Phase Filter. *Journal of E.cardiology*, 22.

Pottala, E. W., & Gradwohl, J. R. (1992). Comparison of Two Methods for Removing Baseline Wander. In *The ECG*. Pub Med National Library of Medicine.

Proenca, H. (2010). Iris recognition: On the segmentation of degraded images acquired in the visible Wavelength. *IEEE Transactions on Pattern Analysis and Machine Intelligence*, *32*(8), 1502–1516. doi:10.1109/TPAMI.2009.140 PMID:20558880

Qian, N. (1999). On the momentum term in gradient descent learning algorithms. *Neural Networks*, *12*(1), 145–151. doi:10.1016/S0893-6080(98)00116-6 PMID:12662723

Radu, P., Srilantzis, K., Howells, V., Hoque, S., & Deravi, F. (2010). *Are Two Eyes Better Than One? An Experimental Investigation on Dual Iris Recognition*. University of Kent.

Rajan. 2012). *Top Ten Big Data Security and Privacy Challenges*. Retrieved from https://downloads.cloudsecurityalliance.org/initiatives/bdwg/Big_Data_Top_Ten_v1.pdf

Rangayyan, R. M. (2002). *Biomedical Signal Analysis*. John Wiley and Sons Publishing Company.

Rani, & Sharma. (2012). Edge Detection in Image Segmentation. *International Journal of Advanced Research in Electronics and Communication Engineering, 1*(6).

Rao. (n.d.). *EHV-AC, HVDC Transmission & Distribution* (3rd ed.). Khanna Publication. Begumudre. (2011). *Extra High Voltage AC Transmission Engineering* (4th ed.). New Age International Publishers.

Riddhi, & Shruti. (2013). A Literature Survey on Face Recognition Techniques. *International Journal of Computer Trends and Technology*, *5*(4), 189–195.

Riedmiller, M., & Braun, H. (1993). A direct adaptive method for faster backpropagation learning: The RPROP algorithm. In *Neural Networks, 1993., IEEE International Conference on* (pp. 586-591). IEEE.

Robertson, D. G., & Dowling, J. J. (2003). Design and responses of Butterworth and critically damped digital filters. *Journal of Electromyography and Kinesiology*, *13*(6), 569–573. doi:10.1016/S1050-6411(03)00080-4 PMID:14573371

Romera, C., & Ventura, S. (2007). A Survey from 1995 to 2005. *Expert Systems with Applications*, *33*, 125–146.

Romero, C., Ventura, S., Eapejo, P. G., & Hervas, C. (2008). Data Mining Algorithms to Classify Students. In *Proceedings of the 1st International Conference on Educational Data Mining.*

Rossi, R. (1992). *Fast FIR Filters for a Stres Test System.* IEEE.

Rumelhart, D. E., & McClelland, J. L.PDP Research Group. (1988). *Parallel distributed processing* (Vol. 1, pp. 354–362). IEEE.

Safavi, A. A., Parandeh, N. M., & Salehi, M. (2010, October). Predicting Breast Cancer Survivability using data mining techniques. In *Software Technology and Engineering (ICSTE), 2010 2nd International Conference on* (Vol. 2, pp. V2-227). IEEE.

Sagiroglu, S., & Sinanc, D. (2013). *Big Data: A Review*. IEEE.

Sahoo, A. K., Sahoo, K. S., & Tiwary, M. (2014). Signature based Malware detection for unstructured data in HADOOP. *IEEE International Conference on Advances in Electronics, Computers and Communications (ICAECC)*. doi:10.1109/ICAECC.2014.7002394

Sahoo, P. K., Soltani, S., & Wong, A. K. C. (1988). A Survey of Thresholding techniques. *Computer Vision Graphics and Image Processing*, *41*(2), 233–260. doi:10.1016/0734-189X(88)90022-9

Saikia, T., & Sarma, K. K. (2014, February). Multilevel-DWT based image de-noising using feed forward artificial neural network. In *Signal Processing and Integrated Networks (SPIN), 2014 International Conference on* (pp. 791-794). IEEE. doi:10.1109/SPIN.2014.6777062

Saini, R., & Narinder, R. (2014). Comparison of various Biometric Methods. *International Journal of Advances in Science and Technology*, *2*(1), 24–30.

Samaria, F., & Fallside, F. (1993). Face Identification and Feature Extraction Using Hidden Markov Models. In G. Vernazza (Ed.), *Image Processing: Theory and Application*. Elsevier.

Samaria, F., & Harter, A. C. (1994). Parameterization of a Stochastic Model for Human Face Identification. *Proc. Second IEEE Workshop Applications of Computer Vision*.

Santhanam, T., & Radhika, S. (2011). Applicability of BPN and MLP neural networks for classification of noises present in different image formats. *International Journal of Computers and Applications*, *26*(5), 10–14. doi:10.5120/3101-4259

Schulze, M. A., & Wu, Q. X. (1995). *Noise reduction in synthetic aperture radar imagery using a morphology-based nonlinear filter*. Digital Image Computing and Applications.

Sharma, & Padda. (2012, February). Configuring an EIGRP based Routing Model. *International Journal of Scientific and Research Publications*, *2*(2).

Shatnawi, A. (2007). Computing the Loop Bound in Iterative Data Flow Graphs Using Natural Token Flow. *International Journal of Computer Information Science and Engineering*, *1*, 819–824.

Shusterman, V. (2000). Enhancing the Precision of ECG Baseline Correction. *Computers and Biomedical Research, an International Journal*, 33. PMID:10854121

Singh & Bhatia. (2010). Automated Conversion of English and Hindi Text to Braille. *International Journal of Computers and Applications*, *4*(6).

Singh, G. K., Sharma, A., & Velusami, S. (2009). A Research Review on Analysis and Interpretation of Arrhythmias using ECG Signals. *IJMST*, *2*(3), 37-55.

Sirovich, L., & Kirby, M. (1987). Low-Dimensional Procedure for the Characterisation of Human Faces. *Journal of the Optical Society of America*, *4*(3), 519–524. doi:10.1364/JOSAA.4.000519

Slaby. (2010). Computerized Braille translation. *Microcomputer Applications*, *1*(13), 107-113.

Sleng & Lau, Y. (1999). Regular feature extraction for recognition of Braille. In *Proceedings of Third International Conference on Computational Intelligence and Multimedia Applications.*

Somasundaram, Shrivastava, & EMC Educational Services. (2009), *Information Storage and Management - Storing, Managing, and Protecting Digital Information*. Wiley India.

Sornmo, L. (1993). Time-Varying Digital Filtering of ECG Baseline Wander. *Medical & Biological Engineering & Computing, 31*(5), 503–508. doi:10.1007/BF02441986 PMID:8295440

Spasov, D., & Gushev, M. (2012). On the Convergence of Distance Vector Routing Protocols.*Proceedings of ICT Innovations 2012.*

Spitters, M. (2000). *Comparing feature sets for learning text categorization.* Academic Press.

Srinath, S., & RaviKumar, C. N. (2013). A Novel Method for Recognizing Kannada Braille: Consonant-Vowels. *International Journal of Emerging Technology and Advanced Engineering, 3*(1).

Stonham, T. J. (1984). Practical Face Recognition and Verification with WISARD. Aspects of Face Processing.

Sung, Liu, & Hwu. (2012). *DL: A Data Layout Transformation System for Heterogeneous Computing.* IEEE.

Sun, W., Li, F., Guo, W., Jin, Y., & Hu, W. (2013). *Store, Schedule and Switch – A New Data Delivery Model in the Big Data Era. In Proceedings of IEEE ICTON* (p. 13). IEEE.

Sun, Y., Chan, K., & Krishnan, S. M. (2002). ECG signal conditioning by morphological filtering. *Computers in Biology and Medicine, 32*(6), 465–479. doi:10.1016/S0010-4825(02)00034-3 PMID:12356496

Superby, J. F., Vandamme, J.-P., & Meskens, N. (2006). Determination of short comings influencing the achievement of thefirst-year university students using data mining methods. In *Proceedings of the Workshop on Educational Data Mining at the 8th International Conference on Intelligent Tutoring Systems (ITS).*

Su, Y., Shan, S., Chen, X., & Gao, W. (2007). Hierarchical Ensemble of Global and Local Classifiers for Face Recognition. *IEEE Transaction on Pattern Recognition, 25*(7), 1885–1895. PMID:19556198

Takacs, B. (1998). Comparing Face Images Using the Modified Hausdorff Distance. *Pattern Recognition, 31*(12), 1873–1881. doi:10.1016/S0031-3203(98)00076-4

Tan, K., Song, J., Zhang, Q., & Sridharan, M. (2005). *A Compound TCP Approach for High-speed and Long Distance Networks.* Microsoft Research, Tech. Rep.

Tan, C.-W., & Kumar, A. (2011). Automated segmentation of iris images using visible wavelength face images. *Proc. CVPR.* doi:10.1109/CVPRW.2011.5981682

Tan, C.-W., & Kumar, A. (2012). A unified framework for automated iris segmentation using distantly acquired face images. *IEEE Transactions on Image Processing, 21*(9), 4068–4079. doi:10.1109/TIP.2012.2199125 PMID:22614641

Tan, C.-W., & Kumar, A. (2014). *Efficient and Accurate at-a-distance Iris Recognition Using Geometric Key based Iris Encoding. IEEE Trans. Information Forensics and Security.*

Tan, T., He, Z., & Sun, Z. (2010). Efficient and robust segmentation of noisy iris images for non-cooperative iris recognition. *Image and Vision Computing, 28*(2), 223–230. doi:10.1016/j.imavis.2009.05.008

Tenenbaum, J. B., De Silva, V., & Langford, J. C. (2000). A global geometric framework for nonlinear dimensionality reduction. *Science, 290*(5500), 2319–2323. PMID:11125149

Thangairulappan, K., Beaulah, J., & Jeyasingh, V. (2012). Face Representation Using Combined Method of Gabor Filters,Wavelet Transformation and DCV and Recognition Using RBF. *Journal of Intelligent Learning and Applications*, *5*(7), 266–273. doi:10.4236/jilsa.2012.44027

The basic procedure based disease detection solution. (n.d.). Retrieved from http://www.planetnatural.com/pest-problem-solver/houseplant-pests/leafminer-control/

The Network Simulator. (n.d.). *NS-2*. Retrieved from http://www.isi.edu/nsnam/ns/index.html

Tickoo, O., Subramanian, V., Kalyanaraman, S., & Ramakrishnan, K. K. (2005). Lttcp: End-to-end framework to improve TCP performance over networks with lossy channels. *Lecture Notes in Computer Science*, *3552*, 81–93. doi:10.1007/11499169_8

Tobagi, F., & Kleinrock, L. (1975). Packet switching in radio channels: Part ii - the hidden terminal problem in Carrier Sense Multiple-Access modes and the busy-tone solution. *IEEE/ACM Transactions on Networking*, *23*(12), 1417–1433.

Toh, C. K. (1997). Associativity-Based Routing For Ad-Hoc Mobile Networks. *Wireless Personal Communications Journal*, *4*(2), 103–139.

Tomiyasu, K. (1978). Tutorial review of synthetic-aperture radar (SAR) with applications to imaging of the ocean surface. *Proceedings of the IEEE*, *66*(5), 563–583. doi:10.1109/PROC.1978.10961

Tomlinson, R. S. (1975). Selecting sequence numbers. *SIGOPS Oper. Syst. Rev.*, *9*, 11-23. http://doi.acm.org/10.1145/563905.810894

Toral, O. A., Ergun, S., Kurt, M., & Ozturk, A. (2014). Mobile GPU-based importance sampling. Signal Processing and Communications Applications Conference (SIU).

Trabzon, P., Du, R., Weber, P., Luszczek, S., & Tomov, G. Peterson, & Dongarra. (2010). From CUDA to OpenCL: Towards a Performance-portable Solution for Multi-platform GPU Programming. tech. rep., Department of Computer Science, UTK, Knoxville Tennessee.

Turk, M., & Pentland, A. (1991). Eigenfaces for Recognition. *Journal of Cognitive Neuroscience*, *3*(1), 71–86. doi:10.1162/jocn.1991.3.1.71

Umarani & Punithavalli. (2010a). Sampling based Association Rules Mining- A Recent Overview. *International Journal on Computer Science and Engineering, 2*(2), 314-318.

Umarani & Punithavalli. (2010b). A study on effective mining of association rules from huge databases. *International Journal of Computer Science and Research, 1*(1).

Usha, D. & Neeru, B. (2012). *Teaching of English in Primary level in Government schools EdCIL*. Retrieved from http://www.ncert.nic.in/departments/nie/del/publication/pdf/English_Primary_level.pdf

Vaccaro, R. J. (1991). *SVD and Signal Processing II: Algorithms, analysis and applications*. Elsevier Science Inc.

Van Alste, J. A., & Schilder, T. S. (1985). Removal of Baseline Wander and Power-Line Interference from the ECG by an Efficient FIR Filter with a Reduced Number of Taps. *IEEE Transactions on Bio-Medical Engineering*, *BME-32*(12), 1052–1060. doi:10.1109/TBME.1985.325514 PMID:4077083

van Nieuwpoort, R., & Romein, J. (2011). Correlating radio astronomy signals with Many-Core hardware. *International Journal of Parallel Programming*, *39*(1), 88–114. doi:10.1007/s10766-010-0144-3

Vassilev, T. I. (2010). Comparison of several parallel API for cloth modelling on modern GPUs. In *Proceedings of the 11th International Conference on Computer Systems and Technologies and Workshop for PhD Students in Computing on International Conference on Computer Systems and Technologies, CompSysTech '10*. ACM. doi:10.1145/1839379.1839403

Wallis, N. (2012). Big Data in Canada: Challenging Complacency for Competitive Advantage. *IDC*.

Wang, F., & Zhang, Y. (2002). Improving TCP performance over mobile ad hoc networks with out-of-order detection and response. In ACM MOBIHOC (pp. 217-225). Lausanne, Switzerland: ACM. doi:10.1145/513800.513827

Wang, J., Wen, J., Zhang, J., & Han, Y. (2010). TCP-FIT: A novel TCP congestion control algorithm for wireless networks. In *GLOBECOM Workshops (GC Wkshps),* (pp. 2065 –2069). IEEE Press.

Wang, F., & Zhang, Y. (2005). A Survey on TCP over Mobile Ad-Hoc Networks. In Y. Xiao & Y. Pan (Eds.), *Ad Hoc and Sensor Networks* (pp. 267–281). Nova Science Publishers.

Webb, A. R. (2003). *Statistical pattern recognition*. John Wiley & Sons.

Weber, Gothandaraman, Hinde, & Peterson. (2011). Comparing Hardware Accelerators in Scientific Applications: A Case Study. *IEEE, 22*.

Weber, R., Gothandaraman, A., Hinde, R. J., & Peterson, G. D. (2011). Comparing Hardware Accelerators in Scientific Applications: A Case Study. *IEEE Transactions on Parallel and Distributed Systems*, *22*(1), 58–68. doi:10.1109/TPDS.2010.125

Webster, J. G., & Clark, J. W. (1978). *Medical Instrumentation-Application and Design*. Houghton Mifflin.

Wei Tan, M., Blake, Saleh, & Dustdar. (2013). Social-Network-Sourced Big Data Analytics. *IEEE Internet Computing*, 62-69.

Weinhaus, F. (2000). Retrieved from http://www.imagemagick.org/Usage/fourier/

Wei, Z.-Z., & Wang, F. (2011). Achieving Resilient Routing through Redistributing Routing Protocols. *Proceedings of the IEEE, ICC*, 2011.

Weng, J., Zhang, Y., & Hwang, W. S. (2003). Candid covariance-free incremental principal component analysis. *Pattern Analysis and Machine Intelligence. IEEE Transactions on*, *25*(8), 1034–1040.

White, R. G. (1991). Change detection in SAR imagery. *International Journal of Remote Sensing*, *12*(2), 339–360. doi:10.1080/01431169108929656

Wiener, N. (1949). *Extrapolation, interpolation, and smoothing of stationary time series* (Vol. 2). Cambridge, MA: MIT Press.

Wireless LAN medium access control (MAC) and physical layer (PHY) specification. (2007, June). IEEE standard 802.11-2007.

Wiskott, L., Fellous, J.-M., Uger, N. K., & Malsburg, C. V. D. (1999). Face Recognition by Elastic Bunch Graph Matching. *Intelligent Biometric Techniques in Fingerprint and Face Recognition*, *11*(5), 355–396.

Wiskott, L., & von der Malsburg, J. C. (1996). Recognizing Faces by Dynamic Link Matching. *NeuroImage*, *4*(3), S14–S18. doi:10.1006/nimg.1996.0043

Woo-seok, J., Hwan-il, K., Byung-hee, L., Kim, Shin, & Kim. (2007). Optimized Fuzzy Clustering By Predator Prey Particle Swarm Optimization. In *Proceedings ofIEEE Congress on Evolutionary Computation*. IEEE.

Wu, Zhu, Wu, & Ding. (2014). Data Mining with Big Data. *IEEE Transactions on Knowledge and Data Engineering, 26*(1).

Wu. (n.d.). *Simulation Based Performance Analyses on RIP, EIGRP and OSPF Using OPNET*. Academic Press.

Wu, Y., & Yang, Y. (1999). A new digital filter method for eliminating 50Hz interference from the ECG. *Zhongguo Yi Liao Qi Xie Za Zhi, 23*(3), 145–148. PMID:12583053

Xiao, X., Hannan, A., Paxson, V., & Crabbe, E. (2000). *RFC 2873: TCP Processing of the IPv4 Precedence Field.* IETF Internet Standard.

Xu, K., Gerla, M., & Bae, s. (2003). Effectiveness of RTS/CTS handshake in IEEE 802.11 based ad hoc networks. *Ad Hoc Networks Journal, 1*(1), 107-123.

Xu, L., Harfoush, K., & Rhee, I. (2004). Binary increase congestion control (BIC) for fast long distance networks. *IEEE Computer and Communications Societies, 4*, 2514-2524.

Xu, S., & Saadawi, T. (2002). Performance evaluation of TCP algorithms in multi-hop wireless packet networks. *Journal of Wireless Communications and Mobile Computing, 2*(1), 85–100. doi:10.1002/wcm.35

Yadav, C., Wang, S., & Kumar, M. (2013). *Algorithm and approaches to handle large Data-A Survey*. arXiv preprint arXiv:1307.5437.

Yan, X., Zhang, C., & Zhang, S. (2005). ARMGA: Identifying interesting association rules with genetic algorithms. *Applied Artificial Intelligence, 19*(7), 677–689.

Zahoor-uddin (1995). Baseline Wandering Removal from Human Electrocardiogram Signal using Projection Pursuit Gradient Ascent Algorithm. *International Journal of Electrical &Computer Sciences, 9*(9), 11-13.

Zhang, X., Ortega-Sanchez, & Murray. (2006). *Text-to-braille translator in a chip*. Paper presented at the 4th International Conference on Electrical and Computer Engineering ICECE, Dhaka, Bangladesh.

Zhang, Y. C., Mao, H. P., Hu, B., & Xili, M. (2007). Features selection of Cotton disease leaves image based on fuzzy feature selection techniques. In *Proceedings of the 2007 International Conference on Wavelet Analysis and Pattern Recognition*. Beijing, China: IEEE.

Zhao, Wu, & Liu. (2014). Dache- A Data Aware Caching for Big-Data Applications Using the Map Reduce Framework. *Tsinghua Science and Technology, 19*(1), 39-50.

Zhao, L., & Yang, Y. H. (1999). Theoretical Analysis of Illumination in PCA-Based Vision Systems. *Pattern Recognition, 32*(4), 547–564. doi:10.1016/S0031-3203(98)00119-8

Zhao, W., Chellappa, R., Phillips, J., & Rosenfeld, A. (2003). Face Recognition: A Literature Survey. *ACM Computing Surveys, 35*(4), 399–458. doi:10.1145/954339.954342

Zhi-Dong, Z., & Yu-Quan, C. (2006). A New Method for Removal of Baseline Wander and Power Line Interference in ECG Signals. *IEEE Conferences on Machine Learning and Cybernetics.*

Zhou, J., Shi, B., & Zou, L. (2003). Improve TCP performance in ad-hoc network by TCP-RC. In *14th IEEE Int. Symposium on Personal, Indoor and Mobile Radio Communications*(pp.216-220). Beijing, China: IEEE.

Zikopoulos, P., & Eaton, C. (2011). *Understanding big data: Analytics for enterprise class hadoop and streaming data.* McGraw-Hill Osborne Media.

Zimmermann, H. (1988). *OSI reference model—The ISO model of architecture for open systems interconnection*. Norwood, MA: Artech House, Inc.

Zschorlich, V. R. (1989). Digital filtering of EMG-signals. *Electromyography and Clinical Neurophysiology*, *29*(2), 81–86. PMID:2707144

About the Contributors

Pradeep Kumar Mallick is an Asst. Professor of Computer Science and Engineering at Balasore College of Engineering and Technology under Bijupatnaik University, India. His research interest is in Data Mining,vSecurity and Image processing and he has published more than 35 technical papers in the international journals and magazines of repute. He was a Gold Medalist in his Master. He is the Editor-in-Chief of the International Journal on Advanced Computer Theory and Engineering (IJACTE) and ITSI Transactions on Electrical and Electronics Engineering, as well as Chairman and Chief Mentor Institute for Research and Development India which is a professional body to encourage researchers and scholars to enhance their research throughput.

* * *

Khwairakpam Amitab was born in Imphal West, Manipur, India, in 1986. He received the B.E. degree in Computer Science and Engineering from the Manipur University in 2009, and M.E. degree in Computer Science and Engineering from the Punjab Engineering College (PEC), Chandigarh, India, in 2011. In 2012, he joined the Department of Information Technology, North-Eastern Hill University (NEHU), Shillong, India as an Assistant Professor. Previously he worked as Assistant Professor in the Department of CSE/IT under Lovely Faculty of Technology and Science, Lovely Professional University, Jalandhar, Punjab. His current research interests include Synthetic Aperture Radar imaging, image processing and soft computing.

Parul Sureshkumar Arora is now Assistant professor Department of Electronics and Telecommunication Engineering, Pune University G.H. Raisoni College Of Engineering & Management Wagholi, Pune, India. She has guided many pg students in her credit.

Shivakumar Baragi received the M.Tech Degree in Digital Electronics from B.V.B.C.E.T, Hubli, VTU University, Belagavi, Karnataka in 2015 and B.E. Degree in Electronics and Communication Engineering from Rural Engineering College, Bhalki, VTU University, Belagavi, Karnataka, India, in 2010. I Worked as Lecturer in M.S. Engineering College, Bangalore during 2010 to 2011. I have presented two papers in 7th International Conference on Electrical, Electronics, Computing and Communication Systems (EECCS'15), Bangalore and 5th National Conference on Electronic Technologies organized by Goa College of Engineering, Goa respectively. Attended National Level Workshop on "Winter School on Biometrics for Secured Authentication Fundamentals and Advances", organized by S.G.G.I.E.T, Nanded.

Akash Kumar Bhoi has completed his B.Tech. (Biomedical Engineering) from the TAT, Bhubaneswar and M.Tech. (Biomedical Instrumentation) from Karunya University, Coimbatore in the year 2009 and 2011 respectively. He is pursuing PhD from Sikkim Manipal University, India. He is Working as Assistant Professor in the Department of Applied Electronics & Instrumentation at Sikkim Manipal Institute of Technology (SMIT), India since 2012. He is member of ISEIS & IAENG, Associate member of UACEE and Editorial Board member of IJAEEE, IJAEEE, ITSI-TEEE, IJECCE & IJCTT and Reviewer of IJET, IJCT, IJBSE, IJMI, AJBLS. His areas of research are Biomedical Signal Processing, Medical Image Processing, Sensor & Transducer and Medical Instrumentation. He has published several papers in national and international journals and conferences. He has also published 3 Book Chapters. He has participated in workshops, seminars and conferences.

Sukant Kishoro Bisoy received the Bachelor's degree in Computer Science & Engineering from (IE, India) and Master's degree in Computer Science & Engineering from *Visvesvaraya Technological University (VTU), Belgaum, India in 2000* and 2003, respectively, and pursuing PhD degree in Computer Engineering from the SOA University, Bhubaneswar, India. He is an Assistant Professor of Computer Science & Engineering Department, C. V. Raman College of Engineering, Bhubaneswar, India. His current research interests are on Ad Hoc Network and Wireless Sensor Network. He has served as Editor of Lecture notes on "Wireless Sensor networks: The recent Challenges". In addition, he has been involved in organizing many conferences, workshop and SDP. He has several publications in national and International conference and given invited talk in many workshops.

Sufal Das was born in Howrah, West Bengal, India, in 1985. He received the B.Tech degree in Computer Science and Engineering from the West Bengal University of Technology in 2005, and M.Tech degree in Information Technology from Tezpur University, India, in 2008. Currently he is pursuing PhD. from North-Eastern Hill Univeristy. In 2010, he has joined the Department of Information Technology, North-Eastern Hill University (NEHU), Shillong, India as an Assistant Professor. Previously he worked as Assistant Professor in the Department of IT under Sikkim Manipal Institute of Technology, Sikkim Manipal University, Sikkim. His current research interests include Data Mining, Big Data Analysis, Machine Learning and Soft Computing. He has published several research papers.

R. Deepika received B.E degree in department of Information science and Engineering from City Engineering College, VTU Belgaum, India in the year 2013.Currently pursuing M.Tech degree in the department of Computer science and Engineering from East West Institute of Technology, VTU Belgaum, India. Area of interest are Image processing and Pattern recognition.

Pertik Garg is presently working with Swami Vivekanand Institute of Engineering and Technology Banur as an Assistant Professor in Department of Computer Science & Engineering from since 4th July 2007. He is pursuing a Ph.D Degree from Punjab Technical University, Jalandhar. His research area is OSPF Network and software Engineering. He is working on Restoration Technique to Optimize Recovery Time for Efficient OSPF Network. He has published more than 10 research papers and presented in national and international conferences/ seminars/ journals. He has published 2-Books and has 9 years of experience in teaching. He has worked on many projects in data synchronization, natural language processes, simulation of mathematical equations and software engineering.

Deepika Ghai received B.Tech degree in Electronics & Communication Department from Rayat Institute of Engineering and Technology, Ropar in 2009, M.tech degree in VLSI Design & CAD from Thapar University, Patiala in 2011 and pursuing Ph.D in Electronics from PEC University of Technology, Chandigarh. Her research interests are digital signal processing and image processing. She has published around 8 journal and conference research papers. She has published one book "VLSI Implementation of Original, Control and Pipeline CORDIC algorithm."

Savita N. Ghaiwat is a student of Department of Electronics and Telecommunication Engineering, Pune University G.H. Raisoni College Of Engineering & Management Wagholi, Pune, India. She published more than 10 papers in International Journals.

Jayshree Ghorpade-Aher is currently working as an Assistant Professor in MAEER'S MITCOE, Department of Computer Engineering, Pune, Savitribai Phule Pune University (SPPU), Maharashtra, India. She has completed her full-time M.E Computers in 2004 from SICTR PICT, Pune and B.E. Computers from Pad. Dr. DY Patil WCOE, Pune, both under the SPPU. She is pursuing her Ph.D. in Computer Engineering. Her research areas include DM, Soft Computing, Bio-informatics, IP and have published about 30+ research papers on topics related to her areas including an IEEE & an Elsevier publication. Awarded *'BEST PAPER AWARD'* by the ACM International Conference, CUBE'12 . She has written a reference book on Computer Networks and published 02 Indian patents. She has received a funding of nearly 04 lacs for research activities from Board of College and University Development, SPPU. She has organized various National & International events involving speakers at international level from various countries. She is involved in the Examination Activities for UG/PG (Subject Chairman), SPPU. She has done the certification for Microsoft Technology Associate – Networking Fundamentals and ISO audit. She is a lifetime member of Computer Society of India.

Santaji Ghorpade is currently working as Senior System Engineer in IBM India Pvt Ltd., Pune, Maharashtra, India. He has done his graduation in Information Technology Engineering from Dr D.Y. Patil COE Akurdi, Pune and post-graduation in Computer Management from Dr Vikhe Patil Foundations CMRD, Pune, Maharashtra, India. He is pursuing his Ph.D. in Computer Management from AIMS, Pune. His research area is Business Intelligence and his interests are, Management Information Systems, Data Warehousing and Data Mining. He has various national and international journal publications and 1 Indian patent published. He has academic as well as professional experience of over more than 12+ years. He also has to his credit Career Counselling and Guidance experience of more than 15 years. He has successfully guided and mentored Final Year Projects of Engineering Students and Graduate.

Ashu Gupta is presently working as Assistant Professor in Apeejay Institute of Management Technical Campus, Jalandhar (Punjab) since August 01, 2001. He received his Ph.D Degree from Punjabi University, Patiala on the topic "Development of Open Source Evaluation Criteria Software for Selection of Simulation Tools used by Automobile Manufacturers in North India". His research area is simulation, sensor networks and software engineering. He has published more than 24 research papers and presented in national and international conferences/ seminars/ journals. Also published 4-Books with International publishers and have 11-years of experience in teaching. He has Life Membership with Computer Society of India, Society for Information Science, Society of Digital Information & Wireless Communication (SDIWC), USA, etc.

Nalini C. Iyer received Ph.D degree in the year 2014 from Visvesvaraya Technological University, Belagavi. Received M. Tech degree in the year 1994 from NITK, Suratkal and received B.E degree in the year 1987 from Karnataka University, Dharwad. Has presented two papers in National conference and 11 International Conference. Published 3 International Papers. Currently working as Head of Instrumentation Technology department, B.V.B.C.E.T, Hubli, Karnataka, India. Worked as Professor in Electronics and Communication Engineering, B.V.B.V.C.E.T, Hubli, Karnataka, India. Has one year Industrial experience and also permanent life member of The Indian Society for Technical Education (ISTE) and I.E.

Neelu Jain received B.E. degree in Electronics and Communication Engineering from University of Roorkee (now IITR) in 1980, M.E. degree in Electronics in 1996 and Ph.D. in Electronics from Panjab University, Chandigarh in 2009. She has been the associate professor of Electronics and Communication Engineering Department at the PEC University of Technology, Chandigarh since 2014. Her area of research includes digital signal processing, image processing and embedded system. She has published around 40 journal and conference research papers.

Manik Kadam is working as the Director for JSPM's JICA, Pune, Maharashtra, India with an experience of 23+ years. He has completed his Bachelors and Masters (M.Sc., M.Phil. M.B.A.) from University of Pune. He has been awarded his Ph.D. in Computer Management by the University of Pune in March 2005. His research interests are MIS, Principles and Practices of Management, Research Methodology, Industrial Organization and Management, Statistical and Quantitative Techniques, Environmental & Physical Chemistry etc. He has 15+ publications in various esteemed journals & conferences. He has co-ordinated the Research Oriented Students Association and various National events. Since last 20 years, he is involved in the Examination Activities for UG/PG (Engg., M.Sc,M.B.A). Also known as a great basketball coach.

Hemanta Kumar Kalita was born in Barpeta, Assam, India. He has received B.E. in Computer Science and Engineering, M.Tech in Information Technology and PhD in Engineering degree from Dibrugarh University, Tezpur University and Jadavpur University, Kolkata respectively. His area of interest includes Wireless Communication, Network Security, Soft Computing and Big Data Analysis. He has more than 15 years of teaching and industrial experience. Currently he is holding the post of Associate Professor in the department of Information Technology, NEHU, Shillong, India. He has one patent and published several research papers.

Debdatta Kandar: Born in 1977 at Deulia, Purba Medinipur, West Bengal, INDIA has received PhD(Engg.) from Department of Electronics and Telecommunication Engineering, Jadavpur University, Kolkata, in the year 2011. He has been awarded 'Young Scientist' award from URSI GA-2005 at Vigyan Bhaban, Delhi. He also worked on a DRDO sponsored project. Mobile Communication, Soft Computing and Radar Operation are the area of specializations. Currently, he is holding the post of Associate Professor in the Department of Information Technology, North-Eastern Hill University.

Bidita Khandelwal did her MD Medicine in 1998 from Assam University. She joined Sikkim Manipal Institute of Medical Sciences (SMIMS) on 16.08.2000 as Assistant Professor in Department of Medicine and since 15.02.2009; she is heading the Department of Medicine. She is life member of API,

IMA, IACM and RSSDI. Other posts held are Chairperson of complaint committee on Sexual Harassment at work place, Chairperson of IEC, Ayurveda Regional Research Institute, Vice chairman API East Zone, Editorial Board member of IJEM, JOHR & SMU Med Journal. Member of Academic Senate of SMU, Member of Sikkim Medical Council, Coordinator post graduate studies and External expert for Board of Study. She is a Member of Research Protocol Evaluation Committee, Publication Evaluation committee, Institutional Ethics Committee, Hospital Management Committee, Infection Control Committee, Promotion Committee, State Task Force, Pharmacovigilance committee. She has special interest in Diabetes Mellitus and has several publications related to it.

Shaila H. Koppad has done her schooling from K.L.E Society's M. R. Sakhare English Medium School Vidyanagar Hubli, Bachelors in Computer Applications from P.C. Jabin Science College, Hubli (affiliated to Karnataka University Dharwad) in 2008 and Masters in Computer Applications from Karnataka University Dharwad in 2012. Since 2012 she is working as Guest Faculty in Bangalore University, MCA Programme, Bangalore. She is also pursuing her Ph.D. under the guidance of Dr. S.Anupama Kumar, Department of MCA, R.V. College of Engineering Bangalore (affiliated to Visvesvaraya Technological University, Belgum). She is Member of International Association Of Engineers and Life Member of Indian Science Congress Association. She may be contacted through e-mail- shaila.koppad@gmail.com.

S. Saravana Kumar, PhD (computer Science), is Professor at Department of Computer Science and Engineering, Sree Vidyanikethan Engineering College, India. He has a decade of teaching and research experience and guided many Ph.D thesis. He is a Senior Member of IEEE (USA) and Fellow, IETE (India). His area of interest includes mobile computing and cloud computing.

Sri P. Sunil Kumar is currently working as Assistant Professor in the Department of Computer Applications, IISIT, Bhubaneswar, India. His research areas include Data Mining, data warehouse, Knowledge Discovery etc.He obtained his Master's degree from I.G.I.T Sarang in 1998, have 17 years of academic and 3 years of research experience. He qualified the UGC-NET (Computer Science and Application) in 2012 when he started publishing articles with IRD, India an unique research organization in Bhubaneswar Odisha. .He has published 3 international publications as leading author and attended number of conferences. He is involved in rural projects of Sri Sathya Sai Organization, Odisha since 1998 which encourages him to publish research papers on ground reality which reflects in his papers.

Arnab Kumar Maji completed his B. Tech and M.Tech in the field of Information Technology in the year of 2003 and 2005 respectively. He is working as an Assistant Professor of North Eastern Hill University, Shillong, Meghalaya, India since 2006. He has published more than 25 numbers of research paper in the field of algorithm, image processing and e-commerce. He is a professional member of ACM India.

Brojo Kishore Mishra has completed his Ph.D in Computer Science from Berhampur University in the year 2012. Currently he is working as an Associate Professor in the department of Information Technology of C. V. Raman College of Engineering, Bhubaneswar. Before joining to this organization he was working as Principal of the MITS Institute of Polytechnic, Rayagada. Now he is the State Student Coordinator, Odisha for Computer Society of India (CSI). He is the life member of CSI, ISTE and member of IAENG, CSTA, ACCS, UACEE professional societies. Also he is the Jury Coordination Committee Member of All IEEE Young Engineers' Humanitarian Challenge (AIYEHUM 2015) project competition, organized by IEEE Region 10 (Asia pacific). His research areas of interest include Data / Opinion Mining, Soft Computing, Big Data & Cloud Computing. He has published more than twenty papers in reputed international journals and conferences.

Mihir Narayan Mohanty has completed his Ph.D in Applied Signal Processing from Bijupatnaik University of Technology, Odisha India. Currently he is working as an Associate Professor in the department of Electronics and Communication Engineering, ITER, SOA University, Bhubaneswar. His research interest is in Data Mining, Applied Signal & Image Processing, Communication Engineering, Devices, Antenna and he has published more than 100 technical papers in the international journals, Conferences and magazines of repute. He has a decade of teaching and research experience and guided many M.Tech Scholars.

Reena Pagare is currently working as Assistant Professor in MAEER's Maharashtra Institute of Technology, Department of Computer Engineering, Pune, Savitribai Phule Pune University (SPPU), Maharashtra, India. She has done her graduation in Computer Engineering in 2001 from MKSSS CCOEW and post-graduation in Computer Engineering in 2009 from SICTR PICT, Pune, SPPU. She is pursuing her Ph.D. in Computer Engineering. Her research interests are Algorithms, Social Network Analysis and Data Mining. She has 20 international journal publications and 2 Indian patents published. She has completed a research project on "Automated Classification of Botanical Herb for Ayurveda" which received funding of 1.6 lacs from Board of College and University Development, SPPU in the year 2013-15. She is FOSS evangelist. Mentoring students for activities related to open source technology in the Department for last 14 years. Organizer of various open source events like FOSSsumMIT' 14, FUDCon' 15. She was the organizer of National Conference on Open Source Technology, FOSSsumMIT' 14 conducted in MAEER's MITCOE during August 2014, which also received funding of 2 lacs from Board of College and University Development, SPPU in 2014-15. She also coordinated for the International Conference on Fedora Users and Developers Conference, Asia Pacific 2015, FUDCon APAC held in June 2015.

Panda, a known name in the arena of academics and & training has a work experience of 17 years as a Lecturer in English at UG & PG Level that includes both general and technical institutions under Utkal University & Biju Patnaik University of Technology (BPUT) respectively. He is Involved and associated with various leading Institutions as a faculty in Spoken English, Soft skill and Personality Development . As Visiting faculty to organizations of repute that include Utkal University Dept.of MBA,Intgrd. MBA, Dept.of MCA and Intgrd. MCA, DDCE Utkal University, Amity University besides other leading technical colleges under BPUT for teaching English and communication skill. He enjoys his liberty, In Spoken English (GD, PD & PI), Linguistics, Phonetics & Stylistic. Contemporary English (Communicative English), Corporate corners, (Business Communication) Motivation, Situation Management, Captions, Concept Building, Leadership in Team Work, Expansion of Ideas and Contribution to News Dailies on subjects that concern the common cause. Prof. Panda is associated with organizations of repute on different capacities: that include ; Researchers association Orissa,cuttack, Advisor to University, Sub-committee on Course Curriculum (BPUT) Youth Hostels Associations of India (YHAI). Nehru Yuba Manch (NYM), He is known for his oratory skills, as an avid reader of Indian ethics and culture and as a trainer of higher order makes him stand apart amid thousands. IDENTITY TRAINING PVT. LTD is proud to have his presence as Director & As A Corporate Trainer that adds quality to the batch of skilled manpower to handle any training assignment under his able guidance.

Prasant Kumar Pattnaik, PhD(computer Science), is Professor at School of Computer Engineering, KIIT University, India. He has a decade of teaching and research experience. He is a Senior Member of IEEE(USA) and Fellow, IETE(India). His area of interest includes mobile computing and cloud computing.

Sateesh Kumar Pradhan is currently working as *Professor & Head* Post Graduate Department of Computer Science & application, Utkal University, Vani Vihar. He has done PhD in the area of "neuron-Based Parallel Algorithms for Solution of Linear Systems and Digital Signal Processing Application". He had organized number of conferences and had more than 30 publications to his credit. Four research scholars have obtained their PhD degree under his able guidance and five of them are currently working under him. He has the privilege of membership in various decision making societies, committees and boards of universities in and outside Odisha. He also heads the responsibility as the member of editorial board of number of publishing organizations.

M. R. Prasad is currently working as Assistant professor in department of computer science and Engineering, JSS Academy of Technical Education Bengaluru. He received his B.E in the year 2004 under VTU Belgaum, India. He got his M.Tech degree in the year 2009 under VTU Belgaum, India. Currently he is pursuing Ph.D under VTU Belgaum, India. His area of interest are Image processing, Pattern Recognition.

Bandariakor Rymbai is M.Tech student in the department of Information Technology of North Eastern Hill University. She successfully published around 05 papers on face recognition in her own credit.

Abhaya Kumar Sahoo has completed his M.Tech in Computer Science and Engineering from KIIT University in the year 2012. He has received the Chancellor's Gold Medal and Vice Chancellor's Gold medal for securing highest CGPA in his M.Tech. Currently he is working as an Assistant Professor in the department of Information Technology of C. V. Raman College of Engineering, Bhubaneswar. Before joining to this organization he was working as Technical Intern in IBM-ISL, Pune. He has received the Young IT Professional award from Computer Society of India-Region IV in the year 2014. He is the Coordinator for NVIDIA GPU Education Center in C. V. Raman College of Engineering, Bhubaneswar. He is the member of IEEE. His research areas of interest include Big Data, Parallel Computing, Data Mining and Image Processing. He has published more than eight papers in reputed international journals and conferences.

Karma Sonam Sherpa has completed his B.E. (Electrical Engineering) from the MREC, Jaipur, and M.Tech. (Power Electronics and Machine Drives) from I.I.T., Kharagpur in the year 1996 and 2003 respectively. He is a doctorate from Sikkim Manipal University. He has been serving SMIT, Sikkim for the last sixteen years. Presently, he is professor in the Department of Electrical & Electronics Engineering and is heading the Department of Electrical & Electronics Engineering and Department of Applied Electronics & Instrumentation Engineering. He is life member of ISTE, IEI and System Society of India (SSI). His areas of interests are Electric Power Distribution System, Power Electronics and Electrical Drives. He has published papers in national and international journals and conferences. He has organized workshop, seminars and conference.

T. M. Shwetha has done her B.E. in Computer Science and Engineering from G.S.S.S. Institute of Technology for Women,Mysore (affiliated to Visvesvaraya Technological University) in 2010 and M.Tech in Computer Science and Technology from Department of Studies in Computer Science, University of Mysore, Mysore in 2012. She has worked on the project "Preparation of Chithradurga District Human Resource Development" Report for Karnataka State from 2012 to 2014 as data analyst. She is also worked on the Project "Public Distribution System and its impact on Food Securities in Karnataka State" since 2013 and she has been working as Guest Faculty in University of Bangalore, Bangalore. She is currently pursuing her Ph.D. under the guidance of Prof. B.L. Muralidhara,Department of MCA,University of Bangalore, Bangalore.

Chetana Srinivas is currently working as Assistant professor in the department of Computer Science and Engineering, at East West Institute of Technology Bengaluru, VTU Belgaum, India. Her research topic is related to Image processing. Her consistent effort in this research made her to perceive Ph.D.

Anita Thengade is working as Assistant Professor, Computer Department, MIT College of Engineering, Pune. She holds Bachelors of Engineering in Computer Science from Dr. BAMU Aurangabad and Masters of Engineering in Computer from Dr. BATU Lonere. Currently she is doing a research in Data Mining, Soft Computing and Satellite image processing. She has 13 years of teaching experience and has taught various subject like DBMS, ADBMS, Computer Graphics, Operating System for UG and PG programs. She has published the 12 paper in National and International conference as well as journal.

Index

F

G

H

I

J

K

L

M

N

O

P